THE ROUTLEDGE INTERNATIONAL HANDBOOK OF SIMMEL STUDIES

The Routledge International Handbook of Simmel Studies documents the richness, variety, and creativity of contemporary international research on Georg Simmel's work. Starting with the established role of Simmel as a classical author of sociology, and including the growing interest in his work in the domain of philosophy, this volume explores the research on Simmel in several further disciplines including art, social aesthetics, literature, theatre, essayism, and critical theory, as well as in the debates on cosmopolitanism, economic pathologies of life, freedom, modernity, religion, and nationalism. Bringing together contributions from leading specialists in research on Simmel, the book is thematically arranged in order to highlight the relevance of his oeuvre for different fields of recent research, with a further section tracing the most important paths that Simmel's reception has taken in the world. As such, it will appeal to scholars across the social sciences and humanities, and to sociologists, philosophers, and social theorists in particular, with interest in Simmel's thought.

Gregor Fitzi is President of the Simmel Gesellschaft. He is the author of *The Challenge of Modernity: Simmel's Sociological Theory* and the co-editor of the three-volume set *Populism and the Crisis of Democracy*. He is editor of the journal *Simmel Studies*.

THE ROUTLEDGE INTERNATIONAL HANDBOOK OF SIMMEL STUDIES

Edited by Gregor Fitzi

Routledge
Taylor & Francis Group

LONDON AND NEW YORK

First published 2021
by Routledge
2 Park Square, Milton Park, Abingdon, Oxon OX14 4RN

and by Routledge
52 Vanderbilt Avenue, New York, NY 10017

Routledge is an imprint of the Taylor & Francis Group, an informa business

British Library Cataloguing-in-Publication Data
A catalogue record for this book is available from the British Library

Library of Congress Cataloging-in-Publication Data
Names: Fitzi, Gregor, editor.
Title: The Routledge international handbook of Simmel studies / [edited by] Gregor Fitzi.
Description: 1 Edition. | New York : Routledge, 2020. |
Series: Routledge international handbooks | Includes bibliographical references and index.
Identifiers: LCCN 2020018872 (print) | LCCN 2020018873 (ebook) | ISBN 9780367277239 (hardback) |
ISBN 9780429297502 (ebook)
Subjects: LCSH: Simmel, Georg, 1858–1918–Political and social views. | Sociology–History. |
Philosophy–History.
Classification: LCC HM447 .R68 2020 (print) | LCC HM447 (ebook) | DDC 301.092–dc23
LC record available at https://lccn.loc.gov/2020018872
LC ebook record available at https://lccn.loc.gov/2020018873

ISBN: 978-0-367-27723-9 (hbk)
ISBN: 978-0-429-29750-2 (ebk)

Typeset in Bembo
by Swales & Willis, Exeter, Devon, UK

CONTENTS

Contents

FIGURES

TABLES

CONTRIBUTORS

Matthieu Amat, PhD, is First Assistant in Modern and Contemporary Philosophy at the University of Lausanne. He published *Le relationnisme philosophique de Georg Simmel: Une idée de la culture* in 2018. He edited, with Fabio d'Andrea, *Simmel Studies: Special Issue: Simmel as Educator*, 1/2019, and *Georg Simmel, Leçons de pédagogie*, 2020.

Arthur Bueno is Lecturer and Research Fellow at the Philosophy Department of the University of Frankfurt and Visiting Professor at the Institute of Psychology of the University of São Paulo. He was an Alexander von Humboldt Postdoctoral Fellow at the Max Weber Centre (Erfurt) and at the University Paris Nanterre.

Andrea Borsari is Associate Professor of Aesthetics at the Department of Architecture, University of Bologna, and recently has taught as visiting professor at UCLA, Copenhagen University, and Ensaplv (École nationale supérieure d'architecture de Paris la Villette). His books include *Mondo, cose, immagini: Sulle forme dell'esperienza estetica* (2018); *Mimicry: Estetica del divenire animale* (2018); and *El tótem y el oso espadachín. Antropología filosófica de la imitación: Helmuth Plessner y Arnold Gehlen* (2007).

Milos Brocic is a PhD candidate at the University of Toronto. His research interests include social theory, political sociology, and culture. His doctoral research draws on Simmel in exploring the relationship between self-expression and contentious politics.

Natàlia Cantó-Milà is Associate Professor in Social Sciences at the Universitat Oberta de Catalunya (UOC) in Barcelona. She gained her PhD at the University of Bielefeld (Germany) with a work on Simmel's relational sociology, and on Simmel's theory of value. Thereafter she went to Leipzig, where she taught sociological theory, social policies, and qualitative methodologies. At the UOC she is responsible for social theory and qualitative methods. She is the editor-in-chief of the journal *Digithum*, an indexed journal specialising in relational sociology. With her research group she leads a research project on the imaginaries of the future of youth. Her main research interests are relational sociology, social theory, sociology of culture, and sociology of emotions.

Barbara Carnevali is Associate Professor at the École des Hautes Études en Sciences Sociales in Paris where she holds a chair in social aesthetics. Her research focuses on the aesthetic dimension of social life, art as a form of knowledge of the social world, and critical theory. Her books include *Social Appearances: A Philosophy of Display and Prestige* (2020).

Gregor Fitzi is President of the Simmel Gesellschaft. After his PhD in Sociology at the University of Bielefeld, he was Assistant Professor at the Institute of Sociology, University of Heidelberg, and Interim Full Professor of Sociological Theory at the University of Bielefeld. Among his recent publications are: *The Challenge of Modernity: Simmel's Sociological Theory* (2019) and, with Jürgen Mackert and Bryan Turner, *Populism and the Crisis of Democracy* (three volumes, 2018).

Paola Giacomoni is Professor of the History of Philosophy at the University of Trento. Her main scientific interests concern the relationship between philosophy and science. She has published numerous essays internationally, several edited books, and five monographs. She was invited as professor and research fellow in Paris and New York.

Austin Harrington is Associate Professor of Sociology at the University of Leeds, UK. His recent publications include *German Cosmopolitan Social Thought and the Idea of the West: Voices from Weimar* (2016) and *Georg Simmel: Essays on Art and Aesthetics* (2020).

Gary D. Jaworski, PhD, is Professor of Sociology and Social Theory (retired) at Fairleigh Dickinson University, Madison, NJ, USA. He is the author of *Georg Simmel and the American Prospect* and other works.

Thomas Kemple, Professor of Sociology at the Department of Sociology, University of British Columbia, is author of *Reading Marx Writing: Melodrama, the Market, and the 'Grundrisse'* (1995), *Intellectual Work and the Spirit of Capitalism* (2012), and *Simmel* (2018); and he is co-editor with Olli Pyyhtinen of *The Anthem Companion to Georg Simmel* (2017), and with Mark Featherstone of *Writing the Body Politic: A John O'Neill Reader* (2020).

Volkhard Krech is Professor of Religious Studies at the Ruhr University Bochum and Director of the Centre for Religious Studies (CERES). Monographs: *Georg Simmels Religionstheorie* (1998); *Religionssoziologie* (1999); *Wissenschaft und Religion: Studien zur Geschichte der Religionsforschung in Deutschland 1871 bis 1933* (2002); *Götterdämmerung: Auf der Suche nach Religion* (2003); and *Wo bleibt die Religion? Studien zur Ambivalenz des Religiösen in der modernen Gesellschaft* (2011).

Monica Martinelli is Associate Professor of Sociology at the Catholic University of Milan (Italy) and member of the Centre for the Anthropology of Religion and Cultural Change. Her scientific research focuses on the study of the sociological classics and their questions about the relationship between the individual and society, applied to contemporary socio-cultural transformations.

Vincenzo Mele is Associate Professor of General Sociology at the University of Pisa, Department of Political Science. He is author of *Metropolis: Georg Simmel, Walter Benjamin and Modernity* (2011), *Aesthetics and Social Theory: Simmel, Benjamin, Adorno, Bourdieu* (2013),

Globalizing Cultures: Theories, Actions, Paradigms (co-edited with M. Vujnovic, 2015). He is editor of the journal *Simmel Studies*.

Ingo Meyer is Senior Lecturer at the University of Klagenfurt, Austria. He was born in 1968, and has studied literature, history, sociology, and philosophy at Bielefeld, Berlin, Bochum, and Bonn. He received his PhD in 2004, and his habilitation in 2015. He has published numerous books and articles on literary realism, Frank Zappa, Georg Simmel, contemporary literature, fine arts, and picture theory.

Andrea Pinotti is Professor in Aesthetics at the State University of Milan. His research focuses on image theories, empathy theories, and German contemporary aesthetics. In 2018 he was awarded the Wissenschaftspreis der Aby-Warburg-Stiftung in Hamburg. He is currently directing an ERC-Advanced project entitled *An-iconology: History, Theory, and Practices of Environmental Images*.

Claudia Portioli is temporary Lecturer at the University of Trento, Italy. She holds a doctorate in aesthetic philosophy (University of Bologna) and has carried out research on Georg Simmel's philosophy of art and theory of knowledge in Italy, Germany, and France. Her publications include Portioli-Fitzi (eds), *Simmel e l'estetica* (2006) and the essay 'War, Culture and *Lebensreform*', *Simmel Studies*, 2/2018.

Olli Pyyhtinen is Associate Professor of Sociology at the University of Tampere, Finland. He is the author of, for example, *The Simmelian Legacy: A Science of Relations* (2017) and *Simmel and 'the Social'* (2010). He also co-edited (with Thomas Kemple) the volume *The Anthem Companion to Georg Simmel* (2016).

Davide Ruggieri, PhD, is Adjunct Professor in Cultural Sociology at the University of Bologna. His main research field tackles the history of sociological theory, Georg Simmel's sociology, critical theory, and relational sociology (particularly the relation of culture/individualisation within the social processes). He conducted research and archive activities abroad in the Universities of Mainz, Frankfurt am Main, Bielefeld, and Munich.

Daniel Silver is Associate Professor of Sociology at the University of Toronto. He received his PhD from the Committee on Social Thought at the University of Chicago. His research interests include social theory, cities, and cultural policy.

Barbara Thériault is Professor at the Département de sociologie and at the Centre Canadien d'études allemandes et européennes at Université de Montréal. She is in charge of the 'Feuilleton' section of the journal *Sociologie et sociétés*, and translates German feuilletons (Simmel, Kracauer, Elias, Leitner) into French.

François Thomas is Associate Professor at the Institute of Philosophy at the University Paris Nanterre (Paris, France). From 2015 to 2019 he was research fellow and teaching assistant at the Institute of Philosophy at the University of Bonn (Germany). His PhD dissertation was on 'The art of translation: Philosophical, ethical, and political translation issues from the historical context of the German Romantics' criticism against the French practice of translation in the 17th and 18th century'. In 2013 he published a monograph on Georg Simmel (*Le Paradigme du comédien*, 2013).

Denis Thouard, Directeur de recherches at the Centre National de la Recherche Scientifique (CNRS), works in Paris (Centre Georg Simmel at the EHESS) and Berlin (Centre Marc Bloch). His topics go from German philosophy (Kant, Schleiermacher) to the whole hermeneutic tradition (from Flacius Illyricus up to Gadamer and Bollack). He has worked and published on Simmel for ten years. His main Simmelian publications are *Réciprocités sociales: Lectures de Simmel* (co-edited with Gregor Fitzi), as an issue of *Sociologies et société* 44, 2012, and *Simmel, le parti-pris du tiers* (co-edited with Bénédicte Zimmermann), 2017.

Monika Tokarzewska is a graduate of German Studies, Polish Studies, and Philosophy at the University of Warsaw. Currently she is an Associate Professor at the Department of German Studies at the Nicolas Copernicus University in Toruń. She published the book *Der Feste Grund des Unberechenbaren: Georg Simmel zwischen Soziologie und Literatur* and numerous texts on aesthetics and society in Simmel's work.

Esteban Vernik is full Professor of Sociology at the University of Buenos Aires, and member of the National Council of Scientific and Technological Research at Gino Germani Institut. His main field of research is sociological theory; among his recent publications are *Georg Simmel, un siglo después* (co-edited with Hernán Borisonik) and Preface to Georg Simmel, *La cantidad estética.*

Patrick Watier is Professor Emeritus of Sociology at the University of Strasbourg. He devoted a number of publications to Simmel's position during World War I. His latest publication: Stebler K., Watier, P. (2018). Simmel: La guerre et l'Europe disparue. *Revue des Sciences Sociales*, *59*: 102–109.

GENERAL INTRODUCTION

Gregor Fitzi

The history of the social sciences is characterised by cycles of oblivion and rediscovery that question the underlying capacity of this realm of knowledge to establish critical autonomy in the face of ongoing societal self-interpretation. The reception of Simmel's works manifests a sequence of silence, veiled criticisms, and renaissance that is a classic example of the gain and loss of autonomy that is common within the social sciences. Sociological theories are easily forgotten because social science is cyclically reabsorbed into the socio-political discourse. Furthermore, given Simmel's consistent philosophical studies, it is even more surprising to note the restrictive reception of his ideas in this domain. Of course, there are some significant exceptions with Albert Mamelet (1914) and Vladimir Jankélévitch (1925) in France, Hans Blumenberg (1976) in Germany, or Antonio Banfi in Italy ([1932] 1986). Yet the interest they accorded Simmel could not establish him as a reference figure for 20th-century philosophy. The engagement of the Simmelian research group in Berlin that gathered around Michael Landmann, Kurt Gassen (1958), and later on Karlfried Gründer, Hannes Böhringer (1976), and Klaus Christian Köhnke (1996), enabled the interest to be kept alive. However, it remained a drop in the ocean of Heideggerism and analytical philosophy. In this regard, the current development of Simmel studies presents a new situation. There is a strong trend to rediscover Simmel's role and importance not only for sociology but also for philosophy, aesthetics, literature, and theatre studies. This handbook addresses these developments.

The historical reconstruction exposes three momentous circumstances that underpin the reasons for the discontinuity, partiality, and specificity in the reception of Simmel's work, as well as his confinement to the role of an outsider in sociology (Coser, 1965), yet also for the later rediscoveries of his thinking: (1) the rupture between the young intellectual generation of the Weimar period and 'classical sociology', (2) Parsons's canonisation of the reference authors of sociology in the late 1940s, and (3) Simmel's rediscovery under the aegis of postmodern thinking in the 1980s.

After World War I, the representatives of 'official sociology' in the Weimar Republic, like Alfred Vierkandt (1923) and Leopold von Wiese (1924-1929), developed Simmel's sociological approach into a formalistic modelling of social reality that could not encounter the interest and the concerns of the younger generation that experienced conflict in the trenches (Stölting, 1986). On the one hand, the institutionalisation of Marxism-Leninism as a state-grounding doctrine in the USSR determined a momentous division between 'classical sociology' and Marxist-oriented social theory. In his influential guide to historical materialism, first published in 1921, Nikolai Bukharin establishes a sharp opposition between 'Marxist sociology' representing the interests of the proletarian class and 'bourgeois sociology' as the ideological reading of modern society for the sake of capitalism (Bukharin, 2012). The lively exchange between the representatives of classical sociology and Marx's social theory thus came to an end and became invisible to the following generations of intellectuals. On the other hand, the efforts to establish the tradition of a 'German line of sociology' by representatives of the conservative revolution in Germany during the late 1920s and 1930s – Hans Freyer, Erik Rothacker, and Andreas Walther – excluded Simmel from the discipline's classical authors because of anti-Semitic and political prejudices (Fitzi, 2015, pp. 61-77; Sontheimer, 1992, p. 118 f.). The later institutionalisation of a sociology that was loyal to the Nazi regime in the 1930s led to the definitive proscription of Simmel's sociology from university teaching (Rammstedt, 1986).

Parsons, for his part, decided to exclude Simmel from the sociological pantheon not only for reasons of career calculations, with the aim of positioning his research programme as an alternative to the Simmel-inspired sociology of the Chicago school (Levine, 1957). As Parsons states in the *Structure of Social Action* (1949, pp. 762, 774; Fitzi, 2015, p. 52 f.), he was highly influenced by the formulation of the tasks of sociology in Freyer's book on sociology as a 'science of reality'. Simmel's sociology as a 'science of the *logos*' could not be part of it (Fitzi, 2015, pp. 417-426). Through the rather uncritical later reception of the sociological canon that was established by Parsons, as well as through the post-1945 institutionalisation of the sociological schools in Germany, the idea that there was 'something wrong' with Simmel's sociology was then carried on unconsciously. Yet, as Simmel already wrote in his diary, his intellectual legacy was like cash that every heir would transform to use according to his nature (GSG 20, p. 261), so that his approach to critical reflection on the ongoing change of modern society has been taken up by the most diverse authors. Foremost among them was the Marxist-oriented intellectual generation of the 1920s that was not satisfied with the Soviet orthodoxy, within and beyond the Frankfurt School (Jay, 1996). Simmelian aspects are thus to be found in the works of Adorno, Benjamin, Kracauer, and many more lesser-known representatives of philosophical and sociological essayism (Braungart & Kaufmann, 2006), including among the other '*fils de Simmel*': Béla Balázs, Carl Einstein, Bernhard Groethuysen, Gertrud Kantorowicz, Theodor Kistiakowski, Max Raphael, Gottfried Salomon-Delatour, and Margarete Susman (cf. Thouard, 2020).

The American reception of Simmel's sociological work demonstrates some other specific aspects. From the beginning, it was strongly anchored in the Department of Sociology at the University of Chicago and lasted for several generations. Albion Small had already asked Simmel in 1895 to become an advisory editor for the *American Journal of Sociology*. During the following years, Small translated eight of Simmel's articles on different topics that were published in this journal until 1910 (GSG 18, pp. 521-536). Robert Ezra Park attended Simmel's lecture on sociology in Berlin in 1899/1900 (GSG 21, pp. 281-344). He contributed later to making the Department of Sociology at the University of Chicago a prominent centre for the diffusion of Simmel's sociology (Levine et al., 1976, p. 179 f.) and established Simmel's work as a foundation stone of the sociological study canon in his *Introduction to Sociology* (Park & Burgess, 1922). In Chicago, over the years many other connoisseurs of Simmel's sociological work were active like Ernest Burgess, Everett Hughes, Louis Wirth, and later Eduard H. Shils and Erving Goffman, as well as Donald Levine (Levine, 1957; Levine et al., 1976, p. 182;

Simmel, 1971). If Parsons did not contribute to the dissemination of Simmel's sociology through his writings, he included him in his early teaching. In the 1930s, he offered an influential course on sociological theory at Harvard, which also considered Simmel's position. Robert K. Merton has traced back the origins of his interest in Simmel to that course, as Levine reports (Levine et al., 1976, p. 183). Merton himself went on to make Columbia University an important centre for the study of Simmel's sociology and influenced its reception by several of his students and above all Lewis A. Coser (ibid.), who became a leading interpreter of Simmel's thought and especially of his conflict sociology (Coser, 1956, 1965). Yet the positioning of the sociological mainstream through the canon of classical authors established by Parsons, which excluded Simmel, led as a reaction to a certain entrenchment of the sociological positions of Simmel's inspiration that produced an official image of Simmel 'the sociologist' to the detriment of the focus on the more philosophical side of his research, above all in American academia (Goodstein, 2017). Later on, a distinguished group of German immigrants created a new wave of interest in Simmel's sociology in the 1940s and 1950s. This generation included among others Hans Gerth, Albert Salomon, Gottfried Salomon-Delatour, and Alfred Schutz, who published and taught on Simmel, as well as Kurt Wolff, who translated and presented different collections of his writings (Simmel, 1950, 1959). In spite of this rich reception history, Simmel's influence on American social thought in general has always been erratic. Moreover, here phases of substantial oblivion also alternated with phases of sudden rediscovery (Jaworski, 1997).

It was only thanks to the untiring engagement of Michael Landmann that the interest in Simmel's oeuvre could be rekindled in Europe after World War II. This commitment eventually set in motion the project of the collected works edition that was carried out by the research team of Otthein and Angela Rammstedt together with Klaus Christian Köhnke and his research team (Gassen & Landmann, 1958; Rammstedt, 2015). Yet every European country showed different historical lines of Simmel reception. In Italy, thanks to the engagement of the philosopher Antonio Banfi, who studied with Simmel in Berlin 1910, an intensive philosophical Simmel reception became established (Portioli, 2012). Since the 1980s in Italy, a younger generation of critical Marxists has turned to Simmel to find an alternative to Marx's interpretation of modernity and defended the idea of Simmel as a left-liberal intellectual (Dal Lago, 1994). In France, in addition to the early sociological reception, above all due to Célestin Bouglé (1896), a philosophical debate arose concerning the translation of Simmel's selected works in 1912 – the *Mélanges de philosophie relativiste: Contribution à la culture philosophique* as a contribution to 'relativist philosophy' (GSG 19, pp. 137-371; Amat, 2018; Mamelet, 1914). The translation was promoted by Henri Bergson and provided by Groethuysen's partner Alix Guillain (Fitzi, 2002, pp. 238-250). Yet, after a longer phase of oblivion, a new reception line was established through the 'polemologic interpretation' of Simmel's conflict sociology, given by the political scientist Julien Freund (1983). The specific effect of this interpretation was related to its conservative political orientation, so that French sociologists tended since then to characterise Simmel as a right-wing liberal intellectual. The divergence between the different political interpretations of Simmel's thought in France and Italy provoked the most astonishing debates in the international conferences ahead.

Yet, the most productive phase of rediscovery for Simmel's work was a result of the encounter of different groups of scholars who were motivated by the start of the enterprise of the Georg Simmel edition in the late 1980s under the guidance of Otthein Rammstedt. The journal *Theory, Culture and Society* played a crucial role in this context (Featherstone, 1991).

Amongst other English social scientists with a Marxist background, David Frisby initiated a longer reception wave that continues until today (Frisby, 1981, 1985, 1992; Harrington & Kemple, 2012). He also inspired other lines of reception in Canada and Finland (Kemple, 2019; Kemple & Pyyhtinen, 2016; Pyyhtinen, 2010, 2018). In France, Patrick Watier has established a solid tradition of sociological Simmel reception in cooperation with the Simmel edition (Deroche-Gurcel & Watier, 2002; Rammstedt & Watier, 1992; Watier, 1986). This work laid the foundations for a pluralist opening of Simmel's reception in France. In November 2015, 25 years after the ambitious project commenced for the publication of the collected works of Georg Simmel, the *Georg Simmel Gesamtausgabe* (GSG) was finally completed. This achievement is due to the dedication of the editor Otthein Rammstedt and his collaborators, above all Klaus Christian Köhnke, Rüdiger Kramme, and Angela Rammstedt. Thanks to the comprehensive edition, the corpus of Simmel's writing is finally accessible and now counts among the classical works at least of sociology. As a consequence, in recent years different innovative lines of Simmel reception have been initiated around the world. In France, a new generation of Simmel scholars established the principle that the reception of classical authors should be independent from the conflicts between the different sociological schools (Thouard & Zimmermann, 2017). With regard to Germany, the research that developed within the team of the Simmel edition has since produced a number of analyses of Simmel's work which highlight the interest of his approach for a number of different issues (amongst others Cantó-Milà, 2005; Dahme, 1981; Dahme & Rammstedt, 1995; Fitzi, 2002, 2015, 2019; Köhnke, 1996; Krech, 1998; Meyer, 2017; Rammstedt, 1998, 2003; Rol & Papilloud, 2009; Tyrell, Rammstedt, & Meyer, 2011). Following the completion of the edition, in Germany there is a stronger interest in a canonisation of Simmel's work that emerges in the publication of a *Simmel-Handbuch* with a sociological focus (Müller & Reitz, 2018), and the preparation of a further handbook project with a focus on the philosophical oeuvre (Bohr et al., 2020). Otherwise, however, and to echo Albion Small's viewpoint (GSG 24, p. 1050), the current 'sociological movement' in Germany seems not to look too intensively to Simmel. On the other hand, however, a strong wave of internationalisation in Simmel research is to be observed. Under the acronym of *Red Simmel*, a Simmelian network has been established in Latin America that is very active with different conferences and publications in Spanish (www.redsimmel.org/; Díaz, 2015; Sabido-Ramos, 2007; Vernik & Borisonik, 2016). Furthermore, *Simmel Studies* has been relaunched as a peer-reviewed journal under the leadership of Enrico Campo, Gregor Fitzi, Vincenzo Mele, and Claudia Portioli (www.erudit.org/en/journals/sst/).

In summary, as in previous years, Simmel's theoretical achievement is nowadays always being rediscovered somewhere, while it is equally neglected elsewhere. This fluid situation raises the provocative question about the pertinence of Simmel's oeuvre in the 21st century. After the end of the Cold War, the world is in a much more undefined, uncertain, and conflict-prone situation. In this context, it became difficult to explain social reality simply from the viewpoint of the sociological paradigms of reification or rationalisation. Apparently, a global liquefaction of normative orders is taking place. Yet, beyond Zygmunt Bauman's diagnosis (2000), tendencies can also be observed to establish 'new', yet in some cases old or at times quite restrictive orders of social reality. A condition of 'solid liquidity' seems to characterise the development of societies that rapidly alternate from phases of liquefaction to periods of rigidity (Fitzi, 2016). Intermittent processes of sociation with strong spatiotemporal delimitations in validity and legitimacy permeate social reality, so that an overall shifting of normative orders becomes dominant (Fitzi, 2015). As distinctive aspects of modernity, the forces of capitalism, economic and financial crises, state power, war, and migration persist. Yet their character gains a higher level of complexity. Simmel's multidimensional oeuvre delivers a number of interpretative keys to deal with this complexity. He painted a multifaceted portrait of the modern age and captured the rapid societal change characterising the transition to the 20th century.

These achievements of Simmel's reflective analyses, along with his sociological, philosophical, and culture critical theory building defines his actuality and furnishes us with different analytical instruments to understand our present era. The task of the present handbook is to offer insights into the richness of the different research areas that start from Simmel's work and focus on very different domains of culture and society. The main emphasis of the project is to concentrate not solely on Simmel's sociological work, but to show what effect his reflections have on various areas of interest. This approach is no coincidence; rather, it is implied by the transformation of international Simmel research in recent decades. This has led to a growing number of high-quality studies that rediscover and shed light on the relevance of Simmel's ideas, not only as a sociologist, but also as a philosopher and as a theorist of culture, literature, theatre, and art.

The *Routledge International Handbook of Simmel Studies* presents a survey of cutting-edge Simmel research by compiling the contributions of leading specialists who have published outstanding research in this field, often in the form of treatises, or whose forthcoming work on Simmel was originally evaluated at conferences and in journal articles. The handbook therefore dedicates special sections to Simmel's oeuvre with particular relevance for the scientific fields in which his importance has become established. Furthermore, the handbook aims to document the paths that Simmel reception took in various regions of the world, so making him a global and multifaceted classical author. The handbook is organised into eight thematic sections that each have the scope to reflect a range of different approaches and contributions. The eight sections are: (1) Biography. (2) Sociology. (3) Philosophy. (4) Art and aesthetics. (5) Literature and theatre. (6) Essayism and critical theory. (7) Topics of debate. (8) Lines of reception. This structure follows the pattern of development of Simmel research to give an appropriate reflection of current research as well as to draw attention to the potential for further analysis and future work.

The handbook's aim is to present the diverse views within a coherent framework of research. Moreover, it seeks in the current *lingua franca* to facilitate access to the complex and often fragmented Simmel research that is invariably in the form of monograph publications rather than in journals, as well as being available in several languages that are not widely accessible. In comparison to existing handbooks, it offers an interdisciplinary approach to the different, often disparate strands of research on Simmel's theoretical heritage. The objective, as far as possible, is to reflect the manifold viewpoints that Simmel's work currently gives rise to. On the one hand, this approach is to present the Simmelian research community with a status report on the complexity of its discourse and to serve as a basis for its future development. On the other hand, the handbook is intended to offer students, teaching staff, and researchers an introductory reference work about the different streams of Simmel's oeuvre that is now available thanks to the Georg Simmel edition that incorporates his collected writings, letters, and biographical documents.

Biography

Otthein Rammstedt's life work should have culminated in a major biographical study about Georg Simmel and his entourage. However, the work on the Simmel edition lasted longer than planned for various reasons. Subsequently, Rammstedt's declining health did not allow for a renewed and consistent endeavour to contribute a definitive account of Simmel's life. The task of presenting Simmel's biography thus falls to a new generation of researchers. Gregor Fitzi's chapter on 'Simmel's life: An unexplored continent' presents the sources, as well as highlights the difficulties and the value of a further comprehensive work on Simmel's biography. New avenues of enquiry open up thanks to the fact that the last volume of the Simmel edition (GSG 24) contains a collection of documents about Simmel's life, while volumes 22 and 23 present the letters as well as short biographies of Simmel's correspondents. The places, the networks, and the lives of prominent personalities who influenced Simmel, can be identified and inquired into. Furthermore, many additional sources, testimonies, and documents about Simmel and his contemporaries can be explored. At the same time, the traditional mythologies can be evaluated with regard to the whereabouts of the lost legacy of Simmel's estate.

Sociology

After decades of recurrent exclusion, disregard, or oblivion, Simmel nowadays counts as one of the 'classics of sociology'. Accordingly, research on Simmel's sociology increasingly follows new avenues of inquiry. In his chapter on 'Simmel's resonance with contemporary sociological debates' Olli Pyyhtinen gives a comprehensive account of the many different ways in which Simmel's ideas play a role for current trends in sociological research. Focusing in particular on economic sociology, urban sociology, and sociology of space, as well as relational sociology, the chapter looks at how new waves of scholarship have stressed the confluence of Simmel's sociological and philosophical concerns, thus making possible not only 'philosophical sociology' but also 'sociological philosophy'. This chapter addresses one of the most intriguing innovative research paths that looks set to pave the way for future work. Davide Ruggieri's 'Relations, forms, and the representation of the social life: Georg Simmel and the challenge of relational sociology as *Lebenssoziologie*' reconstructs the growing interest in Simmel's contribution to relational studies. Yet the dual character of Simmel's sociological theory as 'relational' and 'relationist' underpins the meaning of relation not only as a form of social reality. The chapter thus explores the potential to establish an innovative '*Lebenssoziologie*' that intertwines with contemporary sociological trends, such as presented by Latour, Castells, and Luhmann. Ruggieri concludes with an evaluation of Simmel's contribution to an 'ontology of social emergence', including its ethical implications. In 'Boundaries as relations: Georg Simmel's relational theory of boundaries', Natalia Cantó-Milà examines the theorising about boundaries, borders, limits, and thresholds that accompanied Simmel's whole life and oeuvre. The chapter underlines the metaphorical quality of these notions that serve to approach the limits of the forms of association; yet also of the processes of individualisation, of life and love, and even of the emerging discipline of sociology. Relational boundaries set limits within and between the most diverse societal phenomena. The reconstruction of Simmel's relational theorisation of boundaries, as creators of proximity and distance, openings and closures, thus delivers a set of interpretative keys to analyse the current rapid transformation of social reality. With 'The actuality of a sociological research programme', Gregor Fitzi focuses on the contribution that Simmel gives to a consistent theory of modern society in both the 20th and 21st century. Three main aspects of Simmel's sociological reflection come to the fore. First the analysis of social differentiation that, in contrast to Durkheim, decidedly focuses on the interaction between processes of societal differentiation and individualisation. Then the explanation of the intertwining of these two aspects thanks to a theory of social integration through 'cultural work', which becomes an integral part of Simmel's 'sociological epistemology'. Finally, a theory of the 'qualitative differentiation' of complex societies.

Philosophy

The reflection on Simmel's meaning for philosophy in the 20th century as well as today is the most rapidly growing domain of research in the field of Simmel studies. In 'Relativism: a theoretical and practical philosophical programme', Matthieu Amat retraces the contours of Simmel's well-structured philosophical thought that we sometimes have to read through the lines of his works. The chapter identifies the concepts of relation, interaction, and exchange as the essential core of his philosophical research programme, whose study remains largely neglected, although Simmel explicitly defended it as a 'relativist philosophy'. According to Amat, what connects the different sociological, epistemological, and metaphysical aspects of Simmel's work is his practical intention, so that 'relativism' ultimately means a specific way of philosophising, on whose basis a new 'philosophical culture' can develop. According to Denis Thouard the topicality of Simmel's work lies in its sense for reciprocity, including its complexities and balances. Understanding his philosophy, which he never abandoned while claiming the autonomy of sociology, thus means appreciating his specific 'art of complicating things'. Simmel thinks of the innovation of forms, while knowing how to consider the legacy of tradition, which he theorises from a renewed understanding of the 'objective spirit'. By combining the approaches of historical and 'objective' understanding, Simmel thus helps to break the impasses of hermeneutic philosophy. The chapter shows how this open dialectic manages to avoid the classical pitfalls of scepticism and relativism. Andrea Borsari focuses attention on 'Georg Simmel, Hans Blumenberg, and philosophical anthropology'. In recent decades, a growing interest has emerged in the anthropological propensity of Hans Blumenberg's work. Yet very little attention has been paid to the role that Blumenberg reserves for Georg Simmel's importance in the construction of a philosophical anthropology. Borsari's study helps to fill this gap, by reconstructing the aspects of Simmel's philosophical anthropology that influenced Blumenberg's reflection. They concern the metaphors of money and life; the critique of the friend-enemy distinction; the gestures and myths; the rhetoric and theory of non-conceptuality; and the antinomic character of both philosophers' thought. Gregor Fitzi's analysis of 'Simmel's late life metaphysics' points out the particularity of the 'life and forms' metaphor characterising the late work, and shows its structural relationship to previous research on sociological epistemology. For Simmel, developing a metaphysics capable of presenting itself as science in the Kantian sense meant taking into account the transformation of the modern conditions of life. Philosophical anthropology was no longer possible, unless it was on the basis of a theory of the fragmentation of personality through modern societal differentiation. The path to philosophy thus leads through the understanding of social complexity. The chapter shows how Simmel developed a philosophical approach that designed the only possible metaphysics on this basis.

Art and aesthetics

Simmel's thought has been often criticised for its supposed aestheticised character and lack of systematic method. The research increasingly addresses this kind of misunderstanding. An analysis of the 'artistic' approach in Simmel's gnoseological conception can outline his implicit method of analysing cultural and social phenomena. This is the purpose of Claudia Portioli's chapter on 'Art and knowledge in Simmel's thought and writing style'. It addresses Simmel's genre-related choices and writing style, in order to explore their relationship with his methodological and gnoseological thought. It thus highlights the links between specific aspects of Simmel's theory of knowledge and elements of early German Romanticism. On the other hand, it shows the parallels between Simmel's gnoseological and methodological practice and recent epistemological approaches in human sciences. Barbara Carnevali's and Andrea Pinotti's chapter on 'Social aesthetics' moves in a similar direction. It reconstructs the consistency in Simmel's analysis of the social concretion of aesthetics. The starting point is the role that the senses play in mediating and qualifying social interactions, by giving them a specific 'aesthetic colouring'. The sensory dimension of social recognition is illustrated, on the one hand, with reference to Simmel's sociology of basic sense impressions. On the other hand, the chapter enquires into Simmel's contribution to the reconstruction of the peculiar aesthetic environment of modernity. This is exemplary in urban environments and with regard to the rise of certain fundamental dynamics of contemporary society, such as marketing, consumerism and social media. Ingo Meyer dedicates his chapter 'Philosophy of art' to Simmel's more theoretical aesthetics. In opposition to Nietzsche's or Dilthey's aesthetics approaches, Simmel's aesthetic writings deal with a multiplicity of topics. They range from lifeworld phenomena to the work of artists like Michelangelo, Rodin, Goethe, or Stefan George. Yet the later Simmel develops a specific 'philosophy of art' that is concerned with metaphysical problems. On the one hand, he applies the concept of 'individual law' to the exemplary character of artist's personalities. On the other hand, in a hidden romantic tradition, he understands aesthetic experience as supplementary to religion and science as a means more necessary than ever for curing the pathologies of modern societies. Thomas Kemple's chapter on 'Framing, painting, seeing: Simmel's *Rembrandt* and the sense of modernity' shows in detail how the epochal meaning of the artist's work and personality emerges in Simmel's analysis. His late monograph, *Rembrandt* (1916), does not offer a portrait of the artist's life and times, nor analysis of the formal elements of particular paintings; rather it presents a philosophical meditation on the inner value, unique truth, and lived experience of 'the phenomenon Rembrandt'. Kemple reconstructs how, in Simmel's assessment, Rembrandt's paintings plumb the unfathomable depths of the human soul, opening up unexplored dimensions of perception while imagining new outlooks on life. Hence, the chapter places Simmel's study in the context of his aesthetics of modernity and metaphysics of individuality.

Literature and theatre

Simmel's oeuvre not only offers an interpretative key to conduct sociological and critical analyses of literature as an expression of contemporary culture. It also comprises an original output of literary essays, the '*Momentbilder sub specie aeternitatis*', on highly diverse topics. This particular focus represents one of the most innovative developments in Simmel studies. Monika Tokarzewska's chapter on 'Literary practice and immanent literary theory' is devoted to the literary texts of Georg Simmel. It shows the way in which he navigates between sociology and literature, treating each discipline autonomously. For Simmel, literature is a field of experimentation and a laboratory of thought, where he seeks a new perspective on social reality in its broadest sense. Thereby, he also searches for a new language. Literature is not just an addition to sociology, or to the philosophy of culture. For Simmel, it is governed by its own laws, and thus it allows for the boundaries of imagination and language to be broadened. Paola Giacomoni examines 'The Goethean heritage in Simmel's work'. The chapter aims to indicate the extent of Goethe's presence in Georg Simmel's thinking. Yet it not only evaluates the presence of the educated bourgeois ideas characterising the academic background of the time. It explores the importance of what Simmel called the 'Idea Goethe': the concept of truth, its individual character, and its pragmatic value. Furthermore, Giacomoni examines the question of 'visual thinking' and the notion of 'liminal phenomena' in the works of both authors. The investigation thus suggests a way to determine the significance of 'German classicism' for the formation of Simmel's critical view of modern society. François Thomas' innovative study on 'Simmel: the actor and his roles' focuses on the fact that Simmel is one of the few philosophers to have taken a close interest in the art of acting, by assigning it a central role in his philosophy of art. Yet Simmel's questioning of the actor goes beyond the mere framework of reflection on art and appears as a central theme in the intersection of all the major issues he addresses also in sociology. On the one hand, the reflection on the actor's art mobilises all the conceptual tools that Simmel develops in his other works. On the other hand, the relationship of the individual to his roles, the difficulty of playing a role that does not correspond to one's personality, the theatricalisation of social life in metropolises are themes that feature at the centre of both his theoretical sociology and his analyses of modernity.

Essayism and critical theory

Simmel's approach to social reality and writing has played an important role for the development of critical reflection on modernity and its expression through new languages and journalistic means. Yet his legacy has often also been neglected. Barbara Thériault's 'Georg Simmel and the "newspaper sociology" of the 1920s and 1930s' traces an important reconstruction of Simmel's heritage in the early phases of newspaper essayism. Drawing on feuilleton articles by several authors – among others Siegfried Kracauer, Kurt Tucholsky, Joseph Roth, and Egon Erwin Kisch – the chapter reconstructs what could be labelled a 'newspaper sociology'. Comparing this journalistic production with Simmel's shorter texts, the hidden history of a specific type of sociological writing comes to the fore. It is a style of analysis that thrived beyond the sometimes narrow realm of academic institutions and this section of the handbook reappraises such contributions. Vincenzo Mele's 'Georg Simmel and critical theory' retraces the heritage of Simmel's work within and beyond the so-called 'Frankfurt School'. Adorno's philosophical and sociological essayism, and Kracauer's and Benjamin's culture critical studies would have been impossible without Simmel. However, post-Weimar *Kulturkritiker* always denied the recognition he deserved. Jürgen Habermas' later acknowledgement of Simmel as '*Zeitdiagnostiker*' failed, too, to redress the balance: Simmel is the only classic of sociology to have been excluded from the *Theory of Communicative Action*. The situation improved with the third and fourth generation of critical theorists like Axel Honneth and Rahel Jaeggi. They included Simmel in their theory building. Yet the nature of Simmel's contribution to critical theory remains an open question.

Topics of debate

Simmel's ideas, approaches and theories attract increasing attention in various interdisciplinary debates, including discourses on freedom, religion, nationalism and cosmopolitanism, as well as the modern pathologies of life. The chapters in this section sketch Simmel's position with reference to those debates. Freedom is a crucial theme of modern self-reflection at the intersection between political theory and social sciences. Monica Martinelli's chapter 'Freedom: an open debate' retraces Simmel's contribution to the understanding of this category. Simmel insists on the distinction between the anthropological and the moral issue of liberty. A dual line of reception can thus be reconstructed that reconnects Simmel's work to the recent reflection on liberty, above all by Isaiah Berlin and Zygmunt Bauman. Berlin focuses on the anthropological dimension of liberty and insists on the difference between its negative and positive understanding. Bauman, instead, takes up the centrality of responsibility as the basis of freedom. Simmel's approach can establish a renewed dialectics between these positions. Together with Durkheim and Weber, Simmel builds the trinity of classical sociology of religion. Yet the importance of his contribution to the sociological understanding of religion is still underestimated. Volkhard Krech's chapter on 'Georg Simmel's theory of religion' reconstructs the essential aspects of his reflection on the topic, by distinguishing between his approach to religion in sociology, cultural studies, and philosophy of life. According to Simmel, religion is a sociocultural form that deals with the relationship between social action and social structure. Hence, its emergence has to be understood in analogy to other social phenomena, by distinguishing between the fluid 'religioid' social processes and 'religion' as an established social form in an ideal world of its own. One of the most controversial aspects in Simmel's oeuvre remains his attitude to World War I. Patrick Watier's chapter on 'Georg Simmel: war, nation, and Europe' is dedicated to the critical analysis of this attitude. In 1914, Simmel took a clear stand for the country he considered his homeland just as Durkheim also did in France. The chapter aims to show how a convinced European like Simmel argues in this situation. The reconstruction underlines the importance of emotions and the identification with a national entity that Simmel seemed to share. Yet, to understand Simmel's position, which is not necessarily to endorse it, the chapter also seeks to differentiate between his adhesion to a spiritual (i.e. juridical) entity, on the one hand, and his adhesion to the whole 'being' of an 'imagined community', on the other. With reference to nationalism, Simmel's position on the issue of cosmopolitanism, above all during World War I, seems to be located at the other extreme of the conceptual scale. Austin Harrington dedicates his chapter to 'Simmel's cosmopolitanism'. According to Harrington, it is undoubtedly right to speak of Simmel as a 'cosmopolitan' thinker and in some sense as a theorist of 'cosmopolitanism' in European social thought. Yet, one issue arises. In the few places in which Simmel explicitly deploys the term 'cosmopolitanism', his tone is largely hostile. This requires clarification. During the years of the Great War, Simmel reacts against what might be seen as certain 'thin', 'abstract', or hollowed-out appropriations of cosmopolitan discourse. Otherwise, however, in his work as a whole, he upholds a vision of universalising normative values against the stigmatisation of 'strangers'. The chapter considers both aspects and tries to take stock of the issue. One of the widest debated aspects of Simmel's work is his 'seismographic contribution' to the diagnostic understanding of the modern world. With his chapter on the 'Economic pathologies of life', Arthur Bueno gives a systematic account of Simmel's typology of the hypertrophied and pathological action patterns that surge with the expansion of the monetary economy. He discusses its relevance for the diagnosis of modern society and its forms of psychological suffering until today. The chapter therefore shows how Simmel's early thesis of the colonisation of ends by means – connected to his characterisation of modern experience as 'neurasthenic' – maintains an acute diagnostic capacity for the analysis of the developments in social pathologies in modern times.

Lines of reception

Simmel's work was largely read as a contribution to sociology and its reception on the American continent had specific and complex characteristics that strongly shape perceptions until today. With their chapter on 'Simmel's American legacy revisited', Daniel Silver and Milos Brocic examine the history of Simmel's reception in the United States. After a survey of previous accounts of this legacy, their chapter highlights trends since the 1970s using a mix of computational and traditional methods. If the fundamental view is that Simmel is primarily appreciated for his formalism in sociology, this basic attitude is approached in quite different ways, and claims are often made by competing schools of thought. The reception of Simmel's work more as philosophical sociology remains of marginal relevance for the discipline, although it receives greater attention in cultural studies. In the long run, while a broadly shared interpretation of Simmel's work remains elusive, his legacy continues to be vital. Having established this overall picture, further in-depth analyses give an insight into specific developments. Gary D. Jaworski's chapter entitled 'Goffman, Schutz, and the "secret of the other": on the American sociological reception of Simmel's *"das Geheimnis des Anderen"*' focuses on a particularly significant line of the US American Simmel reception. By employing textual analysis and archival records, which are now available, the essay sheds new light on the ways in which Simmel's ideas on secrecy entered (or did not enter) American sociological thought. Goffman shared Shils's view of secrets as 'destructive'. Yet, his attitude also reveals an affinity with Schutz, who advanced a more positive view of secrets, such as expressed in Simmel's notion of the 'secret of the other'. The case study shows in an exemplary fashion the erratic and selective attitude of the US American Simmel reception.

The reception of Simmel's work in Latin America is characterised by a completely different history. Today, this is one of the regions with the most intensive expansion of Simmel studies. Esteban Vernik reconstructs its historical development in the chapter 'Traces of Simmel in Latin America: modernity, nation, and memory'. In 1923, only five years after the German publication, Simmel's 'Conflict of modern culture' was translated into Spanish in Argentina. The most interesting aspect of its reception was, however, that the Simmelian categories were received in a vitalist vein to establish a definition for the concept of nation that suited Latin American societies. The chapter reconstructs the way in which a fertile field of studies on the idea of nation and memory thus developed under the influence of Simmel's sociological theory until the 1960s when the structural-functionalist foundation of sociology prevailed. Yet, the chapter also shows how the Simmelian approach gained renewed relevance in the 1990s when the reflection on the dictatorship and the need to remember its victims imposed itself on Latin American societies.

Many illuminating contributions to cutting-edge research in Simmel studies were planned for inclusion in the present handbook. Several such proposals, however, could not be realised for myriad reasons within this current collective publication and will undoubtedly make welcome additions to future research. On this note, the outlook is promising for a vigorous development of Simmel studies in the years ahead.

Quotation criteria

The handbook refers throughout to Simmel's original texts – now available in the *Georg Simmel Gesamtausgabe* – by using the acronym GSG followed by the volume number and relevant pages. Scholars who are actively engaged in the global Simmel research community can easily refer from these original texts to the respective translations in their native language. The English translations of Simmel's works are very fragmented, often incomplete and with few exceptions not consistently aligned with the established text of the GSG edition, therefore the following citation strategy has been adopted. The citation of the GSG edition is supplemented with further reference to complete book translations in English or to established single essays editions. Wherever the original English translations are available, as published in volume 18 of the GSG that comprises Simmel's English publications (*Georg Simmel: englischsprachige Veröffentlichungen 1893–1910*), reference is made to GSG 18. For the localisation of further Simmel texts in English translation, we recommend Thomas Kemple's excellent correspondence catalogue to the GSG edition texts published in *Simmel Studies*, vol. 2018/2 (Kemple, 2018).

References

Amat, Matthieu (2018). *Le relationnisme philosophique de Georg Simmel: Une idée de la culture*. Paris: Honoré Champion éditeur.

Banfi, Antonio ([1932] 1986). Il pensiero filosofico e pedagogico di Georg Simmel. In A. Banfi, *Opere, VI: Pedagogia e filosofia dell'educazione*, G. M. Bertin & L. Schirolo (Eds.) (pp. 127–173). Reggio d'Emilia: Istituto Antonio Banfi.

Bauman, Zygmunt (2000). *Liquid Modernity*. Cambridge: Polity.

Blumenberg, Hans (1976). Geld oder Leben. Eine metaphorologische Studie zur Konsistenz der Philosophie Georg Simmels. In Hannes Böhringer & Karlfried Gründer (Eds.), *Ästhetik und Soziologie um die Jahrhundertwende: Georg Simmel* (pp. 121–134). Frankfurt/M.: Klostermann.

Bohr, J., Goslar, T.-F., Hartung, G., & Koenig, H. (2020). *Simmel-Handbuch – Leben-Werk-Wirkung*. Stuttgart: Metzler-Verlag.

Böhringer, Hannes, & Gründer, Karlfried (1976) (Eds.). *Ästhetik und Soziologie um die Jahrhundertwende: Georg Simmel*. Frankfurt/M.: Klostermann.

Bouglé, Célestin (1896). *Les sciences sociales en Allemagne : Les méthodes actuelles*. Paris: F. Alcan.

Braungart, W., & Kaufmann, K. (2006). *Essayismus um 1900*. Heidelberg: Winter.

Bukharin, N. (2012). *Historical materialism: A system of sociology*. London: Routledge.

Cantó-Milà, Natàlia (2005). *A sociological theory of value: Georg Simmel's sociological relationism*. Bielefeld: Transcript.

Coser, Lewis A. (1956). *The functions of social conflict*. London: Routledge and Kegan Paul.

Coser, Lewis A. (Ed.) (1965). *Georg Simmel: Makers of modern social science*. Engelwood Cliffs, NJ: Prentice-Hall.

Dahme, Hans-Jürgen (1981). *Soziologie als exakte Wissenschaft: 1. Georg Simmels Ansatz und seine Bedeutung in der gegenwärtigen Soziologie; 2. Simmels Soziologie im Grundriß*. Stuttgart: Enke.

Dahme, Hans-Jürgen, & Rammstedt, Otthein (Eds.) (1995). *Georg Simmel und die Moderne: Neue Interpretationen und Materialien*. Frankfurt/M.: Suhrkamp.

Dal Lago, Alessandro (1994). *Il conflitto della modernità: il pensiero di Georg Simmel*. Bologna: Il Mulino.

Deroche-Gurcel, Lilyane, & Watier, Patrick (Eds.) (2002). *La Sociologie de Georg Simmel (1908): Éléments actuels de modélisation sociale*. Paris: PUF.

Díaz, Gilberto (Ed.) (2015). *Una actitud del espíritu: Interpretaciones en torno a Georg Simmel*. Bogotá: Editorial de la Facultad de Ciencias Humanas de la Universidad Nacional de Colombia.

Featherstone, Michael (Ed.) (1991). *Theory, Culture and Society*, 8(3), August 1981.

Fitzi, Gregor (2002). *Soziale Erfahrung und Lebensphilosophie. Georg Simmels Beziehung zu Henri Bergson*. Konstanz: UVK.

Fitzi, Gregor (2015). *Grenzen des Konsenses. Rekonstruktion einer Theorie transnormativer Vergesellschaftung*. Weilerwist: Velbrück.

Fitzi, Gregor (2016). Modernity as solid liquidity. Simmel's life-sociology. In T. Kemple & O. Pyyhtinen (Eds.), *The Anthem companion to Georg Simmel* (pp. 59–80). London: Anthem.

Fitzi, Gregor (2019). *The challenge of modernity: Simmel's sociological theory*. London: Routledge.

Freund, Julien (1983). *Sociologie du conflit*. Paris: PUF.

Frisby, David (1981). *Sociological impressionism. A reassessment of Georg Simmel's social theory*. London: Heinemann.

Frisby, David (1985). *Fragments of modernity. Theories of modernity in the works of Simmel, Kracauer and Benjamin*. Oxford: Polity.

Frisby, David (1992). *Simmel and since: Essays on Georg Simmel's social theory*. London: Routledge.

Gassen, Kurt, & Landmann, Michael (1958) (Eds.). *Buch des Dankes an Georg Simmel. Briefe, Erinnerungen, Bibliographie*. Berlin: Duncker & Humblot.

Goodstein, Elisabeth S. (2017). *Georg Simmel and the disciplinary imaginary*. Stanford: Stanford University Press.

Harrington, Austin, & Kemple, Thomas (Eds.) (2012). *Theory, Culture and Society, Annual revue (Special Issue on Georg Simmel), 29*(7/8).

Jankélévitch, Vladimir (1925). Georg Simmel. Philosophie de la vie. *Revue de métaphysique et de morale, 32*, 213-257, 303-386.

Jaworski, Gary D. (1997). *Georg Simmel and the American prospect.* Albany: State University of New York Press.

Jay, M. (1996). *The dialectical imagination: A history of the Frankfurt School and the Institute of Social Research.* Berkeley, CA: University of California Press.

Kemple, Thomas (2018). Bibliography of Simmel's writings in English translation. *Simmel Studies, 22*(2/18), 149–165.

Kemple, Thomas (2019). *Simmel.* Newark: Polity Press.

Kemple, Thomas, & Pyyhtinen, Olli (Eds.) (2016). *The Anthem companion to Georg Simmel.* London and New York: Anthem Press.

Köhnke, Klaus Christian (1996). *Der junge Simmel in Theoriebeziehungen und sozialen Bewegungen.* Frankfurt/M.: Suhrkamp.

Krech, Volkhard (1998). *Georg Simmels Religionstheorie.* Tübingen: Mohr Siebeck.

Levine, Donald N. (1957). *Simmel and Parsons: Two approaches to the study of society.* New York: Arno Press.

Levine, Donald N., Carter, Ellwood B., & Gorman, Eleanor M. (1976). Simmel's influence on American sociology. In H. Böhringer & K. Gründer (Eds.), *Ästhetik und Soziologie um die Jahrhundertwende, Georg Simmel* (pp. 175–228). Frankfurt/M: Klostermann.

Mamelet, Albert (1914). *Le relativisme philosophique chez Georg Simmel.* Paris: Alcan.

Meyer, Ingo (2017). *Georg Simmels Ästhetik: Autonomiepostulat und soziologische Referenz.* Weilerswist: Velbrück Wissenschaft.

Müller, Hans-Peter, & Reitz, Tilman (2018). *Simmel-Handbuch: Begriffe, Hauptwerke, Aktualität.* Frankfurt/M.: Suhrkamp.

Park, Robert E., & Burgess, Ernest W. (1922). *Introduction to the science of sociology.* Chicago, IL: University of Chicago Press.

Parsons, Talcott (1949). *The structure of social action: A study in social theory with special reference to a group of recent European writers.* Glencoe: The Free Press.

Portioli, Claudia (2012). Les chemins de la pensée de G. Simmel en Italie. In *Réciprocités sociales. Lectures de Simmel.* Special Issue of *Sociologie et sociétés, 44*(2), 263–288.

Pyyhtinen, Olli (2010). *Simmel and 'the Social'.* Basingstoke: Palgrave Macmillan.

Pyyhtinen, Olli (2018). *The Simmelian legacy: A science of relations.* London: Palgrave, Macmillan Education.

Rammstedt, Otthein (1986). *Deutsche Soziologie 1933–1945. Die Normalität einer Anpassung.* Frankfurt/M.: Suhrkamp.

Rammstedt, Otthein (1998). Les relations entre Durkheim et Simmel dans le contexte de l'affaire Dreyfus. *L'année sociologique, 48*(1), 139–162.

Rammstedt, Otthein (2003). *Georg Simmels Philosophie des Geldes: Aufsätze und Materialien.* Frankfurt/M.: Suhrkamp.

Rammstedt, Otthein (2015). Zur Geschichte der Georg Simmel Gesamtausgabe. In *Georg Simmel Gesamtausgabe* vol. 24 (pp. 1039–1090). Frankfurt/M.: Suhrkamp.

Rammstedt, Otthein, & Watier, Patrick (1992). *Georg Simmel et les sciences humaines.* (Actes du Colloque G. Simmel et les sciences humaines, 14–15 septembre 1988). Paris: Méridiens Klincksieck.

Rol, Cécile, & Papilloud, Christian (Eds.) (2009). *Soziologie als Möglichkeit. 100 Jahre Georg Simmels Untersuchungen über die Formen der Vergesellschaftung,* Wiesbaden: VS-Verlag.

Sabido-Ramos, Olga (Ed.) (2007). *Georg Simmel. Una revisión contemporánea.* Barcelona: UAM-Azcapotzalco/Anthropos.

Simmel, Georg (1950). *The sociology of Georg Simmel.* Translated, edited, and with an introduction by Kurt H. Wolff. Glencoe, IL: Free Press.

Simmel, Georg (1959). *Georg Simmel, 1858–1918. A collection of essays, with translations and a bibliography.* Ed. by Kurt H. Wolff, with a portrait. Columbus: Ohio State University Press.

Simmel, Georg (1971). *Georg Simmel on individuality and social forms.* Ed. by Donald Levine. Chicago, IL: The University of Chicago Press.

Sontheimer, Kurt (1992). *Antidemokratisches Denken in der Weimarer Republik. Die politischen Ideen des deutschen Nationalismus zwischen 1918 und 1933.* Munich: Deutscher Taschenbuch.

Stölting, Erhard (1986). *Akademische Soziologie in der Weimarer Republik*. Berlin: Duncker & Humblot.

Thouard, Denis (Ed.) (2020). *Les enfants de Simmel*. Belval: Circé.

Thouard, Denis, & Zimmermann, Bénédicte (2017). *Simmel, le parti-pris du tiers*. Paris: CNRS Éditions.

Tyrell, Hartmann, Rammstedt, Otthein, & Meyer, Ingo (Eds.) (2011). *Georg Simmels große Soziologie: Eine kritische Sichtung nach hundert Jahren*. Bielefeld: Transcript Verlag.

Vernik, Esteban, & Borisonik, Hernán (Eds.) (2016). *Georg Simmel, un siglo después. Actualidad y perspectivas*. Ciudad Autónoma de Buenos Aires: Universidad de Buenos, Aires. Instituto de Investigaciones Gino Germani.

Vierkandt, Alfred (1923). *Gesellschaftslehre. Hauptprobleme der philosophischen Soziologie*. Stuttgart: Enke.

Watier, Patrick (Ed.) (1986). *Georg Simmel: La sociologie et l'expérience du monde moderne*. Paris: Méridiens Klincksieck.

Wiese, Leopold v. (1924–1929). *Allgemeine Soziologie als Lehre von den Beziehungen und Beziehungsgebilden der Menschen*. 2 vol. Munich and Leipzig: Duncker & Humblot.

PART I

Biography

1

SIMMEL'S LIFE

An unexplored continent

Gregor Fitzi

Introduction

A comprehensive Simmel biography has yet to be written and this is mainly due to the fact that the source material is too fragmentary. It is valuable to reflect on some factors that explain this situation. Firstly, hardly any information exists about Simmel's life before high-school age. We can rely only on one retrospective description in Simmel's curriculum vitae that introduces his habilitation procedure in 1883. This refers to his secondary-level studies at the Friedrichwerdersches Gymnasium in Berlin (GSG 24, p. 194). Otherwise, Simmel's son Hans gives us some insights into the family history, so some evidence can be localised about the ancestors (Simmel, [1941/42] 2008, p. 10 f.; GSG 24, pp. 649-656). The extensive research for Simmel's *Gesamtausgabe* also uncovered a further series of documents which are now presented in the final volume of the collected works (GSG 24, pp. 141-459).

Simmel was born on 1 March 1858. He lived at the centre of the expanding metropolis Berlin, at the corner of the Friedrich and Leipziger Straße (GSG 24, p. 153), and together with his parents until his father passed away in 1874 (GSG 24, p. 160). Afterwards, he most likely lived with his mother and some of the older siblings. Georg Simmel was the youngest of seven children (Landmann, 1958, p. 11; Simmel, [1941/42] 2008, pp. 12-15). In 1890, Simmel inherited a small estate, which permitted him to start a family and marry Gertrud Kinel (GSG 24, pp. 217, 223). Julius Friedländer, a good family friend, and later presumably the new partner of Simmel's widowed mother, became Georg's guardian after 1874 (ibid.). He was the owner of the publishing house Peters, and the inventor of a procedure to print sheet music in a more convenient way than was traditionally possible (Simmel, [1941/42] 2008, p. 17 f.). 'Uncle Dol', as he was called at home, accumulated a fortune, and decided to leave it in part to the youngest of Simmel's siblings, whose intellectual potential he appreciated.

Simmel's wife, Gertrud Kinel, was a school friend of Sabine Graef, later Lepsius, the sister of Harald Graef, who studied with Simmel. She was a trained portrait painter who practised in Berlin (GSG 23, p. 1187; Landmann, 1958, p. 12; Rammstedt, 1994). From 1882 to 1914, Georg lived in Berlin. From 1890 he was together with Gertrud Simmel and, as of 7 April 1891, with their son Hans (GSG 24, p. 226). Yet they moved about

11 times from one apartment to another (GSG 24, pp. 659-661). This leaves some uncertainty about the reasons for this repeated relocation. One thesis is that, at a young age, Simmel was accustomed to live temporarily in newly built apartments, which became an object for Uncle Dol's real estate investments, in order to check whether everything was in order before realising his return on the investment. This tendency may have led Simmel later to prefer new housing estates where the rents were initially lower. At least, this could also explain the gradual shift to the suburbs that culminated with the move to the scholars' and artists' colony of Berlin West End (Simmel, [1941/42] 2008, p. 49 f.).

The Simmels' constant domestic changes kept in check the amount of household goods that they brought with them, so letters and other documents were probably gradually disposed of. During the Strasbourg period, from summer 1914 to autumn 1918, the family lived in the same apartment at Sternwartstraße 17, today Rue de l'Observatoire, 17 (GSG 24, p. 661). Simmel died here on 26 September 2018. He was buried in Strasbourg's municipal cemetery (Gassen & Landmann, 1958, p. 288; Portioli, 2006; GSG 24, p. 459). After the 11 November 1918 armistice to mark the end of World War I, Simmel's wife Gertrud followed the outflow of remaining German residents and was obliged to leave Strasbourg abruptly around 16 December 1918 (GSG 24, p. 661), since Alsace was reintegrated into the territory of the French Republic. Similarly, when crossing Kehl bridge she could only bring back to Germany a modest part of her household.

Twenty years later, Simmel's son Hans was compelled to emigrate from Nazi Germany to escape anti-Semitic persecution (Simmel, 2008). In keeping with emigration regulations for Jewish citizens at that time, he packed the family's belongings into eight boxes, which should have been sent to the US after their departure from Hamburg's free-trading harbour. However, here we lose every trace of Simmel's estate (Kramme, 1992; Rammstedt, 2004). We do not know if the entire contents of the boxes were confiscated by the Gestapo and resold, as was common practice for the regime (Köhnke, 1996, p. 18; Kramme, 1992, p. 74; Landmann, 1958, p. 14), or if some boxes were burned during one of the many air raids.

Despite this adverse starting point, a number of witnesses and documents are at our disposal, and these may form the basis for a reconstruction of Simmel's biography. By relying on the available sources, Klaus Christian Köhnke provided one of the most complete reconstructions of the life and work of the 'young Simmel' (1996). His method could also be applied to the remaining periods of Simmel's life. In this respect, two main groups of resources should be remembered. On the one hand, there is an important corpus of witness accounts about Simmel, about his life and work, as well as his entourage. First and foremost, the miscellany of personal statements that Michael Landmann gathered in the *Buch des Dankes für Georg Simmel* to mark the centenary of Simmel's birth in 1958 (Gassen & Landmann, 1958) is still fundamental. Landmann's parents Julius and Edith Landmann-Kalischer were close friends of the Simmels in Berlin. Even if the family's archive, including Simmel's letters, were destroyed during World War II, Landmann could fall back on the family's oral anecdotes and memoirs and formulate a first sketch of the 'building stones' for a Simmel biography, which is still the point of departure for every bibliographical work (Landmann, 1958, p. 12). In addition, a most important source of information is the memoirs written by Simmel's son Hans (Simmel, [1941/42] 2008). Before fleeing from Nazi Germany, Hans Simmel wrote a sketch of the family's history using the available documents. Yet his manuscript went missing with the rest of the family's witness accounts on the way to the US. Later, as a physician who was aware that he was going to die because of the consequences of torture during his imprisonment in Dachau, he wrote a second version of his memoirs that is available to us (Landmann, 1958, p. 14).

The second main group of sources for analysis of Simmel's biography is constituted by the materials that are compiled in the complete edition of his works. In November 2015, 25 years after the inception of the ambitious project for publication of the collected works of Georg Simmel, the *Georg Simmel Gesamtausgabe* (GSG) was finally completed (for the history of the GSG cf.: Rammstedt, GSG 24, pp. 1039-1090; Köhnke, 1996, pp. 11-13). This achievement is due to the dedication of the editor-in-chief Otthein Rammstedt and his collaborators, above all Klaus Christian Köhnke, Rüdiger Kramme, and Angela Rammstedt. In this context the changing editorial assistants, and above all the main editors, explored all the possible leads that could reveal further sources of information about Simmel's widely dispersed publications, the letters and documents concerning his life. This workload preoccupied the edition's dedicated researchers in several archives around Europe, and also in Russia, Israel, and the USA. The outcome of the long-standing collective and joint work is presented in the final three volumes of the Simmel edition (GSG 22-24). In particular, volumes 22 and 23, containing the letters that include a biographical note on Simmel's correspondence partners, show how widespread the personal and intellectual networks were that Georg and Gertrud Simmel entertained. Furthermore, in volume 24, all the available documents about Simmel's life are presented, and a number of overviews are provided concerning Simmel's works, lectures, and places of residence. This treasure trove of information is now at the disposal of the scientific community and can become the starting point for different research enterprises. To present an overview of the main groups of the available information, the strategy here is to distinguish between the places, networks, and prominent personalities who influenced Simmel's life.

Moreover, the many different studies published by contemporaries and pupils provide another line of enquiry for Simmel's biography. These deal with the work, yet also with Simmel's status as a 'cultural-historical figure'. Among the noteworthy sources are Gertrud Kantorowicz's short intellectual portrait focusing on the late work in her introduction to Simmel's *Fragments from the Estate* (1923; GSG 20, pp. 473-479). Siegfried Kracauer proposed a sketch of Simmel's intellectual personality as a contribution to the interpretation of the spiritual life in modernity ([1919] 2004). For Simmel's centenary, Margarete Susman drew a portrait of Simmel's 'spiritual figure' that gives an idea of his personality and intellectual relationship to his pupils (Susman, 1959). In addition, a variety of autobiographies or autobiographical novels by individuals who belonged to Simmel's entourage deliver important information about the Simmels. These include Margarete Susman's late memoirs (1966), which in some ways offer the most complete record about Simmel's circle of pupils, who met at the weekly 'jour fixe' in his Berlin living room. Besides that, the two books by Gertrud Simmel's early friend Sabine Lepsius on Stefan George and on artistic life in Berlin around 1900 are fundamental to gain an understanding of the interconnection between the intellectual, literary, and artistic milieus of the West End district, where the Simmels also lived from 1901 (Lepsius, 1935, 1972). Berta Lask's novel, *Silence and Storm*, also deserves a mention, with its autobiographical background in which Max Weber, Emil Lask, and Georg Simmel appear as literary figures of the intellectual world in Heidelberg before World War I (1955). Finally, as Angela Rammstedt has reconstructed, Simmel emerges as a figure in many novels, lyrics, and theatre pieces, which depict the impressions that as widely different authors had of him such as Martin Buber, Michael Josef Eisler, Paul Ernst, Stefan George, Georg Hermann, Kurt Hiller, Margarete Susman, and Kurt Tucholsky (Rammstedt, 1999).

A further set of documents are the many obituaries that were published in 1918 and shortly afterwards (Cf. Gassen & Landmann, 1958, pp. 154-179). The most influential, of course, was Lukács's necrologue in *Pester Lloyd* on 2 October 1918, in which the keyword of 'Simmel's Impressionism' was coined (Lukács, 1991). Frischeisen-Köhler's obituary essay in the *Kant Studien* was also decisive; it established the tripartition of Simmel's work into a positivist, a neo-Kantian, and a life philosophical phase. This perspective was later reproduced uncritically in much of the secondary literature (1919/20).

Places

Simmel's birth certificate clearly states that his birthplace was the house on Leipzigerstraße 82 in Berlin (GSG 24, p. 153). The 'Berlin address book' of the time confirms the information about the family's residence. Hans Simmel relates that this was the house on the north-west side of the crossroads with the Friedrichstraße (Simmel, [1941/42] 2008, p. 16). Yet, the 1846 ground plan for Berlin, which can be consulted in the *Zentral- und Landesbibliothek Berlin*, locates house number 82 on the other side of the street, so the building's exact location still has to be verified. Simmel's father owned the chocolate factory Felix und Sarotti. He was apparently one of the first to bring the art of French confectionery to Berlin, so we must assume that he trained as a pastry chef in France or Switzerland. The company was registered as a supplier to the court (Simmel, [1941/42] 2008, p. 11). Yet, after some good years, the business started to go through a crisis and eventually went bankrupt (ibid., p. 16 f.). A question for further research could be to explore the history of the relationship between Simmel's father and his partners as well as the location of the (still existing) company within the economic landscape of the Prussian capital. Simmel's father apparently later became a building manager and the family started to move around from one apartment to another (GSG 24, p. 658). However, it remains unknown whom he worked for in this context.

In 1901, when Simmel was already a relatively well-known author and university lecturer, he and his wife and son moved to Berlin's West End district (Simmel, [1941/42] 2008, p. 49), first to Lindenallee 13 and from 1906 to Nußbaumallee 14 (GSG 24, p. 660). This was also the address of the family of the portrait painter, Reinhold Lepsius, who was a member of the Berlin Secession and whose wife Sabine was a study friend of Gertrud Simmel. Georg Simmel had already known Reinhold Lepsius for a long while and he was often a guest in his house. Whether or not Simmel was part of the Secession movement, and whether he wrote his essay on *L'art pour l'art* in this context, is still a topic of debate (GSG 13, pp. 9-15). The artistic and literary avant-garde of the day gathered in the Lepsius salon. They included Stefan George, who was a good friend of the family; he lived for a few months in the winter in Berlin's West End, so he regularly spent one evening a week at the Simmels (Simmel, [1941/42] 2008, p. 56 f.). This was until the relationship broke up when George started to structure his circle like a religious sect (Landmann, 1984; Rammstedt, 1999, p. 101 f.).

Simmel's approach to the analysis of modern society was guided by the need to understand what was 'fashionable' (*was it modern?*) in culture and behaviour. In the West End milieu he could cultivate his intensive and critical relationship to the rapidly developing trends of art and literature that helped him to understand the spirit of his time and society. The two studies on George's poetry also developed in this context (GSG 5, pp. 287-300; GSG 7, pp. 21-35; cf. also GSG 23, p. 163 f.). Simmel succeeded, too, in introducing his pupil Gertrud Kantorowicz to the elitist 'George Kreis', so that she was the only woman who published in their journal *Blätter für die Kunst* (Landmann, 1958, p. 12). In the West End district, many areas were still unbuilt, so in leisure time they served as tennis courts, a sport that Simmel enjoyed practising together with his son as well as with Kantorowicz, who also lived in the neighbourhood (Simmel, [1941/42] 2008, pp. 50, 61). Furthermore, several university colleagues lived in the West End, among them Simmel's good friends Ignaz and Anna Jastrow (GSG 23, p. 1168). Jastrow was a political scientist, an expert on labour law and director of the Berlin High School for Commerce, which he co-founded in 1906 (GSG 23, p. 1168). Simmel passionately defended him, so also protecting the honour of the professor's profession, since the sponsor of the High School for Commerce decided to dismiss Jastrow in 1914 as a punishment for also teaching at the Berlin University (GSG 17, pp. 115-118). Despite all these different dimensions of interest in the history of Berlin's West End milieus, where Margarete Susman and Eduard von Bendemann also lived for several years (Susman, 1966, p. 42), there are still no comprehensive studies of the intellectual networks that thrived here at the turn of the century.

The Simmels spent their holidays in different places around Europe. The Swiss Alps were one of the most favoured destinations. Simmel's elder brother Eugen was a passionate climber and published a book about his walks in the Alps (Simmel, [1941/42] 2008, p. 12). Thus, he may have influenced Simmel's choices (ibid., 39). Yet these experiences also animated him to describe what can be seen as one of the first critiques of the tourism industry (GSG 5, pp. 91-95). There was an unequivocal development towards a mass appetite for Alpine holidays with the construction of high mountain railway connections. For Simmel, the rhetoric that transfigured the 'educational value' of the Alpine journeys remained in significant contradiction with the effective cultural impact of these experiences when compared with the classic *grand tour* voyages to Italy. Indeed, it must be said that the travels to Italy left a completely different impression on Simmel. This particularly concerns the sojourns in Florence, where the Simmels found accommodation in the Villa Giovanelli, a former residence of Galileo Galilei, which is located on the hill of San Miniato, from where visitors can enjoy a magnificent view of the whole town (Simmel, [1941/42] 2008, p. 54). Simmel was so impressed by the city, its surroundings, and art treasures that he came several times back to Florence to finish writing his books and considered it the 'homeland of his soul', as he wrote to Edmund Husserl, who asked him for travel advice (GSG 22, p. 570 f.). This deep relationship to the Italian art cities and the contrast to the neurasthenic 'mental life' characterising the whirlwind development of Berlin's industrial megalopolis inspired Simmel's essays on Florence, Rome, and Venice (GSG 8, pp. 69-73; GSG 5, pp. 301–310; GSG 8, pp. 258-263).

Simmel left Berlin in March 1914, as he finally obtained an appointment as a full professor at the Kaiser Wilhelm University in Strasbourg (GSG 23, p. 302). After 29 years, Simmel's lectures ceased in the great hall of the Friedrich Wilhelm University at Unter den Linden, and this came as a shock well beyond the student audience. The lectures had become established as an essential rendezvous in the intellectual life of the German capital, so that journal articles reported on the loss of this 'Berlin tradition' (Gassen & Landmann, 1958, pp. 147-154). In Strasbourg, Simmel started teaching shortly after 20 March 1914 (GSG 23, p. 753). Similar to mainstream European public opinion, he did not expect that little more than four months later he would find himself at the centre of world conflict with its front line at a relatively short distance of 200 kilometres in Verdun. His mind was teeming with projects. He wanted to improve his relationships with French colleagues and especially with Célestin Bouglé, who planned to invite him to Paris as the first German to give a talk at the *Société de philosophie* (GSG 23, p. 300 f.). Furthermore, in June 1914,

Simmel published an essay on Bergson's philosophy in the journal *Die Guldenkammer* (GSG 13, pp. 53-69). Bergson wrote to thank him for the brilliant study and anticipated that he would quote his theories in a future work on the 'social evolution' of humankind (GSG 23, p. 332 f.). Yet, before it came to the publication of *Les deux sources de la morale et de la religion* in 1932, World War I and the ensuing international tensions made it politically impossible for Bergson to mention Simmel (Fitzi, 2002b).

The initial months that Simmel spent in Strasbourg were also interesting because of further developments. On the one hand, the city's intellectual circles that aimed to improve cultural exchange between Alsace and France saw Simmel as a possible partner because of his long-standing role as an advocate for the introduction of French culture in Germany. They tried to establish an exchange with him. Protagonists of this charm offensive were Pierre Bucher, Fritz Kiener, and other intellectuals who gathered around the journal *Révue Alsacienne illustrée/Illustrierte elsässische Rundschau* (GSG 23, pp. 327-329). On the other hand, young German-speaking intellectuals such as René Schickele and Ernst Stadler, who wanted Alsace to play a mediation role in a future united Europe (GSG 23, p. 330), also tried to win Simmel for their cause (GSG 23, p. 338 f.). The development of this intellectual networking in association with Simmel's activity as an intermediary between French and German culture could have brought most beneficial progress for European culture and politics. Yet Simmel's Strasbourg spring was short-lived. When the Austrian declaration of war emerged against Serbia, World War I broke out on 28 July 1914. All the French-German projects came to an abrupt end.

Throughout his life, Simmel was a very active public lecturer, and on such occasions he often presented the first draft of his essays or unpublished chapters of his books (GSG 24, pp. 625-637). These activities often brought him to Vienna, yet also to Mannheim, and many other German cities. During World War I Simmel continued to give his lectures. In 1917, he gave a series of five lectures about 'Philosophical World Views' in Kassel. Although no details have survived about this period, his visit must have played an important role (GSG 24, p. 634). At that time, Simmel had intended to move to Kassel if, in the event of a lost war, he had to leave Strasbourg. During the war, Simmel gave different lectures for the purpose of financing the Red Cross, the associations helping the German prisoners of war, as well as for women's education and the national women's service (GSG 24, pp. 631-637). Yet, from November 1916, he also started to give conferences for the front soldiers. At first, he worked near the French front line in Verdun, then in 1917 in Tournai, in occupied Belgium, and finally in 1918 in neutral Netherlands, in Amsterdam and The Hague. Simmel's topics here were: 'Philosophical worldviews', 'Goethe's worldview', 'The crisis of culture', 'Goethe's love', 'The conflict of modern culture', and 'The problem of the portrait'. Yet the backlash because of these activities in the context of 'patriotic teaching on the Western front', as well as of the presentation of German culture in the neutral countries, has yet to be inquired into (GSG 24, pp. 633-637).

Networks and personalities

In his young years, Simmel was very attentive to the social and political tensions of his time. He wrote about the philosophy of work (GSG 5, pp. 420-444); the psychology and pathologies of modern monetary economy (GSG 2, pp. 49-65; GSG 6, pp. 308-336); socialism and pessimism (GSG 5, pp. 552-559); the women's emancipation movement (GSG 1, pp. 284-294, GSG 17, pp. 39-45; Fitzi, 2019, pp. 31-35); and prostitution (GSG

17, pp. 261-273). In the context of these interests, Simmel developed contacts to a number of socio-political networks and social movements characterising the rapidly developing Berlin industrial metropolis. Köhnke dedicated an important part of his study about the 'young Simmel' to this topic (Köhnke, 1996, pp. 459-473). Furthermore, under the pseudonym Paul Liesegang, Simmel published his contributions for *Vorwärts*, the journal of the Social Democratic party. In this context as well as in his anonymous publications (GSG 17, pp. 193-346), he expressed himself on the topics of the 'social issue' and developed a positive approach to the philosophy of history, which according to Köhnke could not be part of his academic reflection on the question (ibid., p. 460).

In this regard, Simmel's cooperation was crucial with the *Socialwissenschaftliche Studentenvereinigung* (Köhnke, 1996, pp. 432-458). This network of young people who were interested in the study of social issues, and especially its largest group in Berlin, was fundamental for increasing the acceptance and promoting the institutionalisation process of sociology in Germany. Fifteen years later, a conspicuous number of its members became founding members of the German Sociological Association (DGS) (Köhnke, 1996, p. 432 f.; GSG 23, p. 1158 f.). Despite various reconstructions focusing on some aspects and periods related to the activity of the DGS, we still lack an overarching study of its genesis that answers several open questions. These include the issue of the composition of the intellectual milieu that initiated the establishment of the sociological association, its relationship to politics and especially to social democracy, as well as the problem of its internal conflicts. Simmel was deeply committed to ensuring the formation of a professional sociological association and formulated a number of its early invitations (GSG 17, pp. 165-174; GSG 22, pp. 672-677; GSG 24, pp. 299-317). Yet, like his friend Max Weber, he retired from all duties shortly after the DGS was set up in 1909 (Lepsius, 2012; Rammstedt, 1991). A worthwhile research project would be an overall explanation of the background leading up to these decisions.

The *Socialwissenschaftliche Studentenvereinigung* invited Simmel, Max Weber, and Ferdinand Tönnies to give lectures on socio-political topics in Berlin. Between 1894 and 1901 Simmel talked about the 'Psychology of socialism', 'Historical materialism', the 'Sociology of religious affairs' and 'Female Culture' before the *Studentenvereinigung* (GSG 24, p. 625 f.). The Ukrainian social scientist Theodor Kistiakowski (GSG 23, p. 1053 f.) played a prominent role among the organisers of these activities. In 1898, Kistiakowski wrote his doctoral thesis *Gesellschaft und Einzelwesen. Eine methodologische Untersuchung*, which tackles a systematic reconstruction of biologism in the social sciences since Spencer (1876/1882–1885), and subjects it to a neo-Kantian and sociological critique (Kistiakowski, 1899). As a private lecturer and then *Extraordinarius* at the Friedrich Wilhelm University of Berlin, Simmel could not act as a doctoral supervisor. Therefore, several of his pupils completed their PhD in Strasbourg and later in Heidelberg with Wilhelm Windelband, who supported Simmel in this issue. Notably, Kistiakowski followed this path, as did Robert E. Park (1904).

From the beginning of his scientific activity, Simmel was convinced that a science of modern society could only have been possible thanks to a common effort made by a wide group of researchers and not by an individual work of conceptualisation. Around 1893, he planned to establish an international and polyglot journal of sociology (Rol, 2009). His idea was to develop lasting contacts with his colleagues abroad, above all in the USA and France. As a result of these activities in 1895 he became 'advising editor' of the newly established *American Journal of Sociology*. He found an engaged colleague in Albion Small who translated into English eight of the nine papers by Simmel that were published in the journal (GSG 18, pp. 521-536). This connection was particularly important because it established an enduring relationship with the University of Chicago, where one of the first departments of sociology worldwide was set up in 1892; later, it was to become the 'Chicago school of sociology' (Bulmer, 1984). Small's work was subsequently continued by Robert Ezra Park. He attended Simmel's lectures on sociology in Berlin in 1899/1900 (GSG 21, pp. 281-344) and later established Simmel's work as a foundation stone of the sociological study canon in his *Introduction to Sociology* (Park & Burgess, 1922). Moreover, he made Chicago's Department of Sociology a prominent centre for the dissemination of Simmel's sociology (Levine et al., 1976, p. 179 f.). During World War I, Small's open letter to Simmel on public opinion in the US about the war clarified unequivocally that it was naive to assume that only the German government and media did not lie about the conflict (GSG 23, pp. 444-455). The letter had a decisive impact on Simmel's attitude towards World War I, so that he abruptly renounced all his activities to 'explain' to the neutral countries the 'good reasons' for Germany's entrance into war, and went on only to give talks about cultural and philosophical topics (Fitzi, 2018; GSG 24, pp. 631-637).

Simmel's approach to the collective dimension of the sociological enterprise also brought him into contact with his French-speaking colleagues. From the beginning, he closely followed the development of French sociology and wrote reviews on Tarde's *Lois de l'imitation*, 1891 (GSG 1, pp. 248-50), as well as on Le Bon's *Psychologie des foules*, 1895 (GSG 1, pp. 353-360). In this context, Simmel contacted René Worms, who had just become director of the *Institut International de Sociologie* to propose the project of an international sociological journal. Yet Worms was faster and launched his *Revue Internationale de Sociologie* in 1893 (Rol, 2009, 370). In the second year of the journal, Worms published a bad translation of Simmel's article on 'Social differentiation' without asking him for approval of the final text, so that relations came to a breaking point (GSG 19, pp. 9-26; Rol, 2009, p. 374). Nevertheless, a few weeks beforehand Simmel wrote a review to publicise Worms' journal in Germany and his review was published in Schmoller's yearbook (GSG 1, pp. 306-310). In the wake of these experiences, Simmel no longer proposed to offer to Worms his programmatic article on the 'Problem of Sociology'. Instead, his article was published in the leading French philosophical journal, *Revue de Métaphysique et de Morale* (GSG 19, pp. 27-35). This opportunity was due to the fact that Simmel knew several of the revue's editorial colleagues who were in Berlin as visiting scholars and attended his lectures. Among them were Célestin Bouglé and Elie Halevy, who introduced him to the founder and editor of the revue, Xavier Léon (Fitzi, 2002a, pp. 19-32).

Simmel was later involved by Bouglé and Durkheim in the project of *L'Année Sociologique* (ibid., pp. 32-47). At Célestin Bouglé's initial suggestion, in 1896 Durkheim started the editorial enterprise of *L'Année Sociologique* (Besnard, 1979, p. 8). His intention was to work with a notable representative of German social sciences. Bouglé, who was a pupil of both, knew that Durkheim and Simmel shared a common interest in founding sociology as an autonomous discipline by granting it an objective status of research. Yet the cooperation failed, as different studies have reconstructed (Fitzi, 2017; Rammstedt, 1998). Nevertheless, in this case Simmel also positively presented the new sociological journal to the German public in a review (GSG 1, p. 408 f.). The fact that a relationship existed with the internationally most active philosophical and sociological groups in Paris made it easier for him later to intervene in the process of the German translation of Bergson's works (Fitzi, 2002a, pp. 195-228; Simmel, [1941/42] 2008, p. 90). On the other hand, in addition to the early sociological reception, above all due to Célestin Bouglé (1896), a debate arose in France concerning Simmel's selected works translated in French – the *Mélanges de philosophie relativiste. Contribution à la culture philosophique*. The translation was promoted by Henri

Bergson, provided by Groethuysen's partner Alix Guillain, and published in 1912 as a contribution to a 'relativist philosophy' (GSG 19, pp. 137-371; Fitzi, 2002a, pp. 238-250; Mamelet, 1914). Simmel's productive exchange with his French colleagues lasted until the outbreak of World War I which in one day 'destroyed half of his life work', as his son relates (Simmel, [1941/42] 2008, p. 111 f.).

Another important relationship to French culture developed instead on a purely personal basis. Simmel was very impressed by the modernity of Rodin's dynamic sculpture and had published on this topic in 1902 and 1909 (GSG 7, pp. 92-100; GSG 12, pp. 28-36), when he decided to send the studies to the French master. As a thank you, Rodin invited him to visit his studio, so that around 1910 they met twice in Paris and Meudon (Simmel, [1941/42] 2008, pp. 88-90). Simmel worshipped Rodin so much that he dedicated to him an obituary in the middle of World War I, although Rodin had spoken very harsh words against Germany when the war broke out (GSG 13, pp. 307-312). The contact with Rodin allowed Simmel to recommend him to two younger talents who wanted to enter into contact with the artistic milieu in Paris: Rainer Maria Rilke and Max Raphael (Simmel, [1941/42] 2008, p. 89; GSG 23, p. 59 f.).

Beyond the relationship to Rilke and the George circle, including a correspondence with Friedrich Gundolf and Karl Wolfskehl (GSG 23, pp. 1164, 1195 f.), further contacts to the literary world are interspersed throughout Simmel's biography. Three contexts, among others, can be recalled in this respect. In his young years, Simmel dedicated himself to poetry and developed a poetic correspondence with his childhood friend Harald Graef (GSG 23, pp. 1031-1101). As his university career as a philosopher and social scientist then turned out to be very difficult, Simmel seriously considered abandoning academia to become an author. Two biographical episodes bear witness to this possible development. On the one hand, to face the early critique of Nietzsche's philosophy, above all by Ferdinand Tönnies (1897), Simmel decided to approach Nietzsche's sister Elisabeth and to learn more about the unpublished work of the philosopher as well as about the plans for a Nietzsche edition (GSG 22, pp. 234-236, 277). In this context, Simmel wrote a review of Elisabeth Förster-Nietzsche's biography of her brother (GSG 1, pp. 338-346), and of Tönnies' book on the Nietzsche-cult (GSG 1, pp. 400-408). On the other hand, between 1897 and 1907 Simmel collaborated as an author with the journal of the German Art nouveau movement *Die Jugend*. Here he published small articles in the form of aphorisms, by mixing essayistic and literary styles (GSG 20, pp. 347-439). Monika Tokarzewska has given an analysis of Simmel's literary activity and its meaning (2010).

Simmel held a *privatissimus* seminar at home that was attended by selected advanced students including among others Martin Buber, Ernst Bloch, Bernhard Groethuysen (Simmel's favourite pupil according to the son Hans), and the art historians Ernst Gradmann and Gertrud Kantorowicz (Simmel, [1941/42] 2008, p. 61). Margarete Susman, who recounted the atmosphere of these discussions in her memoirs, also attended the *privatissimus* (Susman, 1966, p. 44 f.). Beyond this circle, a wider number of pupils took part in Simmel's lectures. The following among them left us their lecture notes, which are now gathered in volume 21 of Simmel's work edition (GSG 21): Pavel Abramovic, Karl Berger, Ernst Robert Curtius, Kurt Gassen, Georg Heym, Edith Landmann-Kalischer, Adolf Löwe, Harry Graf Kessler, Georg von Lukács, Hugo Nathansohn, Rudolf Pannwitz, Robert Ezra Park, Arthur Ruppin, Gottfried Salomon, Herman Schmalenbach, Kurt Singer, and Margarete Susman. A wider circle of Simmel's pupils can be identified by checking who simply attended his lecturers and referred to his works. According to Köhnke, Simmel's most easily identifiable pupils are Ernst Cassirer, Ernst Bloch, Bernhard Groethuysen, Georg Lukács, and Siegfried Kracauer (Köhnke, 1996, p. 10). In addition, however, many other personalities in Germany and abroad can be understood as 'Simmel's sons and daughters', so that they gradually become the subject of research (Thouard, 2020). Particular attention should also be paid to the women that belonged to Simmel's circle, like Edith Landmann-Kalischer, Gertrud Simmel, Gertrud Kantorowicz, and Margarete Susman. Simmel sustained them in their independent intellectual development and helped them to obtain university qualifications or even PhDs at a time when studying at university was not allowed for women in Germany (Rammstedt, 1994, 1996). A further relationship to one of the most important intellectual women of his time was with Lou Andreas-Salomé, who influenced Simmel's reflection on the issue of love and eroticism (GSG 22, 1037; Fitzi, 2019, p. 114 f.).

During his lifetime, Simmel was engaged in a deep debate with his peers about the essential philosophical issues of their epoch. His correspondence included a 'Who's Who' of philosophy at that time: Richard Avenarius, Henri Bergson, Harald Höffding, Karl Jaspers, Friedrich Jodl, Hermann Graf Keyserling, Edmund Husserl, Moritz Lazarus, Georg Misch, Hugo Münsterberg, Fritz Mauthner, Paul Natorp, Heinrich Rickert, Max Scheler, Herman Schmalenbach, Ernst Troeltsch, Hans Vaihinger, and Wilhelm Windelband. In later years, Simmel was one of the protagonists of the culture philosophical journal *Logos* that was initiated and organised by Rickert's pupils Nikolai von Bubnoff, Sergius Hessen, and Fedor Stepun, under the leadership of Georg Mehlis and Richard Kroner (Kramme, 1995). All these activities that underpin Simmel's philosophical heritage still warrant an overarching reconstruction.

Some mythologies

As is the case with every great narrative, in the field of Simmel research there are also a fair number of metropolitan legends. The most important relate to the whereabouts of certain portions of Simmel's estate. The first episode relates to two lost bags. After Simmel passed away, his wife Gertrud was responsible for the published work, while Gertrud Kantorowicz was the designated administrator of the unpublished estate. One day she was travelling by train and went to the dining car. When she came back, her suitcase had been stolen. Inside was Simmel's almost print-ready manuscript on the 'Philosophy of the Actor', only parts of which had previously been published (Landmann, 1958, p. 14). A further manuscript was lost in a similar way. As Simmel knew that he would die, he asked his wife to destroy all of his unpublished papers. When they went through them, however, he saw his unfinished manuscript 'On Truth' and exclaimed: 'What a pity!' Hence, she asked him to keep the manuscript, if not for publication at least as a memoir for the family – he agreed. She later asked Groethuysen for an expert appraisal and possibly to rework the manuscript for publication (Fitzi, 2002a, p. 269). Yet, it remains unclear what became of the manuscript, since it could not be found in Groethuysen's papers. The story goes that Groethuysen's estate contained a suitcase in which some manuscripts were kept. The daughter of the responsible French estate administrator was repeatedly questioned by Simmel-researchers about the whereabouts of the suitcase. In the end, she was quite upset. Afterwards, the speculation was that Groethuysen's suitcase might have been kept in the archives of the Communist party of France. The manifold enquiries carried out during work for Simmel's complete edition, however, did not lead to any result. The second episode relates to Russia. Firstly, Simmel apparently feared travelling to Russia, but nobody knows why. Was it because of the relatives who lived in St Petersburg and had been involved in some political activities around 1905? (Simmel, [1941/42] 2008, p. 63). Secondly, the Simmel family estate was at least partially auctioned off (Köhnke, 1996, p. 18; Kramme, 1992, p. 74). The editors of Simmel's edition therefore wondered whether some part of Simmel's heritage could have been brought to Russia after the war. Yet investigations in this regard did not yield any results. Nevertheless, if somewhere in future two Rodin drawings with deer should reappear, we will know that Simmel's estate did not get completely lost. The third episode concerns the German emigrants during the Nazi dictatorship. Many of Simmel's friends and correspondents, and at least their daughters and sons, had to escape Germany after 1933. In their family estates there might be letters, photos, or other witness documents concerning the Simmels. Thanks to a courtesy of Cornelia Hahn Oberlander (Vancouver, Canada), Thomas Kemple for example could publish the photo of an open house at the residence of the Jastrows, in 24 Nussbaumallee, Berlin's West End, in 1914, showing Georg and Gertrud Simmel in conversation with Ignaz Jastrow (cf. *Theory, Culture & Society*, 2012, *29* (7/8), 6). It is possible that there are many more things to be discovered in the archives of other personalities and contemporaries from that era who left for the US, Canada, and other countries.

Conclusion

In summary, a great deal of research remains to be done on the unexplored continent of Simmel's life. The correspondence compiled in GSG volumes 22 and 23 offers hints about a number of unexploited or only partially exploited lines of enquiry. A case in point is the exchange between Georg and Gertrud Simmel with Max and Marianne Weber. Otherwise, Simmel's relationship with social or law scientists and often co-founders of the German Sociological Association, with whom he corresponded, still has to be systematically reconstructed. This not only concerns Ferdinand Tönnies, the later president, and Hermann Beck, the manager of the association. It involves, too, Simmel's further correspondents, such as: Georg Jellinek, Robert Michels, Gustav Radbruch, Gottfried Salomon, Gustav Schmoller, Gustav Steffen, Lester Ward, and Howard Brown Woolston. Some of Simmel's works were bestsellers, for example, *Hauptprobleme der Philosophie* (GSG 14, pp. 7-157), which sold 37,000 copies in ten years (GSG 14, p. 476). Thus, another interesting chapter of Simmel's biography would focus on his relationship to the heads of the most important publishing houses of his time in Germany and abroad. This concerns among others his correspondents Wilhelm Crayen (Göschen), Eugen Diederichs, Wilhelm Hertz (Bessersche Buchhandlung), Paul Siebeck (Mohr-Siebeck) in Germany, and Felix Alcan in Paris.

References

Bergson, Henri (1932). *Les deux sources de la morale et de la religion*. Paris: Alcan.

Besnard, Philippe (1979). La formation de l'équipe de l'Année sociologique. *Revue française de sociologie*, *22*(1), 7–31.

Bouglé, Célestin (1896). *Les sciences sociales en Allemagne: Les méthodes actuelles*. Paris: F. Alcan.

Bulmer, Martin (1984). *The Chicago School of Sociology: Institutionalization, diversity, and the rise of sociological research*. Chicago, IL: University of Chicago Press.

Fitzi, Gregor (2002a). *Soziale Erfahrung und Lebensphilosophie. Georg Simmels Beziehung zu Henri Bergson*. Konstanz: UVK.

Fitzi, Gregor (2002b). Société et morale sous l'angle de la philosophie de la vie. Une comparaison franco-allemande. In: F. Worms (Ed.), *Etudes sur les deux sources de la morale et de la religion de Bergson* (pp. 243–264). Paris: PUF.

Fitzi, Gregor (2017). Dialogue. Divergence. Veiled reception. Criticism: Georg Simmel's relationship with Émile Durkheim. In: *Performing the other. Durkheim in Germany*. Special Issue of the *Journal of Classical Sociology, 17*(4), 293–308.

Fitzi, Gregor (2018). Nationalism and Europeanism: Simmel's Dilemma. *Simmel Studies, 22*(2), 125–148.

Fitzi, Gregor (2019). *The challenge of modernity: Simmel's sociological theory.* London: Routledge.

Frischeisen-Köhler, Max (1919/20). Georg Simmel. *Kant-Studien, 24,* 1–51; now also in: P. U. Hein, (Ed.) (1990), *Georg Simmel* (pp. 23–70). Frankfurt/M.: Lang.

Gassen, Kurt, & Landmann, Michael (Eds.) (1958). *Buch des Dankes an Georg Simmel. Briefe, Erinnerungen, Bibliographie.* Berlin: Dunker & Humblot.

Kantorowicz, Gertrud (1923). Vorwort. In: Gertrud Kantorowicz (Ed.), *Georg Simmel, Fragmente und Aufsätze. Aus dem Nachlaß und Veröffentlichungen der letzten Jahre* (pp. V–IX), Ed. by Gertrud Kantorowicz. München: Drei-Masken-Verlag.

Kistiakowski, Theodor (1899). *Gesellschaft und Einzelwesen. Eine methodologische Untersuchung.* Berlin: Liebmann.

Köhnke, Klaus Christian (1996). *Der junge Simmel in Theoriebeziehungen und sozialen Bewegungen.* Frankfurt/M.: Suhrkamp.

Kracauer, Siegfried ([1919] 2004). Georg Simmel. Ein Beitrag zur Deutung des geistigen Lebens unserer Zeit. In: I. Belk. (Ed., with the collaboration of S. Biebl), *Werke, vol. 9.2: Frühe Schriften aus dem Nachlaß* (pp. 139–280). Berlin: Suhrkamp.

Kramme, Rüdiger (1992). Wo ist der Nachlaß von Georg Simmel? *Simmel Newsletter, 2*(1), Summer, 71–76.

Kramme, Rüdiger (1995). Philosophische Kultur als Programm. Die Konstituierungsphase des *LOGOS.* In: K. Sauerland & H. Treiber (Eds.), *Heidelberg im Schnittpunkt intellektueller Kreise: Zur Topographie der 'geistigen Geselligkeit' eines 'Weltdorfes': 1850–1950* (pp. 119–149). Opladen: Westdeutscher Verlag.

Landmann, Michael (1958). Bausteine zur Biographie. In: Kurt Gassen & Michael Landmann (Eds.), *Buch des Dankes an Georg Simmel. Briefe, Erinnerungen, Bibliographie* (pp. 11–33). Berlin: Dunker & Humblot.

Landmann, Michael (1984). Georg Simmel und Stefan George. In: H.-J. Dahme & O. Rammstedt (Eds.), *Georg Simmel und die Moderne. Neue Interpretationen und Materialien* (pp. 147–173). Frankfurt/M.: Suhrkamp.

Lask, Berta (1955). *Stille und Sturm* (vol. I and II). Halle (Saale): Mitteldeutscher Verlag.

Lepsius, Mario R. (2012). Max Weber und die Gründung der Deutschen Gesellschaft für Soziologie. Retrieved from: https://soziologie.de/dgs/geschichte/max-weber-und-die-gruendung-der-dgs#top

Lepsius, Sabine (1935). *Stefan George. Geschichte einer Freundschaft.* Berlin: Die Runde.

Lepsius, Sabine (1972). *Ein Berliner Künstlerleben um die Jahrhundertwende.* München: Müller.

Levine, Donald N., Carter, Ellwood B., & Gorman, Eleanor M. (1976). Simmel's influence on American sociology. In: H. Böhringer & K. Gründer (Eds.). *Ästhetik und Soziologie um die Jahrhundertwende, Georg Simmel* (pp. 175–228). Frankfurt/M: Klostermann.

Lukács, Georg (1991). Georg Simmel. *Theory, Culture and Society, 8,* 145–150.

Mamelet, Albert (1914). *Le relativisme philosophique chez Georg Simmel.* Paris: Alcan.

Park, Robert Ezra (1904). *Masse und Publikum: eine methodologische und soziologische Untersuchung.* Bern: Lack & Grunau.

Park, Robert Era, & Burgess, Ernest W. (1922). *Introduction to the science of sociology.* Chicago, IL: University of Chicago Press.

Portioli, Claudia (2006). La tombe de Simmel dans l'obscurité: ruine ou occasion de mémoire? *Revue de Sciences Sociales, 36,* 150–153.

Rammstedt, Angela (1994). Gertrud Simmel/Kinel - Malerin. *Simmel Newsletter, 4*(1), Summer, 140–162.

Rammstedt, Angela (1996). 'Wir sind des Gottes der begraben stirbt'. Gertrud Kantorowicz und der nationalsozialistische Terror. *Simmel Newsletter, 6*(2), Winter, 135–176.

Rammstedt, Angela (1999) (Ed.). Simmel in der Literatur. Special issue of the *Simmel Newsletter, 9*(1), Summer.

Rammstedt, Otthein (1991). Die Frage der Wertfreiheit und die Gründung der Deutschen Gesellschaft für Soziologie. In: L. Clausen & C. Schlüter (Eds.), *Hundert Jahre „Gemeinschaft und Gesellschaft". Ferdinand Tönnies in der internationalen Diskussion* (pp. 549–560). Opladen: Leske & Budrich.

Rammstedt, Otthein (1998). Les relations entre Durkheim et Simmel dans le contexte de l'affaire Dreyfus. *L'année sociologique, 48*(1), 139–162.

Rammstedt, Otthein (2004). Geschichte des Simmel-Nachlasses 1918 bis 1941. *Simmel Studies*, *14*(1), 93–147.

Rol, Cécile (2009). Die *Soziologie*, faute de mieux. Zwanzig Jahre Streit mit René Worms um die Fachinstitutionaliserung (1893-1913). In: Ch. Pailloud & C. Rol (Eds.), *Soziologie als Möglichkeit. 100 Jahre Untersuchungen über die Formen der Vergesellschaftung* (pp. 367–400). Wiesbaden: VS Verlag.

Simmel, Arnold (2008). Some thoughts on Hans Simmel's Lebenserinnerungen. A son's perspective. *Simmel Studies*, *18*(1), Summer, 137–148.

Simmel, Hans ([1941/42] 2008). Lebenserinnerungen. *Simmel Studies*, *18*(1), Summer, 9–136.

Spencer, Herbert (1876/1882–1885). *Principles of sociology*, 3 vol. London: Williams and Norgate.

Susman, Margarete (1959). *Die geistige Gestalt Georg Simmels*. Tübingen: Mohr Siebeck.

Susman, Margarete (1966). *Ich habe viele Leben gelebt: Erinnerungen*. Stuttgart: Deutsche Verlags-Anstalt.

Thouard, Denis (2020) (Ed.). *Les enfants de Simmel*. Belval: Circé.

Tokarzewska, M. (2010). *Der feste Grund des Unberechenbaren. Georg Simmel zwischen Soziologie und Literatur*. Wiesbaden: VS Verlag für Sozialwissenschaften.

Tönnies, Ferdinand (1897). *Der Nietzsche-Kultus. Eine Kritik*. Leipzig: O. R. Reisland.

PART II

Sociology

2

SIMMEL'S RESONANCE WITH CONTEMPORARY SOCIOLOGICAL DEBATES

Olli Pyyhtinen

Introduction

After having lingered for a long time in disciplinary margins, Simmel is today widely appreciated both as a founding father of sociology and as a source of a great variety of staggering ideas, concepts, and hypotheses for subsequent research. He has also become a key classical reference for relational sociology, network analysis, and for any studies on money, trust, space, or individuality, for example. It therefore no longer holds water to speak of Simmel as a neglected figure whose work would remain largely unrecognized. While a more comprehensive appreciation of Simmel has been gradually growing, his work has also undergone several renaissances. Each renaissance has emphasized different aspects of Simmel's work, reconstructing thus a different Simmel each time, as each generation has read and interpreted his work in its own particular way.

In his lifetime and right after his death, Simmel's work was first given a new life in North American sociology. The early American reception, greatly shaped by Albion W. Small and Robert E. Park, appreciated Simmel in particular for defining the sociological domain and as a classic of urban sociology. Park's student Louis Wirth (1925, p. 219) famously saluted Simmel's metropolis essay as 'the most important single article on the city from a sociological standpoint'. Later Simmel was rediscovered after World War II, when North American sociologists read him, for example, as a classic of small groups, role theory, and conflict theory. The rediscovery was given momentum especially by the publication of *The Sociology of Georg Simmel* (1950), edited by Kurt H. Wolff, which was the first book-length volume containing English translations of Simmel and which significantly promoted the dissemination of Simmel's texts and ideas.

Around that time, in the 1950s, interest in Simmel began to increase in Germany as well, where he had gone from an immensely popular author and speaker to near oblivion just two or three decades after his death. The revival, however, took place slowly. Heinz-Jürgen Dahme (1990) remarked some thirty years ago that the appreciation of Simmel is 'of recent date', and he described the German Simmel reception of the past couple of decades as a '"repression" process' (Dahme, 1990, p. 13, p. 19). While the depreciation of Simmel was also a homegrown product – as former students like Georg Lukács and Ernst Bloch turned away from him and the Frankfurt School lost its connections to Simmel's work – to a certain extent both the post-World War II repression and re-appreciation of his thought are of American influence. The predominance of Talcott Parsons and structural functionalism persistently left Simmel in the margin, until he was re-imported across the Atlantic as a classic of urban studies, role theory, conflict theory, and analyses of small groups (Dahme, 1990, p. 14; Rammstedt, 1994, p. 112; Köhnke, 1996, p. 14 n. 7). On the whole, as Peter-Ernst Schnabel (1974), has shown, the German reception has been very different from the American one. Whereas the North American tradition has, from the outset, typically centred on the operationability of Simmel's theses and on his theory fragments of particular bits and pieces of social reality, irrespective of their connection to the whole of Simmel's work, the German reception is characterized by a more philological and historicist approach, with its focus on situating Simmel's work within the context of the time it was written rather than on the usability of his theses.

Later, in the 1980s and 1990s, Simmel was internationally revived especially as a cultural theorist and a theorist of modernity. This reading of his work owes much to David Frisby (1985), who famously portrayed Simmel as the 'first theorist of modernity', and both in his numerous writings and translations presents Simmel's omnivorous analytical taste for a remarkably wide range of themes and topics, from money to the metropolis, culture, aesthetics, fashion, individuality, the Alpine journey, the ruin, the problem of style, and trade exhibitions, for example.

In this chapter, I examine how the actuality of Simmel's work has been addressed in contemporary discussions and debates. The chapter maps the diffusion of Simmel's ideas across a range of current sociological discussions and debates. Because the influence is very diffused, it is not easy to provide an exhaustive review of it.[1] Recent scholarship stresses Simmel's relevance for a rich variety of themes, such as money, value, taste, and consumption (Poggi, 1993; Dodd, 1994, 2014, 2016; Zelizer, 1994; Gronow, 1997; Sassatelli, 2000; Cantó-Milà, 2005; Lehtonen & Pyyhtinen, 2019); aesthetics (De la Fuente, 2007, 2008, 2016a, 2016b); neoliberalism (Kemple, 2016); gender (Oakes, 1984; Dahme, 1988; Kandal, 1988; van Vucht Tjissen, 1991; Leck, 2000; Witz, 2001); subjectivity (Darmon & Frade, 2012; Lee & Silver, 2012); thirds and tertiality (Fischer, 2000, 2010, 2013; Nooteboom, 2006, Pyyhtinen, 2009, 2018); space (Lechner, 1991; Frisby, 1992, 2001; Schäfers & Bauer, 1994; Ziemann, 2000; Löw, 2001; Schroer, 2006); time (Scaff, 2005); limits and boundaries (Weinstein & Weinstein, 1989; Tester, 1993; Kemple, 2007); emotions (Cantó-Milà, 2016a; Seebach & Núñez Mosteo, 2016; Seebach, 2017; Sabido Ramos, 2019); senses (Swedberg, 2011; Sabido Ramos, 2017); gratitude (Cantó-Milà, 2012); fashion (Nedelmann, 1990; Gronow, 1993; Schiermer, 2009, 2015); secrecy and mendacity (Welty, 1996; Barbour, 2012; Pyyhtinen, 2019); information (Lash, 2005); competition (Burt, 1993); distance and proximity (Cantó-Milà, 2016b); objects and material culture (Miller, 1987; Appadurai, 1988; Pyyhtinen, 2010; De la Fuente, 2016a, 2016b); nature (Gross, 2000, 2001; Giacomoni, 2006); film (Fritsch, 2009); trust (Luhmann, 1979; Accarino, 1984; Möllering, 2001; Jalava, 2006); and building sociological grand theories (Fitzi, 2019). The new wave of scholarship has also rediscovered Simmel as a life-philosopher and refined aesthete (Fitzi, 2002, 2016; Lash, 2005; Pyyhtinen, 2010, 2012, 2017; Goodstein, 2017; Meyer, 2017; Ruggieri, 2017; Amat, 2018; Kemple, 2018; Beer, 2019). Another reason why any attempt at uncovering how Simmel's work has been received, appropriated, and used is met with difficulties is the fact that his influence has remained largely invisible, unacknowledged, and anonymous. Like money – to which Simmel himself compared the legacy he was about to leave – the origin of Simmel's ideas, concepts, and perspectives that have circulated in academia has not always been apparent to the ones using them. His influence has thus been marked as much by invisibility and absence as by visibility and presence. In the chapter, I focus in particular on three fields, where Simmel's work has found resonance and been influential: economic sociology, sociology of space and urban sociology, and relational sociology. Economic sociology tellingly illustrates the peculiar combination of simultaneous presence and absence of Simmel's influence. For the sociology of space and urban sociology, by contrast, Simmel's contribution has been invaluable and impossible to bypass. Finally, out of the several contemporary discussions and debates on which Simmel's ideas has had influence, it is perhaps relational thought that is the most significant (Cantó-Milà, 2005; Pyyhtinen, 2010, 2016, 2017).

Economic sociology

The reception of *The Philosophy of Money* (GSG 6) manifests well the aforementioned simultaneous invisibility and visibility of Simmel's influence. The book was acknowledged internationally. In *The American Journal of Sociology*, for example, there appeared as many as two reviews of it, by first by R.H. Meyer in 1901, followed by a more substantial review by S.P. Altmann in 1903. Nevertheless, for a long time the book remained largely neglected, little understood, and without major scholarly impact. Otthein Rammstedt (2005, p. 9) remarks that 'no scientific discipline has regarded *The Philosophy of Money* as one of its classic texts', and the book has not 'been … accepted by any discipline as fully belonging to its field of analysis', either. As much as amounting to tracing Simmel's actual influence, thinking about the importance of *The Philosophy of Money* could therefore take the form of speculative fiction, a sociological fantasy: what if Simmel, instead of thinkers like Alexis de Tocqueville and Karl Polanyi, had set the agenda for economic sociology? How would the field be different, had scholars paid more attention to Simmel's book? What might the questions asked and the perspectives look like?

The Philosophy of Money has, however, been used in modern economic sociology.[2] For example, in her analysis of the social meanings of money, Viviana Zelizer (1994) starts from Simmel's perspective on the cultural significance of money, yet she emphasizes that his approach needs to be supplemented by stressing the differentiation of multiple monies. Challenging Simmel's idea of money as impersonal and colourless, Zelizer insists that money has various different meanings for different people. Consequently, money is not one, but there exist multiple moneys: inherited money differs from money earned through hard labour, just as a sum of money won in the lottery differs from the money one has made by picking winning stocks. Nor is loaned money the same as stolen money, which in turn differs from money received as a grant, as a donation, or as, say, unemployment benefit (Zelizer, 1994, p. 2 f.).[3]

In *The Social Life of Money* (2014), Nigel Dodd draws explicitly on Simmel, as he examines money as a social form. Dodd explores the social nature of money and how its value and existence is derived from social life, that is, from '*social relations between its users*'. Not only is money a claim on society, but its value rests on the institutions that produce it and on the people who use it. (Dodd, 2014, p. 8 f.). So, analogous to Simmel's question of 'How is society possible?', in his book Dodd asks, 'How is money possible?' (ibid., p. 27). In one of the chapters, Dodd also extensively discusses and makes use of Simmel's idea of perfect money.

Simmel has also been used in the study of consumption. In *The Sociology of Taste* (1997), Jukka Gronow explicates Simmel's contribution to the sociology of taste and consumption.

According to Gronow, Simmel's theory of fashion and his manner of sociologizing the Kantian aesthetics of taste offers significant tools for the analysis of modern consumption. Douglas B. Holt and Kathleen Searls (1994) have argued for the relevance of Simmel's *The Philosophy of Money* for contemporary consumer research, employing the Simmelian notion of consumption to understand in particular consumption goals and lifestyles. Roberta Sassatelli (2000), too, has re-interpreted *The Philosophy of Money* to tease out the analytical potential of Simmel's work on money and his theory of value for the critical sociology of consumption. Simmel's conceptions of value and valuation have also been utilized in valuation studies. Turo-Kimmo Lehtonen and Olli Pyyhtinen (2020) draw on Simmel when analyzing value as enacted in practical relations, as a result of valuation, in the context of dumpster diving. The authors suggest that valuation is not merely a cognitive operation, but it also involves lots of hands-on work, the senses, bodily practices, and various objects and tools.

With regard to senses, Richard Swedberg (2011) sketches an economic sociology of the senses by utilizing Simmel. Swedberg's article exemplifies well how it is not only Simmel's work on money that has proven useful in and for economic sociology, but for instance *Soziologie* (GSG 11), too, contains a number of relevant and fruitful concepts, ideas, and frameworks for analyses of economic phenomena. Roland S. Burt (1993), for example, has famously made use of Simmel's analysis of the sociological significance of third parties in and for social relationships to study the social structure of competition. According to Burt, the structure of a subject's network and the location of one's contacts in the structure may create a competitive advantage. Conceptualizing competition as a triadic structure, Burt draws on Simmel's notion of *tertius gaudens*, 'the third who benefits', to explore how a subject may gain advantage in competition. Following Simmel, Burt suggests that there are basically two *tertius* strategies: being the third between two or more players after one and the same thing (e.g. as a seller between two buyers, thus able to pay their bids against one another), and being the third between players with conflicting demands (Burt, 1993, p. 76). Competition does not therefore concern only the two rivals, but it is a triadic relational configuration in that it also involves a third.

Spatiality and urban sociology

Space has never occupied a central place in sociology. Scholars even speak of a certain kind of 'blindness' (Läpple, 1991, p. 163) and 'forgetting' (Schäfers & Bauer, 1994) when it comes to the relationship that sociological scholarship has had to space. Markus Schroer acknowledges that among classical sociologists Simmel is the one who engaged with spatiality in the most thorough and detailed manner. According to Schroer, Simmel's insights are foundational still today and ever more valuable (Schroer, 2006, p. 60). Frisby (1986, p. 71) notes similarly that Simmel was 'the first sociologist to reveal explicitly the social significance of spatial contexts for human interaction'.

Frank Lechner (1991) suggests that Simmel's engagement with space can be interpreted in three compatible ways: firstly, as a sociological reinterpretation of a Kantian category; secondly, as an addition to Simmel's project of sociology of forms, with an eye on how social relations assume a spatial form; and, thirdly, as contributing to an historically oriented analysis of modernity in that Simmel does not just present us with a catalogue of social forms in space, but he offers us 'ideas on the spatial dimension of modern social structures and the modernization of space itself' (Lechner, 1991, p. 196).

Besides emphasizing Simmel's major contribution to the development of the sociology of space in general, scholars have employed Simmel's ideas in the study of a whole variety of more specific themes, from the spatial relations in world politics (Gazit, 2018), boundaries and borders (Weinstein & Weinstein, 1989; Tester, 1993; Paasi, 2012; see also Cantó-Milà in this volume) to migrants (Bradford & Clark, 2014), for example. A major theme in contemporary sociology and social sciences highly influenced by Simmel's thoughts on space and spatiality is the city. Anthony Vidler (1991), for example, has made an effort to work out a conception of urban space as interdependent with society by drawing from Simmel and his student Siegfried Kracauer. Further, Iain Borden (1997, p. 328) suggests that 'Simmel's conception of space is in keeping with recent urban geographic formulations of space, such as, for example, [Edward] Soja's definition of spatiality as the social quality of socially produced space'. In his article, Borden considers Simmel's thoughts on space and spatiality in the context of the modern metropolis, and he also argues that Simmel fathoms space as a pervasive entity, participating in the continual reproduction of society and cities (Borden, 1997).

Simmel also plays a crucial role in the discussion of the spatial dynamics of metropolitan modernity in Frisby's *Cityscapes of Modernity* (2001) (see also Frisby, 1992). The book, examining modern cityscapes mostly in Berlin, Vienna, and Paris between 1830 and 1930, pursues two parallel readings of Simmel. On the one hand, Frisby reads Simmel's theorizing on modernity in reference to the aesthetic idea of modern experience formulated by Charles Baudelaire. On the one hand, drawing on *The Philosophy of Money*, Frisby examines the modern metropolis as a network woven by the circulation of money. As the overall frame are different forms of experiencing, representing, and structuring modern cityscapes. The front stage is occupied by various social types of figures, from Simmel's stranger, the blasé person, and the adventurer to the *flâneur*, the detective, the researcher, the architect, and the city planner. Through them Frisby tries to illustrate not only the types of people who inhabit urban space but also the nature and inherent tensions of urban modernity.

More recently, Michael Schillmeier (2012) has made use of Simmel's work on urban life together with his sociology of the senses and analysis of the modern money economy to explore how urban relations configure both enabling and disabling scenarios of everyday life. Connecting Simmel's work in a creative manner with insights from actor-network theory, Schillmeier focuses on the entangled coming-into-being of humans and non-humans as actor-networks that constitute and articulate the city. He lays special emphasis on the material practices and inscriptions of money in conjunction with the sensory practices involved to show Simmel's value for urban studies beyond conventional approaches.

Relational sociology

In recent years there has occurred a rise of relational approaches in sociology. The approaches give primacy to relations and dynamic processes over assumedly discrete, static entities such as isolated individual agents and hypostasized structures. The spread of relational ideas can be detected for example in how notions like 'network', 'actor-network', and 'rhizome' have become part of the commonplace social scientific parlance. Scholarship has also addressed the relational aspects of the work of authors like Émile Durkheim (Dépelteau, 2017), George Herbert Mead (Côté, 2018), Niklas Luhmann (Guy, 2018a, 2018b), and Michel Foucault (Pyyhtinen & Tamminen, 2011), and Pierre Bourdieu ([1994] 1998) himself announced that his method of inquiry is 'relational' and insisted that 'the real is relational'. The reawakened interest in Norbert Elias' 'figurational sociology' (see e.g. Dépelteau & Landini, 2017), too, attests to the increasing popularity of relational sociology. It was above all with the publication of Mustafa Emirbayer's (1997) article 'Manifesto for a Relational Sociology' in *The American Journal of Sociology* in 1997 that relational sociology began to take shape as an explicit, self-conscious programme, but in the past decade the programme has gained unprecedented momentum. We can notice this for example in the numerous books and edited volumes published (e.g. Crossley, 2011; Donati, 2011; Dépelteau & Powell, 2013; Powell & Dépelteau, 2013; Donati & Archer, 2015; Pyyhtinen, 2017; Dépelteau, 2018).

Simmel's manner of investigating social reality through relations is in congruence with the recent programmatic calls for relational sociology, and his contribution – along with that of Gabriel Tarde and Marcel Mauss – to initiating a relational approach in sociology has been acknowledged in scholarship. Although relational sociology itself is a far more recent invention, Simmel's commitment to relational thinking was, however, already emphasized in the secondary literature one hundred years ago. In early 20th century France, Simmel was read and appreciated above all as a relativist philosopher. In 1912, a collection of Simmel's essays in French translation appeared under the title *Mélanges de philosophie relativiste* (GSG 19, pp. 137–371). The volume came out a year later than the German collection *Philosophische Kultur* (GSG 14, pp. 159–459), which had been published in 1911. While both volumes focus on philosophical culture (as is clearly announced by the title of the German book and the subtitle *Contributions à la culture philosophique* of *Mélanges*), *Mélanges* has a quite different emphasis compared to *Philosophische Kultur*. Unlike the latter, it is explicitly ordered under the keyword 'relativism'. Gregor Fitzi suggests that while in Germany the notion of 'relativism' bore negative connotations, in France it was not associated with epistemological or ethical scepticism. On the contrary, the expression *philosophie relativiste* had a very positive meaning (Fitzi, 2002, p. 243 f.) It can be summarized with the formula 'relativism is relationism' (Papilloud, 2018, p. 202).

Alfred Mamelet's *Le Relativisme Philosophique chez Georg Simmel* (1914) exemplifies well the early French appreciation of Simmel's relationism. Having appeared originally as four individual essays in issues of *Revue de métaphysique* between 1912 and 1913, Mamelet subsequently collected the papers together into the monograph. In his study, Mamelet interprets relativism within the framework of Kant's transcendental philosophy, and thereby he also sees Simmel's relativism as growing out of Kant's work (Fitzi, 2002, p. 247). Although the book focuses on Simmel as a philosopher, Mamelet touches on Simmel's sociology, too, and links it with his relativist philosophy. As he writes: 'The sociology of Simmel is very clearly governed and directed by his relativist point of view, in particular by the notion of the complementarity and reciprocity of action' (Mamelet, 1965, p. 73). Mamelet sees that Simmel's sociological relativism is 'from the outset, clearly opposed to contemporary French sociology' (ibid., p. 64). He contrasts Simmel's conception of sociology above all to that of Durkheim. For Mamelet, Simmel's sociology has the advantage over Durkheimian sociology that, first, it is not only 'much wider in scope' but, second, it also pays attention to the processes on which social formations are based. As Mamelet remarks, Simmel's sociology does 'not limit itself, as does Durkheim's sociology, to the study of social macrocosms which are objectified, large-scale, synthetic, secondary, and detached from the human interactions from which they derive', but it 'show[s] us the microcosmic structures of society and help[s] us to grasp the detail of the processes of which large-scale institutions … are the result' (ibid., p. 65 f.). Due to its open-ended relation to the world, Mamelet sees relativism as a usable heuristic means.

Nevertheless, *Le Relativisme Philosophique chez Georg Simmel* criticizes Simmel's 'relativism' or relational mode of thought – and all transcendental philosophy in general – especially for being unable to grasp the metaphysical unity of the world.

Mamelet insists that only a philosophical system can achieve this. For him, relativism remains too tightly within the domain of science to build a metaphysics (Fitzi, 2002, p. 248 f.). Mamelet's placement of Simmel's relational approach under Kant's transcendental philosophy is without doubt dubious, for Simmel's relationalism is in no way reducible to it, and Simmel's mature work, especially his life-philosophy, is in fact highly critical of it. Further, it can also be argued against Mamelet that Simmel's philosophical relationalism is primarily concerned with supplementing scientific knowledge by offering an overarching view of the totality of the world. All these problems notwithstanding, Mamelet's study is significant and interesting in that it stands as a testimony of how already some of Simmel's contemporaries engaged themselves with his 'relativism' or relationalism. What is more, it also exemplifies that in France the word 'relativism' was not understood in a negative sense, associated with subjectivism and scepticism (ibid., p. 249), but it was conceived in a manner truer to Simmel, as referring to how relations are constitutive of reality.

Simmel's relational insights have been influential, for example, in social network analysis (e.g. Burt, 1976; Cooper, 2005; Rainie & Wellman, 2012; Chayko, 2015). Scholars have drawn in particular on Simmel's discussion of triads and the role of third parties in relationships when emphasizing the triangular relationship as the elementary unit of networks. No relationship is an isolated unit, but all relations are preconditioned by, connected to, and part of a wider network of relations, and it is the 'third' which epitomizes and opens up this wider dimension of the network (e.g. Callon, 1998; Crossley, 2011). In addition, scholars have utilized Simmel's discussion of the basic triadic forms to articulate different kinds of network configurations in relation to network positions (e.g. Burt, 1993).

Contemporary authors too have emphasized Simmel's major contribution to developing relational thought (see e.g. Cantó-Milà, 2005, 2016b, 2018; Pyyhtinen, 2010, 2016, 2017; Crossley, 2011; Donati, 2011; Ruggieri, 2016, 2017; Papilloud, 2018; see also Ruggieri in this volume). For example, in *A Sociological Theory of Value: Georg Simmel's Sociological Relationalism* (2005) Natàlia Cantó-Milà identifies Simmel's relationalism as the epistemological basis of his theory of value and provides a systematic reconstruction of Simmel's relational manner of thinking. Christian Papilloud (2018) has examined the context, main ideas, and key concepts of Simmel's relational sociology, and, again, Cantó-Milà (2018) has discussed Simmel's notion of forms of 'association' (*Vergesellschaftung*) and apriorities of society as crucial analytical tools for relational sociology. Further, in *Relational Sociology: A New Paradigm for Social Sciences* (2011), Pierpaolo Donati (2011) locates the beginning of relational sociology in Simmel's work. According to Donati, 'with him, it was understood for the first time that the reality of what we call "social" is intimately relational' (Donati, 2011, p. 6).

In *Simmel and 'the Social'* (2010), the author of this chapter examines Simmel's relational understanding of the social in more detail and argues that Simmel's manner of thinking social reality through relations resonates with several relationalist and processualist emphases in contemporary social thought and philosophy. *The Simmelian Legacy: A Science of Relations* (2017) expands this by making the legacy of Simmel's relational thinking more explicit. In the book, I argue that it is above all his relational mode of thought that comprises Simmel's legacy for us, with great potential to enrich our thinking (Pyyhtinen, 2017). What is more, I have also argued that by building on Simmel we can develop a relational, non-reductionist social ontology,[4] which not only acknowledges the fundamental entanglement and interconnectedness of beings but also helps us escape the long tradition of conceiving the world in terms of the micro–macro distinction. Simmel's sociological relationalism is suggestive of an entirely different scalar imaginary vis-à-vis the bi-focal micro–macro and individual–society models. Instead of modelling the world in accordance with a few discrete levels forming a nested vertical hierarchy, it pictures it in terms of infinite chains of manifolds. The manifolds themselves are wholes composed of *Wechselwirkungen* between their parts. The different scalar imaginary also suggests that the world entails an infinite number of layers, not only two, and each of these layers is in principle as real as any other. (Pyyhtinen, 2016, 2017).

Conclusion

In conclusion, contemporary sociological discussions and debates could be said to rely on Simmel in roughly three ways. Firstly, by utilizing in a more or less selective manner Simmel's ideas and formulations concerning specific themes and phenomena. We saw how Simmel has figured as a source of information and inspiration for the analysis of a great variety of topics, from money to senses, emotions, and urban space, for example, and he has been used both in empirical research and theoretical approaches. Secondly, besides being a treasure chest of ideas and observations about particular phenomena, Simmel's work has also been acknowledged for defining the subject matter of sociology. This is what, for example, Albion W. Small, Robert E. Park, and Talcott Parsons appreciated in Simmel. Simmel insisted that sociology should focus on a clearly demarcated problem area: it should study what amounts to society in various socio-historical phenomena, that is, investigate society as such, without further additions (GSG 11). Thirdly, Simmel's actuality has also been stressed by using his work as a source of general theoretical orientations. This manner of incorporation concerns the analytical perspective provided by Simmel.

Perhaps the most salient and significant line of interpretation in contemporary scholarship with regard to this last point, as was suggested above, concerns the relational aspects of his thought. For Simmel, there are no natural unities, but each entity is an achievement, produced in and through relations. There is also no substance to entities other than their relations or, more exactly, their event, their actualization in relations. Relations are one with the essence or substance of a thing. Instead of beginning from static, self-closed entities in a state of rest, Simmel turns attention to their emergence, movement, and stabilization, as well as cessation in and through relations of interdependence. The approach has also political potential, in that it may allow people to realize themselves as active participants in the making of history and society.

All in all, the longstanding perception of Simmel as a marginal of neglected figure no longer holds true. Today, Simmel is widely appreciated, not only for his analyses of particular concrete phenomena, but also for his *mode of thought*. However, notwithstanding Simmel's canonization as a classical sociologist, to some extent he also belongs to a 'counter history' of sociology, offering us ways of escaping the canonized history of the discipline and restructuring the sociological imagination. Indeed, attempts to canonize Simmel, as Goodstein (2017) argues, risk effacing the anomalous aspects of his thought. There is something in Simmel that resists assimilation and provides a shock. By assimilating his work as part of the recognized canon of sociological and cultural theory we may lose what is untypical, strange, transgressive, and most vibrant in and about his work. Simmel's work has to offer insights and a manner of thinking that to this day present a challenge to our preconceived and taken-for-granted notions. In a sense, then, in our adventures into sociological theory we meet Simmel toward the end of the journey, 'coming back from a point we are still struggling to reach' (Duncan, 1959, p. 108). To some extent, the creative and theoretical potential of his work still remains to be discovered.

Notes

1 Schnabel (1974) and Dahme (1981) provide an overview of Simmel's reception in Germany up to the 1970s, and Pyyhtinen (2017) gives an updated version of the reception in the Anglophone, German, and French intellectual worlds. However, a systematic and detailed study into how Simmel figures in contemporary sociology and how he is used is missing. Despite its title, not even the edited volume *Georg Simmel and Contemporary Sociology* (1990) maps the links between Simmel and contemporary scholarship in an encompassing and explicit manner. Rather it only presents new interpretations of his work.

2 In addition, *The Handbook of Economic Sociology* (2005), edited by Neil J. Smelser and Richard Swedberg, acknowledges Simmel as one of the classics of economic sociology and *The Philosophy of Money* as one of the classical works within the field.

3 However, as I have argued elsewhere (see Pyyhtinen, 2017), Zelizer's criticism of Simmel is not entirely accurate or justified. This is because, firstly, Simmel seems to acknowledge the fact that money may have various meanings. For instance, he notes in *The Philosophy of Money* how the same amount of money may differ in nature, depending on whether it belongs to a poor or wealthy person ([1900/07] 1989 GSG 6, pp. 277–81; Simmel, 2004, pp. 219–21). Further, a bit later in the book, Simmel tells how 'the same amount of money in the hands of a stock exchange speculator or a renter, or the State or the large industrialist produces extraordinarily different returns' ([1900/07] 1989 GSG 6, p. 389; Simmel, 2004, p. 293). Secondly, while he admits that it is possible to attach for instance personal, practical, and aesthetic value to money, Simmel stresses that these are renounced or they at least recede to the background when money is used as money ([1900/07] 1989 GSG 6, pp. 173–4; Simmel, 2004, p. 151). As soon as these extra-economic values prevail, money is in a sense withdrawn from circulation and no longer operates as money. Just as 'the unsold commodity is merely a possible commodity, which becomes a real commodity only at the moment of sale', money that is not used for the purpose of buying is money only potentially. It becomes 'real money only at the moment when it buys something' ([1900/07] 1989 GSG 6, p. 150; Simmel, 2004, p. 136).

4 By 'non-reductionism' I mean an analysis that remains immanent to relations and avoids reliance on any transcendent predetermination, such as the micro–macro model that is not only reductionist but also often assumed in advance, something like a transcendental model. Once set in place, it offers itself so naturally to us that it is difficult not to conceive the world along its contours (Marston, Jones, & Woodward, 2005, p. 422; Pyyhtinen, 2015).

References

Accarino, Bruno (1984). Vertrauen und Versprechen. Kredit, Öffentlichkeit und individuelle Entscheidung bei Simmel. In H.-J. Dahme & O. Rammstedt (Eds.), *Georg Simmel und die Moderne. Neue Interpretationen und Materialien* (pp. 116–46). Frankfurt am Main: Suhrkamp.

Amat, Matthieu (2018). *Le relationnisme philosophique de Georg Simmel. Une idée de la culture.* Paris: Honoré Champion.

Appadurai, Arjun (1988). Introduction: Commodities and the politics of value. In Arjun Appadurai (Ed.), *The social life of things. Commodities in cultural perspective* (pp. 3–63). Cambridge: Cambridge University Press.

Barbour, Charles (2012). The maker of lies: Simmel, mendacity and the economy of faith. *Theory, Culture & Society (Annual Review)*, 19(4), 218–36.

Beer, David (2019). *Georg Simmel's concluding thoughts. Worlds, lives, fragments.* Cham: Palgrave Macmillan.

Borden, Iain (1997). Space beyond: Spatiality and the city in the writings of Georg Simmel. *Journal of Architecture*, 2(4), 313–35.

Bourdieu, Pierre ([1994] 1998). *Practical reason: On the theory of action.* Trans. Randal Johnson and Loïc Wacquant. Stanford, CA: Stanford University Press.

Bradford, Simon & Clark, Marilyn (2014). Strangers on the shore: Sub-Saharan African "irregular" migrants in Malta. *Journal of Immigrant & Refugee Studies*, 12(1), 9–26.

Burt, Ronald S. (1976). Positions in networks. *Social Forces*, 55, 93–122.

Burt, Ronald S. (1993). The social structure of competition. In Richard Swedberg (Ed.), *Explorations in economic sociology* (pp. 57–91). New York: Russell Sage Foundation.

Callon, Michel (1998). Introduction: The embeddedness of economic markets in economics. In M. Callon (Ed.), *The laws of the markets* (pp. 1–57). Oxford and Maiden: Blackwell/The Sociological Review.

Cantó-Milà, Natàlia (2005). *A sociological theory of value: Georg Simmel's sociological relationism*. Bielefeld: Transcript.

Cantó-Milà, Natàlia (2012). Gratitude – Invisibly webbing society together. *Journal of Classical Sociology*, *13*(1), 8–19.

Cantó-Milà, Natàlia (2016a). Linking emotions: Emotions as the invisible threads that bind people together. *Sociological Research Online*, *21*(1), 1–4.

Cantó-Milà, Natàlia (2016b). On the special relation between proximity and distance in Simmel's forms of association and beyond. In Th. Kemple & O. Pyyhtinen (Eds.), *The Anthem companion to Georg Simmel* (pp. 81–100). London and New York: Anthem Press.

Cantó-Milà, Natàlia (2018). Georg Simmel's concept of forms of association as an analytical tool for relational sociology. In F. Dépelteau (Ed.) *The Palgrave handbook of relational sociology* (pp. 217–230). New York: Palgrave Macmillan.

Chayko, Mary (2015). The first web theorist? Georg Simmel and the legacy of 'the web of group-affiliations'. *Information, Communication & Society*, *18*(12), 1419–22.

Cooper, Robert (2005). Peripheral vision: Relationality. *Organization Studies*, *26*(11), 1689–710.

Côté, Jean-François (2018). G. H. Mead and relational sociology: The case of concepts. In F. Dépelteau (Ed.), *The Palgrave handbook of relational sociology* (pp. 101–17). Cham: Palgrave Macmillan.

Crossley, Nick (2011). *Towards relational sociology*. London and New York: Routledge.

Dahme, Heinz-Jürgen (1981). *Soziologie als exakte Wissenschaft. Georg Simmels Ansatz und seine Bedeutung in der gegenwärtigen Soziologie. I & II: Simmel's Soziologie in Grundriß*. Stuttgart: Enke.

Dahme, Heinz-Jürgen (1988). On Georg Simmel's Sociology of the Sexes. *International Journal of Politics, Culture, and Society*, *1*(3), 412–30.

Dahme, Heinz-Jürgen (1990). On the current rediscovery of Georg Simmel's sociology – A European point of view. In M. Kaern, B. Phillips, & R. S. Cohen (Eds.), *Georg Simmel and contemporary sociology* (pp. 13–37). Dordrecht: Kluwert.

Darmon, Isabelle & Frade, Carlos (2012). Beneath and beyond the fragments: The charms of Simmel's philosophical path for contemporary subjectivities. *Theory, Culture & Society*, *29*(7–8), 197–217.

De la Fuente, Eduardo (2007). On the promise of a sociological aesthetics: From Georg Simmel to Michel Maffesoli. *Distinktion*, *15*, 91–110.

De la Fuente, Eduardo (2008). The art of social forms and the social forms of art: The sociology-aesthetics nexus in Georg Simmel's thought. *Sociological Theory*, *26*(4), 344–62.

De la Fuente, Eduardo (2016b). A qualitative theory of culture: Georg Simmel and cultural sociology. In D. Inglis & A.-M. Almila (Eds.), *The SAGE handbook of cultural sociology* (pp. 78–90). London: Sage.

De la Fuente, Eduardo (2016a). Frames, handles and landscapes: Simmel and the aesthetic ecology of things. In Th. Kemple & O. Pyyhtinen (Eds.), *The Anthem Companion to Georg Simmel* (pp. 161–184). London and New York: Anthem Press.

Dépelteau, François (2017). Toward a processual-relational adaptation of 'substantialist' sociology: Starting with Durkheim. *Sosiologia*, *54*(4), 410–25.

Dépelteau, François (Ed.) (2018). *The Palgrave handbook of relational sociology*. Cham: Palgrave Macmillan.

Dépelteau, François & Powell, Christopher (Eds.) (2013). *Applying relational sociology: Relations, networks, & society*. New York: Palgrave Macmillan.

Dépelteau, François & Landini, Tatiana (2017). *Norbert Elias and social theory*. New York: Palgrave Macmillan.

Dodd, Nigel (1994). *The sociology of money. Economics, reason and contemporary society*. Cambridge: Polity Press.

Dodd, Nigel (2014). *The social life of money*. Princeton, NJ: Princeton University Press.

Dodd, Nigel (2016). Vires in Numeris: Taking Simmel to Mt Gox. In Th. Kemple & O. Pyyhtinen (Eds.), *The Anthem companion to Georg Simmel* (pp. 121–40). London and New York: Anthem Press.

Donati, Pierpaolo (2011). *Relational sociology: A new paradigm for the social sciences*. London and New York: Routledge.

Donati, Pierpaolo & Archer, Margaret (2015). *The relational subject*. Cambridge: Cambridge University Press.

Duncan, Hugh Dalziel, (1959). Simmel's image of society. In K. H. Wolff (Ed.), *Georg Simmel, 1858–1918. A collection of essays, with translations and a bibliography* (pp. 100–18). Ohio: Ohio State University Press.

Emirbayer, Mustafa (1997). Manifesto for a relational sociology. *The American Journal of Sociology*, *103*(2), 281–317.

Fischer, Joachim (2000). Der Dritte. Zur Anthropologie der Intersubjektivität. In W. Eßbach (Ed.), *Identität und Alterität in Theorie und Methode* (pp. 103–36). Würzburg: Ergon.

Fischer, Joachim (2010). Der lachende Dritte. Schlüsselfigur der Soziologie Simmels. In E. Eßlinger, T. Schlechtriemen, D. Schweitzer, & A. Zons (Eds.), *Die Figur des Dritten. Ein kulturwissenschaftliches Paradigma* (pp. 193–207). Frankfurt am Main: Suhrkamp.

Fischer, Joachim (2013). Turn to the third. A systematic consideration of an innovation in social theory. In B. Malkmus & I. Cooper (Eds.), *Dialectic and paradox: Configurations of the third in modernity* (pp. 81–102). Oxford: Oxford University Press.

Fitzi, Gregor (2002). *Soziale Erfahrung und Lebensphilosophie. Georg Simmels Beziehung zu Henri Bergson.* Konstanz: Universitätsverlag Konstanz.

Fitzi, Gregor (2016). Modernity as solid liquidity: Simmel's life-sociology. In Th. Kemple & O. Pyyhtinen (Eds.), *The Anthem companion to Georg Simmel* (pp. 59–80). London and New York: Anthem Press.

Fitzi, Gregor (2019). *The challenge of modernity: Simmel's sociological theory.* London and New York: Routledge.

Frisby, David (1985). Georg Simmel: First theorist of modernity. *Theory, Culture & Society, 2*(3), 49–67.

Frisby, David (1986). *Fragments of modernity: Theories of modernity in the work of Simmel, Kracauer and Benjamin.* Cambridge, MA: MIT.

Frisby, David (1992). *Simmel and since. Essays on Georg Simmel's social theory.* London and New York: Routledge.

Frisby, David (2001). *Cityscapes of modernity. Critical explorations.* Cambridge: Polity Press.

Fritsch, Daniel (2009). *Georg Simmel im Kino. Die Soziologie des frühen Films und das Abenteuer der Moderne.* Bielefeld: Transcript.

Gazit, Orit (2018) A Simmelian approach to space in world politics. *International Theory, 10*(2), 219–52.

Giacomoni, Paola (2006). Kontinuität der Formen. Georg Simmels Interpretation einiger Begriffe der Naturforschung Goethes. *Simmel Studies, 16*(1), 5–19.

Goodstein, Elizabeth (2017). *Georg Simmel and the disciplinary imaginary.* Stanford, CA: Stanford University Press.

Gronow, Jukka (1993). Taste and fashion: The social function of fashion and style. *Acta Sociologica, 36*(2), 89–100.

Gronow, Jukka (1997). *The sociology of taste.* London and New York: Routledge.

Gross, Matthias (2000). Classical sociology and the restoration of nature: The relevance of Émile Durkheim and Georg Simmel. *Organization & Environment, 13*(3), 277–91.

Gross, Matthias (2001). Unexpected interactions. Georg Simmel and the observation of nature. *Journal of Classical Sociology, 1*(3), 395–414.

GSG 6: Simmel, Georg ([1900/07] 1989). *Philosophie des Geldes. Georg Simmel Gesamtausgabe Band 6.* Eds. David Frisby & Klaus Christian Köhnke. Frankfurt am Main: Suhrkamp.

GSG 11: Simmel, Georg ([1908] 1992). *Soziologie: Untersuchungen über die Formen der Vergesellschaftung. Georg Simmel Gesamtausgabe Band 11.* Ed. Otthein Rammstedt. Frankfurt am Main: Suhrkamp.

Guy, Jean-Sebastién (2018a). Is Niklas Luhmann a relational sociologist? In François Dépelteau (Ed.), *The Palgrave handbook of relational sociology* (pp. 289–304). Cham: Palgrave Macmillan.

Guy, Jean-Sebastién (2018b). Niklas Luhmann before relational sociology: The cybernetics roots of systems theory. *Systems Research and Behavioral Science, 35*, 856–68.

Holt, Douglas B. & Searls, Kathleen (1994). The Impact of modernity on consumption: Simmel's philosophy of money. *Advances in Consumer Research, 21*, 65–69.

Jalava, Janne (2006). *Trust as a decision: The problems and functions of trust in Luhmannian systems theory.* Helsinki: University of Helsinki. PhD thesis.

Kandal, Terry R. (1988). *The woman question in classical sociological theory.* Miami: Florida International University Press.

Kemple, Thomas (2007). Allosociality: Bridges and doors to Simmel's social theory of the limit. *Theory, Culture & Society, 24*(7–8), 1–19.

Kemple, Thomas (2016). Simmel and the sources of neoliberalism. In Th. Kemple & O. Pyyhtinen (Eds.), *The Anthem Companion to Georg Simmel* (pp. 141–60). London and New York: Anthem Press.

Kemple, Thomas (2018). *Simmel.* Cambridge: Polity Press.

Köhnke, Klaus Christian (1996). *Der junge Simmel in Theoriebeziehungen und sozialen Bewegungen.* Frankfurt am Main: Suhrkamp.

Läpple, Dieter (1991). Essay über den Raum. Für ein gesellschaftswissenschaftliches Raumkonzept. In H. Häußermann, D. Ipsen, & Th. Krämer-Badoni (Eds.), *Stadt und Raum. Soziologische Analysen* (pp. 157–207). Pfaffenweiler: Centaurus.

Lash, Scott (2005). Lebenssoziologie. Georg Simmel in the information age. *Theory, Culture & Society, 22*(3), 1–23.

Lechner, Frank J. (1991). Simmel on social space. *Theory, Culture & Society, 8*(3), 195–201.

Leck, Ralph M. (2000). *Georg Simmel and avant-garde sociology. The birth of modernity, 1880–1920.* New York: Humanity Books.

Lee, Monica & Silver, David (2012). Simmel's law of the individual and the ethics of the relational self. *Theory, Culture & Society, 29*(7–8), 124–45.

Lehtonen, Turo-Kimmo & Pyyhtinen, Olli (2020). From trash to treasure: Valuing waste in dumpster diving. *Valuation Studies,* 7(2), 47–69.

Löw, Martina (2001). *Raumsoziologie.* Frankfurt am Main: Suhrkamp.

Luhmann, Niklas (1979). *Trust and power.* Chichester: John Wiley.

Mamelet, Alfred (1914). *Le relativisme philosophique chez Georg Simmel.* Paris: Alcan.

Mamelet, Alfred (1965). Sociological relativism. In L. A. Coser (Ed.), *Georg Simmel* (pp. 64–73). Englewood Cliffs, NJ: Prentice-Hall.

Marston, Sallie A., Jones, John Paul, III, & Woodward, Keith (2005). Human geography without scale. *Transactions of the Institute of British Geographers, 30*(4), 416–32.

Meyer, Ingo (2017). *Georg Simmels Ästhetik, Autonomiepostulat und soziologische Referenz.* Weilerswist: Velbrück Wisssenschaft.

Miller, Daniel (1987). *Material culture and mass consumption.* Oxford, UK: Blackwell.

Möllering, Guido (2001). The nature of trust: From Georg Simmel to theory of expectation, interpretation and suspension. *Sociology, 35*(2), 403–20.

Nedelmann, Birgitta (1990). Georg Simmel as an analyst of autonomous dynamics: The merry-go-round of fashion. In M. Kaern, B. S. Philips, & R. S. Cohen (Eds.), *Georg Simmel and contemporary sociology* (pp. 243–58). Dordrecht: Kluwer.

Nooteboom, Bart (2006). Simmel's treatise on the triad. *Journal of Institutional Economics, 2*(3), 365–83.

Oakes, Guy (1984). The problem of women in Simmel's theory of culture. In G. Simmel (Ed.), *On women, sexuality, and love* (pp. 3–62). Ed. Guy Oakes. New Haven, CT and London: Yale University Press.

Paasi, Anssi (2012). Border studies reanimated: Going beyond the territorial-relational divide. *Environment and Planning A, 44,* 2303–09.

Papilloud, Christian (2018). Georg Simmel and relational sociology. In F. Dépelteau (Ed.), *The Palgrave handbook of relational sociology* (pp. 201–15). Cham: Palgrave Macmillan.

Poggi, Giancarlo (1993). *Money and the modern mind: Georg Simmel's philosophy of money.* Berkeley, CA: University of California Press.

Powell, Christopher & Dépelteau, François (Eds.) (2013). *Conceptualizing relational sociology: Ontological and theoretical issues.* New York: Palgrave Macmillan.

Pyyhtinen, Olli (2009). Being-with: Georg Simmel's sociology of association. *Theory, Culture & Society, 26*(5), 108–28.

Pyyhtinen, Olli (2010). *Simmel and 'the social'.* Basingstoke and New York: Palgrave Macmillan.

Pyyhtinen, Olli (2012). Life, death and individuation: Simmel on the problem of life itself. *Theory, Culture & Society, 29*(7–8), 78–100.

Pyyhtinen, Olli (2015). *More-than-human sociology: A new sociological imagination.* Basingstoke and New York: Palgrave Macmillan.

Pyyhtinen, Olli (2016). The real as relation: Simmel as a pioneer of relational sociology. In Th. Kemple & O. Pyyhtinen (Eds.), *The anthem companion to Georg Simmel* (pp. 101–20). London and New York: Anthem Press.

Pyyhtinen, Olli (2017). *The Simmelian legacy: A science of relations.* Basingstoke and New York: Palgrave Macmillan.

Pyyhtinen, Olli (2018). Das Dritte. In H.-P. Müller & T. Reitz (Eds.), *Simmel-Handbuch: Begriffe, Hauptwerke, Aktualität* (pp. 172–77). Frankfurt am Main: Suhrkamp.

Pyyhtinen, Olli (2019). Confessions of a troubled parrhesiast. Writing as a mode of truth-telling about self in Karl Ove Knausgaard's My Struggle. *Digithum, 24.*

Pyyhtinen, Olli & Tamminen, Sakari (2011). We have never been only human: Foucault and Latour on the question of the anthropos. *Anthropological Theory, 11*(2), 135–52.

Rainie, Lee & Wellman, Barry (2012). *Networked: The new social operating system.* Cambridge, MA: MIT Press.

Rammstedt, Otthein (1994). Georg Simmel. *Soziologie: Mitteilungsblatt der Deutschen Gesellschaft für Soziologie.* Sonderheft, *3,* 103–13.

Rammstedt, Otthein (2005). Foreword. In Natàlia Cantó-Milà (Eds.), *A sociological theory of value: Georg Simmel's sociological relationism* (pp. 9–11). Bielefeld: Transcript.

Ruggieri, Davide (2016). *La sociologia relazionale di Georg Simmel: La relazione come forma sociale vitale.* Milano: Mimesis.

Ruggieri, Davide (2017). Georg Simmel and the 'relational turn'. Contributions to the foundation of the *Lebenssoziologie* since Simmel. *Simmel Studies, 21*(1), 43–72.

Sabido Ramos, Olga (2017). The senses as a resource of meaning in the construction of the stranger: An approach from Georg Simmel's relational sociology. *Simmel Studies, 21*(1), 15–42.

Sabido Ramos, Olga (2019). El análisis sociológico de la vergüenza en Georg Simmel: Una propuesta para pensar el carácter performativo y relacional de las emociones. *Digithum, 23*. DOI: http://doi.org/10.7238/d.v0i23.3148

Sassatelli, Roberta (2000). From value to consumption. A social-theoretical perspective on Simmel's Philosophie des Geldes. *Acta Sociologica, 43*(3), 207–18.

Scaff, Lawrence (2005). The mind of the modernist: Simmel on time. *Time & Society, 14*(1), 5–23.

Schäfers, Bernhard & Bauer, Bettina (1994). Georg Simmels Beitrag zur Raumbezogenheit sozialer Wechselwirkungen. In S. Meyer & E. Schulze (Eds.), *Ein Puzzle das nie aufgeht. Stadt, Region und Individuum in der Moderne* (pp. 45–56). Berlin: Sigma.

Schiermer, Bjørn (2009). Fashion objects: Breaking up the Durkheimian cult. *Distinktion, 10*(2), 81–104.

Schiermer, Bjørn (2015). Fashion victims: On the individualizing and de-individualizing powers of fashion. *Fashion Theory, 14*(1), 83–104.

Schillmeier, Michael (2012). Assembling money and the senses: Revisiting Georg Simmel and the city. In I. Farias & T. H. Bender (Eds.), *Urban assemblages: How actor-network theory changes urban studies* (pp. 229–252). New York: Routledge.

Schnabel, Peter-Ernst (1974). *Die Soziologische Gesamtkonzeption Georg Simmels. Eine wissenschaftshistorische und wissenschaftstheoretische Untersuchung.* Stuttgart: Gustav Fischer.

Schroer, Markus (2006). *Räume, Orte, Grenzen. Auf dem Weg zu einer Soziologie des Raumes.* Frankurt am Main: Suhrkamp.

Seebach, Swen (2017). *Love and society: Special social forms and the master emotion.* London and New York: Routledge.

Seebach, Swen & Núñez Mosteo, Francesc (2016). Is romantic love a linking emotion? *Sociological Research Online, 21*(1), 1–12.

Simmel, Georg (2004). *The philosophy of money.* Third enlarged edition, trans. David Frisby & Tom Bottomore. London and New York: Routledge.

Smelser, Neil J. & Richard, Swedberg (Eds.) (2005). *The handbook of economic sociology.* Princeton, NJ and Oxford: Princeton University Press.

Swedberg, Richard (2011). The role of senses and signs in the economy. *Journal of Cultural Economy, 4*(4), 423–37.

Tester, Keith (1993). *The life and times of Post-Modernity.* London and New York: Routledge.

van Vucht Tjissen, Lieteke (1991). Women and objective culture: Georg Simmel and Marianne Weber. *Theory, Culture & Society, 8*(3), 203–18.

Vidler, Anthony (1991). Agoraphobia: Spatial estrangement in Georg Simmel and Siegfried Kracauer. *New German Critique, 54*, 31–45.

Weinstein, Deena & Weinstein, Michael (1989). Simmel and the dialectic of the double boundary: The Case of the metropolis and the mental life. *Sociological Inquiry, 59*(1), 48–59.

Welty, Gordon (1996). Simmel on 'the lie'. *S: European Journal for Semiotic Studies, 7*(2), 273–98.

Wirth, Louis (1925). A bibliography of the urban community. In R. E. Park, E. W. Burgess, & R. D. Mckenzie (Eds.), *The city* (pp. 161–228). Chicago, IL: University of Chicago Press.

Witz, Anne (2001). Georg Simmel and the masculinity of modernity. *Journal of Classical Sociology, 1*(3), 353–70.

Wolff, Kurt H. (1950). *The sociology of Georg Simmel.* Translated, edited and with an introduction by Kurt H. Wolff. New York: Free Press.

Zelizer, Viviana (1994). *The social meaning of money. Pin money, paychecks, poor relief, & other currencies.* New York: Basic Books.

Ziemann, Andreas (2000). *Die Brücke zur Gesellschaft. Erkenntniskritische und topographische Implikationen der Soziologie Georg Simmels.* Konstanz: Universitätsverlag Konstanz.

3

RELATIONS, FORMS, AND THE REPRESENTATION OF THE SOCIAL LIFE

Georg Simmel and the challenge of relational sociology as *Lebenssoziologie*

Davide Ruggieri

Introduction

Relational Sociology (RS) has come to play a pivotal role on the international stage. Over the course of a movement born almost thirty-five years ago (Donati, 1983), RS has been gradually pervading the different aspects of sociological studies as well as a vast range of fields (Fuhse & Mützel, 2010; Powell & Dépelteau, 2013a, 2013b; Dépelteau, 2018), giving rise to a plethora of worthy innovative ideas, methods, and models: the 'social relation' is considered an extremely key issue in order to comprehend and reshape the idea of a globalised society. Hence, sociology tackles 'social relations' as its own matter, and it takes into account that the very nature of the social realm is relational and interactive due to the 'solid liquid' character of the modern stage (Fitzi, 2016).

Georg Simmel previously stated that sociology, as an independent discipline of humanities, has not discovered any new subject – it only furnishes a new theoretical view on modern individual life with regard to social relations that are more and more determined by the mechanisms of differentiation [*Differenzierung*] and complexity and by the reciprocity factor [*Wechselwirkung*]. As testified by Robert Park, during the *Wintersemester* 1899–1900, Georg Simmel once lectured that his idea of sociology was for him like a 'new key for old smiths' as well as a 'new hammer for old walnuts' (GSG 21, p. 282). This metaphor fits with the conviction that sociology hasn't discovered any new matter of inquiry but it only provides a new 'view' in order to take account of reality (as a social relation).

One surely might wonder if RS is a paradigm under an epistemological point of view: many authors nowadays look at RS as more of a 'turn' (one more turn after the linguistic, cultural, interpretative, narrative, reflexive, and performative turns) than a paradigmatic 'shift' (Cantó-Milà, 2016, p. 12; Vanderberghe, 2018, p. 37 f.). A great number of books and essays testify an impressive and increasing interest into RS, and the epistemological and ontological debate within the international frame on this topic is very intensive. Many amongst the relational authors refer to Georg Simmel as a pioneer as well as a founder of an entire new sector of social studies (Cantò Milà, 2005, 2018; Fuhse & Mützel, 2010; Kemple & Pyyhtinen, 2015; Papilloud, 2018a; Pyyhtinen, 2018; Müller & Reitz, 2018). Additionally, Simmel actually represents a 'relational turn' (Donati, 2011; Ruggieri, 2017) into the sociological studies and within the tradition of the well-known founders of sociology (Werber, Durkheim, Toennies, etc.), as he was committed to considering the relation (as the very 'stuff' of society) in terms of reciprocity [*Wechselwirkung*] as well as the main subject for social sciences.

However, Georg Simmel represents an uncomfortable heritage for the contemporary RS theorists. On the one hand, it depends on the fact that, for the most part, he neither furnished a systematic sociological theory nor demonstrated his theoretical and epistemological premises through empirical cases (as most of the sociological theories actually do). On the other hand, Simmel's theory has been often associated to the 'relativism' *sensu strictissimo* – from Mamelet's (Mamelet, 1914) and Spykman's (Spykman, [1925] 2017) interpretations to the actual bibliographical evidences on this issue (Milson, 2009). Additionally, Papilloud recently suggested considering Simmel's relativism, such as a form of 'relationism', in the sense that social reality is made up of relations (Papilloud, 2018a, p. 202, 2018b). Some scholars have recently demonstrated that Simmel actually maintains a very systematic sociological programme (Schluchter, 2015, p. 9; Fitzi, 2019). Furthermore, Donati remarked that the essential demarcation criterion between *relationist* and *relational* approaches into sociological programmes exactly consists of a non-reductionist bearing of social relations: while many relationist authors blur them according a functionalist, structuralist, or relativist reductive viewpoint, an authentic relational sociology must examine and consider the social *as* relation (Donati, 2017, p. 327 f.).

Simmel's RS surely opposes categorical thinking of 'substantialist' and 'essentialist' approaches (Emirbayer, 1997) to relational thinking, leading the way to contemporary (post) structuralist, interactionist, and 'processual' approaches (Abbott, 2016). In 1997, Mustafa Emirbayer was a pioneer in assessing RS as a specific field within the sociological theories and to assign it a precise physiognomy. He defined the relational perspective as the depiction of the 'social' as dynamic, continuous, and processual (Emirbayer, 1997, p. 281). He particularly distinguished the two 'substantialist approaches': the *self-action* perspectives (that is the Rational Choice theory, Norm following individuals, holistic theories, 'structuralism') and the *interaction* perspective ('variable-centred approach', survey research, and historical comparative analysis). The alternative to these theoretical assumptions (that consider an individual, an organisation, and the society itself as a predefined social unit without defining them) is for him the relational perspective.

In recent times, the sociological interests into 'relational subject' as reciprocity and mutual effect may address the ICTs impact on the social world experience as well as a new impulse for the economical stage. ICTs have been surely changing the very nature of the world we live in. As Luciano Floridi alleged in *The Onlife Manifesto – Being Human in a Hyperconnected Era* (2015), ICTs are not 'mere tools but rather social forces that are increasingly affecting our self-conception (who we are), our mutual interactions (how we socialise); our conception of reality (our metaphysics); and our interactions with reality (our agency)'. He explicitly stated that 'the shift from the primacy of entities to the primacy of interactions' [*assertion IV*] (Floridi, 2015, pp. 2, 7) – it is surely remarkable for the purposes of the following pages. In this regard, the studies on RS can flourish more and more to aid the comprehension of the globalised and digital society, as well as the 'social life' (as reciprocity) within this frame. The idea of a 'cordial economy', arising in recent studies, exactly deals with the critical process that has identified reciprocity and interaction as the determining factors for human cooperation (Bruni & Zamagni, 2013; Patrici, 2018). The same attempt could be addressed regarding the conceptual couple of social and human within the recent debate in the sociological and humanities fields – the redefinition of what is social and what is human is surely extremely topical, as well as the debate dealing with post-humanism (Ferrando, 2013; Al-Amoudi & Morgan, 2018) and new materialism (Bennett, 2010; Devellenes & Dillet, 2018) within the social sciences.

Relational sociology, social relations and the forms of social life

The scope of the following pages is to furnish a relational interpretation of Simmel's theory towards a wide 'theory of forms of social life'. We are surely in debt to Georg Simmel not only because he addressed sociology as a 'science of social relations' (Pyyhtinen, 2018) but also because – particularly in his later essays and volumes – he addressed sociology as a science of those 'forms' in which 'social life' [*soziales Leben*] achieves and fulfils human agency as relation.

Sociology must treat all these issues in a relational way. The relational paradigm focuses upon the *human* lying within the individual and within social institutions as well as non-human issues in order to reveal that what is human in social subjects and in social structures is generated through a reality, that of social relations, which depends on the former, but, at the same time, goes beyond them and exceeds them. 'Although non-material, these social relations are decisive for the unfolding of the human within social life' (Donati, 2011, p. 26). Interaction [*Wechselwirkung*] could be the very key to get access to new forms of cohabitation and co-belonging of social and human life and, more extensively, to get a comprehensive view on the relational scenario between different and opposite issues. According to Simmel, sociology must never renounce being the 'science of being-society of humankind' [*die Lehre von dem Gesellschaft-Sein der Menschheit*] (GSG 2, p. 25), that is similar to how geometry must abstract and comprehend forms of (human) social interaction from the multiplicity and complexity of realm.

The discovery of the very pervasive (metaphysical) principle of interaction [*Wechselwirkung*], inspiring and guiding Simmel's investigations, is an extremely familiar and former issue, which is explicitly recurrent in an academic document (1898) *Anfang einer unvollendeten Selbstdarstellung*:

> I grasped a new concept of sociology by separating the forms of society from the contents (that is, from the impulses, the aims, the objective) contents that become social only when they are received by the reciprocal actions between individuals; I therefore have in my books the study of these types of reciprocal action, as the object of pure sociology. But starting from this sociological meaning of the concept of interaction, it gradually turned to me in an absolutely universal metaphysical principle.
>
> *(Simmel, 1958, p. 9)[1]*

Georg Simmel first provided impulse for the detection of social relations as a reciprocity effect within the modern society frame. Reciprocal interaction generates 'forms' that are embedded in social relations:

> Association [*Vergesellschaftung*] always takes place from a starting point of particular needs, intentions or aims, that is, from highly diverse motivations ranging from material interests to ethically and religiously reflected intentions. Those are 'matters or contents' of social interaction leading human beings to gather together for different forms of action: for each other, with each other and also against each other.
>
> *(GSG 11, p. 18)*

This conviction is very familiar within Simmel's early writings – in his essay *Das Problem der Sociologie* (1894) he sustains that society, in its broadest meaning, manifests itself where more individuals enter into mutual interaction or reciprocal action [*Wechselwirkung*]. The causes and the particular purposes, without one being reached 'association' [*Vergesellschaftung*], represent in a sense the body, the content, which is the material [*das Material*] of the social process. The realisation of these causes and the promotion of these ends determines a reciprocal action and a partnership between its exponents. Additionally, within this reciprocal action the sociologist detects the form [*die Form*] of those born contents: the existence of a specific science of society exactly consists of a possible separation (by virtue of scientific abstraction) of 'contents' and 'forms' (GSG 5, p. 54). This idea is so recurrent that the same schema will be addressed in Simmel's late sociological analysis in his *Grundfragen der Soziologie*, more precisely, in the chapter *Sociability* (Simmel, 1950, p. 40, ff.). Simmel addressed in the fourth chapter of *Grundfragen der Soziologie* the question dealing with the very characteristic conflictual *niveau* between individual life and society (as collective forms and forces, which stand partly outside of individuals and partly are internalised by them) (Simmel, 1950, p. 58). This conflict is surely exacerbated into modernity, due to the more and more complex and differentiated character of social mechanisms.

Axel Honneth recently sustains in his essay *Is there an emancipatory interest? An attempt to answer critical theory's most fundamental question* (2017) that conflicts are an ineliminable feature of all forms of human sociality. He particularly argued the importance of an *Urkonflikt* explaining of the arising of the societal structure. Honneth alleged that critical theory, in this regard, must look and get inspired by Hegel, Dewey, and Simmel as a possible alternative to the *Rousseau-Kantian, Freudian* and *Marxian* views (Honneth, 2017, p. 913).

Finally, we can tackle the question that whatever these forms of social relation are, they can be assumed as *forms of social life*, as Simmel from the very beginning addressed this consideration. Rahel Jaeggi recently brought up this issue in her *Kritik von Lebensformen* (2014) within the frame of a more comprehensive critical theory. Jaeggi suggested that the forms of life should be assumed as 'the cultural and social reproduction of human life', that is, as she alleged afterwards, '*forms of life in the plural*, that is, the different cultural forms that human life can assume' (Jaeggi, 2018, p. 20). Jaeggi found the first trace of the formula *Lebensform* in Eduard Spranger, who assessed a theory on them in the 1920s. She did not mention Simmel, but, for the sake of philological accuracy, Simmel actually talked and argued first and systematically on 'soziale Lebensformen' (at least) in the volume *Grundfragen der Soziologie* (1917). The very exhaustive assertion of what Simmel conceived as a 'form' is stated in that volume – more precisely, when he alleged that: 'Any form (and a form always is a synthesis) is something added by a synthesizing subject' (Simmel, 1950, p. 7) ['*Die Form, die immer eine Verbindung ist, nur von einem verbindenden Subjekt hinzugefügt wird*'] (GSG 16, p. 66). Thus, Simmel furnished a new idea of 'form' in the volume *Lebensanschauung. Vier metaphysische Kapitel* (1918), and he alleged that it is necessarily connected to the inner essence of life (as a flux or stream):

> Life is at once flux without pause and yet something enclosed in its bearers and contents, formed about individualized midpoints, and contrarily it is therefore always a bounded form that continually oversteps its bounds; that is, its essence.
>
> *(Simmel, 2010, p. 9)*

In *Philosophie des Geldes*, Simmel furnished an exhaustive definition of society under the category of interaction and exchange [*Tausch*] and within a semantic frame dealing with the concept of life. He particularly alleged that society is neither to be considered as an abstract entity nor a theoretical fiction; on the contrary, it fills our individual lives:

Society is a structure that transcends the individual [*übersinguläre Gebilde*], but that is not abstract … Society is the universal which, at the same time, is concretely alive [*konkrete Lebendigkeit hat*]. From this arises the unique significance that exchange, as the economic-historical realization of the relativity of things, has for society; exchange raises the specific object and its significance for the individual above its singularity, not into the sphere of abstraction, but into that of lively interaction which is the substance of economic value.

(GSG 6, p. 91)

Scott Lash rightly emphasised the 'formal' turn given by Simmel's questioning on social realm: the very inquiry on '*how* is society possible?' is answered by Simmel under the detection of forms that realise something we call society: 'Kant's initial question is epistemological. Simmel's is ontological. Though there will be an epistemology that follows from it. Forms are what make society possible. These forms that prevent society from disintegrating are functions' (Lash, 2005, p. 5). The fragmentation due to the differentiation process into modernity is finally retrieved through that *objective* synthesis of social forms. As Simmel already sustained in *Soziologie*, within social processes, we catch forms that emerges as autonomous *a priori* synthesis (GSG 2, p. 44 f.), i.e., autonomous from any subjective power. The subjects are rather involved into social processes by virtue of these forms. The 'unity of society' is, in fact, quite different from the 'unity of nature' according to (Kantian) scientific-epistemological criteria. Sociology itself, as independent science amongst humanities, is delimited (under and above) from two distinct fields: metaphysics and epistemology (GSG 2, p. 40; Simmel, 1950, p. 23). Simmel literally alleged that the specific task of sociology is, thus,

considering the abstracted forms that do not so much *generate* social interaction but rather *are* social interaction. Society in a sense that sociology can use is, then, either the overall abstract concept for these forms, the genus of which they are species, or the actual momentary summation of the same.

(GSG 2, p. 18)

The same conviction on the formal inquiry and investigation of social interactions is given by Simmel in *Grundfragem der Soziologie*, as he sustained that society is an 'event' [*Geschehen*] as well as 'the destiny and the form', in which we live and experience [*erleben*] the being connected to other people (GSG 16, p. 70).

From the relational perspective to the *Lebenssoziologie*

In 2003, Liebsch and Staub analysed *Lebensformen* as the primary subject under the viewpoint of humanities in a collective volume (Liebsch & Staub, 2003): it is the scientific result of an interdisciplinary research ('Lebensformen im Widerstreit – Identität und Moral unter dem Druck gesellschaftlicher Desintegration') they were run in 2001.

The first author to explicitly conceptualise *Lebenssoziologie* (what is more, exactly referring to Simmel's sociological theory) is surely Scott Lash, who released in 2005 the essay *Lebenssoziologie: Georg Simmel and the Information Age*. His thesis tries to conciliate some contemporary sociological trends (Latour, Castells and Luhmann) with Simmel's theoretical intuitions. Thus, Lash explicitly affirmed:

Simmel addresses life in terms of social life. This is the originality of his vitalism. For other vitalists, relations between things or between subjects and things are primary.

Relations of perception are primary. For Simmel life is already social. For Simmel social life is literally social *life*. (Lash, 2005, p. 10)

Lash theorises that *Lebenssoziologie* anchors on three main 'vitalist' principles: 'monism, self-reproduction and becoming' – where, by monism, Lash means 'social networks' that is both global and informational (referring to Castells' theory). In the analysis, this theoretical position actually lacks the 'reflexive' relational sphere, which is the human property, giving to 'relations' the social *sigillum*.

In the essay *Zum historischen Verhältnis von Lebensphilosophie und Soziologie und das Programm einer Lebenssoziologie* (2008), Robert Seyfert considered the '*Emergenztheorem*' in Simmel's theory (that is the paradoxical dualism between immanence of life – as a stream – and its transcendence through forms) as the key concept for the construction of a 'Lebenssoziologie' programme, as its possible ontology exactly consists the terms of the 'emergence' (Seyfert, 2007, p. 4688 f.). In 2015, Delitz, Seyfert, and Nungasser further explored this theme, focusing on the three great vitalist (and neovitalist) axes within the sociological tradition: (1) the French tradition: Cornelius Castoriadis, Gilles Deleuze, Georges Simondon and Canguilhem, particularly inspiring and referring to Henri Bergson's philosophy; (2) the German Tradition: Max Scheler, Helmuth Plessner, Arnold Gehlen, rooting on the tradition of philosophical anthropology; and (3) the American tradition: Charles S. Peirce, William James, John Dewey and George H. Mead (Delitz, Seyfert, & Nungesser, 2015, p. 2). It should be noted that the name of Simmel is absent.

As Seyfert clarified in 2018 in the essay *Lebenssoziologie – eine intensive Wissenschaft*, the central question of *Lebenssoziologie* is how to mix organic, inorganic, and artificial elements such that a vital social structure emerges from them (Seyfert, 2018). In this construction of a *Lebenssoziologie* theory, four elements play a pivotal role: (a) emergence – social life as 'heterogeneous stuff' (Seyfert, 2018, p. 374); (b) the *stream* (becoming/growing); (c) the difference as a constitutive medium [*Leben als differenzierende Differenz*] (Seyfert, 2018, p. 387); and (d) intensity (as desubjectivation). The third point is particularly interesting for our discourse: in this regard, Simmel surely plays a worthy role in the sociological tradition and focuses on the relationship between process and form, basically on the formation of social issues from different intertwined (social) *niveaux*. Seyfert alleged that life is not to consider a predetermined form (being); it is rather a 'form of social relations', dropped into a collective structure through elements of all kinds. It is irrelevant that these elements are anthropological, organic, inorganic, or artificial (Seyfert, 2018, p. 375).

In the same volume, there's a very interesting essay, *Leben und Form der Gesellschaft. Zur Lebenssoziologie von Georg Simmel* by Thomas Kron and Pascal Berger; they alleged that Simmel furnishes a wide theory of life since his former publication *Soziologie* (1908) and, thus, explicitly sustained:

> In this very meaning we understand the forms of socialization discussed in Simmel's Sociology as one of several possible forms of unfolding that general, comprehensive vital dualism of life and form.
>
> *(Kron & Berger, 2018, p. 203)*

Kron and Berger focused on the conflict between life and form (and their *analytical* difference) within Simmel's whole work. It is surely relevant for our purposes and extremely inspiring, but what is at the core of the argument we engaged is the strong tie between RS and *Lebenssoziologie* (as detection of all forms of social life) within the whole work of Georg Simmel. From this aspect, his sociology is highly in line with some explicit references amongst the relational sociologists within the contemporary debate. Some of them refer to both 'social life' and 'social relations' as the very matter of sociological inquiry. For instance, Nick Crossley once noted that 'the most appropriate analytic unit for the scientific study of social life is the network of social relations and interactions between actors' (Crossley, 2011, p. 1).

In a footnote in the volume *Relational Sociology. A new Paradigm for Social Sciences*, Donati wrote:

I began this approach to social life with reference to natural rights by commenting on the thought of Toennies (Donati, 1991: Chapter 2) and then locating it in the L of AGIL, interpreting it in a relational manner. (Donati, 2011, p. 56)

Recently, Dépelteau sustained that 'relational sociology offers at least three promises. The first is based on the hypothesis that we can improve our understanding of social life by studying relations between interactants' (Dépelteau, 2018, p. 3). Furthermore, Vanderberghe claimed that 'at the ontological level, [RS] assumes that relations essentially create social life' (Vanderberghe, 2018, p. 39).

Simmel is convinced from the very beginning, i.e., his early writings, that modernity is the new stage for an incessant negotiation (as a processual issue) between individuals and society – the more differentiation process is at work, the more is required from individuals to accept their lives as must be experienced in social terms. This means that individual knowledge and agency, its *niveaux,* are always determined in an interactive and mutual manner: any aspect of individual experience must be traced back to the inner significance of life as process, flux, and, as necessary, interaction and intersection. This idea emerges from Simmel's earlier essay *Über eine Beziehung der Selektionslehre zur Erkenntnistheorie* (1885), where he writes in the first lines: 'For long time it has been shared the assumption that human cognition has sprung from practical necessities toward the maintenance and care of life' (GSG 5, p. 62), and, finally, it recurs in *Lebensanschauung* (1918), when Simmel explicitly stated that, 'In this regard, the cognition is nothing but a scene of life itself, which prepares another scene and thus serves the general vital intention' (GSG 16, p. 257, ff.). In each of its aspects (biological, metaphysical, artistic, sociological, and cultural), life requires mediations, 'forms', which are not only objectifications of the interactive process but also represent autonomous and self-referential worlds. These forms allow individual orientations, so they effectively work on individual lives, placing on a transcendental sphere with regard to the immanent essence of life itself.

In *Main Problems of Philosophy* (released in 1892), Simmel once alleged that reality is the 'world given to us as sum of fragments' (GSG 14, p. 32); hence, the apprehension of reality is referred to the possibility of a unified grasp of the world and oneself. This statement was progressively extended to any kind of 'world' (scientific, moral, aesthetic, religious, etc.), as literally referred by Simmel in his late writings (particularly, in his last volume *View of Life* released in 1918). Humans experience 'worlds' under a social mechanism: fragmentarity gets to unity due to innate and natural tendency to mediate with others through forms (intellectual and mind agency).

In his masterpiece *Sociology. Inquiries into the Construction of Social Forms* (1908), Simmel alleged:

Human interaction is normally based on the fact that the ideational worlds of men have certain elements in common, that objective intellectual contents constitute the material which is transformed into subjective life by means of men's social relations.

(GSG 11, p. 390 f.)

We can trace a theoretical foundation of a *Lebenssoziologie* programme already in the pages of Simmel's *Sociology*, namely, in the famous *Excursus: wie ist Gesellschaft möglich?* of the first chapter. The individuation of three sociological a priori has epistemological effects: Simmel actually attempted to ground his sociological theory already within a *soziale Erkenntnistheorie* in the first chapter of his *Über soziale Differenzierung* in 1890 (GSG 2). Additionally, this is particularly evident if we think to the (puzzling and blurred) meaning he accorded to the second of them: *Ausserdem*, i.e., being socialised depends *moreover* on unsocialised aspects (GSG 11, p. 52, ff.). Thus, Simmel stated:

> The a priori for empirical social life is that life is not entirely social. We form our interrelations under the negative restraint that a part of our personality is not to enter into them, and yet this part has an effect on the social processes in the mind through general psychological connections overall, but furthermore just the formal fact that it stands outside the social processes determines what kind of influence.
>
> *(Simmel, 2009, p. 47)*

This idea recurs in the contemporary debate dealing with not only the relation between what is proper social and what is not but also the relation between society and human. Humanity is something that is always hiding and arising beyond the immanent transactions of social realm – humanity is what determines social relations without getting into them. In *Grundfragen der Soziologie*, Simmel once stated that sociology must actually be an inquiry on 'interactions among the atoms of society. They account for all the toughness and elasticity, all the colour and consistency of social life, that is so striking and yet so mysterious' (Simmel, 1950, p. 10). Humanity is for Simmel neither a 'quantitative supplement' to society, nor the sum of all societies ever, but 'it is an entirely different synthesis of the same elements that in other syntheses result in societies. Mankind and societies are two different vantage points, as it were, from which the individual can be viewed' (Simmel, 1950, p. 63). The dichotomy between humanity and society is not oppositional, but surely fruitful and incredibly worthy for a digital, post-human, and globalised society in its dialectical meaning. As Pierpaolo Donati opined, we might distinguish a *human society*, which is a social realm (form) given by human beings as actors and agents, from a *society of the human*, in which any mediation (*in primis* the technological one) increases and tangles, so that the human must be detected even in contexts where the social relations might not be immediately human (Donati, 2009, 2018).

The arising question could be what kind of ontology must we allow to both humanity and social relations, which we do not have space to discuss here. Within the frame of the new RS addresses, Vanderberghe literally asserted that contemporary authors such as 'François Dépelteau, Andreas Glaeser, Andrew Abbott, Peter Selg, Osmo Kivinen and Tero Piiroinen defend a pragmatist position, but in their radicalism they have already incorporated the neo-vitalist process ontology of Deleuze and Latour' (Vanderberghe, 2018, p. 39). From Bachelard to Levi-Strauss and Bourdieu, he proposes a 'flat ontology' in which everything is in flux and eminently connectable. Moreover, Vanderberghe suggested a workable genealogy for social theorists, namely: Karl Marx, Georg Simmel, Gabriel Tarde, and Marcel Mauss – 'the Relational quartet' (Vanderberghe, 2018, p. 40). Recently, De Landa commented that a fundamental difference between an ontology based on relations between general types and particular instances, which is hierarchical (each level representing a different ontological category: organism, species, and genera), and 'an approach in terms of interacting parts and emergent wholes leads to a flat ontology, one made exclusively of unique, singular individuals, differing in spatio-temporal scale but not in ontological status' (De Landa, 2004, p. 58).

In 2012, Darmon and Frade stressed the idea of a re-evaluation of Simmel's theory under the light of the *Erlebnis* conceptual category: for both authors, Simmel anchored the 'philosophical attitude' in his particularly developed disposition for *Erlebnis*, i.e., the unified pre-conceptual experience of each moment of reality and life, as well as in a particular mode of objectivating this experience (Darmon & Frade, 2012). Furthermore, an attempt to read Simmel's theory under the categories of *Lebenssoziologie* is also provided by Lee and Silver, who stated in this regard (and also towards a relational assessment): 'In Sociology Simmel's relational approach, or "formal sociology," stands in direct contrast to the "organismic" approach. ... Social life consists of the living interactions, constantly being made and remade, that pulse beneath and beyond their "service organs"' (Lee & Silver, 2012, p. 127).

'Leben', pluralism, unity

The first remarkable and systematic attempt to detect a foundation of the so-called *Lebenssoziologie* is given by Simmel in his *Soziologie der Geselligkeit*, which was released in 1910. The discovery of an ontology of the sociable [*Gesellige*] and sociability [*Geselligkeit*] allowed him to focus on what is, at the same time, the very relational and the very living essence of collective forms of human living-together: the pure form of social relation, i.e., the 'forms of social lives' [*Formen des sozialen Lebens*] (GSG 12, p. 177). If society is the collection of the forms of *reciprocal actions* [*Wechselwirkungen*], 'the sum of social relations' as well as any historical form of a given society is 'the historical realm of social relations' (GSG 11, p. 23). The sociologist must treat the social realm that is detaching from institutional forms of human living-together through particular articulations of means/scopes mechanism (subordination, super-ordination, concurrence, contrast, etc.) as well as catching by insight all the pure forms of interactions (coquetterie, adventure, fashion, etc.) that often take place as plays or events. By offering this perspective, Simmel gave a fundamental and naïve impulse for the forthcoming sociology in a twofold meaning – under the former meaning, he represents a reference point for macro-sociologists and common institutional sociology, and under the latter, he is a pioneer for ethno-methodological approaches in sociology, for symbolic interactionism as well as everyday life analysis and qualitative and micro-sociological inquiries.

The 'tragedy of culture' in Simmel's late writings contains worthy intuitions dealing with what cultural objects, human life and social forms may assume. Ferdinand Fellman recently highlighted the meaning of Simmel's trajectory into modernity regarding the relationship between society and culture: they get more and more extraneous to each other, and the very danger for humankind is represented by cultural objects, because they form unintelligible and unpredictable paths for human prediction (Fellman, 2015). Additionally, this aspect deals with individual lives in the digital era, as stated by Floridi. In the 'onlife-world', artefacts have ceased to be mere machines simply operating according to human instructions. They can change states in autonomous ways and can do so by digging into the exponentially growing wealth of data, which is made increasingly available, accessible, and processable by fast-developing and ever more pervasive ICTs (Floridi, 2015, p. 10). This idea basically fits the *New Materialism* motto: 'a materialism in which matter is figured as a vitality at work both inside and outside of selves, and is a force to be reckoned with without being purposive in any strong sense' (Bennett, 2010, p. 62), and, moreover, with Latour's basic assumptions of ANT theory (Latour, 1999), as he was interested from the very beginning in 'not about the "social" but about the associations which allow connections to be made between non-social elements' (Latour, 2003). In all these forms of 'life', the subjectivity of humans is not conceived and not necessarily included: the question is human when individuals will still be interested in searching a meaning, to give a 'form', and to look for unity after (and due to) fragmentarity. Latour conveniently argued for a 'relational' issue, but did not deem it necessary to engage in any 'reflexive' issue (Latour, 2003, p. 36), as for reflexivity or 'reflexive', we must mean – Latour sustained – 'the unintended consequences of actions reverberate throughout the whole of society in such a way that they have become intractable' so that 'we become conscious that consciousness does not mean full control'.

Perhaps, it is the case to recall the 4th assertion of Floridi's *The Onlife Manifesto,* which claims that 'the shift from the primacy of entities to the primacy of interactions', and, particularly, the §4.2 on the *Relational Self:*

> We believe that it is time to affirm, in *political terms,* that our selves are *both* free and social, i.e., that freedom does not occur in a vacuum, but in a space of affordances and constraints: together with freedom, our selves derive from and aspire to relationships and interactions with other selves, technological artefacts, and the rest of nature. As such, human beings are 'free with elasticity', to borrow an economic notion. The contextual nature of human freedom accounts both for the social character of human existence, and the openness of human behaviours that remain to some extent stubbornly unpredictable. Shaping policies in the remit of the Onlife experience means resisting the assumption of a rational disembodied self, and instead stabilising a political conception of the self as an inherently relational free self.
>
> *(Floridi, 2015, p. 10 f.)*

More than one hundred years ago, Simmel clearly set the question in different terms. His opinion on the distinction between subjective and objective issues is still interesting. He considered that there is an essential ontological difference between subjective mind and objective mind (and their corresponding creations). He grasped the intimate paradox of modernity, twisting it around itself like a spiral, and determined a double impulse from it. We feel as if we are all the more constraining the query for individual liberty and the need for social accomplishment through the great pervasive presence of cultural products in our lives. In *Der Begriff und die Tragödie der Kultur* (1911), Simmel writes:

> So the subject confronts art, just as it does law, religion and technology, science and custom: not only now attracted, now repelled by their content; now fused with them as with a part of the self [*das Ich*]; now in estrangement and imperviousness opposed to them, rather it is the form of solidity; of congealed being [*des Geronnenseins*]; of persistent existence with which the spirit, having become object in this way, opposes flowing vitality, inner personal responsibility, the shifting tensions of the subjective soul; as spirit intimately bound to spirit, but precisely therefore experiencing countless tragedies in this profound contrast of form: between subjective life, which is restless but finite, and its contents which, once created, are motionless but timelessly valid.
>
> *(GSG 14, p. 385)*

The 'restlessness' of (social) life is the *pendant* of the 'motionlessness' of forms: the more we will experience the complexity and the intertwined character of modernity through a multiplicity of forms (artistic, technological, social, etc.), the more we will fell the attrition and the uncomfortable aspect of the unavoidable 'tragedy of culture'.

Charles Taylor recently supposed that, in our era, we are experiencing a third wave of 'secularization', which is characterised by an increasing amount of queries for (individual) 'authenticity' due to the strong pluralistic character of society itself – it is like a 'destiny', a natural development. He literally stated that:

The connection between pursuing a moral or spiritual path and belonging to larger ensembles – state, church, even denomination – has been further loosened; and as a result the nova effect has been intensified. We are now living in a spiritual super-nova, a kind of galloping pluralism on the spiritual plane.

(Taylor, 2007, p. 300 f.)

The pluralistic, disenchanted, and differentiated aspect of the modern (and post-modern) social life – in which, according to Charles Taylor, emerges a *buffered self* (opposed to the pre-modern *porous one*) – is also characterised by a sort of 'malaise of immanence' (Taylor, 2007, p. 311), drifting our society to fragility of any (ultimate) meaning, a kind of insignificance of our existences, and monotony and mediocrity of everyday life. Simmel's analysis on this 'grey', *blasé*, and paroxysmal character of modernity (with unavoidable effects on individual lives) is not so far, even if Taylor does not mention him at all.

The relational perspective might finally offer a chance in order to let individual identities be still 'human': in other words, social relations (their interactive and mutual characteristics) might endorse humans as relational subjects (Donati & Archer, 2015; Belardinelli, 2019). With regard to this aspect, maybe Simmel's last appeal to 'The law of the individual' (the last chapter to *Lebensanschauung* book) wanted to exactly point out a new kind of identity stressing the combination of an exceedingly complex social structure, culture, agency, and morals (Amat, 2017, 2018). Simmel alleged that life and its ought are 'symmetric categories', and they are destined to remain opposed and unreconciled due to 'the typical tragedy of the spiritual culture in general' (Simmel, 2010, pp. 100, 103). Simmel deconstructed the false symbiosis between individuality and subjectivity (as well as the false opposition between individuality and legality) in order to anchor the legality of the law of the individual to the inner processuality of life, as he stated in the *Excursus* of this essay. Simmel shifted from the morals of the rational-universal law to the morals of the law of the individual, which is always processual, dynamic, relational in regard to its own contents and then to external individuals and subjects, requiring a 'qualitative differentiation of the ethical conduct' (Simmel, 2010, p. 148). And relational is the inner character of life also because of the indissoluble couple transcendence/immanence:

Transcendence is immanent in life … Life is at once fixed and variable; of finished shape, and developing further; formed, and ever breaking through its forms; persisting, yet rushing onward; bounded and free; circling around in subjectivity, yet standing objectively over things and over itself.

(Simmel, 2010, p. 10)

The 'vitalizing and individualizing of ethicality' in Simmel is given by the conviction that life itself in unity and totality must be considered the only one ethical precept in spite of the necessary (and symmetric) conceptual grasp of the real: if we want to master the real with concepts, Simmel sustains,

we must … allow the gliding and the uninterrupted interrelationships [*Korrelativitäten*] in and between things to congeal into sharply separated pluralities, we must make the continuous discontinuous, and on all sides dam up the endless flow of connections to the next thing, up to the most distant.

Furthermore, plural is the form (and the destiny) of social life, unitary is instead its own core: the individual (vital) ought is derived from life itself as a 'process', as a continuous of being related to itself and, thus, also to otherness. In this regard Hannes Böhringer really hits the nail on the head when he affirms: 'Society as well as life don't have any beginning and any end at all. They are self-supporting networks of relations' (Böhringer, 2018, p. 849).

Note

1 Without further specification, the English translations of Simmel's as well as other texts are by the author.

References

Abbott, A. (2016). *Processual sociology*, Chicago, IL: The University of Chicago Press.

Al-Amoudi, I., & Morgan, J. (Eds.) (2018). *Realist responses to post-human society: Ex machina*. London: Routledge.

Amat, M. (2017). Simmel's law of the individual: A relational idea of culture. *Simmel Studies, 21*(2), 9–143.

Amat, M. (2018). *Le relationnisme philosophique de Georg Simmel. Une idée de la culture*. Paris: Honoré Champion.

Belardinelli, S. (2019). From the person to society and vice versa: What is the use of the relational paradigm? In P. Donati, A. Malo & G. Maspero (Eds.), *Social science, philosophy and theology in dialogue. A relational perspective* (pp. 38–51). Oxon and New York: Routledge.

Bennett, J. (2010). *Vibrant matter. A political ecology of things*. Durham, NC: Duke University Press.

Böhringer, H. (2018). Soziologie und Lebensphilosophie. In H.-P. Müller & T. Reitz (Eds.), *Simmel-Handbuch. Begriffe, Hauptwerke, Aktualität* (pp. 848–853). Berlin: Suhrkamp.

Bruni, L., & Zamagni, S. (Eds.) (2013). *Handbook on the economics of reciprocity and social enterprise*. Cheltenham: Edward Elgar.

Cantò Milà, N. (2005). *A sociological theory of value. Georg Simmel's sociological relationism*. Bielefeld: Transcript Verlag.

Cantó-Milà, N. (2016). Mainstreaming relational sociology. Theory. *The Newsletter of the Research Committee on Sociological Theory*, Summer, pp. 12–15.

Cantò Milà, N. (2018). Georg Simmel's concept of forms of association as an analytical tool for relational sociology. In F. Dépelteau (Ed.) *The Palgrave handbook of relational sociology* (pp. 217–230). Basingstoke: Palgrave Macmillan.

Crossley, N. (2011). *Towards relational sociology*. London: Routledge.

Darmon, I., & Frade, C. (2012). Beneath and beyond the fragments: The charms of Simmel's philosophical path for contemporary subjectivities. *Theory, Culture & Society, 29*(7/8), 197–217.

De Landa, M. (2004). *Intensive science and virtual philosophy*. London: Continuum.

Delitz, H., Seyfert, R., & Nungesser, F. (2015). Was ist »Lebenssoziologie«? Das Leben als Subjekt und Objekt soziologischer Theorie. *Soziologie* (Routinen der Krise - Krise der Routinen. Verhandlungen des 37. Kongresses der Deutschen Gesellschaft für Soziologie in Trier 2014), *35*, 390–399.

Dépelteau, F. (Ed.) (2018). *The Palgrave handbook of relational sociology*. Basingstoke: Palgrave Macmillan.

Devellenes, C., & Dillet, B. (2018). Questioning new materialisms: An introduction. *Theory, Culture & Society, 35*(7–8), 5–20.

Donati, P. (1983). *Introduzione alla sociologia relazionale*. Milano: FrancoAngeli.

Donati, P. (1991). *Teoria relazionale della società. I concetti base*. Milano: Franco Angeli.

Donati, P. (2009). *La società dell'umano*. Genova: Marietti.

Donati, P. (2011). *Relational sociology. A new paradigm for the social sciences*. London: Routledge.

Donati, P. (2017). Quelle sociologie relationelle? Une perspective non relationiste. *Nouvelles Perspectives en Sciences Sociales, 13*(1), 325–371.

Donati, P. (2018). Transcending the human: Why, where, and how? In I. Al-Amoudi & J. Morgan, (Eds.), *Realist responses to post-human society: Ex machina* (pp. 53–81). London and New York: Routledge.

Donati, P., & Archer, M. (2015). *The relational subject*. Cambridge: Cambridge University Press.

Emirbayer, M. (1997). Manifest for a relational sociology. *The American Journal of Sociology, 103*(2), 281–317.

Fellman, F. (2015). Das Ende der Kultur. Wie Georg Simmel den Begriff der Kultur soziologisch dekonstruiert. *Zeitschrift für Kulturphilosophie, 9*(1–2), 79–94.

Ferrando, F. (2013). Posthumanism, transhumanism, antihumanism, metahumanism, and newmaterialisms: Differences and relations. *Existenz, 8*(2), 26–32.

Fitzi, G. (2016). Modernity as solid liquidity. Simmel's life-sociology. In T. Kemple & O. Pyyhtinen (Eds.), *The Anthem companion to Georg Simmel* (pp. 59–80). London and New York: Anthem Press.

Fitzi, G. (2018). Simmel's centenary. A cornucopia of conferences. *Simmel Studies, 22*(1), 171–174.

Fitzi, G. (2019). *The challenge of modernity. Simmel's sociological theory*. London: Routledge.

Floridi, L. (Ed.) (2015). *The onlife manifesto. Being human in a hyperconnected era*. London: Springer.

Fuhse, J., & Mützel, S. (Eds.) (2010). *Relationale Soziologie. Zur kulturellen Wende der Netzwerkforschung*. Wiesbaden: VS Springer.

Honneth, A. (2017). Is there an emancipatory interest? An attempt to answer critical theory's most fundamental question. *European Journal of Philosophy, 25*, 908–920.

Jaeggi, R. (2018). *Critique of forms of life*. Cambridge and London: The Belknap Press of Harvard University Press.

Kemple, T., & Pyyhtinen, O. (2015). *The Anthem companion to Georg Simmel*. London: Anthem Press.

Kron, T., & Berger, P. (2018). Leben und Form der Gesellschaft. Zur Lebenssoziologie von Georg Simmel. In H. Delitz, F. Nungesser & R. Seyfert (Eds.), *Soziologien des Lebens. Überschreitung – Differenzierung – Kritik* (pp. 134–136). Bielefeld: Transcript Verlag.

Lash, S. (2005). Lebenssoziologie: Georg Simmel in the information age. *Theory Culture & Society, 22*, 1–23.

Latour, B. (1999). When things strike back: A possible contribution of science studies to the social sciences. *British Journal of Sociology, 51*(1), 105–123.

Latour, B. (2003). Is re-modernization occurring – And if so, how to prove it? A commentary on Ulrich Beck. *Theory, Culture & Society, 20*(2), 35–48.

Lee, M., & Silver, D. (2012). Simmel's law of the individual and the ethics of the relational self. *Theory, Culture & Society, 29*(7/8), 124–145.

Liebsch, B., & Staub, J. (Eds.) (2003). *Lebensformen im Widerstreit: Integrations- und Identitätskonflikte in pluralen Gesellschaften*. Frankfurt am Main: Campus.

Mamelet, A. (1914). *Le relativisme philosophique chez Georg Simmel*. Paris: Alcan.

Milson, J. (2009). The reflexive relativism of Georg Simmel. *The Journal of Speculative Philosophy (New Series), 23*(3), 180–207.

Müller, H.-P., & Reitz, T. (Eds.) (2018). *Simmel-Handbuch. Begriffe, Hauptwerke, Aktualität*. Berlin: Suhrkamp.

Papilloud, C. (2018a). Georg Simmel and relational sociology. In F. Dépelteau (Ed.), *The Palgrave handbook of relational sociology* (pp. 201–215). Basingstoke: Palgrave Macmillan.

Papilloud, C. (2018b). *Sociology through relation. Theoretical assessments from the French tradition*. Cham: Palgrave Macmillan.

Patrici, C. (2018). *The cordial economy. Ethics, recognition and reciprocity*. London: Springer.

Powell, C., & Dépelteau, F. (Eds.) (2013a). *Conceptualizing relational sociology. Ontological and theoretical issues*. Basingstoke: Palgrave Macmillan.

Powell, C., & Dépelteau, F. (Eds.) (2013b). *Applying relational sociology. Relations, networks, and society*. Basingstoke: Palgrave Macmillan.

Pyyhtinen, O. (2018). *The Simmelian legacy. A science of relations*. Basingstoke: Palgrave Macmillan.

Ruggieri, D. (2017). Georg Simmel and the 'Relational Turn'. Contributions to the foundation of the Lebenssoziologie since Simmel. *Simmel Studies, 21*(1), 43–71.

Schluchter, W. (2015). *Grundlegungen der Soziologie. Eine Theoriegeschichte in systematischer Absicht*, Tübingen: Mohr-Siebeck.

Seyfert, R. (2007). Zum historischen Verhältnis von Lebensphilosophie und Soziologie und das Programm einer Lebenssoziologie. In K. Rehberg (Ed.), *Die Natur der Gesellschaft* (pp. 4684–4694). Frankfurt am Main and New York: Campus.

Seyfert, R. (2018). Lebenssoziologie – Eine intensive Wissenschaft. In H. Delitz, F. Nungesser & R. Seyfert (Eds.), *Soziologien des Lebens. Überschreitung – Differenzierung – Kritik* (pp. 373–408). Bielefeld: Transcript Verlag.

Simmel, G. (1950). *The sociology of Georg Simmel*, Ed. by K. Wolff, Glencoe: The Free press.

Simmel, G. (1958). Anfang einer unvollendeten Selbstdarstellung. In M. Landmann & K. Gassen (Eds.), *Buch des Dankes an Georg Simmel. Briefe, Erinnerungen, Bibliographie* (pp. 9–10). Berlin: Duncker & Humblot.

Simmel, G. (1977). The concept and tragedy of culture. In D. Frisby & M. Featherstone (Eds.), *Simmel on Culture* (pp. 55–77). London: Sage.

Simmel, G. (1989a). *Aufsätze 1887 bis 1890. Über sociale Differenzierung (1890). Die Probleme der Geschichtsphilosophie (1892)*, GSG 2. Frankfurt am Main: Suhrkamp.

Simmel, G. (1989b). *Philosophie des Geldes*, GSG 6. Frankfurt am Main: Suhrkamp.

Simmel, G. (1992a). *Aufsätze und Abhandlungen 1894–1900*, GSG 5. Frankfurt am Main: Suhrkamp.

Simmel, G. (1992b). *Soziologie. Untersuchungen über die Formen der Vergesellschaftung*, GSG 11. Frankfurt am Main: Suhrkamp.

Simmel, G. (1996). *Hauptprobleme der Philosophie. Philosophische Kultur*, GSG 14. Frankfurt am Main: Suhrkamp.

Simmel, G. (2004). *Philosophy of money*. London and New York: Routledge.

Simmel, G. (2009). *Sociology. Inquiries into the construction of social forms*. Leiden and Boston, MA: Brill.

Simmel, G. (2010). *View of life. Four metaphysical essays with journal aphorisms*. Chicago, IL: The University of Chicago Press.

Simmel, G. (2012). *Kollegshefte und Mitschriften*, GSG 21. Berlin: Suhrkamp.

Spykman, N. ([1925] 2017) *The social theory of Georg Simmel*. New York: Routledge.

Taylor, C. (2007) *A secular age*. Cambridge: The Belknap Press of Harvard University Press.

Vanderberghe, F. (2018). The relation as magical operator: Overcoming the divide between relational and processual sociology. In F. Dépelteau (Ed.), *The Palgrave handbook of relational sociology* (pp. 35–58). Basingstoke: Palgrave Macmillan.

4

BOUNDARIES AS RELATIONS

Georg Simmel's relational theory of boundaries

Natàlia Cantó-Milà

The concept of a boundary is **extremely important in all relationships** of human
beings to one another, even though its significance is not always a sociological one.
(Simmel, 1997, p. 142, my emphasis)

[W]e are bounded in every direction, and we are bounded in no direction.
(Simmel, 2010, p. 2)

Introduction

Georg Simmel theorized about boundaries, borders, limits (and thresholds) throughout his
whole life and oeuvre.[1] The theorization about boundaries is one of the most constant (if
not *the* most constant) topic and figure of thought within his oeuvre, if we consider it as
a whole. Furthermore, the concept of boundary increased its importance and centrality
within the Simmelian oeuvre as time went by, reaching a first milestone in the text 'The
Sociology of Space' (GSG 7, pp. 132-183; Simmel, 1997, pp. 137-170) and its later
revision and inclusion in *Sociology*'s ninth chapter on 'Space and the Spatial Ordering of
Society' (GSG 11, pp. 687-790) and culminating in Simmel's last and most beautiful work
The View of Life (1918) (GSG 16, pp. 209-425; Simmel, 2010).

I have differentiated between 'topic' and 'figure of thought', as boundaries were not
always the main subject of Simmel's elucidations when he dealt with them, but a means, i.e.
a figure of thought, through which he approached other issues: be it the limits of the forms
of association, or of sociology as an emerging discipline; be it of exchange or of the process
of constitution of individuality/ies, or even of love and life. In order to think about all these
different subjects, 'boundaries' are necessary. Relational boundaries that set limits between
disciplines, between phenomena, between you and me, between coquetry and provocation,
between competition and assault, between life and inert matter. The boundaries we have
and the boundaries we are, the boundaries we use, the boundaries we set, and the
boundaries we encounter. From our own skin to the frame we design to outline a small

universe painted on a canvas: we are beings of boundaries. These two examples are the beginning of a very long list this chapter will explore and unfold in the forthcoming pages. Thus, the aim of this text is to provide an account of Simmel's relational theorization of boundaries, as creators and markers of proximity and distance, openings and closures.

Theorizing boundaries: the relevance of the concept in Simmel's work

The quote that opens this text shows how Simmel postulated the extreme importance of the concept of boundaries in the human way of relating to the world and to one another. We find in just this one sentence, which is neither particularly long nor complicated (by Simmelian standards), a remarkable amount of information regarding the meaning of the concept of boundaries in Simmel's works. To begin with, Simmel uses the expression 'the concept of'. This is not haphazard. He systematically used this formulation (the concept of/*der Begriff des/ der* ...) when he sought to highlight the theoretical importance of a particular key concept he was about to introduce or elaborate upon. Thus, in the sentence above, and after making a point about the importance of the concept of boundary as a key explanatory concept, he continued by stating its extreme relevance in all human relations – not only the part of these relations which we could regard under the lens of sociology (following Simmel's proposals for sociology as a discipline) (GSG 5, pp. 52-61). Beyond the limits of this discipline, the concept of a boundary allows the theoretician to think of a fundamental condition of the human beings' manifold ways of being-in-the world, being-part-of-the-world.[2]

If we compare Simmel's perspective on the concept of boundaries in the quote above (stemming from 'The Sociology of Space') with the perspective he presented in 'Life as Transcendence', his last written text and the initial chapter of *View of Life*,[3] we will rapidly recognize that by the end of his life Simmel did not think that the concept of boundaries was only of extreme importance when considering human relationships to one another, but he had expanded the scope of importance of this concept so as to reach all relations among living beings, and even to the very conceptualization of life itself.

Of course one may argue that the change of emphasis may be due to the fact that our initial quote stems from a text whose intention was to elaborate on space from a sociological perspective along the lines he had already suggested in his essay 'The Problem of Sociology' in 1894 (GSG 11; GSG 5, pp. 52-61).[4] In contrast, the wider perspective of *View of Life* can be explained by the fact that this latter monograph was neither a sociological book nor a book on sociology, but Simmel's theoretical testament, which he addressed, above all, to philosophy, but whose contributions and elucidations are so deeply transdisciplinary.[5] However, this hypothetical objection regarding the scope of Simmel's reflection on boundaries cannot be dismissed without further attention. Many authors have claimed that many of the seeds that flourished in *View of Life* had already been planted by the time *Philosophy of Money* was written (1900/1907) (Blumenberg, 2012; Harrington & Kemple, 2012; Pyyhtinen, 2018; Kemple, 2019a). Despite sharing this view, it is nonetheless important to focus upon two relevant issues in relation to this point: on the one hand, and despite acknowledging and sharing the idea that many of Simmel's life philosophical thoughts were already more or less implicitly present in this prose before 1908, it is necessary to differentiate between a thought that can be read in-between -lines (especially if we know in which direction the author's thoughts evolved afterwards) and a thought that has been fully developed, and argued at length. On the other hand, and viewed from a current perspective, Simmel's thoughts about life, relationality and boundaries beyond human-to-human relationships are of great relevance today, also for sociology (more-than-human sociology), and social theory in more general terms (Latour, 2005; Pyyhtinen, 2015).

Based on the fact that Simmel's theorization of boundaries is developed the widest and at its best in *View of Life*, we should begin our journey through Simmel's (concept of) boundaries with his last work. It is a very conscious decision, for it is in this text where we can see most clearly how Simmel thought about these curious phenomena of boundaries, which are relational par excellence, beyond disciplinary divisions or specificities, in a truly transdisciplinary way before the term and perspective were on the agenda. Boundaries are relations and regulations of relations (formed relations) made visible, sometimes tangible, experienceable, and whose effects mould the further course of the relations out of which its forming stems. Let us now fully focus on Simmel's proposal for theorizing boundaries from a relational perspective. Why do we claim the paradigm of relationality when thinking of boundaries with and through Simmel?

Following Simmel's relational approach, there are no boundaries where nothing resides beyond them. Boundaries are there to mark a 'this side' and a 'that side' of something. They are thus necessarily relational: their being in between this side and that side makes the existence of this side and that side possible. Without the boundary between them, there would be no two sides, but a continuum. Boundaries break continua (temporal, spatial, relational, vital) in order to establish, frame, tame relationships through it. Without boundaries we would not notice, we would not be aware of, these continuities. Without boundaries we would notice nothing in particular, only an undifferentiated chaos which we could not navigate: 'We are continually orienting ourselves, even when we do not employ abstract concepts, to an "over us" and an "under us", to a right and a left, to a more or less, a tighter or looser, a better or worse. The boundary, above and below, is our means for finding direction in the infinite space of our worlds. We are beings of boundaries, as we are "beings of difference"' (*Unterschiedswesen*, GSG 11, 1992, p. 312); or 'differentiating creatures' as the English translation of 'The Metropolis and Mental Life' suggests (Simmel, 1997, p. 175); or comparing and contrasting beings as he stated in *Philosophy of Money* (Simmel, 2004, p. 83 f.). There is an interconnectedness between these assertions. They seek to emphasize how the setting of boundaries between entities, phenomena or qualities that we see in relation to one another allows us to identify them, strengthen the boundaries and establish clearer relations and comparisons among them. But boundaries are not solely external to us. 'Along with the fact that we *have* boundaries always and everywhere, also we *are* boundaries' (Simmel, 2010, p. 1). Throughout our lives, as long as we are alive, we are boundaries to our own existence, which we keep on overcoming and setting anew. We are boundaries to others, we are boundaries in space and time. And sometimes, when we move across political and social spaces, claiming rights and a possibility of living, we are moving boundaries, moving borders. Yet, when dealing with boundaries Simmel does also not refer himself only to orientation in space (also, but not only). His is a much wider understanding of the concept of 'orientation', which justifies the plural use of 'our worlds': worlds of ideas, concepts, places, time, practices, resources, everyday life and liminal moments – the very concept of liminality refers to the necessary boundaries/thresholds between the profane and the sacred, between finite universes of meaning and everyday life (Turner, 1979). All of them are relational worlds in which no relations are possible without boundaries, and no boundaries are possible without relations.

I have claimed that Simmel's perspective on boundaries is the widest and most complete in *View of Life*. This does not mean, however, that a certain anthropocentric perspective is gone missing from his prose. Despite the fact that the richness and depth of his thoughts have maintained his contributions relevant and 'alive' beyond his own time – they have overcome all boundaries that separate our lives from Simmel's – Simmel himself was born in

1858 and died in 1918. He could not write and think like a man of the 21st century. This is relevant to emphasize, although the message itself needs no further clarification, because it is our job and not Simmel's to take and elaborate on further what we need to think through and theorize what is relevant and necessary for us now. Furthermore, when Simmel, in the very first sentence of 'Life as Transcendence', postulates that human beings need boundaries in each and every dimension of their being and behaviour in order to have a position in the world; i.e. in order to be, or in order to be with meaning, he is thereby not excluding that other living beings may need boundaries too. Or that the Anthropocene may be a boundary we may or may not overcome – it will be overcome, for sure, I am only questioning whether we shall stay at this side or will make it to the other side of this boundary.

On many occasions, what some could view as anthropocentric in Simmel's prose can also be read as humble. He writes from a human perspective, without claiming its exclusive validity, and not even claiming it is the only possible human way of being-in-the-world, and seeing/narrating-the-word. Thus, Simmel's claims about the 'human way' are broad and general, allowing many variations, nuances, and explicit inclusions that allow us to overcome explicit and implicit biases of anthropocentrism (see Pyyhtinen, 2012).

The main claim that Simmel makes regarding boundaries for the human way of inhabiting the world is that without boundaries there is only indeterminacy, no point of orientation, no fixed points (spatial or otherwise) that mark paths or allow trajectories. Fixed points are the result of relations, as are boundaries. In fact, nothing is exempt of being used as a border or boundary in order to mark a limit to be overcome, a position to be established. As we relationally move through existence, we encounter, pick and drop boundaries, which we overcome, or which disappear as new boundaries and new thresholds emerge, which become more meaningful to us than those we let go. Hence, Simmel states the human necessity for boundaries, and the human independence of any concrete boundary:

> [A]lthough the boundary as such is necessary, yet every single specific boundary can be stepped over, every fixity can be displaced, every enclosure can be burst, and every such act, of course, finds or creates a new boundary.
>
> *(Simmel, 2010, p. 2)*

No boundary will stand forever, but there will be boundaries *at least* as long as humanity as we know it exists. Furthermore, and here Simmel clearly overcomes the anthropocentric perspective: there will be boundaries as long as living beings exist, which means, as long as life exists. For boundaries are crucial to any kind of organic life; i.e. to life. The vital need for boundaries, and the potentiality to overcome each particular one of them is crucial to Simmel's argument. He humbly calls this a 'pair of statements', which summarize his whole position on this matter. These two statements are:

> [t]hat the boundary is unconditional in that its existence is constitutive of our given position in the world, but that no boundary is unconditional since every one can in principle be altered, reached over, gotten around – this pair of statements appears as the explication of the **inner unity of vital action**.
>
> *(Simmel, 2010, p. 2, my emphasis)*

We have now reached the point at which an unfolding of the different, and yet so complementary, uses of the concept of boundary in Simmel's texts is possible, and necessary.

We shall begin with the most general use of the concept, i.e. when it comes to specify its relation to the concept of life, as a condition *sine qua non* for life itself; we shall then focus on human life, and will, finally, come to speak about the boundaries of space and time, which are the most common spheres of use of the concept.

Life and boundaries

Simmel's interest for life, from a scientific but above all philosophical and creative viewpoint, grew exponentially in the last decade of his life. This growing interest for the fascinating miracle of life (my expression, not Simmel's) was never compartmentalized in his thought. It spilled over in all directions of his intellectual passions and interests, including the field of aesthetics, pedagogy and, last but not least, sociology. Goodstein has argued how Simmel claimed in his 'Beginning of an Unfinished Self-Presentation' (GSG 20, p. 304 f.) how the principle of *Wechselwirkung* (verbatim translated: reciprocal effect(s)), which was at first mainly crucial to his sociological works, became central to his cosmovision. It became a metaphysical principle through which he sought to understand the world from a relational perspective (Goodstein, 2017, pp. 61-90). We already find traces of relationism (relativism) being presented as the worldview of modern times in *Philosophy of Money*, especially and most explicitly in its first chapter (Simmel, 2004, pp. 101-130).

The principle of *Wechselwirkung*, i.e. the assertion that everything that happens in the world (not only the human world) results from relations, from reciprocal actions and effects, came also to shape the form in which Simmel approached 'life'. Hence, *Wechselwirkung* or reciprocal relations/effects are the other side of the theorization on boundaries. They mutually need and imply each other. The relationship he saw between his sociological principle and the understanding of 'life' is captured in a brief passage of *Fundamental Questions of Sociology* of 1917 (now GSG 16, pp. 59-149), where he argued how central it is for understanding life as well as society to focus on the invisible, continuous relational processes which lie behind the great 'forms' we can observe. They need each other, certainly, but there is more to society than forms, and there is more to life than forms, too. If we only had forms, no boundaries would be overcome, process, change and relations would stop, and everything would be contained, frozen, in fixed forms. Yet forms are not fixed, and boundaries are overcome; life goes on. In Simmel's words:

> To confine ourselves to the large social formations resembles the older science of anatomy with its limitation to the major, definitely circumscribed organs such as heart, liver, lungs, and stomach, and with its neglect of the innumerable, popularly unnamed or unknown tissues. Yet without these, the more obvious organs could never constitute a living organism. On the basis of the major social formations – the traditional subject matter of social science – it would be similarly impossible to piece together the real life of society as we encounter it in our experience. Without the interspersed effects of countless minor syntheses, society would break up into a multitude of discontinuous systems. Sociation continuously emerges and ceases and emerges again. Even where its eternal flux and pulsation are not sufficiently strong to form organizations proper, they link individuals together.
>
> *(Simmel, 1950, p. 9 f.)*

And yet forms are fundamental. If we bring together Simmel's theorization on relationism and his theorization on boundaries, we acknowledge that for him neither social life nor life in general is only the Heraclitan flux, or Bergson's élan vital. Life is indeed flux, but it is also form (Fitzi, 2002). In 'Life as Transcendence' Simmel argues the case for an 'absolute concept of life', (Simmel, 2010, pp. 13, 16) which unites the constant flowing of life with the necessary being formed in order to live. He is aware of the apparent paradox that a definition of life implies which is simultaneously life stream and form. However, in 'Life as Transcendence' he makes a formidable effort to unmask this apparent paradox and turn it into a question of the limits of logic and human reflection when confronted with titanic task of defining and expressing in words (i.e. forms) what life is (Simmel, 2010, pp. 13–16). In this sense, too, language and logic set boundaries which we strive to overcome, just to encounter the next. Simmel brings language and expression certainly beyond most taken-for-granted boundaries, when he approaches life in the following terms:

> Life is at once fixed and variable; of finished shape, and developing further; formed, and ever breaking through its forms; persisting, yet rushing onward; bounded and free; circling around in subjectivity, yet standing objectively over things and over itself – all these contrast are but unfoldings or refractions of that metaphysical fact: the innermost essence of life is its capacity to go out beyond itself, to set its limits by reaching out beyond them; that is, beyond itself.
>
> *(Simmel, 2010, p. 10)*

In a way, we could argue that what some Simmel scholars may have interpreted as a dialectical motive in the work of this author cannot be understood as dialectics but as the 'inner unity of vital action' (see above), which, as long as there is life, sets boundaries that shall be overcome.[6] The setting of these boundaries works by creating individual forms. Forms that are unique for as long as they last (and they may remain materially or in more or less conscious 'memory' as 'more-than-life'). That life can only be life in forms sounds like a paradox, indeed. Simmel uses the term 'paradox' and 'deep contradiction' when attempting to bring the language to its limits in order to describe this 'inner unity' of life, which, abstracted and rationalized to a certain extent, dwells on and expands this duality, expressing itself in the form of two 'ultimate worldshaping principles'. Continuity and change, life and form, constitute together the 'absolute concept of life', which englobes both, as (following Simmel) could not be otherwise. And this would not be possible without boundaries. Boundaries allow individuality to emerge, with its contours and uniqueness. And it lasts for a while, until the boundaries are no more, and new boundaries emerge. Life overcomes boundaries as an individual, until that individual does not overcome them anymore, and it stays at this side of the boundary so to speak, while life keeps on flowing, elsewhere. Forms are individual, not only in the human sense, full of awareness and consciousness (also of one's own forthcoming death). No, all forms are individual, for life materialized as '(t)he hereditary material out of which an organism develops', Simmel claims, 'contains **countless *individual* elements**', and this individuality of each of the elements that compose even the simplest organism result in the fact that **the relationship of the living being to its past is not mechanical**, for it is true for each of these elements that 'the past sequence which leads to *its* individuality can by no means be replaced by another' (Simmel, 2010, p. 6, *emphasis in the original*; **my emphasis**). Form means boundaries/limits, Simmel adds, limits that separate one form from its neighbour, creating a centrifugal force towards these limits that are claimed and reinforced, and a centripetal force towards its centre, providing the '[p]eriphery with a firm hold against dissolution in the flux' (Simmel, 2010, p. 11).

This flux is an undifferentiated stream that needs to become *something* – and there is nothing without form – in order to be. This may sound like a paradox, and yet it is the only way in which the unity of life can exist (Simmel, 2010, p. 16), as '[i]ndividuality is everywhere something alive, and life is everywhere individual' (Simmel, 2010, p. 12). They *must* go together. And Simmel states that the problematization of this fact, of this togetherness – or rather this unity, as togetherness already implies the previous separation in two parts, and the questioning regarding how they can go together at all, is the exception and not the rule. It only emerges as a problem in 'certain culture-historical situations', in which this duality delivers

> itself up as a problem to the intellect, which (because by its character it cannot do other- wise) as an antinomy projects it back even onto that ultimate stratum of life. This stratum is dominated by something which intellect can only call the overcoming of the duality by unity, but which is in itself a third principle beyond duality and unity: the essence of life as the transcendence of itself. In *one* act, it creates something more than the vital stream itself – individual structure – and then breaks through this form that has been etched by a blockage in that stream, which lets the stream reach out beyond its bounds and plunge back again into the ongoing flux. **We are not divided into life free from limits and form made secure by them**; we do not live partly in continuity, partly in individuality, the two asserting themselves against each other. Rather, the fundamental essence of life is precisely that internally unified function which, albeit symbolically and inadequately, I have termed the **transcendence** of itself, and which immediately **actualizes as *one* life what is then split** – by feelings, destinies, and conceptualization – into the dualism of **continuous life flux** and **individually closed form**.
>
> *(Simmel, 2010, p. 13, my emphasis)*

The depicted dualism is therefore a matter of expression, of conceptualization, and of the context in which our lives now develop, of modern human experience. And yet this may not be more than an anecdotical footnote in the book of life, in which an absolute unity between vital stream and form holds. In order to express the relation of the continuous flowing (the so-called vital stream) and the (individual) forms, Simmel coined the concepts of 'more-life' and 'more-than-life' so as to better explain the 'absolute concept of life'. 'More-life' and 'more-than-life' are two aspects or dimensions from which we can view an understand life (Simmel, 2010, p. 13). Without them, there is no life. And they share a fundamental characteristic: the setting and overcoming of boundaries is fundamental to them both.

Life, in order to be life, has to be more-life. For life cannot stand still, it is always becoming, overcoming its own finitude (i.e. its finite boundaries) and setting new boundaries to be overcome. When life stops overcoming boundaries, when the stream of life stops overcoming itself in the forms it inhabits, and hence going beyond its boundaries, life ceases to be. When no boundaries are crossed, that which was alive, that concrete individuality that was alive, is no more.

> [S]o long as life is present at all, it begets vitality, because sheer physiological self- maintenance involves continual regeneration. This is not one function that it exer- cises among others; rather, insofar as it does this it is its life. If, as I am furthermore convinced, death is immanent in life from the outset, this, too, is a stepping out of life beyond itself. While remaining in its center, life stretches out toward the

absolute of life, as it were, and becomes in this direction more-life; but it also stretches out toward nothingness, and just as it persists and yet increases itself in *one* action, so also it persists and declines in *one* action, *as* one action.

(Simmel, 2010, p. 13 f.)

Birth and death are the thresholds of life, and are seen in close, 'deep', relationship with each other. Birth and death as boundaries themselves. They are already/still part of the life of the individual form who has been born, is alive, and dies, but they connect the existence of this concrete individuality with a beyond, which cannot be lived by the same individuality. Life overcomes this boundary as well, but that concrete form, through which life was lived, does not. New forms will emerge in its place, through new births, towards new deaths (Simmel, 2010, p. 14; Kemple, 2019b).

If we now focus our attention upon the question of the 'more-than-life', we will have to acknowledge that at this point is where a certain anthropocentric bias partially colours Simmel's conceptualization of life, as he explains the 'more-than-life' from a human viewpoint only, and linking it to human creativity. We will come back to this point in our next section, when we focus explicitly and specifically on Simmel's observations about human life.

Human life through boundaries

Without arguing that only humans can become individualized, Simmel does argue in *View of Life* that the human form of individuality is perhaps the most complete, aware and, above all, *creative*. As has been stated above, no form of life is a mere mechanical reproduction of its elements, as each of these elements is indeed individual, and, in this sense, formed, bounded and therefore unique and special. And yet, the paradox of life (between life streaming and form) becomes particularly interesting when Simmel focuses upon this paradox in relation to human life: We

[c]onceive life as a continuous stream proceeding through successive generations. Yet the bearers of this process (i.e., not those who have it, but those who **are** it) are individuals (i.e. closed, self-centered, unambiguously distinct beings). Although the stream of life flows through – or more accurately, *as* – these individuals, it nevertheless dams up in each of them and becomes a sharply outlined form. Each individual then asserts itself as a complete entity, both against other individuals of its kind and against the total environment with all its contents, and it does not tolerate any blurring of its periphery.

(Simmel, 2010, p. 9, emphasis in the original, *my emphasis)*

This idea of the individual protecting and claiming his or her boundaries relationally against a society that at the same time makes these boundaries possible echoes with what Simmel argued in the second and fourth chapters of *Fundamental Questions of Sociology* (GSG 16, pp. 59-149), when he dealt from different angles with the relation 'individual-society'.

Life is caught up in forms, forms that allow individuality, boundaries and limits that mark where I begin, where you end, and make the bridge possible that we cross to communicate, to touch, to consciously create a 'together'. The 'sharply outlined forms' of our human individualities, which we assert and strive to keep bounded throughout our lives, constitute the contested limits of the self, of ourselves.[7] And, as Simmel claims in so numerous occasions, no limits are forever:

> Since life's further flowing is incessant all the same – since the persisting centrality of the total organism, of the 'I', or its more relative contents, cannot nullify the essential continuity of the flowing – the idea arises that life pushes out beyond the given organic, or spiritual, or objective form; that it overflows the dam.
>
> *(Simmel, 2010, p. 9)*

> The limits of myself, of herself, your limits, are the dam of this so precious individuality which cannot and will not last. And yet these individualities are as much part of life as the continuous flowing. Life is flux and boundedness, the stream and the forms, shaped as 'individualized midpoints'.
>
> *(Simmel, 2010, p. 9)*

When dealing with the 'more-than-life' Simmel argues that we encounter it in human creativity, in the capacity to create something which comes from us, but which is not us, and whose existence becomes independent from us from the very moment of its creation. This is not restricted to geniuses, like Rembrandt or Goethe, who, furthermore, in their creative endeavours are *almost* capable of letting us 'touch', 'feel', that absolute concept of life in which the vital streaming and the form are united, beyond or before the awareness and problematisation of dualities (i.e. without logical boundaries between them) (Simmel, 2010, p. 16). No, the creative processes, the imagination, Simmel refers to at this point are in all of us, and are 'us'. And they allow us to produce from/in our lives something whose existence becomes independent from ours from its very initial moment, and which nonetheless has emerged from the creative individual spirits (of course always in interrelation with each other) (Simmel, 2010, p. 14 f.).

Simmel makes here a parallelism between the creation of more-than-life from the creative human spirit and the 'creation' of offspring (so often misunderstood as 'reproduction' in so many spheres of our lives). Our offspring are, as the products of our creative spirits, independent beings, in spite of having been originated from no other potency than ours, human beings and their parent(s). Paralleling thus this process of producing a new being, and of being born as a new independent being (in the sense of an individual form with his/her own boundaries), Simmel argues:

> [s]o too the creation of an independently meaningful content is immanent to life at the level of the spirit. The fact that our ideas and cognitions, our values and judgments stand completely beyond the creative life in their meaning, their objective intelligibility and their historical effectiveness – this is the exact characteristic of human life. Just as life's transcendence, within the plane of life itself, of its current, delimited form constitutes more-life (although it is nevertheless the immediate, inescapable essence of life itself), so also its transcendence into the level of objective content, of logically autonomous and no longer vital meaning, constitutes more-than-life, which is inseparable from it and is the essence of spiritual life itself.
>
> *(Simmel, 2010, p. 16)*

At this point, and dealing as we are with boundaries, it may be an appropriate moment to question the clear-cut boundary that Simmel establishes between 'more-life' (from the renewal of cells to the birth of offspring) and 'more-than-life' (from the economic and legal system, to the forms of association and cultural production). Perhaps the boundary between 'more-life' and 'more-than-life' is less clear-cut and strict than some paragraphs of 'Life as

Transcendence' (and Simmel's thematization of this issue in general) invite us to assume. Of course, when Simmel speaks of the birth of offspring, he is arguing along the lines of strict organic reproduction. However, also here I claim that the century of scientific investigations that separates us from him has allowed us to problematize if there is anything like 'strict organic reproduction', without *forms* of care, relation, proximity (sensorial and otherwise), among so many others. This certainly applies to the birth of new individual living beings, but if we pay close attention to the thesis of epigenetics, it may go well beyond it. In a way, it seems that in all aspects and ambits of life boundaries are always porous (more or less, but porous all the same), and set to be overcome.

If we focus on the way in which Simmel speaks about the *forms* in which the past lives beyond itself, and reaches out to us, to our present and to the bit of future that is present in our present, he speaks of the two forms in which this may happen: as objectifications and as memories (Simmel, 2010, p. 7). The first, the objectifications, are 'traditional' more-than-life: those products of human creativity that are born from us, but which become independent from us, stable and fixed forms as soon as they and us are separated. Thus, as soon as I write this sentence, as soon as this chapter is sent, as soon as this handbook is published, these very words have an existence unattached from my own. In this way our creative imagination and incarnated culture produce objects, parts of the objective culture, which will stare back at us from their impassibility of forms when we are no longer ourselves, but, if we are still alive, have become someone else. And will remain there once we are gone. The second, the memories, are known to be more processual. We may not only remain in a non-alive way, in a non-material (related to our own bodies, not to materiality in general) in the products we have created, which have come to enlarge the sphere of objective culture in a way or another, but also in the memories that live not in the books, laws, techniques we have co-created, but in the minds, in the spirits of those who remember us, and also in their bodies – in their habitus, in their tastes and dispositions, in the colour of their eyes and the ways they move their hands. And here we see already the more-life and more-than-life entangling and becoming one; their boundaries blurring in the individual form of another being. For offspring is never only more-life (and I am not implying that more-life is not much!), but an individual and unique form that embraces life fully, contains and channels life in all its modes, modulations and aspects.

The boundaries of time

[T]he **reality of life** at any moment carries its past within it in a very different way from that of a mechanical phenomenon.

(Simmel, 2010, p. 6, my emphasis)

In 'Life as Transcendence' Simmel argues that it is only in life, which he defined as a 'mode of existence', where time can exist and make sense. Time exists (only) for living beings, and in a very particular way for human beings, for whom the experience of time is a way of consciously and experientially making sense of the changes of relations, of matter, of states. Human beings have a peculiarity among the living beings, an 'original phenomenon', which is their self-awareness. The 'I' exists as an I and a me, it confronts itself, and makes itself object of its knowing, observing, even feeling; but, moreover, it can also observe itself as a third party. In humans, Simmel argues, life has reached the stage of consciousness (*Geist*). We do not need to discuss again the question of the boundary of consciousness – whether humans are the only conscious ones and to what an extent. But it is clear that Simmel attaches to the level of human consciousness the analysis of the ways in which life can carry its past into its present: through objectification in concepts and structures as well as through memory. In memory, '[t]he past of the subjective life not only becomes the cause of the life of the present, but also continues over into the present with its contents **relatively** unchanged' (Simmel, 2010, p. 7, my emphasis).

The past, in our memory, lives in us and has made us into what we are in the present. Yet this past has not disappeared completely in the process. It has made it to the other side of the temporal boundary that separates past from present. Hence,

> [t]he sphere of actual, present life stretches all the way back to the moment of its formation. Of course, the past as such does not thereby rise from the grave; but because we comprehend an experience not as a present thing, but rather as one that is attached to some moment in the past, our present is not focused on one point, as is that of a mechanical existence, but is, so to speak, extended backward. At such instances we live beyond the moment back into the past. It is similar with our relation to the future, which is no way adequately characterized by defining man as the 'goal-setting' being.
>
> *(Simmel, 2010, p. 7)*

In this way, our experience of life (or life as an experience) does not take place in a strict present tense, but this present, while being present, has so to speak a foot in the past and a foot in the future. Experienced time overcomes boundaries of measured time. In parallel to the division of the concept of life as life stream and forms, which Simmel claims to be more related to our understanding and logical thinking than to the reality of life itself, a similar phenomenon takes place in relation to the human conceptualization of time, which is '[d]isrupted and crystallized into the logical differentiation of three grammatically separate tenses' (Simmel, 2010, p. 7).

This disruption and crystallization of the three forms of time, the tenses (past, present and future), turns the continuum of time into three watertight compartments, setting clear boundaries to time: past – present – future. The present becomes a fine, subtle and thin line, the past is 'a long before' that is closed, unreachable, and the future becomes an opening to the unknown, to an afterwards. These crystallizations, as Simmel terms them to emphasize their rigidity, make our thoughts, words, experiences of time conceal the immediate continuity and fluidity of the boundaries between past-present-future. Simmel contrast these crystallizations with the past which is alive in the present life process, and the 'immediate continuous stretching of itself [of the life process] into the future' (Simmel, 2010, p. 7). Thus he argues that

> (t)he future does not lie ahead of us like some untrodden land that is separated from the present by a **sharp boundary line**, but rather **we live continually in a border region that belongs as much to the future as to the present**.
>
> *(Simmel, 2010, p. 7 f., my emphasis)*

This differentiation between sharp boundary lines and border regions is of a great analytical significance. While in the way in which we think of, conceptualize and measure abstract time, we work with clear-cut boundaries (sharp boundary lines), experientially we live in an extended and stretching time (border region), which carries the past, keeping it partially alive and present (while losing/forgetting many pieces of information, experiences – contents – in the process) and living with a foot already in the future. Thus our present life is extended from a preserved/ remembered past towards a future that, paraphrasing Luhmann, 'cannot begin' (Luhmann, 1976), as we're already living towards it, in it.

When we speak of and from the experience of life (and not of a conceptualization of time), the precise division of past, present and future does not and cannot hold. This clear-cut division follows the mechanistic model, which the opening quote of this section speaks about in order to differentiate it from 'the reality of life' (Simmel, 2010, p. 8). Time, presented through these clear-cut boundaries between past, present and future, is not real.

> Time is real only for life alone. … Time is life seen apart from its contents, because life alone transcends in both directions the atemporal present-point of every other reality and only thereby realizes, all by itself, the temporal dimension (i.e., time).
>
> *(Simmel, 2010, p. 8)*

In order to elaborate further on the difference between the temporal conceptualisation as divided in three tenses in its 'full logical strictness' and the reality of time within life (or time in 'the reality of life'), Simmel postulates that the 'mechanical' present

> [d]oes not encompass more than the absolute unextendedness of a moment; it is as little time as the point is space. It denotes exclusively the collision of past and future, which alone make up amounts of time; that is, time as such. But since the one is no longer, and the other not yet, reality adheres to the present alone; this means that reality is not at all something temporal; the concept of time can be applied to reality's contents only if the atemporality they possess as present has become a 'no more' or a 'not yet', at any rate a nothing. **Time is not in reality, and reality is not time**. We acknowledge the force of this paradox, however, only for the logically observed object. The subjectively lived life will not adjust to it; the latter is felt, no matter whether or not it is logically justified, to be something real in a temporal dimension. Common usage indicates this, if in an inexact and superficial way, by understanding of the term 'present' not only the mere punctuality of this conceptual sense, but also always a bit of the past and a somewhat smaller bit of the future. (These 'bits' vary greatly in size according to whether the present in question is of a personal or political, cultural or geological nature).
>
> *(Simmel, 2010, p. 6)*

There is a continuity in the mode of existence of life, the past and the future are not pushed towards the realm of the unreal, and they are not disconnected from each other by a logical separation: the past exists into the present, and the present exists into its future, and this is life; i.e. the overcoming of boundaries in 'growth, procreation, and the spiritual processes' (Simmel, 2010, p. 8). We set the limits in time between the tenses, just to overcome them, to live in a tense that our grammar does not contemplate and does not speak about (and thus does not allow us to speak about).

If we focus on the 'border region' between past and present, we have to deal with issues of forgetting and preserving/remembering (as objectifications or memories). Forgetting and preserving/remembering live towards the present and both shape it. The present we inhabit and incarnate is not only shaped by the part of the past that lives in us, through us, as memories and objectifications, but also *as* us: the 'us' we have become through what has been kept, but also that which has been lost − what is forgotten and lost also shapes our present being (like erosion shapes the shore and the cliffs, as much as the sand, water and rocks that remain).

If we focus on the border region between present (already shaped by and counter-intuitively pregnant with the past) and the future, we encounter the issue of uncertainty: of living towards the unknown and, to a considerable extent, the unknowable. Simmel illustrates this point with the example of the chess player:

> We are all like the chess player in this regard: if he did not know with a reasonable degree of probability what consequences would result from a certain move, the game would be impossible; but it would also be impossible if this foresight extended indefinitely.
>
> *(Simmel, 2010, p. 2)*

Simmel addresses here the limit between the knowable and not-knowable, foreseeable and unforeseeable. However, he addresses it with one of the easiest examples. Most relational contexts in our lives (and in life in general) are less patterned and ruled than a chess game. Life does not evolve in a controlled context in which only certain moves are possible, times are structured, and boundaries are marked by squares of black and white. Of course, Simmel is very well aware of this fact, and claims that the border between knowledge and ignorance is not the only fact that 'makes our life what we know it to be'. It is also the border between preserving/remembering and forgetting, creating and reproducing, imagining and expressing, proximity and distance. Furthermore, Simmel adds, the relation between knowing and not knowing changes as life goes by, and as the relational constellations in which we partake change (Simmel, 2010, p. 2). The perspective on these relational constellations also changes to our eyes (to our senses in general, to our comprehension and experience) when we move across social and spatial positions. Social mobility, migration, transitions in gender (performative) identities can all be understood, and meaningfully analyzed, as processes of boundary making and boundary breaking, of boundary crossing (the boundary does not need to break, sometimes it stands, but we have made it to the other side – like in cases of social mobility (upwards or downwards). The same applies to our relational and more or less mobile position within concrete social fields.

The boundaries of space

With these last examples we have started to transit the boundary between the section on the boundaries of time and our final section: on the boundaries of space, physical as well as social. They are not essential, but, as all boundaries and borders, relational. Boundaries are fluid, a condensation of reciprocal relations of proximity and distance which consolidate the proximity within the bounded territory and emphasize the distance with what lies beyond it. The claim that boundaries are fluid is not meant to be a tasteless, or even sarcastic, comment in front of the many human beings who die trying to cross a border, or when considering the many migrants, the so-called 'illegal migrants' who make it to the other side – thus crossing the border that was erected to keep them at distance – at a cost perhaps so much higher than they had ever imagined. It means that the boundary that regulates who shall live or shall die, who shall pass or shall remain on the other side, is a boundary that has not always been there, and more than likely will not always be there. It is a relational boundary that is formed and holds, with all available mechanisms of power applied to reinforce it precisely because (and not despite of the fact that) it is surmountable. Any boundary can be crossed, any boundary can be overcome. But sadly, that does not mean that anybody can cross it at any time. The regulation of movements (fluxes) and relations is the fundamental reason for the emergence of spatial boundaries in the first place.

The *place* where physical boundaries emerge and crystallise is also not an essential characteristic of the landscape or of the boundaries themselves (Massey, 2005). It is again a relational process in which humans and non-humans are relationally involved. The mountains, the rivers, the seas and lakes, economic and political interests, biopolitics and geopolitics, desires and necessities, wars and hunger all in interrelation with one another end up forming borders that will sometimes or even often be crossed, and one day will be burst.

If we focus on the significant example of political boundaries, we can argue their crucial role in emphasizing distance instead of proximity in their attempt to regulate the mobility of living beings (plants, animals, and if we want a separate category for us, also humans) and non-living beings, some viewed as merchandise, others viewed as trash, others incontrollable and often unseen (like air, rain or radiation). All these boundary crossers can be classified (and treated accordingly) as 'legal' and 'illegal', 'desired' or 'undesired', 'benign' or 'dangerous'. Of course, not all borders and boundaries that are projected upon space are incarnated and make 'place' with the same intensity and condensed power as political boundaries. These have life-shaping and life-changing consequences.

There are boundaries between rooms (living-rooms and dormitories, kitchens and offices), with entries regulated by doors that can be open and invite our crossing or closed, marking a beyond that cannot be seen. These everyday life boundaries frame and form different activities that are expected and anticipated to be located within their walls/doors, and which regulate and organise practices as well as relationships.

There are also invisible, movable boundaries around our bodies ('they' move as 'we' move). Depending on circumstances, conventions and context, these invisible boundaries have a narrower or wider diameter, which marks that personal space that *should* only be crossed in intimacy. There are boundaries we set by closing our eyes, or by looking down or away, to protect ourselves from being read into, from being connected to another person, a stranger in the metropolis, a boss, a lover. There are boundaries we set by using our headphones in public transport, or that are set for us, like for example when teenagers enter the room wearing headphones but with their music so loud that you know there is no use in talking to them: the border is 'on'. We set boundaries by putting clothes on our bodies, some emphasizing the distance, others advertising the porosity of the boundary, playing with it. Our interrelations are a continuous interplay with boundary setting and boundary overcoming, proximity and distance.

The theoretical elucidations Simmel offered to his readers regarding the processes of boundary setting in relation to the continuum that goes from close proximity and remote distance reside mostly in the above mention essay 'The Sociology of Space' (GSG 7, pp. 132-183) and *Sociology*'s ninth chapter (GSG 11, pp. 687-790) as well as in the essays 'Metropolis and the Life of the Mind' (Simmel, 1997, pp. 174-185) and 'Bridge and Door' (Simmel, 1997, pp. 170-174). While in the essay Simmel argues more along the lines I have just discussed above regarding the invisible boundaries we set to our senses in order to channel interrelations and stimuli derived from a high density of humans and non-humans inhabiting together a relatively small and crowded place, in *Sociology* he focuses more on the way in which boundaries are set in order to claim power, territories, or affiliations. In this sense, the ninth chapter of *Sociology* focuses on paradigmatic examples of institutions according to the way they deal with their boundaries and the processes of setting limits and borders. Thus, he identified two poles of the continuum regarding the way these institutions set their relationship to space through the way they determine and fix their borders: on the one side of the continuum we find the state, which requires clear-cut borders upon space so that no two states can occupy together the same territory. On the other side of the continuum we find the 'church', understood as a religious community which can be spread 'all over the place' and sets its boundaries along the community of believers. Thus, the believers are, in a way, the boundaries of the religious community. Within the same believer no two religions can coexist and claim the same amount of faith and commitment from her, and yet the person next to her can be the boundary of another religious community. In the middle between these two poles of the continuum we have the municipality, or the guilds within a particular city. In the case of the municipality the boundaries are clear, and, notwithstanding there is an 'area of influence' (intellectual, political, economic) which expands, Simmel argues, in 'waves'.

Considering the relation of the human being (and the human body) to the surroundings, i.e. considering the position of the human being relationally, Simmel argues how the overcoming of the boundaries set by our senses have completely changed the view we have of the world, how we relate to one another, and how we position ourselves (and are positioned) in this new universe – made possible by the overcoming and setting of (new) boundaries. In one of the most beautiful paragraphs of 'Life as Transcendence', we have been able to overcome what we see with our naked eyes thanks to the telescope and the microscope. We could add, from our current perspective, how we are also able to see each other from unsurmountable distances for our plain senses, through webcams and videos and streaming, how we have been able to overcome the speed at which our legs can carry us from here to there by trains, cars, airplanes, even rockets. We have been able to overcome the boundaries set by our ears through the telephone, and now with mobile technologies and the Internet. We can even listen to and see each other as we chat with each other across oceans, thus creating spaces of interaction where physical proximity is not requires any longer. Touch and smell are somewhat far behind, at the moment. But efforts are being made to overcome these boundaries too.

I would like to conclude these explorations and reflections on Simmel's concept of boundaries/limits/borders (*Grenzen*) with a renewed calling of attention to the centrality of this concept within a relational paradigm: whatever boundary we cross or push forward has an effect on us, changing our relational position within a constellation which is, in the most continuous tense, in a process of continuously becoming. In a moment like ours, it may be wise therefore to close this text by recalling Simmel's words helping us become aware of the consequences of the boundaries we cross and push. We are surrounded by boundaries and limits, we cross some of them, individually and collectively. Others remain simply potentially crossable, but we move towards another direction, or at least we think we do. But this would be a topic for a different chapter. Let us invite Simmel to close this chapter, by simultaneously inviting the reader to link Simmel's words to the contemporary challenges we are facing with an Anthropocene that many of us look at as boundary which we hope we will be able to cross hoping that, on the other side, we will have a chance to create new boundaries that will make, at least for a while, our world more liveable, retaining our 'cosmic diminution', which certainly can help us with its humbling echoes, but cherishing the relational threads that allow us to become who we are becoming by setting us boundaries and giving us resources to cross them.

[W]e regard ourselves in a hitherto unheard of cosmic diminution. As we push our boundaries out into the realm of the measureless, our relations to such vast spaces and times press us back in our consciousness to the magnitude boundary of an infinitesimal point.

(Simmel, 2010, p. 4)

Notes

1 I conceive the concept of *Grenze* in German as meaning borders, limits and boundaries at the same time. In this text, if I do not need to specify one of these three meanings, I shall use the English word 'boundary/ies' as the wider translation of the concept of '*Grenze/n*'.

2 What we understand as 'sociology' has changed since 1908, not the least because of the reception of Simmel's works. Precisely from this scholarly perspective we should acknowledge that a part of the beyond-sociology which Simmel thematizes in the quote, as a further and crucial relational dimension of humanity, has been worked upon, and captured in the magnificent formula 'more-than-human' sociology, proposed by Pyyhtinen (Pyyhtinen, 2015).

3 In relation to the title of Simmel's works in English, I follow Elizabeth Goodstein's (2017) rightful critique and recommendation to leave the 'the' behind: in *(The) Philosophy of Money* as well as in *(The) View of Life* – thus emphasizing the Simmelian position that seldom there is only one standpoint on such important matters as life or money (and through it contemporary society in all its complexities and spheres) (See GSG 6 & GSG 16).

4 For a comparative perspective on Simmel's three versions of 'The Problem of Sociology' (GSG 5, 1992, pp. 52-61; GSG 11, 1992; GSG 16, 1999, pp. 59-149), see Cantó-Milà (2019, pp. 139-150).

5 Opening now a discussion about the transdisciplinary character of Simmel's contributions and oeuvre in general would lead to hundreds of pages, which have already been written by others. See for instance (Goodstein, 2017; Pyyhtinen 2018; Fitzi, 2019; Kemple, 2019a).

6 Thus, for instance, while (Landmann, 1958; Weinstein & Weinstein, 1993; Schermer & Jary, 2013; Goodstein, 2017), among others, Willi Goetschel has emphasized how Simmel avoided the term dialectics and sought to move beyond it. In his words: 'Simmel pointedly refrains from the use of the term dialectic. In fact, there is only one instance, as far as I can see, where dialectic appears in Simmel's writing in the title of a text. It is a newspaper article from September 28, 1916 in the Berlin paper Der Tag, in its "Illustrated Section." In the middle of the First World War the essay's title "Die Dialektik des deutschen Geistes" ("The Dialectic of the German Spirit") exudes a rather pessimist tone that the text's subdued tenor confirms (GSG 13, 224–230). Dialectic, we can say, presents for Simmel a somber notion that signals risk, danger, and possible disaster and destruction' (Goetschel, 2019:135, my emphasis).

7 In relation to the conceptualization of the 'self' I would like to quote from Simons' 2019 essay: 'The self is associated with a process that mediates between the world and life. It exhibits a desire for forms, but at the same time it is also compelled to transgress any and all boundaries' (Simons, 2019, p. 110). This essay examines Simmel's concept of forms and boundaries, relating it to Goethe in a way that has not been done before, and opening many new insights to Simmel scholars.

References

Note: Georg Simmel's collected works – in German – are cited following the standard abbreviation GSG (Georg Simmel Gesamtausgabe).

Blumenberg, H. (2012). Money or life: Metaphors of Georg Simmel's philosophy, Trans. R. Savage. *Theory, Culture and Society*, 29(7–8), 249–262.

Cantó-Milà, Natàlia (2016). On the special relation between proximity and distance in Simmel's forms of association and beyond. In Th. Kemple & O. Pyyhtinen (Eds.), *The Anthem companion to Georg Simmel* (pp. 81–100). London and New York: Anthem Press.

Cantó-Milà, Natàlia (2019). On Simmel's relativism and the foundations of a relational approach. *The Germanic Review: Literature, Culture, Theory*, 94(2), 139–150, DOI: 10.1080/00168890.2019.1585668

Fitzi, Gregor (2002). *Soziale Erfahrung und Lebensphilosophie. Georg Simmels Beziehung zu Henri Bergson.* Konstanz: Universitätsverlag Konstanz.

Fitzi, Gregor (2016). Modernity as solid liquidity: Simmel's life-sociology. In Th. Kemple & O. Pyyhtinen (Eds.), *The Anthem companion to Georg Simmel* (pp. 59–80). London and New York: Anthem Press.

Fitzi, Gregor (2019). *The challenge of modernity. Simmel's sociological theory.* Oxon and New York: Routledge.

Goetschel, Willi (2019). Form and relation: Difference and alterity in Simmel. *The Germanic Review: Literature, Culture, Theory, 94*(2), 125–138, DOI: 10.1080/00168890.2019.1585667

Goodstein, Elizabeth (2017). *Georg Simmel and the disciplinary imaginary.* Stanford, CA: Stanford University Press.

GSG 5 (1992). *Aufsätze und Abhandlungen 1894–1900.* Georg Simmel Gesamtausgabe vol. 5. Eds. Heinz-Jürgen Dahme & David Frisby. Frankfurt am Main: Suhrkamp.

GSG 6 (1989). *Philosophie des Geldes.* Georg Simmel Gesamtausgabe vol. 6. Eds. David Frisby & Klaus Christian Köhnke. Frankfurt am Main: Suhrkamp.

GSG 7 (1995). *Aufsätze und Abhandlungen 1901–1908 vol. I.* Georg Simmel Gesamtausgabe vol. 7. Eds. Angela Rammstedt Rüdiger Kramme & Otthein Rammstedt. Frankfurt am Main: Suhrkamp.

GSG 11 (1992). *Soziologie: Untersuchungen über die Formen der Vergesellschaftung.* Georg Simmel Gesamtausgabe vol. 11. Ed. Otthein Rammstedt. Frankfurt am Main: Suhrkamp.

GSG 13 (2000). *Aufsätze und Abhandlungen 1909–1918 vol. II.* Georg Simmel Gesamtausgabe vol. 13. Ed. Klaus Latzel. Frankfurt am Main: Suhrkamp.

GSG 16 (1999). *Der Krieg und die geistigen Entscheidungen; Grundfragen der Soziologie; Vom Wesen des historischen Verstehens; Der Konflikt der modernen Kultur; Lebensanschauung.* Georg Simmel Gesamtausgabe vol. 16. Eds. Gregor Fitzi & Otthein Rammstedt. Frankfurt am Main: Suhrkamp.

GSG 20 (2004). *Postume Veröffentlichungen; Ungedrucktes; Schuldpädagogik.* Georg Simmel Gesamtausgabe vol.20. Eds. Torge Karlsruhen & Otthein Rammstedt. Frankfurt am Main: Suhrkamp.

Harrington, Austin, & Kemple, Thomas (2012). Introduction: Georg Simmel's 'Sociological Metaphysics': Money, Sociality, and Precarious Life. *Theory, Culture & Society, 29*(7–8), 7–25. DOI: 10.1177/0263276412459087

Schermer, Henry, & Jary, David (2013). Interaction, form and the dialectical approach – Simmel's analytical conceptual framework. In Id. *Form and dialectic in Georg Simmel's sociology. A new interpretation* (pp. 17–46). London: Palgrave Macmillan.

Kemple, Thomas (2019a). *Simmel.* Cambridge: Polity.

Kemple, Thomas (2019b). Simmel's sense of adventure: Death and old age in philosophy, art, and everyday life. *The Germanic Review: Literature, Culture, Theory, 94*(2), 163–174, DOI: 10.1080/00168890.2019.1585670

Landmann, M. ([1958] 1993). Bausteine zur Biographie. In K. Gassen & M. Landmann (Eds.), *Buch des Dankes an Georg Simmel. Briefe, Erinnerungen, Bibliographie. Zu seinem 100. Geburtstag am 1. März 1958* (pp. 11–33). 2. Aufl. Berlin: Duncker & Humblot.

Latour, Bruno (2005). *Reassembling the social: An introduction to actor-network theory.* Oxford: Oxford University Press.

Luhmann, Niklas (1976). The future cannot begin: Temporal structures in modern society. *Social Research, 43*(1), 130–152. Retrieved from www.jstor.org/stable/40970217.

Massey, Doreen (2005). *For space.* London: Sage Publications.

Pyyhtinen, Olli (2012). Life, death and individuation: Simmel on the problem of life itself. *Theory, Culture & Society, 29*(7–8), 78–100. DOI: 10.1177/0263276411435567

Pyyhtinen, Olli (2015). *More-than-human sociology: A new sociological imagination.* Basingstoke and New York: Palgrave Macmillan.

Pyyhtinen, Olli (2018). Das Dritte. In H.-P. Müller & T. Reitz (Eds.), *Simmel-Handbuch: Begriffe, Hauptwerke, Aktualität* (pp. 172–177). Frankfurt am Main: Suhrkamp.

Pyyhtinen, Olli, & Tamminen, Sakari (2011). We have never been only human: Foucault and Latour on the question of the anthropos. *Anthropological Theory, 11*(2), 135–152. DOI: 10.1177/1463499611407398

Simmel, Georg (1950). *The Sociology of Georg Simmel.* Ed. by Kurt H. Wolff. New York: The Free Press.

Simmel, Georg (1997). *Simmel on culture: Selected writings.* Ed. D. Frisby & M. Featherstone. London, Thousand Oaks, CA and New Delhi: Sage.

Simmel, Georg (2004). *The philosophy of money*. Third enlarged edition, trans. D. Frisby & T. Bottomore. London and New York: Routledge.

Simmel, Georg (2010). *The view of life. Four metaphysical essays with journal aphorisms.* Trans. J. A. Y. Andrews & D. N. Levine. Chicago, IL: University of Chicago Press.

Simons, Oliver (2019). Simmel's poetics of forms. *The Germanic Review: Literature, Culture, Theory, 94*(2), 101–113, DOI: 10.1080/00168890.2019.1585665

Turner, Victor (1979). Frame, flow and reflection: Ritual and drama as public liminality. *Japanese Journal of Religious Studies, 6*(4), 465–499. Retrieved from www.jstor.org/stable/30233219.

Weinstein, Deena, & Weinstein, Michael (1993). *Postmodernized Simmel.* London: Routledge, DOI: 10.4324/9781315823348

5

THE ACTUALITY OF A SOCIOLOGICAL RESEARCH PROGRAMME

Gregor Fitzi

Introduction

There are some aspects of Simmel's approach to the foundation of sociology as an autonomous science that are particularly topical in an age that is confronted with an ongoing dissolution of institutional and normative societal contexts and the renewed strength of political ideologies. Simmel grounds his sociological research programme on a methodologically led critique of societal self-description that induces the reification of societal processes into ontological subjects with an intrinsic claim of legitimacy. Instead, social science should explain the processes that establish macrosocial structures and grant their reproduction. This should be accomplished through a reconstruction of the relationships of 'reciprocal influence' (*Wechselwirkung*) between the two fundamental dimensions of social reality: social action and social structure. This methodological move puts the question of 'social validity' (*soziale Geltung*) at the centre of sociological research. There is no theorem of 'social emergence' as a result of which the existence of social structures or systems can be taken for granted, so that the task of sociology could simply consist in their description (Sawyer, 2005). On the other hand, modern societies are not simply conceived of as liquefying constructions (Bauman, 2000). Rather, it is the dynamics of complex societies that constantly establish new social forms and dissolve others that constitutes the subject matter of sociology. Yet the enduring unfolding of societal 'solid liquidity' has to be reconstructed by inquiring into the manifold ways in which the opposing logics of social action and social structure match, so making society possible (Fitzi, 2016). Grounded on this approach, Simmel's sociology enables us to address the central problems of modern societies, their normative pluralism, their qualitative differentiation, and their discontinuous structuration. In order to understand how Simmel achieves these goals it is therefore worth focusing on three main theoretical streams of his sociological research programme. These are: (1) the theory of the parallel differentiation of social structure and agency; (2) the theory of social integration through cultural work; and (3) the theory of qualitative societal differentiation.

Parallel differentiation of social structure and agency

As a positive science, for Simmel, sociology can progress only if it differentiates itself from the ongoing self-description of society. The latter is usually formulated in terms of social ontology that endows abstract entities like statuses, classes, societies, states, churches, or political parties with the character of social actors. In the social sciences there is, then as now, a tendency to uncritically adopt the customary concepts of social ontology by treating them as analytical categories of scientific research. This fosters the reproduction of societal self-description in different guises under the label of social sciences. *On Social Differentiation* - Simmel's first sociological work, published in 1890 - makes a decisive contribution to the dismantling of the hypostatised categories, which are compiled from societal self-description and become accepted within the scientific discourse (GSG 2, pp. 109-295). The advantages of a deontologisation and normative neutralisation of sociological categories become clear by comparing Simmel's approach with the early systematisation of the grounding concepts of sociology in Tönnies' *Community and Society* that was published only three years before, in 1887. Tönnies' theory proposed a juxtaposition of two structural concepts of society, 'community' (*Gemeinschaft*) and 'society' (*Gesellschaft*), that were historically grounded in the pre-modern and modern time, by founding them on two variations of the human will: a more organic one (*Wesenwille*) and a more interest-oriented one (*Kürwille*). The opposition of the concepts maintained a latent normative nuance, so that they could be easily reinterpreted in an ideological manner during the political turmoil of the Weimar Republic, as Plessner showed in 1924 in his critique of *Gemeinschaft*.

In opposition to that, in *On Social Differentiation*, Simmel moves to a completely different terrain of sociological theory-building. His research programme assesses the contrasting forms of social relationship and the different types of personality as successive degrees of a biunivocal process of social differentiation, intervening between social structure and agency. This approach dissolves the ontological concepts put forward in terms of traditional social theory and supplies an assessment of the processes that lead from undifferentiated to more complex states of social reality. The forms of social structure and the typologies of individuality, which characterise pre-modern and modern societies, become variations of the interplay between the respective constitutive elements in more or less differentiated social environments. Simmel's sociology thus makes the processes of 'reciprocal action' (*soziale Wechselwirkung*) its object, by taking into account the dynamic and relational aspect of social reality. Its task is to trace back the reified orders of society to their founding social relationships and position them on a development axis that ranges from their undifferentiated to highly differentiated arrangements.

The first step to founding sociology as a positive science thus emerges as a critique of the hypostatised concept of society. Simmel rejects the methodology of sociological holism that defines social structures or systems as autonomous agencies with the character of social subjects. Yet Simmel's approach in *On Social Differentiation* is also a criticism of methodological individualism that leads back all societal phenomena to the action of single individuals (GSG 2, p. 126 f.). In the normative perspective of modern political theory, society's existence is traced back to the individuals who supposedly participate in the social contract. Yet, extending this methodological approach to sociology is problematic insofar as the concept of the individual also constitutes an abstract idea. Its notion hypostatises the complex flow of contradictory motives shaping individual life to an ontological category. Accordingly, to grant sociology the dignity of a positive science, it must be methodologically founded on a paradigm that goes beyond both the classical approaches of social and political theory (Fitzi, 2017b). The sociological research focus must be redirected towards the 'interplay between social actors' (*soziale Wechselwirkung*) that is located between the two ontological extremes of the concepts of society and the individual.

The unity of the research object (*Gegenstand*) of social science must be considered, therefore, as the result of the dynamic relationship between its parts (GSG 2, p. 129). Society is treated as the sum of reciprocal actions among individuals and social groups, so that sociology must assess their dynamic regularities and establish the typologies of their recurring forms. Accordingly, not every social interaction becomes a matter for sociology, which incorporates only the interrelations shown to persist beyond the participation of the single individuals concerned. Simmel's early approach to establishing sociology as a positive science thus allows for sketching out a typology of social forms and seems primarily to give a contribution on the theory of social structure. Nevertheless, the third chapter of *On Social Differentiation* presents an analysis of the parallel differentiation processes of the social group and the individual personality (GSG 2, pp. 169-198). Simmel can show that social agency, too, is the result of an interplay between the various facets of personality related to the different social circles in which the individual participates (GSG 2, pp. 237-257). This epistemological approach, which combines differentiation and individualisation theory, gives scope for the dismantling of the customary ontological concepts of individual and society in terms of relations of reciprocal action (*Wechselwirkungsbeziehungen*) by linking these to the overarching process of social differentiation.

As Simmel explains in societal-historical terms, there is no consistent separation in undifferentiated societies between individuals and the social group. Social relationships are governed by a dense 'collective consciousness' that uniformly shapes individuals' ways of being, acting, and thinking. With the quantitative development of the social group, however, social bonds attached to the single person loosen up. As a rule, one can state that the smaller the social group, the less the potential for the individual to develop relationships beyond the original community of affiliation. Conversely, the higher the number of relationships that the individuals entertain, the easier it is for them to emancipate from each of them (GSG 2, p. 140). Thanks to their social structure, smaller social groups can be easily integrated, although individuals must accomplish more for the community. With increasing social differentiation, due to the multiplication of the functional roles society requires, the interdependence between all individuals intensifies, yet the personal bonds weaken. This widens the scope of liberty when maintaining social relationships beyond one's original background. Individuals now take part in very different 'social circles' and thereby interconnect the most disparate domains of society (GSG 2, pp. 237-257).

Nonetheless, for Simmel, the differentiation of social structure proceeds not without a parallel process that differentiates the individual's personality (GSG 2, pp. 169-198). Consequently, the development of social structure and individual agency must be assessed in terms of their reciprocal relationship. The rise of modern individuality is a function of the quantitative extension of the social group and depends on the quantity of social circles that the individuals are engaged in (GSG 2, p. 239). By acting in differentiated societies, individuals become the 'crossing point' of highly diverse social circles, so that their particular combination structures their personality in a completely original way. Individuals do not live any more in simply concentric social circles, like a family that is part of a clan, a village, a nation and so on (GSG 2, p. 241). In parallel, they entertain complex networks of relationships in professional, economic, political, religious, or leisure circles that involve highly diverse groups of persons. Thus, individuals' liberty when living in complex societies is given by the fact that the social circles that they participate in are less and less concentric and establish a growing complexity of culture (GSG 2, p. 239). Their combination represents the coordinate system for individuals' social relationships and becomes increasingly personal depending on which new circles are added. The quantitative development of social differentiation thus leads both to a qualitative differentiation of social structure and to a process of stronger individualisation.

Hence, a multiplicity of parallel realisations of social networks with various meanings join in the same societal space (GSG 2, pp. 237-257). Mirror-inverted, as it were, the individual personalities become a matrix of the different specialised social domains that the social actors are engaged in. Their quantitative complexity turns out to be of qualitative importance. Only single fragments of the personality are now connected with the different social circles, thus making the individuals increasingly more independent from each other than would otherwise be the case in undifferentiated societies. By the same token, individuals are more heavily dependent on the number of different relationships that they are engaged in, and their personality is more deeply fragmented. The modern condition of life is thus character-ised by a wider sphere of liberty, yet also by higher risks of alienation. Modern individuals try to relate the fragments of their personality as well as the different social roles, which they have to play, in a meaningful synthesis. The dynamics of the social circles, however, fills the personality fragments with ever-new meanings and expectations, so making the task a never-ending process and exposing individuals to a feeling of disorientation and senselessness.

Indeed, for Simmel the social differentiation process also involves a further aspect. Each domain of society gradually produces an autonomous logic whereby each culture sphere becomes independent from the next and triggers a qualitative differentiation of society. In the beginning, individuals merely specialise in the different functions, which the process of the social division of labour demands, to realise their life goals. Afterwards, society's qualita-tive differentiated domains develop a powerful influence and select the individual attitudes they need to reproduce their objective logic. Thus, the means of social action become goals, while the process of social differentiation leads to the reification of the social structure (GSG 2, p. 247). With this evolution, however, the integration of modern society is confronted with an issue that cannot be solved on a purely structural level: in other words, 'system inte-gration' does not suffice (Lockwood, 1964). For Simmel, a society consisting solely of func-tional systems would break apart (GSG 11, p. 33). Only as long as the 'creativity of social action' weaves new relationships between the objectified social circles can complex societies be socially integrated. This performance of the social agency occurs in the everyday dynam-ics of social reality construction; individuals retain in their hands the multitudinous threads of their social belonging, thus ensuring the cohesiveness of the social fabric. Every individual brings forth a different version of the process of interweaving the various social circles, so making it possible to achieve the social and systemic integration of highly differentiated societies.

For Simmel, the creativity and the rhythm of social action thereby replaces the need for normative integration in complex societies. Thus, in contradistinction to Parsons (Parsons, 1967), no functional *ersatz* of 'collective consciousness' or 'collective accountability' is needed to integrate highly differentiated societies (GSG 2, p. 139 f.). On a level of structural analysis, the ongoing social differentiation makes it impossible to achieve any normative integration of society because the manifold and constantly changing combinations of social circles, which social agency produces, can hardly be reduced to an overlapping common pattern. What holds together the social groups is rather the increased frequency of social exchanges that substitutes their missing homogeneity. This is a topic that Simmel will develop further, in the closing chapter of his *The Philosophy of Money* under the headline of the 'tempo of life' (*Tempo des Lebens*) (GSG 6, p. 696 f.). From the perspective of the ana-lysis of social action, rather than establishing overlapping solidarity bonds that hold social actors together, here social agency produces an infinitude of faint lines of relation with intermittent character, so granting social integration. If some social threads tear, the social fabric on others will endure and social agency will build new ones. Only if the majority were lost over a longer period would this lead to a crisis of social structure (GSG 2, p. 142 f.). From a methodological viewpoint, highly differentiated societies, therefore, cannot be seen as a 'social building' that is statically founded on clearly defined patterns of social action. Instead, they must be assessed as an 'organic fabric' that further exists thanks to its ongoing dynamics of building, severing, and rebuilding social relationships.

Social integration through cultural work

The central concept of Simmel's sociology is 'sociation' (*Vergesellschaftung*) and this is defined as a process of 'reciprocal social action' (*Soziale Wechselwirkung*) that relates two or more actors to each other and takes place in the most manifold forms (GSG 11, p. 19). Therefore, Simmel's *opus magnum,* published in 1908, is entitled *Sociology. Inquiries into the Forms of Sociation* (*Soziologie. Untersuchungen über die Formen der Vergesellschaftung*) (GSG 11; Simmel, 2009). The focus of Simmel's sociology is an investigation of the different domains of social reality and a presentation of a typological reconstruction of the social forms that establish their core. Yet the unique aspect of this research programme is its specific perspective. Traditional sociology concentrates on macrosocial formations, which already have the status of autonomous structures, so that societal self-description reifies them to ontological entities. Macrosocial organs and systems like statuses, classes, states, churches, unions, or political parties, however, constitute neither the whole nor the most specific component of social reality. Countless microsocial, apparently negligible forms of relationship and interactions persist between social actors, which make the existence of macrosocial formations possible.

Using a metaphorical analogy with modern biology, Simmel points out in this regard that sociology deserves more than a mere descriptive morphology of the organs of society. Indeed, sociology must inquire into the 'societal connecting tissues' holding macrosocial formations together and so preventing society from breaking apart into a multiplicity of discontinuous systems (GSG 11, p. 33). This methodological perspective tackles the problem that generally the microsocial formations are not already consolidated into supra-individual formations that are visible to the naked eye. Rather, they call for a distinct methodological approach. Conversely, the inquiry into such formations reveals society '*in status nascens*', that is, in its day-to-day building process whereby sociation ties are constantly established, loosened and substituted by new ones (ibid.). Simmel's sociological approach makes this processual moment of sociation its central research focus. The historical beginnings of the social formations are not the main point of interest, but rather the relentless everyday dynamics producing the fine elements of sociation, which empirically grant the considerable flexibility of highly differentiated societies.

Considered from a systematic viewpoint, one can say that Simmel's sociological research programme, his 'sociological epistemology' answers the question of how coordination is possible between social structure and social action by outlining different consecutive methodological steps (GSG 11, pp. 13-62). Firstly, it distinguishes between the matter and form of social reality by filtering out of the manifold social phenomena the persistent forms of sociation and so establishing their typology (GSG 18, pp. 465-497). Formal sociology then establishes a morphology of the preservation mechanisms of social groups by showing how social forms reproduce themselves (GSG 18, pp. 83-140). Subsequently, by founding sociology on a processual conception of sociation, Simmel traces back macrosocial formations to the microsocial strands of sociation that permit their everyday existence. Finally, this analytical procedure leads formal sociology to formulate a further and decisive question. This question characterises the supplementary sections of the *Sociology* of 1908, the 'excurses' that Simmel wrote to bring together in a coherent treatise the many sociological studies that he had published since 1898 (GSG 11, p. 898). Sociology must examine the 'conditions of possibility' for sociation that allow the social actors to become the bearers of macrosocial formations by 'holding in their hands' the fine strands of sociation, which they entertain in the most diverse social circles. The crucial requirement for a theoretical account of how social action and social structure can converge empirically - seen from a systematic viewpoint, the matter of 'social validity' - thus leads to the heart of Simmel's sociological epistemology. He gives an exposition of this matter in the excursus of *Sociology* on 'How is Society Possible?' (GSG 11, pp. 42–61; English: GSG 18, pp. 498–518). This text is the final product and the most significant effort of theoretical synthesis in Simmel's whole sociological research programme. It provides the basis for his entire subsequent work on sociology of culture (Fitzi, 2019, pp. 89-117) and sociological anthropology (GSG 16, pp. 209-425) that the secondary literature usually misconstrues as turning away from sociology.

In the excursus, the various themes are intertwined of the parallel social differentiation of the social group and personality, the role of social actors as crossing points of social circles as well as the function of social action creativity for the subsistence of social structure. However, Simmel remains true to his strict formal methodology of analysis that places in parenthesis the motivation sphere of social action and omits it from the sociological inquiry into reality. One could argue here that Simmel fails to compile a sociological theory of validity, or at least of the legitimation of macrosocial formations through social action. Because, in contrast to Weber's understanding of sociology, formal sociology does not concentrate on the motivational sphere of social action (Weber, 1921). However, this observation is misleading. The uniqueness of Simmel's sociological epistemology lies precisely in its grounding a theory of social validity by maintaining the methodological focus of sociology exclusively on the forms of sociation and by setting aside the manifold motivations and goals that influence social action. In strict epistemological terms, Simmel poses the question about the 'conditions of possibility' that allow the social actors to become bearers of their social relationships. In this way, sociological methodology responds to the question concerning the convergence of social action and social structure, by going beyond the conventional approach of moral sociology, which concentrates on the motivational sphere of social action.

Firstly, the persistence of macrosocial formations is traced back to the microsocial formations that make them possible in everyday societal dynamics. In a second step, these minor forms of reciprocal action are explained in terms of their empirical validity by determining the 'forms of consciousness' (*Bewusstseinsformen*) that permit the social actors to become bearers of the multiplicity of social relationships which they keep in different societal domains. The epistemological reason for excluding from the inquiry the specific individual or collective motivations, goals, or value orientations that accompany the sociation processes is that they are too variable to explain the persistence of the social forms. This approach to the analysis of social reality is in line with Kant's epistemological method of setting aside everything that is contingent to shed light on the conditions of existence (the a priori) of the phenomena that have to be explained. Yet, the difference and the methodological problem here is that the object of sociology is characterised by particularities that make a simple extension of Kant's approach impossible and demand a distinct foundation of sociological epistemology.

Accordingly, the aim of Simmel's sociological epistemology is to trace the 'categories of consciousness' that allow for the convergence of social action and social structure in the everyday praxis of social actors. All societal processes indeed take place 'in the mind' of the social actors, thus intertwining their motivations and goals in social action. If this were not the case, society would look like a lifeless puppet show (GSG 11, p. 35). All the same, the analytical perspective of sociological epistemology is not compelled to concentrate on the psychological layer of the motivation of social action. Sociology aims not at discovering the rules of the psychological processes accompanying social interaction (Fitzi, 2017a). Rather, it seizes the formal configurations of consciousness, which characterise the knowledge of being involved in social relationships. A consciousness that allows social actors to become and remain their bearers.

Simmel applies Kant's so-called 'regressive method' as a founding gesture of sociological epistemology to examine the 'conditions of the possibility' of social reality (Kant, 1783, pp. 253–383). From the overall consciousness of 'being part of social relationships', sociological epistemology sorts out everything that constitutes the contingent and fluctuating motivation of social action. Thus, Simmel can trace social reality back to formal knowledge structures of its experience in the minds of social actors. Epistemologically, this sets out the 'conditions of existence' for the objects of the social world (GSG 11, p. 37). These formal knowledge structures must be seen as the apriorities of social life because they are proven to exist independently of each specific content with which they are empirically associated. This is demonstrated by applying the regressive analytical method to social reality. Sociological epistemology can work out the social character of formal knowledge structures necessary to permit social reality's existence, because its focus is not the contents of consciousness of isolated social actors. Instead, it inquires into their reciprocal connection with respect to the category of sociation. Sociological epistemology is thus by no means a variation of subject-philosophy. It poses the question about what happens in the consciousness of social actors when they are engaged in sociation processes with each other. It examines the formal knowledge structures that are necessarily present to make possible the processes of sociation. In summary, the cognitive interest of sociological epistemology focuses on the question of how society is possible as an 'objective form of subjective consciousnesses' (GSG 11, p. 41).

Throughout the process of reciprocal cognition between social actors, the other actor can never be fully known as a counterpart. So it is necessary for the social actor to construct a picture of his counterpart by generalising and to some extent creating a stereotypical view by using the partial information available. The way in which the picture emerges of the social counterpart depends on the degree of social distance between social actors. The process is led by the need to obtain a stable image of the 'other' as a reliable partner of social interaction by constructing the same as the 'consistent type of himself' (GSG 11, p. 47). For Simmel, this generalising and stereotyping process between social actors must be seen as the first a priori of sociation. Yet social actors are subjects of experience; they cannot be reduced to simple objects of perception. In other words, the personality of the other can never be completely grasped. Certain typifications and stylisations intervene to compensate for the insufficient knowledge that social actors have about each other. The socially guided perception of the other thus exercises an exonerating action with regard to sociation processes: the social actors now react in an intuitive, mechanical and often unconscious way to the complexity of the social world. Every actor appears to be the social stereotype of himself, thus fitting into expectations of that social circles in which he is engaged (GSG 11, p. 48 f.). Beyond every fragmentation of modern social actors in highly differentiated societies, social counterparts thus become stylised to abiding characters that allow the perpetuation of social relationships.

This analysis enables Simmel's sociological epistemology to provide an original response to the classical question of sociological theory, which Parsons declared as the 'double contingency' problem (Parsons & Shils, 1951, p. 16). Social actors do not stabilise their social relationships by referring to mutual normative orientations, but by constructing stereotypical images of each other and their interrelations. A multiplicity of typologically generalised representations of social reality that are the product of the stereotyping process of social perception delivers the basis for the constructed image of society as the sum of ongoing social relationships. Yet given the fact that social reality is seen from an infinite number of alternative viewpoints, social actors are confronted with an array of stereotypical images of themselves and their relationships. They must satisfy the various expectations of the social circles that they are engaged in. The key question is then how social actors can handle the multiplicity of their social identities, so that they manage to participate in the sociation processes. On the one hand, the expectations of social circles merge into social role patterns that the social actors must conform to. On the other hand, social structures also provide the actors with the instruments for their self-fulfilment within social reality. The convergence of social structure with social action therefore depends on the creative performance of the social actors that links these aspects together. Yet social actors do not merely coincide with their social roles, but also exist and perform independently of them. This makes them a factor of contingency for sociation processes. Every member of the social group is not only a part of it, but must also be seen as an individual who exists for his own sake (second precondition a priori of sociation, GSG 11, p. 51). Moreover, a precondition for participating in the processes of sociation is to maintain a meaningful relationship between both elements, yet without succumbing to alienation or, at the other extreme, falling into blasé social autism. The characterisation of sociation forms, in the sense of 'being outside' of the majority of social ties, allows Simmel to develop his classical analyses of figures of social exclusion such as the 'poor' or the 'stranger' (GSG 11, pp. 512-555, 764-771; Simmel, 2009, pp. 409-442, 601-605). The same tension-fraught relationship between being socialised and being on one's own, however, applies to every social relationship.

Simmel's epistemological theory-building concerning the integration between the socialised and non-socialised facets of the social actor's consciousness thus introduces his sociological theory of social validity. Its main assumption is that each social actor is the point of intersection and the bearer of a network of sociation processes that contributes to society's persistence. Yet individuals are not only part and function of society. There is an essential line of tension and conflict which characterises all sociation processes and affects the personality of the individual social actors. Not only must they contend with the fragmentation of their personality in highly differentiated societies, but they must also deal with the antagonism between its socialised and non-socialised domains. Consequently, in order to integrate complex societies, a repeated creative performance is required of the individual social actors to overcome the conflict between the different domains of consciousness, or in the terms of cultural sociology between objective and subjective culture. Simmel's sociological epistemology shows that this performance cannot be taken for granted as the outcome of a habit or custom, which social actors acquire during primary and secondary socialisation, and then continuing to supervise all sociation processes. Instead, the creative performance that relies on the socialised and non-socialised domains of the personality occurs on a different basis every day. This circumstance constitutes the decisive challenge for social life in rapidly changing and highly differentiated modern societies. The creative performance of social action is not automatism. Rather, it is founded on the capacity of the consciousness to relate its different socialised and non-socialised flows of experience in a synthesis that makes sense for the social actors. This performance that produces social meaning can receive the most varied existential, ethical, political, or religious validations. According to Simmel's methodology, however, sociological epistemology focuses exclusively on the formal structure, which characterises the creative performance of social action, that is, on the competence of social actors' consciousness in relating the socialised and non-socialised realms of life experience in whatever meaningful synthesis. This formal structure, which founds the consciousness of being engaged in sociation processes, constitutes the third condition a priori for the existence of social relationships (GSG 11, p. 58 f.). Only on this basis can social actors become the bearers of the network of sociation processes that they are involved in, because they can deliver the creative performance to shape the social meaning that holds them together.

Simmel's conception of the sociological a priori ends with a theory of the socially determined cultural work that social actors must perform to be part of society. For this purpose, he embeds the culture theory of *The Philosophy of Money* in his later sociological epistemology (GSG 6, pp. 617-654). Culture becomes a grounding category of sociology. The cultural accomplishments of the social actors are recognised as *the* performance that coordinates social action and social structure. Accordingly, culture can neither be conceived as a reflex or consequence of the economic relations of production (Marx), nor of the social relationships (Durkheim). Instead, culture must be seen as a structural factor of society that grants its stability, plasticity, and change within the everyday process of building and legitimating the social fabric. If the cultural work done by social actors represents the decisive factor for enabling highly differentiated societies to hold together, develop, and change, then the sociological inquiry into the manifold cultural expressions that characterise modern societies becomes an absolute priority of every research agenda. After 1908, Simmel's endeavours focus on the manifold cultural expressions of modernity and show how the logic of the sociological a priori can be applied to the different domains of culture.

Qualitative differentiated society

Under the influence of Parsons, contemporary sociology refers to 'functional differentiation' as the modern form of societal differentiation (Parsons, 1951). The idea is that society develops different domains that are specialised in delivering a particular performance to the rest of society, so that each societal sphere can be assigned to a specific 'function of society' as a whole. Society is seen as a living organism that consists of a number of organs that cooperate in assuring the life and wealth of the whole, as was already argued by the biology-inspired sociology of the 19th century (Schäffle, 1875-1878; Spencer, 1876/1882–1885). Classical sociologists like Durkheim, Simmel, or Weber had a quite different understanding of modern societal differentiation. Their attention remains focused on the fact that highly differentiated societies tend to give rise to societal domains that follow an autonomous logic and do not accept the leading function of any particular domain. The process is regarded as a contingent societal phenomenon that does not follow any natural law, including the laws of evolutionary biology. Thus, classical sociologists make no axiomatic assumptions about the relationships between the different societal domains and refuse to subordinate sociological research to pre-cast metaphors borrowed from other scientific domains. Neither the biological-functional character of society as a living being, nor a predetermined harmony between societal domains, nor conflict, nor the prevalence of one domain, like religion, politics or economy over and above the other, can be turned into the unscrutinised axiomatic premise of sociological theory. Whatever relationships persist between the different societal spheres is a question that must be cleared on an empirical level of inquiry. Hence, classical sociological theories are theories of 'qualitative societal differentiation' but not of functional differentiation. The particular aspect of Simmel's approach to this issue is given by the fact that he always develops a theory of the parallel differentiation of social structure and social action by inquiring into the manifold conditions a priori of their relationship.

Similarly to Max Weber (MWG I/19, pp. 479-522; Weber, 2004), Simmel develops his analysis of qualitative social differentiation in the context of a study on religion, i.e. in *Die Religion*, which he wrote in 1906 on the request of his pupil Martin Buber for the series *Die Gesellschaft* (Simmel GSG 10, pp. 39-118, 409-414; Simmel, [1941/42] 2008, p. 61). In highly differentiated societies, as Simmel's theory of culture shows (GSG 5, pp. 560-582), social life is subordinated to a number of external powers. The result is a wide fragmentation of the personality of social actors, whose different spheres are led by the autonomous logic of respective social circles. Apparently, and this was the result of the analysis in *The Philosophy of Money,* there is no escape from the modern fragmentation of the social actor (GSG 6, p. 446 f.), so that Simmel still writes about the 'Fragmentary Character of Life' in August 1916 (GSG 13, pp. 202-216). From a different perspective of analysis, however, Simmel shows that the creativity of social action has the potential to overcome the modern human condition by regrouping all the content of life experience in the context of a particular approach to the world. This attitude, which aims to make sense of life experience, is also an expression of the cultural work that is addressed by the third a priori of sociation (GSG 11, p. 58 f.). Furthermore, this approach does not grant an automatic reversal of the fragmentation of modern life, although it can overcome it under specific conditions. According to Simmel, social actors can choose a 'predominant logic' for governing *their* social action, so that the fragmented content of social reality is reordered under the particular perspective of art, religion, economy, politics or other logics (GSG 10, p. 42). The grasp of social action from the point of view of a specific logic represents a modality for realising the third a priori of sociation with consequences that also influence the order of social structure because the intersection of the different social circles, where the social actor is active, acquires a completely different meaning. Consequently, the number of social actors who orient towards a specific logic of action also mainly determines the way in which society is structured.

In *Die Religion*, Simmel focuses on the perspective that religion casts on world and action, yet a similar assessment applies to each qualitative differentiated domain of modern society. The allocation of the totality of the world fragments to a particular perspective depends on the subjective logic of social action. According to the analysis of the third a priori of sociation, the mind constitutes the connecting force that relates to each other the disparate contents of consciousness that characterise life experience within complex societies. Following the most diverse impulses, emotions, and choices, social actors let a specific qualitative nuance of consciousness predominate and paint life-contents with a specific colour. Hence, not only the objectified logics of the qualitative differentiated domains in complex societies attempt to draw their specific complexion over the totality of social reality, but also the subjective nuances of consciousness that motivate the social actors. The logics of social structure and social action enter into a reciprocally determined and more or less conflictual relationship on the level of qualitative societal differentiation. Accordingly, from the perspective of the social actor, if religion, art, politics, or the economy constitute the keynote of existence, the different domains of society, i.e. their disparate contents, must organise around it.

Nevertheless, this approach to social action does not lead to the sole reign of one qualitative differentiated logic over the whole of qualitative differentiated social reality. Rather, it simply points to the expression of all its possible contents 'through its language'. Qualitative societal differentiation persists, but it is subjectively subsumed under a predominant logic of social action. This applies notably to religion that conveys all world contents through its language, even if its oddest result is a 'negation' of the secular world orders (GSG 10, p. 46). Yet, the same dynamics involves the logic and language of every societal domain, if it becomes the overall focus of social action. Thanks to a particular approach to life experience, all the disparate contents of the world come to expression under its control by relating the manifold domains of social action under a common point of view. Different meaningful 'stances to world and life' (*Attitüden zu Welt und Leben*) immediately fall into a relationship of competition claiming the same right of shaping all the disparate contents of qualitative differentiated societies. Yet which approach prevails on social action depends on the attitude of the single actors, who decide which logic will lead their cultural work, so relating together the world fragments by following a specific logic of the third a priori of sociation.

Accordingly, the task of sociology is to reconstruct how social action produces its different logics, and how these become autonomous by constituting objective domains of social structure. For these reasons, Simmel's cultural sociology provides an action theory based on an explanation of the continuous establishment, depletion and change of qualitative social differentiation in complex societies. Different subjective logics lead social action by producing the objects of different domains of socially determined experience, and following the scheme of the sociological a priori. The products of the cultural work then gather to form clusters of the objective culture and develop an intrinsic logic, which claims to be followed by the social actors (GSG 5, pp. 560-582; GSG 6, pp. 617-654). Social action stances, however, can differently relate the objectified contents of social life by following diverse logics. The result is permanent tension between the subjective logic of action creativity and the objective logic of social structure, which characterises qualitative differentiated societies and builds the core of Simmel's sociological theory of culture. Complex societies never develop one static and perennial hypostasised social structure, whose functioning can be traced back to a pre-cast metaphor borrowed from other scientific domains. Rather, they consist of multiple, alternative, and competing perspectives about the shaping of social structure that fight for predominance. The dynamics of qualitative societal differentiation, therefore, must be reconstructed empirically and cannot be subsumed under axiomatic assumptions about the relationship between the different societal domains. The goal of Simmel's middle phase of work starting around 1908 was to show how the tension-fraught dynamics between the logics of social action and social structure develops in the different cultural spheres.

Simmel's sociological assessment of the societal spheres of the economy, social life and politics suggests that he is a representative of the theory of social reification in Marx's sense. A pessimistic tone in the diagnosis of modernity emerges several times in *The Philosophy of Money*, so the idea of the unescapable 'tragedy of culture' seems to build the core of Simmel's sociological theory - as its most feuillettonistic formulation suggests (GSG 12, pp. 194-223). Social actors are overstrained by the autonomisation of objective culture, thus making the recomposition of the logic of social action with that of social structure only seem possible at the price of a commercialisation of values, constraint of the rule of intersubjectivity and outvoting of political minorities. This negative vision of societal development seems almost to relate Simmel to Weber's most pessimistic utterings about bureaucratic petrification, the 'iron cage' of modern life and the problem of the 'last man' (MWG I/18, p. 488). Yet, in this respect, it must be noted on the one hand that both Simmel and Weber underline the circumstance of an ongoing dialectic within modern society with the outcome that every diagnosis of its trend towards development does not imply an automatism of its evolution. On the other hand, however, Simmel's sociological assessment of the societal domains such as religion, art, and eroticism shows that in his eyes, and regardless of every reification, the creativity of social action has the potential for achieving a transformation of society's existing structures. In accordance with the logic of the third a priori of sociation, if a specific cultural stance becomes the leading orientation of social action, its creativity can overcome the fragmentation of the different domains of life that is provoked by the modern qualitative differentiation of society.

Each cultural principle can become the dominant approach for shaping life conduct by producing overall semantics that guides social action and expresses all the contents of the world in its language, including those originating from other domains of qualitative differentiated societies. In terms of the logic of the third a priori of sociation, the everyday cultural work of social actors unifies the manifold contents of the world under a particular perspective by selecting, interpreting, and relating them to each other through common semantics. Society remains fragmented, as long as the qualitative differentiation of society occurs on the structural level of the autonomisation of different reified societal domains organised around an objective logic. They appear in an increasing 'self-referential entropy' because everyday cultural work does not actualise societal semantics, while their compartments stagnate. Objective and subjective culture fall apart and their conflict jeopardises the persistence of the social fabric, as the theory of the social a priori shows (GSG 11, pp. 42-61). Yet if the creativity of social action relates the disparate objective contents of life experience from the point of view of a particular cultural attitude, reification processes can be overcome by a new shaping of social reality. The transformation of societal semantics occurs in competition between different and at times opposing cultural principles. Any question concerning how many different 'attitudes to life and the world' strive for objectivation as well as which one seems to prevail can only be answered empirically. For Simmel, the main difference between the objective shaping of the world, along the lines of the reified logic of the societal domains, and its subjective reshaping through social action, lies in the fact that the first produces a world of cultural fragments, whereas the second unifies them into a meaningful totality. This is the importance of the everyday cultural work of social action in qualitative differentiated societies. Its creative potential realises the requirements of the third a priori of sociation from the perspective of a particular principle of culture, by granting the coordination of social action and social structure.

A central topic here is art. Art fosters a creative recombination of the fragmented content of modern life experience, thus allowing for subjective and objective culture to merge in an innovative and meaningful synthesis. The creative power of art thus permits a new ordering of the world, whose elements are generally maintained in reciprocal indifference or conflicted relationship. The cultural work of art is based on the same logic as the everyday creativity of social action, which follows the logic of the third a priori of sociation. Yet for Simmel the synthesis of world elements from the perspective of art manifests a particular quality, because its creative work becomes an end in itself. Art represents the unifying activity of the consciousness that relates subjective and objective culture in a way that is completely released from its practical means. Cultural work is carried out for its own sake and contributes to the production of a new reality, thus showing in a concrete sense that even in highly differentiated societies it is possible to accomplish the cycle of culture. Artistic creativity therefore offers a model for innovative cultural work and societal change, which in Simmel's eyes could transform the imperative of the third a priori of sociation into an instrument of emancipation.

References

Bauman, Zygmunt (2000). *Liquid modernity*. Cambridge: Polity.

Fitzi, Gregor (2016). Modernity as solid liquidity. Simmel's life-sociology. In Th. Kemple & O. Pyyhtinen (Eds.), *The Anthem companion to Georg Simmel* (pp. 59–80). London: Anthem.

Fitzi, Gregor (2017a). Dialogue. Divergence. Veiled reception. Criticism. Georg Simmel relationship with Émile Durkheim. *Journal of Classical Sociology, 2017*(4), 293–308.

Fitzi, Gregor (2017b). Ni holisme, ni individualisme. La troisième voie de la sociologie chez Simmel. In D. Thouard & B. Zimmermann (Eds.), *Simmel, le parti-pris du tiers* (pp. 89–112). Paris: Éditions du CNRS.

Fitzi, Gregor (2019). *The challenge of modernity. Simmel's sociological theory*. Abingdon and London: Routledge.

GSG: Simmel, Georg (1989-2015). *Georg Simmel Gesamtausgabe*. Ed. by Otthein Rammstedt et al. Frankfurt/M.: Suhrkamp, 24 volumes, quoted here as GSG followed by the volume number.

Kant, Immanuel (1783). *Prolegomena zu einer jeden künftigen Metaphysik, die als Wissenschaft wird auftreten können*. Riga: Hartknoch, now in: *Kants Werke* (Akademie-Ausgabe), vol. 4.

Lockwood, David (1964). Social Integration and System Integration. In G. K. Zollschan & W. Hirsch (Eds.), *Explorations in social change* (pp. 244–257). London: Houghton Mifflin.

MWG: Weber, Max (1984–). *Max Weber Gesamtausgabe*. Tübingen: Mohr Siebeck. Quoted here as MWG followed by the volume number.

Parsons, Talcott (1951). *The social system*. Glencoe: The Free Press.

Parsons, Talcott (1967). Durkheim's contribution to the theory of integration of social systems. In Id., *Sociological theory and modern society* (pp. 3–34). New York: Free Press.

Parsons, Talcott & Shils, Edward A. (Eds.) (1951). *Toward a general theory of action*. Cambridge, MA: Harvard University Press.

Plessner, Helmuth (1924). *Die Grenzen der Gemeinschaft. Eine Kritik des sozialen Radikalismus*. In Id. (1981), *Gesammelte Schriften*, vol. 5. *Macht und Menschliche Natur* (pp. 7–133). Frankfurt/M.: Suhrkamp. English: Id. (1999). *The limits of community: A critique of social radicalism*. New York: Humanity Books.

Sawyer, Keyth R. (2005). *Social emergence. Societies as complex systems*. Cambridge: Cambridge University Press.

Schäffle, Albert (1875-1878). *Bau und Leben des socialen Körpers. Encyclopädischer Entwurf einer realen Anatomie, Physiologie und Psychologie der menschlichen Gesellschaft mit besonderer Rücksicht auf die Volkswirthschaft als socialen Stoffwechsel*, 4 vol. Tübingen: Laupp.

Simmel, Georg (2009). *Sociology: Inquiries into the construction of social forms*. Leiden: Brill.

Simmel, Hans ([1941/42] 2008). Lebenserinnerungen. *Simmel Studies, 18*(1), 9–136.

Spencer, Herbert (1876/1882–1885). *Principles of sociology*, 3 vol. London: Williams and Norgate.

Weber, Max (1921). *Soziologische Grundbegriffe*. Now in Id. (2013) *Max Weber Gesamtausgabe I/23 Wirtschaft und Gesellschaft. Soziologie. Unvollendet. 1919–1920* (pp. 147-215), Ed. by K. Borchardt, E. Hanke & W. Schluchter. Tübingen: Mohr Siebeck, English: Weber, Max (2002). *Basic concepts in sociology*. New York: Citadel Press.

Weber, Max (2004). Intermediate reflection on economic ethics of the world religions. In S. Whimster (Ed.), *The essential Weber. A reader* (pp. 215–244). London: Routledge.

PART III

Philosophy

6

RELATIVISM

A theoretical and practical philosophical programme

Matthieu Amat

Introduction

Is a relativist philosophy possible? In 1883, Windelband answered this question in the negative, in both epistemological and moral terms. In 'Critical and genetic method' (1915), he presented relativism as the inevitable consequence of the genetic method in science, whether this method be naturalistic, psychological, or historical. Relativism would thus be the outcome of all 'philosophies' which fail to account for the objective validity (logical, ethical, or aesthetic) of their objects. The stakes are also moral:

> Relativism is the 'philosophy' of the blasé person who no longer believe in anything, or of the cosmopolitan gamin who shrugs his shoulders at everything and making cheeky joked and finds it right to talk one way today and another way tomorrow.
>
> *(Windelband, 1915, p. 117)*

Relativism is the expression of psychological types favoured by 'modern life', the metropolis, its profusion and excitement of all kinds. The relativist is the man that Nietzsche brought to the 'land of culture', full of colours and smeared with signs from all eras and all countries (Nietzsche, 1967, eKGWB/Za-II-Bildung).

Nine years later, in his habilitation thesis, Rickert described relativism as a *contradictio in adjecto*: in affirming that 'there is no truth', 'a relativist who considers his opinion to be true does not know what he thinks'. Relativism cannot be a 'philosophical' or 'scientific point of view'. It is 'the product of a time that does not dare to face the problem of truth' and poses indeed a moral problem (Rickert, 1892, pp. 74–77).

Yet it was to Rickert that Simmel entrusted, in 1896, his desire to deliver 'in the course of the decade', a 'theory of relativism' (GSG 22, p. 214) and, two years later, to constitute, under the name of 'relativism', a 'theory of value' (ibid., p. 292). In fact, Simmel shared the critique of contemporary relativism to a large extent: the *Philosophy of money*, for example, deepens Windelband's insights on the blasé attitude and the nervous anxiety 'that drives modern man from socialism to Nietzsche, from Böcklin to impressionism, from Hegel to Schopenhauer' (GSG 6, p. 675; Simmel, 2004, p. 490). Simmel's relativism will have to mark his distance from what could be called a 'bad' relativism: the target of neo-Kantians but also a figure of what

Nietzsche calls nihilism: the feeling that 'the world looks *valueless*' or 'that there is no truth …[;] this, too, is merely nihilism' (Nietzsche, 1967, eKGWB/NF-1887, 11[99]; Nietzsche's emphasis).

The Simmelian relativism aims precisely to be a new theory and guarantee of value and truth. In a fragmentary text drafted in the early 1910s, possibly composed to introduce the French volume *Mélanges de philosophie relativiste* (GSG 20, p. 549 f.), Simmel writes:

> The historical dissolution of everything substantial, absolute, eternal into the flow of things, into the historical changeability, into the only psychological reality, seems to me to be secured only against an unfounded subjectivism and scepticism, if one replaces those substantially fixed values with the living reciprocal action of elements, which are again subject to the same dissolution into infinity. The central concepts of truth, of value, of objectivity, etc. presented themselves to me as reciprocal actions, as contents of a relativism, which now no longer meant the sceptical loosening of all consistencies, but precisely the securing against them by means of a new concept of consistency (Philosophy of Money).
>
> *(GSG 20, p. 304)*

Simmel continues, stating that relativism is both a 'principle of knowledge' and a 'cosmic principle', thanks to which the 'substantial and abstract image of the unity of the world' can be replaced 'with an organic reciprocal action' (ibid., p. 305). Relativism appears as a genuine philosophical programme, assuming and even completing the functional turn in contemporary thinking and culture, but without falling into the 'sceptical dissolution' of any objectivity.[1]

Probably because of persistent misunderstandings about the nature of relativism – as the correspondence with Rickert shows in particular (cf. GSG 23, pp. 637–639) – Simmel rarely uses the term after the 1900 *Philosophy of money*, where we find the most complete exposition of relativism. However, in a 1916 letter to Rickert, Simmel continues to defend his relativism, as an 'entirely positive metaphysical worldview, that has as little to do with scepticism as does the physical R[elativism] of Einstein' (GSG 23, p. 638). Anyhow, we believe that it remains the more comprehensive term to approach the ensemble and unity of intent of Simmel's work. Let us now consider the multiple dimensions of this theoretical but also practical programme, as well as some aspects of his genesis.

1890–1900: towards relativism

How can values be both relative and absolute?

According to a letter to Rickert dated May 10, 1898, the main task of 'relativism' is to constitute a 'theory of value'.

> The concept of value seems to me to contain … a *circulus vitiosus*, because we always find, when we follow the relationships far enough away, that the value of A is based on the value of B, while that of B is based on that of A. I could be satisfied with it …, if not, just as undoubtedly, absolute and objective values would require recognition. … I am convinced that I can only stick to my relativism if it is able to solve all the problems posed by absolutist theories.
>
> *(GSG 22, p. 292)*

How can the values be both relative and absolute? This problem will be solved in the first chapter of the *Philosophy of money*. But it is the result of ten years of reflection, of which we will summarise some steps.

Value is a cardinal concept at the end of the 19th century, especially in German philosophy. In Lotze's 'value idealism', the values fill, in a post-Hegelian context, the gap between the metaphysical needs and the results of science (Lotze, 1884–1888, p. iv; cf. Schnädelbach, 1983, pp. 206–218.). Their mode of being (or quasi-being) is neither subjective (in a psychological sense) nor objective (in a physical or metaphysical sense), but ideal. They have a *validity* (*Geltung*) that imposes itself on the conscience without strictly *being* (Lotze, 1989, § 316). This grammar strongly influenced many theories of ideal objects at the turn of the century, in particular Windelband's and Rickert's theories of value and, through them, Simmel's reflections on value.

In fact, when saying that 'there are values that require recognition', Simmel quasi quotes Rickert. Simmel read Rickert's *Object of knowledge. Contribution to the problem of philosophical transcendence* as soon as it was published (1892). The book influenced him strongly and inaugurated a long dialogue between the two philosophers (cf. GSG 22, p. 77 f., p. 214; GSG 23, p. 619). In his habilitation thesis, Rickert shows that any claim to knowledge depends on the possibility of the position of 'values' being endowed with 'absolute validity': 'in each knowledge, a value is recognized' (Rickert, 1892, pp. 58, 60). Only this can give our judgement a 'character of necessity' (ibid., 90). Judgement is a psychological fact, but its necessity or validity is transcendental. This distinction between the judgement (as psychological fact) and his content (likely to have an objective validity) comes from Lotze's *Logic* and is an anti-psychologist and anti-relativist *topos* at the turn of the century. Like his neo-Kantian colleagues, or like the Husserl of the *Logical investigations* (1993, p. 4), Simmel defends in 1900 this distinction between genesis and validity. However, at the same time he claims, somehow, the relative character of values.

In the 1890 review of Eucken's *Lebensanschauungen*, Simmel states that 'a new image of reality requires new scales of value'. The question is to know what sort of values can be defended when faced with the 'evolutionist', 'materialist and mechanical character of the modern worldview' (GSG 1, pp. 276–279). Against attempts to save 'ideals emanating from outdated worldviews' or lamentations of a crisis and the lack of values, Simmel demands 'an elevation and extension of the notion of value', in order to liberate it from 'rigidity and isolation' (ibid., p. 277). The challenge is less to create new values than to promote a new way of thinking about value.

The *Introduction to the science of morals* (1892–1893) is an important step in this endeavour. The book intends to be a 'critique of the fundamental concepts of ethics', in a 'purely genetic' perspective (GSG 3, p. 10 f.). The so-called 'objective, ideal meaning of values' is dissolved in order to lay the foundations for a true science of moral phenomena (GSG 4, p. 19). Simmel proposes his own version of historicisation and relativisation of moral values, among the many others advanced in the 19th century.

However, the book contains the seeds of a relativisation of another kind, structural rather than historical. It is no longer a question of dissolving moral concepts into the multiplicity of psychological and socio-historical relations, but of revealing that they are relational structures which contain a logical circularity. Duty is a means to an end, but is recognised as a duty if it becomes an end in itself (GSG 3, p. 36); we must want what is good, but we define good through what we must want (ibid., p. 57). The list is long; Simmel tirelessly emphasises all circularities, demonstrating the impossibility of founding morality, whether on 'a priori principles' or on 'ultimate ends' (ibid., p. 308 f.).

These developments are of considerable importance for the future theory of value. However, as evinced by the letter cited above, the outline of such a theory was to be deemed unsatisfactory. To overcome the gap between relativist sensibility (in both the historical and the structural sense) and the lesson that he receives from Rickert, Simmel will need Nietzsche's mediation.

The crucial text is the 1896 essay 'Nietzsche, a moral-philosophical silhouette'. The essay is devoted to Nietzsche's 'moral philosophy' and 'theory of value'. Simmel begins by presenting the genealogical critique of 'altruistic and democratic values' (GSG 5, p. 116 f.). But what interests him is that 'on this historical-psychological basis' are built 'systematic axiological concepts'. 'The systematic starting point of this theory of value' is found in the concept of 'distance between people' (ibid., p. 118). More than a social or historical fact, this distance is the 'unconditional, logical-conceptual condition of any value within society' (ibid., p. 119). Indeed, we cannot speak of a value of an 'average level', which 'is neither high nor low, but the basis from which we can measure the high and low' (ibid.). The value of a whole – whatever it be: social, psychological, aesthetical, etc. – can be measured only from its highest point, i.e. its internal distances. A 'pure objectivity in the measurement of value' is thus made possible (ibid., p. 120).

Simmel elevates the '*Pathos der Distanz*' to an axiomatic rank: it is the condition of possibility of the experience of value (cf. Lichtblau, 1984). Value certainly has historical, psychological, and sociological conditions, but is not an expression of these conditions. It is the quality of a living relational structure. Nietzsche salvages the objective character of value without resorting to any transcendence or setting a 'final goal' for life. He shows that the philosophy of life is not condemned to axiological relativism. Simmel will follow this Nietzschean path, but will complement the perspective on life with a perspective on culture, that is on the question of life's objectifications. As the 1918 *Lebensanschauung* claims, in its 'immanent transcendence', life is not only 'more-life', constant intensification of itself, but also 'more-than-life', objectification of itself (GSG 16, p. 215 f., 229–232). Relativism must reflect this problematic relationship.

The functions and provenance of reciprocal action

Let us now turn to the second main concept in the building of Simmel's relativism: reciprocal action (*Wechselwirkung*). It is often considered first and foremost as a sociological concept. But it is also and first an epistemological and even a metaphysical concept.

Reciprocal action appears in the first chapter of the 1890 *Social differentiation*, 'A theory of knowledge for the social sciences'. Against all 'residual Platonism', and adopting motives from the phenomenalism of Mach or Vaihinger, Simmel claims that there is no 'real unit', neither substantial nor ideal. All universal and substantial notions have to be dissolved into individual atoms and functional relations. 'Society' is neither an entity *per se* nor a mere sum of individuals, but the 'sum of its members reciprocal actions' (GSG 2, pp. 126–130). The 'soul' is not an 'unitary substance' but 'a complex of representations' (GSG 3, p. 245). 'Man' is a state of 'relative stability of certain traits' in a biological and historical evolution (GSG 4, p. 45). In the *Philosophy of money*, Simmel writes that 'the contents of life … are … split up into so many small parts; their rounded totalities are so shattered that any arbitrary synthesis and formation of them is possible' (GSG 6, p. 366; Simmel, 2004, p. 278.). Are we not in a maximal relativism without any stability and criterium of objectivity? Simmel introduces a principle that was not acknowledged by the positivist:

[T]here is only one reason that provides at least a relative objectivity of unification: the reciprocal action of the parts. We can qualify each object as unitary in proportion to the intensity with which its parts are in reciprocal dynamical relations.

(GSG 2, p. 129)

Atom, cell, individual, society are thus relative units stabilised by reciprocal actions. As an epistemic category, reciprocal action guarantees objectivity criteria and avoids the reduction of the world to an amorphous plane without quality. To that extent, it has features of a metaphysical or cosmological idea. 'We have to admit, as a regulative world principle, that everything is in some way in a reciprocal action with everything, that forces and reciprocating relationships exist between every point of the world and every other' (ibid., 130).

The convergence of the epistemic and cosmologic functions as well as the lexicon of the 'regulative' invite a Kantian reading. The 'Transcendental analytic' makes reciprocal action the third category of relation, which synthetises those of substance and of causality (Kant, 1900–, Ak, III, p. 138). Within the framework of schematism theory, it becomes a regulative scheme which organises the whole experience: 'all substances, as far as they can be perceived as simultaneous in space, are in a universal reciprocal action' (ibid., p. 180), to the point that 'the unity of the universe, in which all phenomena must be linked, is clearly a consequence of [this] principle' (ibid., p. 185).

Lotze, who was appointed to the Berlin University in 1880 but died the following year, could also have played a great and more direct role. We know that Simmel intended to give a lecture on Lotze's 'practical philosophy' during WS 1886/87 (Köhnke, 1996, p. 194). In Lotze's 1879 *Metaphysics*, the 'connexion of things' is conceived in terms of a metaphysical reciprocal action, understood as an inner relationship of a unique substance. Only this hypothesis would conciliate 'the world's richly coloured course' with its unity (Lotze, 1912, pp. 105, 112, 140). This synthesis of Leibnizian and Spinozian features prefigures some aspects of Simmel relativism, 'in which the significance of each element affects everything else' and which is 'closer than one … thinks to … Spinoza's philosophy' (GSG 6, p. 120 f.; Simmel, 2004, p. 116 f.).

Lotze gives his metaphysics a functional formalisation: the being (M) becomes a function of all its elements (M = φ (A, B, R)). If one were to change, each of the others would in turn be modified (Lotze, 1912, p. 141). Metaphysics takes note of the contemporary turning point from substance towards functions. We will later evoke Herbart's 'relationship method', whose influence on Lotze and, through Lazarus, on Simmel, is capital. Another Herbartian legacy is crucial, by which reciprocal action reveals its psychological and sociological fecundity. 'By Herbart and his school dissolving the life of the soul into the mechanics of the individual representations, the reciprocal action of representations takes the place of the ego as a being and a movement, and a process of emergence of representations takes the place of the will as a faculty of the soul' (GSG 4, p. 141).

Against the idealist concept of 'pure self', Herbart argues that 'the self is nothing else and can only be the meeting point of changing representations' (Herbart, 1964, p. 132). Herbart discovered, according to Simmel, the 'functional character' of the psychic (GSG 21, p. 123). Decisive is Moritz Lazarus' – the 'most influent' among Simmel's teachers (Böhringer & Gründer, 1976, p. 249) – extension of Herbart's psychology towards *Völkerpsychologie*. Lazarus assigns to psychology the task of describing not only the 'reciprocal actions' that determine the 'circle of representations' of the 'individual mind', but also the reciprocal actions between the individual minds and the 'big circles of representations' (language, science, religion) that constitute the 'objective mind' (Lazarus, 2003, p. 15 f.). It prefigures Simmel's sociology but also, as we will see later, his relativist theory of objectivity and culture.

With the 1894 essay 'The Problem of Sociology' the reciprocal action scheme becomes a form. What is 'specifically social' is not exactly the reciprocal actions, but their forms (domination, subordination, concurrence, imitation, etc), which are likely to be separated from their contents and develop relatively independently (GSG 5, p. 54 f.). Simmel speaks in Kantian terms of *a priori* of society; de facto, these forms are a condition for the possibility of the social experience, in the double sense that they make society *and* sociology possible.[2] In addition, it becomes conceivable that types of forms other than social forms emerge from the reciprocal actions, forms which would correspond to other dimensions of cultural life.

Here should be mentioned a last heritage, that of Schleiermacher, who described 'sociability' as a 'fully determined and accomplished reciprocal action connecting all members [of society]' and as 'the true character of society in terms of its form' (Schleiermacher, 1984, p. 169).[3] The concept is not only descriptive, but also prescriptive: 'everything must become a reciprocal action' (ibid., p. 170). To be formative, it must, for instance, be possible to describe the transmission of an idea as a reciprocal action (cf. Thouard, 2007, p. 68). This neo-humanist *topos*, which will have a decisive place in Simmel's description of pedagogical relations (Amat, 2019), is generalised in the *Philosophy of money*: 'what appears at first a one-sided activity is actually based upon reciprocity: the orator appears as the leader and inspirer to the assembly, the teacher to his class, the journalist to his public'. This is the condition for such relationships to ensure that 'the sum of value is greater after than before' (GSG 6, p. 59; Simmel, 2004, p. 79). Reciprocal action not only describes a relationship, it measures the quality of that relationship.

Relativity as objectivity: relativism as a theory of value

It is up to the *Philosophy of Money*'s first chapter, 'Value and Money', to articulate the reciprocal action scheme and the problem of value.

The emergence of economic value: a paradigm

The method used in the first and second sections of the chapter is difficult to follow. We are constantly oscillating between 'historical-genetic' and 'objective-logical' perspectives (GSG 6, p. 74; Simmel, 2004, p. 88). Let us consider the economic exchange. It is obvious that historical, psychological and sociological conditions make it possible, but after having considered some of them, Simmel asks to consider the 'inner and so to speak systematic meaning of the concepts of value and exchange' (p. 74; p. 88). Exchange is a reciprocal action, not only between the participants but also, in a way, between the objects that are exchanged. 'This reciprocal balancing, through which each economic object expresses its value in another object, removes both objects from the sphere of merely subjective significance. The relativity of valuation signifies its objectification' (p. 56; p. 77).

The value of objects is more an expression of the reciprocal measurement of objects by each other than an expression of subjective evaluation. In situations where economic circuits are poorly developed, the weight of this objective moment remains limited, but the more they are developed, the more this weight grows. The value is thus 'objective', but not in the sense that it is a quality of the object, just as a line has no length by itself but 'gains the quality of length only by comparison with others' (p. 66; p. 83). Length is objective because it is relative: 'definite standards have grown out of the innumerable comparisons of length, and they form the basis for determining the length of all tangible objects' (p. 67; p. 84). Units of measurement (as money) are crystallisations of comparisons. Just as length, value is neither a subjective fact, nor an object's real determination, nor an abstract idea, but a form and expression of a relation: the 'lively interaction' is the 'body of economic value' (p. 91; p. 99).[4] The value's mode of being is not that of 'abstract generality', but that of an 'universal endowed with concrete life' (ibid.).

This 'life' is ambivalent. We speak here of reciprocal action between objects, through a process that tends to become autonomous from social and personal life: 'the objects circulate according to norms and measures that are fixed at any one moment, through which they confront the individual as an objective realm' or 'realm of values' (p. 55; p. 76). The relativist theory of value opens up a critique of social and life's forms, which questions the distance between life and its objectifications. Here is where the influence of Marx's critique of value and of 'commodity fetishism' makes an appearance. Henceforth, the problem that the relativism has to solve becomes a trilemma: it is a question of reconciling relativity with objectivity, but also with life, that is, as we will see, individuality. Before addressing this challenge, we still have to consider the extension of the relativist theory of value or objectivity.

Truth as a 'relational concept': the relative and the absolute

The 'objective realm' of economic values offers a formal model designed to extend to all spheres of objectivity – which does not mean economic reductionism. The third section of the chapter develops the case of the truth-value-indexed 'realm of theory' (GSG 6, p. 103; Simmel, 2004, p. 106). Truth is relative in two ways, which should not be confused. First, 'we are convinced that all representations of what exists are functions of a specific physical and psychological organization' (p. 100; p. 104). The truth of a representation then designates its 'reliability, expediency and accuracy'. To that extent, 'there are as many basically different truths as there are different organizations and conditions of life' (p. 102; p. 105). Simmel defends here a pragmatic and biologised Kantianism that leads to an anthropological relativism. The main point is the following: 'Once these modes of representation have been finally established as expedient through selection and cultivation, they form among themselves a realm of theory that determines, according to inner criteria, the inclusion or exclusion of every new representation' (p. 103; p. 106). The 'whole system of geometry' depends on our 'physio-psychological organisation', but 'the rules of geometry are built upon each other according to a strict inner autonomy'. Through the progressive objectification of our representations of space, one discovers some 'inner criteria' that are 'completely independent of [their] physical realization' and impose themselves on the mind (p. 102 f.; p. 105).

It is now in a very different sense that 'truth is ... a relative concept' (*Verhältnisbegriff*) (p. 100; p. 104): not relative to an evaluation centre, but as 'a relation of representations to each other' (p. 103; p. 106).[5] The 'theoretical consciousness' that is formed as a correlate to the 'realm of theory' discovers the possibility of infinitely extending the relationship by deduction or by going back to the presuppositions. But the whole system is not based on an *a priori* or evident truth:

No matter what proposition we have discovered as the ultimate one, standing above the relativity of all other propositions, it remains possible that we shall recognize this one too as being merely relative and conditioned by a superior one. ... [C]onsequently, in order to avoid dogmatic thought, we have to treat each position at which we arrive as if it were the penultimate one.

(p. 96; p. 101 f.)

Theoretical consciousness cannot lay definitive logical foundations. Its objects are indefinitely determinable, through the actualisation of the virtual relationships that surround them as a halo. It is not to be deplored, but the very form of our knowledge. 'Cognition is thus a free-floating process, whose elements determine their position reciprocally, in the same way as masses of matter do by means of weight' (p. 100; p. 104).

Just as there is no sense in talking about a weight of the entire universe, so there is no sense in talking about an absolute, fundamental, or isolated truth. 'It is then perfectly acceptable that our image of the world "floats in the air," since the world itself does so' (p. 100; p. 104). In the *Lebensanschauung*, Simmel will speak of a 'cosmos of science', alongside other 'cultural cosmos' of economics, of art, of religion, etc (cf. Amat, 2015).

With this relativist (relationist) concept of truth, the series of conditions is open at both ends but 'curves in a circle'.[6] 'Reciprocity of proofs is the basic form of knowledge, conceived in its perfect state' (p. 100; p. 104). At the end of the 'Doctrine of Essence', Hegel describes the transition from causality to reciprocal action, in similar terms, as a 'withdrawal of infinite progress into a relationship closed in itself' (Hegel, 1979, p. 300). But in Simmel, the circle can be closed and totalised no more than the series has a first or last term. The circle of reciprocal action has more of Lotzean functionalism and the Herbartian 'relationship method', according to which 'no predicate x is inherent in y, but y is a function of x' (Herbart, 1964 (§ 180), p. 41). This is also true of 'foundations': we should 'think the foundation as a multiple that determines itself reciprocally' instead of thinking it 'as *a* thought' (Herbart, 1964 (§ 187), p. 57). In that spirit, Simmel states that: 'There is originally in the world of practice no single value, any more than there is originally in the world of consciousness a number "one". ... [T]he "two" is prior to the "one"' (GSG 6, p. 76; Simmel, 2004, p. 89).[7]

This generalised relativity certainly means the end of a certain figure of the absolute, but also surmounts the opposition of the relative and the absolute. Relativism does not replace absolute values with relative values.

The relativistic view has often been considered as a degradation of the value, reliability and significance of things, regardless of the fact that only the naive adherence to something absolute, which is here questioned, could put relativism in such a position. ... [I]t is the contrary that is true; only through the continuous dissolution of any rigid separateness into interaction do we approach the functional unity of all elements of the universe, in which the significance of each element affects everything else.

(GSG 6, p. 120; Simmel, 2004, p. 116)

Each value determination, each figure of objectivity, virtually envelops the infinity of reciprocal actions, in its 'immanent limitlessness'. Relativism is 'the scheme of genuine infinity in activity' (p. 121; p. 117).

Relativism as the description and ideal of individuality

Money and the immanent critique of modern culture

Since relativism does not build on a foundation, it has to start 'in the middle', with a given reality, from which it will try to pull the wires of the interlacing relationships. In principle, every starting point is possible, because of the 'functional unity of all elements in the universe'. It would thus be possible to 'fin[d] in each of life's details the totality of its meaning' (GSG 6, p. 12). However, some details have a specific heuristic fertility, as shown for example by the essays on the metropolis (GSG 7, pp. 116–131), the handle (GSG 7, pp. 345–350) or on Rodin's sculpture, which expresses 'the essence of modernity' (GSG 14, p. 346). But the best way to penetrate the forms of life and their objectifications in a modern culture appeared to Simmel to be money.

Money is the only cultural formation that is a *pure force*, that has completely rejected all substantial carriers out of it, that is absolutely symbolic. From this point of view, it is the most characteristic phenomenon of our time, where *dynamics* has taken the direction of all theory and practice. This is not in contradiction with the fact that it is a *pure relationship* (and precisely in this characteristic of our time), not including any specific content. Because strength is really nothing more than a relationship[8] (GSG 20, p. 295).

Money is the 'sublimation (*Sublimat*) of relativity' (GSG 6, p. 124; Simmel, 2004, p. 119).[9] As part of the system, it *has*, like each of the economic goods, a relativity. As an element outside the system, it *is* this relativity.[10] Money symbolises value conceived as function and not as substance. It exemplifies paradigmatically the fact that value is an expression and a quality of relationships.[11]

But money is not only a symbol of a 'pure relationship' in general. It finds its symbolic power also in the 'detail' of its concrete figures. Through analogical (and not causal) operations that cannot be questioned here (cf. Frisby, 1984), money's movements and figures symbolise the style of modern life in its ambivalences: fluidisation of all contents, objectification and levelling processes, acceleration of life's tempo, depersonalisation, cynicism … Relativism seeks the way between the Charybdis of rigidification of life and the Scylla of a dissolving mobility, between dogmatism and radical scepticism. Along the thread of money, he proceeds to a description of the modern lifestyle which is also its immanent critique, revealing the points where life's mobility is impeded or, on the contrary, leads to unproductive trepidation or uneasiness. This critique diagnoses a lack of relationship between the subjective and objective poles, between life and its objectification. Relativism must therefore revitalise this relationship, in order to avoid the modern oscillation between sterile subjectivisms and alienating objectifications. To that end, it tries to propose a new conception of individuality.

How can values be both objective and individual?

The experience of value, not as feeling but as recognition of validity, implies the preliminary establishment of distance between the subject and the object. Positioning itself, so to speak, in a lateral way, relativism can now consider this distance for itself. It recognises it as something 'objective' and as part of the value determination, since it 'is established by real obstacles and necessary struggles, by gain and loss' (GSG 6, p. 51; Simmel, 2004, p. 74). Yet we have argued that value is the expression of a relationship between objects. In fact, value depends on reciprocal determinations deployed on a plane and an axis: the plane on which the object finds its place in the object system, and the axis determining the relative position of the subject with respect to the system. The price of a good on a market does not yet include the price to pay for access to that market. The expenses to be incurred are individually determined, but are not 'subjective'. They should not be confused with the sentimental 'subjective surplus' by which one object is desired more than another (p. 79; p. 91). It is by abstraction that the value is reduced to a strictly relational-structural validity. A completed relativism has to integrate the subject's position, which excludes any 'confusion between individuality and subjectivity of value' (p. 50; p. 73).

In the second section of Chapter 4, Simmel describes an 'utopian' pricing situation, the realisation of which would satisfy the 'ideal of fairness' (pp. 425–427; pp. 318–319). It would be a matter of forming prices by considering 'the personal assets of the consumers' (p. 425; p. 318). The price of taxes, a fine, a medical consultation or any commodity would vary according to individual resources. It could be a performance of money: as a universal equivalent – and thanks to its lack of quality – it can 'objectify the most individual factors' and 'adequately express at every sale all the individual circumstances'. Yet, 'individuals' circumstances, too, are objective facts' (p. 427; p. 319). Economically, it would be a 'completion of … trade', but it expresses, more fundamentally, 'a philosophical view of the world':

> We first become conscious of objectivity through its absolute contrast with the subject. … Only the higher level of intellectual development encompasses once more the comprehensive concept of objectivity which includes the subject within it. It no longer requires the immediacy of the contrast to be fixed and clear, but rather it raises the subject to a component part of an objective view of the world.
>
> *(GSG 6, p. 428; Simmel, 2004, p. 320)*

This 'comprehensive objectivity' is no longer that of the Kantian theory of knowledge, but the construct of a relational ontology that recognises individual configurations of being. Objectivity does not face the subject, but integrates him so that his concrete individuality is restored. Simmel summarised his intention in his diary, writing that '[his] problem' is 'Objectification of the subject or rather: Desubjectification of what is individual' (GSG 20, p. 262). By means of an analogical use of economic categories, we have given a concrete figure to this operation. The question is how this 'desubjectification' of the individual is possible in other areas of culture and for modern life in general.

The individualisation of truth and the law of the individual

Simmel regularly associates this project of reintegrating subjectivity into a higher objectivity with Goethe's name, prolonging the anti-idealistic readings of his work. According to the 1912 *Goethebuch*, Goethe's ideal consists in 'allowing oneself to be, so to speak, crossed by the existing, in order to be part of its objectivity' (GSG 15, p. 184). This 'existing' can be conceived as 'real or ideal', that is, as nature but also as culture (p. 183). Goethe points to 'the idea and growth of our self as a unitary value complex', constituted from the elements of the 'scientific, artistic or social value systems' (p. 21).

The chapter entitled 'Truth' clearly indicates the relational and individual – that is: not alienating – character of this objectification, by defending an individualisation of truth. The truth of a 'representation' depends on 'the meaning that *the existence of the representation in our consciousness* has for our lives' (p. 34). 'Representation' and 'consciousness' should not be understood in an idealistic sense, but in the realistic sense inherited from Herbart and Lazarus. Representation has worth as an 'element of life itself'. Its 'truth value' also concerns 'the living function which is exercised within the developing complex of the soul' (p. 35). In other words, it expresses the quality of the reciprocal actions between the elements that constitute the 'complex of the soul'. Since 'soul' or 'life' are always already embedded in the 'whole being', this is not a subjective or solipsist conception of truth.

> Truth is, so to speak, the relation between a man's life and the world totality in which it takes place. It is not truth according to its logical content ... but because the thought, no less than our physiological structure or our feelings, is a man's *being*, which has its own correctness or non-correctness, as an actual quality, cause or consequence of the global rapport of this man to the world.
>
> *(GSG 15, p. 38)*[12]

Just as money could ideally measure the value of a good by considering its 'objective' and 'subjective' determinations at the same time, so a relativist notion of truth should express not only the reciprocal determinations of objective contents in the 'realm of theory', but also the subject's position, that is his particular and determined perspective on these contents. According to this second-order point of view, truth is indeed a question of meaning rather than of logical validity. This individualisation of truth is also an 'ontologisation', since truth is the 'quality' of a man's 'being' or 'life' or, more precisely, of a relational structure whose poles are called 'life' and 'world'.

The concept of individual law could be interpreted in this direction.[13] Facing the 'strangeness or sterilizing distance from life' of moral principles (GSG 16, p. 353; Simmel, 2010, p. 104), the *Lebensanschauung*'s last chapter, 'The Law of the Individual', presents a clear relativist programme: 'redissolution of these rigid, quasi substantialising objectifications', to recover 'the flowing relations, the functional, holistic linkages of the life-unity to which [these objectifications] belong' (p. 413; p. 146). To that end, 'the false fusion between individuality and subjectivity must be dissolved, just like that between universality and lawfulness' (p. 410; p. 143 f.).

'[T]he ultimate authority' above all action would be this question: 'is it then *my* duty, does it belong to the objective-ideal configuration of *my* life?' (p. 407; p. 141). This is often interpreted in a pre-existential way, like a decision and resolution that engages me, or in a neo-romantic way, as if this law were the ideal of a pure inner development, which would somehow be prefigured in an intimate core of our personality. In both cases, the question of the 'objective-ideal configuration' of life seems to us to be neglected and the relativist principle that the 'two' is prior to the 'one' is forgotten. 'Individuality that lives in the form of the Ought is not something ahistorical, non-material' (p. 409; p. 143).

> This Ought – when it is recognized as a form of each individual life coordinated with its actuality-form – accepts all possible linkages external to itself ...; for all ties, demands, impulses – whether social or fateful, rational or religious, or stemming from the thousand conditions of the environment – surely influence this life itself; duty is determined according to the filling and forming that life experiences from these.
>
> *(p. 404 f.; p. 140)*

Anything that determines life in its concreteness, every dimension of experience, determines its individual duty. Being 'the citizen of a specific State' plays a part in determining the individual law, for example, by imposing a military service (p. 410; p. 144). At issue is not a general ethical principle, which demands that a citizen must serve the State, but a concrete ethical determination of life. It may be that some concrete circumstances provide good reasons for the anti-militarist, so that his life would acquire more meaning and value by deserting. Individual law is the well-understood categorical imperative, that is, individualised: the lack of a priori determination of what duty is made of is the condition for the possibility of taking into account the concreteness of the situation, of the singular relationship of the individual to the objective arrangement and to himself (pp. 404–407; pp. 140-142). To that extent, individual law is the ideal norm of a relation, the ideal of maximising life's meaning by increasing the reciprocal actions between all the spiritual and cultural contents that constitute it, at each moment, but also temporally, since life, as consciousness and memory, implies a reciprocal action with its own past (GSG 14, p. 353).

What is it like to be relativist? Relativism as philosophical life

Relativism appears now as a relational ontology of cultural life, that provides both objective-descriptive and evaluative criteria, taking particular consideration of individual forms of life.[14] But relativism would also like to promote individuation through its own practice, by means of the effects it has on the subject that 'relativises'.

A functional metaphysics

We have shown that the relativist concept of truth integrates the subject's position. Let us now consider this position 'from the inside', starting by the process of knowledge.

> [R]elativism with reference to the principles of knowledge may be formulated in the following way: the constitutive principles that claim to express, once and for all, the essence of objects, are transposed into regulative principles which are only points of view in the progress of knowledge. ... [O]ur understanding must proceed *as if* things behave in such and such a way.
>
> *(GSG 6, p. 106; Simmel, 2004, p. 108)*[15]

Principles of knowledge – be they metaphysical positions (e.g. monism and pluralism), intellectual operations (e.g. analysis and synthesis) or scientific methods (e.g. deductive or inductive) (pp. 107–112; pp. 109–114) – have only a heuristic value, guiding research toward an indefinite synthesis movement. The determination and synthesis of the given works in the 'as if' mode. The expression is borrowed from Kant's 'Transcendental Dialectic' (1900–, Ak, III, p. 445). The 'as if' is neither a degree of probability nor a useful fiction, as Hans Vaihinger claims, which Simmel contests in his *Kant* (GSG 9, pp. 25–26). The 'as if' has a kind of objective validity, since it is 'a scheme of the [supreme] regulatory principle of the systematic unity of all knowledge' (ibid.). With the 'as if', Kant 'turned the curse of metaphysics into a blessing' (GSG 9, p. 26), he 'save[d] the value of the absolute and the transcendent by placing it entirely in its function: to give meaning, to put in order, and to guide in the relative and the empirical' (p. 196 f.). Through the generalisation of the 'as if' principle, relativism is a kind of functional metaphysics, in which, to speak in Kantian terms, there are only differences in degree between the categories of understanding and the ideas of reason. This brings us to a second principle:

> If the constitutive assertions ... are changed into heuristic assertions ... this makes possible the simultaneous validity of opposing principles. The true unity of apprehension is secured only by such a dissolution of dogmatic rigidity into the living and moving process. Its ultimate principles become realised not in the form of mutual exclusion, but in the form of mutual dependence, mutual evocation and mutual complementation.
>
> *(GSG 6, p. 107; Simmel, 2004, p. 108)*

Lukács (1958, p. 174) made Simmel 'the most significant representative of methodological pluralism' of his generation. He is indeed, but the essential point is not the equal legitimacy of the principles but their 'mutual dependence', their 'organic relationship in the form of alternation' (GSG 6, p. 112; Simmel, 2004, p. 111). Simmel takes the example of 'historical' (i.e. individualising) and 'generalising method': 'Any economic phenomenon can only be clearly deduced from a particular psycho-historical constellation. But such a deduction always implies certain connections in the form of laws' (p. 111 f.; p. 110 f.). Both perspectives are therefore required. Assertions that are contradictory in terms of contents may have an internal relation that is expressible not in terms of objective validity, but on the second-order level of meaning (cf. Millson, 2009, pp. 198, 202): 'relativity, i.e. the reciprocal character of the meaning of norms of knowledge' (GSG 6, p. 111; Simmel, 2004, p. 111).[16] A principle has meaning only through its opposition and co-determination with another principle.

Kant saw in the conflict of reason with itself its 'most remarkable phenomenon' and what rouses it from its 'dogmatic sleep' (1900–, Ak, III, p. 338). Conflict 'cultivates reason by making it consider its object from two points of view' (ibid., p. 487). However, it would be in the interest of reason to finally supress it. Simmel, on the contrary, values unconditionally this antithetical form of thought and 'state of perpetual balance' (ibid., p. 329). Against the 'philistine prejudice' according to which 'all conflicts and problems are there to be solved', he regularly states that conflict is a 'school through which the self is formed' (GSG 16, p. 206). The position is neither dogmatic (the conflict is not settled), nor sceptical (there is no suspension of judgement), nor critical (the conflict is not reduced to an appearance), but relativist (the conflict is a form of unity, since the two parties depend on each other). J. Cohn saw in Simmel 'the master of the dialectic attitude' (Cohn, 1923, p. 51); its dialectic is, however, 'without reconciliation' (Landmann, 1968, p. 16).

Traugott Oesterreich (1923, p. 417) described Simmel's philosophy as a 'relativist reformulation of criticism'. Oesterreich thinks about the relational theory of objectivity that relativises Kant's theory of *a priori*. We take this formula on our own account, but only if we extend it to Kant's understanding of metaphysics, as regulative ideas that are necessary to build a 'cosmic concept' of philosophy, an 'architectonic system' understood as 'culture of human reason' (1900–, Ak, III, p. 542 f.). In a context of specialisation, where philosophy tends to be reduced to a theory of knowledge, Simmel underlines the need for a philosophy in its cosmic concept, which recovers its practical vocation (cf. e. g. GSG 17, p. 328 f.; GSG 22, pp. 289, 941). Relativism aspires to be such a philosophy, but emancipated from teleology, systematic ideals and every foundational programme.

Relativism as expression and cultivation of life

Relativism has another specific epistemic virtue. Among the 'great epistemological principles', it is the only one that can be applied to itself without contradiction (GSG 6, p. 116; Simmel,

2004, p. 114). Dogmatism is based on certainty but cannot serve as a base for certainty itself; scepticism, by defending the thesis that it is impossible to reach the truth, contradicts itself; criticism wants to identify the conditions of objectivity from experience, but 'it is impossible for it to prove that the experience itself is valid' (p. 117; p. 115). Relativism, in contrast, 'is not destroyed by the fact that its validity is only relative'. Not only does it practice and justify the indefinite movement from one principle to another, but it admits the relative validity of other methods or principles of knowledge, in particular of 'absolutist or substantialist principles' (ibid.). Simmel underlines the fertility of the 'unilateral determined worldview' of the great dogmatic philosophers, 'genius creators', which offer new contents to philosophy (GSG 14, p. 165; Simmel, 1997, p. 30). Reflecting back on itself, the mind, as a relativist, should understand that these dogmatic principles have worth as heuristic principles.

Finally, relativism is the only principle of knowledge that truly integrates 'the basic fact of self-awareness', conceived not as self-position but as the experience of the infinite relativity of any position (GSG 6, p. 118 f.; Simmel, 2004, p. 115 f.). Relativism 'makes it possible to express adequately the manner and method of our understanding in its real relation to the world' (p. 106; p. 108) and then expresses a fundamental structure of life. The *Philosophy of Money*'s 2nd edition of 1907 proposes some examples of reciprocal dependence relating directly to the conduct of life: sometimes we aim and value rest, sometimes maximum excitement; sometimes individualisation, sometimes social participation, etc. Between these parties, 'our most intimate feeling oscillates' (p. 108; p. 109).

> It seems ... the very challenge of life, to experience joy and sorrow, strength and weakness, virtue and sin as a living unity, each one being a condition of the other, each sacred and consecrating the other. We may seldom be aware of the general principle in these opposing tendencies, but they determine our attitude towards life.
>
> *(ibid.)*

Not only epistemological oppositions are relative, but also value oppositions. Simmel's position here differs from that of Max Weber, who sees value positions as irreducible decisions (Weber, 1992, pp. 104–105). Simmel's relativism is not a decisionism.

It is in the 'Introduction' to *Philosophical Culture* that the formative virtue of relativism appears most clearly. The term 'relativism' is not used, probably for reception reasons that we have already mentioned. But the *Mélanges de philosophie relativiste* that were published in France the following year contains the same introductory text and are subtitled '*Contributions à la culture philosophique*'. 'Philosophical culture' thus designates the practical dimension of the relativist programme. Simmel diagnoses and defends a 'turning point from metaphysics as dogma to metaphysics as life or function' (GSG 14, p. 165; Simmel, 1997, p. 30). The relativist alternation of metaphysic principles is directly defended in terms of life:

> There is a contradiction [between the principles] only in their dogmatic crystallisation and not in the mobility of philosophical life itself, the individual path of which can be characterised as personal and unified, no matter what its turns and bends.
>
> *(GSG 14, p. 164; Simmel, 1997, p. 35)*[17]

Philosophical culture is a form of *Bildung* that unifies, as a process and not by its content, the plurality and the conflict of perspectives. It gives a determination to the famous definition that we find in 'The Concept and Tragedy of Culture' (an essay that constitutes a chapter of the *Philosophical culture*): 'culture is the path from closed unity through developed diversity to developed unity' (GSG 14, p. 387). This diversity is also the one of the objects: philosophical culture is an 'intellectual mobility ... in which ... connected to the broadest variety of actualities, all possible currents of philosophy run' (GSG 14, p. 165; Simmel, 1997, p. 35).[18] This mobility is exercised on concrete objects, on what the *Philosophy of Money* called 'life's detail'. It is indeed a practice of relativism, as post-foundational philosophy, that starts from what is concretely given in objective culture.

It is worth quoting the last lines of *Schopenhauer und Nietzsche*, which present the relativist *Bildung* as an extension and deepening of the soul. Simmel asks if a synthesis between Schopenhauer and Nietzsche's evaluation of life is possible.

Their unity is possible only in a dimension that is distinct from the one of their objective content: in the subject who considers them both. Feeling the oscillation of the spiritual existence in the spacing between the terms of the opposition, the soul extends itself – despite or rather thanks to the fact that it does not feel obliged to any of the parties – to the point where it embraces and enjoys the desperation and the jubilation of life as poles that measure its proper extension, its proper force and the fullness of its form (GSG 10, p. 408).

Here we find the determination of value as inner distance, which is now summoned to measure the extension of the soul. In 'The Conflict of Modern Culture', published in 1918, Simmel noted that, for the first time in European history, we lack 'a global ideal of culture' (GSG 16, p. 200; Simmel, 1997, p. 80), that is, a living form which could organise the objectified contents of culture in order to form and orient ourselves. As philosophical culture, or metaphysics as life, relativism attempted to fill this void, yet without proposing a new totalising conception of the world, but instead suggesting a way to play with all the possible worldviews, get a sense for their internal relations and, in doing so, extend the experience and meaning of life.

Conclusive remarks

In 1899, Eisler's *Dictionary of Philosophical Terms* only considers, in the article 'Relativismus', the 'doctrine of the relativity of all knowledge, i.e. the dependence of its validity on consciousness'. It refers to sophists and sceptics. However, there is an openness towards theories of knowledge that could be said to be relational but not sceptical: Herbart is mentioned, who teaches that 'we actually live in relationships and need nothing else' (Eisler, 1899, p. 645 f.). In the 1904 edition, the article is expanded, and relativism is specified. It can be 'subjective' (sceptical or sophistic), but also 'objectivist' (as in Goethe's description of 'real' relationships between substances and faculties), 'critical' (as in transcendental philosophy) and 'metaphysical' (like in Hegel, 'within the system of the absolute'). Nietzsche and Simmel are mentioned as representatives of relativism, unfortunately without further clarification (Eisler, 1904, p. 253).

In fact, Simmel's relativism, which is 'subjective' only in some aspects of the early work and in the consideration of some provisional pragmatic determinations of objectivity,[19] stands at the intersection of the other dimensions noted by Eisler. It is *objectivist* or to a certain point *realist* – as a relational ontology that pretends to describe the concrete configurations of life – *critical* – as he questions the value and validity of experience, as a 'relativist reformulation of criticism' but also as an immanent critique of cultural configurations – and *metaphysical* – as a regulative principle and unsystematic 'cosmic concept' of philosophy. But we must not forget that this theoretical enterprise is ultimately defended as a way of practicing philosophy and a figure of philosophical life and culture, in the context of a modern culture that oscillates between processes of massive objectification and of dissolving functionalisation.

Notes

1 It may be preferable to speak of *relationism* or *relationalism* (Amat, 2018, p. 27; Cohn, 1925, p. 125 f.; Pyyhtinen, 2018, pp. 22–27; Vandenberghe, 2002). However, to avoid formal complications regarding the quotations, we will use Simmel's term here.
2 The literature on the sociological dimension of Simmel's relativism is abundant. See e. g. Cantó Milà (2005); Pyyhtinen (2018, pp. 30–47); on Simmel's interpretation of *a priori*, see Adolf (2002).
3 Quoted by Christian (1978, p. 118). It is likely that Dilthey, who described society as 'interplay of reciprocal action' (Dilthey, 1959, p. 37), served as an intermediary.
4 Translation slightly amended.
5 On these 'pragmatic' and 'coherentist' descriptions of truth, see Steizinger (2015).
6 Translation slightly amended.
7 Translation slightly amended.
8 Here again we see what Simmel owes to Nietzsche and his relational concept of force.
9 Translation slightly amended.
10 On this 'Doppelrolle' see Flotow (1995, pp. 93–98).
11 To go further, see Schlitte (2012).
12 Simmel's emphasis.
13 There is no question of exhausting this much discussed and multi-faceted concept here. See Lotter (2000); Lee and Silver (2012); Amat (2017) and Fitzi (2019, pp. 153-156).
14 An impersonal or collective reality can be considered as an individuality; see the reflections on history (e.g. GSG 9, p. 386).
15 Simmel's emphasis.
16 Translation slightly amended.
17 Translation amended.
18 Translation slightly amended.
19 For a more pragmatic reading of Simmel's relativism, which nevertheless tries to accommodate its different dimensions, see Steizinger (2020).

References

Adolf, H. (2002). *Erkenntnistheorie auf dem Weg zur Metaphysik. Interpretation, Modifikation und Überschreitung des kantischen Apriorikonzepts bei Georg Simmel*. Munich: Utz.

Amat, M. (2015). Kulturphilosophie als Kosmologie. Das Beispiel Georg Simmels. *Zeitschrift für Kulturphilosophie*, 1–2, 257–270.

Amat, M. (2017). Simmel's law of the individual: A relational idea of culture. *Simmel Studies. New Series*, 21(2), 41–72.

Amat, M. (2018). *Le relationnisme philosophique de Georg Simmel. Une idée de la culture*. Paris: Honoré Champion.

Amat, M. (2019). Pedagogical implications of Simmel's relativism. The Strasbourg lectures on pedagogy. In M. Amat & F. D'Andrea, (Eds.), *Simmel as educator. Special issue of the Simmel Studies. New Series*, 23(1), 147–182.

Böhringer, H., & Gründer, K. (Eds.) (1976). *Ästhetik und Soziologie um die Jahrhundertwende: Georg Simmel*. Frankfurt (Main): Klostermann.

Cantó Milà, N. (2005). *A Sociological theory of value, Georg Simmel's sociological relationism*. Bielefeld: Transcript.

Christian, P. (1978). *Einheit und Zwiespalt: zum hegelianisierenden Denken in der Philosophie und Soziologie Georg Simmels*. Berlin: Duncker & Humblot.

Cohn, J. (1923). *Theorie der Dialektik. Formenlehre der Philosophie*. Leipzig: Meiner.

Cohn, J. (1925). *Geschichte der Philosophie, vol. VII: Die Philosophie im Zeitalter des Spezialismus*. Berlin and Leipzig: Teubner.

Dilthey, W. (1959). *Gesammelte Schriften, vol. I: Einleitung in die Geisteswissenschaften. Versuch einer Grundlegung für das Studium der Gesellschaft und der Geschichte [1883], vol. 1*, B. Groethuysen (Ed.). Stuttgart and Göttingen: Teubner.

Eisler, R. (1899). *Wörterbuch der Philosophischen Begriffe und Ausdrücke*. Berlin: Mittler & Sohn.

Eisler, R. (1904). *Wörterbuch der Philosophischen Begriffe und Ausdrücke*, 2 vol. Berlin: Mittler et Sohn, vol. 2: O-Z.

Fitzi, G. (2019). *The challenge of modernity. Simmel's sociological theory*. New York and London: Routledge.

Flotow, P. v. (1995). *Geld, Wirtschaft und Gesellschaft. Georg Simmels Philosophie des Geldes*. Frankfurt (Main): Suhrkamp.

Frisby, D. (1984). Georg Simmels Theorie der Moderne. In O. Rammstedt & H.-J. Dahme (Eds.), *Georg Simmel und die Moderne* (pp. 9–79). Frankfurt (Main): Surhkamp.

Hegel, G. W. F. (1979). *Werke, vol. 8: Enzyklopädie der philosophischen Wissenschaften im Grundrisse 1830, 1, Die Wissenschaft der Logik. Mit den mündlichen Zusätzen*. Frankfurt (Main): Surhkamp.

Herbart, J. F. (1964). *Allgemeine Metaphysik nebst den Anfängen der philosophischen Naturlehre. Zweiter, Systematischer Teil* (1829). In Id., *Sämtliche Werke* (pp. 1–388), K. Kehrbach (Ed.), Langensalza, 1887–1912, reprinted in 1964, vol. 8. Aalen: Scientia Verlag.

Husserl, E. (1993). *Logische Untersuchungen, vol. 2: Untersuchungen zur Phänomenologie und Theorie der Erkenntnis, I [1900]*. Tübingen: Max Niemeyer.

Kant, E. (1900–). *Gesammelte Schriften, 'Akademieausgabe', (Ak.)*. Königlich Preußische Akademie der Wissenschaften/Deutsche Akademie der Wissenschaften zu Berlin/Akademie der Wissenschaften zu Göttingen, 29 vol. Berlin: Reimer/de Gruyter.

Köhnke, K.-C. (1996). *Der junge Simmel in Theoriebeziehungen und sozialen Bewegungen*. Frankfurt (Main): Suhrkamp.

Landmann, M. (1968). Einleitung des Herausgebers. In G. Simmel (Eds.), *Das individuelle Gesetz. Philosophische Exkurse* (pp. 7–29). Frankfurt (Main): Suhrkamp.

Lazarus, M. (2003). Ueber den Begriff und die Möglichkeit einer Völkerpsychologie. In M. Lazarus (Ed.), *Grundzüge der Völkerpsychologie und Kulturwissenchaft* (pp. 3–26). K. C. Köhnke (Ed.). Hamburg: Meiner.

Lee, M., & Silver, D. (2012). Simmel's law of the individual and the ethics of relational self. *Theory, Culture & Society, 29*(7/8), 124–145.

Lichtblau, K. (1984). Das 'Pathos der Distanz'. Präliminarien zur Nietzsche-Rezeption bei Georg Simmel. In O. Rammstedt & H.-J. Dahme (Eds), *Georg Simmel und die Moderne* (pp. 231–281). Frankfurt (Main): Surhkamp.

Lotter, M.-S. (2000). Das individuelle Gesetz. Zu Simmels Kritik an der Lebensfremdheit der kantischen Moralphilosophie. *Kant-Studien, 91*(2), 178–203.

Lotze, R. H. (1884–1888). *Mikrokosmus. Ideen zur Naturgeschichte und Geschichte der Menschheit. Versuch einer Anthropologie*, 3 vol. Leipzig: Hirzel.

Lotze, R. H. (1912). *Metaphysik. Drei Bücher der Ontologie, Kosmologie und Psychologie*. Leipzig: Meiner.

Lotze, R. H. (1989). *Logik. Drittes Buch. Vom Erkennen (Methodologie)*, G. Gabriel (Ed.). Hamburg: Meiner.

Lukács, G. (1958). Georg Simmel [1918]. In K. Gassen & M. Landmann (Eds.), *Buch des Dankes an Georg Simmel* (pp. 171–176). Berlin: Duncker & Humblot.

Millson, J. A. (2009). The reflexive relativism of Georg Simmel. *The Journal of Speculative Philosophy, New Series, 23*(3), 180–207.

Nietzsche, F. (1967) *Digital critical edition of the complete works and letters* (www.nietzschesource.org/#eKGWB). Based on the critical text by G. Colli and M. Montinari, and edited by P. D'Iorio. Berlin/New York: de Gruyter.

Oesterreich, T. K. (1923). *Friedrich Ueberwegs Grundriss der Geschichte der Philosophie, 4. Teil. Die deutsche Philosophie des 19. Jahrhunderts und der Gegenwart*. Berlin: Mittler & Sohn.

Pyyhtinen, O. (2018). *The Simmelian legacy*. Basingstoke: Palgrave MacMillan.

Rickert, H. (1892). *Der Gegenstand der Erkenntnis. Beitrag zum Problem der philosophischen Transzendenz*. Fribourg: Wagner.

Schleiermacher, F. (1984). Versuch einer Theorie des geselligen Betragens. In Id., *Kritische Gesamtausgabe, I/2* (pp. 163–184), G. Meckenstock (Ed.). Berlin and New York: de Gruyter.

Schlitte, A. (2012). *Die Macht des Geldes und die Symbolik der Kultur. Georg Simmels Philosophie des Geldes*. Munich: Fink.

Schnädelbach, H. (1983). *Philosophie in Deutschland 1831–1933*, Frankfurt Main: Suhrkamp.

Simmel, G. (1997). *On culture.* D. Frisby & M. Featherstone (Eds.). London, Thousand Oaks, CA and New Delhi: SAGE.

Simmel, G. (2004). *Philosophy of money.* Trans. T. Bottomore & D. Frisby. London and New York: Routledge.

Simmel, G. (2010). *The View of Life. Four Metaphysical Essays with Journal Aphorisms.* Trans. J. A. Y. Andrews, with an introduction by D. N. Levine & D. Silver. Chicago, IL and London: University of Chicago Press.

Steizinger, J. (2015). In defence of epistemic relativism: The concept of truth in Georg Simmel's Philosophy of money. *Proceedings of the 38th international Ludwig Wittgenstein-Symposium in Kirchberg. Contributions of the Austrian Wittgenstein Society,* XXIII, 300–302.

Steizinger, J. (2020). Georg Simmels Bekenntnis zum Relativismus. Historische und systematische Überlegungen. In G. Hartung (Ed.), *Der Philosoph Georg Simmel* (forthcoming). Freiburg: Karl Alber.

Thouard, D. (2007). *Schleiermacher. Communauté, individualité, communication.* Paris: Vrin.

Vandenberghe, F. (2002). Relativisme, relationnisme, structuralisme. *Simmel Studies, 12*(1), 41–84.

Weber, M. (1992). Wissenschaft als Beruf. In Id., *Gesamtausgabe,* I: *Schriften und Reden,* vol. 17: H. Baier, M. R. Lepsius, W. J. Mommsen, W. Schluchter & J. Winckelmann (Eds.), *Wissenschaft als Beruf (1917/1919). Politik als Beruf (1919)* (pp. 49–111). Tübingen: Mohr Siebeck.

Windelband, W. (1915). Kritische oder genetische Methode. In Id. *Präludien. Aufsätzen und Reden zur Philosophie und ihrer Geschichte,* vol. 2, (pp. 99–135). Tübingen: Mohr.

7

THE ART OF COMPLICATING THINGS

Denis Thouard

The topicality of Simmel's work – notwithstanding all the criticisms that can be made about its unfinished nature, the unnecessarily intertwined mode of writing, at times the vagueness and the refusal of scientific terminology – lies in its sense for reciprocity, as well as in its complexities and balances. Simmel never abandoned philosophy while claiming the autonomy of sociology. He considered both the sui generis dimension of the social fact and its individual reality, allowing us to overcome quarrels that, in France, have long blocked sociological reflection. He thinks of innovation and the creation of forms while knowing how to consider the deposit of tradition, which he theorises from a renewed understanding of the 'objective spirit'. In the hermeneutic field, it thus allows to overcome the opposition between a critical approach concerned with the author's intention, and an ontological approach, favouring the self-deployment of tradition (Gadamer, 2004). By combining the approaches of historical and 'objective' understanding, it helps to break the impasses of hermeneutic philosophy. Simmel retained the meaning of ambivalence from Hegelian thought, but he was able to avoid enclosing it in a complete logic. Does his open dialectic bring him closer to scepticism or relativism? Let us say that he was first and foremost attentive to the ambivalences of the phenomena, that he endeavoured, both for historical knowledge and for sociology, to achieve an approach as objective as the field of research each time allowed.

The bias of the third party

Simmel is not satisfied with simple oppositions. He is not a classical spirit, in love with symmetries. However, as he indicates about the human face, such symmetries minimise individuality (GSG 7, p. 40). Moreover, the focus is on characterising the individual. His mode of questioning involves a sceptical aspect that calls into question established concepts and inherited categories. The plurality of perspectives on an object becomes self-evident. He keeps his distance from dogmatism.

This attitude develops into a logic of its own invention. If logic is partly linked with cosmology, the world presupposed by Simmelian logic is a world of contingency, in which something new can arise. The category of the 'third' is of decisive importance for this reason: it assumes that being cannot be reduced to the possible.

The world is mobile and unpredictable. The category of becoming is necessary to think about processuality. It is important to reintroduce continuity and nuance into thought. The hold of history in the 19th century, but also the setting in motion of all sciences in the face of the evidence of slow evolutions attested by the life sciences, the *longue durée* that encourages a more unitary outlook and all these elements are shared constraints. Simmel assumes their persistence in their radicalism.

Rather than oppositions between fixed substances, Simmel tends to grasp middle-terms, passages, new forms. His thought thus shows the imprint of the Hegelian dialectic, yet without being obliged to adopt, too, the whole system, its aim was to think of movement and of becoming it. Simmel hardly ever quotes Hegel, but familiarity with the dialectical turn of thought is evident in his ideas. Rather than opposing being with nothingness, he engages in the future that fluidises this first opposition. On the other hand, he does not follow Hegel in his synthetic movement, nor in his systematic fulfilment, but rather he adheres to contradiction. We could talk about a 'dialectic without reconciliation' (Landmann, 1987, p. 16). For example, he was very interested in the concept of 'objective spirit', whose analytical validity he probed in itself, regardless of its position within the Hegelian system. Between the subjective, psychological world and the world of ideals, this allows us to think of the social as a third world.

On the one hand, the realm of thought is made up of oppositions like the social world of conflict; on the other hand, there are always terms, gradients, partial synthesis, which encourage us to move away from a dualistic logic. For if the oppositional structure reproduces itself on several levels, it is also because it is functional and not substantial. This is why Simmel intends not to lock himself into a dualistic pattern of thought, so that he would oppose, for example, mind to matter, superstructure to infrastructure, individuals to society. Such an approach also complicates the idea of class struggle or domination, which loses its absolute character, by repeating itself at different levels of analysis.

The variation in scale, practised from his first great book, *Introduction to Moral Science (1892–93)*, avoids the absolutisation of moral characters, as shown by the treatment of selfishness and altruism (GSG 3, p. 4). The discussion must always be resumed at new expense, at the different levels where it arises. Darwin's inspired perspectives do not invalidate the conceptual work of philosophers, including the Kantian lineage, but rather encourage them to be taken up in a different way. Naturalist and social approaches thus relativise each other.

The tension maintained expresses the rejection of a comfortable dualism. Simmel seeks to identify a third position that is not an Aristotelian happy medium,[1] but an approach that renews and updates Kant's critical position. Legitimate aspirations of conflicting views should be allowed. The plurality of perspectives is not a defect, but rather a wealth. However, it is by thinking of his own time that Simmel exudes the new ground of a pluralism of coexistence, born of the contemporaneity of contradictory yet legitimate aspirations. If modern political thought was based on the pact of individuals establishing political society, this approach has been challenged by the thoughts of history, which have seen in peoples, in collective ensembles, the true actors of political life. These two perspectives are true, but neither can claim to eject the other. Modern natural law has forged many concepts used for the interpretation of modern states, especially in their democratic forms. At the same time, these constructions often failed by their abstraction and universalism, ignoring concrete conditions of realisation. It is time, Simmel thinks, to sketch out a new articulation of these requirements.

He does not approach it directly from a political point of view, but from a sociological viewpoint. It is, in particular, by analysing the rise of individualism in modern societies that his ideas emerge from two contrasting forms, which together are the engine of social dynamics: the concern for equality that makes everyone want to be 'like' others, and the no less keen concern for difference, which is that everyone wants to be caught up in their irreplaceable singularity. The two aspirations seem so incompatible that the very thought of a 'society' seems absurd. And yet, Simmel shows that one can think of social beings without reducing them to their 'sociality', but by acknowledging a non-social part.

This look at society can be based on a whole tradition of analysis, from moralists to novelists. Let's take Molière's *The Misanthrope*. Alceste claims recognition of his individuality, without making any concessions to the forms of ordinary civility. His word is, 'I want to be distinguished' (*Misanthrope*, v. 63, 2013). He makes himself unpopular. Philinte, and indeed all the other characters in the play, plead for the compromise that makes coexistence possible, even pleasant: let us not impose on others our being at all times, but let us arbitrate between our social existence and our intimate existence. Alceste can easily, with his proto-romantic nature, call society false, hypocritical, corrupt. There is, Molière suggests, a little wisdom in this adaptability. At the same time, the desire to be recognised in one's uniqueness can secretly lie in everyone. Society is the transaction incessantly renegotiated between these attitudes. It imposes a third-party logic, since it condemns neither to complete hypocrisy nor to absolute authenticity. Transparency would be totalitarian, and this is the consequence that we would have to draw from the Simmelian analyses, which insist precisely on the importance of secrecy and the unsocialised part of our lives. But pure ceremonial convention would be an empty shell in which individuals would suffocate. The analyses of *Sociology* (GSG 11), but also of 'sociability' (GSG 12, pp. 177-193), illustrate Simmel's nuanced position. In its own way, it takes up the opposition of the freedom of the Ancients to that of the Moderns in the liberal tradition, albeit interpreting it as a social logic and not only as an ideological one. It maintains that social existence cannot be established on a single dimension (Berlin, 1966; Constant, [1819] 1988).

Another of Simmel's famous analyses allows us to experience the analytical scope of this approach: the 'psychology of flirtation' (1909), which is a reflection on seduction (GSG 12, pp. 37-50). The quintessential flirtatious character, to stick to our example, is Célimène. This young widow enjoys herself in the middle of a court of admirers, all of whom she is careful not to drive away, though without giving anything to any of them. She maintains ambiguity about her preferences to keep some freedom of action. Alceste claims an exclusive love and directly attacks the strategy of seduction. In this respect, he claims that the one he loves conforms to his ideal of the romantic relationship which is exclusive: 'Madam, you have to choose' (*Misanthrope*, v. 1603). He does not see the scope of Célimène's social survival strategy. If every 'yes' of the flirt contains a 'no', because it must suggest a deferred hope, and if each 'no' implies a 'yes', because no rebuff should be too definitive (as it must be spared the future), it is not necessarily out of stupidity, lightness or inconsistency, even out of immorality! It is that in the social game the woman suddenly freed from marriage has precarious but real room for freedom, which she knows she should not waste in dizzy performance. Simmel's comments on the art of seducing are, notwithstanding their formal character, part of a reflection on the female condition, in turn, part of a reflection on the culture and weight of male patterns imposed on the dominant culture. Not everything is like this in Simmel's work, and some passages on 'women' cause one to smile and sometimes provoke indignation. However, the formal resources of his analyses go beyond positions that could be lent to him. We are reminded that he received the shock of the Ibsen theatre and that he was involved with women's causes (GSG 17, pp. 39-45, 326 f.).

However, far from reducing flirtatious to feminine behaviour, Simmel deploys its scope, recalling all those situations where the alternative repels us and where we would rather unite the 'yes' and the 'no', or even take them simultaneously (GSG 12, p. 49). At the same time, he gave the flirt a self-portrait, which earned him the nickname 'philosopher of perhaps' from Ernst Bloch (1969):

> All the attractions of a for and against simultaneous, perhaps, prolonged restraint of the decision, which allows to enjoy the two exclusive aspects of each other in the realisation, – all are not merely specific to the flirt of the woman with the man, but come into play with thousands of other content.
>
> (GSG 12, p. 49)

Logic and social ontology

If we must deal subjectively or psychologically with the question of indecision, in objective or sociological terms this implies rather a consideration of the third-party logic of social action. Where an abstract logic opposes the subject and the predicate, social logic must consider a triangular relationship: X makes Y in relation to Z. The actor is never lonely but taken in a context that reflects his perception of himself. Simmel's apprehension of the social is not based on society or the constitution of society by individuals according to a mysterious mechanism, but – almost phenomenologically – on the reciprocal relationship of at least two individuals. As each person changes his behaviour, even insensitively, according to that of the other, or even the simple gaze of the other, we are dealing with a social phenomenon. In other words, we have entered a three-term logic. This dimension transforms the very forms of thought. It was accepted by Fichte and Hegel under a logic of recognition, but it was also deployed by Peirce under the species of semiotics. Simmel does not elaborate particularly on the formal side of these remarks, but his investigation of social relations is part of this research and under the sign of the third party.

The institution, the symbol, the social form are third parties that prevent dualities from becoming too polarised and being transformed into irremediable conflicts. It is also the primary function of fashion, understood by Simmel as an institution and even a 'machine to produce society'. The theme of conflict that affects societies finds a possible resolution in fashion. It is to be understood as one of those 'social institutions' whose 'resolutions that never-lasting welcome the persistent antagonism in the external form of a cooperation' (GSG 10, p. 11). Fashion is a social operator that articulates the aspiration for equality with the penchant for differentiation. These two claims are as legitimate as each other.

As such, the city of Paris seemed to offer him the most accomplished realisation of the concept of fashion:

> It is in Paris that fashion shows the greatest gap and the greatest reconciliation of its two components. Individualism, the adaptation to personal clothing, is much deeper than in Germany; but in this one observes strictly a certain broad framework of the general style, of the current fashion, to the point that the singular phenomenon never comes out of the general, but is nevertheless always noticed.
>
> (GSG 10, p. 15)

The two modern passions of equality and individuality are thus compatible. They make possible the excesses of extreme conformism as well as extravagance. Fashion brings them together.

But its synthesis also tends to produce an immobility, because the constant change that is the internal law of fashion is so fast that it is directionless. The speed of the tempo required by this incessant change, on the other hand, exerts strong pressure on individuals, an 'appalling enslavement' (GSG 10, p. 32), which is like the ransom of the gain in individual freedom conquered by democratic societies. Fashion would present one of the structures that liberate by enslaving: individual choices remain possible, but under the condition of the acceptance of a common order that imposes a framework on them. The figure of the *fashion victim* is evoked by Simmel as the pinnacle of alienation, but alienation is not resorbable. We are dealing with a graduation in which a variety of individual behaviours can find themselves realised on the basis of 'no'. Conciliation provided by the social institution is never free from conflict: it is an organisation of conflictual relations.

Simmel analyses the phenomena that structure the new forms of societies based on the principle of equality stated during the Enlightenment and which the advent of a generalised monetary 'capitalist' economy was to impose in practice. These institutions deal with a new economy of time that is both accelerated and disconnected from the historical outlook. Such perception of time offers an illusory change. In order to think of a more accomplished individuality, Simmel examined the differences in temporalisation in his latest writings, and incorporated in part the Bergsonian analyses of duration. In any case, his analysis is never based on hardened oppositions such as between society and community, individual and society, but rather on an apprehension of ambiguities and tensions at work in phenomena.

The role of the third party is never that of a synthesis, but an articulation of differences. Fashion becomes an important phenomenon in an egalitarian urban society, because it preserves conflicting aspirations for conformism and singularity. It does not claim to resolve or dissolve these tensions but observes how socialisation is constantly recomposed against trends that undermine it.

In a narrow sense, social forms ensure the maintenance of a society understood as perpetual self-constitution, working with conflicts, as an infinite negotiation of diversity with itself. They make it possible to coordinate diversity over time. They focus first on morals, i.e. on an area that ranges from ways of life and habits to moral and legal norms and up to established institutions. These forms are all part of social normativity to some degree. They temper individual and collective action and give it a framework that guarantees its effectiveness and compatibility. Their study is the primary subject of sociology. It therefore takes a cross-sectional look at society, attentive to the functions that ensure its maintenance and transformation. The cardinal question that is asked, which is at the same time the fundamental mystery, is: how do social forms maintain themselves?

Social forms are thought of by Simmel in terms of their genesis, that is, from below, and they begin as soon as a gesture or habit is formed. As soon as by virtue of an action a form is manifested in its repetition or its imitation, we are dealing with a third-party structure that immediately exerts its hold over the act. In the case of habitual action, the social form discharges the actor of some of the creative investment and allows him to go further. Automation frees by binding. The basic gestures that establish a common culture, from the walk to the greeting, are based on these learnings. It could also be exemplified by language, which is first spoken in us, and yet we appropriate ourselves by a spontaneity of our own that makes us access the performing matrix: we can invent phrases that were never said. These forms are what can rightly be called 'institutions' because they refer to a primary inventiveness. This is the meaning that Merleau-Ponty repeats in his courses at the Collège de France, when he talks about 'these events of an experience that give it lasting dimensions, against which a whole series of other experiences will make sense, will form a continuation thinkable or a story' (Merleau-Ponty, [1968] 2015, p. 61). He also notes the ambiguity of these conditions of progress: 'The sedimentation that makes us go further also means that we are threatened by hollow thoughts, and that the sense of origins is emptying' (ibid, p. 167).

In terms of their history, social forms and institutions at large thus refer to the norms that govern social action in practice and give it the regularity necessary to maintain it. We can also call such norms 'disciplines' in the sense that each time they are processes related to learning, for example, examining the use of time that social cohesion itself depends on, but these norms are by no means the systematic effect of a state coercion! However, they are also sensible stock deposits or the treasure trove of meanings. Here, language can serve as a model for this type of form that introduces additional mediation in relation to the functionalist regulation of social action. A meaning is conveyed in a statement uttered in a context. The resumption of this statement in a different context will affect the primary meaning, in the sense that an arbitration will be necessary between two versions of that meaning, depending on the first or the second context. However, beyond situations where language is used purely deictically or pragmatically, a statement that is somewhat complex refers to a meaning that can be reconstructed independently of its contexts of speech. These meanings can be taken up and they give rules for action, as the laws of the past can standardise society. But they may also contain more individual meanings, such as works of art; they encourage their implementation, such as technical objects, or even technological systems; they are universal as well as the forms of knowledge. Without it being possible to envisage the diversity of these achievements that together constitute culture, namely society taken from the point of view of its transformation, these forms also arise as third terms between different moments. They allow the passage – bridge and door – between generations as well as between individuals. In addition to the social forms that are the subject of *Sociology,* they could be compared to the symbolic forms of Cassirer.[2] It is the world of all the works that requires hermeneutics.

Balanced hermeneutics

Simmel was neither a philologist nor a historian. Yet his approach of works is based on his reflection on history, in turn, giving him his epistemological framework and his philosophy of culture that deals with the structure of the contents.

The epistemology of historical knowledge underlines a double difficulty for the historian: his object is not given to him. He must rebuild it from what remains of sensible actions. There are still traces that are the physical signs of past events. However, the historian's approach can confirm the object by ordering these traces in relation to meaningless assumptions.

This attitude confronts two dangers: on the one hand, it could lead to idealism that loses the link to past reality. To counter the danger of historicism making historical processes the equivalent of a second nature that determines nothing less than the first sequence of events, Simmel had asked the Kantian question concerning the conditions of the possibility of knowledge and that these are also the conditions of history. Was there not a risk of returning history to the knowledge that we were absorbing? Simmel, however, insisted on the 'physical movements of the individual' (gestures, mimes, sounds) from which to constitute a complex form of reconstitutive knowledge (GSG 9, p. 239). The other danger was symmetrically a form of naturalism hidden in psychologism that its early formulations did not exclude clearly enough. If knowledge is linked to our ability to understand the perspective of actors by reliving their emotions and thoughts, on the grounds that the unity of the human psyche guarantees its possibility, we lose the critical dimension of the process to finally follow Dilthey's solution, which is more truly psychological than hermeneutics. However, if the ability to 'feel' by varying degrees the psychic states of the actors of history is required as a necessary process of subjectivation, since the historian is not dealing with abstractions, then this moment is involved in the processes of reconstruction that forms part of a critical methodology.

After 1900 and its accentuation of the hermeneutic dimension of historical knowledge, if Dilthey develops his account of a methodology articulated in the three moments of *lived* experience, *expression* and *understanding*, it is because there was a need to correct the merely anthropological and ultimately psychological understanding. Dilthey's later introduction of the *objective spirit* had the function of stabilising the cultural world by explaining the possibility of its objectification. He would rely on a concept already used by Simmel and one of their common inspirations, Moritz Lazarus. However, these corrections made by Dilthey did not allow to continually give primacy to the psychological identification on reconstruction. Simmel's approach is to amend the imaginative variation that renders the actors' point of view, while controlling the always hypothetical reconstruction of the sequences of the past. He thus contrasts Dilthey's view with a principle that limits the scope of hermeneutics: the You. The object of the historical interpretation is an unassimilable You, which preserves its share of secrecy and the unknowable, just as actors involved in social interactions have the 'right to secrecy' (GSG 8, 115). Reconstructions are therefore only hypothetical. This critical dimension expresses the singularity of socio-historical knowledge, the object of which is still a subject. A fundamental conceptual opposition allows Simmel to articulate this dual dimension: it distinguishes *historical* understanding, which as much as possible renders the aim of the actors in the situation of origin, from the *objective* understanding, which involves the whole dimension of meaning that is carried by the acts or works of the actors without being attributable to them in particular. This distinction, which appears to be different from the first texts, finds explicit wording in the 1918 article 'On Historical Understanding'. Simmel makes of the You the 'original phenomenon' (*Urphänomen*), that critically limits every historical understanding. It can no longer be an empathetic identification with the actors' aim, but a heuristic fiction. The aim of the actors, *the intentio auctoris*, is an impregnable dimension of historical, but also socio-cultural understanding in the general meaning of the works. Without resorting to an expensive ontological hypothesis that would return this meaning to a destiny, so seeing in individuals only the spokesmen of a message that would transcend them, Simmel takes seriously the heterogeneous genesis of cultural meanings. If this approach considers the role of the first witnesses, listeners, interpreters (the 'reception') and the interpretive tradition that develops from them, it stops short of reducing the acts or spiritual works. The two dimensions of understanding are to be taken together, correcting each other. In this way, Simmel proposes a model of historical intelligence that intends to integrate the different semantic formations appearing throughout history in a contingent way. Without situating himself in a history of hermeneutic positions, Simmel corrects Dilthey's psychologism by articulating the individual interpretive-reconstructive act to the complex structure of the historical world (or 'world of the spirit' in Diltheyan terms). This approach maintains the actors' point of view as an essential dimension of reconstruction, but far from reducing the significance of historical sequences, such as an excessively rationalistic view of human action would tend to, it takes into account the random compositional effects due to the convergence of multiple series in the production of the event. This is not explained by a preconceived idea, more or less prophetic, but in a relative and limited way by a study on contexts and by interpretive choices.

What has been sketched here with regard to historical knowledge finds its counterpart in the problem that Simmel develops to account for cultural objects. In other words, we refer to the whole of what constitutes the objective spirit, that is, everything that implies a physical trace and shareable and shared aims of meaning: works, institutions, technical objects, symbolic forms, etc.

The question of culture appears in Simmel's thought as a problem that is on the philosophical agenda of his contemporaries: how to broaden the criticism of reason to historical phenomena? Is history, the world of movement and uncertainty, susceptible to a form of knowledge of its own? This is Dilthey's question, but this is also the query that philosophers who draw inspiration from Kant take up from Windelband. Culture also opened up the spectrum of historical interests that for too long were focused on great men, battles and event history: with breakthroughs towards a cultural history (Jacob Burckhardt, Karl Lamprecht), the landscape was radically transformed. Whether they are called historical sciences or cultural sciences, this field is awaiting appropriate reflexive treatment. Simmel fits into this debate first in terms of the epistemology of history, but also by opening up his questioning to the variety of the world of culture.

Cultural objects are temporal objects. Coming from the production and cooperative activities of men, they have a consistency of their own: a form and a structure. They have a consistent objectivity. No one can change them as they see fit. The constraint of the work, such as that of technical invention or institution, is necessary through continuous co-optation that does not necessarily depend on an explicit sanction, as in the case of the legal standard.

It may seem bold to put together objects that refer to practices, orders of value, and phenomena that are so different. However, Simmel's systematic position commits him to do so, alongside the detailed treatment of certain objects like the vase cove that would be emblematic. There is a common structure belonging to cultural objects that allows us to speak of a 'philosophy of culture'. These objects correspond to the ways in which human beings construct a habitable universe by depositing in objective forms or structures the effects of mankind's practice.

Simmel notes that these forms, which are initially the expression of a practice, also have an objective existence due to the materiality of the form. In the case of conventions, this materiality may consist only of the continuation of the tacitly renewed agreement between the actors over time. Because of this objectification, they have an objectivity. However, this objective marks a fixation, a stop in the accompaniment of practices that take place over time. Inevitably, therefore, there comes a time when a contradiction arises between the forms to serve the action and the demands of the action. This disparity corresponds to the structure of the crisis of culture, a crisis that can go as far as tragedy. The latter term means that productions, which should facilitate action, eventually prohibit it.

To what extent is this pathological form of cultural development inescapable? At the end of his article on the 'tragedy of culture', Simmel recalls that the mind 'countless times' manages to accomplish the work of assimilation of cultural content (GSG12, p. 223). But sometimes the subjective effort of appropriation exceeds its strengths, either because the number of works is too large or their complexity implies a concentration difficult to find in the modern world. There is then an encystment. The form that allowed a gain in abstraction becomes an obstacle. The works and institutions in which the memory of practices and knowledge accumulated over generations were deposited became opaque, illegible. The result is an immediate relapse into a naivety not sought for itself, but inevitably resulting from the multiplication of relationships and the dispersion that it entails.

Simmel's philosophy of culture did not develop a system, even if 'open' like Rickert's, of different cultural forms. The variety is such that the attempt would not have made sense. The cultural objects discussed in his essays, such as fashion, the frame, the bridge, the jug, open up a multiplicity of cases. They appear within their own normative worlds as a result of the work of culture. Law, technology, art or eroticism thus separate themselves from the course of life in order to establish a proper order of meaning, materially dependent on common, yet autonomous conditions governed by a particular legality.

Art is one of these areas, which is of decisive importance for the philosophy of culture, since the works of art are more individualised than others. Simmel included man from his aesthetic studies in his collection *Philosophical Culture* (*Philosophische Kultur*, 1912 - GSG 14, pp. 159-459). Its hermeneutics can be read indirectly.

Simmel produced several typical studies which exude the contours of a 'Philosophy of Art'. Although he could not complete this in his later years in a study that he was developing (which was lost), we can sketch his ideas in a thematic reconstruction. His examination focuses on the fields of urban planning (rather than architecture), sculpture and painting. He also considers the performing arts from the viewpoint of the actor. There is some analysis of poetics, although it is only briefly represented.

His three studies on the cities of Rome, Venice and Florence are part of an aesthetic approach: they are read as works of art, having no assignable author, yet producing a singular aesthetic satisfaction. The text on Rome in particular reflects on this paradox which is representative of cultural objects in general: they have no author in the sense that they are anonymous, too numerous, replaced and continued by others to the point that they are collective works. Nonetheless, they produce the impression of a purpose, for we consider them as if a design had presided over their elaboration. Cities are therefore part of a kind of uncoordinated architecture. It would be futile to apply intentional hermeneutics to them, and yet it makes perfect sense to try to interpret them.

The same cannot be said of the works of sculpture, of which Simmel examines two great illustrations in detail: Michelangelo and Rodin. He strives to capture in them moments when an art defined by a certain style switches to liberation. The most massive and formal art, a paragon of classicism, becomes in these two artists the place of a struggle between flight and gravity. A contradictory movement motivates these works. The unfinished business reinforces the sense of contradiction, even tragic, that holds Simmel back. It is the surpassing of form that interests him in Michelangelo's work, in other words the transition to a new plastic language. Rodin, for his part, seems to him to implement modern mobility, introducing the unfinished as a principle of creation, redefining the space around the work. In both cases, Simmel focuses on artistic projects that transcend the conditions that made them possible. The work is not magnified for itself, as it would be for any classicism, but instead it includes the dynamics of its own negation. Thus, clearing a space that transcends it, it indicates the possibility of forms that are unpleasing, inviting their transgression.

The study of painting focuses on the work of Rembrandt, which is the subject of the major book on art. Simmel tracks down the way the artwork establishes its own space and even unearths a temporality within it that thwarts the *ut pictura poesis*. It is now the instantaneous art of the figuration of forms that is likely to suggest an immanent duration, an ageing that captures the figures in the portraits, starting with that of the painter himself who speaks apart in his self-portraits. The analysis of the portraits, but especially of the gaze in the portraits, seeks to fix this attention: Simmel sees it as a 'look without space', exuding an immanent transcendence. Such a look is no longer expressive, it does not even symbolise infinity. It opens up another dimension.

The performing arts are represented by studies about the actor, who brings a perspective to the theatre where it is firstly the actualisation of an objective deposit that matters. The actor's play is paradigmatic of the relationship we have to objective culture, since theatre exists only at the crossroads of these two non-existences: the traditional, the texts, on the one side; and on the other, the performance that produces them in a new way. Simmel relies on stage play to suggest the cultural and collective dimension of any work that inevitably results from collaboration between eras, no less than between authors and audiences. If the public did not participate in art, would there be art? Music and dance are not discussed. He could not write the proposed work on Beethoven, but it is evoked when he addresses the question of the late work. From this connection with other artistic genres, one can assume that his words would have been no less differentiated.

Finally, there is no accomplished poetics, especially if we agree that the book dedicated to Goethe does not consider the poet! Or that the long and developed article on Dante feeds a psychological purpose! However, the attendance of Stefan George led him to write some studies on this poet that clearly dwell on the meaning of his interpretation of poetic works. Art is based on a form of feeling that passes through abstraction. Creation and the reception of the artwork do not refer to a personal feeling, but extend the personal element towards objective validity. The work establishes 'an order beyond the mere personal self' (GSG 5, p. 289). Simmel uses the terms 'ascension' (*Aufstieg*), 'turning point' (*Wendung*) that could almost be translated by 'conversion' (GSG 5, p. 293). It characterises this phenomenon by the production of an 'incredibly strict legality of forms' under a 'super-personal necessity'.

Yet it is precisely this dimension of the verbal work of art that is evident in George. Set in an evolution of forms, Simmel thinks he sees here, after 'art for feeling' and 'art for art', the dimension of the objective expression of art: 'We feel the subjective element that arises in us as an objective element which belongs to the work itself' (GSG 7, p. 29).

Theoretical texts such as the one on 'The Aesthetics of Gravity' or 'The Legality of the Work of Art' allow us to trace the contours of a Simmelian aesthetic, which provides the principles of a suggestive hermeneutics that may have been influential for many readers of Simmel during the 20th century.

Complexity and reflection

The general turn of Simmel's thinking is not analytical, but problematic. It introduces the dimension of possible alternatives to its treatment of the object. For this reason, imaginative variation and aesthetic modelling have a systematic role in this approach. In a relative world, that is, where all things are interconnected without an ontological order of dependence or causal relationships, three-term logic is more operative than the dichotomous process. As an object that is both historical and possibly endowed with meaning or value, it is all the more necessary to problematise the mode of knowledge. This involves the commitment to go beyond the mere recognition of a generalised 'reciprocal relationship'.

By placing more emphasis on the dimension of succession, Simmel approached forms from the point of view of history and the philosophy of culture. The general model he proposes provides a framework for understanding the particular status of cultural objects which could be said to be subjectivities of the past. The question of their updating is also that of their interpretation in necessarily collective practices. Cultural objects condense practices, as works of art condense time and thus access greater individualisation. At least, this aspect particularly interests Simmel. The works are created in time; they resist time by taking shape and dissolve this form by capturing a singular temporality.

By addressing the field of social and cultural ontology, Simmel challenges inherited categories and conventional approaches in favour of original questioning. The studies in sociology and cultural philosophy (which frame a general hermeneutics of symbolic objects) are an integral part of this overall problem. Through his acknowledgement of the complexity of its objects and the invention of new modes of treatment, which are respectful of their socio-cultural ambiguity, Simmel seeks to meet the challenge of modernity in all its complexity. To that extent, and without dealing directly with hermeneutical purposes, he reveals a new issue in the hermeneutical debate that remains attractive and inspiring until today. Interpretation does not only have to seek intentional meaning, which would be too restrained. Nor does it need to obtain a broad explanatory model of socio-historical phenomena (such as historical, sociological or evolutionist laws) – that would be too far removed from what is to be explained. But by allowing these two hermeneutical claims to intersect, he offers a sober way of dealing with such complex things as societies – and men – are.

Notes

1 Aristotle, especially in his ethical writings, holds that virtue is at the same distance from two excesses.
2 In the three volumes of his *Philosophy of Symbolic Forms* (1923–1927), Ernst Cassirer developed an extension of critical philosophy to the field of culture, apprehended from the expressive forces of the mind: access to symbolisation was a decisive performance of liberation and abstraction, but it takes place in and by the sensitive form (Cassirer, 1953). Cassirer details the process for forms of language, myth and scientific knowledge. Comparison with plural and plural worlds of Simmel's self-norms is already made by Michael Landmann (1976, p. 4).

References

Berlin, Isaiah (1966). *Two concepts of liberty. An inaugural lecture delivered before the University of Oxford on 31 October 1958*. Oxford: Clarendon Press.

Bloch, Ernst (1969). Weisen des 'Vielleicht' bei Simmel (1958). In *Philosophische Aufsätze, Gesamtausgabe 10* (pp. 57–60). Frankfurt: Suhrkamp.

Cassirer, Ernst (1953). *The philosophy of symbolic forms (1923–1927)*. New Haven, CT: Yale University Press.

Constant, Benjamin ([1819] 1988). De la liberté des Anciens comparée à celle des modernes. The liberty of the ancients compared to that of the moderns. In B. Fontana (Ed.), *The political writings of Benjamin Constant* (pp. 309–328). Cambridge: Cambridge University Press.

Gadamer, Hans Georg (2004). *Truth and method*, 2nd rev. ed. (1st English ed., 1975), revised translation by J. Weinsheimer and D. G. Marshall. London and New York: Crossroads.

Landmann, Michael (1976). Georg Simmel: Konturen seines Denkens. In H. Böhringer & K. Gründer (Eds.), *Ästhetik und Soziologie um die Jahrhundertwende: Georg Simmel* (pp. 3–17). Frankfurt a.M: Klostermann.

Landmann, Michael (1987). Einleitung. In G. Simmel (Ed.), *Das individuelle Gesetz* (pp. 7–29). Frankfurt am Main: Suhrkamp.

Merleau-Ponty, Maurice ([1968] 2015). *Résumés de cours. L'institution; la passivité (cours au Collège de France 1954–1955)*, prefaced by Claude Lefort. Paris: Belin.

Molière (2013). *Le Misanthrope*. Ed. by J. Chupeau. Paris: Gallimard.

8

GEORG SIMMEL, HANS BLUMENBERG, AND PHILOSOPHICAL ANTHROPOLOGY

Andrea Borsari

Introduction[1]

In the last two decades, an increasingly extensive survey of the anthropological propensity of his thought has emerged in the research on the work of Hans Blumenberg (1921–1996).[2] But, even after the publication of his voluminous dossier on phenomenological anthropology, represented by the posthumous book *Beschreibung des Menschen*, very little attention has been paid to the role that Blumenberg himself reserved for the importance that Georg Simmel could have played and can have in the construction of a philosophical anthropology, different from those that the decades after his death would later have realized.[3] The study presented here aims therefore to fill such a gap, at least in broad terms. It thus proceeds to reconstruct the various aspects that Simmel's anthropological penchant contains according to Blumenberg's reading. First of all, through an examination of the key passage *from money to life in the metaphorological analysis* of the dynamics within the thinking of the Berlin philosopher. It then focuses on the *modes of 'description of man'* made possible by him, such as the function of sight, gaze, and face in anthropogenesis, the importance of distancing processes from reality, the discovery of indirect paths, of transposing oneself into the other and of imagination, and countermoves aimed at confronting anthropological contingency and producing a tentative and, at the same time, impossible 'consolation'. Thirdly, this study deepens understanding the different genesis of the anthropological condition and the political sphere, as well as the different levels of knowledge presupposed by the Blumenbergian judgement on the *barbaric character* of decisions, based on the central category of the political according to Carl Schmitt, the *friend-enemy distinction*. Subsequently, the analysis also surrounds *the gestures, the mythical occurrences, and the explosive metaphorics* through which various places in Simmel's work focus on the corporeal relationship between empirical level and theory: on value as a functional specification of significance and on life as a self-affirmation of an unlikely reality, as well as on the possible misunderstandings in the expression of human beings at the limit between expressibility and inexpressibility. Fifthly, the opposition between persuasion and oppression, as a central instance of an *anthropological approach to the actuality of rhetoric*, finds its specificity in the Simmelian category of 'role' and in its passage from a theatrical background to the dimension of personal identity. At the same time the *theory of nonconceptuality* makes use of the impossibility of reducing the figural dimension to a simple auxiliary and temporary construction in the logical-conceptual definition process, in order to affirm the luxurious constitution of human beings and the role of metaphor as an element uniting within the anthropogenesis the reference to reality and the reference to possibility. Finally, the chapter concludes by retracing the more general *antinomic character* common to the movement of thought both in Blumenberg and in Simmel, starting with the analysis of the *philosophy of life* of the latter and of some samples taken from his *aesthetics*, such as the specifically human performance of joining and separating, style as a synthesis of universal and individual, the coexistence in the work of art of a centripetal thrust and a centrifugal push, and the paradoxical convergence of the individual and the law. And it comes to find the angular point of encounter with the Blumenbergian 'anthropological antinomy' in the 'law of contrast' (*Gegensatz*), which seems to regulate in its various modulations and prevalences the different phases of the Simmelian thought and, certainly, his contribution to the philosophical anthropology proposed here.

Money or life

It is thanks to Hans Blumenberg that we can consider Georg Simmel as one of the few authors to be included in the philosophical canon after Nietzsche, thanks to his *Philosophy of Money*[4] and, although such a judgement undoubtedly remains very controversial, it has certainly increased in the last thirty years the number of those willing to share it, both in the vast sphere of the social sciences as well as in philosophy in the strict sense (Meyer, 2008, p. 399 f.). However, the reader who delves into the Blumenbergian laboratory entitled to the 'description of man' will be astonished to discover the unprecedented figure of Georg Simmel 'anthropologist'. Moreover, a Simmel to be read as an unfinished figure of a philosophical anthropology that could have been expected at 'another level' with respect to everything that under such a banner would have been produced during the twenties of the last century (Blumenberg, 2006, p. 625).

To Simmel, and to the consistency as well as internal consistency of his work, Blumenberg himself had nevertheless dedicated the extensive metaphorological study on 'money or life' in which he proposed to trace the imaginal thread of the immanent dynamics generated by the contrast between the polarities of solidification and liquidity, form and dissolution, institution and freedom, levelling and individualization (Blumenberg, 2012 [1974]). In the plural tension and the multiple transition so modulated between money and life is included a large section of Simmel's research, following to that reversal of the genetic relationship that hides the metaphorical density as secondary in the exposition where Simmel comes to talk about life having already found the metaphor of money, the replacement of stable and substantial values with the living reciprocal action of elements that in turn are subject to the same 'dissolution into the infinite' (Blumenberg, 2012 [1974], p. 254). With the vision of the potential objectivity of the subjective that is realized in the world of the totality of human actions as

> to build a world that may be acquired without conflict and mutual oppression, to possess values whose acquisition and enjoyment by one person does not exclude that of another, but opens the door a thousand times for him to acquire such values as well.
>
> *(Simmel, 1978 [1900], p. 291)*

Simmel arrives early – ten years before the Cassirer of *Substance and Function* – at a functional representation of objectivity itself and at the detachment from every naturalism and the principle of conservation related to it (Blumenberg, 2012 [1974], p. 254). Even in normative terms, 'Simmel retains a crucial schema of *The philosophy of money*, namely the binding of objectivity, whether that of values or of norms, to the idea of totality, whether that of subjective valuations or of individual vital actions'; and he can therefore formulate the 'individual law' as 'a function of the total life of the individual personality' (Simmel, 1918, quoted in Blumenberg, 2012 [1974], p. 255). By virtue of his ability to avoid 'hard' theoretical formulations, Simmel proceeds from the descriptive level to the highest degree of universality, always depicting the energy thus invested in the same way as in his concept of life the propensity to formal consolidation and rigidification of forms each time it withdraws again from the 'resulting sedimentations' towards the indeterminacy of 'formless liquidity' (Blumenberg, 2012 [1974], p. 255). It is possible, however, to find 'profit and loss' in the transition from the early metaphorics of money to the late concept of life, so that the shift from the philosophy of money to the philosophy of life is reflexively a paradigm of the philosophy of life. That which in money can still be grasped in descriptive terms as an intertwining of 'a gain in possibility with a loss in reality, of entitlement with of renunciation', as 'emancipation of the individual at the cost of functionalization of its qualities', still dissolves at the level of life in the attribution of generic determinations only as 'the fateful and unpacifiable restlessness of life in each of its realizations, its inclination and its resistance to formal rigidification' (Blumenberg, 2012 [1974], p. 258). On the other hand, money already contains the withdrawal of the disappointing reality in the suspension of pure possibility, since it, as 'absolute medium', is able to realize 'the possibility of all values as the value of all possibilities'. As the concept of life brings this metaphor to fulfilment 'only abstracting from the fact of the finitude of individual lives, it is only elevated to the hypostasis of a substance that expresses itself in them merely superficially' (Blumenberg, 2012 [1974], p. 261). Unlike theological metaphysics, only anthropology 'can afford to insist on the attraction of pure possibilities and to speak of the disappointment of accomplished reality' (Blumenberg, 2012 [1974], p. 259).[5]

The description of man

At the heart of the anthropological assumption of the Simmelian thought – of the 'Simmel anthropologist' from which we have taken the steps – we will find the nucleus identified on the empirical and anthropogenetic level by an equal need to find an escape route when we end up in a blind alley and that – transposed into the sphere of a dynamic essence of the human being centred on the research of *Trost*, of consolation – becomes 'a form of distancing from reality, in the extreme case, of loss of reality', through the recourse to the virtues of distance and 'pure expressiveness' to elaborate something like the pain one could not escape from at will (Blumenberg, 2006, p. 626 f.).[6] If *Trost* is not intended here as a quieter (*Quietiv*) of the incapacity to modify his own condition, but as a correlative of a being who could not be helped by the quantum of pain to which he or she is destined and consequently finds himself at the limit of the inconsolable, it will have to be reconnected to the structure by digressions and indirect ways (*Umwege*) of culture and to the paradoxical need for compensation of a being who thus obtains the 'excess of sensitivity of the imaginary' capable of treating the absent as present and of living in the absence of foundation of contingency (Blumenberg, 2006, pp. 630–643). The awareness of the anthropological contingency, of the fact that the same individual could have been or become another, shows the casual or 'inconvenient' character of identity and radicalizes the sense of 'exchange of roles', the original or primary phenomenon at the base of human capacity to 'transpose into other', depict him/her and impersonate him/her, which also the Simmelian philosophy of the actor correctly identifies (Blumenberg, 2006, p. 650 f.). Visibility, the fact of being able to be seen, like a bodily-visible being, comes to constitute the basic relation of the human condition in which the social experience is defined as entering into a relationship with the other through an effect of reciprocity, an interchangeable reciprocal action, symbolized by looking at each other in the eyes (it cannot be taken with the eye without giving at the same time) and elaborated through the notion of *Wechselwirkung* derived from Simmel's *Sociology* (Blumenberg, 2006, p. 871 f.).

The definition of 'sociology of the eye' has been used in this regard, but it is even more urgent to underline again, with Hans Blumenberg and against its trivialization, the philosophical and anthropological importance of the Simmelian acquisition for the definition of reality itself. The same discussion of Simmel's 'sociology of the senses' (Simmel, 1908b, pp. 722–742) and of the differentiation between sight and hearing leads to the enhancement of the inhibitory and indirect way of each culture, which is primarily digression through the others, and to highlight the indirect structure of self-consciousness that captures the stranger through internal experience and the self from the outside, as an 'artefact of the experience of the stranger' (Blumenberg, 2006, pp. 875–881). In the sociology of the senses – observes Blumenberg in his *Höhlenausgänge* – Simmel is confronted with the 'nature of cave' typical of the big city. This is the place of distance, where what is absent is available in the same way as what is present, and abstraction, a diminished substitute for magic, which constitutes a sort of 'acoustic cavern', a screen against everything that it does not produce and does not recognize as reality. In addition, it disadvantages everything that in terms of experience and relationship cannot be produced and acquired exclusively through sight.

> Still before Kafka and Wittgenstein – he writes – in 1908 Simmel uses the metaphor that is found in this noise shielding, in the restriction to the mere sight, without the possibility of listening, in the modern metropolis on all sides surrounded by closed doors.
>
> *(Blumenberg, 1989, pp. 76–81)*

Even the face, on the basis of Rembrandt's late self-portraits analysed by Simmel as the story of the depositing of the depth of a life in the subtlety of colour, thus makes it possible to understand a human being 'already at his appearance without waiting for his action', contributing more generally, to a 'culture of understanding' against the 'barbarity of friend-enemy decisions' (Blumenberg, 2006, p. 873 f.).

The barbarity of friend-enemy decisions

It therefore seems possible to ascribe to Simmelian ancestry in a philosophical-anthropological key at least a substantial part of Blumenberg's critical posture with respect to the Schmittian theory of the political, caught in its nucleus of a 'friend-enemy' relationship, as has been shown in the dossier published the year after the *Description of man* and entitled to the relations between Blumenberg and Carl Schmitt (*Briefwechsel 1971–1978 und weitere Materialien*, 2007). From it emerges, in fact, the ascertainment of the different genesis, 'heterogonie', of 'friend' and 'enemy', and first possible motivation for the barbarism[7] cited:

'enmity is a political category, friendship is an anthropological category', although both are comparable based on time parameters. To an immortal being, with infinite time available, it would not be difficult to frame all the others 'on the same categorial level, starting from an indifference as painless as friendly'; lacking, however, such an assumption, 'it is necessary to decide quickly for the enmity, while for the friendship it can be decided along a much more extended period' (Blumenberg & Schmitt, 2007, p. 222). The 'totality of the consequences of the immediate decision [*Schnellentscheidung*], with all the preventive aspects and the subsequent burdens [*postoperativen Lasten*]' (ibid.) will thus constitute the political. Starting, then, from spatial parameters, the 'scene of recognition' develops itself: 'the enemy is presumably anyone approaching' (ibid.). The mode of 'recognition' (*Erkennung*) takes place according to the meeting of the reciprocity of the gaze after Simmel that has already been seen at work in the *Description of man* and is taken up again here, again in an anthropogenetic key, in the text on visibility (*Sichtbarkeit*, Blumenberg & Schmitt, 2007, pp. 218–222):

> visibility becomes an anthropological category only through the link it establishes with the ambivalence of the friend-enemy relationship. ... What does not exist outside of humankind is the *uncertainty* that [Ungewißheit *darüber, ob*] the act of being seen as actualization of visibility means danger or help, loss or gain, or if it requires escape or assignment to the other [*Zuwendung*].

It is therefore on the perceptive level that the act of recognition takes place, precisely 'in the organic perception' (*in organischer Wahrnehmung*), in a univocal way and through 'specific characteristics and information': 'Friend or enemy is, in any case, *a* kind *of being others* [*eine Gattung* der anderen]; this is always predetermined by pure recognition from the external aspect [*Aussehen*] (or other sensory qualities)' (Blumenberg & Schmitt, 2007, p. 218).

The unsustainable character of the Schmittian opposition – and, as Simmel already recalled in his *Sociology*, the 'barbaric' in the Greek sense indicates that with which there is a 'non-relation' [*Nicht-Beziehung*] (Simmel, 1908b, p. 770) – derives from the heterogeneity of the genetic plans that it contains and it results from the lack of assumption of the anthropological and perceptive-sensitive dimension in the recognition of the enemy, and of its spatial and temporal conditions, 'so that due to this possible past, which can extend to the scene of recognition, the anthropological category can invalidate [*außer Kraft setzen*] the political one' (Blumenberg & Schmitt, 2007, p. 222). Still resorting to a kind of dialectic of the Simmelian foreigner, as he writes in his *Sociology*:

> the unity of distance and closeness, which every relationship between men involves, is here arrived at a constellation that can be formulated shorter in the following terms: distance in the relationship means that the near subject is far away, while being a foreigner means that the distant subject is near.
>
> *(Simmel, 1908b, p. 765)*

For the 'Feind' (enemy) assumed as 'jeder, der sich nähert' (everyone who approaches), Blumenberg explains how 'foreigners, in the radical sense of their exotic aspect, they appear in an extremely undifferentiated way' and that 'in order to prevent damage that may occur later, humanity is set to qualify the foreigner as a presumed enemy' (Blumenberg & Schmitt, 2007, p. 223). While the fact that this recommendation no longer has any reason to exist does not put these well-established mechanisms out of business as quickly as if it could be done without. Up to the actualizing consequences: 'If Europe dismantles its internal borders, in all probability its external borders become even more impermeable' (ibid.). And, still in connection with the spatial dimension, the narrowing of the field produced by the distant neighbour:

> The world has certainly become smaller, but this only strengthens the disruptive force [*Brisanz*] of the non-recognition micro-decisions [*Mikroentscheidungen der Nichterkennung*] that occur within it. Undefined anguish in front of others has grown, and this means that this narrow world is virtually more racist than before.
> *(Blumenberg & Schmitt, 2007, p. 223 f.)*

The landscape that opens up to modernity is therefore the one 'stiffened in unsolvable elements', in 'dilemmas that must be maintained', or rather we are faced with an 'anthropological situation' whereby, even in the case of trust, far from being the result of 'measures' adopted, it 'is all the more reliable the less we know how it was created' (Blumenberg & Schmitt, 2007, p. 224). On the other hand, the adoption of the universal quantifier 'everything is …' incurs in a nihilistic fallacy, even in the case of the assumption of the sciences of the spirit (*Geisteswissenschaften*) 'everything is language' (then 'everything is nothing'), or in the 'limit case' of 'rhetorical intensification' with anthropological value of the 'we want everything' (*wir wollen alles* or *vogliamo tutto*) on which the anthropology *in nuce* condensed in *Die Sorge geht über den Fluß* (cf. Blumenberg, 2010 [1987], pp. 13–15) has insisted (Blumenberg & Schmitt, 2007, p. 225). Once the fog of uniformation has thinned out, the Goethean *farbige Abglanz* [refracted colour or coloured reflection] does not take over, but 'the product of the decay of all monisms' and of 'all the last units', a 'dualism':

> the recurrence of reason when it seems having come very close to its purpose: the One – and here, almost as if we could not keep it, there is already the Other. At the peak of the success of his system, Platonism generates gnosis, while the monotheism of salvation produces the dualism of predestination and reprobation.
> *(Blumenberg & Schmitt, 2007, p. 225 f.)*

The critical consequences for political theology therefore flow into the impossibility of turning to politics or anthropology:

> What theology deals with is the project of an instance that can *neither* be anthropologized *nor* politicized: God is not friend of anyone, nor an enemy of anyone. And yet it is precisely for this reason that you pull it, to pull it to one side or the other, to occupy the artefact of precarious balance.
> *(Blumenberg & Schmitt, 2007, p. 226)*

At its peak, the dualism instigated by the absolute makes visible the 'asymmetry of the products: the enemy is not the antagonist of the friend, the political is not, in complete disjunction, the negation of the anthropological' (ibid.). Neglecting to consider the anthropogenetic dimension of kinship, to which friendship refers – in linguistic terms, the friend is equated with the relative (*Blutsverwandten*) and therefore chosen in a 'very narrow context' – one ends up losing sight of the public dimension to which instead the 'political' refers and to which the 'private' is opposed. And this conflation will be subjected to a critique analogous to the contemporary – 'not by chance' – Heideggerian 'analytic-existential dualism of the single life, articulated in authenticity-inauthenticity'; as in that, in fact, in the 'friend-enemy dualism of which Carl Schmitt speaks in the *Concept of the Political* [*Begriff des Politischen*] ... one *is existentially something other* than the other' (ibid.).

Gestures, myths, explosive metaphors

Bringing them together under the common denominator of 'gestures of the loss of reality [*Wirklichkeitsverlust*]' to the gesture of Edmund Husserl noted by Helmuth Plessner, who in extending his walking stick 'in an unsurpassable vivid manner ... represented the intentional act', (Blumenberg, 2010 [1987], p. 35), Blumenberg captures the aporias of the philosophy of life in stylized form in Simmel's gestures described by his student Ludwig Marcuse. The gestures 'accompanied what was said and almost unnoticeably marked the secret wish to communicate something not yet expressed' (Blumenberg, 2010 [1987], p. 33). Specifically, the philosopher is remembered as he holds lectures, as if from that situation we could see revealed something of the tension that is already implicit in the concept of such a philosophy, through two gestures 'that should be imagined in relation to each other'. The first consists of 'how he, bobbing up and down on the exposed side of the lectern, drilled the sharpened pencil into the air – into an invisible matter, as it were', interpreted by Marcuse as 'the gesture of the passionate analytical thinker'. The second gesture, which is considered most important, is thus outlined:

> he left the exposed edge of the lectern; the outstretched pencil pointed sunk between his fingers; and with his head lowered he silently crossed back to the other side of the lectern – until he got a grip on himself and was able to continue the lecture.

Moreover, commented by Marcuse, observing that: 'In this silent second of forgetting himself, he inwardly annulled what he had just investigated' (ibid.). In turn, Blumenberg comments squarely:

> Simmel's many readers all recognize this turning point in so many of his arguments, when he goes beyond the supposedly last attainable formulation, observes the results he just produced on the counter-pole of possibilities and relativizes it. It was the same in the live performance of the teacher: he left behind what has just been but could only silently promise how to go beyond .
>
> *(Blumenberg, 2010 [1987], p. 34)*

We are also faced with 'the "immeasurable tragedy" of philosophical thinking' which invests both the philosopher and the philosophical enterprise that crosses it, questioning the relationship between theory and empirical reality and at the same time exposing its generative oscillation:

> he appears to be condemned to 'fall into his own arms' in order to prevent himself from exhausting his logical consistency. Simmel's thought process seems to be able to become optically perceptible: one saw his pleasure in analysis even in the thin air of the most subtle reality [*subtilster Realität*] or of what is no longer reality [*Nicht-mehr-Realität*], a reality that therefore could be cruelly and inconsiderately yanked back to the ground of empirical facts. Therefore, before he became

a '*Lebensphilosoph* [life philosopher]', Simmel has tested himself with the philosophy of a topic that offers some of the greatest resistance to thought: the philosophy of money.

(Blumenberg, 2010 [1987], p. 34)[8]

In the analysis of the mythical figure of Sisyphus, from the point of view of the elaboration of myth, Blumenberg evokes the Simmelian definition of 'significance' (*Bedeutsamkeit*) in connection with the dimension of value in the *Philosophy of money*:

> Objects are not difficult to acquire because they are valuable, but we call those objects valuable that resist our desire to possess them. Since the desire encounters resistance and frustration, the objects gain a significance that would never been attributed to them by an unchecked will.
>
> *(Simmel, 1978 [1900], p. 67)*

Thus, Blumenberg comments, the value is 'a specific functional form of significance', as it tends to the 'objectification of the comparison' and thus of the 'possibility of exchange', without ever entirely giving up 'the subjective element that is contained in the "felt" value of something that is desired' (Blumenberg, 1985 [1979], p. 76). Therefore Sisyphus is read in *Work on Myth* as a 'mythical figure of futility [or uselessness: *Vergeblichkeit*]' in which we could grasp even at a late date, 'and perhaps only then', 'the importance of not being occupied and possessed by reality only, and only by a single reality at that' (ibid.). Still in the analysis of the myth, Blumenberg notes that significance is 'a defence against indifference' and becomes 'a resistance to the tendency toward a condition of higher probability – of diffusion, of erosion, of entropy'. And from this comes the role that it acquires in the philosophy of life, or 'it portrays life as the self-assertion of reality that resists probability' (Blumenberg, 1985 [1979], p. 109). As well as the possibility of defining it as 'the form in which the background of nothing [*des Nichts*], as that which produces anxiety, has been put at a distance, whereby, without this "prehistory," the function of what is significant remains uncomprehended, though present' (Blumenberg, 1985 [1979], p. 110).

The use of 'explosive metaphorics' (*Sprengmetaphorik*) in Simmel is also placed at the boundary between 'expressibility and inexpressibility'. Where, for example, in an annotation of his posthumous *Diary* he takes up the *via negationis* of Cusano to connote the Nietzschean concept of 'eternal return of the same':

> the world process seems to me like the turning of an enormous wheel – in the way, to be sure, that is presupposed by the eternal return. Not however with the same result – that at some point the same thing really repeats itself; for the wheel has an infinitely large radius.
>
> *(Blumenberg, 1996 [1979], p. 91)*[9]

Or, in the form of a misunderstanding, in the case of the Kantian conception of freedom 'as a necessary presupposition of reason', in which one can recognize the 'danger of using an absolute metaphorics' and nothing has been gained by learning that 'the synthesis of the representations itself is "already" an action of the understanding': 'this misunderstanding ... already plays a role in Simmel's much-admired interpretation of Kant and subsequently in his attempt, in his philosophy of history, to derive arguments against deterministic historicism from it' (Blumenberg, 1996 [1979], p. 101 f.). However, observes Bumenberg, the 'human beings' would make their history freely, or more freely, because the synthesis of their representations is an 'action of their understanding': 'this is just the misleading effect of an absolute metaphor that has been taken literally' (Blumenberg, 1996 [1979], p. 102).

Anthropological rhetoric and nonconceptuality

Blumenberg had also referred to Simmel's thought to clarify, in his *Anthropological approach to the actuality of rhetoric* (1987 [1971]), the characteristics of the persuasion in opposition to the oppression, given that the former presupposes that 'one shares a horizon' (which is not given in the relationship with the barbarians, where the use of force prevails), as well as the 'allusions to prototypical material, and the orientation to the metaphor, to the similitude [*an der Metapher, am Gleichnis*]' (Blumenberg, 1987 [1971], p. 436). In particular, according to Simmel, the metaphor of 'roles' is so productive because 'life is "an early form of the dramatic art"' and these metaphors

> no longer having to do with the implication that it is a question of illusion, of a theatrical double life, with and without masks, with and without costume, so that one would only need to expose the stage and the actors in order to catch sight of the reality and put an end with the theatrical intermezzo.
>
> *(Blumenberg, 1987 [1971], p. 442)*

In fact, Blumenberg comments: 'the "life" of which Simmel speaks is not only incidentally and episodically an "early form" of the dramatic art; rather, "being able to live" and "define a role for oneself" are identical' (ibid.). And he adds, in the first person:

> I assert that not only is this discourse of 'roles' metaphorical, but the process of definition that goes with the role concept – a process upon which the conscious-ness of identity depends, and which it can be damaged – is itself rooted in meta-phor and is asserted and defended, both internally and externally by metaphor.
>
> *(ibid.)*

He argues this way that:

> the 'agreement' that has to be the goal of all 'persuasion' ... is the congruence – which is endangered in all situation and always has to be secured afresh – between one's role consciousness and the role expectations that others have of one.
>
> *(ibid.)*

It can be noticed that Simmel converges in Blumenberg's reading also on the reflection that identifies an autonomous space for nonconceptuality (*Unbegrifflichkeit*) and leads to the impossibility of reducing the figural and metaphorical dimension to a simple auxiliary and temporary construction on the path of logical-conceptual reduction. Already with money 'the generality and lack of content' become a 'real power', 'whose relation to all the con-trary qualities of the objects transacted and to their psychological constellations can be equally interpreted as service and as domination', thus unfolding a lucid analysis of the power of abstraction, as the 'tragedy of human concept formation', or the process by which 'the higher concept, which through its breadth embraces a growing number of details, must count upon an increasing loss of content' (Simmel, 1978 [1900], p. 220). The metaphor is then brought to completion in the concept of life, as has been mentioned, through abstraction from the 'fact of finitude of individual lives' and its assumption as a hypostasis of a 'substance', which in such lives manifests itself only on the surface (Blumenberg, 2012 [1974], p. 261). Until the crudeness of the disenchantment with which Simmel compares the fruit of his life, his spiritual heritage, to the cash money divided among his many heirs, 'of which each invests his own part in a manner consistent with his nature, without being interested in the origin of that inheritance' (Simmel, 1923a, p. 261). It will be precisely the elaboration of a 'theory of nonconceptuality' – which became accessible only in relatively recent times but was composed by Blumenberg in the same years as the essay on Simmel – to point out as the 'ancient unspeakable', the 'individuum ineffable', does not coincide at all with 'the linguistically indescribable or with the unnameable', but to be identified, 'precisely because it is readable in the individuum', with 'the unattainable through the concept as correlate of the substance' (Blumenberg, 2007, p. 134), not without returning to the 'abstract conjunction of the concept and the negation' operated by Simmel and on the 'union of the functions of the concept and of the metaphor where there is an overflowing increase of the negation in the metaphor' connected to it (Blumenberg, 2007, p. 103). Compared to Schopenhauer, a general reference term for Simmel's conception of abstraction itself, it will also be pointed out that the concept is not a 'surrogate' nor a 'fulfilment' of reason, understood as 'reduced, abstract, colourless, mathematical plant of the whole world', but it is a 'gap open' for the intentions of reason itself and, *anthropogenetically*, its origin will be sought in human being as 'the being that orients, abandons the surrounding environment of perception and goes beyond the horizon of his senses, being characterized by the *actio per distans*' (Blumenberg, 2007, p. 9). It is referring to the 'luxurious' constitution of human beings, however, that operates the metaphor, removing the lack of 'being lacking' from the 'bottom of a surplus', from the 'exaggeration beyond the horizon of the necessities of life', as this horizon, 'separates possibility and reality':

> the metaphor joins the primary habit of referring to reality and the secondary one of referring to possibility: said even more formally, the metaphor is the instrument of a world of expanding relationships that has abandoned the not necessary regulations to the language and the biological mechanisms of the environment, and that in the meantime has become accustomed to the obvious and usual institutions of the lifeworld.
>
> *(Blumenberg, 2007, p. 116)*

Antinomicity, philosophy of life and aesthetics

Moreover, in Blumenberg's book *Care crosses the river* (*Die Sorge geht über den Fluß*, 2010 [1987]) Simmel is still evoked with regard to the nautical metaphor, with which, in 1912 responding to the letter of Marianne Weber to whom he dedicated his book on Goethe, he defines the new horizon of his own work and, with it, the relationship between the individual life and the stream or current of the life. The book represents, in fact, the conclusion of an entire phase of his work and it is now time to orientate elsewhere: 'Here a gesture of great self-confidence commences: "Now I tack my sail and seek untrodden land" ... "Admittedly, the journey will certainly come to an end before it reaches the coast"' (Blumenberg, 2010 [1987], p. 85). This is followed by Blumenberg's comment:

Andrea Borsari

Life offers life no other chance than that of the fragment one possibility to life, that of the fragment. Life's contingency reveals shows what the individual and its finitude are all about: a life ends, life goes on – there are no arrival on the shores of the *terra incognita*.

(ibid.)

And Blumenberg adds:

Simmel oriented himself by means of the metaphor of flowing life developed by Bergson. He doesn't put to sea, he doesn't arrive; he only changes the direction of the sail – he has always been on the high seas. ... There will be no harbour, but also no island where one could shipwreck before reaching the goal.

(Blumenberg, 2010 [1987], p. 86)

Misfortune mates, 'comrades' who believe they can 'make themselves at home on the ship so that they ultimately think that the ship itself is the new land' are wrong, because in this way they misunderstand the situation and while making claims to a system, they always want a totality (ibid.). The alternative, 'if the ship does not have to become a house', can only be death – 'there is no doubt that Simmel is thinking about death' – as an 'indispensable complement to the philosophy of life':

life can only preserve itself through the death of each of its 'delegates', none of whom have a claim *to be* it, only to take part in it – the final *methexis* [participation] in the remnant of all ideas, the end of Platonism in the nonconcept of 'life'. One has to die on board.

(ibid.)

It must be clear, Blumenberg specifies, that this 'imply neither a longing for death desire nor a death drive', as it represents instead 'an unwillingness towards every new totality, uneasiness with unities of the type that Gestalt-theory or the systematics of symbolic forms had to offer or intended to offer'. Therefore,

'life' gives itself form and shape [*Form und Gestalt*] but not without the proviso of taking it back, of melting it down [*Vorbehalt der Zurücknahme, der Einschmelzung*], as if the supply of substance is too meagre to be able to leave it at what already exists. As the author of the *Philosophy of Money* knows, death is an economy of life, of the substance that is always and essentially in too short a supply.

(Blumenberg, 2010 [1987], p. 86)

When he investigates the indefiniteness of the concept of life in the genesis of the theory of the lifeworld (*Theorie der Lebenswelt*, 2010) and through the passage that, as the Simmelian formulation at the conclusion of his *Rembrandt* indicates, leads from the philosophy of life to the philosophy of existence, it appears clear to Blumenberg that at stake here is a sort of 'reoccupation' (*Umbesetzung*) of positions from 'metaphoric' to 'metaphysical' and therefore that the concept of 'life in an absolute sense' already in Simmel's *Rembrandt* appears as 'no more in some kind of contrast with the form, but it arises as itself, with its own form linked only to itself and inseparable from itself' (Blumenberg, 2010, p. 20 f.).[10]

If we assume a conception of the aesthetics that includes both the philosophical reflection on art and the wider perceptive-sensitive relationship with the world, that it is precisely the work of Georg Simmel that may have first authorized to think in its entirety, it becomes possible to choose some samples of the Simmelian work as an illustration and specification of his anthropological approach in the aesthetic field, in accordance with Blumenberg's reading.[11]

Starting from the human performance of joining and separating on which the powerful Simmelian metaphorical field of the bridge and the door is concentrated, one can examine them in the light of their congruence with those that are defined as specifically human performances: 'Only the human being in front of nature has the ability to unite and divide, thanks to this way of proceeding on the basis of which everything is always the presupposition of the other' (Simmel, 1909, p. 55). In the anthropological perspective of the genesis of the specifically human ('the human performance *as* human performance'), in fact, we get to circumscribe the gradient of an 'image of the border point [*Bilde des Grenzpunktes*] of man', superior to the indifference of direction contained in the conjunction of two points of the bridge, as 'the richest and most vital meaning' of the door, 'life outside of the limitations of a being per se isolated towards the unlimited' and 'complete difference of intention' between entering and going out (Simmel, 1909, p. 58). What it 'makes sensible', which confers a sensitive configuration without reducing it to a conceptual abstraction, is the character of the human being (*Mensch*) as a 'boundary being that has no boundaries' (Simmel, 1909, p. 60). With the twofold rejection of the *actor*'s task as a mere actualization of a text and as an imitative mechanical transposition of reality, we then grasp an 'actorial aptitude' (*schauspielerische Attitude*) which accompanies human beings in their unitary 'being-so' world and makes the 'role' a Goethean 'original or primary phenomenon' (*Urphänomen*) that offers a sensitive configuration – visible and audible – to the elements of life through performing (Simmel, 1912, p. 314) and approximates the 'essence of art' as an elaboration in a form of the 'contents of the existence' to reach the single unit (Simmel, 1912, p. 309). In this approach to the relationship between actor and reality, the underlying motif of the Simmelian critique of the *naturalistic* posture in the theory of art is also highlighted, which makes the work entirely dependent on its '*terminus a quo*' in the reality and neglects the creative efficacy of the artist capable of building worlds and objectifying an autonomous 'third' between contents and people (Simmel, 1923b, pp. 229, 240).

On the other hand, it shows all the limits of abstraction and rationalism calculating the purism of the *art pour l'art* which escapes the organic connection between the elements and the whole of life, with respect to which the work of art constitutes an indirect way towards and through the whole, while the artistic point of view is constantly stimulated by the contradiction between the need to consider this work 'a world of its own' and the need to see it as 'a wave in the current of life' (Simmel, 1914, p. 15). To the polarity between individual and universal, between the common and generalizing power, on the one hand, and the capacity of singular concretion in image, on the other hand, it is also possible to bring back the notion of style, in the midst of the First World War also bent on servicing a clash of cultures, which reflects this opposition to the outside, where it fully embodies the pole of the universal in the double sense of 'typical-abstract' and 'social being' (Simmel, 1918, p. 318), and to its own interior, as a unifying individual style, a 'particular and individual expression of life', since, as Simmel had written in the capital text on the subject, 'style is a principle of generality, with which the principle of individuality or is mixed, or removes or represents it' (Simmel, 1908a, p. 376). The less the work of art draws on the 'timeless compactness of the life result of the in itself satisfied phenomenal form', and instead leads to expression 'the progress of life itself as it continually regenerates itself on the impulse of its own drive forces' (Simmel, 1918, p. 319), the more it moves away from the polarity of the style and ends up asserting itself 'beyond beauty', as in the exemplary case of Rembrandt, where we do not find any 'abstractable [*abstrahierbares*] scheme that transcends individual entities' and 'every image has only its form' (Simmel, 1918, p. 315). Finally, an analogous law of contrast with relative 'dialectics without conciliation' (Landmann, 1968, p. 16) is the sphere of normativity, declined as an 'individual law' of no less normative force and rigour than the universal and composed starting from a parallel of ethics and aesthetics, according to which 'only the individual unitary whole of my life can determine how I should behave', just as 'only the work of art can be a law unto itself' (Simmel, 1917–18, pp. 387, 386). While the general concepts are able to grasp only 'isolated *contents*' (Simmel, 1917–18, p. 386), from the reciprocal normative efficacy that the parts of a work of art exercise on each other results in the objectification of an individual configuration in which idea and law tend to coincide in actual reality, still in connection with the Goethean sense of the primary or original phenomenon (*Urphänomen*) as the convergence of theory and phenomenon and with the sensible rendering of something otherwise abstract.

In conclusion, it is possible to focus through the essays here considered on some of the main points that mark, also in the aesthetic-anthropological field, an insistent prefer-ence for aporetic solutions and against 'the prejudice according to which all conflicts and problems are there to be resolved' (Simmel, 1918b, p. 207). It also becomes possible to bring them back to that inclination to let the 'antinomies' subsist, in accordance with the everyday attitude of the life world (Ritter, 1974, p. 16), precisely to a sort of 'law of contrast', which is itself taken as a constitutive element of the Simmelian cognitive enterprise.[12] An antinomic propensity that in turn ends up bringing us back to the long-term *instance* that animated Hans Blumenberg's research as an 'anthropological antinomy' and that in the form of a reconstructive hypothesis of Georg Simmel's thought on philo-sophical anthropology provided the perspective from which to carry out this reappraisal.

Still conclusively, it also becomes possible to ask whether the reconstruction proposed here of the various tangential points to the recognition of a Simmel anthropologist in the work of Hans Blumenberg has arrived at a definition that justifies the attribution of having contained the nucleus of a philosophical anthropology that could have been better than those that would later be followed with this denomination. If Blumenberg has taken up the acquisitions of Alsberg, Gehlen and Plessner at various points (see Fischer, 2008, pp. 435-441), there is no doubt that the emphasis he places on the Simmelian anthropological elem-ents circumscribed here is aimed at delineating and tends to coincide with at least a part of the contribution by Blumenberg himself to an innovative philosophical anthropology. Sum-ming up, in fact, he insists on the relation between elementary tropisms and life forms in metaphorology, on the possible redescriptions of anthropogenesis by virtue of the distancing through sight, gaze, face and the ability to transpose into another through the imagination, like anthropological countermoves to cope contingency. He also insists on the bodily rela-tionship between the empirical level and the theoretical level with its articulations in the gestural sphere of the connection with reality, in mythical occurrences and explosive meta-phors, on the critique of the conflating – and therefore barbaric – genesis of the anthropo-logical and historical plans of the distinction friend-enemy, as well as on the relationship between persuasion and apprehension that arises from an anthropological approach to rhet-oric and from the revaluation of the figural dimension of nonconceptuality. If, more gener-ally, this vision leads to the overthrow of the usual conception of a lacking being in a wealthy one, i.e. in a luxurious constitution, and to the construction of anthropology starting from the permanence of force fields produced by the tension of antinomic terms, it seems possible to affirm, finally, that this second level and relational dimension, full of possibilities and that emphasizes the possible, represents the original way to remove anthropology from any essentialism and, at the same time, the distinctive and peculiar legacy of the Simmelian lesson for Blumenberg in view of an anthropology that could have been and that he tried on his own.

Notes

1 All quotations from texts written in languages other than English, if not referring to a printed translation, are in author's translation.
2 See, at least, Borsari (1999), Heidenreich (2005), Klein (2009), Müller (2005), Trierweiler (2010), Moxter (2011).
3 See Blumenberg (2006) and Borsari (2010).
4 As Blumenberg explains, the *Philosophy of Money*: 'is one of the few written after Nietzsche that belongs (or will turn out to belong) in the canon', Blumenberg, 2012 [1974], p. 258).
5 On Blumenberg's interpretation, see Krech (1993, pp. 6, 9-12), who identifies the development of an anthropology in Simmel's passage from money to life.
6 Under the title of 'consolation', Blumenberg repeats almost literary the Simmelian aphorism of the posthumous *Diary* ('The human is a being in search of consolation', Simmel, 1923a, p. 272 [*Der Mensch ist ein trostsuchendes Wesen*]): 'Humans are creatures in need of consolation' (Blumenberg, 2010 [1987], p. 106 [*Der Mensch ist ein trostbedürfiges Wesen*]).
7 In his *Die Sorge geht über den Fluß*, Blumenberg had marked as barbarism the lack of consideration of the detour or indirect way (the 'full use [*Ausschöpfung*] of the world' is only 'a side benefit' of the 'culture of detours'): 'In the strictness of its exclusions, the supposed "art of living" that takes the shortest routes, is barbarism' (Blumenberg, 2010 [1987], p. 96).
8 See Jürgen Habermas for whom Blumenberg's propensity for anecdotes reveals a literary model that includes the rooting of the theory in the lifeworld and in a contextualizing way tries to discover the truth in the metaphorical nature of the story, and who suggests that 'Blumenberg's inclination to the anecdotal betrays a literary model, perhaps Georg Simmel' (Habermas, 1992, p. 225). On the close link between the interest in the anthropological dimension and its anecdotal interpretation, see Zill (2014, p. 39) et seq. On gestures in Simmel, see Waizbort (2000, p. 582-588).
9 Here Blumenberg is quoting Simmel (1923a, p. 263).
10 Here Blumenberg is quoting Simmel (1916, p. 510). See also Blumenberg (2010, p. 124-125).
11 For a recapitulation of the studies on Simmel's aesthetic, see Meyer (2017).
12 For the development of this perspective, see Borsari (2018).

References

Blumenberg, H. (1985 [1979]). *Work on myth*. Trans. R. M. Wallace. Cambridge: MIT Press.
Blumenberg, H. (1987 [1971]). An anthropological approach to the contemporary significance of rhetoric. Trans. R. M. Wallace. In K. Baynes, J. Bohman & Th. McCarthy (Eds.), *After philosophy: End or transformation?* (pp. 429–458). Cambridge: MIT Press.
Blumenberg, H. (1989). *Höhlenausgänge*. Frankfurt am Main: Suhrkamp.
Blumenberg, H. (1996 [1979]). Prospect for a theory of nonconceptuality. Trans. S. Rendall. In H. Blumenberg (Eds.), *Shipwreck with spectator: Paradigm of a metaphor for existence* (pp. 81–102). Cambridge: MIT Press.
Blumenberg, H. (2006). *Beschreibung des Menschen*, Ed. by M. Sommer. Frankfurt am Main: Suhrkamp.
Blumenberg, H. (2007). *Theorie der Unbegrifflichkeit*. Frankfurt am Main: Suhrkamp.
Blumenberg, H. (2010). *Theorie der Lebenswelt*, Ed. by M. Sommer. Frankfurt am Main: Suhrkamp.
Blumenberg, H. (2010 [1987]). *Care Crosses the River*. Trans. P. Fleming. Stanford: Stanford University Press.
Blumenberg, H. (2012 [1974]). Money or life: Metaphors of Georg Simmel's philosophy, Trans. R. Savage. *Theory, Culture and Society*, *29*(7–8), 249–262.

Blumenberg, H., & Schmitt, C. (2007). *Briefwechsel 1971–1978 und weitere Materialen*, Ed. and with a postface by A. Schmitz and M. Lepper. Frankfurt am Main: Suhrkamp.

Borsari, A. (1999). *L'«antinomia antropologica». Realtà, mondo e cultura in Hans Blumenberg* [The 'anthropological antinomy': Reality, world and culture in Hans Blumenberg]. In A. Borsari (Ed.), *Hans Blumenberg. Mito, metafora, modernità* (pp. 341–418). Bologna: Il Mulino.

Borsari, A. (2010). *Il Simmel antropologo della* Beschreibung*: una noterella* [The anthropologist Simmel in Blumenberg's *Description of man*: A short note]. In D. Giordano & A. Fragio (Eds.), *Hans Blumenberg. Nuovi paradigmi di analisi* (pp. 323–327). Roma: Aracne.

Borsari, A. (2018). *Aisthesis, esposizioni e istantanee* [Perception, exibitions, snapshots] – *Georg Simmel*. In A. Borsari, *Mondo, cose, immagini. Sulle forme dell'esperienza estetica* (pp. 101–135). Bologna: Bononia University Press.

Fischer, J. (2008). *Philosophische Anthropologie. Eine Denkrichtung des 20. Jahrhunderts.* Freiburg and München: Alber.

Habermas, J. (1992). *Postmetaphysical thinking: Philosophical essays.* Transl. W. M. Hohengarten. Cambridge: Polity Press.

Heidenreich, F. (2005). *Mensch und Moderne bei Hans Blumenberg.* München: W. Fink.

Klein, R. A. (Ed.). (2009). *Auf Distanz zur Natur. Philosophische und theologische Perspektiven in Hans Blumenbergs Anthropologie.* Würzburg: Königshausen & Neumann.

Krech, V. (1993). 'Geld oder Leben' oder 'Geld zum Leben'. Anmerkungen zu zwei Rezeptionsvarianten der Philosophie des Geldes. *Simmel Newsletter, 3*(2), 174–179.

Landmann, M. (1968). Einleitung des Herausgebers. In G. Simmel, *Das individuelle Gesetz. Philosophische Exkurse* (pp. 7–29), Ed. by M. Landmann. Frankfurt am Main: Suhrkamp.

Meyer, I. (2008). 'Jenseits der Schönheit'. Simmels Ästhetik – originärer Eklektizismus? In G. Simmel, *Jenseits der Schönheit. Schriften zur Ästhetik und Kunstphilosophie* (pp. 399–437), Ed. and with a postface by I. Meyer. Frankfurt am Main: Suhrkamp.

Meyer, I. (2017). *Georg Simmels Ästhetik. Autonomiepostulat und soziologische Referenz.* Weilerswist: Velbrück Wissenschaft.

Moxter, M. (Ed.). (2011). *Erinnerung an das Humane. Beiträge zur phänomenologischen Anthropologie Hans Blumenbergs.* Tübingen: Mohr Siebeck.

Müller, O. (2005). *Sorge um die Vernunft. Hans Blumenbergs phänomenologische Anthropologie.* Paderborn: Mentis.

Ritter, H. (1974). Contribution to the discussion (*Aus der Diskussion*) to M. Landmann, *Georg Simmel: Konturen seines Denkens*. In H. Böhringer & K. Gründer (Eds.), *Ästhetik und Soziologie um die Jahrhundertwende: Georg Simmel* (pp. 12–17). Frankfurt am Main: V. Klostermann.

Simmel, G. (1908a). Das Problem des Stiles. In G. Simmel (1993). *Gesamtausgabe, 8, Aufsätze und Abhandlungen 1901–1908*, vol. II (pp. 374–384), Ed. by A. Cavalli & V. Krech. Frankfurt am Main: Suhrkamp.

Simmel, G. (1908b). Soziologie. Untersuchungen über die Formen der Vergesellschaftung. In G. Simmel (1992). *Gesamtausgabe, 11*, Ed. by O. Rammstedt. Frankfurt am Main: Suhrkamp.

Simmel, G. (1909). Brücke und Tür. In G. Simmel (2001). *Gesamtausgabe, 12, Aufsätze und Abhandlungen 1909-1918*, vol. I (pp. 55–61), Ed. by K. Latzel. Frankfurt am Main: Suhrkamp.

Simmel, G. (1912). Der Schauspieler und die Wirklichkeit. In G. Simmel (2001). *Gesamtausgabe, 12, Aufsätze und Abhandlungen 1909–1918*, vol. I (pp. 308–315), Ed. by K. Latzel. Frankfurt am Main: Suhrkamp.

Simmel, G. (1914). L'art pour l'art. In G. Simmel (2000). *Gesamtausgabe, 13, Aufsätze und Abhandlungen 1909–1918*, vol. II (pp. 9–15), Ed. by K. Latzel. Frankfurt am Main: Suhrkamp.

Simmel, G. (1916). Rembrandt. Ein kunst-philosophischer Versuch. In G. Simmel (2003). *Gesamtausgabe, 15, Goethe, Deutschlands innere Wandlung, Das Problem der historischen Zeit, Rembrandt* (pp. 305–515), Ed. by U. Kösser, H.-M. Kruckis & O. Rammstedt. Frankfurt am Main: Suhrkamp.

Simmel, G. (1917–18). Gesetzmäßigkeit im Kunstwerk. In G. Simmel (2000). *Gesamtausgabe, 13, Aufsätze und Abhandlungen 1909–1918*, vol. II (pp. 382–394), Ed. by K. Latzel. Frankfurt am Main: Suhrkamp.

Simmel, G. (1918a). Germanischer und klassisch-romanischer Stil. In G. Simmel (2000). *Gesamtausgabe, 13, Aufsätze und Abhandlungen 1909–1918*, vol. II (pp. 313–320), Ed. by K. Latzel. Frankfurt am Main: Suhrkamp.

Simmel, G. (1918b). *Der Konflikt der modernen Kultur. Ein Vortrag* (1918). In G. Simmel (1999). *Gesamtausgabe, 16* (pp. 183–207), Ed. by G. Fitzi & O. Rammstedt. Frankfurt am Main: Suhrkamp.

Simmel, G. (1918c). *Lebensanschauung. Vier metaphysische Kapitel.* München and Leipzig: Duncker & Humblot.

Simmel, G. (1923a). Aus dem nachgelassenen Tagebuche. In G. Simmel, (2004). *Gesamtausgabe, 20, Postume Veröffentlichungen. Schulpädagogik* (pp. 261–296), Ed. by T. Karlsruhen & Otthein Rammstedt. Frankfurt am Main: Suhrkamp.

Simmel, G. (1923b). Zum Problem des Naturalismus. In G. Simmel (2004). *Gesamtausgabe, 20, Postume Veröffentlichungen. Schulpädagogik* (pp. 220–248), Ed. by T. Karlsruhen & Otthein Rammstedt. Frankfurt am Main: Suhrkamp.

Simmel, G. (1978 [1900]). *The Philosophy of Money.* Trans. T. Bottomore & D. Frisby. London: Routledge.

Trierweiler, D. (Ed.). (2010). *Hans Blumenberg, anthropologie philosophique.* Paris: Presses Universitaires de France.

Waizbort, L. (2000). *As aventuras de Georg Simmel.* São Paulo: Editora 34.

Zill, R. (2014). Anekdote. In R. Buch & D. Weidner (Eds.), *Blumenberg lesen. Ein Glossar* (pp. 26–42). Frankfurt am Main: Suhrkamp.

9

SIMMEL'S 'LATE LIFE METAPHYSICS'

Gregor Fitzi

Philosophy in times of complex societies

In the introductory chapter of *Soziologie* in 1908, Simmel formulates in unequivocal terms the answer to the question of how a philosophy may be possible under the terms of the human condition in modernity. The quantity and quality of social relationships, which individuals are compelled to entertain in complex societies, change their way of life so dramatically that the assessment of every issue concerning humanity has to be grounded on a theory of society (GSG 11, p. 13 f.). Consequently, any kind of philosophical anthropology in the classical sense is no longer practicable, unless it takes the form of a sociology of human life. The classical philosophical questions of epistemology, ethics, social and political philosophy, yet also of aesthetics, and cultural theory must be faced from a renewed viewpoint. As Marx had argued before with regard to the economic production process, the underlying conditions of life had changed in an irreversible way through the political and industrial revolutions of the late eighteenth century (Marx, 2000, pp. 46-63). Yet, for Simmel the change to the structure of society, as well as the fragmentation of agency in modern times, applied to every domain of qualitative differentiated societies, and not only to the economy (GSG 5, pp. 560-582).

Simmel's entire *oeuvre* can be regarded as an effort of theory-building that is dedicated to the task of understanding the classical philosophical questions in the light of the ongoing transformation of society. He developed an epistemology, a critical theory of culture, an anthropology, a social ethics, and an aesthetics, which take into account the modification of the basic conditions of human life in modern society (Fitzi, 2019). For the interpreter of Simmel's work the task is thus, on the one hand, to understand which are the elements of this theoretical effort, and, on the other hand, to explain its philosophical meaning. Philosophy can no longer be grounded on the traditional philosophical dichotomies between subject and object, identity and diversity, tradition and progress, deontology and libertinism or community and society (GSG 14, pp. 7-157). Modernity is always an ambiguous mixture of these different 'phenomenal occurrences of reality', so that its development can only be grasped by analysing their points of intersection (GSG 14, pp. 159-459). Accordingly, theory must develop an analysis of the reciprocal action between subjective and objective spirit in order to develop a *Realphilosophie* of the existing and steadily changing world (GSG 6, pp. 617-654).

From the beginning of his academic career, Simmel engaged in a series of research projects on social differentiation, monetarisation, culture reification, urbanisation, neurasthenia, fashion, and women emancipation. This analytical work 'on the concept' delivered two major results. On the one hand, it reconstructed the framework of modern culture and society, that is, of the conditions of the possibility of human life in complex societies. Yet, on the other hand, these sociological researches profoundly modified Simmel's epistemological and philosophical positions. In modernity, individuals are compelled to manage an increasing number of social relationships that are related to the different social circles in which they participate. Accordingly, their personality becomes strongly fragmented in manifold facets that follow the logic of the different reified domains of society (GSG 2, pp. 169-198). The coordination of the different streams of social activity and the attempt to make sense of what Weber called a 'conduct of life' thus becomes increasingly complex (Weber, 1992; GSG 11, p. 59). In modern qualitative differentiated societies, alienation thus affects individuals not only as members of the capitalist production process but also in every other societal domain. The individual's personality as well as the social relationships face an increased rhythm and acceleration of social life, which establish an entropy for the subjects of social action, be they individual or collective (GSG 6, p. 696 f.). Furthermore, modernity implies a multiplication of random social contacts, which individuals have with the mobile mass of their peers, yet without accessing the spatiotemporal resources to rationalise and stabilise these latent social relationships. The result is an increasing passivity towards the reified structures of social interaction due to the need to neutralise the emotional impact, the intensity, and the acceleration of social life.

These are the theses of Simmel's study on monetary economy, *The Philosophy of Money* (GSG 6), which he resumed in the renowned study on the 'The Metropolis and Mental Life' (GSG 7, pp. 116-131). Here the meaning of Simmel's philosophical research programme to face modernity by developing social science comes clearly to the fore. The shifting spatial distance between individuals in urbanised societies induces an intensified production of symbolic social distance that becomes a major instrument for regulating social relationship. A process of stereotypisation gains the upper hand and easily leads to the development of reductive and prejudicial images of the other, because the interaction partners are diminished to the function that they are supposed to play in a particular social setting (GSG 11, p. 47). The formation of structured social relationship, in which individuals invest themselves in a more comprehensive way, is hindered by the accelerated rhythm of social interaction. Increasingly, the social fabric develops an 'intermittent character', so that individuals avoid investing energies in particular configurations of the social order and tend to adapt passively to their ongoing change. Accordingly, the question arises as to how an epistemological research project, which does not want to capitulate in view of the complexity of modern society, can give a theoretical account of these 'deep transnormative condition' of social life (Fitzi, 2015).

In the epistemological debate of the second part of the nineteenth century from Auguste Comte to Edmund Husserl, the ongoing fragmentation of society is perceived as a specialisation and loss of unity of modern sciences. Knowledge seems to take shape by simply following the autonomous logic of the different qualitative differentiated domains of science, so that a unitary conception of knowledge, or 'philosophy' in Simmel's definition, becomes impossible (GSG 14, pp. 7-157). The great efforts to grant a synthesis of the whole of human knowledge, which characterised the research projects of Transcendental Philosophy and German Idealism, look like shadows of a lost age. In 1883 Dilthey formulated his influential answer to the question of a philosophical foundation for the modern sciences - especially for the fast-paced emergence of the human, historical and social sciences - in the form of a programme for the 'grounding of a science of society and history'. A chronological assessment of Simmel's publications reveals that he consistently attempted to achieve Dilthey's desideratum of research. Yet his engagement with this question also led him to a significant epistemological turn, as the comparison between the two editions of the *The Problems of the Philosophy of History* demonstrates (GSG 2, pp. 297-421; GSG 9, pp. 227-419).

The epistemological challenge of a 'science of society and history' became to understand how socio-historical reality is produced by human agency and conversely how its institutionalised structures act back on it. By enquiring into this topic, Simmel realised a momentous epistemological finding, as he relates in the excursus on 'How is society possible?' for the introductory chapter of *Soziologie* (GSG 11, pp. 42-61). In contradistinction to the knowledge process, which produces the human image of nature, in the social sciences researchers do not first integrate the basic elements of their perception of reality into a synthesis of knowledge. The scrutiny of sociocultural reality deals with contents that are already the product of a synthetic process of knowledge *between* the social actors. This allows for formulating a distinction between natural and sociocultural sciences, which avoids the ontological and psychology-led traps that characterised the debate about the 'sciences of the spirit' between Dilthey, Rickert and Windelband (Dilthey, 1883; Rickert, 1896–1902; Windelband, [1894] 1924).

According to Simmel, the difference between natural and socio-historical reality depends on the fact that 'nature', following Kant's approach, consists in a product of knowledge that an epistemic subject accomplishes by relating in a synthetic judgement the objective contents of its perception of reality. In contrast, culture is the product of the socio-historically determined interaction between different human subjects. The elements of knowledge of a 'science of society and history' thus have a complex synthetic character and the epistemic subject finds them already accomplished. This makes socio-historical knowledge a metaknowledge that necessitates a completely different epistemology. An epistemology of society and history that switches from the level of inquiry into the relationship between subject and object of knowledge to that of the relationship between different subjects of knowledge, which produce socio-historical reality. Accordingly, it has to adopt the perspective of the acting individuals instead of adopting the observer perspective.

This methodological move leads to the central dilemma of 'sociological epistemology' and shows how different Simmel's answer to the question of the humanities and social sciences is in comparison to Dilthey's one. Society is an 'objective representation of subjective minds' (GSG 11, p. 41), so that in complex societies 'life does not simply comprehend life'. The cycle between expression and comprehension is mediated by an increasing social distance, an acceleration of the tempo of social life and the consequent stereotypisation of the fellow individual. Individuals do not perceive each other by means of a natural psychology, but rather through the intermediation of sociocultural forms, which continually produce images of the others as well as of the social relationships. The crucial question for sociological epistemology becomes thus how to identify the forms of sociocultural intermediation that empirically produce the complex research object of social sciences. Simmel's answer to the question is that to describe the processes of reciprocal perception, which regulate social interaction, research in the humanities and social sciences has to focus on the 'meaning' that they have for social relationships, rather than on the psychological processes that accompany them. This in turn represents the beginning of 'sociological epistemology' as an alternative answer to Dilthey's epochal question about the 'philosophical grounding of a science of society and history'.

In this perspective Kant's so-called 'analytical-regressive method' ([1783] 1968, p. 276, footnote), plays the decisive role for the development of sociological epistemology. By sorting out all the contingent aspects characterising the sociocultural shaping of inter-action, sociological epistemology methodologically traces back the most basic 'conditions a priori' that every social interaction presupposes. The discussion of the three sociological a priori - which Simmel presents in the excursus on 'How is society possible?' - consti-tutes the result of this research programme (GSG 11, pp. 42-61). Sociology becomes the 'science of society and history' that deals with the tension-fraught encounter between the incompatible logics of social action and social structure and describes its manifold culturally mediated forms, permitting the existence of socio-historical reality as an 'objective represen-tation of subjective minds'. Based on the results of sociological epistemology, Simmel man-ages to develop a theory of 'qualitative societal differentiation', by elaborating analytically the sociocultural a priori that regulate the existence of different societal domains. The separ-ate surveys dedicated to this issue included in order of appearance: economy, law, politics, religion, art, and the erotic (Fitzi, 2019, pp. 89-122). At the end of these manifold research efforts, Simmel succeeded in relating them in an overarching theory of sociocultural activity, which characterises the human being as 'limit-setting animal', in the sense of Hegel's concept of *Tätigkeit* (Lukács, 1986).

The 'late life metaphysics'

Simmel's late work phase has conventionally been explained as a product of the intellectual vogue of life philosophy, the 'fashionable cultural phenomenon' of the *Belle Époque* that cir-culated widely in Paris and as far as Germany (Rickert, 1920). Simmel was interested in Schopenhauer's and Nietzsche's philosophy of life and wrote a monograph about their philosophical conceptions in 1907 (GSG 10, pp. 167-408). Furthermore, he played a decisive role in the introduction of Bergson's philosophy in Germany by organising an authorised translation of his works (Fitzi, 2002, pp. 195-228; GSG 13, pp. 53-69). Simmel's final book, *The view of life* (GSG 16, pp. 209-425), was a contribution to the epistemological paradigm of philosophy of life. However, it was also designed as a critique of its mono-dimensional orientation that derives all existence from the idea of the eternal flow of the stream of consciousness. Simmel presents an alternative to Bergson's conception of *durée* as being the common denominator between consciousness and the natural world (Fitzi, 2002, pp. 265-285). Instead, the common characteristic of natural, psychic, and societal life is seen in the opposition between processes that construct and dismantle life forms. Cells, organisms, psychic processes, cultural contents, and social structures rise and flourish by giving them-selves individual forms (GSG 16, pp. 222-235). Yet, there is a specific threshold where cells split, organisms reproduce themselves or die and psychic processes, cultural contents and social structures decline, or lose influence on reality, and are substituted by new ones. These intermittent processes of 'growth through form building' and 'loss of form', permitting new growth, constitute for Simmel the deepest metaphysic dimension of reality in the sense of Kant's 'grounding conditions of its possibility'.

Following Kant, philosophy had to abandon the study of the unknowable 'reality-in-itself' in favour of the inquiry into the structures a priori of the mind that determine the nature of experience, in order to establish metaphysics 'as a science' (Kant, [1783] 1968). Accordingly, Simmel developed sociological epistemology that grasped the intersubjective structures a priori of the mind that determine 'modern social experience'. Based on this achievement, 'metaphysics as a science' could not rest on a conception of the 'universal and necessary' transcendental structures of the mind, regulating human knowledge and thereby human life experience as a whole. Simmel's sociology of culture provided case studies of the a priori orienting social action in the different domains of culture that constitute modern societies (Fitzi, 2019, pp. 89-117). Manifold 'attitudes to life and the world' exist that can potentially shape the entirety of the contents of experience. Yet, the objective domains of culture evidence a strong tendency to autonomisation, develop innate logics, impose their rules on the creativity of social action, and result in a conflict between objective and subjective culture (GSG 5, pp. 560-582). Consequently, the question arises as if individuals can handle the fragmentation of their personality and overcome the reification of the social world under the societal conditions of modern life (GSG 11, pp. 42-61). This interest grounded Simmel's research programme for his so-called late life metaphysics, which started with a reflection on a sociologically well-informed philosophical anthropology (GSG 16, pp. 212-218).

Human individuals do not simply fit into the natural world, like animals, yet tear themselves away, facing nature, demanding, violating and being violated. This basic dualism of human nature gives rise to history, yet also the 'tragedy of culture' (GSG 12, pp. 194-223). In modern societies, however, no assessment is possible of anthropological issues without developing a theory of society (GSG 11, p. 13 f.), as Simmel remarked with implicit reference to Marx's critique of classical German anthropology in the theses on Feuerbach.[1] A foundation project was necessary that linked together the different strands of analysis, which Simmel provided in *Sociology* (GSG 11) and in the studies on qualitative differentiated society (Fitzi, 2019, pp. 89-117). Because of his premature death, Simmel could not advance his late research project as much as he had intended to. Yet, *The view of life* (GSG 16, pp. 209-425) gives an idea of what it had possibly become, as Kantorowicz writes in the introduction to *Fragments from the Estate* (1923; GSG 20, pp. 473-479).

The key to formulating an anthropological concept linking together the different spheres of life, lies in the interpretation of the 'limit character' *(Grenzcharakter)* of human life experience of the world, circumscribing its potentially unlimited scope (GSG 21, pp. 988-1011). This attitude requires significant efforts at shaping the relationship between opposite principles of reality, so that a mixture of formlessness and forming impetus constantly moulds human life. Accordingly, the human approach to world can be grasped only through a category appreciating the 'limit-setting attitude' that differentiates human beings from other organisms, and cannot be identified with the pure flow of 'experienced temporality', as Bergson's concept of *durée* suggests (Bergson, [1889] 1997). A life metaphysics that is aware of the cultural and societal dimension of human life in modernity must take into account that human beings steadily provide portions of the never-ending extension of their 'experienced temporality' with sociocultural forms in order to instil them with meaning (GSG 16, p. 212). This creative attitude is constitutive for human life and cannot be discarded as an expression of modern alienation, as Bergson does. Human life experience becomes meaningful within certain spatio-temporal and existential limits, whereas without any shaping it remains a meaningless flow of psychic impressions.

This is the core of Simmel's critique toward Bergson's philosophy of *durée*, whose theoretical backdrop lies in the particular way in which he transformed the terms of Kantian epistemology to develop a science of society (Fitzi, 2002, pp. 55-129; GSG 11, pp. 42-61). Individuals are not only confronted with social stereotypes (first sociological a priori) and feel that they do not seize the entirety of their individuality (second sociological a priori), but in order to participate in sociation they also need to recompose both aspects of their life experience in a synthesis that overcomes their condition of alienation (third sociological a priori). Fleeing from the dynamics of sociation to seek shelter in the intimacy of the deep flow of psychic perception (*durée*) must therefore be considered as a pathology of modernity, along with the blasé attitude, so forcing the creativity of social action to capitulate to alienation (GSG 6, p. 335 f.). Hence, the proper 'motion impulsion' of human life lies not in experienced temporality, but rather in the process of the continuous setting and overcoming of individual sociocultural limits of experience (GSG 16, p. 213). Not the unstoppable flow of temporality, but moulding life experience and constantly transgressing every limit confer on human life its motive for motion. This stance is constitutive for the anthropological difference: in contrast to the reactive, instinct-driven relationship to the environment of the animal, human beings continuously 'produce their world', by giving a meaningful shape to portions of life experience. They delimit the extension of their perception flow by producing sociocultural forms. However, they cannot rest throughout on single forms because they are conscious of their limiting character and feel the incentive to go beyond them and produce new ones in the never-ending cycle of social life's creativity.

In *The view of life* (GSG 16, pp. 209-425), Simmel aimed at founding the theoretical and methodological approach for his 'science of society and history' (GSG 16, p. 238). Thus the assessment of the manifold sociocultural a priori, enabling individuals to participate in different societal domains, flows into research about the deeper layer of preconditions that permit the rise of their manifold variety. Sociological anthropology takes the shape of a research project about the 'a priori of the a priori' of social action in the different domains of qualitative differentiated societies. If the individual objects of experience can be led back to specific conditions of possibility for experience, their sum can revert to the grounding conditions of possibility for the manifold human experience of the world. Explaining its unitary, yet equally contradictory nature, producing, dissolving, and again producing sociocultural life forms, first requests consideration of both dimensions of 'life and forms', focussing on the anthropological structure of life experience. In a second step, starting from the results of sociological anthropology, a 'general theory of life' can be developed that addresses its different manifestations and highlights the similar dynamic of producing, dissolving and again producing life forms in all biological, cultural, and societal domains of life (GSG 16, p. 222 f.).

A sociologically well-informed anthropology

As an acting animal, the 'position' (*Stellung*) of the human being towards the world is characterised by the circumstance that in every dimension of his life he finds himself caught between two opposing constraints. Accordingly, consciousness orientates itself at a formal structure of existence that is always comprehended between a before and after, back and forth, over and under, better and worse, and so on. Two rows of experience flowing in opposite directions depart from every life content, so building a system of coordinates for every aspect of life. These 'delimitations of experience' represent the means whereby human beings find their way in the infinite spatiotemporal extension of their world experience, so that they have limits always and everywhere and, therefore, also 'are limit' (GSG 16, p. 212). Accordingly, only a dynamic category of 'limit-building' permits an understanding of the human way of life as 'beings of the limit'. Nonetheless, that the human structure of life experience is grounded on its manifold temporal delimitations, represents only the first layer of Simmel's anthropological limit category. Human life experience is characterised by its dual nature of having a static and a dynamic modality that are mutually dependent, so that every single action includes a delimiting aspect and its mode of overcoming. If the existence of limits of experience is indispensable for the subsistence of human life, the individual limits are steadily overcome. Yet, every act of overcoming also implies the creation of a new limit, so that its principle is never suspended. Only because humans are conscious about their condition of being constantly delimited are they capable of overcoming single sociocultural forms that shape their life and, equally, of establishing new forms beyond them. Hence, this anthropological attitude must be considered as the origin for the 'dialectics of the cultural forms' which characterises human history (GSG 13, pp. 217-223).

To formulate his anthropological conception more precisely, Simmel develops a specific 'life-philosophical' terminology. Human life must be considered, on the one hand, as being 'more-life' because its creativity continuously endeavours to break out from its existing limits, by shaping sociocultural relationships anew. At the same time, however, human life is also 'more-than-life' because to carry out its creativity it needs to establish new sociocultural forms whereby it can pursue it goals. Therefore, human life can subsist only, if it manages to come to terms with the dynamic process of the steady creation, overcoming and renewed creation of sociocultural forms that make social action possible (GSG 16, p. 232 f.). On the basis of these theoretical arguments, Simmel could eventually extend the scheme of the sociological a priori to the theoretical paradigm of sociological anthropology and thus also to his critical conception of life philosophy by founding the unitary category of life as a synthesis between the dynamic ideas of 'more-life' and 'more-than-life'.

Life in itself is only possible as a dynamic conflict between life and form. This open-ended dialectics concerns life as an overarching concept, yet above all sociocultural life. Accordingly, in *The view of life* Simmel develops a cultural-sociological 'world-theory' that addresses the sum of the shaping forms which are capable of collecting the variety of the contents of experience under a single a priori, by giving them different meanings. Thanks to this theoretical approach, Simmel reconstructs the origins of different spheres of culture, which become autonomous societal domains, by analysing their origination from different stances of the human behaviour. They constitute the manifold human ways of 'having a world' (GSG 16, p. 236 f.). As the numerous studies in cultural sociology already showed, there are different competing logics, which are capable in principle of shaping the infinity of possible contents of experience. Yet, Simmel's sociological anthropology goes one step further: it endeavours to demonstrate that the different logics that produce competing cultural spheres correspond to the 'leading functions of consciousness' which organise the human approach to the world. The different spheres emerging through cultural work are closed in themselves; they do not allow for overlaps because their respective logic is incompatible, albeit each one tends to be capable of expressing the totality of world contents in its language. The question thus becomes how to explain their genesis.

Once the products of the creative process of social action are present, they become autonomous and join the reified domains of objective culture following a particular logic. Hence, according to its meaning, every content of consciousness 'belongs' to a different objective context with which the individual must come to terms to live in qualitative differentiated societies (GSG 16, p. 243). The affiliation of culture contents to different objective worlds appears thus to be the result of an artificial cutting out of portions of the consciousness flow in the way Bergson underlined in his analyses of experienced temporality (Bergson, [1907] 1994, p. 273). Nevertheless, individuals perceive them as 'their contents' of consciousness. A sociological anthropology must therefore reconstruct the ways in which culture contents are generated by the meaning-giving activity of social actors. They cannot be discarded as a defective development of human life. Rather, they must be explained in terms of their genesis and autonomisation process, until they become reified societal structures and claim recognition by further social action.

To this end, Simmel develops a theory of the 'anthropological preforms of culture' that characterise the human approach to the world, and assesses the sociocultural mechanisms that lead their transformation into reified cultural forms. The metaphor that he proposes to define this process is that of the 'axial rotation' (*Achsendrehung*) in the relationship between life and forms (GSG 16, p. 245). The objective cultural world emerges from cultural preforms, which were originally produced to serve the vital needs of human life. Yet, societal dynamics makes them independent to the point where they compel the latter to serve their purposes. The different domains of culture arise thanks to the manifold activity of the individuals, so that in its immediacy the single cultural contents appear in their embryonal form and strongly differ from the manifestations of the reified cultural world. Yet, the cultural functions that social life produces for its purposes gain momentum; they crystallise to autonomous cultural spheres and finally become independent. To be part of it, any further cultural product must therefore conform to the established sociocultural canons of life, so that creativity must serve extraneous purposes.

Thanks to the causal bi-directional approach of sociological anthropology, Simmel provides a theory for the ongoing institutionalisation of the societal world. Yet, he does so by revealing its deep-rootedness within the human approach to life. The function of the sociocultural institutions is regarded as being neither positive nor negative in principle, but structurally ambivalent. Human coexistence needs sociocultural forms to subsist; yet also for making possible individual self-fulfilment within society. On the one hand, sociocultural forms thus represent as many means of self-realisation both for single individuals as well as for the creativity of social action. On the other hand, however, sociocultural forms become a straitjacket for the further development of creative sociocultural forces, so that human coexistence constantly takes the form of a latent conflict and open-ended dialectic between two opposite tendencies of sociocultural life (GSG 16, pp. 181-207). Accordingly, the task of sociological anthropology is to reconstruct the embryonal preforms that permit the development and the reproduction of the various sociocultural domains such as art, religion, law, science, and so on (GSG 16, p. 245 f.).

Simmel develops an exemplary assessment of some selected 'preforms of culture', whose genesis shall be analysed, in order to explain the validity of cultural forms. Different anthropological approaches to world shape social action before the 'axial rotation' of life transforms them in reified cultural forms. In this context, science as the cultural domain of society that gains particular relevance in modernity moves to the forefront of the analysis (GSG 16, p. 256). In contrast to knowledge in general, science is only possible on condition that cognitive activity becomes independent from the immediate needs of human and societal life. Science is thus grounded on the circumstance that socially recognised methodological procedures exist, so allowing for the establishment of legitimised knowledge with which social action must comply, and implies an overturning of practical mechanisms of knowledge, which customarily lead social action (GSG 16, p. 265). Establishing the objective status of scientific truth requires a complete 'axial rotation' of the original relationship between knowledge and social action, so that social life no longer determines subjective knowledge, but rather must conform to the legitimised results of scientific research as an autonomous societal domain.

The development of technology in modern times, thus enhancing the scope of the human perception of the world beyond its biological limits, conditions a tension-fraught relationship between objective and subjective knowledge and alienates the individuals from their customary relationship to the world. The employment of technological instruments of knowledge empowers sensorial perception many times over, so that it no longer has any self-evident relationship to the biologically given context of the human experience of the world (GSG 16, p. 215). Hence, modern science and technology burst the anthropologically determined limits of life experience by enhancing objective legitimised knowledge, yet also by conferring a specific modern nuance of uncertainty on the feeling of life.[2] As a consequence, a specific sort of cultural work in the sense of the third a priori of sociation must be delivered to grant the coordination of the anthropologically determined attitude to the world with the legitimised contexts of objective scientific knowledge (GSG 11, p. 59).

What stays in the focus of the *Lebensanschauung* is once more the issue of the coordination between the objective dimension of the societal processes that is embodied in sociocultural forms and the subjective functioning of social action. Yet here the approach is to revert to sociological anthropology by concentrating on the tension-fraught relationship between the creativity of social action, which characterises the preforms of culture, and the multiplicity of the institutionalised modalities of 'owning the world' (*Welthaben*) in a qualitative differentiated society. This tension not only arises within the domains of science and technology, yet also in the remaining sociocultural spheres, including art, which for Simmel remains in an ideal-typical contrast to the natural sciences that reconstruct the world as absolute continuity, as a restless movement and as a constant flow of the world material (GSG 16, p. 266). In contrast to this view of the world produced by natural sciences, which informs Bergson's conception of experienced temporality (Bergson, [1889] 1997), for Simmel the human attitude towards the world depends on the necessity of shaping the unlimited contents of perception in different forms, by creating all the various sorts of sociocultural objects that constitute the subject matter of cultural sociology.[3] According to this acknowledgement, art must be considered as the most significant domain of culture. Thanks to the process of artistic creativity, the human attitude of 'giving form' to the world develops to its most advanced degree of perfection and becomes an end in itself. Thus the 'preforms of creativity' must be detected that give rise to the autonomous societal domain of art.

The modalities of the 'vision of the other' that develop within reciprocal social action provide the embryonal forms of the different established genres of art production. In contrast to the representation of the world in natural sciences, the 'practical vision' of everyday life breaks through the continuity of matter and highlights definite objects from the endless flow of existence (GSG 16, p. 266 f.). By assessing the modalities of the vision beyond their use in everyday praxis, one comes across the creative work of the fine arts, whose performance consists in elevating the content of sensorial perception into a persistent form. For in art it becomes an end in itself to shape and mould the contents of experience. The creative process of the fine arts can, thus, be regarded as a continuation of the natural vision process, provided that it no longer constitutes a function of the life process, but rather operates on its own to realise the purposes of artistic creativity. The artist's vision distinguishes itself because it occurs not for the sake of its content, but its form. As artistic shaping of world material, it produces perception contents, albeit only for the purposes of the creative process.

Human individuals as 'sighted beings' are as much fragmentary artists as they are embryonal scientists as subjects of knowledge. Yet, the transition from the vital preforms to the cultural forms occurs in both cases because of an 'axial rotation' of the causal relationship between life and forms. In the studies on portrait painting and poetry, Simmel remarks that the 'consciousness of the other' characterising social interaction becomes an autonomous cultural form in art (GSG 5, pp. 287-300; GSG 7, pp. 21-35, 321-332; GSG 13, pp. 370-381). In *The view of life*, he adds to this analysis a reconstruction of the inverse causal relationship, so converting cultural forms back into preforms of perception. A comparative assessment of the effect of art not only on the observer of paintings but also on the listeners of poetry, drama, and music highlights in which relationships mature cultural forms remain with their respective preforms of human perception (GSG 16, p. 274 f.). Accordingly, the eminent social meaning of art consists in the fact that it performs an intermediary role in the relationship between subjective and objective culture in both directions of the 'axial rotation' of life. It produces objective contents of culture and contributes to their reification as autonomous domains of society. Yet it also allows for their translation anew into preforms of culture by building a bridge to subjective culture in the process of receiving when the observer of fine art, the spectator of drama or the listener of music in some way follows the artist on his creative route. To borrow Simmel's terms: the work of art not only incorporates vital energies in itself to reproduce its form, but it also operates like a bridge that leads back from the forms to life. This double performance of the arts not only stirs the cycle of culture, but it also contributes to the integration of society by realising the coordination between the objective cultural forms and the preforms of social creativity in the sense of the third a priori of sociation (GSG 11, p. 59).

The reciprocal action between autonomous cultural forms and correlated preforms characterises poetry and drama in an eminent way. Their vital preforms not only consist in linguistic expression. They are also grounded on a specific interior shaping of the vision that permits poetic creativity. In principle, this expression of art operates no differently than the countless acts of consciousness whereby the individuals adapt perception to the goals of social life by gaining from its unsteady flow a consistent and reliable image of the world objects and interaction partners. Poetry arises from the generalisation and typification of social reality influenced by the first a priori of sociation (GSG 11, p. 47). However, it does so by styling fragmentary knowledge of the imagined other into an artistic image of his personality (GSG 16, p. 279). In his creative work, the poet operates for the sake of perfection in the expressive form and not for the purposes of practical social life. The artistic and literary representation of the fellow human individual find their prototype in social modalities of the perception of the other. Yet they can only succeed as art forms if a complete 'axial rotation' of the vital expediency in shaping the image of the fellow human individual takes place. This allows for the realisation of the artistic intent of creating a typological human character as an end in itself (GSG 16, p. 280 f.).

During his analyses in *The view of life*, Simmel underlines that the three a priori of sociation constitute the fundamental preforms for the artistic representation of the other, thus promoting the rise of art as an autonomous domain of qualitative differentiated societies. Sociological epistemology and cultural sociology so link together in a unitary theory of the sociocultural human lifeform within the perspective of sociological anthropology. This theory-building constitutes Simmel's final answer to Dilthey's appeal (1883) for a coherent foundation for the study of society and history, in the form of a sociological-anthropological theory of culture in qualitative differentiated societies.

The scholarly reception of Simmel's late achievements was minimal and mostly mistaken. Post-1918 the intellectual mainstream in Germany and abroad only read the label of Simmel's intellectual testament: *The view of life*. Accordingly, the book was pigeonholed under 'life philosophy', designated as one of the passing fashions of the *Belle Époque*. Rickert, who was an objective witness of this development and a good friend of Simmel, came to his defence, albeit from a critical point of view (1920, pp. 64-70). He highlighted the difference between the theoretical project of *Lebensanschauung* and the fashionable streams of philosophical *belles-lettres* before and after World War I. However, this did not suffice to grant a favourable reception for Simmel's sociological anthropology.[4]

A sociologically well-informed ethics

According to the central assumptions of sociological anthropology, Simmel's idea of 'individual law' represents the mature formulation of his long-lasting examination of the ethical question concerning the relationship between the individual and society in complex societies. This reflection accompanied Simmel's analytical-descriptive assessment of the modern individuation processes since the study on *Social Differentiation* (GSG 2, pp. 169-198). The higher margins of freedom for the individuals in complex societies find their counterpart in the fragmentation of the personality that is motivated by modern cultural conflict. To have a life conduct means in this context that the individuals have the capacity to link, in a meaningful synthesis, the different and to some extent contradictory social roles, which they perform (GSG 11, p. 59). The reconciliation of normative conflicts resulting from the opposition between the objectified logics of different societal domains can hardly be granted by existing lifestyles, so that the cultural work, which has to be performed to constitute ethical individuality, becomes increasingly important.

Kant's categorical imperative calls for a disavowal of all subjective interests and individual needs, by ensuring the conformity of behaviour to a universal rule, to which everybody would be able to conform in the same situation (Kant, 2015; cf. GSG 9, pp. 7-226). Yet, in social-ethical terms, the categorical imperative seems to contribute rather to the substantial heteronomy of the modern moral subject, than to its emancipation from normative alienation. It forces him to accept the power of the conflicting normative orders characterising the established domains of qualitative differentiated societies. In Kant's deontological perspective, not only are egoistic inclinations criticised, but also the self-fulfilment of individuality is rejected as something immoral, along with the humanist ideals of the German classicism, and above all Goethe's way of life (GSG 17, pp. 7-270). Yet, for Simmel in complex societies these limitations of the creativity of social action have to be seen critically, because here the moral subjects are called upon to be consistent, by realising a meaningful subjective synthesis of their normative commitments. As a consequence, if the individuals were unable to realise their fulfilment, this would not only have negative consequences for his consistency, but also for the persistence of the social fabric.

The fact that no ethics emerge that are capable of shaping anew the individual's life conduct in complex societies, and of overcoming the socially determined heteronomy of the moral subject, depends for Simmel on the traditional ethical way of thinking. From this perspective, life and duty are seen as ontological entities. They belong to separated orders of reality, so that ethical consciousness is conceived of as a succession of disjointed decisions that are divorced from the remaining life process. Yet, an empirical view of ethical life shows that things do not follow this logic. The contents of moral judgement and the formulations of obligation are a direct expression of the individual's real life and cannot be added to externally by following some abstract, general rules (GSG 16, p. 349). Empirically normative acts emerge from the specific individual context of life of moral subjects, so that duty does not prevail in contrast to individual life. Rather, duty is a modality of life performance, thus making possible an autonomous normative legislation of individuality. The problematic aspect of Kant's concept of ethical autonomy lies in the fact that it splits the individual into two opposing domains by playing off sensuality against rationality, and supposing that only the latter can constitute the true moral subject (GSG 16, p. 355).

Simmel's project for grounding a social ethics of the autonomous moral subject in complex societies thus focuses on overcoming the Kantian dualism between individual life and obligation. The 'individual law' aims at reconciling the creative impulses of the modern complex personality with the ethical principle of obligation towards the community, by making the biographies of great artists to exemplary expressions of this process (GSG 15, pp. 7-270). Self-fulfilment and the commitment to the normative expectations of the different social circles would no longer remain in a relationship of reciprocal exclusion. The precondition for Simmel's social-ethical project, however, is represented by the emancipation of individuality from all traditional ideals of moral conformity. The individuals have to give themselves an ethical law and make self-fulfilment the principal purpose of moral life. So the personality can be shaped as though it were a work of art, by cyclically overcoming its current form for a new one, and making the struggle for qualitative individuality the purpose of social ethics (GSG 7, pp. 49-56; GSG 16, p. 367).

As long as ethics was founded on the idea of 'quantitative individuality', as an ideal of freedom from external coercion, self-limitation of the scope of single actions in the terms of Kant's categorical imperative and the idea of respecting the freedom of the fellow human became a necessary and pivotal point of social ethics. Yet, if the concept of the qualitative self-fulfilment of individuality represents the starting point for developing social ethics, the continuous process of moral life shaping can no longer be regarded as a sum of disconnected single actions. The ethical law of individuality can only be constituted as a reflection about its comprehensive dynamic unity and not as the result of an accidental succession of normative decisions, induced by categorical imperatives, which mirror the logics of the different societal domains. Thus, on the one hand, the individual conduct of life becomes again – as it was in the religious ethics (Weber, 1992) – the object of a consistent ethical project. On the other hand, however, the ethical life conduct does not provoke the triumph of hedonistic amoralism or blasé artistic egoism, as Simmel observed them in his diagnosis of the Wilhelmine age (GSG 18, pp. 167-202).

Individual law is firmly anchored in the 'obligation-history' of individuality, so that moral judgement must always take it into account (GSG 16, p. 392 f.). The ethical way out of the spatial conflict between the different normative orders of qualitative differentiated societies, thus must be found in the 'temporal depth' of individual moral life. In determining the normative path for the self-fulfilment project of the individuality, moral subjects have to be absolutely free. In doing this, however, they do not find themselves in an ethical vacuum, but within a network of constitutive ethical obligations that they contracted during previous ethical life and that demand to be consistent. For Simmel, realising a positive synthesis between these obligations and the self-fulfilment of the individuality represents the regulative ideal of modern societal life. Beyond the dichotomy between the subjective moral and the objective ethical obligation, a third dimension of life conduct thus becomes decisive: the objective obligation that the normative history of individuality represents for present moral judgement (GSG 16, p. 408).

With this formulation of 'individual social ethics', Simmel provides a persuasive alternative to the consumerist hedonism of the *Belle Époque*, by simultaneously offering a path for overcoming the normative alienation of the moral subject in qualitative differentiated societies. Individuals should be free to develop themselves and so would become conscientious members of their society. In this respect, Simmel proposes an ethical programme that is comparable with Durkheim's conception of so-called 'moral individualism', even if it is grounded on completely different moral assumptions (Durkheim, 2002). Accordingly, already in the first version of 'Individual Law' of 1913 (GSG 12, pp. 417-470), Simmel regarded the feeling of national belonging as an ethical corrective for a potentially unlimited tendency towards individualisation and cosmopolitanism. In order to construct itself in complex societies, individuality must overcome the condition of alienation produced by the ongoing process of societal differentiation. The multiple facets of the personality are narrowly tied to the different social domains, which are founded on autonomous and at times contradictory logics, and become increasingly fragmented. Individuality therefore risks resulting in a simple addition of the social roles, to which the actors are committed. To overcome this condition, modern moral subjects must take the shape of a project, giving sense to the entire personality in accordance with their 'individual law'.

This is the perspective that Simmel's social ethics adopts to provide a way out of the levelling process reducing modern individuality to a simple epiphenomenon of the social mechanism. There is, however, an objective limit to the autonomisation project of the individual law. It consists in the existential debt, which the individuals contracts vis-à-vis the community that made possible their birth, growth, and education, and the nation-state, of which they are the citizens. These ties cannot be simply forgotten or cut, rather they have to be taken into account to construct the ethical project of the individual law. The idea of 'normative temporality' thus represents the most decisive compensation of Simmel's profoundly liberal social ethics in communitarian terms. At the time of the first publication of the essay on 'Individual Law', before World War I, Simmel already exemplified this conception of social ethics by resorting to the analysis of the relationship of an antimilitarist to the motherland (GSG 12, pp. 417-470). The objectivity of the individual law is so deeply rooted in the temporal sequence of life that the call of the homeland to the service of arms would also apply to an antimilitarist. He is a citizen of the nation-state and cannot take leave of the debt he contracted vis-à-vis the political community, even if from a moral viewpoint he has the right to refuse the use of arms (GSG 12, p. 458; GSG 16, p. 409). Under the semblances of the nation, thus, the ethical history of the individuality appeals to him with an ethical objectivity that he cannot deny, without calling into question at once his own existence. The outbreak of World War I confronted Simmel with the full gravity of this conception of political obligation. On the one hand, he was aware that the war instantly destroyed half of his life work, as represented by the relationships of scientific cooperation, which he developed with his French colleagues (Simmel, [1941/42] 2008, p. 111). On the other hand, the emergence of strong feelings of national solidarity led him to hope for an ethical renewal through the experience of the war. The 'mammonism' that dominated pre-war Germany and imposed the evaluation of all worldly items as commodities seemed to come to an end. In the course of the war, Simmel completely changed his mind and realised that his 'individual law' had to be rebuilt on a completely new basis (Fitzi, 2018). This initiated his reflection on the ideal of Europe that could constitute an alternative to the fixation of the individual law on the individual's debt toward the nation (GSG 13, pp. 112-116). Passing away on September 26, 1918, six weeks before the armistice, Simmel did not have the time to develop further his conception of ethical life (GSG 24, p. 459).

Notes

1 Marx's and Engels' *German Ideology* was not published during Simmel's lifetime. Thus it is to be assumed that he took notice of Marx's Theses, published in Engels' book on Feuerbach (1886).
2 In *The Human Condition*, Arendt would later reformulate this viewpoint as the modern conflict between the world as it appears and as it is explained intellectually ([1958] 1998, p. 248 f.).
3 This aspect can be seen as the 'Kantian Element' that subsists in Simmel's 'late metaphysics'. To this point cf. Fitzi (2002, pp. 265-285).
4 The only exception is Plessner's research on *The stages of organic life and the human being*, [1928] 1975), cf. Fitzi (2019, pp. 139-143).

References

Arendt, Hannah ([1958] 1998). *The human condition.* Chicago, IL: University of Chicago Press.

Bergson, Henri ([1889] 1997). *Essai sur les données immédiates de la conscience.* Paris: PUF.

Bergson, Henri ([1907] 1994). *L'évolution créatrice.* Paris: PUF.

Dilthey, Wilhelm (1883). *Einleitung in die Geisteswissenschaften. Versuch einer Grundlegung für das Studium der Gesellschaft und der Geschichte, vol. 1; now Id. (1959). Gesammelte Schriften, vol. 1.* Stuttgart: Teubner.

Durkheim, Émile (2002). *L'individualisme et les intellectuels.* Paris: Mille et une nuits.

Engels, Friedrich (1886). *Ludwig Feuerbach und der Ausgang der klassischen deutschen Philosophie.* (Mit Anhang: Thesen über Feuerbach verfasst von Marx 1845). Stuttgart: Dietz.

Fitzi, Gregor (2002). *Soziale Erfahrung und Lebensphilosophie. Georg Simmels Beziehung zu Henri Bergson.* Konstanz: UVK.

Fitzi, Gregor (2015). *Grenzen des Konsenses. Rekonstruktion einer Theorie transnormativer Vergesellschaftung.* Weilerwist: Velbrück.

Fitzi, Gregor (2018). Nationalism and Europeanism: Simmel's dilemma. *Simmel Studies, 22*(2), 125–148.

Fitzi, Gregor (2019). *The challenge of modernity. Simmel's sociological theory.* Abingdon and London: Routledge.

Kant, Immanuel ([1783] 1968). *Prolegomena zu einer jeden künftigen Metaphysik, die als Wissenschaft wird auftreten können.* Riga: Hartknoch; now *Kants Werke* (Akademie-Ausgabe), vol. 4, (pp. 253–383). Berlin: De Gruyter.

Kant, Immanuel (2015). *Critique of practical reason (1788).* A. Reath & M. J. Gregor (Eds.). Cambridge: Cambridge University Press.

Kantorowicz, Gertrud (1923). Vorwort. In Simmel, Georg. *Fragmente und Aufsätze. Aus dem Nachlaß und Veröffentlichungen der letzten Jahre* (pp. V–IX), ed. by Gertrud Kantorowicz. München: Drei-Masken-Verlag.

Lukács, Georg (1986). *Der junge Hegel und die Probleme der kapitalistischen Gesellschaft.* Berlin, Weimar: Aufbau-Verlag.

Marx, Karl (2000). *Selected writings.* Oxford and New York: Oxford University Press.

Plessner, Helmuth ([1928] 1975). *Die Stufen des Organischen und der Mensch. Einleitung in die philosophische Anthropologie.* 3. unv. Aufl. Berlin and New York: De Gruyter.

Rickert, Heinrich (1896–1902). *Die Grenzen der naturwissenschaftlichen Begriffsbildung. Eine logische Einleitung in die historischen Wissenschaften.* Tübingen: Mohr Siebeck.

Rickert, Heinrich (1920). *Die Philosophie des Lebens. Darstellung und Kritik der philosophischen Modeströmungen unserer Zeit.* Tübingen: Mohr Siebeck.

Simmel, Georg (1989-2015). *Georg Simmel Gesamtausgabe.* Ed. by Otthein Rammstedt et al. Frankfurt/M.: Suhrkamp, 24 volumes, quoted here as GSG followed by the volume number.

Simmel, Hans ([1941/42] 2008). Lebenserinnerungen. *Simmel Studies, 18*(1), 9–136.

Weber, Max (1992). *The protestant ethic and the spirit of capitalism.* London: Routledge.

Windelband, Wilhelm [1894] 1924. Geschichte und Naturwissenschaft (Straßburger Rektoratsrede 1894). In Id. *Präludien. Aufsätzen und Reden zur Philosophie und ihrer Geschichte* (pp. 136–160). Tübingen: Mohr.

PART IV

Art and aesthetics

10

ART AND KNOWLEDGE IN SIMMEL'S THOUGHT AND WRITING STYLE

Claudia Portioli

Introduction

Simmel's references to art as a methodological source and model for other fields of know-ledge appear in his gnoseological thoughts on history as well as in his sociological and philo-sophical investigations. Parallels between art procedures and methods of knowledge have bewildered or even alienated those scholars who consider that social sciences as disciplines must follow the model of natural sciences and are expected to apply strictly codified methods to social or cultural phenomena in order to find social or psychological laws that are univer-sally valid. A similar reaction came from philosophers[1] who conceive the task of philosophy as the construction of systems of thought that tend to absolute and to universal principles that are able to explain the totality of reality and/or significant aspects thereof. From that perspective, Simmel has often been accused of aestheticism, romantic elitist disengagement, subjectivism (Hübner-Funk, 1976), and of creating a sociology for aesthetes (Von Wiese, 1910). Frisby (1986) criticised Simmel for being unable to investigate the origins of mod-ernity because his 'aesthetic' methodology prevented him from going beyond the analysis of the processes.

The following episode will hopefully help to understand the importance of analysing the gnoseological implications, not only of Simmel's references to the artistic method or his fre-quent parallels between artistic procedures and other aspects of historical knowledge, but also of his writing style. During his farewell lecture[2] as Professor Emeritus, Otthein Rammstedt, the German editor of the complete edition of Simmel's work, recalled that when he had pre-sented the project for the complete edition twenty years earlier, Habermas had objected that Simmel did not have the 'Format' to be considered a classic of sociology.[3] What did Habermas mean by this? He could allude to Simmel's theoretical consistency as a sociolo-gist, but also to the stylistic textual genre that befits the field of sociology. Or perhaps Habermas was using '*Format*' to designate an ideal model or scientific method of analysis with which Simmel, according to him, did not comply.

The following pages will address the relationship, on the one hand, between art and knowledge and, on the other, between gnoseological thought and writing style in Simmel's work, shedding light on their implications for his theory of knowledge and methodological praxis. Indirectly, these pages will also offer a possible answer to the question of '*Format*'.

Before proceeding, let me clarify a point regarding Simmel's aesthetics. The often neglected relevance of the gnoseological implications of the relationship between art and knowledge in Simmel's thought should not suggest that this dimension is representative of the totality of Simmel's aesthetics. As a matter of fact, the latter includes different spheres such as philosophy, theory and history of art,[4] aesthetics as analysis of sense perception,[5] aesthetics as a reflection on the gnoseological and methodological aspects of art and its procedures,[6] and aesthetics as analysis of the social impact of aesthetic phenomena in modern ordinary life.[7] A further sphere of Simmel's aesthetics could also include his creative texts.[8] Scholars, especially in the past, tended to overlap the different spheres of Simmel's aesthetics by trying to trace them back to a unitary sociological interpretation of Simmel's work.

Art and knowledge in Simmel's thought

Simmel addresses various issues pertaining to the theory of knowledge and points out the gnoseological value of aesthetic aspects, especially with regard to the fields of history and sociology, in the following writings: *Das Problem der Soziologie* (The Problem of Sociology) (1894);[9] *Soziologische Aesthetik* (Aesthetic sociology) (1896); *Philosophie des Geldes* (Philosophy of money) (1900); *Kant* (1904); *Die Probleme der Geschichtsphilosophie* (The problems of philosophy of history) (1905/1907); *Kant und Goethe* (Kant and Goethe) (1906/1916); and *Vom Wesen des historischen Verstehens* (On the essence of historical understanding) (1918).

Before addressing the meaning and implications of Simmel's parallels between artistic and historical, philosophical, and sociological methods, let me summarise a few key aspects of Simmel's theory of knowledge, starting with his specific conception of *a priori*, which differs from that of Kant: according to Simmel, *a priori* principles of knowledge can be identified neither from a quantitative nor from a qualitative point of view, as it happens in Kant's theory. Moreover, unlike Kant, Simmel does not restrict his investigation of *a priori* to the knowledge of nature in general, but extends it to the whole historical and psychological world, because – as Simmel argues – it was also worth to be investigated in its preconditions a priori (GSG 9, p. 45). Even though Simmel shares the latter point with the neo-Kantian philosophers Windelband and Rickert, his conception of *a priori* differs both from their view and from Kant's.[10] In particular, according to him, *a priori* principles are historically determined and have a hypothetical (GSG 16, p. 302) and empirical-historical character (GSG 6, pp. 112-113). In other words, they cannot be provided with universal and necessary validity. In *Philosophie des Geldes*, Simmel claims that no normative content can ever imply eternal immutability: on the contrary, normative contents have a temporal validity and are linked to historical circumstances (GSG 6, p. 98). They are transformed into heuristic assertions and provided with pure methodological meaning (ibid.). Furthermore, in *Kant* (1904), Simmel argues that necessity and universality are no longer essential characteristics of knowledge and that the idea of an unfinished gnoseological development is more appropriate to the spirit of the time (GSG 9, p. 38 f., 43). A second aspect of Simmel's gnoseological thought is his relative-relational notion of truth, which he explains in *Philosophie des Geldes*[11] (GSG 6, p. 116): according to him, this relativistic conception of truth does not imply any kind of scepticism, as he argues in a letter to Rickert of 15 April 1916 (GSG 23, pp. 636-639).

Simmel's theory of knowledge also presents recurring parallels between the procedures of art and the dynamics of understanding, especially but not exclusively in the field of history and a new way of conceiving philosophy. Simmel also draws attention to the inevitable social and psychological conditioning of the work of the researcher. At the same time, he stresses the importance of the individual/subjective creativity of the historian (GSG 9, p. 293) when selecting the material of investigation and when elaborating persuasive interpretations. In this regard, Simmel speaks of a 'synthesis of the imagination' (*Synthesis der Phantasie*) (GSG 9, p. 274) that underlies historical descriptions. This aspect testifies to his awareness of the inevitable 'subjective' character of historical interpretations. In particular, Simmel argues that the work of a historian is comparable to that of an artist (GSG 9, p. 297) or of a poet (GSG 9, p. 298) in terms of how they interpret and organise facts in order to attain a coherent image of a psychological process.

Simmel's idea that scientific and artistic activities both imply a transformation of the material or the givenness of phenomena with which they work is reminiscent of some of the arguments of the art theoretician Conrad Fiedler (1887) in his *Der Ursprung der künstlerischen Tätigkeit* (The origin of artistic activity). Moreover, in *Die Gesellschaft als Kunstwerk* (Society as an artwork) (1999), Barbara Aulinger addresses the influence of art history on Simmel's sociology and highlights that several aspects of Simmel's work already appear in the writings of Herman Grimm, Simmel's professor of art history in Berlin. In addition to Grimm and Simmel's shared interest for Goethe and Michelangelo, Aulinger also mentions passages in which Grimm anticipates concepts such as that of reciprocal action, thematises the role of clothing fashion in the great city, and even anticipates a comparison between the activity of writing history and the artistic work (Aulinger, 1999, pp. 102-107).

Simmel highlights that each field of knowledge develops different criteria of validity, none of which are mutually exclusive (GSG 9, pp. 276, 360, 375). He also draws attention to the fact that historical interpretations, just like scientific theories, were elaborated in specific periods and are therefore temporary. This circumstance implies that they need not to be conceived as absolute or definitive, but on the contrary as open to possible reviews. Regarding historical phenomena, Simmel excludes the possibility of establishing deterministic laws (GSG 9, p. 313 f.): historical material is constituted by unique and individual events whose complexity prevents them from being decomposed into elemental parts or explained through deterministic cause-effect connections (GSG 9, p. 312). To Simmel, the notion of individual causality, as possibility of thought, seems methodologically more appropriate to historical sciences (GSG 9, p. 315). Historical laws are simplifications of complex material, and validity cannot be applied outside of the case at hand (GSG 9, p. 315). When it comes to knowing historical processes, historical laws have at best a heuristic and provisional character (GSG9, p. 90 f.).

Simmel's previous considerations evoke, in some respects, Windelband's distinction between idiographic and nomothetic sciences (Windelband, 1904, p. 12), which characterised his position within the methodological debate about the differences between sciences of the spirit and natural sciences. According to Windelband, history belongs to idiographic sciences, as its contents are singular, determinate events. Beyond this similarity, Simmel's gnoseological position differs from Windelband's in that Simmel speaks of historical laws even if he does not conceive them as universal or nomothetic, but only based on hypothetical and individual causality. Moreover, in his essay *Das Probleme der Soziologie* (1894), which became the introductive chapter of *Soziologie* (1908) (GSG 11, pp. 13-62), Simmel does not mention the pursuit of social laws as one of the tasks of sociology. He also argues that, although we must be aware that social interactions presuppose psychological processes, sociology does not necessarily result in the formulation of psychological laws (GSG11, p. 36).

Simmel also compares the way in which scientists develop a unitary method to the way in which an artist gives form to his/her own style. In the praxis, he argues, scientists (except for mathematicians) intertwine a plurality of methods in an individual way; they also resort to historically established methods and combine them through their own particular way of observing. This practice, Simmel notes, presents similarities with that of great artists (GSG 9, p. 359 f., footnote) who feed their personal style with the styles and techniques of previous artists and currents. Klaus Lichtblau has drawn attention to the importance of recognising Simmel's specific methodological pluralism in order to prevent scholars from misleading interpretations that, in the past, have produced labelling such as Hegelianism, positivism, neo-Kantianism, formalism, and impressionism, each of which has revealed its limits (Lichtblau, 1993).

On the whole, Simmel's gnoseological thought shows a constant attention for the complexity of the real and for the limits of the knowledge in general. He also points out the selective character in terms of choice and subjective interest (deprived of negative connotation) that characterises the unitary element, the categories and the issues on which the different fields of knowledge are grounded (GSG 9, pp. 276, 390).

Concerning the question of the sense of history, Simmel refers to the key role of feelings, especially the 'feeling of interest' and the 'feeling of importance' (GSG 9, p. 379 f.). In particular, he considers the following hypothesis: a phenomenon is designated as historical when it induces in the individual an accentuation of feelings, namely a reaction in terms of interest which is probably due to the fact the individual perceives those phenomena as having more consequences, from a quantitative point of view, than others (ibid., p. 381).

According to Simmel, feelings also play a role in relation to truth. In particular, in *Philosophie des Geldes*,[12] he argues that, from a psychological point of view, the holding of something as true is a feeling that accompanies the contents of representation (GSG 6, p. 625 f.).

The latter considerations seem to reflect specific aspects of Goethe's gnoseological view through which, according to Simmel, it was possible to overcome a few limits of Kant's theory of knowledge. In particular, Goethe believed that human beings 'know' not only through the intellect (as argued by Kant), but through their whole selves: in other words, all the elements of their life, such as their artistic imagination, love, sense of beauty, take part in the understanding process, along with their intellect and sensory perception (GSG 9, p. 28).

Lastly, Simmel's considerations in the 'Preface' of *Philosophie des Geldes* are particularly relevant to the topic of this paper (GSG 6, pp. 9-14). In those pages, Simmel not only formulates his aim to integrate materialistic analysis by going beyond a mono-causal model of explanation, but he also explicitly distances himself from the traditional philosophical aim to address the totality of existence, whereby philosophy often reveals its own limits by offering less than promised (GSG 6, p. 12). It is precisely in order to overcome this problem that Simmel refers to the artistic method. Unlike traditional philosophy, art seems to achieve more than expected precisely by addressing a single and limited theme, such as a portrait or a mood (ibid.). Similarly, Simmel begins his analysis with circumscribed aspects of the problem (money and economic life), and then develops them on a more general level. In his 'Introduction' to *Philosophische Kultur* (1911), he notes that when an absolute metaphysical principle is adopted in order to explain reality, a large number of superficial or isolated phenomena of life remain excluded from the all-encompassing interpretation that this principle should guarantee (GSG 14, p. 163). As an alternative, Simmel proposes to replace any claim to an all-embracing explanation of reality with a free and flexible metaphysical impulse, capable of addressing every possible content and open to a potentially unlimited range of objects (GSG 14, p. 163).

Romanticism and the gnoseological creative power of art

In order to overcome the intellectualism and the specific limits of Kant's gnoseological theory, one of the main models acknowledged by Simmel is Goethe's view and practice of knowledge. As mentioned above, according to Goethe, all the aspects and faculties of a human being and of his/her life (love, sense of beauty, intellect, sensory perception, etc.) are active in the knowledge process. This conception of knowledge, rooted in the '*Sturm und Drang*' movement, anticipates a few key aspects of the gnoseological approach developed by the main representatives of the early German Romanticism. In that context, unlike in Kant, art takes on a gnoseological function along with feeling and intuitive intellect. As it happens with other theoretical references of his thought, Simmel, however, does not limit himself to passively adopt the concepts or methodological instruments of his predecessors, but rather re-elaborates and combines them in a new and personal way for the purposes of his own research and epistemological thought (Goodstein, 2017, p. 6). According to Simmel, in a similar fashion to artists, researchers develop a unitary style of method, which is actually composed by a personal combination of a plurality of methods which are intertwined, especially in the praxis of knowledge (GSG 9, pp. 359, 360, footnote).

Furthermore, Goethe's considerations on the violence represented by an intellectualistic approach to nature, as in Kant's philosophical theory (GSG 10, p. 136), find a parallel in Simmel's observations in the 'Preface' of *Probleme der Geschichtsphilosophie*, where he highlights two forms of violence that threaten the modern human being. The first is a form of knowledge based on a mechanistic view of nature that reduces the soul to the same blind necessity of a falling stone, while the second is a form of historical knowledge which considers the soul as a simple point of intersection of social threads (GSG 9, p. 230).

Simmel's debt to Classical-Romantic thought was probably underestimated by critics (Giacomoni, 1995, p. 92). However, while sharing some aspects of the gnoseological thought and practice of the German Romantics, Simmel's purposes are different. As shown by his conception of truth, Simmel does not feel '*Sehnsucht*' for attaining the absolute essence of nature or true reality by means of art, intuitive intellect and feeling, unlike Romantic authors such as Novalis or Hölderlin.

Before addressing how Simmel's method concretely works, at least in many of his essays, let me mention two additional parallels between Simmel's gnoseological thought and practice and early German Romanticism: the role of the fragment in the part/whole relation and the resort to experimental forms of writing. Here again, however, differences subsist beyond similarities. To German Romantic authors such as Novalis or Friedrich Schlegel, fragments are expressions of finite portions or aspects of reality. For instance, Novalis identifies possible manifestation of the infinite in common objects of ordinary life (Givone, 1994, p. 62). In Simmel's analysis, the fragment rather represents the starting point for approaching cultural and social phenomena, including in ordinary life, which may reveal their impact and relevance on a broader scale, especially in a context such as the modern world, characterised by constant changes and transformations.

Furthermore, it seems to me that in Simmel's texts, the fragment is connected to his experiments with new forms of writing. On the one hand, to German Romantic authors such as Friedrich Schlegel or Novalis, such experiments were meant to develop reflexive forms of poetry that increasingly tended toward prose, thereby subverting the previous system of textual genres in order to express, in a personal and creative way, the problematic relationship between finite and infinite (Givone, 1994, p. 56). Friedrich Schlegel, in 'Fragment 116', published in the magazine *Athenäum*, claimed Romantic poetry aimed to be progressive and to merge different textual genres (Schlegel, 1991, p. 31 f.). In Simmel's case, experimenting with new forms of writing means above all to make extensive use of the essay format, which appears more adequate to shaping provisional form of understanding, especially if compared to the treatise. Simmel's use of the essay form, at least in a good part of his work, appears to me to be a choice that consistently puts into practice his theoretical[13] development of gnoseological issues, for instance in *Kant*, *Probleme der Geschichtsphilosophie*, and *Philosophie des Geldes*. Furthermore, as Rammstedt (1991) reminds us, Simmel also experimented with forms of creative writing such as fairy tales (GSG 17, pp. 387-389; GSG 20, p. 302 f.), short poetic compositions, aphorisms, jokes, fragments and short stories, often witty and ironic in tone. Most of these texts were published in the journal *Jugend* between 1897 and 1907 under the title *Momentbilder sub specie aeternitatis*, anonymously or signed with the initials of his full name (GSG 17, pp. 347-440; Rammstedt, 1991). What is the value of wit and irony in these short texts, considering that these two qualities are among the main rhetorical and stylistic strategies used by German Romantics? In early Romanticism, the resort to wit and irony seems to signal an awareness of the paradoxical and contradictory character of the real (Rella, 1997, p. 34 f.). The latter aspect is also present in Simmel, although with a further connotation: they become a means to take distance from and question the belief in absolute values or in definitive interpretations of the world (Rammstedt, 2006, p. 106). To German Romantic authors, irony expresses (among other things) the awareness that a finite form such as poetry will never be able to capture the infinite, which in their view corresponds to truth and nature (Givone, 1994, p. 56). At the same time, this awareness prevents them neither from constantly searching for new ways of capturing the infinite, nor from 'laughing'/ironising on their own limits. Regarding Simmel's creative experiments, in *Georg Simmels Ästhetik* (2017), Ingo Mayer analyses Simmel's poem 'Nur eine Brücke', anonymously published in the journal *Jugend*. According to Mayer, this text can be interpreted as a philosophical poem disguised as an intimate love poem. Simmel – probably alluding to Shelling's conception of the absolute identity of Subject and Object represented by Nature – playfully expresses his idea of the requested unity of '*Stimmung*' (state of mind) and form as inseparable by '*der ästhetischen Individuation*' (Mayer, 2017, pp. 239-243). If Mayer's interpretation of Simmel's text as a philosophical poem is plausible, then it represents another aspect of Romantic origin, i.e. the increasing philosophical character of poetry, and most of all its tendency to reflect on its own creation process. On the whole, therefore, it seems to me that Simmel's debt to the Romantics does not concern their specific views on truth, nature, God or their longing for the absolute: these elements would actually conflict, among other things, with Simmel's relativistic-relational notion of truth and with his conception of understanding as a process which can never and nowhere be considered concluded (GSG 9, p. 43; Faath, 2006). Simmel's debts toward Romanticism appear to me rather to concern the stimuli he received and further re-elaborated for his own thought and methods. One of these stimuli could be represented by the gnoseological value that Romantic authors attributed to art. As seen in the above-mentioned passages, however, to Simmel this aspect does not literally mean knowing through art, but rather looking at how art works in order to find suggestions and strategies for overcoming the limits of all-embracing and systematic approaches of philosophy or other theoretical approaches. A second stimulus has to do with the Romantic tendency to create similarities and see correspondences between different aspects of reality that are not immediately visible or evident (Rella, 1997, p. 35). This aspect could find a parallel in Simmel's frequent resort to analogy as a possible instrument for highlighting single aspects of phenomena that could not be explained in terms of cause-effect relations without doing violence to their complexity.

Furthermore, the self-reflexivity of the creation process which, according to Mayer, underlies Simmel's 'Nur eine Brücke' evokes both a characteristic of Romantic poetry and another recurring element of Simmel's work, namely gnoseological reflexivity and self-reflexivity. This aspect is addressed not only in the 'Preface' of *Philosophie des Geldes*, as highlighted by Goodstein (2017, p. 209), but also in the first chapter of *Soziologie* and in *Probleme der Geschichtsphilosophie*.

Essay and writing style: gnoseological implications

In the first chapter of *Soziologie*, Simmel writes that in new fields of human sciences (at the time, sociology was one of them), the scientific praxis often involves a certain degree of instinctive procedure, as its norms and motives will become conceptually clearer only in a later phase. Besides, he observes that a scientific work that would face new tasks through a completely codified methodology would be condemned to sterility (GSG 11, p. 30). Moreover, in the first footnote of the same chapter, Simmel highlights the following aspects of his *Soziologie*: its fragmentary and incomplete nature; the random choice of the addressed problems and of the exemplifications; and the heterogeneity of the tackled themes (ibid.). He also clarifies that this book represents only the beginning and outline of a much larger work, and notes that any systematic completeness would be a self-illusion (GSG 11, p. 31). Goodstein observes that Simmel uses the 'I' form in the end of the 'Preface' to *Philosophie des Geldes* (Goodstein, 2017, p. 210). The same goes for the above-mentioned footnote of *Sociology*. By doing so, Simmel declares his awareness of the provisional character of the results of his research and takes responsibility for it: rather than an error, this provisional character is part of an on-going process of understanding. I believe that the fact that Simmel inserts gnoseological thought within scientific works in new branches of human sciences – such as sociology was at Simmel's time – is consistent with his considerations in *Probleme der Geschichtsphilosophie* about the widespread lack of interest in gnoseological thought within specialist research (GSG 9, p. 359).

Prefaces, footnotes, and introductions to his main works therefore appear as significant places in which Simmel often manifests self-reflexivity on his methods and procedure. Another case in point is his 'Introduction' to *Philosophische Kultur* – a kind of 'philosophical manifesto' (Weingartner, 1962, p. 159, footnote) in which Simmel expresses the need to transform both the conception and practice of metaphysics, and suggests a possible turn from metaphysics as dogma to metaphysics as life and function.

Coming back to Simmel's comments about the fragmented character of *Soziologie*, contained in the above-mentioned footnote of the first chapter, the single chapters of this work could be considered as autonomous essays addressing specific themes, although within a general and coherent project. As Otthein Rammstedt points out in his 'Editorischer Bericht', most of the chapters of *Soziologie* had been published before the publication of the whole book in 1908 (GSG 11, pp. 877 f., 895-898). Hence I suggest considering as 'essays' not only the excursus of *Soziologie*, as Rammstedt does (Rammstedt, 2006, pp. 103–105), but also the single chapters of the book.

Recently, Elisabeth Goodstein (2017, 2019), starting from the analysis of *Philosophie des Geldes* and of its reception, has suggested that Simmel develops a modernist and self-reflexive philosophical method that transcends disciplinary boundaries. The characteristics and potentialities of this approach, she argues, have been obscured and ignored because of the way in which the disciplines of sociology and philosophy have been constructed, especially in the Anglo-American and Anglophone sociological and philosophical tradition. It affected the reception of Simmel's sociological and philosophical thought. According to Goodstein, the canonisation of *Philosophie des Geldes* as a sociological work, regardless of its original designation as philosophical, explains the lack of interest in the text on the part of the philosophical community. This may explain why, in her view, the text 'became perhaps the most important, mostly unread theoretical work of the 20th century' (Goodstein, 2019, p. 176). In particular, she argues that Simmel develops a new modernist form of philosophy, capable of facing the dissolution of absolute values and truths. This new approach – often misinterpreted by critics within the Anglo-American tradition and Anglophone literature – concerns not only the 'theoretical significance of everyday phenomena such as gender, urban life, fashion' and technology in society (Goodstein, 2017, p. 336), but also how Simmel enacts this new form of philosophy in his works.

With respect to Simmel's gnoseological thought, it is therefore worth analysing what the stylistic characteristics of Simmel's writing reveal about his methods, his way of producing knowledge and the role of the essayistic form in many of his works.[14] From a rhetorical-stylistic perspective, the following elements of Simmel's texts seem to me particularly relevant. The first is the frequent use of the conditional tense, whose function appears to be to attenuate the assertive value of the utterances. The second is the resort to the locution '*als ob*' ('as if'), reminiscent of the useful 'fictions' addressed by Hans Vaihinger in *Philosophie des 'als ob'* (The philosophy of 'as if') of 1911 (Vaihinger, 2008). The third element is the above-mentioned use of analogy as a rhetorical figure that highlights connections between aspects of phenomena that cannot be explained through deterministic cause-effect relations. Finally, there is the frequent use of the adverb 'perhaps' ('*vielleicht*'), through which Simmel usually introduces general interpretative hypotheses and highlights the provisional nature of his interpretations. In this regard, it is particularly revealing that in one of the gnoseological passages of *Philosophie des Geldes*, Simmel explicitly encourages us to rephrase our more general assertions pertaining to knowledge by introducing them with the expression 'as if' (GSG 6, p. 106).

Let me now mention two examples in which Simmel makes use of some of these stylistic and rhetorical strategies in order to downplay any claim to universal validity. Both examples concern the hypothesis of an empirical-historical genesis of the category of 'beautiful'. In his writing 'Soziologische Aesthetik' (1896), Simmel introduces with 'perhaps' the key argument through which he addresses the question of the origin of beautiful: a possible genetic relationship between beautiful and what individuals perceived as useful in a remote and forgotten past (GSG 5, p. 208). Four years later, in order to illustrate the objectification process of categories such as value in *Philosophie des Geldes*, Simmel re-proposes his hypothesis on the origin of the category of beautiful in a paragraph titled '*Analogie*: der ästhetische Wert' (cursive mine) and makes use of the conditional form when resuming his basic thesis, namely a forgotten relationship between useful and beautiful (GSG 6, pp. 15, 46).

An additional typical element of Simmel's writing style can be linked to the notion of 'reciprocal action', one of Simmel's key concepts from both a methodological and a gnoseological point of view. I am speaking of Simmel's long and complicated phrases, rich in subordinate clauses. This stylistic characteristic may have to do with Simmel's effort to make connections explicit and to keep together the different perspectives and the various – sometimes contrasting – aspects of the analysed phenomenon. This stylistic element therefore appears to show both the plurality of the identified factors and their deep connection and interaction, in accordance with Simmel's heuristic gnoseological notion of reciprocal action. I also suggest that his long and complicated phrases reflect Simmel's aim to deal with different – sometimes conflicting – points of view on various aspects of reality. Moreover,

Simmel's long syntactic constructions, rich in subordinate clauses, allow him to express the ambivalent character of most of the phenomena that he investigated. I therefore believe that it is possible to speak of the transposition, on a stylistic level, of Simmel's perspectivism.

Among the principal German authors who discussed the theory of the essay form, Lukács (1972) and Musil (1978) describe it as a hybrid textual genre, halfway between art and science. Furthermore, the essay is often characterised as having the fragment-character. Its flexible textual form can both adhere to the experience and overcome its partiality by tending towards a theoretical dimension, but without presuming to achieve a total and absolute explanation of reality (Adorno, 1972, p. 75). Simmel's essays not only present many of these aspects, according to Andrea Pinotti (2010b), they also develop a dialectical method of analysis that is deeply rooted in the philosophical tradition; this approach allows the readers to go beyond the characterisation of impressionism often associated with Simmel's work.

According to Rammstedt, Simmel's conception of the part/whole issue changed along with the modifications of his notion and practice of the essay, which is linked to theory (Rammstedt, 2006, p. 115, 2008, p. 21 f.). Furthermore, Simmel's essays appear to be characterised by a provisional form of understanding, as shown by the qualifications that he often adds to his titles: '*Fragment*', '*Silhouette*' (silhouette, outline), '*Skizze*' (outline), '*Studie*'[15] (study), '*Vorstudie*' (preparatory study, preparatory sketch) and '*Versuch*' (attempt, experiment). This suggests a substantial difference between the gnoseological meaning of Simmel's use of the essayistic form and Lukács' conception of the function and value of essay. In the last part of his *Über Wesen und Form des Essays* (On the Nature and Form of the Essay) (1910), Lukács argues that the essay is a means toward the final aim of constructing a system: it represents an anticipation of the system, the penultimate step before reaching it (Lukács, 1972, p. 46 f.). Unlike Lukács, Simmel's use of the essayistic form seems to express and reflect, on a stylistic and structural level, both his way of understanding and producing knowledge and his gnoseological thought,[16] which emphasises the limits of an all-embracing and systematic explanation of reality. In this sense, Simmel's essay practice appears closer to what Musil writes in the fragment 'Über den Essay', namely that the essay tries to create an order by connecting thoughts: it does not offer a total solution, but particular solutions, and goes on exploring (Musil, 1978).

Rammstedt (2006, p. 115) notes that issues such as the part/whole relation, relativism, reciprocal action, and dialectics are present not only on a theoretical level in Simmel's thought, but also on a practical level in his essays, where Simmel examines them in depth by representing objects and social beings (Rammstedt, 2006, p. 115). In his final considerations, Rammstedt adds that the extent of the essayistic form in Simmel's oeuvre remains an open question. Actually, the list of fifty identified essays (Rammstedt, 2006, pp. 103-105) could be extended if one considers the essay not only as textual genre, but also as methodological practice (Rammstedt, 2006, p. 115). One could argue that *Philosophie des Geldes* was written through an essayistic methodology, especially if one thinks of Simmel's methodological considerations in the preface (ibid.). The same could be said of 'Über Kunstausstellungen' (On art exhibitions) (1896). Nevertheless, if we define the essay merely as a textual genre, one must acknowledge that Simmel also made use of other genres. My suggestion is that Simmel's approach – in works such as *Philosophie des Geldes* or *Soziologie* – could be described as an open systematics, insofar as it does not contradict the essayistic method, but incorporates it even when the textual form is different from that of an essay. This happens, for instance, in *Soziologie* or *Rembrandt*, significantly subtitled *Ein kunstphilosophischer Versuch* (An attempt/experiment in the philosophy of art). Making reference to a previously unknown note of

1916 (GSG 24, p. 71), in which Simmel analyses his own life and work, Rammstedt (2008, p. 22) draws attention to the fact that Simmel himself associates *Philosophie des Geldes* with essays such as 'Brücke und Tür' (Bridge and door) (GSG 12, pp. 55-61), 'Der Henkel' (The handle) or 'Die Ruine' (The ruin) (GSG 14, pp. 278-286), precisely from a methodological point of view. In all these cases, Simmel attempts to show that under the surface of any portion of reality or objects – a handle, a frame, a door, a ruin – lies a canal that connects it to metaphysical depth (GSG 24, p. 71; Rammstedt, 2008, p. 22).

Simmel's 'artistic' method at work

I will now analyse Simmel's 'Über Kunstausstellungen' (1890)[17] as a concrete illustration of the possible relations between stylistic choices, argumentative line/structure and his theory of knowledge. First of all, I should emphasise that art exhibitions, the subject of this essay, were not self-evidently relevant in Simmel's time. The choice of exploring this topic therefore appears to be 'subjective', not in the sense of superficial or arbitrary, but because the focus on this fragment of modern reality as worthy of attention and investigation ultimately depends on the particular sensitivity of the beholder. It is the interest of the observer which leads him to investigate this specific phenomenon. The aim of the author is to show the meaning of this phenomenon by analysing its repercussions on the fruition of art works on the one hand, and on perception in general on the other. Simmel highlights the meaning of art exhibitions as a new kind of experience that stimulates and involves the senses of the audience in an unprecedented way. He also sees them as a small-scale image of the transformations of sensations and perception in modern life. The procedure adopted by Simmel to express this meaning is far from logical or deductive. Having considered a number of common complaints about the general decline in the quality of art exhibitions, Simmel analyses on a phenomenological level the psycho-physic and mental processes which characterise this new type of aesthetic experience (art exhibitions), both in their negative and positive impact on the viewers. He also identifies the novelty of this phenomenon in the radical transformation of the perceptive experience that it induces. Simmel concludes by emphasising the paradigmatic and symbolic character of this experience and its connection, by analogy, to more general changes in perception taking place in the modern time. Simmel suspends his judgement on the phenomenon and argues that its effective extent and scope will be understood only in light of future developments.

On the interpretative level, it seems to me that the way in which Simmel circumscribes the subject of his analysis is represented by the creative power of the researcher's subjectivity. As mentioned above, according to *Die Probleme der Geschichtsphilosophie* (GSG 9, p. 274), in history creativity constitutes the positive contribution of subjectivity to the definition of the research topic and to the understanding process. What is relevant, in 'Über Kunstausstellungen', has been established on the basis of the intuition, sensitivity and feeling of the scholar, similarly to Goethe's approach. I suggest calling this first phase of Simmel's approach the moment of 'subjective relevance': in this phase, the reader's attention is drawn on the basis of a choice oriented by the interest and subjective sensitivity of the researcher. The second phase is that of 'phenomenological analysis' of the effects and implications of the investigated phenomenon. In this second phase, Simmel usually emphasises ambivalent aspects, which cannot be qualified as only positive nor as exclusively negative. Actually, he often shows how their value changes according to the perspective from which they are considered. Furthermore, as Klaus Lichtblau observes in the 'Introduction' to the collection of Simmel's writings *Soziologische Ästhetik* (Lichtblau,

1998), Simmel often highlights a relevant aspect or on-going transformation, whose extent generally goes beyond the analysed phenomenon. This aspect could be regarded as the third phase of his approach. The last element is the absence of a final evaluation: what we generally find instead, is an openness to possible future developments and to possible revisions of the heuristic interpretation that he has elaborated.

Let me briefly mention a few key elements that allow to understand in which sense it is possible to speak of an 'artistic' method in Simmel. Firstly, I should stress that the expression 'artistic' method is not to be taken literally: Simmel is not claiming that sociological and/or cultural phenomena can be investigated through art. While artistic topics have also been the subjects of Simmel's investigations, this aspect concerns more specifically his philosophy of art. Secondly, on the praxis level, one can speak of an 'artistic' method in Simmel mainly for those texts written in an essayistic form (even when they are later included in a wider work). Thirdly, on a theoretical level, the 'artistic' method refers especially to the elements of Simmel's gnoseological thought that concern the human sciences: the role of sensitivity, feeling, intuition, the subjective conditioning of the researcher in defining his/her interest and selection of the material, the creative and shaping power of his/her subjectivity in the understanding process, the more or less deliberate use of a plurality of methods that come together in the scholar's personal research style, and the explicit reference to the advantages of the artistic method in *Philosophie des Geldes*. The emphasis on these aspects does not justify, in my view, the charge of aestheticism raised against Simmel's theory and practice of knowledge.

'A posteriori' validity – an interpretative hypothesis

Although Simmel consciously abandons the pretension of founding the validity of his thesis/ interpretations on logical-rationalistic demonstrations in which the data only play an instrumental role, it does not imply his giving up any claim to validity. This is an interesting gnoseological outcome of Simmel's method and essayistic style: instead of verifying the validity of an interpretative hypothesis by making reference to the pre-established criteria of a theoretical normative system, Simmel recurs to what I would call '*a posteriori* verification'. In other words, he directly delivers his interpretations in an essayistic form to the readers. In this regard, the qualification '*Versuch*' that often accompanies the titles of Simmel's essays becomes particularly meaningful: to begin with, it represents the original German term for 'essay'. '*Versuch*' can be translated both as 'attempt' and as 'experiment'. This second option is particularly revealing: '*Versuch*' emphasises not only the provisional character of the results (along with other linguistic indicators such as '*vielleicht*'), but also the very fact that what the readers receive is an 'experiment', an 'attempt' of interpretation which is waiting for a confirmation, although never a definitive one, an interpretation which could be applied to further phenomena. The reader community becomes an instrument for intersubjective validation. Validity therefore depends on the fact that the readers may find those interpretations persuasive on the basis of what they evoke in them and of their own experiences and questions about reality.

With regard to the use of the term '*Versuch*', Ludwig Rohner (1972, p. 15 f.) recalls that Herman Grimm (Simmel's art history professor in Berlin) deplored the substitution of the German word '*Versuch*' with the English term 'essay' around the middle of the 19th century. According to Leopoldo Waizbort (2006, pp. 38-48), the proximity between Simmel and Grimm could help us better understand Simmel's use of essayistic writing. In 'Über den Essay und seine Prosa' (1952), Max Bense highlights the experimental character of the essay form (Bense, 1972) – a feature that also applies to Simmel's essayistic writings.

Art, knowledge, and writing style – further possible developments

The fact that the writing style is not a neutral act, but a practice that also involves political and epistemological implications has been highlighted and problematised in some approaches of the human sciences, for instance in the debate and epistemological turn that followed the publication of *Writing cultures* (Clifford & Marcus, 1986) in the field of anthropology. Similarly, in sociology, Alessandro Dal Lago argues that the problem of writing, made of linguistic, stylistic and genre-related choices, constitutes an autonomous dimension of the scientific work (Dal Lago, 1987, p. 40 f.). In particular, he points out that at the end of the 19th century – when sociology was trying to become an autonomous science – sociologists resorted to stylistic and rhetorical devices taken from more authoritative sciences in order to legitimise their own scientific character (ibid.). In *Sociology as an Art Form* (1976), Robert Nisbet highlights the role of creativity for both the artist and the sociologist, and notes that the latter resorts to creative imagination in order to elaborate schemas which give sense to the collected data. Nisbet, like Simmel, speaks of thinking and working styles in physics, biology, and sociology as well as in literature and other art forms. In the sphere of philosophy, the epistemologist Paul Feyerabend (1984) argues in *Wissenschaft als Kunst* (Science as an Art Form) that science and other forms of knowledge present different styles that correspond to different criteria of validity. He also suggests that what the art historian Alois Riegl says in relation to art, namely that in art there is neither decay nor progress, is also valid in relation to knowledge. This is probably why Simmel takes inspiration from the artistic methods not in order to completely abandon any rationalistic approach, but in order to integrate them and overcome their limits by developing a personal style of knowing that is aware of its own limits. In the article 'Le paradigme esthétique (la sociologie comme art)', the sociologist Michel Maffesoli (1986) draws on Simmel's approach and stresses the need to integrate the sociological methods of rational analysis with the 'aesthetic paradigm of knowledge', an expression by which he designates an epistemological approach open to a plurality of methods of knowledge, also coming from outside sociology.

If the analysis of the stylistic, linguistic, and textual genre contributes – along with the investigation of Simmel's gnoseological thought – to exploring his way of conceiving and practicing knowledge, further tasks could be undertaken and other aspects investigated. On the one hand, I envisage the possibility of distinguishing, within Simmel's body of work, among different types of essayistic writings, depending on their aims: producing understanding in a new field or about phenomena that have not yet been investigated, or experimenting with a textual form in order to shape a particular '*Stimmung*' (state of mind) elicited, for instance, by the image of a city like Rome, Florence, or Venice. About this notion, Mayer (2017, p. 236) observes that '*Stimmung*' was one of the central categories of German aesthetic culture in Simmel's time. On the other hand, I believe that the changes in Simmel's writing style must be diachronically analysed in order to shed light on their possible connection with parallel transformations in his theory of knowledge. In this regard, Harro Müller's (2019) recent analysis of the modifications of linguistic characteristics, argumentative structure and stylistic elements in Simmel's late writings is quite revealing. In particular, Müller observes a shift from polysemy to monosemy in Simmel's wartime texts: typical expressions generally associated with Simmel's gnoseological perspectivism, such as '*sowohl als auch*' ('both ... and', 'as well as'), '*vielleicht*' ('perhaps'), '*sozusagen*' ('so to speak'), and the use of parallels and analogies all tend to disappear. In some of Simmel's late texts appear expressions such as '*entweder oder*' ('either ... or'), which according to Müller emphasise the category of decision. Further in-depth analyses in this direction may shed new light on aspects of Simmel's thought and work which maybe have not been completely disclosed.

Notes

1 From a philosophical point of view, Andrea Pinotti observes that Simmel's essays and his more extensive works (such as *Soziologie* (1908)) may disappoint those philosophers who adhere to architectural strictness and methodical procedure (Pinotti, 2010b, p. 12).
2 Held on February 2003 at the University of Bielefeld in Germany.
3 See also Habermas (1996).
4 See, among others, Faath (1998); Aulinger (1999); De Simone (2002); Pinotti (2010a); Mayer (2017).
5 See, among others, Borsari (2006); Portioli (2008); Pinotti (2009); Carnevali (2017).
6 See, among others, Frisby (1986); Faath (1998); Aulinger (1999); Karlsruhen (2006); Portioli (2006); Vozza (2006).
7 See, among others, Frisby (1986); Lichtblau (1998); Squicciarino (1999); Fitzi (2006); Mele (2006); De la Fuente (2008); Matteucci (2012); Carnevali (2017).
8 See, among others, Rammstedt (1991, 2008); Tokarzewska (2010); Mayer (2017).
9 A later version of this essay became the first chapter of *Soziologie* (1908).
10 On this topic, see, among others, Faath (1998, pp. 39-44) and Banfi (1922). On the notions of *a priori* in Simmel's sociological and historical thought in the context of cultural and social sciences, and of '*Verstehen*' ('understanding') in the context of the hermeneutic tradition, see Lichtblau (1993).
11 For a further analysis of Simmel's thought on truth, see also the chapter 'Wahrheit' (Truth) in *Goethe*, GSG 15, pp. 32-60.
12 Henceforth, the indications of the pages of Simmel's works will make reference to the German edition of the complete works of Simmel (*Georg Simmel Gesamtausgabe*, here GSG). I will consequently use the German titles of Simmel's works.
13 According to Otthein Rammstedt, Lukács' 'Über Wesen und Form des Essays' can help us understand that the formal configuration of Simmel's essays is interdependent with his gnoseological approach (Rammstedt, 2006, p. 109 f.).
14 For a deep analysis of the relationship between thought, writing style and method, see Nasi (1999, pp. 81–113). By focusing on the essays of the Italian philosopher and literary scholar Luciano Anceschi, Nasi also highlights the need of understanding the writing style through a flexible and open method of investigation which can be linked to the tradition represented by Socrates, Montaigne, and Simmel (ibid., p. 112).
15 For a different interpretation of the value of these qualifications in relation to Simmel's later use of the term 'essay', starting from 1900, see Rammstedt (2006, pp. 103, 108 f).
16 Especially with reference to his theory of knowledge as it emerges in the following works: *Kant*, *Probleme der Geschichtsphilosophie* (II and III edition), *Philosophie des Geldes*, and *Soziologie*.
17 By choosing this text, I extend the list of Simmel's essays initially suggested by Rammstedt (2006, pp. 103-105). It seems to me that this text already presents most of the aspects that appear to be constitutive – from a methodological, structural and stylistic point of view – of Simmel's essay in *Philosophische Kultur. Gesammelte essais* of 1911 (GSG 14). Rammstedt argues that Simmel began using the essayistic form around 1900, in connection with the publication of his short writings and creative texts in the journal *Jugend* between 1897 and 1900. This experience presumably played a key role in Simmel's shift to the essay form (Rammstedt, 1991, 2008, p. 10).

References

Adorno, T. W. (1972), Der Essay al Form. In Rohner, L. (Ed.) (1972). Deutsche essays. Prosa aus zwei Jahrhunderten, Bd. 1. München: dtv, pp. 61–83.
Aulinger, B. (1999). *Die Gesellschaft al Kunstwerk. Fiktion und Methode bei Georg Simmel*. Wien: Passagen Verlag.
Banfi, A. (1922). Il relativismo critico e l'intuizione filosofica della vita nel pensiero di G. Simmel. In G. Simmel (Ed.), *I problemi fondamentali della filosofia* (pp. 3–31), (Translation and Introduction by Antonio Banfi. Preface by Fulvio Papi). Firenze: ILI (reprint 1972).
Bense, M. (1972). Über den Essay und seine Prosa (1952). In Rohner, L. (Ed.) (1972). Deutsche essays. Prosa aus zwei Jahrhunderten, Bd. 1. München: dtv, pp. 48–60.
Borsari, A. (2006). Ausstellung/Esposizione. Su aisthesis e forma in Georg Simmel. In C. Portioli & G. Fitzi (Eds.), *Georg Simmel e l'estetica. Arte, conoscenza e vita moderna* (pp. 197–226). Milano: Mimesis.

Carnevali, B. (2017). Social Sensibility. Simmel, the Senses, and the Aesthetics of Recognition. *Simmel Studies*, *21*(2), pp. 9–39.

Clifford, J., & Marcus, G. E. (Eds.) (1986). *Writing Cultures*. Berkeley, CA: University of California Press.

Dal Lago, A. (1987). Introduzione. In W. Lepenies (Ed.), *Le tre culture* (pp. 9–23). Bologna: Il Mulino.

De la Fuente, E. (2008). The art of social forms and the social forms of art: The sociology-aesthetics nexus in Georg Simmel's thought. *Sociological Theory*, *26*(4), pp. 344–362.

De Simone, A. (2002). *Filosofia dell'arte. Lettura di Simmel*. Lecce: Milella.

Faath, U. (1998). *Mehr-als-Kunst. Zur Kunstphilosophie Georg Simmels*. Würzburg: Königshausen & Neumann.

Faath, U. (2006). L'intima essenza del conoscere, mai e in nessun luogo conclusa. In C. Portioli & G. Fitzi (Eds.), *Georg Simmel e l'estetica. Arte, conoscenza e vita moderna* (pp. 43–54). Milano: Mimesis.

Feyerabend, P. K. (1984). *Wissenschaft als Kunst*. Frankfurt a. M.: Suhrkamp.

Fiedler, C. (1887). *Der Ursprung der künstlerischen Tätigkeit*. Leipzig: Verlag von S. Hizel.

Fitzi, G. (2006). Espressionismo e post-espressionismo nella diagnosi della modernità. In C. Portioli & G. Fitzi (Eds.), *Georg Simmel e l'estetica. Arte, conoscenza e vita moderna* (pp. 197–208). Milano: Mimesis.

Frisby, D. (1986). *Fragments of Modernity*. Cambridge, MA: The MIT Press.

Giacomoni, P. (1995). *Classicità e frammento: Georg Simmel goethiano*. Napoli: Guida.

Givone, S. (1994). *Storia dell'estetica*. Roma and Bari: Laterza.

Goetschel, W. & Silver, D. (Eds.) (2019). *Interdisciplinary Simmel, The Germanic Review: Literature, Culture, Theory* (Vol. 94, No. 2). London: Routledge.

Goodstein, E. (2017). *Georg Simmel and the Disciplinary Imaginary*. Stanford: Stanford University Press.

Goodstein, E. (2019). Thinking the boundaries: Georg Simmel's phenomenology of disciplinarity. In W. Goetschel & D. Silver (Eds.), *The Germanic Review: Literature, Culture, Theory* (Vol. 94, No. 2, pp. 79–92). London: Routledge Taylor & Francis Group.

Habermas, J. (1996). Georg Simmel on Philosophy and Culture: Postscript to a Collection of Essays, (Eng. translation by Mathieu Deflem). *Critical Inquiry*, *22*(3), pp. 403–414.

Hübner-Funk, S. (1976). Ästhetismus und Soziologie bei Georg Simmel. In H. Böhringer & K. Gründer (Eds.), *Ästhetik und Soziologie um die Jahrhundertwende* (pp. 44-58). Frankfurt am Main: Klostermann.

Karlsruhen, T. (2006). La percezione della spiritualità e il suo significato nella sensibilità. In C. Portioli & G. Fitzi (Eds.), *Georg Simmel e l'estetica. Arte, conoscenza e vita moderna* (pp. 79–97). Milano: Mimesis.

Lichtblau, K. (1993). Das Verstehen des Verstehens. Georg Simmel und die Tradition einer hermeneutischen kultur- und Sozialwissenschaft. In T. Jung & S. Müller-Doohm (Eds.), *»Wirklichkeit« im Deutungsprozeß. Verstehen und Methoden in den Kultur- und Sozialwissenschaften* (pp. 27–56). Frankfurt a. M.: Suhrkamp.

Lichtblau, K. (1998). Introduction. In G. Simmel (Eds.), *Soziologische Ästhetik* (pp. 7–33). Bodenheim: Philo.

Lukács, G. (1972). *Über Wesen und Form des Essays. Ein Brief an Leo Popper*. In Rohner, L. (Ed.) (1972). Deutsche essays. Prosa aus zwei Jahrhunderten, Bd. 1. München: dtv, pp. 27–47.

Maffesoli, M. (1986). Le paradigme esthétique (la sociologie comme art). In P. Watier (Ed.), *La sociologie et l'expérience du monde moderne* (pp. 103–120). Paris: Méridiens-Klincksieck.

Matteucci, G. (2012). *L'artificio estetico: Moda e bello naturale in Simmel e Adorno*. Milano: Mimesis.

Mayer, I. (2017). *Georg Simmels Ästhetik*. Weilerswist: Velbrück Wissemschaft.

Mele, V. (2006). Introduzione. In G. Simmel (Ed.), *Estetica sociologica* (pp. 7–42), translated by U. Hoffman & V. Mele. Roma: Armando.

Müller, H. (2019). Beobachtungen zu Georg Simmels Schreibszene, Schreibfeld und zu späten Schriften. In W. Goetschel & D. Silver (Eds.), *The Germanic Review: Literature, Culture, Theory* (Vol. 94, No. 2, pp. 79–92). London: Routledge Taylor & Francis Group.

Musil, R. (1978). Über den Essay. In *Tagebücher. Gesammelte Werke*, II (pp. 1334–1338). Reinbek bei Hamburg: Rowohlt.

Nasi, F. (1999). Fenomenologia e stile nella scrittura di Luciano Anceschi. In F. Nasi (Ed.), *Stile e comprensione* (pp. 81–113). Bologna: CLUEB.

Nisbet, R. (1976). *Sociology as an Art Form*. London, Oxford and New York: Oxford University Press.

Pinotti, A. (2009). Nascita della metropoli e storia della percezione: Georg Simmel. In M. Vegetti (Eds.), *Filosofie della metropoli. Spazio, potere, architettura nel pensiero del Novecento* (pp. 119–152). Roma: Carocci.

Pinotti, A. (2010a). Trittico rembrandtiano. Burckhardt, Simmel, Warburg. *Materiali di Estetica*, *1*, pp. 330–344.

Pinotti, A. (2010b). Dingsuche. Der Essayist Georg Simmel. In M. Pirro & M. M. Brambilla (Eds.), *Wege des essayistisches Schreibens im deutschsprachigen Raum (1900–1920), Amsterdamer Beiträge zur neueren Germanistik*, (pp. 11–27). Amsterdam and New York: Rodopi.

Portioli, C. (2006). Gli stili della conoscenza: questione di metodo? Simmel e Feyerabend. In C. Portioli & G. Fitzi (Eds.), *Georg Simmel e l'estetica. Arte, conoscenza e vita moderna* (pp. 129–148). Milano: Mimesis.

Portioli, C. (2008). La fascination des sens par la marchandise entre anesthésie et hyperesthésie. *Revue de Sciences Sociales, 40*, pp. 50–59.

Portioli, C. & Fitzi, G. (Eds.) (2006). *Georg Simmel e l'estetica. Arte, conoscenza e vita moderna*. Milano: Mimesis.

Rammstedt, O. (1991). On Simmel's Aesthetics: Argumentation in the Journal Jugend. 1897–1906. *Theory, Culture and Society, 8*, pp. 125–144.

Rammstedt, O. (2006). Il saggio in Georg Simmel. Un tentativo di avvicinamento. In C. Portioli & G. Fitzi (Eds.), *Georg Simmel e l'estetica. Arte, conoscenza e vita moderna* (pp. 101–116). Milano: Mimesis.

Rammstedt, O. (2008). La 'littérature de l'anse' de Georg Simmel. Une approche de l'essai. *Société, 101*, 7–22.

Rella, F. (1997). *L'estetica del Romanticismo*. Roma: Donzelli.

Rohner, L. (Ed.) (1972). *Deutsche essays. Prosa aus zwei Jahrhunderten*, Bd. 1. München: dtv.

Schlegel, F. (1991). *Philosophical Fragments*. P. Firchow (trans.). Minneapolis, MN: University of Minnesota Press.

Squicciarino, N. (1999). *Il profondo della superficie. Abbigliamento e civetteria come forme di comunicazione*. Roma: Armando.

Tokarzewska, M. (2010). *Der feste Grund des Unberechenbaren: Georg Simmel zwischen Soziologie und Literatur*. Wiesbaden: Springer.

Vaihinger, H. (2008). *The Philosophy of 'as if'*. London: Routledge.

Von Wiese, L. (1910). Neue sociologiche Literatur – Kritische Literaturübersichten. *Archiv für Sozialwissenschaft und Sozialpolitik, 31*, pp. 882–907.

Vozza, M. (2006). Simmel tra estetica ed epistemologia. In C. Portioli & G. Fitzi (Eds.), *Georg Simmel e l'estetica. Arte, conoscenza e vita moderns* (pp. 55–77). Milano: Mimesis.

Waizbort, L. (2006). *As aventuras de Georg Simmel*. São Paulo: Editora24.

Weingartner, R. H. (1962). *Experience and Culture. The Philosophy of Georg Simmel*. Middlettown, CT: Wesleyan University Press.

Windelband, W. (1904). *Geschichte und Naturwissenschaft: Rede zum Antritt des Rectorats der Kaiser-Wilhelms-Universität Strassburg, geh. am 1. Mai 1894*. Strassburg: J. H. Ed. Heitz (Heitz & Mündel).

11

SOCIAL AESTHETICS

Barbara Carnevali and Andrea Pinotti

Introduction

This chapter examines the contribution of Georg Simmel's ideas towards the development of a philosophical approach defined as *social aesthetics*. The expression designates an area of aesthetics that targets society and social phenomena. Social aesthetics is thus the *study of the aesthetic dimension of society*, occupying the semantic space between the field of studies that focuses on the realm of sensation and perception (*aisthesis*), baptised 'Aesthetica' by Alexander G. Baumgarten in the mid-eighteenth century, and that pertaining to the theory of art – major and minor arts – as well as those techniques used to shape and transform the sensible world.[1]

Simmel's unique approach to the social world can be traced back to the 'Sociological aesthetics' outlined in his essay bearing the same name (Simmel, [1896a] 1968). This method was then applied in many of his works, including his masterful analysis of the modern *Lebensstil* (lifestyle) in *The philosophy of money* (GSG 6, pp. 591-716) and his pioneering essays on fashion (GSG 18, pp. 355- 386) and sociability (GSG 12, pp. 177-193). As this paper will demonstrate, social aesthetics is one of the fundamental traits of Simmel's philosophical perspective, and perhaps his most original and interesting contribution in view of contemporary debates. Yet the concept has been ignored for too long, treated with embarrassment by scholars, and even harshly contested due to its presumed tendency towards 'aestheticization' (see paradigmatically S. Hübner-Funk, 1976): an accusation which suggests the nullification or subordination of the material and economic aspects of social reality, something that Simmel has never claimed. On the contrary, one of the fundamental principles of his method, clearly defined in the preface to the *Philosophy of money*, is *Wechselwirkung* – the infinite reciprocity and interplay of material and ideal dimensions – so that neither the former nor the latter can be considered the exclusive cause of social phenomena (GSG 6, pp. 9-14). In order to dispel this misunderstanding from the beginning, it is worth citing Simmel directly:

> Every interpretation of an ideal structure by means of an economic structure must lead to the demand that the latter in turn be understood from more ideal depths, while for these depths themselves the general economic basis has to be sought, and so on indefinitely.
>
> *(Simmel, [1900] 2004, p. 54)*

Another prejudice that has prevented the correct reception and re-evaluation of Simmel's social aesthetics is the theory's alleged affinity with postmodern thought.[2] According to the proponents of this postmodern reading, this erroneous association was not only due to Simmel's propensity to aestheticise reality, but also stems from the unsystematic, fragmentary, and even 'deconstructionist' nature of his approach. Again, this is an interpretative mistake that can be debunked through careful re-examination of Simmel's method, which is more closely aligned with 'modernist' philosophical style (Goodstein, 2017). Simmel's approach exists within an irreconcilable dialectic, perpetually caught between the denunciation of the socio-cultural fragmentation of his time and the longing for an impossible totality. Aesthetics plays an important role in this struggle, offering the only possible path to modern synthesis (Simmel, [1900] 2004, p. 54).

Once freed from these interpretative obstacles, social aesthetics can be re-read as an essential component of Simmel's line of thinking - especially in light of contemporary cultural and economic transformations, in which aesthetic and social dynamics have become increasingly intertwined. For this reason, Simmel's approach is being revived today by a new generation of sociologists (de la Fuente, 2007; Mele, 2011). This chapter extends beyond the philosophical aspirations of this burgeoning contemporary scholarship to promote a more intimate dialogue between the fields of philosophical anthropology, aesthetics, and social philosophy.

Foundations of social aesthetics: the formal approach

The theoretical foundations for Simmel's social aesthetics can be found in two essays: 'Sociological aesthetics', dated 1896 (GSG 5, pp. 197-214), and 'Sociology of the senses', published as an autonomous essay in 1907 (GSG 8, pp. 276-292) and then recast in the 1908 *Sociology* as an excursus (GSG 11, pp. 722-742). A comparative reading of these two texts shows how Simmel's original approach is much more solid and coherent than normally believed. In fact, the two essays can be considered as exemplary illustrations of two complementary developments in social aesthetics: a *formal* one, which focuses on the relationship between social forms and aesthetic forms - mostly on the level of analogy, but a continuous reciprocal conditioning between the two spheres is also implied; and a *sensory* one, centred on the role that the senses play in conditioning the relationships between social subjects, endowing them with sensible qualities and influencing them through the dynamics of taste.

In 'Sociological aesthetics', Simmel analyses the polarity between two aesthetic attitudes. The idea of a conflict between two basic, oppositional tendencies moving towards identity or difference runs throughout his work as a metaphysical presupposition and functions as a structuring principle for all social phenomena. In his 1896 essay, this conflict juxtaposes *aesthetic pantheism* (*ästhetischer Pantheismus*), a perspective that views all things as an expression of the same beauty, with *aesthetic individualism* (*ästhetischer Individualismus*), a theory that espouses beauty as an attribute of singularity. As aesthetic individualism emphasises differentiation, ranking, and the value of individuality, this viewpoint is very much a product of the modern mind-set.

On a sociological level, these aesthetic approaches correspond, in Simmel's view, to the strong opposition between two political forms: socialism and individualism. Socialism manifests a predisposition towards aesthetic symmetry, expressing order, rationality, and equality between the parts of a whole, in which the intellectual component predominates. (In this context Simmel makes some observations about the connections between visibility, symmetry, and surveillance that we can now interpret in the spirit of Michel Foucault's work.)

Contrarily, individualism upholds the independence of the parts with respect to the whole, giving preference to aesthetic forms that are more anarchic and deregulated. As far as Simmel's concept of aesthetic individualism is concerned, it can be enlightening to mention developments in later works, such as his 1901 essay 'Two forms of individualism' (GSG 7, pp. 49-56). By articulating the principle of dualistic differentiation within the bounds of modern individualism, Simmel distinguishes between an eighteenth-century individualism of Kantian inspiration, 'a quantitative' individualism which focuses on the 'type' of the human being in general, i.e. which of his or her qualities the individual shares with everyone else; and a romantic or 'qualitative' individualism, clearly exemplified by Nietzsche's work, that gives prominence to the enhancement of difference and singularity. By virtue of their inherent reference to the dialectic 'general/singular', both forms of individualism are tied to the topic of 'style', the concept in which, as it will be explored in more detail below, Simmel's formal approach to social aesthetics culminates. It is romantic individualism, however, that drives modern individuals to seek an original form in order to realise their unique identity, to express their singular qualities and to create their 'individual law'. This also applies to the production of works of art and other aesthetic products in which the ego's difference is exteriorised. Simmel's diagnosis continues to be relevant today because it resonates with what has been formulated by Charles Taylor (1989) as the romantic 'expressivist turn', the modern alliance between ethics and aesthetics, in which authenticity is inseparable from 'originality', and its expression in aesthetic form. It is also extremely valuable to understanding the contemporary kinship between aesthetic media (i.e. social media) and contemporary forms of individualism.

Another relevant topic outlined in 'Sociological aesthetics' is that of the dialectic 'closeness/distance' between art and life. Realist forms of art, such as literary naturalism, retain their proximity to the lifeworld, because they represent its features in a mimetic way; stylised forms are more distant. The theme of distance is connected to the notion of autonomy with regard to the aesthetic dimension and constitutes one of the fundamental Kantian assumptions inherited by Simmel: by virtue of its 'disinterest', the aesthetic experience distances itself from the practical needs of life; when this distance extends beyond a certain threshold, the aesthetic experience transcends necessity, allowing for 'free play'. The dialectics of 'closeness/distance' and 'freedom/necessity' overlap with a third dialectic – that of *content* and *form*: the more the formal element predominates (i.e. style), the more removed the aesthetic experience becomes from life and the more it is liberated from necessity. Simmel's essay 'The sociology of sociability' (Simmel, [1910] 1997) illustrates this mechanism in a paradigmatic way: social interaction is motivated by 'contents' that serve the purpose of life (erotic instincts, material interests, religious beliefs, and so forth) and that create relationships of dependency and mutual trade between people - clear examples of *Wechselwirkung*. When the interaction is made autonomous from the 'contents' (such as those listed above), the 'form' becomes an end in itself: sociability (*Geselligkeit*) is born, opening the door to pleasure of being together without a specific purpose.

This notion of aesthetic autonomy stems from eighteenth-century episteme, which defines the aesthetic field in opposition to the economic, practical field, and it is, according to many points of view, out-dated. This is not the place to address this issue in depth, but it is worth mentioning a tension that is present throughout Simmel's work between two different conceptions of aesthetics (Mayer, 2017): aesthetics as a 'free' condition, as 'Art' in the idealistic and romantic meaning of the word, and aesthetics as a subsidiary dimension, that exists and is 'useful' in the lifeworld. It is this second meaning that holds the diverse potentialities of social aesthetics.

The sensory approach

In 'Sociological aesthetics', applying his principle of *Wechselwirkung*, Simmel defiantly overturns the Marxist idea of an 'ultimate' determination of aesthetic forms by economic means, suggesting that tastes and predilections can provide a kind of aesthetic predisposition towards specific social forms. Simmel declares that '[t]he social question' (i.e., in the language of the nineteenth century, the set of economic and political issues raised by the industrial revolution and the new organisation of labour) 'is not only an ethical question, but also an aesthetic one' (Simmel, [1896a] 1968, p. 74). He illustrates this principle in a remark that introduces his sensory approach in social aesthetics. The discomfort that the cultivated bourgeoisie resents when sensing the sweat of workers is an unconscious obstacle to social reform: this 'aesthetic bias' could be more relevant in politics than it is to the dominant classes' unwillingness to renounce luxury and privilege. The profound role that unpleasant and pleasurable sensory impressions play in influencing social relations will be developed more extensively by Simmel in the 'Sociology of the senses'. By invoking this precise example of stench that he found to be so meaningful, Simmel will re-define the 'social question' as a 'nasal question' (*eine Nasenfrage*) (Simmel, [1907b] 1997, p. 118).

'Sociology of the senses', full of insights that deserve to be more fully developed in light of recent advances in philosophy of perception, media, and sensory studies, sketches the project of a *social aesthesiology* (twenty years after Simmel, this idea re-emerged in the philosophical anthropology of Helmuth Plessner: Fischer, 2015). Simmel investigates the role that the senses play in shaping social relations, not only by allowing individuals to reciprocally connect with each other and to interact, but also by profoundly influencing the nature of their bonds: the senses create a unique 'aesthetic impression', a specific sensible quality that Simmel describes using an explicitly aesthetic lexicon, as the 'colour' (*Färbung*) of a relationship, its exclusive sensorial and emotional totality. Thanks to a two-fold capacity to transfer content and, at the same time, to form and qualify it, the senses can be considered the 'aesthetic *a priori*' of society. (And thus, also 'somatic *a priori*', given that human beings are sentient subjects with a body: our bodies are the vehicle through which we experience our relationships with the world and with others.) Although the eye dominates Simmel's theories on social sensibility, because of the public and sharable nature of visual perceptions and the perfect reciprocity implicit in the mutual glance, the fabric of social relations is in no way exclusive to sight. All the senses have this property: hearing, touch, and smell (oddly, taste is not considered by Simmel). Each of the senses 'colours' our relationships with other people and with the external world in accordance with its specific characteristics of sense organ and with the specific environmental conditions, historical and cultural, in which the perception takes place.

The core of Simmel's aesthesiology is a reflection on the peculiar 'double intentionality' of sense impressions. From a subjective point of view, indeed, sense impressions present themselves as 'our' sensations and provoke reactions of pleasure or displeasure inside us, accompanied by the feeling of a rise or drop in vital energy. In this case, perception matters because of its *aesthetic value* (pleasure) not its knowledge value. From an objective point of view, sense impressions become a means to acquire information about the nature of things and people. From this simple distinction Simmel draws important conclusions regarding social *aisthesis*. Our knowledge of other people is never completely purified of sensible impressions: on the contrary, it is closely dependent on what we perceive and feel about them – their appearance, their voice, their scent and the 'atmosphere' that seems to accompany them, in short, on what Simmel defines as the 'reaction of feeling to the sensible image [*sinnliches Bild*] of a person' (Simmel, [1907b] 1997, p. 111). Our relationship to others is thus a *taste* for others,

173

a subliminal inclination to like or dislike them – what Simmel also calls *sympathy* and *antipathy*. This is an original 'aesthetic way' to tackle the question of *Anerkennung* (recognition), the typically Hegelian term that Simmel himself had recourse to (Simmel, [1908a] 1997, p. 206). Social status is not guaranteed by an abstract, rational, and moral acknowledgement, but is rather the product of an aesthetic appreciation – 'I like/I dislike' – in accordance with individual taste. Simmel's insights outline a theory of social communication as seduction ('a will to please') as well as a conception of power defined by the capacity to influence social interactions by aesthetic means, both of which deserve to be further developed through an in-depth comparison with Pierre Bourdieu's idea of 'distinction' as 'a social critique of the judgment of taste' (Bourdieu, 1984; Carnevali, 2017).

In other words, according to Simmel, *aisthesis* is the precondition through which all the cognitive and practical dimensions of social interaction must pass. Their differentiation into separate spheres is shaped and conditioned beforehand by the aesthetic dimension. This explains, among other things, why the arts that transform appearances and influence social perception (publicity, staging, advertising, rhetoric, and erotic seduction) hold so much weight in social and political dynamics.

Adornment and fashion

Far from being merely identified with anatomical constitution and delimited by bodily boundaries, the sensible (i.e. aesthetic) image of a person embraces a wide constellation of things which, although objectual, are intimately hybridised with the subject, and can be ontologically defined as a *Wechselwirkung* of objectivity and subjectivity (Portioli, 2018): tattoos, clothes, and ornaments. These three classes of entities (which correspond to as many social practices) can be gathered under the collective name of 'adornment' (*Schmuck*), and differ along a scale according to their relative closeness to the body (Simmel, [1908a] 1997, p. 208).

Using powerfully energetic imagery, Simmel characterises the interaction of body and adornment as a 'human radioactivity', in the sense that 'every individual is surrounded by a larger or smaller sphere of significance radiating from him; and everybody else, who deals with him, is immersed in this sphere' (Simmel, [1908a] 1997, p. 207). This energetic potential also explains the typical recourse to precious stones and metals in adornment, because of their capacity to attract the gaze by virtue of their glitter. Among all adornments, jewels are endowed with a special power of social magnification, and for the most elementary reason: not only are they superfluous (hence functionless) and expensive (hence distinctive), they also shine – they are 'brilliant'. In turn, they illuminate the wearer and create a halo effect that literally illustrates the law of the irradiation of the sensible. Brilliance is one of the most overused metaphors of social recognition that exists, for that matter: the brilliant person is the one who manages to be the most noticed and most remembered.

Adornment is thus a paradigm of social-aesthetic value. What human beings seek in the quest for recognition is this, above all: they want to please and to be perceived. By evoking a popular formula circulating in contemporary culture, we could associate Simmel's ideas with an economy of attention (Lanham, 2006; Citton, 2017) in which value is produced by the ability to attract attention and to be seen – to '*cause a sensation*'. In the struggle for perceptibility, adornment is neither a superfluous nor a redundant habit; on the contrary, it acquires the modal status of necessity (playing with words, we could define it a 'necessary accessory'): 'People adorn themselves for others. Adornment is a social need' (Simmel, [1900] 2004, p. 175). In the practice of adornment, two opposite and contradictory tendencies find their paradoxical convergence: 'One adorns oneself for oneself, but can do so only by adornment for others' (Simmel, [1908a] 1997, p. 206). On the one hand, adornment is exquisitely ego-istic, since it is intended to exalt the individual's unique character; on the other hand, adornment is essentially altruistic, a gift to others to please them. Once again, Simmel, avoiding a deterministic approach, opts for a co-determination of two factors - the tension between being-for-oneself and being-for-the-other, two reciprocal poles encapsulating the ends and means.

Adornments may also be viewed in the context of the dialectical relationship between *old* and *new*: if old clothes adjust to the body and the personality of the individual who wears them, new clothes impose their shape upon the person: they are elegant, but less individual, more stylised. In this respect they are more similar to jewels, especially the ones made of metal, which perpetually retain their newness. As wearable and detachable accessories, jewels expand a person and hint towards super-individual horizons. Herein lies the reason why jewels must never be considered proper works of art, but rather remain humbly categorised as handicrafts: as artworks they would compete with and therefore oppose the individuality of the person they are intended to serve.

The 'old/new' dialectic culminates in fashion, the most characteristic social phenomenon of modernity. Fashion satisfies two contradictory needs that embody the metaphysical con-flict between the forces already exposed in 'Sociological aesthetics': imitation and homologa-tion on the one hand, distinction and differentiation on the other. It divides social classes from one another, and unifies each social class within itself. Predictably, Simmel recoils from a deterministic explanation: 'Connection and differentiation are the two fundamental functions which are here inseparably united, of which one of the two, although or because it forms a logical contrast to the other, becomes the condition of its realization' (Simmel, [1905] 1997, p. 189).

Simmel gave the first sociological account of fashion: he insisted on an essential anti-thetical battleground between higher and lower social strata, where the latter run after the former in order to appropriate their lifestyle, inducing the former to quickly adopt a new fashion in order to maintain their distinction from the broad masses. With respect to the complexity of contemporary sub-cultures, this aspect is understandably worn out and fre-quently contested by fashion studies.

Frame and display

The essentially servile aspect of adornment also applies to non-human ornaments, as is evi-dent in the paradigmatic example of the picture frame. This apparently peripheral device (that Kant had dismissed as a *parergon*, a mere supplement external to the artwork, in para-graph 14 of his *Critique of judgment*), performs an essential double function: on the one hand, it unifies all the various elements of the pictorial representation into a coherent composition, using its centripetal force to attract the viewer's gaze within its bounds; on the other hand, it accurately separates art from real life, representation from reality, acting as an unbridgeable stream surrounding the island-like picture. In doing this, the frame must not aspire to an artistic value *per se*, which would jeopardise the task of magnifying the artistic value of the work it surrounds: 'Just as the frame for a soul can only be a body, but not itself a soul, so a work of art which exists for its own sake cannot emphasize and support the autonomous existence of another such work' (Simmel, [1902] 1994, p. 14 f.). Frames perform a crucial dialectical operation: separating and connecting. In the domain of the visual arts, they embody a function which constitutes, on a general level, the rhythm of society and of life itself. This social function of framing (further investigated by Erving Goffman's 'frame analysis': Goffman, 1974) is particularly evident in the phenomenon of fashion, which Simmel explicitly compares to the frame, and in the phenomenon of display, as a determinant of aesthetic value.

In a short essay 'The Berlin trade exhibition' (1896) on the industrial exhibition of Treptow, that can be read along with 'Über Kunstausstellungen' (1890), an account of Berlin's artistic scene (Borsari, 2006), Simmel reflects on the exhibition (*Ausstellung*) as an aesthetical form and defines the emergence of a new aesthetic value in modernity: the 'shop-window quality of things' (*die Schaufenster-Qualität der Dinge*). This value, also known as *display value* in the tradition of anti-capitalistic criticism of modernity, provides the missing link in the *Wechselwirkung* between aesthetics and economics.

According to Simmel, the production of goods, in the realm of free competition and the predominance of supply over demand, ensures that objects tend to reveal a seductive aspect that functions to the detriment of their utility. In order to attract the interest of a buyer, further appeal must be added to the object's use value. This enhancement is often accomplished by the way the object is arranged and presented for public viewing. Simmel defines this characteristic as 'putting into form', an 'aesthetic *superadditum*' that takes place through arrangement and display. The ability to give a more pleasing visual appearance to things that are useful, a talent prevalent in Eastern and Roman cultures, here stems from the struggle to win over the buyer. That which is inherently lacking in grace is made graceful:

> The banal attempt to put things in their best light, as in the cries of the street traders, is transformed through the interesting attempt to confer a new aesthetic significance by displaying objects together – something already happening in the relationship between advertising and poster art.
>
> *(Simmel, [1896b] 1997, p. 257)*

Simmel shows how the form of display transforms the value of presented material: an object can be depreciated by a neighbouring one possessing better qualities, but it can also stand out to its own advantage. Equality and uniformity prevail simultaneously due to an environment in which the same objects are displayed together. However, at the same time, a principle of individualisation is also established: on the one hand, the whole becomes the summation of the exhibition; on the other hand, the whole remains the single object. The sensory effect on the viewer, who is subjected to a disordered hodgepodge of sensory stimuli, is amplified by the whole. According to Simmel's analysis, the viewer reacts with either hyper-excitation or blasé indifference (as we shall see in the final part of this chapter, there is thus a profound similarity and reciprocity between the exhibition form – introduced by industry, capitalism, and art exhibitions – and the urban modern sensory form). The experience of visitors to an exhibition is marked by superficial attention, by the distracted glance of the *flâneur*, who superficially glides over things.

In addition to the activities of the window dresser and the phenomena of publicity and advertising, explicitly highlighted by Simmel, this form of aesthetic value creation via display crystallises today in one of the most representative professions of the creative economy: the exhibition 'curator', a figure who has become increasingly important in the contemporary artistic and media scene (O'Neill, 2012). The primary function of a curator is clearly a socio-ontological one: the institutional framing, which, according to George Dickie, who reinterprets Arthur Danto's concept of *Artworld* by recasting it in sociological terms, consists of transfiguring the object, endowing it with the status of 'work of art', by the very decision to exclude it from the everyday world and display it in a gallery (Dickie, 1974). But a curator is also an expert who endows any object with an aesthetic surplus value by meticulously staging its parts, the space and the exhibition mode (regardless of whether the object in question already possesses an aesthetic value, as in the case of artworks): by putting one thing next to another and also by knowing how to enhance it through proper lighting, the choice of time and place, the right background, and so forth. Because of its individualising and influencing power, the 'exhibition form' can be compared with the equally value-enhancing form of style.

Style

'Style' is a central concept in Simmel's method, as the topic bridges together his ideas about aesthetics related to art theory, his theory of sensibility and, more generally, his reflections on culture and on life itself. With regard to the theory of art, Simmel is indebted to *Kunst-wissenschaft*, the science of art developed around the turn of the century in German-speaking countries, especially Heinrich Wölfflin's formalistic version. With regard to the philosophy of culture, Simmel inherits his ability to extend his observations about the specific artistic gesture to the more general domain of life from Nietzsche.

Both aesthetic pathways - the specific and the general - are intimately intertwined, converging upon a wide array of psychological, sociological, epistemological, and metaphysical issues. Such wide-ranging perspectives are able to intermingle because Simmel's concept of style is imbued with a crucial and ubiquitous dialectical tension, that between individuation and typicity - yet another fertile example of the metaphysical conflict expressed in 'Sociological aesthetics'. At first sight, style and individuality occupy two opposite poles on the spectrum of artistic expression:

> The decisive thing is this: style is always that type of artistic arrangement which, to the extent it carries or helps to carry the impression of a work of art, negates its quite individual nature and value, its uniqueness of meaning.
>
> *(Simmel, [1908b] 1997, p. 211)*

Thus, style opposes the uniqueness both of the artist and of the artwork: the latter can be copied from an original, but is essentially different from an object of applied and industrial arts (*Kunstgewerbe*), which is a replica from a model (here, style means the character, mark, label, or brand of a company).

However, Simmel's insistence on uniqueness (a property subsequently echoed in Walter Benjamin's characterisation of the auratic artwork) conflicts with his 'exception to the rule': that great artistic personalities (he mentions Botticelli, Michelangelo, Goethe, and Beethoven as examples) also express style through their unique genius in representing the world. Better said, they *are* their style, whereas their epigones *have* the style of the master they imitate. 'Saying that style is the man himself' – argues Simmel implicitly quoting Buffon – 'is well justified, even more clearly in the sense that the man is the style' (Simmel, [1908b] 1997, p. 212). Style, in other words, operates both as a *principium dividuationis* and as a *principium individuationis*: it expresses unity in diversity both among different personalities and artworks belonging to a super-individual plane (school, epoch, culture ...) and among the creative manifestations of a single genius personality. If in the former case style functions as a universal law, in the latter the ethical concept of the 'law of the individual [*individuelles Gesetz*]' (GSG 12, pp. 417-470; Simmel, [1918b] 2010) becomes aesthetically homologous with the religious-artistic notion of the 'type of an individual [*Typus eines Individuums*]' (Simmel, [1907a] 1997).

By virtue of the generalising effect of style, the fundamental contrast between typicisation and individuation needs to be more subtly nuanced: these are not poles of a rigid contraposition, but rather dialectical factors of a relational process: typicisation works within individuality as the unifier of the multiple manifestations of a single personality. At the same time, style individuates 'a form encompassing the most diverse contents, in which we recognize these contents as belonging to the same period, people, or state of mind' (Simmel, [1918a] 2007, p. 48). Typicisation and individuation are immanent reciprocal moments of a dialectical interaction (*Wechselwirkung*). The very same interaction which, on a meta-level, is instituted between style and styles as within a theme of which only particular variations are given. As Simmel himself acknowledges, 'style is a principle of generality which either mixes with the principle of individuality, displaces it or represents it' (Simmel, [1908b] 1997, p. 212). Such dialectic informs the sociological implications of style and stylisation: far from being the mere façade of social status, which exists prior to its symbolic representation, style also shapes the social order, producing classifications and symbolic hierarchies.

Among all the historical instantiations of style, two play a decisive role in Simmel's approach: classical art (of ancient Greece or of the Italian Renaissance), and its cultural opposite, Germanic art, spanning from the Middle Ages to Rembrandt (its highest representative). These are not just specific styles, but seem to embody two opposite fundamental attitudes in the very question of style: classical art, in which the law of typicisation is predominant, emphasises the general, the universal, the equal to the detriment of its irreducible individuality; Germanic art, on the contrary, finds its unity in an expressive modality aiming to represent individuality rather than the adherence to form and type.

Finally, from this historical example, we arrive at the more general 'form/life' dialectic. The interaction between these two notions generates a symbiosis that imbues the entire Simmelian philosophy: classicism aims to present form in the appearance of life; contrarily, Germanic art seeks to present life in the appearance of form. Where in classical art every individual vital manifestation is subsumed to the super-individual form, the kind of universality which is revealed in Germanic art represents the totality of a single life, according to what Simmel calls an '*immanent* generalization' (Simmel, [1916] 2005, p. 95). Classical art seeks the a-temporal being, universality, the distilled result of a process; Germanic art aims to render the becoming, the whole of an entire individual life condensed in a single present moment.

Far from being confined to 'racial' and geographic determinations of style (at the time, the 'Italia vs. Germania' stance was commonplace, and shared by many *Kunstwissenschaft* authors), Simmel's argument also embraces historical development, addressing in particular the role of style in modernity. The modern epoch would trigger the X-ray-like quality of Simmel's observations: 'What drives modern man so strongly to style is the unburdening and concealment of the personal, which is the essence of style' (Simmel, [1908b] 1997, p. 216). The modern radical intensification of subjectivism and individuality pushes individuals to seek a moderating response in the stylised design of home furnishing and clothes. This also explains the tendency of modern man to live among antiquities, objects that are expression of one epoch's style and of one homogeneous time-character. Style, intended here as the stylisation of forms of life, operates as a mediator between the individuals and their social milieu.

For an investigation of the relationship between modernity and the drive towards stylisation we return to chapter six in *The philosophy of money*, significantly titled 'The style of life' (Simmel, [1900] 2004, pp. 433–518): here the predominant feature of the modern lifestyle is identified as the point of intersection between monetary culture, intellectuality, and stylisation. These three tendencies can be viewed as three responses to the 'intensification' (*Steigerung*) of the nervous life provoked by the progressive enhancement of stimuli characteristic of the metropolitan milieu. Just as the intellect can take refuge in the concept in order to counteract the irreducible particularities of a single phenomenon, so too money analogously obliterates the differences among things, levelling their peculiar incommensurable features in the anonymous expression of a monetary value. This lack of character is precisely what is pursued by stylisation. Correspondingly, the subject experiencing a monetised and conceptualised world becomes decolourised, anesthetised, blasé.

Social history of *aisthesis*

The analysis of lifestyle in a specific socio-historical context, namely the *modern* one, introduces us to a key point in Simmel's theory: the historicisation of the aesthetic *a priori*. While accepting the idea that sensibility is determined by conditions of space and time, Simmel rejects the static universality of these forms, pleading instead for their dynamic differentiation. The human being is not to be conceived of as a sentient creature whose sensible spatio-temporal forms are seemingly fixed, as Kant's *Critique of pure reason* claimed. On the contrary, such conditions change correlatively according to the ways and the environments in which people live, and their mutation can be historically described: 'The fact that these forms should possess universality and necessity remains ideally valid, but is no longer as relevant and decisive for the modern man as it was for Kant. We have become more modest' (GSG 9, p. 38; translation by Andrea Pinotti).[3] Simmel adds a further element to his profession of modesty, one that is also derived from Kant, namely the law of *Wechselwirkung*. Extending this law to all domains of human experience, Simmel calls for a reciprocal action between subjective experiential forms and the concrete environment in which they operate, so that formal *a priori* and the historical world become intertwined in a co-constitution and co-determination.

The modern urban landscape, as it was taking shape in Berlin around the turn of the century, provided Simmel with the ideal testing ground for his complex constellation of ideas. His famous 1903 essay 'The metropolis and mental life' represents the most effective distillation of this approach; at the same time, it ties in with his investigations on lifestyle conducted in studies ranging from *The philosophy of money* to the later phenomenology of the 'Sociology of the senses'.

The metropolis essay outlines a veritable aesthesiology of the city, focusing on the habits of perception of its inhabitants: the repeated shocks, the fear of contact, the *blasé attitude*, the conditioning of intersubjective relationships through intellectuality and the monetary economy, the dialectics of proximity and distance: all themes that would exert a crucial influence on critical urban studies, starting from Siegfried Kracauer's Weimar essays on the urban types or Walter Benjamin's pages on Baudelaire and on Paris.

The methodological fulcrum of Simmel's urban aesthesiology draws upon his dialectical conception of the relationship between surface and depth:

> From each point on the surface of existence however closely attached to the surface alone one may drop a sounding into the depth of the psyche so that all the most banal externalities of life finally are connected with the ultimate decisions concerning the meaning and style of life.
>
> *(Simmel, [1903] 1997, p. 177)*

In the big city, the surface layer is represented by the ordinary phenomena of daily life, characterised by a frantic rhythm and hectic overstimulation; the depth is represented by the effect of these elements on the *Geistesleben*, the internal life of the human beings. A paradigmatic example is the pedestrian crossing in the midst of chaotic traffic, which consumes a huge amount of conscience energy to be properly managed and differentiated: a condition that Simmel synthesises in his formula 'intensification of nervous stimulation' (*Steigerung des Nervenlebens*) (Simmel, [1903] 1997, p. 175).

What appeared to Baudelaire as a 'fourmillante cité' ('ant-swarming city') is understood by Simmel as an urban jungle in which the life-struggle of archaic humanity is renewed in modern form. Now, instead of confronting the forces of nature, the individual must face the levelling powers of society, the impact of traditions, cultural conventions, economy, and technology. Once again, we encounter the dialectical tension between individuation and generalisation, a veritable a priori in Simmel's social theory.

The intellect, thanks its capacity to neglect the individual properties of a single phenomenon by subsuming it in a superior general class of phenomena (the concept), becomes the defensive organ of urbanites who try to protect themselves from the overwhelming attack of external impressions. In this argument we can grasp Simmel's dialectical analysis in all its subtlety: in order to protect their singularity, the individuals' only recourse is to rely upon an anti-individual faculty, the intellect. In qualifying the said organ as the 'least sensitive and quite remote from the depth of the personality' (Simmel, [1903] 1997, p. 176), Simmel's words can be read in dialogue with Nietzsche and Freud. The former characterised intellective conceptualisation as a function that transcends individuality: 'We obtain the concept, as we do the form, by overlooking what is individual and actual' (Nietzsche, [1873] 1992, p. 83). The latter argued that 'for every excessive intrusion into consciousness there is a corresponding amnesia' (Freud, [1895] 1966, p. 350), thus identifying oblivion as a defensive strategy of conscience against the stimulation overflow.

The most powerful ally of intellect is monetary economy as the standardised condition of metropolitan life, and this happens precisely because, like the intellective concept, money overlooks individuality: 'Money is concerned only with what is common to all: it asks for the exchange value, it reduces all quality and individuality to the question: How much?' (Simmel, [1903] 1997, p. 176). Universal calculability and objective neutrality are the correlatives of the monetisation of life. As we have seen before, Simmel rejects a deterministic interpretation of the relationship between intellectuality and money economy in terms of cause and effect. Instead he addresses their mutual interaction: the metropolitan way of life offers the most favourable *humus* for reciprocal determination.

The direct aesthesiological consequence of this reciprocity is the emergence of a specific anthropological urban type: the *blasé* person. This subject is characterised by an incapacity to properly react to new sensations, by 'the blunting of discrimination' towards the differences among things. The objects, regardless of their individual colour, appear to him 'in an evenly flat and grey tone', on the background of a universal 'discolouration' of the world (Simmel, [1903] 1997, p. 178). On the level of sociability, the metropolitan *habitus* tending towards indifference easily slides into a reserved demeanour, and the reserved stance, in its turn, into antipathy and antagonism. It would nevertheless be wrong to interpret such an attitude as an anti-social one: dissociation can be considered one of the basic forms of socialisation.

A deterministic model becomes inadequate when one tries to understand the blasé attitude: the blasé figure's blunted and decolourised sensibility is not only the effect of the urban hyper-stimulation, but its cause as well. The diffused blasé *habitus* triggers a reaction, provoking attitudes which aim to pierce the callous skin of urbanites and to overstep the threshold of insensitivity: extravagance, mannerism, caprice, and preciousness. The need for a progressive intensification of stimuli is most evident in the high-speed pace at which fashion changes:

> Changes in fashion reflect the extent of dullness of nervous impulses: the more nervous the age, the more rapidly its fashions change, simply because the need for the appeal of differentiating oneself, one of the most important elements of all fashion, goes hand in hand with the weakening of nervous energy.
>
> *(Simmel, [1905] 1997, p. 191 f.)*

The acceleration of the urban tempo is strictly connected to the reduction of spatial distances provoked both by constant external contact with a large population of people and by massive developments in transportation: 'In general, with the increase in culture, the long-distance effects of the senses become weaker and their local effects become stronger; we become not only short-sighted but short-sensed in general' (Simmel, [1907b] 1997, p. 119).

As shown above, Simmel may be considered as a pioneer in the study of the historicity of perception and a forerunner in his own right of a constellation of thinkers who have variously articulated this idea in the twentieth century: Walter Benjamin is probably the main contributor to its popularisation, claiming in his famous essay on artwork that 'the era of the migration of peoples, an era which saw the rise of the late-Roman art industry and the Vienna Genesis, developed not only an art different from that of antiquity but also a different perception' (Benjamin, [1935-1936] 2008, p. 23). Among his sources he mentions Paul Valéry's *The conquest of ubiquity*, in which we read that 'for the last twenty years neither matter nor space nor time has been what it was from time immemorial' (Valéry, [1928] 1964, p. 225). But he might very well have quoted Simmel on this point.

Conclusions

More than a century separates us from Simmel's revolutionary ideas: it behoves us to update them in the spirit in which they were generated rather than applying them to the letter. Thus, we must strive to modernise his theory in a way that incorporates recent advances in cultural sociology and media and as well as sensory and urban studies. Simmel's project can be continued by examining how our contemporary sensorium has been profoundly modified by technological, media, and artistic innovations such as television, cinema, design, and the internet. As Simmel foresaw in the writings we have commented on, aesthetics has become a primary tissue in today's social fabric, interweaving itself with communication, with the dynamics of power and economics, with the processes of valorisation and exchange (see Heinich, 2005, 2012; Karpik, 2007; Reckwitz, 2017, 2020): just consider the role that phenomena such as marketing and advertising, self-display and 'influencing' on the social media play in shaping our daily life. These current conditions, engender new forms of 'aesthetic experience', affecting all social fields - in particular the middle-class lifestyle - that have nothing to do with the romantic experience of the autonomy of art. Far from defining itself as a foreign sphere removed from the lifeworld, the aesthetic dimension re-engages itself with social reality. Or rather, it shows that it has never really emancipated itself from it. Simmel's social aesthetics offers a valuable tool to address these issues, not only because of his specific intuition about display value, framing or individual stylisation, but also, and above all, because of his ability to grasp the intimate complicity of aesthetics with social life.

Notes

1 The same idea could be paraphrased as 'aesthetics of the social'; however, social aesthetics is preferable because it sounds analogous to 'social philosophy'. The expression has been used by scholars whose perspective, in some respects, converges with the one presented here, as 'everyday aesthetics'. See particularly Berleant (2005).
2 Criticism against Simmel's theories varies according to the context of their reception. The German interpreters were the first, in the wake of Lukács, to launch an accusation against aestheticism, while the Anglo-American reception of Simmel's social aesthetics, first addressed in the work of David Frisby, was strongly mediated by cultural studies, and has been receptive to postmodern readings. The French reception, in turn, has been severely hampered by the influence of Marxist thought, by Durkheim's and Bourdieu's diffidence toward Simmel's sociological method, and by the postmodern, 'Dionysiac' reading by Michel Maffesoli. The Italian reception, on the other hand, was moderated by the Frankfurt School: Simmel is mostly read as a critical theorist and the precursor to Benjamin and Kracauer.
3 In this respect, Simmel's perspective is to be considered against the more general background of the deep somatization of Kant's transcendentalism that occurred during the second half of the nineteenth century thanks to the work of psycho-physiologists such as Fechner, Wundt, Helmholtz, and the zoologist von Uexküll who subsequently extended this organicistic approach to the entire animal world.

References

Benjamin, W. ([1935–1936] 2008). The work of art in the age of its technological reproducibility. In M. W. Jennings, B. Doherty & Th. Y. Levin (Eds.), *The work of art in the age of its technological reproducibility, and other writings on media* (pp. 19–55). Cambridge, MA: Harvard University Press.
Berleant, A. (2005). Ideas for a social aesthetics. In A. Light & J. M. Smith (Eds.), *The aesthetics of everyday life* (pp. 23–38). New York: Columbia University Press.
Borsari, A. (2006). *Ausstellung/Esposizione*. Su aisthesis e forma in Georg Simmel. In C. Portioli & G. Fitzi (Eds.), *Georg Simmel e l'estetica. Arte, conoscenza e vita moderna* (pp. 197–208). Milano: Mimesis.
Bourdieu, P. (1984). *Distinction: A social critique of the judgment of taste*, trans. by R. Nice. Cambridge, MA: Harvard University Press.
Carnevali, B. (2017). Social sensibility. Simmel, the senses, and the aesthetics of recognition. *Simmel Studies*, *21*(2), 9–39.
Citton, Y. (2017). *The ecology of attention*. Cambridge and Malden: Polity Press.
de la Fuente, E. (2007). On the promise of a sociological aesthetics: From Georg Simmel to Michel Maffesoli. *Distinktion: Journal of Social Theory*, *8*(2), 93–112.
Dickie, G. (1974). *Art and the aesthetic: An institutional analysis*. Ithaca, NY: Cornell University Press.
Fischer, J. (2015). Simmels Sinn der Sinne. Zum 'vital turn' der Soziologie. In H. K. Göbel & S. Prinz (Eds.), *Die Sinnlichkeit des Sozialen. Wahrnehmung und materielle Kultur* (pp. 423–440). Bielefeld: Transcript Verlag.
Freud, S. ([1895] 1966). Project for a scientific psychology. In J. Strachey (Ed.), *The standard edition of the complete psychological works of Sigmund Freud*, vol. 1 (pp. 281–397). London: The Hogarth Press and the Institute of Psychoanalysis.
Goffman, E. (1974). *Frame analysis: An essay on the organization of experience*. Boston, MA: Northeastern University Press.
Goodstein, E. S. (2017). *Georg Simmel and the disciplinary imaginary*. Stanford: Stanford University Press.
Heinich, N. (2005). *L'élite artiste. Excellence et singularité en régime démocratique*. Paris: Gallimard.
Heinich, N. (2012) *De la Visibilité. Excellence et singularité en régime médiatique*. Paris: Gallimard.
Hübner-Funk, S. (1976), Ästhetizismus und Soziologie bei Georg Simmel. In H. Böhringer & K. Gründer (Eds.), *Ästhetik und Soziologie um die Jahrhundertwende: Georg Simmel* (pp. 44–70). Frankfurt: Klostermann.
Karpik, L. (2007). *L'économie des singularités*. Paris: Gallimard.
Lanham, R. A. (2006). *The economics of attention: Style and substance in the age of information*. Chicago, IL: University of Chicago Press.
Mayer, I. (2017). *Georg Simmels Ästhetik: Autonomiepostulat und soziologische Referenz*. Weilerswist: Velbrück Wissenschaft.

Mele, V. (2011). Origin, meaning and relevance of Simmel's sociological aesthetics. In V. Mele (Ed.), *Sociology, aesthetics, and the city* (pp. 31–57). Pisa: Pisa University Press.

Nietzsche, F. ([1873] 1992). On truth and lies in a nonmoral sense. In D. Breazeale (Ed.), *Philosophy and truth. Selections from Nietzsche's notebooks of the early 1870's* (pp. 79–91). New Jersey and London: Humanities Press.

O'Neill, P. (2012). *The culture of curating and the curating of culture(s)*. Cambridge: The MIT Press.

Portioli, C. (2018). La performance des objets chez Simmel. *Revue des sciences sociales, 59,* 110–115.

Reckwitz, A. (2017). *The invention of creativity: Modern society and the culture of the new,* trans. by Steven Black. Cambridge: Polity Press.

Reckwitz, A. (2020). *The society of singularities,* trans. by Valentine A. Pakis. Cambridge: Polity Press.

Simmel, G. ([1896a] 1968). Sociological aesthetics. In P. Etzkorn (Ed.), *The conflict in modern culture and other essays* (pp. 68–80). New York: Teachers College Press.

Simmel, G. ([1896b] 1997). The Berlin trade exhibition. In D. Frisby & M. Featherstone (Eds.), *Simmel on culture* (pp. 255–258). London: Sage.

Simmel, G. ([1900] 2004). *The philosophy of money.* London and New York: Routledge.

Simmel, G. ([1902] 1994). The picture frame. An aesthetic study, trans. by M. Ritter. *Theory, Culture and Society, 11*(1), 121–133.

Simmel, G. ([1903] 1997). The metropolis and mental life. In D. Frisby & M. Featherstone (Eds.), *Simmel on culture* (pp. 174–185). London: Sage.

Simmel, G. ([1905] 1997). The philosophy of fashion. In D. Frisby & M. Featherstone (Eds.), *Simmel on culture* (pp. 187–206). London: Sage.

Simmel, G. ([1907a] 1997). Christianity and art. In H. J. Helle (Ed.), *Essays on religion* (pp. 65–77). New Haven, CT: Yale University Press.

Simmel, G. ([1907b] 1997). Sociology of the senses. In D. Frisby & M. Featherstone (Eds.), *Simmel on culture* (pp. 109–120). London: Sage.

Simmel, G. ([1908a] 1997). Adornment. In D. Frisby & M. Featherstone (Eds.), *Simmel on culture* (pp. 206–211). London: Sage.

Simmel, G. ([1908b] 1997). The problem of style. In D. Frisby & M. Featherstone (Eds.), *Simmel on culture* (pp. 211–217). London: Sage.

Simmel, G. ([1908c] 2009). *Sociology: Inquiries into the construction of social forms,* 2 vols., trans. by A. J. Blasi, A. K. Jacobs, & M. Kanjiranthinkal. Leiden and Boston, MA: Brill.

Simmel, G. ([1910] 1997). The sociology of sociability. In D. Frisby & M. Featherstone (Eds.), *Simmel on culture* (pp. 120–129). London: Sage.

Simmel, G. ([1916] 2005). *Rembrandt: An essay on the philosophy of art,* trans. by A. Scott & H. Staubmann. New York and London: Routledge.

Simmel, G. ([1918a] 2007). Germanic and classical Romanic style, trans. by A. Harrington. *Theory, Culture & Society, 24*(7–8), 47–52.

Simmel, G. ([1918b] 2010). *The view of life: Four metaphysical chapters with journal aphorisms,* trans. by A. Y. Andrews & D. N. Levine. Chicago, IL: University of Chicago Press.

Taylor, C. (1989). *Sources of the self: The making of modern identity.* Cambridge, MA: Harvard University Press.

Valéry, P. ([1928] 1964). The conquest of ubiquity. In *The collected works,* trans. by R. Manheim, vol. 13 (pp. 225–229). London: Routledge & Kegan Paul.

12

PHILOSOPHY OF ART

Ingo Meyer

Simmel and the fine arts[1]

Contrary to the other founding fathers of modern sociology, Émile Durkheim and Max Weber, Georg Simmel devoted a considerable amount of his writings, especially during his later period, to various problems concerning the fine arts. While his brilliant studies on jewellery, sociology of the senses, flirtation, etc., still find a broad echo in the social sciences and neighbouring disciplines, to name only Walter Benjamin, Theodor W. Adorno, Siegfried Kracauer, and, in more recent times, authors like Tilman Allert and Rainer Paris, his contributions to the philosophy of art remain rather unknown. Art historians read his *Rembrandt* (Wyss, 1985), intended as a sum of his reflections; Goethe enthusiasts love and analyse his monograph of 1912 (Voßkamp, 2009; Geulen, 2014), while phenomenologists make use of his essay on landscape (Smuda, 1986). But without a doubt, for sociologists, where Simmel rightly is still known best, these texts – speculative, permanently touching metaphysical spheres – definitely have little to offer (Müller, 2018, p. 53 ff.).

To avoid misunderstandings, firstly, the common 'tripartite periodization', originally suggested in an obituary by Max Frischeisen-Köhler (1919/20) to distinguish an early evolutionist Simmel from the Neo-Kantian and from late Simmel, as a philosopher of life, now seems obsolete.[2] Indeed, already by 1899 and before any so-called 'turn', in a review of a book by the Belgian symbolist Maurice Maeterlinck he calls for identifying the 'meaning of life' (GSG 1, p. 419)[3] in a 'philosophy of life' (ibid.). Rather more convincingly, recent research has instead stressed the unity of Simmel's tasks from the outset (Orth, 2015, p. 244); his main emphasis on sociology for several years is due to biographical circumstances and disciplinary demands – he always regarded himself as a philosopher (GSG 22, p. 342) but felt that only he himself could constitute 'formal sociology' at this time.

For an academic philosopher in the German *Kaiserreich*, Simmel was astonishingly well informed about classical and contemporary literature, e.g. he was willing to skip the entire Latin tradition in favour of English classics like 'Milton, Shakespeare, Hume, Swift, Byron, Carlyle, Emerson' (ibid., p. 348). For a few years, he was a friend of Stefan George's and Paul Ernst's; he had read Dante, Stendhal, Oscar Wilde, and Arthur Schnitzler; he knew Schiller's theoretical attempts, Zola, Dostoevsky, Tolstoy, even Russian romantics like Lermontov and the 'insider tip' Hölderlin (GSG 16, p. 410; GSG 7, p. 21). Anonymously, he published several poems and literary 'miniatures' for a while around 1900 (in GSG 17, 347-440; cf. Tokarzewska, 2010), but Simmel seldom wrote about philosophical aesthetics as a kind of pure theory. Nevertheless, in the early 20th century he did so twice – 'Kant und die moderne Aesthetik' of 1903 (GSG 7, pp. 255-272) and 'Schopenhauers Aesthetik und die moderne Kunstauffassung' of 1906 (GSG 8, pp. 87-107). These contributions shall be viewed as attempts to come to terms with his ideas, or as two different ways of self-understanding for ulterior purposes, namely, Simmel's own philosophy of art. His article on Schopenhauer tries to separate the main insights from his rigid pessimism. Simmel correctly stresses the 'intrinsic value of the aesthetic situation', mostly missed by German philosophers (ibid., p. 104), and founds what still is a contemporary (Bohrer, 1981; Seel, 2000) definition of aesthetic experience: the fine arts search for 'the meaning of *appearance* and appearance of *meaning*' (GSG 8, p. 106). The text devoted to Kant's aesthetics mocks his philistine style but concludes with two important results: aesthetic experience has nothing to do with beauty – beauty belongs primarily to the life-world, e.g. to physiognomics and design (GSG 7, pp. 262, 268), but the work of art represents a potentialised order, a perfect unity 'which reality never offers' (ibid., 262). Simmel cannot accept Kant's intricate construction called *Critique of Judgement* but he admits that Kant at least found, though not entirely convincingly, a way to connect subjectivity 'with the meta-individual common ground' (ibid., 271). De facto, Simmel transforms Kant's 'disinterested pleasure' here into a non-Kantian 'finest extraction of life' (ibid., p. 269) as the second insight, which means that at this point Simmel loosens up aesthetics' dependence on the obsolete mimesis concept. Art is not about illusion, probability, or even simple 'correctness', but via a compressed form that merely shares minimal structural homologies with reality, the artwork offers a strange combination of 'intensity of meaning' (GSG 8, 405) and emotional significance (*Gefühlsbedeutung*, GSG 10, p. 285; cf. GSG 6, p. 166).

In parallel to this, Simmel defends another, even more intricate combination while highlighting aesthetic effects (*Wirkungsästhetik*) in a Kantian manner and, at the same time, places emphasis on the 'closeness' (*Geschlossenheit*) of the work of art, i.e. a strong Hegelian tradition.[4] Nietzsche's case is different. It is an error to link Simmel's reflections on the philosophy of art to those of Nietzsche (Lichtblau, 1984, pp. 232, 259); though he read *The Birth of Tragedy*, his idea of art is quite distinct from Nietzsche's 'dionysic/dionysian?' concept as the joyful 'destruction of the principium individuationis swelling from the deepest foundations of mankind, even nature itself' (Nietzsche, 1980, p. 28). Moreover, Simmel drops 'shine' as a basic concept, which was over-exaggerated by Nietzsche, when he talks of 'redemption in shine' by aesthetic experience (ibid., p. 44). Shine, Simmel suggests, implies an already existing reality, so with shine no one can ever defend the piece of art's autonomy (GSG 20, p. 194). From the beginning to the end, for Simmel, Nietzsche always remained a moral philosopher.[5] Simmel paid little attention to 'minor', nowadays almost forgotten figures dealing with aesthetics. The relation to his Berlin colleague Wilhelm Dilthey was never easy (Köhnke, 1996, p. 355 f., 374 f.); later, Simmel blamed his conception of '*Erlebnis*' as a merely refined, but still mechanistic 'milieu' theory (GSG 15, p. 26 f.). Whether or not he read Neo-Kantian contributors like Johannes Volkelt or Jonas Cohn, then Theodor Lipps with his theory of empathy or Karl Groos with his then influential game theory, remains a matter of speculation (Meyer, 2008, p. 403 f.). We are better informed about his reading of art history and art theory from more obvious influences such as Alois Riegl, Konrad Fiedler, Richard Muther, August Schmarsow, Bernard Berenson, Adolf von Hildebrand, and others (GSG 15, p. 366 f.; GSG 20, p. 243; GSG 21, p. 349; GSG 22, pp. 416, 982). Heinrich Wölfflin, the founder of a formalistic art history, was a Berlin colleague too, and Simmel sometimes went to his courses, but in a letter in 1941 Wölfflin himself summarised Simmel's interpretations on the visual arts as 'too sophisticated' (Wölfflin, 1982, 475).

In sharp contrast, Simmel's preoccupation with music is disguised. Hermann Helmholtz refused his dissertation *Psychologisch-ethnologische Studien über die Anfänge der Musik* of 1881 (GSG 1, pp. 5-89) and later, for Simmel, in keeping with a romantic tradition, music is something 'insular' (GSG 20, p. 266), non-communicable. Rudolf Pannwitz and Margarete Susman remember a very close, but intimate relation to music (Gassen & Landmann, 1958, pp. 236, 280). Occasionally, music appears Schopenhauerian-like as an 'image of the world's absolute fate' (GSG 10, p. 295) and as Simmel wrote in his last years to Susman on 9 December 1916, he planned an essay on Beethoven (GSG 23, p. 717), which obviously had to be cancelled.

Nevertheless, Simmel's first attempt to understand the meaning of art systematically is in his *Philosophy of Money* (GSG 6). Art, Simmel emphasises, is a sphere of its own which puts reality at a distance – to make it accessible. In a very romantic way,[6] Simmel remarks:

> All arts change our natural and spontaneous scope on reality. On the one hand, we are getting closer to its own and profound meaning in a more immediate relation, beyond reality's cold veneerings the arts tell us about a soulful being we are feeling familiar with. On the other hand, any art brings us into a distance from the immediate character of things, it levels down stimuluses and spans a veil between us and reality, like a fine mist around distant mountains.
>
> *(GSG 6, p. 658 f.)*

It is also remarkable that here Simmel tries to relate the evolution of fine arts with that of society. Phenomena like naturalism, aestheticism, '*Nervenkunst*', etc. *correspond* to social developments such as differentiation and acceleration:

> I believe that this secret unrest which moves modern men from socialism to Nietzsche, from Böcklin to impressionism, from Hegel to Schopenhauer and back not only is caused from being busy and excited, but vice-versa is just an expression of our most internal state, a lack of something definite in the core of our soul.
>
> *(GSG 6, p. 675)*

Later on, Simmel only admits on one further occasion that art has something to do with society when he takes Rodin's 'meta-impressionism' as proof of society becoming fragmented and accelerated at the same time (GSG 14, p. 347).

The arts' main feature, as Simmel is convinced from the beginning, is to present a thoroughly closed unity; as he variously phrased it – 'not of this earth', a 'universe on its own', or even as a 'diaphanous universe' (GSG 7, p. 262; GSG 16, p. 267; GSG 15, p. 492; GSG 20, p. 233 etc.). In this way, art becomes something quite opposite to society, e.g. to be demonstrated via the fact that Simmel cannot imagine aesthetic production as teamwork. Of course, motifs and inspirations take their impetus from society, the lifeworld, or even from life itself, but they are transformed into something completely different, a *form* now independent of its origins,[7] 'in the arts, form is an end in itself' (GSG 16, p. 267). Contrary to any reductionism, art always has to express something individual, for Simmel, via its sheer existence, it even qualifies as an antidote to modern division of labour (GSG 6, p. 629 f.; GSG 14, p. 414). It should be clear that his position is not applicable to avant-garde and postmodernist conceptions; as far as a history of ideas is concerned, Simmel's basic convictions belong, roughly speaking, to the era from the

'*Goethezeit*' to van Gogh, whom he tends to rank even higher than his beloved Rodin (GSG 14, p. 337 f.).

But to understand the late Simmel's view on art besides fascination with artists as such, one has to consider his idea of religion, philosophy, and the arts as complementary approaches to 'life' itself in modern societies. For Simmel, even if science, religion, and the arts collaborate, or at least work simultaneously in structural homologies allowing representation of world inside the world, a remnant will nonetheless remain. He speaks about a '*Wirklichkeitswelt*' (GSG 16, p. 239) as a residual and, strangely enough, he is convinced that the true metaphysical problem is not the 'beyond' but our immediate impressions, facts, presence – actual *being*:

> Not what lies behind scientific representations, the obscure, the 'thing in itself', the fugitive is beyond recognition, but the immediate, concrete image, the things' surfaces presented to us. Not beyond science, but on this side of being cognition fails. We wrongly interpret the fact that we cannot apply on concepts what we see, feel, and experience, that we cannot build *what actually is* into epistemic forms, as if behind these contents of forms should stand something hidden.
>
> *(GSG 20, p. 262 f., my emphasis)*

Thus, Simmel states not only that there is no 'pure' insight even in everyday life, communication, and interaction, but that the soul of man is the 'greatest attempt ever with unfit means' (ibid., 268) – problems are not meant to be solved, they primarily pave the way for getting in touch with reality (GSG 16, p. 206). It is our fears and failures which are responsible for any decisive reaction.

Obviously, here the arts are intended to take over. Simmel says that they are also capable of capturing the entire being (GSG 14, p. 20), though with a slight but important difference to philosophy: 'the artist has the power to do what the logician is not able to: to expand a concept without diluting its content' (GSG 20, p. 266; cf. GSG 6, p. 280 f., as the 'tragedy of all concept building'); he broadens intension and extension at the same time. This is implied when Simmel generally speaks of 'symbolisation as the founding essence of any art' (GSG 7, p. 189): visuality, representation, fiction, and even reference as such prove that to set *forms*, meaning is possible. For Simmel, exactly this is the 'wonder' of human spirit, or the secret paradox behind doing culture – always just modelling a fragment, a glimpse, a selection in order to represent *world*. Form is possible suggests that meaning is possible. In the fine arts, one can observe this proceeding in the purest way, not bothered by the struggles and tasks of everyday life. Therefore, I decided to call Simmel's late, and definitely metaphysical, point of view 'world-founding art', a '*Weltgründungskunst*' (Meyer, 2017, p. 246): this approach serves as a supplement, counterpoint, and correction to philosophy, while the latter depends on mere concepts. As a demonstration of how to eliminate contingency during its production, turning mass into quality, every piece of art shows what we all do in everyday life, but on a lower, mostly unconscious level: we act, produce, decide, construct, avoid, and fail; we have to live our life with all its consequences. In *The View of Life*, again with hidden references to romanticism (Novalis, in this case), Simmel emphasises that we are all 'pre-existential' painters, poets, and so on (GSG 16, p. 275); it is just about 'a gradual difference' (ibid., p. 270). In this light, I understand arts in Simmel's late texts as the 'shop window of metaphysics' (Meyer, 2017, p. 344); here, any sensitive individual can observe best what it means to be a '*Kulturwesen*', as philosophical anthropology puts it a decade later; in a *pars pro toto*, here we can *see* best what we *do*.[8] So, in contrast to Hegel's

(1986, p. 25 f., 141 f.) famous notion of the modern loss of relevance of the arts, for Simmel, in modern societies the arts will become more and more important. This is his last word in his aesthetics as metaphysics of freedom, and at the same time an explanation of the 'individual law', a concept not accidently generated from Simmel's earliest Rodin exegesis in 1902 (GSG 7, p. 93).

Philosophy of art

With regard to Simmel's late philosophy of art, his books on *Goethe, Rembrandt*, and his essay on Michelangelo (GSG 14, pp. 304-329) seem most remarkable. One must not expect literary criticism or formal analysis; primarily, *Goethe* is Simmel's full-blown, book-length application of the individual law,[9] there is no philological interpretation of famous works. In the first half, Simmel even mostly quotes from Goethe's 'scientific' works. Simmel wants to outline the 'idea' (GSG 15, p. 9) or even 'philosophy Goethe' (GSG 10, p. 126), which is objectifying the individual, a lifelong self-shaping into form (GSG 15, p. 76). Simmel explains this 'idea' with one of Goethe's own favourite concepts which is morphology (ibid., pp. 88, 148 f.; cf. Meyer, 2017, p. 117 f.). The substantial core of Goethe's attitude to life, creating an entirety by exploring fields of action and production as much as possible, is to borrow another of Goethe's own, almost sacred terms: *Tätigkeit*, in the attempt to incorporate subjects such as 'truth', 'love' (i.e. women), science, and so forth as completely as possible. Paradoxically, he always keeps his identity during its transformation toward personal enrichment. Everything in the great chain of beings – Goethe definitely was *welt-fromm* – is important; everything is part of the entire life, 'organism' is a symbol of the world, and 'world' is a symbol for organism (GSG 15, p. 79). Simmel affirmatively quotes Goethe and Eckermann's exchange of 2 May 1824, when Goethe claimed that all his production was merely meant symbolically and that he did not care much whether he made pots or bowls (ibid., p. 160 f.). If this were to be taken seriously, a massive problem would arise concerning the ontology of art in the sense that there would be no significant difference between reality and arts. For Goethe, however, it did not matter because, in his view around 1800, the work of art is as real as reality is beautiful. However, for Simmel's philosophy of art, this represents its latent, but most virulent problem.

All the same, Simmel concludes that: 'He [Goethe] belongs to the ones who really came to an end, without any rest' (ibid., p. 269), and thus he demonstrated a way in which 'the absolute normal is capable to fill in the dimensions of real grandeur' (ibid., p. 270).[10]

Nonetheless, compared with such a harmonistic view of Goethe, Simmel's 'Michelangelo' essay seems more contemporary – he once told Rainer Maria Rilke that this was his best essayistic achievement so far (GSG 23, p. 478). Simmel's opinion is that the great Renaissance artist *misses* his individual law because he fails to separate artistic perfection from his enduring search for religious transcendence. Things, or more precisely, the Neo-Kantian 'spheres of values', are already differentiated in early modern contexts, so Michelangelo commits a category mistake: art *cannot* deliver redemption and religion has nothing to do with aesthetic perfection – you cannot have your cake and eat it, but Michelangelo definitely wanted to (GSG 14, p. 318 f.). So, as corresponding phenomena, in Michelangelo's late works Simmel discovers permanent variations of motifs of a tragic void, a radical and astonishing *negativity* (ibid., 315).

Simmel's famous book *Rembrandt* is very different to these slightly obsolete attempts; it was intended as a sum of his reflections on art. There is not a single word about the Dutch master's life, nor is there any remark on the Baroque era. Simmel did not want to publish the first edition with illustrations: he regarded it as philosophy, not as an 'art book', which led to a long struggle with Kurt Wolff, the publishers, in 1916 (GSG 23, p. 668 ff.). Simmel is concerned here with fundamental problems of producing and perceiving a piece of art: the most famous contribution, which is still worth reading, is his question in the 'Excursus: What do we *see* in a piece of art?' (GSG 15, pp. 402–501). Unfortunately, his answer can only satisfy halfway: yes, spectators apply motion and meaning 'onto the canvas', thus completing movements just presented in a particular, fixed situation, a still. Via the imagination, we see what we actually *do not see*, but instead of working out a kind of context-based aesthetic semantics, e.g. using the latent/manifest difference, Simmel drifts into a one-way street claiming a fundamental gap between reality and the arts. However, then he is trapped by ontological circularities. Reality and art, Simmel proposes, are 'two coordinated potentials of form for an identical content', he talks of an 'equivalent or a parallel between the real and the artistic shape' (GSG 15, p. 496 f.), and so consequently, he either has to reject the autonomous state of the arts or has to claim at least two different realities. Furthermore, even with his speculation on 'total behaviour' and 'total perception' (ibid., pp. 50, 329) as corresponding principles in production and reception – once again, a romantic conception that was probably unknown to Simmel[11] – he cannot explain how we *do* understand the represented, how we feel and empathise with persons being portrayed. It does not help to summon our view of 'a totality of life' (GSG 15, p. 353) when we see Rembrandt's late portraits; of course, Simmel here implicitly depends on the latent idea of a preordained harmony, if not on the 'book of nature'.

To make clear how a portrait can show traces of life, of one's own history (*Lebensvergangenheit im Bilde*, ibid., pp. 351–359), Simmel uses a chiastic figure, 'by spiritualizing sensuality, one is allowed to sensualize spiritualized viewing' (ibid., p. 351). He admits that he argues circularly but insists that in fact something historic, intelligible is given 'momentarily' by merely watching a picture that simply represents, say, an aged body. Those who cannot agree will never identify any hermeneutic fusion of horizons (ibid., 352), one has to get rid of any analytical task. The point is to understand as 'active viewing' (ibid., p. 353) of 'life transcending mere instant moments' (ibid., p. 355). Thus, Simmel switches from a piece of art's unity to the beholder, and basically he comes close to generating aesthetic meaning as a process. What appeals to us is not a fixed composition of colours on canvas, rather merely our everlasting attempts to imply meaning as a 'process of life' *correspond* to the represented 'stream of becoming' (*Werdensströmung*, ibid.). In this way, the 'view of total life' is possible (ibid., p. 353): 'Rembrandt's representations of human life each permit to see a life's totality' (ibid., p. 363) – evidently, viewing is a function of vitality, Simmel has described it as creative, even pre-artistic (ibid.; GSG 16, p. 275). However, we are not really convinced. These are just summoning, not unfolding arguments. He transposes the predestined harmony into something strangely immemorial;[12] he over-aggregates his concepts and generally lacks any development of a kind of aesthetic semantics, although he knows about the – highly contemporary (Gumbrecht, 2004) – relevance of moods, feelings, and intensities for aesthetic experience.[13] One can best detect the late Simmel's helplessness when he frequently labels the most intricate problems as varieties of 'basic phenomena' (*Urphänomene*, GSG 15, pp. 68, 139; cf. GSG 16, p. 162) rather than decomposing them carefully step by step.

In his most ambitious chapters, however, Simmel is obviously wrong. He operates with an ontological splitting when he claims that artworks present contents without reference (ibid., pp. 496, 499 f.) and implicitly presumes understanding as based on some preordained harmony. In a particular way, the first presumption seems similar to Husserl's idea of an *epoché*, i.e. to regard simply 'phenomena' without questioning their validity (Husserl, 1976, p. 54 ff.), but this will not work either. The second assumption is no help at all. Even measured by Simmel's own complexity to argue, the venture must fail to claim that arts and reality are situated on the same ontological level: when they act on equivalent levels, yet art is autonomous, why can they treat 'identical' contents? These contents have to be already formed, which implies a superior, meta-level, or an 'invisible hand'. Moreover, when art is 'not of this earth', a perfect unity on its own, how can we listen when it speaks to us? Simmel underestimates the ontological problem and, due to the period when he was writing, he does not elaborate upon any concept of aesthetic media which could emit or rather provoke meaning. Incidentally, the problems he put on the agenda are still virulent. Recently, a broad and ongoing debate has shown that even contemporary art historians do not yet know how to conceptualise time represented by a picture (Grave, 2014), or which ontological status they own – and we still do not know what a picture actually *is*[14] (cf. Meyer, 2017, p. 256 ff.). Simmel's excursus therefore remains useful as a starting point to show what kind of problems are implied when dealing with meaning, pictures, and imagination.

However, some of Simmel's most interesting ideas on the arts are widely dispersed across his numerous writings and notes, often when he is not directly preoccupied with metaphysical questions. To view is construction; it is to omit something, always being based on pattern dependency – in this way, he anticipates James J. Gibson's theory of cognitive extraction (GSG 16, p. 270; cf. Gibson, 1979, pp. 147, 238 ff.) which became prominent via Ernst H. Gombrich's *Art and Illusion* (2002, p. IX, 185, 277 f.). He reflects on Aby Warburg's 'pathos formula' before it was even labelled this way (GSG 8, pp. 264–275; cf. Warburg, 1992). Also, Simmel recognises the 'lyrical ego' as a textual phenomenon not congruent with the empirical author; years later, his friend Margarete Susman was to introduce this concept to philology (GSG 7, pp. 31 f., 331 f.; Susman, 1910, p. 16 f.). Furthermore, Wolfgang Iser's 'implicit reader' is to be found, here, it is indeed called 'ideal spectator' (GSG 15, p. 391 f.; cf. Iser, 1972, p. 7 f.). Though not a phenomenologist, like Husserl and his disciples, Simmel's occasional sense for structural principles concerning the reception of art is astonishing. On a more generalised level, and since the preludes to the *Philosophy of Money*, Simmel already deals with the idea of the arts as a compensation to deficits of the life-world, which was made famous decades later by philosophers Joachim Ritter and Odo Marquard, both without any contact to Simmel's tradition (GSG 5, p. 202; Ritter, 1974, p. 131 f.; Marquard, 1994). Besides, Simmel invents the idea of 'polycontextural' aesthetic disciplines when he suggests that the arts appear completely different when regarded from 'external' points of view like religion, science, politics, law etc. (GSG 8, p. 368 f.; cf. Plumpe & Werber, 1995, p. 20). And vice versa, similar to the late Niklas Luhmann, Simmel asks how reality appears when the arts once do exist (GSG 6, p. 658; GSG 17, pp. 353-356; Luhmann, 1995, p. 231). But the ultimate Simmel changes his approach again. Like Nelson Goodman (1984, pp. 87, 132) did at a later date, in *The View of Life* Simmel claims not only two but multiple 'worlds' on the same epistemic level and distinguishes them from a 'world of reality' (*Wirklichkeitswelt*, GSG 16, p. 239). Goodman was harshly attacked for ontological nonsense. Simmel in *Rembrandt* talks of a 'dark, substantial being', which grounds both life and forms as opposite to it (GSG 15, p. 385), though he makes no further mention of it two years later in *The View of Life*. Additionally, there are still only a few investigations into Simmel's relationship to Husserl beyond their personal friendship (Backhaus, 1998, 2003) – did he probably intend something similar to the latter's famous life-world as a basic, undeniable structure from which any possible knowledge evolves (Husserl, 1963, pp. 49, 124 ff.)? Here, with an accusation that is consistent from Richard Hamann to Georg Lukács' obituary in 1918 to David P. Frisby, one must truly regret Simmel's merely 'impressionistic' remarks instead of his coming to terms systematically (Hamann, 1907, p. 217; Gassen & Landmann, 1958, p. 172; Frisby, 1981, pp. 69 f., 87).

But finally, and probably in a 'typically German' manner, the ultimate Simmel cannot resist explicitly melting together the once separated ethics and aesthetics. In his 'Normativity in the Artwork' of 1918, Simmel becomes extremely speculative: each great piece of art, in its combination of elements towards a whole, can show or *visualise* how an eminent life shall happen (GSG 13, p. 393). It seems contradictory that suddenly Simmel ignores his own programme of radical aesthetic autonomy. Yet possibly, the temptation was over-whelming to suggest a more convincing program than the Kantian idea to model the aes-thetic effect as a mere *virtual* analogy between epistemic and moral judgements, between theoretical and practical reason, as executed in the *Critique of Judgement* as the 'subjective general' (KdU B XLVI, 20, 26). In one of his latest essays, Simmel's obvious motivation was to do it better.

Reception

As Jürgen Habermas (1991, p. 161) put it, Simmel's influence is widespread, but mostly anonymous. First of all, as a theorist, at times when modern tendencies were blamed by Emperor Wilhelm II as 'gutter art', he publicly backed aestheticism and *Jugendstil* emphasis of the indispensable autonomy of art, yet this was not based on a preference for *l'art pour l'art* but *'l'art pour la vie'* (GSG 13, p. 15). Furthermore, in about 1900 nearly all rebirths of metaphysics with a strong aesthetic foundation depended on Simmel. Close disciples, like Lukács in his early book title of 1911 *Die Seele und die Formen*, acknowledge their debts to Simmel, but even the late Marxist Lukács still relies on Simmelian categories, besides Hegel (Ludz, 1963, p. 63), when he talks of 'intensive totalities' and the relevance of forms throughout his dogmatic writings. Most leftist thinkers struggled with Simmel's influence, since Ernst Bloch simply invented Simmel in uniform during World War I, by shouting out chauvinistic slogans (Rammstedt & Meyer, 2006, p. 194 f.). Walter Benjamin's dependency on Simmel becomes clear when one scrolls through his notes on the *Passagenwerk*, even his concept of allegory can be read as heavily determined by Simmel (Meyer, 2017, p. 295 f.). Theodor W. Adorno, who always blamed Simmel for simply bad metaphysics, took over – like Benjamin – the motif of 'constellation' and 'crystallization': to think inductively, cen-tring arguments around a topic more than catching it conceptually (Adorno, 1973, pp. 326, 335). Max Raphael, who was introduced to Rodin by Simmel, demands 'absolute shaping' in his dissertation *From Monet to Picasso* (Raphael, 1989a, pp. 34, 69), thus exaggerating Sim-mel's mostly negative view on new tendencies in the fine arts such as futurism and expres-sionism. Yet, even after his Marxist-materialistic turn, Raphael's reflections on the ontological status of a work of art and his emphasis of its 'organic unity' still evolve from Simmel (Raphael, 1989b, pp. 330, 319 f.; Meyer, 2017, p. 282 ff.).

The most beautiful reminiscence on Simmel is supplied by Wilhelm Worringer whose famous dissertation *Abstraction and Empathy* of 1908 was initially read as a justification of expressionism.[15] Worringer reported that he only had to see Simmel from afar at the Troca-déro, Paris, at Easter-time in 1905, to get the main idea of his book like a lightning bolt (Worringer, 1996, p. 9 f.).[16] Yet it is easy to detect his factual inspiration based on the early Simmel's talk of art as capable of bringing reality close to us (empathy) and/or putting it at a distance (abstraction) (GSG 6, p. 658 f.; cf. Worringer, 1996, pp. 47, 52, 69, 189). Funnily enough, Worringer's dichotomy had an influence on Simmel, who immediately obtained a typescript of Worringer's book (GSG 23, p. 40). Unfortunately, a few years later he used it to develop his own infamous concept of 'German style' being the only true inventive one (abstraction) in contrast to 'Roman style' as mere mimetic (empathy) (GSG 13, p. 316 f.; GSG 15, p. 507 ff.).

Recent studies of Simmel's philosophy of art provoke mixed feelings. Barbara Aulinger (1999, p. 16) claims that Simmel's *sociology* is directly inspired by contemporary art historians such as Adolf von Hildebrand, Alois Riegl, and Konrad Fiedler, but her conclusions remain tentative (ibid., pp. 110, 120, 136). Oliver Schwerdt adopts Hannes Boehringer's thesis, according to Simmel, of the functionality that money brings to the value of things and applies it to Dadaism: aleatoric concepts and nonsense poetry now represent functionality on an aesthetic level (Schwerdt, 2012, pp. 17, 43 f.), thus illustrating and at the same time solving Simmel's diagnosis of a 'tragedy of culture' (ibid., 52, 65 f.). It should be noted that interpretations of this kind derive from a 'with Simmel and against him' style: for instance, on the one hand, he did not ever admit teamwork as a productive means in aesthetics (GSG 6, p. 629); on the other hand, nor could he recognise any similarities between the economic and the aesthetic sphere (ibid., p. 361f.): the work of art is strictly opposed to any kind of functionality (GSG 13, p. 390).

Although aesthetics have rediscovered that metaphysics is mainly a domain of the fine arts (Wyss, 2007, p. 157), for contemporary purposes, Simmel's attempts seem hard to revitalise. Once Simmel was right when he insisted on the autonomous state of the arts, stressing their particular sphere of 'values'. Due to his small amount of too 'simple' concepts (Adorno, 1974, p. 558 f.), his writings lack any kind of technical means that are conducive for interpretation. Nevertheless, he was able to complete a formal analysis of poetry, as he showed in a review devoted to Paul Ernst's *Polymeter* (GSG 1, p. 410 ff.). Simmel's views on Rembrandt or Michelangelo are not meant to apply to other artists, let alone his ignorance of any historical interest. There is no chance of generalising his insights, nor of using them as a 'tool kit'. There is no methodological reflection. For Simmel, who did not believe in the comparability of philosophers or artists (GSG 14, p. 34ff.), this approach was merely consistent. However, even the much acclaimed realisation of a specific artwork as a unity, as *form*, has not become much clearer. It remains, with Simmel, a 'wonder'. However, what is missing is something similar to a workshop report, though metaphysical, too, in the manner of Paul Cézanne, Hugo von Hofmannsthal, or Paul Valéry, who made several such contributions around 1900. Albeit not in the style of an artist, Simmel always insisted on the philosophy of art's licence to free speculation (GSG 21, p. 143) – one has to love it, or leave it.

Notes

1 Unless specified otherwise, all English quotes are the author's translation.
2 Levine (2007) suggests focusing more on 'form' and the Kant/Goethe dichotomy as a key to systematise Simmel's œuvre as a whole.
3 Quotations after Georg Simmel, *Gesamtausgabe*, ed. by Otthein Rammstedt (with GSG), 24 vols., Frankfurt/M.: Suhrkamp, 1989–2015.
4 One has to wonder that at no point does he explicitly deal with Hegel's classicist aesthetics. Incidentally, I am convinced that Simmel did not read Hegel extensively before 1905. This is not easy to prove, although it could be demonstrated indirectly via several transcriptions made by students during his lectures over the years, as collected in GSG 21. The only Hegel exegesis published during Simmel's lifetime is in his *Main Problems of Philosophy* of 1910, GSG 14, p. 66 ff. Strangely

enough, in his lectures, Hegel's aesthetics seem not 'important enough' to Simmel, GSG 21, p. 391.

5 Obviously, Simmel does not qualify as a 're-reader'. Opinions on other philosophers, once set down in writing, are repeated for decades in various contexts.

6 Reminiscent of metaphors in Shelley's *Defence of Poetry*, his 'Sonnet (Lift not the painted veil)' and Schopenhauer's 'veil of Maja'.

7 Simmel's many different meanings of 'form' in sociology, philosophy and aesthetics warrant a semantic analysis which has not been written yet. For a focus on sociology that is still instructive, cf. Steinhoff (1924/25).

8 Simmel preferred the visual arts for his conclusions; he rather seldom wrote about literature.

9 This was recognised early by Niehues-Pröbsting (1981, p. 107).

10 For Simmel, Goethe was not a genius or at least exceptionally skilled; he just had considerable luck (and was clever enough) to fully live out his interests.

11 Philipp Otto Runge spoke of 'Totalanschauung' and 'Totaleindruck' as a precondition of creative imagination, cf. letter to unknown person 1807/08, letter to Clemens Brentano of 5 December 1809, Runge (1938, pp. 125, 227).

12 Incidentally, hermeneutics did not yet advance a step further. Even Henrich (2007, p. 192), has to admit: 'In expressions, which is the first that attracts understanding, there always is to feel something from the whole life … But the entire context is not accessible like a singular and immediate expression'.

13 On aesthetic semantics, (cf. Hogrebe, 1980; Meyer, 2013). In his famous article, Frege (1969, p. 45), talks of 'Sinnfärbung', but we do not know whether Simmel even knew the colleague's name.

14 Some contrary positions are Boehm (1995, 2007) (hermeneutics); Mitchell (2005) (discourse), Brandt (1999) (analytical), Bredekamp (2010) (culturalism).

15 'Abstraction' is meant as a powerful type of doing art in early cultures, 'empathy' is reserved for mature (and rather decadent) eras, cf. Worringer (1996, pp. 69f, 81).

16 There is some doubt about Worringer's story, Kittlitz (2012, p. 83). However, around Easter 1905, Simmel in fact stayed in Paris – to meet Rodin. A close reading could easily show how deeply Worringer is influenced by Simmel's concepts, cf. Meyer (2017, p. 109f).

References

Adorno, T. W. (1973). Die Aktualität der Philosophie (1931). In Id. *Gesammelte Schriften*, vol. 1 (pp. 325–344), Ed. by R. Tiedemann. Frankfurt/M.: Suhrkamp.

Adorno, T. W. (1974). Henkel, Krug und frühe Erfahrung. In Id. *Noten zur Literatur* (pp. 556–566), Ed. by R. Tiedemann. Frankfurt/M.: Suhrkamp.

Aulinger, B. (1999). *Die Gesellschaft als Kunstwerk. Fiktion und Methode bei Georg Simmel*. Wien, Passagen.

Backhaus, G. (1998). Georg Simmel as an eidetic scientist. *Sociological Theory*, 16, 260–281.

Backhaus, G. (2003). Husserlian affinities in Simmel's later philosophy of history: The 1918 essay. *Human Studies*, 26, 223–258.

Boehm, G. (Ed.) (1995). *Was ist ein Bild?* Munich: Fink.

Boehm, G. (2007). *Wie Bilder Sinn erzeugen. Die Macht des Zeigens*. Berlin: Berlin University Press.

Bohrer, K. H. (1981). *Plötzlichkeit. Zum Augenblick ästhetischen Scheins*. Frankfurt/M.: Suhrkamp.

Brandt, R. (1999). *Die Wirklichkeit des Bildes. Sehen und Erkennen – Vom Spiegel zum Kunstbild*. Munich: Hanser.

Bredekamp, H. (2010). *Theorie des Bildakts. Frankfurter Adorno-Vorlesungen 2007*. Berlin: Suhrkamp.

Frege, G. (1969). Über Sinn und Bedeutung (1890). In Id. *Funktion, Begriff, Bedeutung. Fünf Studien* (pp. 40–65), Ed. by G. Patzig, 3rd ed. Göttingen: Vandenhoeck & Ruprecht.

Frisby, D. P. (1981). *Sociological impressionism. A reassessment of Simmel's social theory*. London: Heinemann.

Gassen, K., & Landmann, M. (Eds.) (1958). *Buch des Dankes an Georg Simmel. Briefe, Erinnerungen, Bibliographie. Zu seinem Geburtstag am 1. März 1958*. Berlin: Duncker & Humblot.

Geulen, E. (2014). Nachlese: Simmels Goethebuch und Benjamins Wahlverwandtschaftenaufsatz. In J. Maatsch (Ed.), *Morphologie und Moderne. Goethes 'anschauliches Denken' in den Geistes- und Kulturwissenschaften seit 1800* (pp. 195–218). Berlin and Boston, MA: de Gruyter.

Gibson, J. J. (1979). *The ecological approach to visual perception*. Boston, MA: Houghton Mifflin.

Gombrich, E. H. (2002). *Kunst und Illusion. Zur Psychologie der bildlichen Darstellung (1960).* 6th ed. Berlin: Phaidon.

Goodman, N. (1984). *Weisen der Welterzeugung.* Frankfurt/M.: Suhrkamp.

Grave, J. (2014). Der Akt des Bildbetrachtens. Überlegungen zur rezeptionsästhetischen Temporalität des Bildes. In M. Gamper & H. Hühn (Eds.), *Ästhetische Eigenzeiten in Kunst, Literatur und Wissenschaft* (pp. 51–71). Hannover: Wehrhahn.

Gumbrecht, H. U. (2004). *Diesseits der Hermeneutik. Über die Produktion von Präsenz.* Frankfurt/M: Suhrkamp.

Habermas, J. (1991). Georg Simmel über Philosophie und Kultur. Nachwort zu einer Sammlung von Essays (1983). In Id. *Texte und Kontexte* (pp. 157–169). Frankfurt/M.: Suhrkamp.

Hamann, R. (1907). *Der Impressionismus in Leben und Kunst.* Köln: DuMont.

Hegel, G. W. F. (1986). *Vorlesungen über die Ästhetik I.* Werke vol. 13, Ed. by. E. Moldenhauer & K. M. Michel. Frankfurt/M.: Suhrkamp.

Henrich, D. (2007). *Denken und Selbstsein. Vorlesungen über Subjektivität.* Frankfurt/M.: Suhrkamp.

Hogrebe, W. (1980). Semantische Ästhetik. *Zeitschrift für philosophische Forschung, 34,* 18–37.

Husserl, E. (1963). *Die Krisis der europäischen Wissenschaften und die transzendentale Phänomenologie (1935). Husserliana* vol. VI, Ed. by W. Biemel. The Hague: Nijhoff.

Husserl, E. (1976). *Ideen zu einer reinen Phänomenolgie und phänomenologischen Philosophie (1913). Husserliana* vol. III/1, Ed. by K. Schuhmann, The Hague: Nijhoff.

Iser, W. (1972). *Der implizite Leser. Kommunikationsformen des Romans von Bunyan bis Beckett.* München: Fink.

Kittlitz, W. V. (2012). Das Gespenst des Psychologismus. Erwin Panofsky über Riegl und Worringer. In N. Grammacini & J. Rösler (Eds.), *Hundert Jahre 'Abstraktion und Einfühlung'. Konstellationen um Wilhelm Worringer* (pp. 79–92). Munich: Fink.

Köhnke, K. C. (1996). *Der junge Simmel – in Theoriebeziehungen und sozialen Bewegungen.* Frankfurt/M.: Suhrkamp.

Levine, D. N. (2007). Soziologie und Lebensanschauung. Zwei Wege der 'Kant-Goethe-Synthese' bei Georg Simmel. *Simmel Studies, 17*(2), 239–263.

Lichtblau, K. (1984). Das 'Pathos der Distanz'. Präliminarien zur Nietzsche-Rezeption bei Georg Simmel. In H.-J. Dahme & O. Rammstedt (Eds.), *Georg Simmel und die Moderne. Neue Interpretationen und Materialien* (pp. 231–281). Frankfurt/M.: Suhrkamp.

Ludz, P. (1963). Marxismus und Literatur. In G. Lukács, *Schriften zur Literatursoziologie* (pp. 19–68), Ed. by P. Ludz, 2nd ed. Neuwied: Luchterhand.

Luhmann, N. (1995). *Die Kunst der Gesellschaft.* Frankfurt/M.: Suhrkamp.

Marquard, O. (1994). Krise der Erwartung – Stunde der Erfahrung. Zur ästhetischen Kompensation des modernen Erfahrungsverlustes. In Id. *Skepsis und Zustimmung. Philosophische Studien* (pp. 70–92). Stuttgart: Reclam.

Meyer, I. (2008). 'Jenseits der Schönheit'. Simmels Ästhetik – originärer Eklektizismus? In G. Simmel (Ed.), *Jenseits der Schönheit. Schriften zur Ästhetik und Kunstphilosophie* (pp. 399–437). Frankfurt/M.: Suhrkamp.

Meyer, I. (2013). Notizen zur gegenwärtigen Lage der Ästhetik. *Merkur, 67,* 191–204.

Meyer, I. (2017). *Georg Simmels Ästhetik. Autonomiepostulat und soziologische Referenz.* Weilerswist: Velbrück Wissenschaft.

Mitchell, W. J. T. (2005). *What do pictures want? The lives and loves of images.* Chicago, IL: Chicago University Press.

Müller, H.-P. (2018). Einführung. In H.-P. Müller & T. Reitz (Eds.), *Simmel-Handbuch. Begriffe, Hauptwerke, Aktualität* (pp. 11–90). Frankfurt/M.: Suhrkamp.

Niehues-Pröbsting, H. (1981). Das 'individuelle Gesetz' in der Kunst. Georg Simmels Ästhetik der Lebensphilosophie. In U. Franke & V. Gerhardt (Eds.), *Die Kunst gibt zu denken. Über das Verhältnis von Philosophie und Kunst* (pp. 100–114). Münster: Wölk.

Nietzsche, F. (1980). *Die Geburt der Tragödie aus dem Geist der Musik (1871).* In G. Colli & M. Montinari (Eds.), *Kritische Studienausgabe,* vol. 1 (pp. 7–156). Munich: DTV.

Orth, E. W. (2015). Georg Simmels Metaphysik als Ironie des Lebens. *Zeitschrift für Kulturphilosophie 9: Schwerpunkt Simmel, 2015*(1–2), 241–256.

Plumpe, G., & Werber, N. (1995). Umwelten der Literatur. In G. Plumpe & N. Werber (Eds.), *Beobachtungen der Literatur. Aspekte einer polykontexturalen Literaturwissenschaft* (pp. 9–33). Opladen: Westdeutscher Verlag.

Rammstedt, O., & Meyer, I. (2006). Eine Episode wird zum Trauma: Bloch bei Simmel. *Simmel Studies*, *16*(2), 183–213.

Raphael, M. (1989a). *Von Monet zu Picasso. Grundzüge einer Ästhetik und Entwicklung der modernen Malerei (1913)*, Ed. by K. Binder. Frankfurt/M.: Suhrkamp.

Raphael, M. (1989b). *Wie will ein Kunstwerk gesehen werden? 'The Demands of Art'*, Ed. by K. Binder. Frankfurt/M.: Suhrkamp.

Ritter, J. (1974). Die Aufgabe der Geisteswissenschaften in der modernen Gesellschaft (1963). In Id. *Subjektivität. Sechs Aufsätze* (pp. 105–140). Frankfurt/M.: Suhrkamp.

Runge, P.-O. (1938). *Schriften, Fragmente/Briefe*, Ed. by E. Forsthoff. Berlin: Friedrich Vorwerk.

Schwerdt, O. (2012). *Geld und Unsinn. Georg Simmel und der Dadaismus. Eine systematische Studie zu relativistischer Philosophie und Kunst*. Leipzig: Euphorion.

Seel, M. (2000). *Ästhetik des Erscheinens*. München: Hanser.

Simmel, G. (1989–2015). *Gesamtausgabe (GSG)*, Ed. by O. Rammstedt, 24 vols. Frankfurt/M.: Suhrkamp.

Smuda, M. (1986). Natur als ästhetischer Gegenstand. Zur Konstitution von Landschaft. In Id. (Ed.), *Landschaft* (pp. 44–69). Frankfurt/M.: Suhrkamp.

Steinhoff, M. (1924/25). Die Form als soziologische Grundkategorie bei Georg Simmel. *Kölner Vierteljahreshefte für Soziologie*, *4*, 215–259.

Susman, M. (1910). *Das Wesen der modernen deutschen Lyrik*. Stuttgart: Strecker & Schröder.

Tokarzewska, M. (2010). *Der feste Grund des Unberechenbaren. Georg Simmel zwischen Soziologie und Literatur*. Wiesbaden: VS Verlag für Sozialwissenschaften.

Voßkamp, W. (2009). 'Diese Rastlosigkeit von Selbstentwicklung und Produktivität'. Georg Simmels Goethe-Buch. *Simmel Studies*, *19*(1), 5–19.

Warburg, A. (1992). Dürer und die italienische Antike (1906). In Id. *Ausgewählte Schriften und Würdigungen* (pp. 125–130), Ed. by D. Wuttke, 3rd ed. Baden-Baden: Koerner Verlag.

Wölfflin, H. (1982). *Autobiographie, Tagebücher und Briefe*, Ed. by J. Gantner, Basel: Schwabe.

Worringer, W. (1996). *Abstraktion und Einfühlung. Ein Beitrag zur Stilpsychologie (1908)*. Dresden: Philo Fine Arts.

Wyss, B. (1985). Simmels Rembrandt. In G. Simmel (Ed.), *Rembrandt. Ein kunstphilosophischer Versuch* (pp. VII–XXXI). München: Matthes & Seitz.

Wyss, B. (2007). *Die Wiederkehr des Neuen*, Ed. by S. Walther. Hamburg: Philo Fine Arts.

13

FRAMING, PAINTING, SEEING

Simmel's *Rembrandt* and the sense of modernity

Thomas Kemple

Introduction

Social theory finds its focus and reaches its limits in the human encounter with otherness. In facing what is *singular* about ourselves and others, we become connected to one another, realizing how we are more or less the same (in the sense of the Greek *homo*); how groups attract and repel each other, or conflict with and complement one another as opposites (*hetero*); and how individuals relate to or distinguish themselves on the basis of what belongs to them as uniquely their own (*auto*). Since emerging as a field of inquiry in the 19th century, social theory has pursued the knowledge of sociality and sociability, in part by acknowledging the otherness of the other (*allo*). Classical theories of the social world consider how actions are oriented to or taken over in the process of becoming familiar or foreign, of transforming the strange into the intimate, or of making what at first seems typical into something unique. A striking feature of the social theory of Georg Simmel lies in how he does not restrict himself only to investigating the forms of association (*Vergesellschaftungsformen*) between individuals, or the contents of interactions (*Wechselwirkungen*) between human collectives (Kemple, 2007). He goes further to develop what we might call a theory of *allosociality*, an understanding of the *thresholds of existence* through which non-human being surpasses human culture and the points where life itself extends into more-life or even more-than-life (Simmel, 2010, p. 13; Pyyhtinen, 2018, pp. 102-24). Simmel's writings are at once sociological in their concern with understanding the human condition and philosophical in meditating on the aesthetic, ethical, and metaphysical limits of life itself (Goodstein, 2017, pp. 249-95).

The boundaries between these aspects of Simmel's work are especially evident in his 1916 monograph *Rembrandt*, subtitled 'an essay in the philosophy of art'. In this underappreciated and supremely challenging late work, Simmel is not primarily concerned with providing a sociological account of the aesthetic breakthrough achieved in the Dutch Golden Age, or in assessing how Rembrandt's work resisted the Baroque style dominant in mid-17th century Europe, as would an art critic and historian (Schama, 1999). Nor is he mainly interested in examining the influence on Rembrandt of the Reformed Church in Holland, the significance of Amsterdam's Jewish community at the time, or the expanding hegemony of the

United Provinces in the capitalist world economy, as would a cultural and intellectual historian (Neumann, 1902). Rembrandt's personal circumstances likewise receive only passing mention, when they are noted at all, such as the personal tragedies of the deaths of his children and his beloved Saskia, his financial hardships from bad investments and overspending, his mentorship of younger artists in his workshop, and his membership in artistic guilds. In contrast to conventional sociologies of the modern art world, and of the field of painting in particular, Simmel does not dwell on the social conditions, historical transformations, and individual inspirations that informed Rembrandt's distinctive 'aesthetic gaze', or how this way of seeing the world was institutionalized in schools and salons, promoted through patrons and merchants, or acknowledged by critics and collectors as constituting a distinctive artistic style, standard, or 'nomos' (Becker, 1982 p. 35; Bourdieu, 1993, p. 223, 2017). Rather than asking 'why Rembrandt, and why in the Netherlands of the early 17th century?', Simmel's questions centre on the 'inner significance [*seelische Bedeutung*]' of Rembrandt's works, and on the 'felt values [*Wertempfindungen*] that we [viewers] associate with his art as such, quite independently of the conditions of its coming into being' (Simmel, 2005, p. 1; GSG 15, p. 307).

Simmel's stated objective in this study need not distract us from situating his arguments within the life-philosophy (*Lebensphilosophie*) and aesthetic writings of his later years, in particular his concern to develop a social theory of individuality freed from the constraints of both naturalism and conventionalism (Scott & Staubmann, 2005; Fitzi, 2019, p. 109 f.). In what follows I explore how Simmel focuses on what is unique and original about Rembrandt's work and the emerging *sense of modernity* his art exemplifies. Simmel is best known for developing a general theory of the modern age in terms of the intersecting social circles of the metropolis and the cultural dynamics of the money economy (Fitzi, 2019, pp. 7–39). In the 'Excursus on the Sociology of the Senses' from the chapter of *Sociology* on 'Space and the Spatial Ordering of Society', for example, he analyses in 'microscopic' detail how connections and interactions between individuals are mediated through the eye, above all in the social act of seeing and being seen by others. Among other topics, he considers how the social space of the modern metropolis transforms our worldview by altering how often or how long we are exposed to the gaze of others:

> Before the development of buses, trains, and streetcars in the nineteenth century, people were not at all in a position to be able or to have to view one another for minutes or hours at a time without speaking to one another.
>
> *(Simmel, 2009, p. 573)*

In the Rembrandt study, by contrast, Simmel shifts his focus from the *spatial* ordering of modern social life to examine how the sense of sight is engaged in the visual arts and expresses something distinctive about the *temporal* experience of the modern individual. For Simmel, 'Rembrandt' is not just the name of an artistic genius who transcended the times in which he lived, but also an emblem for what is new in our experience of individuality. Rembrandt's work, rather than the man, is therefore an expression of something unique about the times we ourselves are living through.

Framing the human condition

Artists or artworks cannot be understood entirely apart from the cultural temperament, historical conditions, and personal dispositions of the world that first gave them life. Rembrandt is generally known for the profound empathy he conveyed for the human condition, as seen from the particular perspectives of the poor, the propertied, the young, and the ageing who populate his work. Likewise, his works are distinguished by a particular style that stands out against the backdrop of his age. In one of Simmel's last essays, on Germanic and classical Romanic artistic styles, he considers how the overall character of an artwork can express the general mood of a period or the pervasive sensibility of a people, drawing comparisons between northern and southern Europe. (Like the Rembrandt study, this essay was written during his time in Strasbourg, where the two cultures meet and mix.) In Mediterranean antiquity and the Italian Renaissance, artists aimed to create lucid panoramas with geometrical precision, or vivid scenes depicting the rational unity of lives lived in public. By contrast, the artists of northern Europe are more concerned with portraying private and intimate worlds, 'the life always of the individual human being, which can proceed only through this one canal' (Simmel, 2007, p. 49). In an almost aphoristic way he argues that, 'where classicism seeks to present form in the appearance of life, Rembrandt sought to present life through form' (ibid.). Rembrandt's art turns away from a consideration the general features of beauty configured as a timeless unity and dwells instead on the unique personality, fate, and 'inner universality' of individuals who exist 'as a wave within a greater flux that can be felt only at a particular instant in time' (Simmel, 2007, p. 5). Rembrandt can be described as a painter of singular actions and instants, each following its own individual law, rather than as a monumental artist of transcendent forms reflecting a universal ideal.

In the 'Preface' to the Rembrandt book, Simmel describes his method as one that departs from the 'low road' that examines the historical conditions allowing a work to be classified in a certain way, on the one hand, or that analyses only particular combinations of form, composition, colour, and subject-matter, on the other hand. Extending this spatial metaphor, he describes the latter approach, which picks apart the elements of a work of art and examines their spatial juxtaposition, as remaining somehow 'in front of' the work of art without really entering into the emotional response or inner effect it has on the viewer. His own philosophical approach, by contrast, begins from 'behind' by locating the 'existence and experience' of the work of art within 'the movements of the soul, the height of conceptuality … and the depths of world-historical antitheses' (Simmel, 2005, p. 2). In other words, his aim is to evoke the singular experience and impression 'emerging out of or standing above' Rembrandt's work. Perhaps with one of Rembrandt's most well-known group portraits in mind (**Figure 13.1**), he contrasts this philosophical attitude with the analytical treatment of art, which he compares to the technique of dissecting bodies and souls on canvas: 'But no more than a living being can be animated from the dismembered limbs on a dissection bench can a work of art, reassembled out of such elements, be recreated and thereby rendered intelligible' (Simmel, 2005, p. 2). Like the hand of the corpse in the scene of Dr Tulp's anatomy lesson, which directs the gaze of the men in attendance - and by extension the viewer - to the anatomical atlas in front of them, Simmel argues that a strictly aesthetic analysis cannot explicate the experience of wonder and insight evoked by Rembrandt's paintings. At most, Simmel admits (2005, p. 3), the pages of his own essay can recall the overall emotional effect on the viewer, without breaking this body of work apart into its elements.

In a short piece from 1905 on 'The Aesthetics of the Portrait', Simmel attempts to account for how sensory and psychic elements are blended together in the art of portrait-painting, which is based on 'the capacity of visible aspects to express something invisible, something like a soul' (GSG 7, p. 322). In *The Anatomy Lesson* this animating principle is dramatized and intensified in the juxtaposition of clothed bodies and a naked corpse, and in the play of facial expressions with one another, rather than in any suggestion that there is some invisible essence behind any of these aspects of the scene (which in any case would be

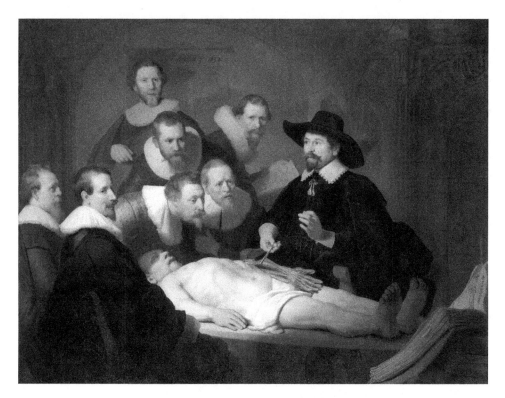

Figure 13.1 Rembrandt. The Anatomy Lesson of Doctor Nicholaes Tulp (1635)
Mauritshuis Online Catalogue. *Source*: https://commons.wikimedia.org/wiki/

impossible for the dead man!). As the novelist W. G. Sebald (1998, pp. 13-17) remarks about this painting, it is odd that the dissection does not begin in the customary way by opening up the abdomen, but rather with the hand of the corpse of the criminal (the typical specimen for anatomical demonstrations at the time). However, the arm seems too elongated and might even be purposefully presented as a double of the right hand of the dead man, the doctor, or even the painter himself. Like a manicule on the margins of a medieval manuscript, the dead man's hand seems to be gesturing to the medical textbook at the foot of the dissection table. In fact, the scene graphically depicts a significant moment in the history of modern medicine, when the gaze of science was turning away from the eye of God and penetrating 'autopsicly' beneath the surfaces of Creation to inspect the inner tissues and explore the complex structures of the human body (O'Neill, 1995). In contrast to Descartes, whose anatomical studies in Amsterdam at the time aimed at rendering perception transparent, with light 'reading through the geometry of bodies' (Foucault, 1973, p. xiii), Dr Tulp and his audience seem poised to descend into the dark folds of the flesh, as if on the verge of discovering the obscure workings of life itself, and thus the very nature of our mortality.

Although Simmel does not invoke this historical and cultural framework, he implicitly situates Rembrandt's art on the threshold of the modern revolution in aesthetic techniques and everyday perception, a revolution that is accompanied by a fundamental shift in the ethical view of human beings and the scientific study of life. This larger cultural context is invoked more explicitly in the opening pages of his last book, *The View of Life*, where Simmel

(2010, pp. 1-6) suggests in broadly philosophical terms that the very nature of human beings is to transcend limits, and that a defining feature of the modern age lies in the technical capacity to break through boundaries. In particular, he notes that the expansion of the sensible world through the invention of the telescope and the microscope in the early modern period has given rise to a new awareness of our boundedness as human beings, and at the same time has propelled our drive to burst through all limitations. Where the telescope brings far-away worlds into close proximity and renders the invisible visible, the microscope discloses the fine details of minute structures that disrupt our natural perception of space and disorient our sense of time. To illustrate this point, he cites a long passage from 'a most thoughtful biologist', who imagines how a fictional creature with eyes like 'the structure of a giant telescope' might view the world (Simmel, 2010, p. 4). Such a being could be expected to have a longer lifespan, produce very different kinds of objects, or conceive of time and space in ways that unsettle or surpass human perception and capacities. Simmel's unacknowledged source here, the baron Felix von Uexküll's 1913 essay collection *Bausteine zu einer biologischen Weltanschauung* (Elements of a biological worldview), considers the world of animal perception in a way that abandons the conventional anthropocentric perspective of the life-sciences (Agamben, 2004, p. 39). In the essay Simmel quotes from, Uexküll (1913, p. 141) describes an 'emerging worldview' (*kommende Weltanschauung*) already evident in modern physics and the avant-garde artistic movements of his day. Just as Uexküll considers how animal perspectives on the world as well as innovations in optical technologies displace ordinary human-centred worldviews, Simmel reflects on how Rembrandt uses colour, canvas, and paint-bush to frame the human condition and the experience of the modern individual in new and often uncanny ways. Although artwork 'closes itself off against everything external to itself as a world of its own', as Simmel (1994, p. 11) argues in an essay on the picture frame, in Rembrandt's work this closure also opens up another perspective on life and new ways of experiencing the world.

Painting the self

To reiterate, Simmel approaches Rembrandt not as a critic, historian, or sociologist of art and aesthetics, but as a life-philosopher concerned with the outer limits of existence and the inner experience of mortality. In the 'Preface', he uses an optical analogy to describe his philosophical method of meditating on 'the phenomenon of Rembrandt' (*die Erscheinung Rembrandts*). Rather than analyzing the craft of the artist in detail or examining the man and his times, his art-philosophical experiment or essay (*kunstphilsophische Versuch*) will attempt 'to lower a plumb line through the immediate singular, the simply given, into the depths of ultimate spiritual-intellectual meanings' (*von dem unmittelbar Einzelnen, dem einfach Gegeben das Senkblei in die Schicht der letzten geistigen Bedeutsamkeiten zu schicken*) (Simmel, 2005, p. 3; GSG 14, p. 309). In contrast to his other writings, this 'plumb line' or probe will be not be lowered from the surfaces of the metropolis and or the money economy (on Simmel's use of this analogy in 'The Metropolis and Mental Life' see Kemple, 2018, pp. 100-102). Instead, he treats the artwork as an entry point into the modern worldview and as a pathway to the inner experience of the modern soul. Ironically, the vibrancy and vitality of Rembrandt's figures derive as much from their lively settings – in taverns, battles, lecture theatres, and historical scenes, or caught up in quieter moments of working, studying, reflecting, or resting – as from the absent presence of death that inhabits their life from the outset. Death provides 'the colouration and shaping of life', and is therefore the inner and ever-present subject-matter of Rembrandt's paintings (Simmel, 2005, p. 74). Using the language of his life-philosophical writings, he describes how Rembrandt handles the tragic character of death not as a mournful or sorrowful affair, but rather as emerging exuberantly out of the law and meaning of each of life's moments (Simmel, 2005, p. 76, 2010, pp. 63-70).

Rembrandt is perhaps best known for the many ways he portrays his ageing body and his own mortality, without vanity or pretence and thus as sincerely as he does any other subject. 'Death only reaches macroscopic visibility at the moment of death', Simmel (2005, p. 71) asserts, making a point that is graphically exemplified in *The Anatomy Lesson*. Otherwise, in the course of our daily activities, death shapes the meaning of life unnoticed and colours each moment in silence. The metaphysical significance of this idea is illustrated in Simmel's reflections on Rembrandt's famous series of self-portraits (**Figures 13.2 and 13.3**). With each attempt at painting himself in a certain pose, mood, or character, Rembrandt trains his eye to see himself as an other, as if to regard the inside from the outside or to make the invisible visible. This technique evolves through the course of his career, as Simmel notes in his discussion of how Rembrandt represents typical features of the human form while also showing them to be unique to a particular person, including himself. For example,

Figure 13.2 Rembrandt. Rembrandt and Saskia in the Scene of the Prodigal Son (ca 1637)
Google Cultural Centre; *Source:* https://commons.wikimedia.org/wiki/

Figure 13.3 Rembrandt. Self-Portrait as Zeuxis (ca 1662)
The Yorck Project; *Source:* https://commons.wikimedia.org/wiki/Rembrandt/1656-1669#/media/

> if one looks carefully at the Dresden self-portrait with Saskia, his unadulterated joy of life appears a little artificial, as if it came momentarily to the surface of his nature, whose depth, however, is malformed by grave, inescapable fates reaching from afar.
>
> *(Simmel, 2005, p. 74)*

By contrast, in the famous self-portraits as he grows old Rembrandt expresses a genuineness and a spontaneity that break through the compulsive impetuousness and staged exuberance of youth. These later works convey the sobering and palpable presence of the 'inescapable fates' in their immediacy and with almost frightening clarity:

> [W]hen, by way of comparison, we look at the laughing self-portrait of the Carstanjen collection (of thirty-four years later) ... the laughing is unmistakably something purely momentary having, so to speak, come about as a coincidental combination

of life-elements, each one of which is quite differently tuned. The whole is as if infused by, and oriented toward, death.

(Simmel, 2005, p. 74)

Rembrandt's paintings of his ageing self display the accumulation of changing facial features, emotions, situations, and experiences making up a life that has lived to the fullest but is still in the process of becoming. And yet between these self-portraits, Simmel (2005, p. 74) concludes,

> exists a quite uncanny similarity: the grin of the old man appears only as the further development of that youthful joy and as if the element of death in life, which in this joy had withdrawn itself into the deepest most invisible, strata, has now been driving up to the surface.

Rembrandt's self-portraits, like his paintings of old people, express what Simmel (2005, p. 12) calls 'the secret of life': the paradox that each moment expresses something of the whole of life and yet is simultaneously unique and irreducible to any other.

In Simmel's view, Rembrandt indulges in luxuriousness, sumptuousness, and pompousness, but also focuses his gaze seriously and soberly on faces and bodies that have been worked over by ageing, fatigue, and vulnerability. These two self-portraits capture moments of rapture and joy, as if to arrest these moments in time under the aspect of eternity (*sub specie aeternitatis*, a phrase Simmel sometimes uses in silent homage to Spinoza). In each, he achieves this effect through the art of accentuation, in particular by casting himself somewhat unflatteringly in the role of a legendary character – as the prodigal son of the New Testament, squandering his fortune in brothels and taverns; and as the painter Zeuxis from Greek antiquity, who supposedly died laughing when an elderly woman asked him to paint her portrait in the guise of Aphrodite. Simmel (2005, pp. 79-81) goes on to note that, for Rembrandt, a person's 'character' can hardly be given once and for all but is instead revealed gradually over time and through experience in the course of a life. Between these two self-portraits, the lust for luxury seems to have turned from the impulse to relish in an extravagant scene furnished with lavish objects into a more austere meditation on the unique the features of a face radiating outward. Despite the contrast between these self-characterizations, each veers into a kind of 'caricature', in the sense that Simmel describes this artform in a short piece published a year after the Rembrandt study. What at first seems to be trivial or artless can be understood as a sign of the ultimate place of humans between the limitless powers of divinity on the one hand, and the finitude of animal existence on the other. In exceeding the desire to achieve organic equilibrium between the parts and the whole of life, the artist of caricature and characterization exposes something essential in the nature of the human being as a 'breaker of boundaries' and 'creature of exaggeration' (GSG 13, p. 244 f.).

In an essay on 'The Problem of the Portrait' published the year he died, Simmel offers some further reflections on how 'the painter's eye' extracts a unity out of the fragmentary character of life by enhancing the effects of form and lighting or by foregrounding and backgrounding figures. The painter emphasizes one-sidedly and in a deliberate way what each of us perceives automatically and grasps holistically without thinking. 'Not through our eyes alone as isolated anatomical instruments but only as whole unitary beings do we perceive other whole human beings. Our five senses are merely the canals through which our whole perceptual capability flows' (GSG 13, p. 372). Since the visual faculty working alone can only comprehend reality from a single angle or in pieces, the art of portraiture can be said to entail 'the completion of the sense of sight as such, the elaboration of pure appearances in their appeal and inner necessity for us' (ibid.). In contrast to the precise geometric proportions achieved in classical Greek and Renaissance art, or the ornamental principles of form and decoration exemplified in ancient or Egyptian art forms, Rembrandt's paintings attain a certain unity by selecting from life's diverse, fluctuating, and fragmentary features and reducing them to the world of a single sense, the faculty of sight (GSG 13, p. 379). In Simmel's estimation, Rembrandt is indeed the painter of modern life, but not just in the sense that Baudelaire (1972, p. 403) used this expression in the 19th century to describe the artist who depicts 'the transient, the fleeting, the contingent' along with 'the eternal and the immoveable'. Rembrandt is also the painter of modern individuals turning inward on themselves, and his self-portraits in particular offer a glimpse into what an inward journey into the depths of one's own soul might look like.

Seeing the other

In the course of discussing Rembrandt's religious art, which follows the chapters on the representation of the soul and the expression of individualization, Simmel enumerates the qualities of inwardness, religiosity, and light (*Seelenhaftigkeit, Religiosität, und Licht*) that distinguish his portrayal of both biblical and everyday scenes. The persistence of religious values in his works – especially their manifestly Protestant and pious concerns – would seem to constitute a stumbling block in any attempt to establish Rembrandt's modernity. Whether focusing on saintly or ordinary moments of personal devotion, revelation, and contemplation, Rembrandt's most accomplished paintings represent actions and experiences as emotional and soulful outpourings that proceed *sub specie religionis* (Simmel, 2005, p. 115). Although Rembrandt can indeed be called 'the painter of the soul', these spiritual qualities are not conveyed as illustrations of theological dogmas or of a mystical climax originating from some transcendent source, but rather through his steadfast attention to people in the flesh as they go about their everyday lives. In Simmel's view, Rembrandt's art is 'metaphysical' only in the sense that he conveys 'a value outside time [*ein überzeitlicher Wert*] that is borne exclusively by the inwardness of these temporal individuals' (Simmel, 2005, p. 130; GSG 15, p. 576). Sensuous and earthly phenomena are infused with mysterious and religious meanings that radiate outward from within the life of the figures, and from a source that is somehow immanent in the work of art itself.

These points are developed in an excursus that Simmel inserts into his discussion of how light provides the medium through which Rembrandt conveys this sense of soulfulness and religiosity. Elaborating on the question 'What Do We *See* in a Work of Art?', Simmel (2005, pp. 142-151; GSG 15, pp. 492-501) does not focus on the play of light and shadow or the combination of colours that allow a painting to represent something. Somewhat surprisingly, he answers the question through an extended discussion of Rembrandt's skill as a draughtsman and his remarkable talent in elevating etching to a true art form. Despite having no overtly religious content, Rembrandt's early drawing of his mother comes under particular scrutiny, specifically the detail of 'a fur collar that is a true miracle [*ein wahres Wunder*] of the art of etching' (Simmel, 2005, p. 142; GSG 15, p. 492; **Figure 13.4**). We 'see' the fur not because it is 'telegraphically' transported to us as a fragment of reality via the surface of the canvas, but nor do we 'supplement' what has been left out with something we supply from our memory. Rather, this sketch succeeds so brilliantly because it is self-sufficient as a work of art, subsisting in a world of its own at the same time as it draws from a sphere of reality and perception that is distinct from the artistic realm. Simmel describes this paradox in

Figure 13.4 Rembrandt. The Artist's Mother (1628)

Metmuseum.org; *Source:* https://commons.wikimedia.org/wiki/File:The_Artist%27s_Mother-_Head_
and_Bust,_Three-Quarters_Right_MET_MM4848.jpg

terms of the relative autonomy and mutual influence of the sphere of aesthetic perception
with respect to the realm of reality:

> The *artistic* vision and the arrangement of the configuration [*Gebilde*] that, in those
> three-dimensional and practical contexts [*Zusammenhängen*] is a 'real' fur collar,
> emerges – in terms of its origin, form, and sense – in a precisely autochtonous way
> within the artistic spirit and its creative categories, just as the three-dimensional fur
> collar does within all other genetic and correlative elements by which we label it
> 'real [*wirklichen*]'.
>
> *(Simmel, 2005, p. 145 f.; GSG 15, p. 495)*

Without claiming that the world of art is either dependent on or entirely separate from
the world of reality, Simmel argues that the 'wonder' of the fur collar lies in how the
lines follow the powers and laws of drawing while still belonging to the plane of actuality: 'Appearance still belongs to reality, just as a shadow still belongs the physical world,
because it is only through the latter that it exists' (Simmel, 2005, p. 148). In a sense,
each realm speaks its own language, with art translating the 'mother-tongue' of reality
into its own terms, but without 'redeeming' or 'overcoming' reality through a kind of
magic trick.

Like the question Simmel (2009, pp. 40-52) asks in the famous excursus from the first chapter of his monumental *Sociology*, 'How is Society Possible?', his answer to the question 'What Do We *See* in a Work of Art?' hinges on a Kantian understanding of how knowledge, perception, and representation cannot provide an exact copy, record, or replica of reality. The painting or drawing does not just convey the corporeal presence of the original, as in a photograph, a movie, or some other mechanical reproduction. Instead, the material reality of the image articulates the vision of the artist while at the same time reflecting back on and appealing to the observing eye of the viewer. The drawing of a fur collar cannot replicate a real fur collar in the way that a photograph reproduces light and shadow in realistic proportions through chemical and mechanical means (see Kemple, 2018, pp. 12-17 for a discussion of the earlier excursus, and p. x for a photograph of Simmel's wife Gertrud wearing a fur collar). As if to anticipate what Roland Barthes (1981, pp. 94–96) would later call the *punctum* of the photographic image, Simmel fixes on a detail in Rembrandt's drawing that punctures through the field of cultural interest (the *studium*), like the hand of the corpse gesturing toward the medical text in *The Anatomy Lesson*. In constantly refining his technique over time, Rembrandt has learned to see that every object and each feature has its own splendour – the collar as much as the veil, the eyes as much as the smile, all lovingly portrayed with the hand of the artist. As Jean Genet (2003, p. 87) describes this layer of the work, 'Rembrandt's secret' lies in how 'each face has value and that it refers – or leads – to one human identity that is equal to another'; and in Simmel's (2005, p. 6) formulation: 'the entire human being … is inherent in each separate experience'. With age and practice, Rembrandt channels his existence into the activities of his gaze and his hand, so that the canvas itself, even more than the figures depicted on it, becomes the substance of his passion to behold the whole of life.

At one point early on in the study, Simmel (2005, p. 38) observes how Rembrandt is less concerned with capturing the being (*Sein*) or essence (*Wesen*) of a subject than he is with seeking out the coming-into-being (*das Gewordensein*) of the person portrayed. The representation of movement and individual development are therefore distinctive features of Rembrandt's technique and immanent qualities of the work itself. With this observation in mind, Simmel (ibid.) asks, 'what is it then that moves within the picture?' In the cinema, the images themselves move while the spectators remain an immobile mass public settled into their seats with their attention fixed on the screen (see Frisch, 2009, pp. 131-142 on the historical context of these remarks). As in the moving picture, the painting breaks away from the three- (or four-) dimensional reality of the subject or scene by creating its own self-sufficient world on a material surface, and by framing and fixing a new reality on a two-dimensional plane. Referring to himself in the third person, Simmel (2005, p. 38) notes that while the painted figure itself does not move, something within 'the viewer Simmel' moves through his exploration of the painting and by completing the gesture immanent in the work, both before and after the moment represented. In short, the imagination of the viewer moves within the work and subsists on its own beside or in front of the work, each co-existing and overlapping with the other. The achievement of Rembrandt's art lies not in how it realizes a static form imposed from without, as in earlier artistic styles, but in how it appeals to a dynamic originating from inside 'the totality of life in its perceptive function' (Simmel, 2005, p. 42).

* * *

Throughout his reflections on the 'phenomenon of Rembrandt', Simmel's concern is not to provide a portrait of the artist and his times, to analyze the formal aesthetic elements of his work, or even to treat it as an historical document of early modernity. At the risk of seeming old-fashioned or narrow-minded, his aims are decidedly philosophical in examining the nature of the truth represented by and expressed in the work of art itself. More broadly, he considers how 'Rembrandtian art' expresses a distinctive *sense* of modernity and opens up a new experience of individuality. Thus, Simmel's task is also personal and even autobiographical in exploring a dimension of the life of the mind (*Geistesleben*) that at first appears to be very different from the metaphysical questions and sociological problems that preoccupy him elsewhere. In this regard, *Rembrandt* the book is also a kind of self-portrait, a mirror-image of Simmel's own inner ideals, passions, and beliefs, but refracted through the relatively foreign medium of painting. In contrast to his study of Goethe published a few years earlier, where literature, drama, and science are held up as expressions of the supreme values of life, and even as elements of his own personal 'confession', Rembrandt's art of pictorial representation appears here as merely *analogous* to Simmel's own elusive style of philosophical writing (see Kemple, 2019, on the contrasting case of Goethe). Rather than presenting an ideal to be emulated or a model for *saying* the truth with the pen, as in a philosophical essay or a sociological treatise, the work of art portrays the life of the individual with the paintbrush, *showing* something about the human condition by highlighting certain aspects of life over others.

In the final pages of the Rembrandt study, Simmel (2005, pp. 155-162; GSG 15, pp. 505-515) sketches some general speculations on the human capacity to create and to fashion (*Schöpfertum und Gestaltertum*). Where the artists of classical Greece limited themselves to moulding, reworking, and *forming* a given material by multiplying and augmenting certain features of reality over others, Rembrandt, Shakespeare, Beethoven and others in the modern Germanic tradition succeeded in *producing* something new out of the deepest sources of their own personal existence:

> The principle of life, as of individuality, in the meaning granted to it here [and especially in Rembrandt's work] resists the separation of form from the totality of being [*Seinstotalität*], even if this form is not inherited but is completely original: a self-production.
>
> *(Simmel, 2005, p. 159; GSG 15, p. 511)*

In other words, these artists defy the temptation to conform to 'valid' aesthetic standards or the compulsion to adapt to prevailing artistic conventions, insisting instead on expressing the creative unity of form and substance even at the risk of appearing strange, clumsy, or inaccessible. It is as if for them 'the truth' somehow lies both within and outside the work of art, or rather beside and around it as a byproduct, frame, and *parergon* that touches on, enters into, and cooperates with the process of creation itself (Derrida, 1987, p. 54). Despite this unique achievement, Simmel (2005, p. 162; GSG 15, p. 515) insists, a philosophical study can only separate (*scheiden*) out what is distinctive about these contrasting aesthetic styles rather than decide (*entscheiden*) between them.

As I have pointed out elsewhere (Kemple, 2018, pp. 153-166, 2019), Simmel often seems to suggest that modernity can be pictured as a kind of *adventure*, a leap out of the customs, habits, and patterns of previous periods of history into a risky, unprecedented, and unknown world. In an essay from 1911, he suggests that the cultures of modernity seem to expand the range of adventures and the intensity of experiences that anyone might have, whether by choice or by force: from colonial expeditions to commercial enterprises, and from foreign travel to love affairs (Simmel, 1997, p. 223 f.). The modern artwork turns the trajectory of the adventure inward and downward by plumbing the unfathomable depths of the human soul, opening up unexplored dimensions of perception, and creating new outlooks on life. Like a work of art, an adventure must have a clear beginning and a definite end, a frame that tears experience away from what came before and from what comes after. Just as gamblers, conquerors, dreamers, and lovers may risk life and limb, adventurers of the spirit (*Geist*) such as philosophers and artists often combine a certain presence of mind with wonton self-abandonment. But where the adventure usually ends at some point of return, the art-work may persist in its own realm and even break away from the identity of the person who created it. And while the adventure often involves an encounter with 'something alien, untouchable, out of the ordinary', the artwork might dwell instead on the familiar, the tangible, and the everyday. In any event, to the extent that modernity may be singled out as 'an incomparable experience' from the total context of historical life that came before it, it might be called the age of adventure, the philosopher its prophet, and the artist its visionary.

References

Agamben, Giorgio (2004). *The OPEN: Man and animal*, trans. Kevin Attell. Redwood: Stanford University Press.

Barthes, Roland (1981). *Camera lucida: Reflections on photography*, trans. Richard Howard. New York: Hill & Wang.

Baudelaire, Charles (1972). The painter of modern life. In P. E. Charvet (Ed.), *Selected writings on art and artists* (pp. 390–435). London: Penguin Books.

Becker, Howard S. (1982). *Art worlds*. Berkeley, CA: University of California Press.

Bourdieu, Pierre (1993). Manet and the institutionalization of anomie. In R. Johnson (trans.), *The field of cultural production: Essays on art and literature* (pp. 238–253). Cambridge: Polity Press.

Bourdieu, Pierre (2017). *Manet: A symbolic revolution*. Trans. Peter Collier, Margaret Rigaud-Drayton. Cambridge: Polity Press.

Derrida, Jacques (1987). *The truth in painting*, trans. Geoff Bennington and Ian McLeod. Chicago: The University of Chicago Press.

Fitzi, Gregor (2019). *The challenge of modernity: Simmel's sociological theory*. London: Routledge.

Foucault, Michel (1973). *The birth of the clinic: An archaeology of medical perception*, trans. A. M. Sheridan. New York: Vintage Books.

Genet, Jean (2003). Rembrandt's Secret. In Ch. Mendell (trans.), *Fragments of the artwork* (pp. 84–90). Redwood: Stanford University Press.

Goodstein, Elizabeth S. (2017). *Georg Simmel and the disciplinary imaginary*. Redwood: Stanford University Press.

Frisch, D. (2009). *Georg Simmel im Kino: Die Soziologie des frühen Films und das Abenteuer der Moderne*. Bielefeld: Transcript.

Kemple, Thomas (2007). Allosociality: Bridges and doors to Simmel's social theory of the limit. *Theory, Culture & Society, 24*, 7–8.

Kemple, Thomas (2018). *Simmel*. Cambridge: Polity Press.

Kemple, Thomas (2019). Simmel's sense of adventure: Death and old age in philosophy, art, and everyday life. *The Germanic Review: Literature, Culture, Theory, 94*(2), 163–174.

Kemple, Thomas (2019). The tragic-comic lives of theory: Values of a Simmelian existence, *Digithum, 4*, 10–20.

Neumann, Carl (1902). *Rembrandt*. Berlin: Spemann.

O'Neill, John (1995). Foucault's optics: The (in)vision of mortality and modernity. In Ch. Jenks (ed.), *Visual culture* (pp. 190–201). London: Routledge.

Pyyhtinen, Olli (2018). *The Simmelian legacy*. Basingstoke: Palgrave Macmillan.

Schama, Simon (1999). *Rembrandt's eyes*. London: Allen Lane.

Scott, Alan, & Staubmann, Helmut (2005). Editors' introduction to Georg Simmel, *Rembrandt: An essay in the philosophy of art*. London: Routledge.

Sebald, Winfried Georg (1998). *The rings of Saturn*, trans. Micheal Hulse. New York: New Directions Books.

Simmel, Georg (1989-2015). *Georg* Simmel *Gesamtausgabe*. Ed. by Otthein Rammstedt et al. Frankfurt/M.: Suhrkamp, 24 volumes, quoted here as GSG followed by the volume number.

Simmel, Georg (1994). The picture frame: An aesthetic study, trans. Mark Ritter. *Theory, Culture & Society*, *11*(1), 11–17.

Simmel, Georg (1995). Ästhetik des Porträts. In Rüdiger Kramme, Angela Rammstedt, Otthein Rammstedt (Eds.), *Georg Simmel Gesamtausgabe*, Band 7 (pp. 321–332). Frankfurt-am-Main: Suhrkamp.

Simmel, Georg (1997). The adventure. In D. Frisby and M. Featherstone (Eds.), *Simmel on culture* (pp. 221–232). London: SAGE.

Simmel, Georg (2000a). Über die Karikatur. In Klaus Latzel (Ed.), *Georg Simmel Gesamtausgabe*, Band 13 (pp. 244–251). Frankfurt-am-Main: Suhrkamp.

Simmel, Georg (2000b), Das Problem des Porträts. In Klaus Latzel (Ed.), *Georg Simmel Gesamtausgabe*, Band 13 (pp. 370–381). Frankfurt-am-Main: Suhrkamp.

Simmel, Georg (2003), *Rembrandt. Ein kunstphilosophischer Versuch*. In Uta Kösser, Hans-Martin Kruckis, Otthein Rammstedt (Eds.), *Georg Simmel Gesamtausgabe*, Band 15 (pp. 305–515). Frankfurt-am-Main: Suhrkamp.

Simmel, Georg (2005). *Rembrandt: An essay on the philosophy of art*, A. Scott and H. Staubmann (trans). London: Routledge.

Simmel, Georg (2007). Germanic and classical Romanic style, trans. A. Harrington. *Theory, Culture & Society*, 24, 7–8.

Simmel, Georg (2009). *Sociology: Inquiries into the construction of social forms, Volume 1*, A. J. Blasi, A. K. Jacobs, M. Kanjiranthnikal (trans). Leiden: Brill.

Simmel, Georg (2010). *The view of life: Four metaphysical essays with journal aphorisms*, trans. J. A. Y. Andrews, D. N. Levine. Chicago: University of Chicago Press.

Uexküll, Jakob Baron von (1913). *Bausteine zu einer biologischen Weltanschauung*. München: F. Bruckmann.

PART V

Literature and theatre

14

LITERARY PRACTICE AND IMMANENT LITERARY THEORY[1]

Monika Tokarzewska

Sociology and literature – two cultures?

When we consider the relationship Georg Simmel has with the arts, the visual arts will be our first association. Simmel wrote about artists such as Rembrandt, Michelangelo, Rodin, and Leonardo da Vinci; to some of them, he dedicated several studies. In his essays, we find numerous key metaphors and symbols referring to the visual arts such as the ornament, the ruin, the picture frame, and fashion. In the reception of Simmel, associations with literature are not so obvious although he devoted a number of articles and an important book to Goethe, and several essays to Goethe and Stefan George (Simmel, GSG 7, pp. 21-35; GSG 8, pp. 293-297; GSG 12, pp. 9-21, 316-323, 324-333, 334-350, 351-361, 369-373, 374-380, 388-416; several essays in GSG 13, GSG 15, pp. 7-270). It is even less obvious and more unusual to look at Simmel as a writer, and yet we find quite a few literary texts among his works: poems, prose miniatures and aphorisms, and also the so-called 'fragments', referring to the tradition of early German Romanticism.

Moreover, Simmel, as a sociologist and philosopher of culture, favoured the essay, located on the perimeters of literature; Simmel, an essayist, was probably discussed most often. Literature, however, permeates Simmel's entire output, which manifests itself not only in his style but also in the composition of his texts. One can view *Sociology*, from 1908, as a montage technique of composition (Tokarzewska, 2010, pp. 155–168). The famous 'excursuses' function within the chapters through the logic of analogy, contrasting to the main text and to each other. And yet a glance at the rather modest secondary literature confirms that the subject of 'Simmel and literature' is still waiting for a true discovery.

The recently completed edition of his collected works, an impressive project by an international team led by Otthein Rammstedt, facilitates navigation through Simmel's output.[2] This edition is a grand aid, especially for researchers dealing with the hitherto unknown aspects of this work, for example, Simmel as a writer, a journalist, a polemist, or even an epistolologist (GSG 22 and 23). While his classic books such as *Philosophy of Money*, *Sociology*, and *The View of Life* have been readily available for years, his literary texts, letters, reviews, and polemics, dispersed in magazines and archives, remained largely beyond the researchers' field of view. The collected works restore balance, complement our view of Simmel, or perhaps even change it a little. Volume 20 contains texts never published during his lifetime; these include 'fragments', located between philosophy and literature, collected under the common titles of *Über die Liebe, Aus dem nachgelassenen Tagebuche, Aus der nachgelaßnen Mappe 'Metaphysik'*; it also includes aphorisms and a few fairy tales. In volume 17, we find short literary texts written by Simmel for the *Jugend* magazine, which was published in Munich. They had fallen into oblivion because Simmel did not sign them with his surname, but just his initials. Christian Wehlte collected them and published them as a volume in 1998 (Simmel, 1998). In the collected works, we receive their critical edition for the first time. They have a different character and we find poems, aphorisms, fairy tales, and miniature prose works among them. In the studies on Simmel, the heading given to Simmel's texts printed in several issues of the magazine, '*Momentbilder sub specie aeternitatis*' (Snapshots sub specie aeternitatis), began to play the role of a quasi-title to the entire series, created in 1897–1907 (Frisby, [1981] 2013, pp. 102-131). The word 'snapshot', ('*Momentbild*'), functions as their hallmark, as well as the specific name of a literary genre created by Simmel and continued by Ernst Bloch, Walter Benjamin, and Theodor Adorno.

It is the 'snapshots' that undoubtedly also make Simmel a writer. But how can one place his literary work in the context of the entire output? Do they constitute an intellectual exercise and a kind of escape from 'serious' scholarly articles? Is it important to keep in mind, however, that their author is one of the founding fathers of sociology as an academic discipline, so should they be considered in this context, with questions about interrelationships? I suggest the latter. To me, the sociology question seems to be particularly important, because the period in which the 'snapshots' were created coincides with the years in which Simmel worked on both his monumental *Sociology*, the monograph published in 1908 (GSG 11), and on his *Philosophy of Money* published in 1900 (GSG 6).

The sociology of literature is a well-known and practised field of research, although it seems not very popular nowadays. In general, it is not preoccupied with literary texts themselves, but rather their functioning in society and on the market (Meyer, 2013, p. 5), and this aspect is of no interest to us at the moment. In contrast to this approach, little has been published on the immanent relations of literature and sociology, and only rare publications tackle mutual interactions between the literary and scholarly discourse of sociologists or, more broadly, scholars who also write literature.[3] Literariness is usually perceived as an obstacle in academic discourse; distorting its objectivity, it introduces ideology and raises suspicions about the author's intention to seduce the reader through emotions instead of logical arguments. While the question of a narrative is still important for some historical research, in principle, sociology does not care for its own writing styles; sociological research assumes the transparency of style.

In Simmel's time, the separation of sociological and literary discourse was not at all obvious, and sociology emancipated itself only by recognizing its own potential. By analogy to Charles Percy Snow, who once wrote about 'two cultures', humanities and sciences (Snow, [1959] 2002), Wolf Lepenies put 'three cultures' into the title of his classic book (Lepenies, 1985).[4] He presented the birth of sociology as the third culture, which was born between the paradigm of exact, experimental, and natural sciences, together with their ideal of scientism and the search for objective laws, so important in the nineteenth century, on one extreme; on the other, there was literature, describing and interpreting individual situations and fate (Lepenies, 1988).

It was nineteenth-century literature by Balzac, Flaubert, Zola, Henry James, and other authors that portrayed modern society in a masterful and innovative way, inventing new narrative styles. The pioneers of academic sociology such as Marx referred to Balzac's novels as a social analysis. The first sociologists, in turn, even those focused on pure science, reached for examples from literature, like Durkheim quoting Goethe, Musset, Lamartine, and Chateaubriand in his study on suicide. Through its immersion in the German bourgeois culture, the sociology of even such an 'unliterary' writer and thinker as Max Weber has much in common with the world of townspeople portrayed in the works of Thomas Mann (Lepenies, 1988, pp. 87, 297-312). Lepenies does not mention Ferdinand Tönnies, another of the founding fathers, who was inspired by Theodor Storm's novels (Fechner, 1985). Since Lepenies concentrates exclusively on Western Europe, specifically on France, England, and Germany, we will not find in his texts figures like Florian Znaniecki, the author of *The Polish Peasant in Europe and America*, who began his intellectual career as a poet and is the author of *Cheops*, a poem about ancient Egypt (Thomas & Znaniecki, 1918; Znaniecki, 1903).[5]However, Lepenies is interested not so much in sociologists practising different styles of writing; in principle, what interests him are these different 'cultures'. He writes about literary intelligentsia and 'intelligentsia devoted to the social sciences' (*'literarische und sozialwissenschaftliche Intelligenz'*) (Lepenies, 1988, p. 1) remaining in a creative contact or conflict. In France, the institutionalization of sociology at universities was important, forcing one to distance oneself somewhat from a literary way of writing; according to Lepenies, the problem of institutionalization was not particularly important in England, where the new discipline was developing outside academia. In Germany, it was important for sociology to establish a relationship with historical sciences. German literary intelligentsia is represented here by Thomas Mann and above all Stefan George, with his circle of followers, who demonstratively and with contempt distanced themselves from the mass and the superficial, which were associated with modern society, and thus from sociology.

While writing his book, Lepenies did not know of Simmel's literary texts, so he could not ask himself about Simmel's (as a writer and sociologist) attitude towards George. This disrupts the image of mutual distance. In his vision of sociology, Simmel distanced himself from social policy, but he was constantly inspired by the aesthetics and the notion of aesthetic distance, which was also crucial for George's poetry. It suffices to recall the genesis of money in the *Philosophy of money* or an essay on the Alps. As we know, for many years Simmel and George also maintained good personal contacts, particularly intense just in the period when the Berlin scholar published in *Jugend* magazine and, at the same time, worked on *Sociology* and *Philosophy of money*. Simmel is not, therefore, an exception when it comes to the interpenetration of sociology and literature in the early stages of the existence of the former, but rather shares this feature with his intellectual peers. What is less typical is the fact that his creative inspirations are closer to the literary style of George, broadly understood, than to Balzac's social realism or Flaubert's naturalism.

Between scientific method and artistic perspective

The *Jugend* journal, which was published in Munich, was a publication of the literary avant-garde of its time. Among authors publishing in it were Rilke, Brod, Dehmel, Hofmannsthal, Hesse, Schnitzler, and Wedekind. The first issues also include musical additions in the form of sheet music including, for example, Richard Strauss's songs. Attention was also given to its visual aspect, represented by sophisticated illustrations. Its publishers, Hirthe and Ostini, made the *Jugend* magazine both ambitious and intended for broad circles of a culturally sensitive audience (Rammstedt, 1988; Frisby, [1981] 2013; Kemple in Simmel, 2012). This project, therefore, combined elitism with egalitarianism. The *Jugend* has become an icon of the era; after many years, recalling the role he played, Walter Benjamin emphasizes that the magazine did not promote pessimism in the spirit of fin de siècle but wanted to combine art with life and inspire artistic activities (Benjamin, [1930–31] 1985, p. 153).

Certainly, the profile of this magazine appealed to Simmel. His literary texts, especially short prose, are a bridge between his own experience and the world of forms and concepts. Many of his 'snapshots' spring from situations that, with a high degree of probability, can be said to have happened to Simmel: it may be some remark during a social conversation, his son's comments on something that struck him, or his own school time memories. Usually, he uses the first-person for narration in his texts, which may prompt the reader to identify it with Simmel himself. However, they never have an autobiographical character; they quickly stray from a personal note and become a starting point for considerations, which allows their author to capture a more general reflection about the world and people.

Simmel's literary texts, in particular his prose miniatures, are mostly about some interpersonal reality; they have sociological meaning. We can read in them observations about human behaviour and characters, about the values they represent, and even about social concepts (such as the Utopian programme of absolute justice, ironically illustrated in a fairy tale called *Roses. A social hypothesis* ['Rosen. Eine soziale Hypothese']) (GSG 17, pp. 357-361), and about desires, fascinations, dreams, and wishes. The latter are usually fulfilled in a way surprising to the one who expressed them - revealing deeper, hidden layers of their personality. Many texts and aphorisms speak about the elementary and at the same time the most complicated interpersonal interactions: love, lies, indifference, and one's maturity and immaturity to enter into relationships and escape from them. Often these escapes end tragically; for example, this happens to the heroine of one of the tales from the series *On fulfilled wishes. Two very similar fairy tales* ('Von erfüllten Wünschen. Zwei sehr ähnliche Maerchen') (GSG 17, pp. 387-389). A narcissistic girl fixated on me-my-myself sinks into the dark depths of this 'me', like the abyss of an ocean. In this prose, one can recognize a characteristic feature of Simmel's sociology, focused on interpersonal reality in microscale. However, this is not sociological discourse nor is it sociology dressed in a literary costume. Simmel's snapshots, aphorisms, and fragments have their autonomy as works of art and follow the logic of their own artistic form, although sometimes a more general world reflection is interwoven into their artistically depicted worlds, reminding one perhaps of the style of the famous Simmelian essays.

The title of Simmel's magazine column in *Jugend*, '*Momentbilder sub specie aeternitatis*', concisely and aptly captures the essential feature of his writing practice. The first step, and at the same time the foundation of his text, is often an element of the surrounding reality. These elements include, for example, somebody's remark on a topic during a conversation (GSG 17, p. 423), a funny comment from his son returning from school (GSG 17, p. 381), an allusion to a text he read (GSG 17, p. 427), and even skate marks left on ice by an amateur skater, noticed during a walk (GSG 17, p. 398). These elements then become the starting point for a reflection. They get related to essential matters: to fate, our belief or disbelief in God and to various values, to the complex world in which we live, where we seek sense and happiness, often without success. (Happiness as a desire without which the social world would lose all its dynamic is the subject of several of Simmel's stories.) Quite often, Simmel derives deep thoughts and observations from a completely trivial event, thus provoking the reader to appreciate trivial matters.

However, Simmel does not want the casual to lose its random character and be dissolved in generalisations. The detailed and the general are to blend into one, and the aim of an artist is to give such perspective to a detail, as if to rotate it in the light so that a hidden more general meaning can be seen in it. Of course, at this point there comes to mind Simmel's well-known metaphor from his essay *Metropolis and mental life*:

> from each point of the surface of being, however much it may appear to have merely grown in and out of this surface, a plumb line can be dropped into the soul's depth such that of the most banal superficialities are in the end bound to the final determinations of the meaning and style of life via indications of direction.
>
> *(GSG 7, p. 120; transl. Scott & Staubmann, 2005, p. xiii)*

It is not a search for generality along the same path which science takes. In *Sociology*, Simmel looked for social forms or some regularities in interpersonal interactions. These regularities recur historically and geographically, even though they are always 'embodied' in the social particulars. Earlier, before working on *Sociology*, Simmel studied the philosophy of history. Wolfgang Lepenies emphasizes that, in Germany, it was often a discipline that had to be methodologically addressed by sociology, still looking for its methods. In an article *The Problem of Sociology* ('Das Problem der Sociologie') published in 1894 (so a bit before Simmel started writing for the *Jugend*), Simmel juxtaposes history with sociology and reflects on the methods of cognition typical of both of them (GSG 5, pp. 52-61). The historian's role is to abstract: the laws of history are not contained in the events themselves; they are the result of a reflection of a historian who, by his choices, determines what was important in the context of a problem under examination, and how events could stem from one another or determine one another (GSG 5, p. 60). A year later (1885), Simmel published in *Die Zukunft* an essay called *Böcklin's landscapes* ('Böcklins Landschaften'), dedicated to the painting of symbolist Arnold Böcklin. In this essay we find the formula '*sub specie aeternitatis*' taken from Spinoza, which was also used later in the *Jugend* (Frisby, [1981] 2013, p. 105). According to Simmel, this formula shows how an artist looks for generality and deeper meaning. This is how it works:

> Spinoza demands of the philosopher that he view things sub specie aeternitatis. That is to say, purely according to their inner necessity and significance, divorced from the contingency of their here and now.
>
> *(GSG 5, pp. 96–97; transl. in Rammstedt, 1994, p. 76)*

A perspective such as the one we can see in Böcklin's paintings allows deeper meanings to manifest in the objects themselves. Thus, it is a different practice of achieving generalization than looking for principles modelled of the laws of nature. Certainly, Simmel thought intensely about this problem; the similarities and, above all, the differences between the scientific and artistic methods drew his closest attention. Among his aphorisms, we find the following: 'The artist is capable of doing what the logician is not: to extend a concept without it losing content' (GSG 20, p. 266; transl. Swedberg & Reich, 2010, p. 33). In the artistic method, he was attracted to the possibility of preserving the sensual presence of a thing or a situation, which is often lost in an abstraction of scientific narrative. Of course, the Berlin-based professor is a child of his era and an heir to a certain specific understanding of art; Böcklin refers to the same broadly understood symbolism and elitism. He could, however, appreciate and carefully observe the tendencies in contemporary art that were rather alien to him. This is evidenced by an interesting review of Gerhardt Hauptmann's naturalistic play *The weavers* ('Die Weber') (GSG 17, pp. 26-28). However, what definitely distinguishes Simmel-the-writer from Böcklin or Stefan George is, first of all, his great taste for what is trivial, routine, and seemingly insignificant and, secondly, his irony. Both of these things protect Simmel's prose miniatures from excessive sublimeness.

Between an aphorism and a 'snapshot'

Simmel's literary work represents several genres, among which prose miniatures and aphorisms stand out (Richard Swedberg and Wendelin Reich estimated that Simmel created some 300 of them) (Swedberg & Reich, 2010). This proves that these genres were closest to Simmel. The few poems in his output, written mostly in a post-Romantic and ironic style in the spirit of Heine, are rather insignificant. His snapshots usually have a special structure; they are neither traditional short stories nor novellas. Their plot is usually quite reduced; there is almost no action in them; their construction is determined by other elements, for example, a certain situational element. I will develop this thought further below.

Simmel himself qualified some of his prose miniatures genologically as 'fairy tales' (Märchen). They are also characterized by a reduced plot and only a small number of heroes, in accordance with the tradition of this genre. There also appear the names of literary genres invented by Simmel himself for the needs of a given text. The aforementioned fairy tale about roses has a sub-title of 'social hypothesis' (*'eine soziale Hypothese'*). No such genre exists in prose; Simmel indicates that he is aware of the originality of his prose, moving between literature and sociology, and wanted to emphasize this specificity. 'Hypothesis' belongs in scientific activity; thus defining a literary text, Simmel shows that fictional texts can be treated a bit like experiments that can provide us with knowledge about society. There is a lot of irony in this because, in this particular fairy tale, a certain community decided to introduce equality and justice in rose growing. All the residents of a village had equally beautiful roses in their gardens thanks to the creation of some right conditions. Any envy among neighbours would cease, but this reform failed, and the conclusion drawn from this experiment was: people would always notice a difference between their own and other people's situations, and thus there would always be a reason for social unrest. This will always be true, even though the text is humorous fiction. Some of Simmel's literary and para-literary texts can be described as complex aphorisms (as per Swedberg & Reich, 2010, p. 25) or seen as 'fragments', a genre created by early German Romantics and located between literature and philosophy.

All the genres which Simmel made use of were influenced by his special interest: various forms of 'societalization'.[6] The interpersonal theme gives them a special Simmelian bend. Most of the general, wise statements which are distant from the subject of interpersonal relations can be found in his aphorisms but, in my opinion, there are exceptions there too. Simmel often uses paradox and antithesis, typical of this genre. By way of example, we can cite the following: 'Among the people who work on their opus, there are few who are worked on by their opus' (*'Unter den vielen Menschen, die an ihrem Werk arbeiten, sind wenige, an denen ihr Werk arbeitet'*) (GSG 20, p. 281) or 'The first duty of love is not to claim the right to it' (*'Die erste Pflicht der Liebe ist, kein Recht aus ihr zu Machen'*) (GSG 17, p. 352). Simmel tries to exploit the most important feature of aphorism - the compression of sense in a very short form. Swedberg and Reich consider this property to be the main reason for Simmel's interest in aphorism (Swedberg & Reich, 2010, p. 28). An author practising the aphorism exercises the discipline of style. However, one must not forget about the performative effect of aphorism on the reader: if it is well written, it does not convey thoughts directly but does it in a surprising and intriguing way. This motivates the reader to be active and think. In contrast to an activity to which the recipient is stimulated by other genres, such as a short story, a novel, or a theatrical play, an aphorism encourages and provokes intellectual activity, above all. A story and a novel can move us through the presentation of heroes' fates or evocative descriptions of nature, or a presentation of a fantastic world. An aphorism and romantic 'fragment', in many respects similar to it, play with the meaning of words, encouraging us to ask questions about what we call and how we can define the world around us. Thus, this activity is closest to that of a scientist seeking a language to describe new phenomena.

The above-cited aphorism of love juxtaposes the seemingly contradictory notions of '*Recht*' (the right to) and '*Pflicht*' (a duty), showing their paradoxical closeness when we refer to love. Thanks to this, it reveals the extraordinary paradox of this feeling, both fleeting and constituting the basis of a serious relationship with another human being. It turns out that the aphorism, at first seemingly distant from a sociological analysis, contains Simmel's characteristic perspective: love here is not an individual's emotional experience, but a form of 'societalization', unique through the way in which 'law' is connected with 'duty'.

On the other hand, in Simmel's sociological and cultural studies, we can find numerous sentences that could be taken out of them and treated as aphorisms. However, here we deal not only with the similarity of style in texts belonging to different kinds of discourse. Simmel treated some of his well-formulated sentences as aphorisms. In a famous essay called *Fashion*, we come across this sentence: 'We may define it [the fashion – M.T.] as the child of thought and thoughtlessness' ('*Man möchte sie das Kind des Gedankens mit der Gedankenlosigkeit nennen*') (Simmel, [1905] 1957, p. 542 and GSG 10, p. 10) Almost the same sentence can be found in the series of aphorisms which Simmel published in the *Jugend* (GSG 17, p. 370). Which came first? A text about fashion that gave birth to an aphorism later or one neatly captured thought from which Simmel drew the entire essay? It is difficult to say.[7] Still, Simmel's style in his academic work shows some quest for aphorism. Sentences in his essays are usually rather lengthy, often complex; they thoroughly analyse the subject, highlighting it from many perspectives. They give the impression of one's communing with thoughts developing live in front of the reader's eyes. Short and condensed wordings suddenly woven together, which are de facto aphorisms, sum up a given stage of reflection, give the text some rhythm, and organize the argument.

Simmel's numerous prose miniatures end with an intriguing sentence. Sometimes this point, when extracted out of context, could be treated as an aphorism, either without change or with only small additions. A good example is the ending of a story called *The most irrelevant; a moral dilemma* ('*Das Gleichgiltigste. Ein moralisches Dilemma*'). An interlocutor says in conversation, 'Since when have you lived at the end of this century? Are you still unaware that the heart of the matter is in what is the most irrelevant?' (GSG 17, p. 369). This statement could serve as an aphorism about the intellectual mood of the fin de siècle era when the traditional hierarchies of things became relative. In the context of a story, these points usually have the role of flipping the current argumentation in a surprising way and showing a new perspective on a problem or situation. Sometimes, irony follows surprise. In *Beyond beauty* ('*Jenseits der Schönheit*') we have a hero referred to as 'our friend' who expresses quite controversial views in a long monologue. Despite the relativism that possessed the intellectual world, in that friend's opinion, there remained the last undisputed ideal: the ideal of beauty. However, this is a deceptive ideal, because it is responsible for competition and race in society. If it were replaced by a cult of ugliness, harmony would eventually prevail. At the end of the story, the narrator takes the floor and informs us that 'friend', proud with his idea, stood up and went to a mirror to see the first messiah of the new gospel of ugliness: 'Deeply moved by the solemnity of this new gospel, and from an irrepressible desire to be its first blood-witness, our friend got up and took a look in the mirror' (Simmel, 2012, p. 269; GSG 17, p. 356).

The *Beyond beauty* miniature shows very well some of the formal features specific to Simmel's prose. Among the 'snapshots', we can find a number of texts that are built around a conversation which takes place in company gathered in a salon or similar place. This situation is usually only sketched; it never becomes an independent topic within the story. We have to guess at it in *Beyond beauty*: the story begins with the friend's monologue suggesting that all ideas have been used. The reader knows, however, that he is dealing not with first-person prose, because the monologue is in quotation marks from the first sentence, so is the quote. The narrator, who uses the third person, manifests his presence only after some time. He briefly informs the reader, '[t]hus reflected our friend, heavy of heart' (Simmel, 2012, p. 267; GSG 17, p. 353). Surely the friend did not speak to himself, so there must be a social gathering in the background. Maybe they are all in a living room, the one Simmel and his wife Gertrud had in his Berlin house, which intellectuals and artists would visit. Simmel is also the author of an essay entitled *Sociology of sociability* ('*Soziologie der Geselligkeit*'), in which there is a 'sociability game' which takes place in a casual salon conversation, where different people and different views meet on a neutral ground; he interprets it as 'societalization' in a pure form (Simmel, [1911] 1949).

The reader becomes a witness to 'our friend's' literal quotation, as if one were a participant in the meeting and a member of some group. He observes the protagonist giving a speech and then sees the full final scene in front of a mirror, which is full of irony. The narrator does not have to add much; the hero becomes a comic figure by himself. The source of humour is the contrast between the solemn tone of the monologue and the fact, which is easy to guess, that the friend is not particularly attractive and, therefore, his seemingly unselfish concept of making mankind happy is not entirely unselfish. Readers, presented with such a final point, distance themselves from the hero; their attention is redirected from the friend's abstract speculation, which is detached from reality, to his human weaknesses and his complexes, hidden under the rhetoric of concepts, and to his corporeality.

In Simmel's other stories, we also encounter life confronted with theory. It seems to be one of the most important motifs of his literary work. In one of the fairy tales, a wizard grants the wish of a young man who wants his body to be free from gravity (GSG 17, p. 388 f.). When saying goodbye, the boy receives a riddle from the sorcerer, a mysterious sounding quatrain. He is told that the weight of his body would come back when he solved this riddle. The solution to the puzzle is the word 'you', and it is revealed in the least opportune moment for the hero. Taking advantage of his weightless condition, he was sliding on very thin ice on a lake when he spotted a female stranger on the other side. Fascinated by her looks, he shouted to her, 'You!', the ice broke under him, and the water swallowed him forever. Simmel uses the force of gravity as a metaphor: freeing the hero of his weight, he also frees him of reference to the earthly. The desire to glide in the skies of abstraction and free oneself from everything that can be symbolized by the force of gravity, tying one to the ground, turns out to be a pernicious illusion of freedom. Numerous heroes of Simmel's prose miniatures can be said to lack the 'embodiment' of their theories, wishes, and dreams. When they break away from reality, they turn out to be defenceless against the burden of interpersonal relations. It does not only have to be about love. Herbert, the hero of another story, was lucky enough to have a logical advantage in all the disputes he entered. This made him lonely.

In Simmel's views expressed and mentioned in 'Snapshots', one can find an analogy or allusions to the ideas of his contemporary world. They are not, however, accounts of existing worldviews, but more so their ironic versions. They are characterized by reduction and exaggeration; they are often reduced to absurdity and produce a comical effect. This idea is illustrated very logically by the hero of the *Metaphysics of laziness* ('*Metaphysik der Faulheit*') (GSG 17, pp. 392-397), that the main idea of mankind is to be lazy. Without laziness, there would be no inventions. This refers to an article by Paul Lafargues on work (Lafargue, 1883). One can also find it in the story of roses where top-down attempts were made to introduce a social utopia consisting in getting everyone in their garden to have roses that are not different from those of the others'. Here you can hear the echoes of popular socialist and communist utopias or polemics with ideas of an ideal state, many of which have been known to the history of thought since Plato. In all these cases, we deal with some idea or thought system referring to reality which is transformed in a literary way. Simmel exaggerates the role of a feature, which is ridiculous or absurd in terms of common sense and makes it a central idea. The worldviews and ideas proclaimed by the heroes in Simmel's prose are not to be taken seriously, but they are part of the world depicted in the work - they are subjects themselves and play a certain role in the literary world. The reader does not identify with them, nor does the narrator, who is very sparingly present; we look at ideas and social ideas of values as if from the outside, often wondering or smiling, as if they were presented on stage in a theatre. Theories and views do not exist in Simmel's literary world abstractly, as such. They are the elements of social reality - people exchange them; they are born in a conversation; they are spoken in front of others. The characters want to surprise others or to impress them. Words and ideas belong to people and, together with their 'owners', are part of an interpersonal interaction. It was certainly impossible for Simmel to find this approach in science; this must have come from literary discourse.

Simmel's situation in the years of cooperation with the *Jugend* vis-a-vis literary and sociological discourse

At a time when Simmel published his literary texts in the *Jugend*, his situation was both special and difficult. Studying his correspondence from these years, it is noticeable at once that the central elements of his situation included, on the one hand, an unstable professional situation: he could lecture at the Berlin university but did not receive the position of a full professor (Ordinarius) although he was probably the most popular lecturer. His classes were financed by the auditors and offered in the largest hall to accommodate a larger audience, including interested listeners who were not his university students. From his letters, we learn about his ongoing efforts to obtain a professorship in Berlin or another city. Partly from Simmel's own comments and partly from third parties, we know about the dislike that some of his academic colleagues had towards the popular lecturer (GSG 22, pp. 118-120, 280 f.). On the other hand, this is the period of Simmel's growing popularity in the international academic world. He writes a lot, he meets his contemporary academic celebrities like Durkheim and plans to start a new international sociological journal. A book called *Philosophy of money* is published in 1900; *Sociology* gradually emerges and is published somewhat later in 1908. In general, Simmel found his most intensive and productive exchange of ideas coming from outside of academia. In those years, regular guests at his house included Stefan George, Rainer Maria Rilke, and Lou von Salome. One can assume that the company of poets inspired Simmel in his own work. The more he felt isolated at his university, the more important such contacts were to him. We do not know, however, whether his literary output was the topic of conversations in Simmel's home. His texts in the *Jugend* were signed only with his initials, so we can guess that Simmel did not want to be perceived as a writer in his intellectual circles. Among his fellow professors, he had the opinion of a scholar but was also a controversial man, anyway. We do not have Simmel's complete correspondence, but we have quite numerous letters from this period: the only reference to 'Snapshots' (and in general to his own literary texts) is in just one letter to Heinrich Rickert (GSG 22, p. 304 f.).

In his sociological activity, Simmel felt both lonely and exceptional. Busy with the emerging plans for the creation of a sociological journal, as early as January 19, 1893, in a letter to Friedrich Jodl, he wrote about a discipline that was just being born (GSG 22, p. 83 f.). He had no interest in the subject of social policy; instead, he favoured research on 'forms of societalization' (*Formen der Vergesellschaftung*), which were his own original idea. In another letter to Jodl, he wrote a day later that this new emerging science did not need only those who had already declared themselves to be sociologists, but above all, it needed cultural historians, comparative linguists, and art historians (GSG 22, pp. 85–87). In letters to Célestin Bouglé, who was also his friend, we find his words about the 'uncertain and obscure status which sociology still has' (GSG 22, p. 111). All this indicates that Simmel saw sociology as an open project, open not only to ideas but also to new styles of writing and new languages for the recognition of reality, which fostered the development of two discourses: scholarly and literary.

Texts that he contributed to 'Sociology' were articles initially published in journals and magazines. They owed their internal consistency and the fact that they belong together as one not just to a common thread and a unified train of thought but to the references to a common perspective, which is the Simmelian idea of sociology as a special way of perceiving the world. Society is not an object, but an action, happening in interpersonal relations.[8] In literary texts, Simmel took a similar perspective, but he sought its expression in specifically literary forms. The pace of observation and writing were similar in both cases, determined by the circulation of magazines.

Simmel's immanent literary theory?

Let us return to the question about the relationship between sociology and literature from the beginning of this text. In the case of Simmel, this relationship is unobvious at first glance. We do not deal here with Balzac or Flaubert, who describe the bourgeois society of mature capitalism in Paris or, for example, with Bolesław Prus, a Polish novelist, presenting Warsaw as a social panorama in the second half of the nineteenth century (Prus, 1890). In fact, as we have seen, in Simmel's writings there is a close relationship between literature and sociology. Simmel himself realized that he left behind special and multifaceted output for which he would not have heirs, but which would appeal to many readers.

Simmel did not develop his own theory of literature, nor did he make theoretical commentary on his own or someone else's literary output. The remarks which can be found in the texts about Stefan George or Goethe are too infrequent, and are not expressed in the classical language of literary theory. Perhaps it would be much easier to reconstruct his theory of fine arts on the basis of, for example, essays on Rembrandt or Michelangelo, as well as the theory of applied and decorative art (essays on the ornament, or the essay on jug handle). However, after analysing Simmel's literary output, one could try to establish a certain theory of literature, which is immanently contained in this body of work. I believe that it would be most appropriate to state that literature from Simmel's perspective is, without losing its autonomy, a statement rooted in society. For Simmel, it is also a laboratory of thought. Literature does not reflect society in a realistic style, as if in a mirror, to use Stendhal's expression (Stendhal, [1830] 1998, p. 371). As we have seen, Simmel makes a conscious departure from realism. For example, his favourite literary genres include fables. Reduction is often found among the 'devices' frequently used by him. (I use the term 'device' in the meaning given to it by Russian formalists, Viktor Shklovsky in particular

(Shklovsky, [1917] 2015).) Reduction relates to the worldviews as presented in the works (they are focused on a single aspect), character personalities (they are determined by a single feature, a single life objective, or a single dream), as well as the represented world (which is represented in a very sparing manner). As far as aphorisms and fragments are concerned, there is a sparsity of form present at the very core of these genres. Certainly, Simmel is not concerned about the faithful representation of the social panorama of phenomena. However, I believe that he understood literature as a way of writing that allows for certain mechanisms of social reality to be reached, which can only be revealed in the language of literature where fantasy is included, together with building model worlds and situations. Łukasz Afeltowicz, summarizing the results of research conducted by Bruno Latour and Karin Knorr-Cetina on the topic of science and technology in the modern society, writes that the success of life sciences is closely linked to the institution of the laboratory (Afeltowicz, 2012). The laboratory enables to 'reduce the complexity of the world, isolate certain factors, learn about their functioning and manipulate them' (Afeltowicz, 2012, p. 90). In laboratories, we are dealing 'not with nature, but with purified, processed, often artificially created fragments of the world' (Afeltowicz, 2012, p. 90 f.). The research on nature would be impossible outside the laboratory because of the vast complexity of the world. Social reality is enormously complex. Simmel acts in his literary texts as if he were building a kind of laboratory. What happens if people are deprived of the idea of happiness? What happens if, instead of beauty, ugliness becomes the most important idea? Experiments of this kind are not a part of the common scientific discourse; however, they broaden our social imagination and the boundaries of our language.

Notes

1 I would like to express my grateful thanks to Gregor Fitzi for the invitation to work on common research project devoted to Simmel, to Natàlia Cantó-Milà and all the participants in the Simmel conference in Portbou (2018) for interesting discussions, and to Karol Sauerland for reading the text and for critical and very helpful comments about it. I would also like to thank Krzysztof Strzemeski most warmly for his invaluable help in the translation of the article and quotations from Simmel's texts into English. Last but not least: I always thank with cordial gratitude Professor Otthein Rammstedt and the late invaluable Angela Rammstedt, who supported me in everything that concerns Georg Simmel.
2 Simmel, G. *Gesamtausgabe in 24 Bänden*, edited by Otthein Rammstedt, Frankfurt/Main: Suhrkamp. The last volume of the Gesamtausgabe was published in 2015.
3 Exceptions include the interesting study of Daniel Grummt (2016).
4 The English translation of the title does not preserve this expression.
5 Ratajczak discusses Znaniecki's literary origins in an interesting way (Ratajczak, 2016).
6 There are various propositions for the translation of a key term of Simmel's, 'Vergesellschaftung', into English. I have decided on the solution proposed by Olli Pyyhtinen (Pyyhtinen, 2010, p. 178).
7 The aphorism in *Jugend* was published earlier (June 4, 1898) than the version of the essay on fashion published in 'Moderne Zeitfragen' (1905). The first essay on fashion ('*Zur Psychologie der Mode*'), published 1895 in 'Die Zeit', does not contain this particular sentence.
8 The fact that relationism is one of the deepest foundations of Simmel's thinking about the world and society, and that Simmel's interpretation in this spirit holds a new potential, is most intensely pointed out by Natalia Cantó-Milà (2005).

References

Afeltowicz, Ł. (2012). *Modele, artefakty, kolektywy. Praktyka badawcza w perspektywie współczesnych studiów nad nauką*. Toruń: Wydawnictwo Naukowe Uniwersytetu Mikołaja Kopernika.

Benjamin, W. ([1930–31] 1985). Aus dem Tagebuch einer Verlorenen. In R. Tiedemann & H. Schweppenhäuser (Eds.), *Walter Benjamin. Gesammelte Schriften*. Vol. 6 (pp. 152–157). Frankfurt am Main: Suhrkamp.

Cantó-Milà, N. (2005). *A sociological theory of value. Georg Simmel's sociological relationism*. Bielefeld: Transcript.

Fechner, R. (Ed.). (1985). *Der Dichter und der Soziologe. Zum Verhältnis zwischen Theodor Storm und Ferdinand Tönnies. Referate der Arbeitstagung im November 1984 in Husum*. Hamburg: Ferdinand-Tönnies-Arbeitsstelle am Institut für Soziologie der Universität Hamburg.

Frisby, D. ([1981] 2013). Snapshots 'sub specie aeternitatis'? In D. Frisby (Ed.), *Sociological impressionism. A reassessment of Georg Simmel's social theory* (pp. 102–131). New York: Routledge.

Grummt, D. (2016). SozialwissenschaftlerInnen und KünstlerInnen? Das Beispiel lyrischer SoziologInnen. In M. Kauppert & H. Eberl (Eds.), *Ästhetische Praxis* (pp. 395–420). Wiesbaden: Springer VS.

Lafargue, P. (1883). *Le droit à la paresse*. Paris: Henry Oriol.

Lepenies, W. (1985). *Die drei Kulturen. Soziologie zwischen Literatur und Wissenschaft*. München: Carl Hanser Verlag.

Lepenies, W. (1988). *Between literature and science: The rise of sociology*. Cambridge: Cambridge University Press.

Meyer, I. (2013). Protosoziologie: Stendhals Interaktionismus und die agonale Konzeption der Geselligkeit. *Internationales Archiv für Sozialgeschichte der Literatur, 38*(1), 1–30.

Prus, B. (1890). *Lalka*. Warszawa: Gebethner i Wolff.

Pyyhtinen, O. (2010). *Simmel and 'The social'*. London: Palgrave.

Rammstedt, O. (1988) Zur Ästhetik Simmels. Die Argumentation in der 'Jugend' 1897-1906. *Beiträge der Georg Simmel-Gesellschaft, 22*(1), 1–26.

Rammstedt, O. (1994). On Simmel's aestetics: Argumentation in the journal 'Jugend' 1897-1906. In D. Frisby (Ed.), *Georg Simmel. Critical assessments*. Vol. 3 (pp. 66–82). London and New York: Routledge.

Ratajczak, W. (2016). Znaniecki poeta. *Humaniora. Czasopismo internetowe, 13*(1), 69–81.

Scott, A., & Staubmann, H. (2005). Editor's introduction: Georg Simmel on Rembrandt – Understanding the human beyond naturalism and conventionalism. In A. Scott & H. Staubmann (Eds.), *Georg Simmel. Rembrandt – An essay in the philosophy of art* (pp. xi–xix). London: Routledge.

Shklovsky, W. ([1917] 2015) Art, as device. Translated and introduced by Alexandra Berlina. *Poetics Today, 36*(3), 151–174.

Simmel, G. ([1905] 1957) Fashion. Translated by anonymous. *The American Journal of Sociology, 62*(6), 541–558.

Simmel, G. ([1911] 1949) The sociology of sociability. Translated by E. C. Hughes. *American Journal of Sociology, 55*(3), 254–261.

Simmel, G. (1998). *Momentbilder – Sub Specie Aeternitatis: Philosophische Miniaturen*, Ed. by C. Wehlte. Heidelberg: Manutius.

Simmel, G. (2012). Selections from Simmel's writings for the journal 'Jugend'. Selected and translated by T. A. Kemple. *Theory, Culture & Society, 29*(7/8), 263–278.

Snow, Ch. P. ([1959] 2002). *The two cultures*. Cambridge: Cambridge University Press.

Stendhal (Beyle, M. H.) ([1830] 1998) *The red and the black. A chronicle of the nineteenth century*. Translated by C. Slater. Oxford: Oxford University Press.

Swedberg, R., & Reich, W. (2010) Georg Simmel's aphorisms. *Theory, Culture & Society, 27*(1), 24–51.

Thomas, W. I., & Znaniecki, F. (1918). *The polish peasant in Europe and America. Monograph of a immigrant group*. Boston, MA: The Gorham Press.

Tokarzewska, M. (2010). *Der feste Grund des Unberechenbaren. Georg Simmel zwischen Soziologie und Literatur*. Wiesbaden: VS Verlag für Sozialwissenschaften.

Znaniecki, F. (1903). *Cheops. Poemat fantastyczny*. Warszawa: J. Fiszer.

15

THE GOETHEAN HERITAGE
IN SIMMEL'S WORK

Paola Giacomoni

Introduction[1]

Georg Simmel, sociologist of the metropolitan lifestyle, philosopher of modernity, money, and fragment, was deeply inspired by German philosophy of the classical period. In spite of the particular style of his learning and the results of his research, his interest in, and passion for the German culture of the late 18th century played a decisive role in his philosophy and sociology. Throughout his career, Simmel devoted to the subject numerous essays in journals, and articles in newspapers. Moreover, a series of lectures on Kant was published in 1904 (GSG 9, pp. 7-226), followed by a comparative study – *Kant und Goethe* – in 1906 (GSG 10, pp. 119-166), and the magnificent monograph on Goethe in 1913 (GSG 15, pp. 7-270).

The importance of Kant's thought to the theoretical backbone of Simmel's philosophy is well known. However, less attention has traditionally been paid to the role of Goethe's legacy in Simmel's thought – the man himself, and his work, both of which provided Simmel with constant inspiration (Giacomoni, 1995, 2002, 2006). The multitude of quotations from Goethe found throughout his writing have been considered, too often simply ornamental. Today this issue has been seriously tackled in several high-quality studies, though they mostly focus on Goethe's concept of life, leaving morphology on the background (Bleicher, 2007; Levine, 2012; Harrington, 2016; Weik, 2017; Amat, 2018, pp. 341–369). This chapter will focus on Goethe's methodological *practice* in order to show its influence – one out of the many – on Simmel's work.

Simmel's enormous interest in Goethe's poetry and works of natural science, as well as in his personality in general, led him to recognise an original research method and line of thought (though it had very little success with Goethe's contemporaries) (Amrine, Zuckert, & Wheeler, 1987). His profound knowledge of Goethe's works – the poems, natural science, and correspondence – brought him extremely, though paradoxically, close to the 'Olympic' poet and his scientific and philosophical attitude, and allowed him to travel a road that clearly bore the imprints of both Goethe and Kant's passage.

It is well known that Goethe's study of nature focused principally on the morphology of living phenomena, the animal form and plant metamorphosis (Giorello & Grieco, 1998; Moiso, 2002; Richards, 2002; Breidbach, 2006; Cislaghi, 2008; Pfau, 2010), as well as on his famous theory of colours. Simmel precisely identifies Goethe's approach to phenomena: he was neither a *Naturforscher*, nor a *Naturphilosoph*, but a *Naturschauer* (GSG 15, p. 61).[2] The poet conceived his study of Nature as being, on the one hand, firmly connected to the visible experience of phenomena, to their manifold and comparative observation, while – on the other hand – exploring the natural world not merely as a simple aggregate of data, but rather as a set of *forms*.

This approach can, I believe, profitably be employed to comment upon the first outlines of the '*Idee Goethe*' as they are revealed in Simmel's 1913 monograph. The paradox that we discover is the following: in the sociological works and, to some extent also in the philosophical texts, Simmel starts from an analysis of modernity which highlights the questions of desubstantification, the loss of a clear centre, the multiplying of possible perspectives on society, and on the world. In other areas of his work, particularly those in which aesthetics plays the pivotal role, or in the explicitly *lebensphilosophisch* texts, the unitary metaphor of the organism again becomes a crucial reference point and the influence of Goethe is clearly manifest. And, finally, to what extent is Goethe a resource and a mirror for Simmel both as philosopher and sociologist of modernity? Therefore, we must ask ourselves: was Simmel using Goethe to create a pre-modern picture - that of a *Universalgelehrte* - which, since he hardly distinguished at all between different fields of study, could roam freely from one to another?[3] Or does his remarkably frequent referencing of Goethe stem from a sense of affinity with an author who - although he never described himself as a philosopher – allowed Simmel to maintain a critical distance from the classical 19th century tradition? To what extent is Goethe a resource and a mirror for Simmel both as philosopher and sociologist of modernity?

A fruitful truth

'*Im Anfang war die Tat*'

Let me begin to answer this question by analysing the way in which Simmel presents Goethe's concept of truth. Goethe, Simmel affirms at the beginning of the second chapter of his *Goethe* monograph, was convinced that the theoretical positions we choose to adopt are linked to our specific individual characteristics. In fact, Goethe argues against the idea that knowledge is a simple mirroring of an objectively given truth, in which the cognitive process as a living expression of individual subjectivity is absolutely denied, and claims that, on the contrary, the knower must be understood in dynamic terms: truth is seen not as an absolute fact, to which one adapts, but as a product of the human spirit. This active, productive aspect of truth is very much part not only of Goethe's poetic and narrative output but also, as we shall see, of his investigations of Nature. His approach appeared to Simmel significantly different from the 19th century philosophical tradition and the positivism of the middle of the century in particular, which – indeed – had little time for Goethe's research methods.

There are clear echoes here of the *Hauptprobleme der Philosophie*, in which philosophy is defined by Simmel as 'a temperament expressed by a certain world view' (GSG 14, p. 26). Here we have a concept of knowledge as largely dependent on how it arises in the subject; this does not, however, mean reducing its significance to the singularity of the person who produced it, as the way in which Simmel analyses Kant, Schopenhauer and Nietzsche clearly demonstrates. These philosophies, according to Simmel, express the type of man in which they are embodied, and not each thinker's empirical experience; in this sense, each philosophical system is to be interpreted as a *unicum*, but does not thereby lose its validity or objectivity. These questions are taken up again in *Lebensanschauung*, where truth is linked to context, to 'transvital worlds', which are held to be free, in the sense that they are independent of teleological human action.

Simmel's analysis reveals unusual elements of the '*Idee Goethe*'. He claims that Goethe believed there to be as many truths as there are individuals, and that truth is the relationship between the life of a man and the totality of the world in which he finds himself (GSG 15, p. 32). A relevant key to understanding Goethe's concept of truth is his emphasis on its pragmatic character, as abundantly exemplified not only in his writings on nature (Goethe, [1947] 2019) but also in *Maximen und Reflexionen* (Goethe, 1982, 12, pp. 365-550), and in the letters (Goethe, 1986). The fruitful nature of truth is fundamental to Goethe. Simmel quotes: 'I have observed that I consider a thought which is fruitful for me to be true, and that such a thought connects with my other thoughts and thus nourishes me' (GSG 15, p. 33).

Was fruchtbar ist, allein ist wahr, Goethe says in the poem *Vermächtnis* (Goethe, 1982, 1, p. 270). Commenting on this statement, Simmel underlines the undeniable pragmatic flavour of truth, although he points out that this is very definitely not utilitarian pragmatism, an approach absolutely alien to Goethe, who sees knowledge in relation to the totality of a man's life, which it either benefits or undermines. Knowledge cannot be conceived in isolation, detached from the general context of the life, to which it is related (Amat, 2018, pp. 358-369).

Goethe's statements about the pragmatic nature of knowledge are many, and surprising; his avoidance of the aprioristic has often been noted. This is, indeed, inevitable when he reflects on the necessary requirements in each and every cognitive situation, and on the different possible *Vorstellungsarten* on any one phenomenon (Kuhn, 1967; Kleinschnieder, 1971; Giacomoni, 1993; Breidbach, 2006). These themes are developed particularly in Goethe's scientific writing, in which he reflects generally on his working methods – without ever actually defining any clear methodology – and on the way in which he approached natural objects. For example, dealing with the various – and often contradictory – hypotheses about a particular subject (Neptunism and volcanism in geology, epigenesis and preformism in biology, atomism and dynamism in relation to the concept of matter, etc.) he argues that they were not necessarily mutually exclusive, but could be freely used according to the needs of a particular aspect of research. In the essays *Vorarbeiten zur Morphologie* (Goethe, [1947] 2019, I, 10, pp. 50-63) and *Über die Notwendigkeit von Hypothesen* (Goethe, [1947] 2019, I, 10, pp. 35-36) as well as in his late essay on the Cuvier-Geoffroy debate (Goethe, 1982, 13, pp. 219-250), Goethe's statements are very definite. If two conflicting hypotheses exist to explain a particular question, the correct attitude – he admits - is to bear both in mind while engaged in one's research, rather than opting for one alone, and discarding the other.

Both hypotheses are – at some level – compatible *Vorstellungsarten*, although it is undoubtedly difficult to juggle them both efficiently in our minds as we endeavour to understand the natural world, and to know - moment by moment - which point of view to choose, rather than obstinately limiting oneself to one or other perspective (Goethe, [1947] 2019, I, 10, p. 55).

There is not just a single point of view on natural phenomena and, as a result, we can choose the most appropriate one according to the situation, Goethe claims. We ought to adopt the perspective, which seems to be the most effective: truth is not given as a datum to be passively accepted. These are not statements of a naïve realist; they express a very refined, unusual and innovative scientific attitude that Simmel could appreciate as a modern trait. The capability to choose the right perspective and be ready to change it according to the context shows an incredibly open-mindedness. Simmel understands it deeply, although he always emphasises Goethe's tendency towards a global and metaphysical unity of multiple viewpoints.

Experience and experiments

'Ein Phänomen ist ein Glied einer großen Kette'

The same orientation is shown about experience and experiment in science. In his famous essay *Der Versuch als Vermittler zwischen Objekt und Subjekt* (Goethe, 1982, 13, pp. 10-21), Goethe talks about scientific experiment, referring in particular to *Beiträge zur Optik* (Goethe, [1947] 2019, I, 3, pp. 6-53), in which he proposes an ordered sequence of experiments and observations in relation to how we perceive colours, based upon which he forms a hypothesis about their origin. These texts clearly demonstrated a work method, a style of observation, which held much of interest to Simmel. In particular, the claim that the individual nature of knowledge does not contradict the requirement that experiments must be repeatable and become intersubjective, as the following definition clearly explains:

> We speak of an experiment when we take experiences of our own or of others, deliberately reproduce and present again the phenomena that arose, both those that came about fortuitously and those that appeared through the artifice of the experiment.
>
> *(Goethe, 1982, 13, p. 14)*

And:

> since everything in nature, especially the more common forces and elements, is in eternal action and reaction, we can say of every phenomenon that it is connected to countless others, just as a radiant point of light sends out its rays in all directions. Once we have carried out an experiment, we cannot be careful enough to examine other bordering phenomena and what follows next. This is more important than looking at the experiment in itself. It is the duty of the scientist to modify every single experiment.
>
> *(Goethe, 1982, 13, p. 17f.)*

The observation of a phenomenon from all possible points of view permits the scientist to reach well-grounded conclusions, untainted by bias. (Goethe, 1982, 13, pp. 23-25) The experiments – most of which were carried out by using a prism, and whose results are presented in a series of diagrams (Goethe, [1947] 2019, I, 3) - serve as an excellent illustration of Goethe's way of working. The observations are carried out looking at the colours from different perspectives, modifying and varying the first, basic experiment in which colours appear at the edges of a white surface when it is set against a darkly coloured background, and vice versa. This was the way in which the colours had appeared to Goethe the first time he used a prism – not as the splitting up of white light into the colour spectrum, as Newton had described it in his *Optics*. The many variations on the basic experiment - the gradual changing of the conditions, the reversing of the relationship between light and dark, the different distances at which the observer stood, the different relative sizes of the bright and the dark surfaces - all led in the same direction. They demonstrated a specific colour sequence, a specific order of colours, which seemed to confirm the preliminary hypothesis, which was later to lie at the heart of Goethe's *Farbenlehre* (Goethe, 1982, 13, pp. 314-523).

The operational nature of Goethe's attitude is thus fundamental: he does not merely contemplate the phenomenon before him, he *acts* upon it, changing the conditions in which it occurs, its position and that of the observer, and he shows it to others in order to have as many confirmations as possible of the hypothesis upon which the experiments are based. Knowledge is not simply a reflection of the world, but nor is it just the fusion of subject and object – as Simmel states particularly in *Kant und Goethe* – or an unveiling of the true essence of Nature, the laws of which are just passively accepted. Knowledge is a complex, sophisticated, elaboration: a conscious manipulation - through both experiment and the analysis of data - which allows, at the same time, a consciously creative identification of the form of a phenomenon, based on the comparison of different possible perspectives on it. In this sense, knowledge is fruitful: *Fruchtbarkeit* was one of Goethe's determining criteria for a valid theory, not so much as regarded its a posteriori utility or applicability, but in relation to the results obtained through a certain sequence of - both manual and mental - operations.

Simmel's interpretation neatly captures the originality of the 'perspectivist' aspect of Goethe's approach and sometimes makes it even more radically relativistic. Goethe's precise epistemological observations, however, often assume a metaphysical hue in Simmel's thought. Simmel clearly identifies the extraordinarily modern openness in Goethe's scientific method, although in many passages of the 1913 monograph he simply tends to attribute it to Goethe's 'temperament' and to a metaphysical approach to the phenomenal world, which is hard to find in Goethe's writings.

The many possible perspectives on any one phenomenon converge and form a circle, a new and compact unity in which all the different points of view of the whole of humanity combine to give rise to a functional organism – and not to an aggregate. These can, ultimately, attain a truth, which is no longer relative, or emphatically sceptical, but rather grounded in objects and their various ways of appearing. Simmel, in his interpretation, is more inclined to synthesise than was Goethe, who – in contrast – left the field of hypothesis much more open, as evidenced by the famous maxim:

In New York there are ninety different Christian confessions, each and all acknowledge God and the Lord in their own particular way without being at loggerheads with one another. We must get as far as that in nature study, and indeed in every branch of research; for what sense is there in everybody talking about liberal attitudes and yet wanting to prevent, others from thinking in their own way and having their own say?

(Goethe, 1982, 12, n°709, p. 466)

Simmel's characteristic claim of a necessary 'pluralism of principles' in the field of knowledge, one of his philosophical and methodological key notes, is not always – as one would have expected – a direct reflection of the Goethean position from which it - indirectly - drew its inspiration. Simmel does not always see the more 'innovative' strand of Goethe's thought as essential to either his own theories; it is often, rather, interpreted within the framework of the metaphysics of unity, which he considers to dominate Goethe's reflections (Giacomoni, 2006).

We must also remember the relevance of the philosophical perspective of Simmel's final period, which culminated in *Lebensanschauung*. Here, Simmel posits a dialectic between life and the forms that connects the vitality of life with the idea that this vitality can only find expression by producing independent 'worlds' or forms, and that these forms then appear to be autonomous - detached from their origin, and often in conflict with it. The reciprocal relationship between man and the world brings about a dialectic between life and form, certain key elements of which Simmel seeks in Goethe.

As Gregor Fitzi (2002), Fitzi (2016), and Elizabeth Goodstein have stressed (2016), today this point of view can be understood not as a metaphysical remnant, but as a still valid tool for the analysis of contemporary complex societies. In contrast to the rigid systems of Weber and Parsons, Simmel's more flexible theory depends on its very capacity to set the scene, within a dynamic framework, for the presence of specific - stable, crystallised forms, which are, however, neither abstract nor definite, but rather continually re-definable within the flow of life.

These concepts can be reinterpreted today as appropriate tools for the analysis of the 'liquid' society: in fact, life and money are both metaphorically presented by Simmel as liquid. At the same time, forms also possessed some elements of precise, institutional definiteness, albeit subject to continuous transformation. The liveliness and originality of Goethe's approach are clearly revealed by Simmel; even though the latter's metaphysical perspective – paradoxically – tends to obscure its freshness.

Visual thinking and morphology

'Eine zarte Empirie'

As Donald Levine reminds us, Lewis Coser used to exclaim: 'If you want to understand Simmel, you have got to understand Form. Form! Form! Form!' (Levine, 2012, p. 30).

The role of the aesthetic element is explicit in Simmel's scientific attitude since *Die Philosophie des Geldes* (GSG 6). Its connection to the world of sensory knowledge and to the concept of form in Goethe's writings is also evident. Bleicher underlines the role of *Anschauung* as a 'key-term that encapsulates Goethe's way of "seeing" the object of study' (Bleicher, 2007, p. 144). It encompasses, among others, the meanings of 'beholding', 'looking at', 'gazing', 'contemplating', 'perceiving the core', 'intuition'. Goethe speaks of a 'delicate empiricism' (*eine zarte Empirie*) (Goethe, 1982, 12, n° 509, p. 435) that does not overlap with the classic empiricist tradition. We have to deal with the complex concept of seeing forms, which brings us closer to the *Gestaltpsychology*. Alongside the wide array of sources inspiring Simmel's thought,[4] Goethe's morphology intimately leaves a mark on Simmel's way of thinking.[5]

Before delving into the subject, a preliminary clarification about lexicon should be made: Goethe is well aware that, in ancient Greek, 'form' is either termed '*morphé*' or '*eidos*': '*morphé*' is the outline, the visible external profile of an object, in opposition with essence, its internal significance. In German, this concept usually corresponds to '*Gestalt*'. '*Form*' indicates the organisation of a phenomenon that relies on a general – yet not universal – order. It refers to something at the same time specific and diversified: the scaffolding of a structure. It usually translates '*eidos*' and its opposite is matter. Its original semantic meaning (from *oida*) is also related to the domain of vision. Both meanings are not separated in Goethe's lexicon; in his inventive writing style he often uses them synonymously (Pörksen, 1988). The visible extension of an object not only has a precise outline and an aesthetic style, but also a structure and an internal organisation. This organisation implies a part-whole relationship, which can be identified both in the perceptual phenomenon and in the corresponding idea (Cassirer, [1916] 1991; Wilkinson,

1951; Arnheim, 1969; Amrine, Zuckert, & Wheeler, 1987; Giacomoni, 1993; Moiso, 2002; Breidbach, 2006).

The word '*Bildung*' is another key word in Goethe's writings, as he explains in *Die Absicht eingeleitet*, introducing *Die Metamorphose der Pflanzen* (Goethe, 1982, 13, p. 55). *Bildung* clarifies the non-static meaning of form. Both concepts are dynamically meant, in a sense that refers to metamorphosis: the complex passage from a form to another. Yet it is better to avoid interpreting it in a Darwinian sense (Weik, 2017, p. 339) – as such expressions as *Urpflanze* and *Urtier* may apparently allow us hypothesise (Richards, 2002). As we will show, Goethe is thinking about the possibility to modify a model while observing the manifold variations in natural phenomena. The question is: how do we get to see forms? Can we consider vision as a sense that provides us not only with real perceptions, but also with ideas, avoiding exotericism?

In the *Exkurs über die Soziologie der Sinne* in the *Soziologie* of 1908 (GSG 11, pp. 722-742), the mutual gaze is indicated as 'the immediate and purest interactive relationship': it does not demand the necessity of a stable and durable form, a spirit's objectification. As Simmel phrases it, 'the most vital interactivity, however, in which the eye-to-eye look intertwines human beings, does not crystallise in any kind of objective formation' (GSG 11, p. 723).

In social relationships, there is no need to crystallise the sense of sight in an objective form. In this case, the human and social world consists of actions that occur instantly, without leaving a lasting trace. The eye-to-eye look is an immediately reciprocal relation. The mind remains in a subjective state and completely disappears 'at the least diversion of the glance'. The whole interaction ends there, in the intensity of a moment that is essential to increase or decrease the distance between people. The look is one of the most significant human events and not an object, according to Simmel. The eye-to-eye look creates an atmosphere, a *Stimmung,* which has not only an expressive effect, but also a heuristic function. Without being a stable and objective form, it can be the point of departure of several forms of relationships, including those that seem to be their opposite, such as the conflict and the secret.

This analysis is a sort of zero-degree in Simmel's sociology. He is always on the search for definite and objective social forms and specific types of behaviour (Thouard & Zimmermann, 2017, pp. 113-133), creatively following Kant's and Weber's methods. Are these forms something 'visible'? Is the spirit's objectification – e.g., money and such types as the stranger, the poor, the blasé – something that can be really perceived, in a way similar to that of Goethe, when he observes the skull of animals or the organ of plants? The difference is striking, but there is something in common.

Simmel writes in *Goethe* monograph:

> Insofar as the form is visibly given, it is granted with full reality, which cannot merge from non-visible instances. Still, whenever the view (*Blick*) is correctly focused, the underlining idea is also visible … Immediate intuition (*Anschauung*), whose pure and essential dimension is determined by natural senses (*Sinnlichkeit*) alone, provides us with 'forms', unachievable by either the concrete analytics of elementary sciences or the abstract synthetics of speculation.
>
> *(GSG 15, pp. 62, 66)*

Simmel's emphasis on form as immediate perception is always accompanied and enriched by several of Goethe's quotations. The most celebrated states:

Everything factual is already theory: to understand this would be the greatest possible achievement. The blueness of the sky reveals the basic law of chromatics. Don't go looking for anything beyond phenomena: they are themselves what they teach, the theory.

(Goethe, 1982, 12, n° 488, p. 432)

Both in nature and in society forms are not mere data: they are the result of a creative research conducted from different standpoints. Form is embraced by Goethe using 'an exact sensory imagination' (*eine exakte sinnliche Phantasie*) (Goethe, 1982, 13, p. 42), aimed at identifying an invariant within the multifarious empirical phenomena. Form is a twofold entity: on the one hand, it is a whole obtained by organising empirical data; on the other hand, it singles out specific elements, such as the different forms of social relationship. When considered from several perspectives, both natural and social phenomena can be organised in specific forms. For his *Metamorphose der Pflanzen* (1790), Goethe passionately and even obsessively collects and observes many different kinds of plants, including during his journey to Italy; his hypothesis is that a common organisation – the form 'leaf' – can be identified in a series of variations in every single organ of the plant. Form is neither individual nor simply general: according to Goethe, the 'transcendental leaf' (Goethe, [1947] 2019, I, 10 p. 52) is never an empirical leaf or a platonic idea, but the result of a detailed comparison between the different plant organs that show an identical structure, from the seed to the flower and the fruit, including the reproductive parts. It is an invariant that does not exist as such, but is a useful tool to interpret that field of phenomena in terms of metamorphosis.

Simmel is well acquainted with the details of this morphological method, which inspired him in many of his works, in spite of the classical bifurcation of *Naturwissenschaften* and *Geisteswissenschaften*. Conflict, subordination, secret, and discretion are forms of social relationships that can be selected by taking a close look on social behaviours while searching for some specific patterns. In order to define conflict as a form of social interaction, for instance, a non-conventional talent for observation is needed. He explicitly, albeit metaphorically, speaks of 'intuition', not in a metaphysical sense, but as a 'specific angle of vision' (*eine besondere Einstellung des Blickes*) (GSG 11, p. 29) that allows a distinction between the concrete phenomenon and its form. Different examples of conflicts are examined in *Soziologie* – aversion, animosity, hostility, war, '*Schadenfreude*', antagonism in marriage – in which a specific aspect is intensified and used as a marker. This aspect is capable of outlining a recognisable structure. In fact, Simmel regards the opposition between two people or more as a kind of relationship – where all the voices have the same right and subordination is avoided – and not its end.

Nevertheless, in order to throw a bridge from the empirical data to a form, one must be capable of insight. In an old but still valuable essay, Friedrich Tenbruck (1959) underlines the importance of the form-matter relationship – in Aristotelian-Kantian sense – in *Das Problem der Soziologie* (1908), the revised and extended version of the essay of the same title of 1894. Simmel emphasises that form and matter are 'inseparable in reality', though 'separated in scientific abstraction' (GSG 11, p. 19). The method used by Simmel – Tenbruck claims – is not strictly empirical-inductive. Abstraction is expounded in a radical sense as:

extracting or extricating from reality something which is not a directly observable and common element in it. ... Although it starts with the social-historical reality, it must finally rely on something else for selecting and exaggerating features of that reality, in order to bring out the inherent, structural order of the elements involved. ... Certain elements go together, they 'fit'. This 'objective' cluster can refer to simultaneous elements or to a sequence of elements.

(Tenbruck, 1959, p. 74f., 79, 84)

Ideal-types of Weber's sociology are an evident source of inspiration for Simmel, according to Tenbruck. No objections (Giacomoni, 1978), yet Simmel's sources are manifold. Goethe's morphology always keeps on running in the background. Writing about his method, Goethe uses the fascinating but ambiguous statement 'the eyes of the mind' (*die Augen des Geistes*) (Förster, 2001). However, in Goethe's practice of science, it does not refer to either a mystery or an illumination; on the contrary, it indicates a research habit that considers a collection of objects from several points of view, taking different perspectives, and finally identifying an invariant among the multiple data. In this case, form is at the same time specific and not individual (Giacomoni, 1993). In a sense very close to Tenbruck's reading, some singular aspects emerge as markers of a group of phenomena and characterise it as a form. This is effectively exemplified in Goethe's essay on the osteological type, in which he refers to the length of the snake's body that prevents it from having side organs and the magnificent wingspan in birds to the detriment of body size. A single part plays a crucial role in the form of an organism. If we compare different organisms by using the 'eye of the mind', on search for constant and variable elements, we can identify the transformation of nature, the differentiation of species and varieties, leaving aside accidental and not significant details (Goethe, 1982, 13, pp. 175–180). Simmel understands it very well and applies it to the level of perception in *Lebensanschauung*:

> Every optical perception signifies immediately a selection from unlimited possibilities; within every immediate visual field we emphasise (for reasons having to do only in exceptional cases with the mere optical) always particular points only; perception leaves a host of thing outside of them, as though not there at all, and even in each particular object there are innumerable sides and qualities our gaze passes over. ... The material of our world of visual perception is in fact not what is really there, but rather a residuum left over after the omission of countless possible components – and this certainly determines in very positive fashion the formations, associations, and unitary structure of the world. Thus, if a noted modern painter said that drawing is omission, then this truth presupposes another: seeing is omission [*Sehen ist Weglassen*].

> *(GSG 16, p. 56)*

Aesthetic forms

'Schönheit ist Vollkommenheit mit Freiheit'

In Simmel's aesthetic writings this Goethean understanding of perception is even more evident. The ability of seeing is of indisputable importance in art. In the essays on art and on portrait the visual approach is crucial. The first meaning of 'aesthetic' is *aisthesis*, sensory perception, a kind of knowledge in which a selective seeing is essential.

What does seeing a form mean in this case? First of all: parts and whole. The relationship between part and whole is a key element in Simmel: the proclivity to think of being a whole as well as being part of a whole are the two most significant tendencies of the human mind, whose relationship can be complementary as well as opposite. This is the cornerstone of all his sociological research and the key-category of his aesthetics.

Parts-whole relationship is also evident in all of Goethe's naturalistic writings. For instance, in a short intervention on Lavater's *Physiognomische Fragmente* 1775 (Goethe, [1947] 2019, I, 10, pp. 1-5), he analyses some *silhouettes*: the profile of a face just emphasises some of its lines and not all traits; facial expressions, its colours and its singularities are overlooked. Only lines matter. In this context, it is crucial to take into account the respective role of and the specific interaction among single parts: a high forehead is usually combined with a particular line of the nose, the shape of a chin is strictly related to that of the mouth. All these features constitute a form in the sense of *morphé*, in accordance with his reflection on the metamorphosis of plants. Comparison shows nuanced similarities and differences, yet the transformation of form is easy to distinguish for a skilled beholder. The general impression is produced by the reciprocal action of these formal elements and provides us with a sophisticated tool of comparison. Typical combinations of features at a high degree of abstraction are displayed: e.g. Newton's and Socrates' face. Even animal skulls display typical combinations of lines according to the animal living habits (Giacomoni, 1993, pp. 25–46).

The face is defined by Simmel as 'the geometrical locus, as it were, of the inner personality' (GSG 7, p. 39). Emotions leave lasting traces on the face that identify the permanent character, the persistent inwardness of a person. It is something super-personal, a form, and, as such, it implies a certain grade of symmetry. The face 'does not act' as the other parts of the body: it speaks a language of abiding embodied symbols; a specific form of interaction between the single parts (not significant in themselves) and the whole enables the expression of a recognisable type.[6]

At the same time, the part-whole relationship makes the most fluid flow of individual inner life directly visible: in this sense, symmetry is eluded. Individuality is thus put into play, not as form, but rather as distance from a general scheme (Giacomoni, 1997). Individuality is always anti-symmetric: it is the measure of the distance from a geometrical rule – the scaffolding of form. It implies the possibility of an infinite number of sudden passages from a form to another as well as from an expression to another. 'The face is the most remarkable aesthetic synthesis of the formal principle of symmetry and that of individuality' (GSG 7, p. 40).[7]

To illuminate this point, Simmel establishes a comparison between the Italian portrait and Rembrandt's art (GSG 15, pp. 323–327). The Italian portrait stems from the search for form and social rank: its universality is evident also in its technical perfection. It represents a role, a type: a knight, a craftsman, a nobleman, but not an individual. For this reason, it is enigmatic. It does not represent a living and unique character in its irreplaceable richness, but a social type or a role. Conversely, Rembrandt's art aims to paint individuals, even a single aspect or an instant of an individual life (see Titus' portrait and the famous etching of Rembrandt's mother). And for this reason, definite forms and neat lines are eluded. The dynamics of life is displayed in his paintings and etchings, although not directly, but through the specific logic of the world of art.

And again: '*Zeichnen ist Weglassen*' (GSG 15, p. 493). When we ask ourselves 'What do we *see* in a work of art?' (GSG 15, p. 492), the answer cannot be simply: reality. Art refers to a completely different context of significance that occurs in an independent objectivity, that of the artistic realm. In the case of the famous etching of Rembrandt's mother wearing a fur collar 'we do not see a fur collar at all' (GSG 15, p. 494). As a real object, outside the work of art, the collar is the outcome of a synthetic and cognitive act, which is not merely visual: we deal with tactile perceptions, activities, practical occurrences, categorisations, psychic factors, etc. Conversely, as a work of art, the fur collar only consists of few strokes of ink: a merely optical stylisation, not to be compared with the real object. Art forges another realm, a self-sufficient sphere, with its own grammar, its creative categories and significance. The work of art builds up a different perspective, which is neither mirroring nor in contact with reality: the same object (the fur collar) can be expressed in two different languages, both grounded on their respective set of values. The selective organisation of parts consolidates a unity that belongs to the art as a new sphere of reality, as a new world (GSG 15, pp. 492-501).

Truth and error: liminal phenomena

'Eine tätige Skepsis'

Form is the unity of parts and whole. However, a gap between experience and science can be detected, especially in Goethe's late writings, such as *Bedenken und Ergebung* (Goethe, 1982, 13, p. 31). In this sense, Simmel brilliantly captures Goethe's interest in liminal phenomena, in the elements which, when changing from one form to another, become distorted or turn into actual anomalies. The anomalous is, for Goethe, a result of transformation, of the constant movement and plasticity of life, not a random - mysterious, or even inexplicable – product of chance. When one of the characteristics of a living being becomes overly dominant and distorts the being's original form – even to the point of rendering it unrecognisable – that initial form appears unidentifiable or actually bogus, and – indeed – to have broken the rules that govern it. However, when considered within a continuous series of transformations, the anomalous allows us to see the totality of a Nature in constant – although not random or irrational – transformation: the normal and the abnormal are only relative points of view, meanings and functions are in constant flux.

Simmel mentions how important it is to pay attention to the *Mißbildungen*, as Goethe calls abnormal or monstrous forms (GSG 15, pp. 134-136), which he examines in *Metamorphose der Pflanzen,* for example; here, irregular formations, such as the proliferated rose, assume a clear heuristic value. Nature's powerful creative impulse sometimes finds moments, in its transformations, which seem 'to grow slack, irresolutely leaving its creation in an indeterminate, malleable state'. But he immediately adds that 'our observations of this metamorphosis will allow us to discover what is hidden in regular metamorphosis, to see clearly what we can only infer in regular metamorphosis' (Goethe, 1982, 13, p. 65). The shift from one form to another necessarily involves a process of deformation in which the old form seems to vanish before the new one has clearly revealed itself.

The *Mißbildungen* should thus be understood as phenomena intrinsic to a transition from one form to another, rather than as mere errors of Nature. The proliferated rose is such a case: its abnormal form demonstrates - to the bodily eyes - the morphological and structural affinity between the vegetative and reproductive parts of the plant, which could only be detected with the 'eyes of the mind' in normal forms. For the relativist/ organismic Goethe portrayed by Simmel, truth clearly cannot be set up against error. Irregular formations are not 'wrong' but – on the contrary – are significant instances which reveal the other side of metamorphosis, that of the momentary distortion or deformation inherent in the necessary passing away of an old - and birth of a new - form.

Nor are cognitive errors considered simply as mistakes - to be corrected, rejected, excluded. Many of Goethe's *Maximen* deal with this concept of error (Goethe, 1982, 12, nn° 293-339). An individual point of view may be objectively erroneous, but it is never superfluous, never junk to simply be ignored: it constitutes a glimpse of the truth, it is not merely wrong, or definitively, unquestionably, useless. Moreover, as has often been pointed out, Goethe, who believed that no way of thinking had a monopoly on the truth, was not a proponent of the method of exclusion. In this sense, his thought can be described as essentially 'theatrical' – in all spheres, from the literary to the scientific, he allowed both protagonist and antagonist to take the stage, regardless of the fact than he would then side – to a greater or lesser extent – with one or other of the 'actors' (Giacomoni, 2000). The recognition of alterity, of a multiplicity of possible truths, is, of course, a typically Goethean gesture. The following (much quoted) maxim is an excellent example of Goethe's concept of truth as always approximate, never a definite solution:

> It is as certain as it is wonderful that error and truth spring from the same source; frequently, therefore, error must not be attacked because this would also mean attacking the truth.
>
> *(Goethe, 1982, 12, n°310, p. 407)*

The methodology adopted by Goethe in his scientific papers has been re-examined in recent decades, revealing new – maybe unexpected – elements of modernity. The father of the *Bildungsroman* still has some surprises in store for us, which Simmel – although he captured them with great acuity - enveloped in veils of metaphysics, thus inevitably somewhat obscuring their significance. Goethe was not, of course, the source of Simmel's main sociological or philosophical ideas. Nevertheless, it is clear that he perceives many of his own most innovative perspectives to be profoundly connected to certain Goethean ideas.

Simmel often points out that, according to Goethe, the passage from a form to another takes place without conflict. In Goethe's eyes, form is not a rigid crystallisation of the flow of life. Everything occurs spontaneously, with no obstacles and no opposition, as Simmel frequently notes in his 1913 monograph. But we have seen that anomalies cannot be eluded. They are essential in the interpretation of nature in its variety of phenomena and transformations. Liminal passages allow metamorphosis and are not immediately connoted by a tragic outcome; they are modifications of a common pattern that generally characterises that realm. Liminal phenomena are crucial for Simmel: they transgress categories and build bridges between disciplines. The stranger as an in-between figure is their paradigm (Goodstein, 2016, 2017), though internal tensions often make those figures fragile, instable, and full of contradictions. This aspect has been often emphasised, particularly if we consider Simmel's last writings. However, form-life dialectic is no longer to be interpreted as simply 'contaminated with metaphysical residues and in need to reframing to be used for twentieth-century social science' (Goodstein, 2016, p. 31): it can be a useful tool to decipher the complex phenomena of contemporary society (Fitzi, 2019, pp. 135-138).

Considering Simmel's whole work, the transformation of forms in sociological, economic, aesthetic, and philosophical contexts shows a positive dynamics: from the solidity of a form to the liquidity of the flow of life the passage can be tragic, but it is not necessarily a threat to life (Weik, 2017, p. 341): it is first of all a physiological reshaping of reality. Social institutions change their form sometimes abruptly sometimes gradually, thus adapting to the subsequent step of the social life. If this passage can be seen in analogy with a metamorphosis, we can conclude that Goethe's way of thinking, together with many others voices, is always on the background of Simmel's philosophical and sociological perspective.

Notes

1 If not specified otherwise all English quotes are the author's translation.
2 Simmel was very early convinced of the paramount philosophical importance of Goethe's work: 'Goethe's philosophy' was among the subjects for his trial lesson at the University of Berlin in 1885 (Gassen & Landmann, 1958, p. 21).
3 An issue addressed in one of the first reviews of the book (Havenstein, 1914).
4 D. Levine (2012, p. 36) states that Simmel's engagement with Goethe is related to life and to form, although, we have to reconcile the influence of both Goethe and Kant on this subject. He emphasises the 'plurality of views' that Simmel's work encompasses.
5 I do not claim that Goethe's morphological method is the only source of Simmel's concept of form or the main inspiration of his formal sociology and philosophy. It would be a one-sided interpretation, overlooking the paramount role played by Kant and Weber, among others.
6 In *Das Problem der Soziologie* (GSG, 11, pp. 25-29) Simmel repeatedly uses the analogy with geometrical figures: specific polygons and spheres result from the different combinations of lines. *Morphé* and *eidos* are combined together.
7 The obsession with symmetry, the need for an architectonic of knowledge is exactly the point of Kant's system which is judged 'obsolete' and remote from modern perspective of an infinite development in the 1896 essay *Was ist uns Kant?* (GSG 5, 145-177).

References

Amat, M. (2018). *Le relationnisme philosophique de Georg Simmel. Une idée de la culture.* Paris: Honoré Champion Éditeur.

Amrine, F., Zuckert, F., & Wheeler, H. (Eds.) (1987). *Goethe and the sciences. A reappraisal.* Dordrecht, Boston, MA, Lancaster, and Tokyo: Reidel.

Arnheim, R. (1969). *Visual thinking.* Berkeley, CA and Los Angeles, CA: University of California Press.

Bleicher, J. (2007). From Kant to Goethe. Georg Simmel on the way to *Leben. Theory, Culture and Society, 24*(6), 139–158.

Breidbach, O. (2006). *Goethes Metamorphosenlehre.* München: Fink.

Cassirer, E. ([1916] 1991). *Freiheit und Form. Studien zur deutschen Geistesgeschichte.* Hamburg: Meiner.

Cislaghi, F. (2008). *Goethe e Darwin. La filosofia delle forme viventi.* Milano: Mimesis.

Fitzi, G. (2002). *Soziale Erfahrung und Lebensphilosophie. Georg Simmels Beziehung zu Henri Bergson.* Konstanz: UVK.

Fitzi, G. (2016). Modernity as solid liquidity. In Kemple, T. & Pyyhtinen, O. (Eds.), *The Anthem companion to Georg Simmel* (pp. 59–80). London and New York: Anthem Press.

Fitzi, G. (2019). *The challenge of modernity: Simmel's sociological theory.* London and New York: Routledge.

Förster, E. (2001). Goethe and the 'Auge des Geistes'. *Deutsche Vierteljahrsschrift für Literaturwissenschaft und Geistesgeschichte, 75,* 87–101.

Gassen, K., & Landmann, M. (Eds.) (1958). *Buch des Dankes an Georg Simmel.* Berlin: Duncker & Humblot.

Giacomoni, P. (1978). Max Weber e l'ambiguità del 'Verstehen'. *Rivista di filosofia, 12,* 420–450.

Giacomoni, P. (1993). *Le forme e il vivente. Morfologia e filosofia della natura in J.W. Goethe.* Napoli: Guida.

Giacomoni, P. (1995). *Classicità e frammento. Georg Simmel goethiano.* Napoli: Guida.

Giacomoni, P. (1997). Individuum und Typus bei Simmel und Goethe. *Simmel Newsletter, 7*(1), 17–24.

Giacomoni, P. (2000). Polarità e individualità nel 'Tasso' di Goethe. *Materiali di estetica, 3,* 171–186.

Giacomoni, P. (2002). Georg Simmel on life and force: Between Goethe and Kant. In Tymieniecka, A. T. (Ed.), *Analecta Husserliana,* vol. 74 (pp. 51–70). Dordrecht, Boston, MA, and London: Kluwer.

Giacomoni, P. (2006). Kontinuität der Formen: Georg Simmels Interpretation einiger Begriffe der Naturphilosophie Goethes. *Simmel Studies, 16,* 5–19.

Giorello, G., & Grieco, A. (Eds.). (1998). *Goethe scienziato.* Torino: Einaudi.

Goethe, J. W. (1982). *Werke. Hamburger Ausgabe,* 14 vol. Trunz, E. (Ed.) München: Beck.

Goethe, J. W. (1986). *Briefe. Hamburger Ausgabe.* Trunz, E. (Ed.) München: Beck.

Goethe, J. W. ([1947] 2019). *Die Schriften zur Naturwissenschaft,* im Auftrag der Deutschen Akademie der Naturforscher Leopoldina. Matthei, R., Troll, W., & Wolff, L. (Eds.). Weimar: Böhlaus. 2 Abt., 11 vol.

Goodstein, E. (2016). Sociology as sideline: Does it matter that Georg Simmel (thought he) was a philosopher? In Kemple, T. & Pyyhtinen, O. (Eds.), *The Anthem companion to Georg Simmel* (pp. 29–58). London and New York: Anthem Press.

Goodstein, E. (2017). *Georg Simmel and the disciplinary imaginary*. Stanford: Stanford University Press.

Harrington, A. (2016). Goethe and the creative life. In Kemple, T. & Pyyhtinen, O. (Eds.), *The Anthem companion to Georg Simmel* (pp. 183–190). London and New York: Anthem Press.

Havenstein, M. (1914). Chamberlains und Simmels 'Goethe'. *Preußische Jahrbücher, 155*, 270–291.

Kleinschnieder, M. (1971). *Goethes Naturstudien*. Bonn: Bouvier.

Kuhn, D. (1978). Grundzüge der goetheschen Morphologie. *Goethe Jahrbuch, 95*, 199–211.

Levine, D. N. (2012). Soziologie and Lebensanschauung: Two approaches to synthetizing 'Kant and Goethe' in Simmel's Work. *Theory, Culture and Society, 29*(7/8), 26–52.

Moiso, F. (2002). *Goethe. La natura e le sue forme*. Milano: Mimesis.

Pfau, T. (2010). 'All is leaf': Difference, metamorphosis, and Goethe's phenomenology of knowledge. *Studies in Romanticism, 49*, 3–41.

Pörksen, U. (1988). 'Alles ist Blatt'. Über die Reichweite und Grenzen der naturwissenschaftlichen Sprache und Darstellungsmodelle Goethes. *Berichte zur Wissenschaftsgeschichte, 11*, 133–148.

Richards, J. R. (2002). *The romantic conception of life: Science and philosophy in the age of Goethe*. Chicago, IL and London: Chicago University Press.

Simmel, G. (1971). *On individuality and social forms*. Levine, D. N. (Ed.). Chicago, IL and London: The University of Chicago Press.

Simmel, G. (1989-2015). *Georg Simmel Gesamtausgabe (GSG)*. Rammstedt, O. (Ed.). Frankfurt a. M.: Suhrkamp.

Simmel, G. (2005). *Rembrandt. An essay in the philosophy of art*. Scott, A. & Staubmann, H. (Eds.). New York and London: Routledge.

Simmel, G. (2009). *Sociology. Inquiries into the construction of social forms*. Blasi, A. J., Jacobs, A. K., & Kanjiarathinkal, M. (Eds.). Leiden and Boston, MA: Brill.

Simmel, G. (2010). *The view of life. Four metaphysical essays with journal aphorisms*. Andrews, A. Y. & Levine, D. N.. (Eds.). Chicago, IL and London: The University of Chicago Press.

Tenbruck, F. (1959). Formal sociology. In Wolff, K. H. (Ed.), *Georg Simmel, 1858–1918. A collection of essays, with translation and a bibliography* (pp. 61–99). Columbus: The Ohio State University Press.

Thouard, D., & Zimmermann, B. (Eds.) (2017). *Le parti-pris du tiers*. Paris: Centre national de la recherche scientifique.

Weik, E. (2017). Goethe and the study of life: A comparison with Husserl and Simmel. *Continental Philosophy Review, 50*, 335–357.

Wilkinson, E. (1951). Goethe's conception of form. *Proceedings of British Academy, 37*, 175–197.

16

SIMMEL

The actor and his roles

François Thomas

Georg Simmel is one of the few philosophers to have taken a close interest in the art of acting and to have assigned it a real importance in his philosophy of art. Simmel devoted four articles to the art of the actor, which he considered to be the art form that raised the most difficult problems (cf. *Zur Philosophie des Schauspielers*, 1923, GSG 20, p. 202). But the question of the actor goes beyond the mere framework of reflection on art and appears as a central theme in Simmel's work; indeed, it lies at the intersection of all the major issues he addresses. On the one hand, reflection on the actor's art mobilizes all the conceptual tools that Simmel develops in his other texts (relativism, law of the individual, philosophy of life, etc.); on the other hand, the relationship of the individual to his roles, the difficulty of playing a role that does not correspond to one's personality, the theatricalization of social life in metropolises, are themes lying at the centre of both his theoretical sociology and his important analyses of modernity.

It was an original problematization of the relationship between the actor and his roles that lent the theme of the actor its centrality in Simmel's thought. We will first specify his new approach to acting before addressing Simmel's sociological reflections on the notion of social role and the dramatization of social life in large cities. Finally, we will come back to Simmel's aesthetic analyses of acting itself.

The ordinary enigma and the new problem of the actor

According to Simmel, 'the enigma of the actor, as we usually imagine it' is that of metamorphosis: 'how can a determined, singular personality suddenly become another person, very different, or many others?' (*Zur Philosophie des Schauspielers*, 1908, GSG 8, p. 428). How does the actor manage to disappear behind his role, to be forgotten or annihilated (Rousseau), in order to give the spectator the illusion that the character himself is present on stage? This question runs through philosophical reflection on the theatre, from Plato to Nietzsche, via Diderot, Rousseau, Hegel (and even Sartre). But, according to Simmel, the activity of actors on the stage should no longer be understood in these terms at the turn of the 20th century. Instead, it is necessary to consider the coexistence of the role and the actor, and no longer the disappearance of the one for the benefit of the other.

Simmel's reflection takes into account the emergence of great theatrical stars and the slow emancipation of the actors' art since the end of the 18th century. According to Simmel, the actor is no longer a simple 'puppet' in the poet's hands, something deployed in the service of the text (cf. *Zur Philosophie des Schauspielers*, 1908, GSG 8, p. 425). In his articles, Simmel mentions Elonora Duse, Tommaso Salvini, Joseph Kainz, Alexander Moissi, Sarah Bernhardt, etc. How should one define the specific art of these actors and what makes them true artists and creators? The spectator who goes to the theatre at the beginning of the 20th century no longer expects the actor to disappear behind his character. As Simmel points out, he does not seek to forget the singularity of the actor and the originality of his performance in order to see only fictional beings. He does not go to the theatre simply to see *Phèdre* or *Hamlet*, but rather a particular interpretation of these characters by a particular actor. Conversely, he does not simply attend the actor's performance without taking into account the role and text that the actor is supposed to play. Simmel's reflections are to be compared to Proust's descriptions in *A la recherche du temps perdu*, when the narrator goes to the theatre to attend a performance of Racine's *Phèdre*, in order to grasp the nature of La Berma's talent, the fictional equivalent of the French actress Sarah Bernhard. (See Proust, 1987, p. 441, 1988, p. 347.)

How should one conceive this union of objectivity (the role and the text) and subjectivity (the actor's original personality)? This, for Simmel, is the problem of dramatic art. According to him, the interpretation on stage does not derive either from the text or from the individual nature of the actor or from reality (as if the scene were set in 'real' life), but from the law that a particular role imposes on a particular actor. The actor's relationship to his role is for Simmel an exemplary case of the 'law of the individual'. According to his personality, his physique, etc., and according to the role he has to play, each actor must find the original and singular way in which he has to interpret the role (cf. *Zur Philosophie des Schauspielers*, 1908, GSG 8, p. 425). Different interpretations of the same role by different actors, however opposed they may be, can nevertheless appear equally 'right' and each can reveal the character in its truth. There is no single, universal criterion that would emerge from reading the text and abstractly determine what the 'true' interpretation of a role should be. This does not mean, however, that all interpretations are equal, or that it is sufficient for the actor to follow his spontaneity and impose an entirely subjective interpretation of the character. It makes sense to talk about a 'false' interpretation. But since we cannot refer to an ideal and literary law, it is this 'law of the individual' that serves as a criterion. An interpretation is false when the actor fails to find or realize the requirement that the role imposes on his nature as an artist, or when no relationship is conceivable between the actor and the role. For many actors, Simmel writes, 'Hamlet is what colour is to a colourblind' (cf. *Zur Philosophie des Schauspielers*, 1923, GSG 20, p. 211). By this 'relativistic' or relational conception, it is possible to defend the plurality of interpretations, while maintaining a form of objectivity and avoiding the 'relativism' according to which all interpretations would be admissible.

We could summarize the aesthetic problem of the actor's art as follows: how can an actor appropriate a role, so that he plays this role perfectly and reveals himself through his acting? Such a formulation of the problem makes it possible to broaden the scope of the analysis, insofar as playing a role, not deceiving or lying (such as Tartuffe playing the false devotee), is then not the prerogative of the actors alone, but is part, according to Simmel, 'of the functions that constitute our concrete life' (*Zur Philosophie des Schauspielers*, 1923, GSG 20, p. 203). Our daily and social life is made up of roles that we interpret, which guide both our gestures and our words, and which correspond more or less to our original personalities. Simmel's reflections on the art of the actor converge here with his sociological theories: with his analyses of the conditions of possibility of society and socialization, as well as his reflections on modernity. What effects does life in large cities, the monetarization of exchanges, the division of labour, have on the individual's relationship to his or her social roles?

Conditions of possibility of social life

'We are all actors ... in however fragmentary a way', Simmel writes in one of his articles on theatre (*Zur Philosophie des Schauspielers*, 1923, GSG 20, p. 204): 'playing a role – not as pretence or deception, but as pouring one's personal life into a form of expression that we find somehow already existing, traced in advance – this belongs to the functions that constitute our actual, concrete life' (GSG 20, p. 203).

The notion of playing a role is at the heart of the first chapter of *Sociology*, in which Simmel questions what he calls the 'a priori forms of socialization', i.e. the conditions of possibility of any social interaction. The first of these a priori forms, Simmel writes, is that 'we see the other more or less as the result of a generalization' (GSG 11, p. 47). We perceive the other first of all as a 'representative', a 'type', and not as an individual in all his uniqueness. On the one hand, we never have access to what makes up his identity, his 'pure being-for-itself' (*reines Fürsichsein*, GSG 11, p. 48). We only have fragmentary knowledge of others, however close our relationship to them. Yet on the other hand, as Simmel points out, our experience of others is never a mere perception of 'juxtaposed fragments'. In approximately the same way that, according to Kant (GSG 11, p. 50), understanding shapes the diverse given in intuition into an object, we transform the incomplete vision that we have of beings or things into a totality and construct a unified image of others. In social life, this leads us to perceive individuals by first associating them with the roles they play. 'We do not see the other simply as an individual, but as a colleague, as belonging to the same regiment or as a fellow party member ... Everywhere, social generalization conceals features of reality' (GSG 11, p. 50). But at the same time, we know that an individual cannot be reduced to the role he plays and that his way of playing his social role depends on everything that he is in addition. The perception of others includes an awareness of a gap between the role and the person. We designate the other 'according to an implicit type, with which his pure being for himself [*reines Fürsichsein*] does not coincide' (GSG 11, p. 48). We first perceive the role or function, but this role is always interpreted in a certain way, just as, in the theatre, we do not simply see the role but always an interpretation of it.

> We know that the civil servant is not only a civil servant, the trader not only a trader, the officer not only an officer. ... In the eyes of all those who meet him, this extra-social being, that is, his temperament, his particular destiny, his interests and the value of his personality, even if all this only slightly alters the essence of his activities as a civil servant, as a trader, as a soldier, always gives him a particular nuance, so that his social image is woven with extra-social imponderables.
>
> *(GSG 11, p. 51)*

This is the second a priori form. One might think that these roles played in everyday life are above all shackles that prevent personality from expressing itself, that individuals are forced to play roles with which they do not identify and which prevent them from 'being themselves' – as if social life constituted an alienation of our authentic self. Such a claim, however, is reminiscent of the dove in the *Critique of Pure Reason*, which thinks that it would fly more easily if it were to encounter no air resistance. We can only develop our personality through the mediation of an objective, external content that we appropriate to a greater or lesser degree. In other words, what is subjective can only be realized, become effective, by inserting itself into an objective form. We need to pour our inner life into an external form, without which this inner life itself could not unfold or express itself. This is the meaning of Simmel's quote, according to which 'playing a role – pouring one's personal life into a form of expression that we find somehow already existing, traced in advance – this belongs to the functions that constitute our actual, concrete life' (*Zur Philosophie des Schauspielers*, 1923, GSG 20, p. 203).

We perceive others first of all through the role they play because every individual inserts himself into existence only by means of a role or a form that is already traced out, in which his own personality finds expression. But the two poles of person and role cannot be absolutized. There is not, on the one hand, our true being and, on the other, a role that would exist in itself, without any interpretation: the two poles are relative to one other. 'We inevitably represent something that, deep down, we are not' (*Zur Philosophie des Schauspielers*, GSG 20, p. 203). We cannot simply oppose an authentic inner and an apparent surface, as if there were the characters we played publicly, and the 'true face' (see H. Plessner 'Der Kampf ums wahre Gesicht', in *Grenzen der Gemeinschaft*, *Gesammelte Schriften V*, 1981, pp. 58-78) that we would reveal in private, or for ourselves alone, once all the masks of social life had fallen. An individual's personality only appears through the roles he or she plays, whilst always being more than, or something besides, the roles he or she plays.

In this respect, playing a role is a constitutive act of our social life. One might think that acting is a secondary activity, which involves distinguishing between real (or serious) actions and actions that are performed, which repeat or imitate the former. But acting is not imitating, the act of the actor is not an act of reproduction. This is one of the major points of Simmel's theatrical aesthetics. Acting is at the heart of human activities. We only become ourselves by playing. In this regard, Simmel reinterprets Schiller's thesis in his *Letters on Aesthetic Education* that man is only fully a human being when he plays (15th Letter, Schiller, 1993, p. 131).

Simmel's sociology, starting with these reflections on the notion of social role, seeks to preserve a space for the individual and individual freedom. Simmel does not think in terms of social determinism, but makes the notion of *Wechselwirkung* one of the key notions of his sociological thinking. Simmel insists on the idea that the actor is not the puppet of his role. In his book on the philosophy of history, he uses the same image to emphasize the idea that man is not a puppet at the hands of historical, social, or economic laws.

This theoretical model, presented at the beginning of *Sociology*, also provides Simmel with a framework for analysing different pathologies of the social and modern world. This dialectic of the subjective and the objective involved in the fact of 'playing a role', this complex balance between an individual and his roles, is threatened by the evolution of social life in large modern cities, the monetarization of exchange, the division of labour. Simmel describes the experience of modernity as an experience of fragmentation ('We are fragments, not only of the general human being, but also of ourselves', *Soziologie*, GSG 11, p. 49): on the one hand, the gap between personality and its roles widens, and on the other hand, personality itself tends to be reduced to the sum of the roles played by the individual, which are ever more numerous and diverse.

Origins of the society of the spectacle

Social life in large cities tends to become a game of roles and masks, behind which the personality of the actors increasingly disappears. Economic relations make individuals increasingly dependent on a growing number of other individuals and their services. Yet what people are in addition to or outside of their activity, what they are as individuals, plays almost no role in these interactions.

> The modern division of labour permits the number of dependencies to increase just as it causes personalities to disappear behind their functions, because only one side of them operates, at the expense of all those others whose composition would make up a personality.
>
> *(Philosophy of money, Simmel, 2004, p. 297)*

The function appears as an ideal form, autonomous, independent of its own supports. We increasingly engage with the postman, the policeman, the tram driver, without worrying about the individuality that embodies these roles. Individuals become interchangeable; we pay for a service.

> The human being, as a producer, a buyer or a seller, as an economic agent, comes closer to the ideal of absolute objectivity ... individual life, the tonality of the global person are absent from economic activity, and people are only the vectors of a balance achieved according to objective standards ... and everything that has no place in this pure objectivity has also disappeared in practice.
>
> *(Soziologie, GSG 11, p. 52)*

This is why money and the division of labour lead to a growing impersonalization of social life and exchange. However, there is something positive about this process, as Simmel points out, since the depersonalization of exchange gives us a new form of independence. 'We are compensated for the great quantity of our dependencies by the indifference towards the respective persons and by our liberty to change them at will' (*Philosophy of money*, Simmel, 2004, p. 298). In short, we have never been so free, if freedom is to be understood as independence from the will of others. But the negative side of this freedom is that 'under certain circumstances, one never feels as lonely and as deserted as in the metropolitan throng' (The Metropolis and Mental Life, *Die Großstädte und das Geistesleben*, GSG 7, p. 126).

On account of the division of labour, the different functions or tasks performed by the individual mobilize only one aspect of his or her personality. Specialization thus increases the gap between the individual and his roles and accentuates the impression of fragmentation of the self. This trend is further amplified by what Simmel calls 'social differentiation'. In pre-modern societies, individuals belonged to a small social group (often the family circle). In modern and industrial societies, individuals belong to a plurality of social circles, especially in large cities. Sociability is diversifying. On the one hand, the individual once again acquires greater independence and freedom; but on the other hand, it reinforces the feeling of fragmentation between the different spheres of his social life. The modern individual struggles to synthesize his social roles and the more private and intimate spheres of his life. He finds it increasingly difficult to determine what constitutes the unity of his self, the unity of the different characters he plays in these different spheres, as if he no longer recognizes himself in his roles.

This fragmentation is further aggravated by what Simmel calls the 'domination of object-ive culture'. In the sixth chapter of the *Philosophy of Money*, entitles 'The Lifestyle', Simmel has this phenomenon depend directly on the division of labour (*Philosophy of Money*, Simmel, 2004, p. 463):

> The sense of being oppressed by the externalities of modern life is not only the consequence but also the cause of the fact that they confront us as autonomous objects ... Modern man is so surrounded by nothing but impersonal objects that he becomes more and more conditioned into accepting the idea of an anti-individualistic social order. ... Cultural objects increasingly evolve into an inter-connected enclosed world that has increasingly fewer points at which the subjective soul can interpose its will and feelings.
>
> *(Philosophy of Money, Simmel, 2004, p. 465)*

In response to this depersonalization of human relationships, certain inhabitants of large cities use a wide range of strategies to attract the attention of others. In search of his lost self, the modern individual develops a need to distinguish himself and to draw attention to himself. In his analysis of modern large cities, Simmel therefore studies the different phenom-ena of theatricalization of social life. His reflections on fashion, coquetry, urban architecture, and the phenomena of histrionism, describe the emergence of a 'society of the spectacle'. Simmel is interested in anything that reveals an effort to give existence and visibility to the self. One of his most famous studies is devoted to adornment: 'The radiance of finery, the sensual attention it arouses, confer on the personality such an extension or intensification of its sphere that it is, so to speak, more when adorned with finery' (*Psychologie des Schmuckes*, GSG 8, p. 387).

The individual is thus torn between, on the one hand, a need to affirm himself, to differ-entiate himself – according to Simmel, this 'individualism' which pushes the individual to affirm his singularity can be traced back to German Romanticism – and, on the other hand, a multiform process of depersonalization, pluralization, and fragmentation of the self, whose coherence the individual no longer manages to perceive.

In this context, we can see the potential importance and significance of the figure of the actor. The actor is indeed the one who embodies, or seeks to embody, this requirement of self-accomplishment, this synthesis of objective and subjective. The actor on stage is entirely in his role. 'There is no art in which production and the whole personality are linked in such a tight unity', says Simmel of theatrical art in his articles on 'women's culture' (GSG 12, p. 272; GSG 14, p. 442).

We can therefore understand the growing fascination in the 19th century with this figure who seems to devote his life to achieving what modern man fails to. With the proliferation of theatres in large cities in the second half of the 19th century, the development of the press, but also the development of democratic individualism (cf. de Tocqueville, 1981), great theatrical stars appeared, who, like Sarah Bernhardt in France, sometimes became sig-nificant national figures. Actors became real social figures, whose individuality, adventures and passions fascinated the ever-increasing number of people who went to the theatre (cf. Duvignaud, 1965). In Henry James' expression in the novel *The Tragic Muse* (1961, p. 298), the actor is 'the great modern personage'.

Simmel's analyses shed light on the social importance assumed by the actors, but he also seeks to identify the philosophical and metaphysical significance of the theatrical art of his time; more precisely, in the context of the tragedy of culture and the philosophy of life.

'The interpretation of this art, he wrote in 1912, flows into the great current of the modern understanding of the world' (*Der Schauspieler und die Wirklicheit*, 1912, GSG 12, p. 315).

Towards the philosophy of the actor

Simmel's articles on theatre seek to determine what constitutes the actor's own art. However, this means, above all, recognizing the performance of actors as an art in its own right. Three conceptions are to be rejected, according to Simmel: the first reduces the actor to being only the 'puppet of the role'; the second sees the actor's task as that of imitating or reproducing reality; the third believes that the actor should only play himself or be himself on stage. In these three conceptions, the proper artistic dimension of the actor's work disappears.

At the turn of the 20th century, theatre was still often perceived as a literary art form, in which only the author was considered the true artist, and only the written text was considered a work of art. Yet the character, as it appears in the written play, is not a complete human being. A great indeterminacy remains, which leaves room for the actor's interpretation and allows him, by bringing his own individuality onto the stage, to bestow a sensible existence on the literary character. The text itself does not fully determine in advance the interpretation of the role. The text opens a space in which the actor's art can unfold and completely different interpretations of the same role can emerge.

Simmel insists on the fact that the actor does not bring the character into reality (*Verwirklichung*), but into the realm of the sensual (*Versinnlichung*), as he says with reference to Schiller (cf. *Der Schauspieler und die Wirklichkeit*, 1912, GSG 12, p. 309). The actor transforms the reality into a work of art. Simmel's reflections on theatre correspond to his more general critique of realism and naturalism in art. Naturalist theatre, which claims to reproduce reality as faithfully as possible, misunderstands itself and forgets that it is much more than a pure and simple imitation of reality. An important concept in Simmel's reflections on aesthetic is that of 'stylisation': any theatrical scene, however realistic it may be, is based on choices of perspective and gives reality an artistic form (whether it is the set, the actor's approach, the representation of time, etc.). This is why it is important to distinguish the art of the imitator from that of the actor. The latter does not reproduce reality, but creates a new world (cf. *Der Schauspieler und die Wirklichkeit*, GSG 12, p. 311).

Rejecting the idea that the actor's task is to transform himself and disappear behind a multitude of characters and rejecting the conception of theatre as an art of imitation allows Simmel also to reject the long tradition, stretching from Plato to Rousseau, of considering theatre as a false and morally dangerous art. Far from considering the actors to be immoral and depraved individuals (Rousseau, for example, described the actor as one who can play all roles, except for the noblest of all, that of man, whom he abandons, 2003), Simmel conceives the art of the actor on the model of the 'beautiful soul' as defined by Schiller in his essay on *Grace and dignity* (2005). This 'beautiful soul' refers to

> a nature that only has to follow its perfectly spontaneous instincts, which have no need to be modified, in order to fully satisfy the moral imperative. But it does not thereby obey an external law but the ideal requirement that corresponds precisely to its being in a given situation.
>
> (*Zur Philosophie des Schauspielers, 1908, GSG 8, p. 427*)

It is the same for the actor whose personality immediately matches the imperatives of the role. His whole being is immediately in harmony with the requirements of the role. His general task is thus, fundamentally, to improvise despite having repeated the role hundreds of times (cf. *Zur Philosophie des Schauspielers*, GSG 20, p. 206). The actor recreates on the stage a role learned by heart, giving new life to the objective content that constitutes the text which has detached itself from the author's subjectivity.

The actor's art then becomes the very image of the 'transcendence of life'. The written role emancipates itself from the life that created it and becomes an autonomous content that the actor's subjectivity appropriates in turn. When he performs, the actor is both other than himself and more than himself: he blossoms and surpasses himself by interpreting a role that is at first foreign to him. 'The most important inner manifestation of the transcendence of life: at every moment life is all life, and at every moment another life. The art of acting!' (*Zur Philosophie des Schauspieler*, 1923, GSG 20, p. 219). The affirmation that acting is a true art form and that actors no longer have to be considered as the mechanical puppets of the role corresponds more deeply, for Simmel, to a change of world-view: 'What is at work here is the great theme with which our time is building a new worldview: the replacement of the mechanism by life' (*Der Schauspieler und die Wirkilichkeit*, 1912, GSG 12, p. 315).

It is interesting to compare Simmel's reflections with those of a contemporary, the famous English actor and director Edward Gordon Craig. In 1908, the year of Simmel's first article on theatre, Craig published his reflections on 'The actor and the *Über-Marionette*'. Following Diderot and his paradox, Craig made the art of puppetry the model for understanding the nature of the theatre. The comparison between actors and puppets aims to remove the question of interiority and to free the actor from the problem of the externalization of feelings. Craig's reflections are amongst the first in the early 20th century on the importance of the stage director in the theatre. Craig considers the director as the real artist, the one who holds all the threads of the show. For Craig, the figure of the actor, as it appeared in the 19th century, already belongs to the past, and the 'renaissance' of theatrical art is based on the 'renaissance of the stage director' (Craig, 1905, p. 148).

Simmel, on the contrary, does not seem to have perceived the growing importance of the figure of the director, of which he makes no mention in his texts on the theatre. His philosophical and sociological analyses of modernity lead him to focus all his attention on the art of acting and to present the actor as a particularly special figure. While the modern soul lives in tears and anxiety, the actor, through his art, unifies his personality and gives it coherence and style. In the context of the conflict between life and modern culture, where lifeless cultural contents multiply and overwhelm the individual who can no longer breathe life into them, the actor seems to triumph over this tragedy of culture, overcoming the division of the subjective and the objective, bringing opposites together:

> The actor, purely and single-mindedly obedient to the inherent laws of his art, forming all the demands of nature and poetry in accordance with these laws, will nevertheless satisfy those demands precisely in the measure in which his autonomous artistic act is perfected; and, precisely insofar as his actor's art is completed, it will enlighten us in the deepest sense about the real way of the world, the actor's personality, and the play itself, and like all great art it will thereby give us a presentiment and a pledge that the elements of life, in their ultimate ground, do not lie side by side, as utterly indifferent and unconnected as life itself would make us believe.
>
> *(cf.* Zur Philosophie des Schauspielers, *GSG 20, p. 213)*

Insofar as 'there is no art in which production and the totality of personality are linked in such a narrow unity', the actor, who artistically shapes all dimensions of the sensible world (*Der Schauspieler und die Wirklichkeit*, GSG 12, p. 308 f.), seems to accomplish this general task of art in the richest and most profound way.

References

Craig, E. C. (1905). The art of the theater. The first dialogue. In: E. C. Craig (1957). *On the art of the theatre* (pp. 137–181). 5th edition. London: Heinemann.

Craig, E. C. (1908). The actor and the *Über-Marionette*. In: E. C. Craig (1957). *On the art of the theatre* (pp. 54–94). 5th edition. London: Heinemann.

Craig, E. C. (1911) *On the art of the theatre*. London: Heinemann.

Duvignaud, J. (1965). *L'acteur, esquisse d'une sociologie du comédien*. Paris: Gallimard.

James, H. (1961). *The tragic muse*. New York: Dell publishing co.

Plessner, H. (1981). Der Kampf ums wahre Gesicht. In: H. Plessner, *Gesammelte Schriften V*, G. Dux, O. Marquard, & E. Ströker (Eds.) (pp. 58–78). Frankfurt am Main: Surhkamp.

Proust, M. (1987). *À la recherche du temps perdu. À l'ombre des jeunes filles en fleurs*. J.-Y. Tadier (Ed.). Paris: Gallimard/Pléiade.

Proust, M. (1988). *A la recherche du temps perdu. Le Côté de Guermantes I*. J.-Y. Tadier (Ed.). Paris: Gallimard/Pléiade.

Rousseau, J.-J. (2003). *Lettre à d'Alembert sur les spectacles*. M. Buffat (Ed.). Paris: Garnier-Flammarion.

Schiller, F. von (2005). On grace and dignity. Translated by J. V. Curran. In *Schiller's 'On grace and dignity' in its cultural context: Essays and a new translation* (pp. 123–170). J. V. Curran & C. Fricker (Eds.). Rochester and New York: Camden House.

Schiller, F. V. (1993). Letters on the aesthetic education of man. Translated by E.M. Wilkinson & L.A. Willoughby. In: F. von Schiller. *Essays* (pp. 86–178). D. O. Dahlstrom & W. Hinderer (Eds.). New York: Continuum.

Simmel, G. (1989-2015). *Georg Simmel Gesamtausgabe*. O. Rammstedt. Frankfurt am Main: Suhrkamp, here cited with GSG.

Simmel, G. (2004). *The philosophy of money*. 3rd edition. D. Frisby (Ed.). Translated by Tom Bottomore and David Frisby. London and New York: Routledge.

Thomas, F. (2013). *Le paradigme du comédien. Une introduction à la pensée de Georg Simmel*. Paris: Hermann.

de Tocqueville, A. (1981). *De la démocratie en Amérique*. F. Furet (Ed.). Paris: Garnier-Flamarion.

PART VI

Essayism and critical theory

17

GEORG SIMMEL AND THE 'NEWSPAPER SOCIOLOGY' OF THE 1920s AND 1930s

Barbara Thériault

'And I read and read and, exhausted, I give up thirty-three times and start from the beginning again and am taken out, unconscious ... Holy Simmel! Of course, one cannot say everything in a simple manner, but one can simply say it' (Tucholsky, [1926] 1985, pp. 398, 400 [my translation]).[1]

Be it in a positive or negative fashion, Georg Simmel was – and Kurt Tucholsky is here but one example of this – a reference for a generation of thinkers: they reviewed his conferences and lectures, articles and books, as well as posthumous collections of essays in newspapers and magazines.[2] Simmel himself wrote, especially around 1900, a lot of essays, which were published in newspapers and, between 1897 and 1907 in the weekly *Jugend*. Otthein Rammstedt (2006) has pointed out that an important part of his work is made out of essays, or excursus, about singular themes (letters, discretion, adornment, the secret, the Alps, see also Simmel's miscellany in GSG 17; Tokarzewska, 2010; Thouard, 2012).[3]

We find this form and similar themes again in the 1920s and 1930s when journalists, amidst a booming newspaper industry (Jost, Utz, & Valloton, 1996, p. 144), 'went about their tricky trade [*ihr kniffliges Handwerk trieben*] in the rarified atmosphere [*in der dünnen Luft*] of the sociology of the time' (quoted in Bussiek, 2011, p. 175). If we are to believe the author of this 1926 quote, *Frankfurter Zeitung* editor Friedrich Sieburg, there existed what could be called a 'newspaper sociology' in the feuilleton, or cultural pages. Feuilletons were brief, often ironical texts with a sociological twist; they dealt with contemporary themes in a more literary fashion, not unlike the essay tradition attributed to Simmel (see also Adorno, [1958/1974] 1984; Habermas, [1983] 1986). Today's readers find in the feuilleton of the time a 'Simmelian feel', and are left to wonder about the author's influence on journalists of the 1920s and 1930s.

To help me tackle the subject, I summoned an imaginary professor, a construct born of the multiple feedbacks I received while investigating this topic and who will serve – in the tradition of the feuilleton – as an alter ego, one providing both critical and encouraging comments.

What does he think of my endeavour?

Liebe Frau Thériault, das ist ein hochspannendes Thema! Es gibt dazu so gut wie nichts an Sekundärliteratur.[4]

***

Such an attentive reader of Simmel as Otthein Rammstedt (2006) knew, for one, that it was a difficult question. After pointing to the importance of newspaper publications in Simmel's work, he backs out. It is, he argues, hazardous, if not impossible, to assess Simmel's actual impact on his time. Relinquishing the task, he sets himself instead to delineate Simmel's conception of the essay. If it is indeed difficult to identify Simmel's influence on newspaper sociology (was he the first to work in such an essayistic, both sociological and philosophical, fashion?), would it not be possible, I wonder, to lay out some specific traits of the journalistic feuilleton style of writing, in order to gauge the extent of Simmel's contribution?

In this journey across journalistic writings, I draw on feuilletons by several authors – mostly Siegfried Kracauer (1889-1966), but also Kurt Tucholsky (1890-1938), Joseph Roth (1894-1939), and Egon Erwin Kisch (1885-1948), among others – all writing, at the same period, short articles that are neither novels nor scientific treatises. There are of course numerous variations in style between them, which they themselves are wary to stress: Kracauer is more empirical, sociological in his analysis, and he is most remembered for his essays.[5] Tucholsky has a highly sarcastic tone, while Kisch practiced what would today be called 'literary reportage'.

Both observers and practitioners of the feuilleton highlight the tensions between essays, feuilletons, and reportages. While the latter, for instance, were not much valued, they gained popularity and prestige at the beginning of the 20th century. Yet, as Erhard Schütz (2017, p. 47) rightly points out, the reportage would not have become what it was without the techniques experimented in the feuilleton that had developed from the 1860s and 1870s on. While being critical of each other,[6] the genres actually borrowed elements from one another and shared what Hildegard Kernmayer calls a 'poetics of the in-between' ('Poetik des Dazwischen'): the playful staging of the approximative, the 'by-the-way', ephemeral, and temporary (Kernmayer, 2017, p. 66).

As a sociologist, I see in the texts published in German newspapers in the 1920s and 1930s the journalistic feuilleton writing at its finest, and Simmel's most palpable influence.[7] In the following pages, I aim to delineate patterns, which I could then compare to Simmel's shorter texts, in the hope I will learn about the feuilleton tradition and maybe, along the way, unearth fragments of a specific type of sociological writing's hidden history; a style of writing that thrived, at least for a time, beyond the sometimes narrow realm of academic institutions.

Schreiben Sie das auf, Frau Thériault![8]

***

During the 1920s and 1930s, when those I would call 'newspaper sociologists' participated in public events – be it a commission, a conference, a theatre play, a sports event, a radio show, an exhibition, a reading, or even the arrival of a new train – they were at least as much interested in the spectated as in the spectators. They paid attention to what was officially going on, on stage, but even more to the audience, the public, and the material environment surrounding them.[9] Incidentally, '*Publikum*' (public), or alternatively '*Menge*' (crowd) are some of the words Kracauer uses most in his feuilletons.[10]

Stimmt! Im 'Dichter im Warenhaus' erwähnt Kracauer nur einmal am Ende den Namen des Dichters, Heinrich Mann; er beschreibt vielmehr das Publikum und den Veranstaltungsort.[11]

After briefly describing an event that, more often than not, they had been tasked to cover, the newspaper sociologists literally turned their gaze toward the public. They changed perspectives. While remaining aware of their individuality (Srubar, 1992, p. 43), they sided with the public and observed it from different angles: they picked exemplary cases, who were then used as representatives of a strata or a phenomenon. By writing in the first person singular, they did not elevate themselves above the objects of their inquiry; rather, they saw themselves as part of a – mostly impoverished and economically precarious – public. They never stood outside the portraits they sketched – rather like a modern-day group selfie.

Such portraits are not unlike Simmel's texts: snapshots, fragments of a society, that draw on different types of material put together to build a kind of mosaic: a competition, films, advertisements, and newspaper adds, everyday objects (palm trees, suspenders). They often zoom in on a detail; Roland Barthes (1980) would refer to the *punctum*, something which stands out, an everyday observation that serves as a starting point for a cultural analysis, an opportunity for an exploration into something deeper.[12] The feuilleton writers often assume, like Simmel in his short texts, the existence of an underlying metaphysical dimension, of something bigger hiding under the inconspicuous surface-level expressions of daily life.

One thing we must keep in mind is that newspaper articles were just one of the possible outlets for those authors, and probably not their most valued. For professional writers, the feuilleton was often considered a mere livelihood (Kernmayer & Schütz, 2017, p. 122).[13] Parts, excursus, or parenthesis of longer texts would be published in a newspaper and later reworked and reprinted in the more valued form of a novel or a treatise (as was the case for Simmel's *Sociology* [GSG 11] or, alternatively, a collection of essays such as *Philosophische Kultur* [GSG 14, pp. 159–459]).[14] And although Simmel probably did not see himself as a journalist and is rarely if ever depicted as such, his publications in newspapers can partly account for his – in the academic sociology and philosophy often decried – 'style', the so-called lack of system and references.[15]

***

When depicting reality, the feuilleton writers favour a particular background: the metropolis, often a busy street corner in Berlin (Jäger & Schütz, 1994).

Ja, ja, der Aufsatz von 1903 'Die Großstädte und das Geistesleben' ([1903] 1995) ist natürlich unumgänglich, wenn man Simmels Einfluss auf die Soziologie betrachtet. Dazu hat Srubar und viele andere im Übrigen auch geschrieben. Und es fällt mir ein, kennen Sie Lindners Buch 'Aus dem Geist der Reportage'?[16] Er bringt den Journalismus und Simmels Aufsatz mit der frühen amerikanischen Soziologie des gleichen Zeitraums in Verbindung.[17]

'Metropolis and Mental Life' (GSG 7, pp. 116–131) seems to have opened new research fields for Simmel's contemporaries: the individual tendencies in the context of the urban and monetary economy, as seen from the everyday life – the *detail* and the *small*. On many occasions, Simmel argues away from the objects of the social sciences of his time: not only the political or economic spheres, the law, the family or the church, but – say – the society of two individuals (GSG 8, pp. 348–354) or of the senses (GSG 8, pp. 276–292), and about the present time. Straying like he did, he helped shape the sociological – and journalistic – eye (Srubar, 1992, p. 42).[18]

While the feuilleton writers are concerned with daily life in the city, they pictured other scenes than the Simmelian ones, scenes of their time. They went outside the bourgeois décor (a particular form of sociability and intimacy, a type of discretion, of gender relations that one finds in several pieces collected in *Soziologie* and *Philosophische Kultur*), and into the new middle of society of their time, the salaried masses, to write about offices, department stores, leisure activities, and what they considered as refuges (cafés, dancing halls and variety bars, cinemas, amusement parks), but also employment offices and labour courts.

Ja, genau, wie die Selfies, die auch Teil der Massenkultur sind, vielmehr so als bei Simmel, der weder als 'demokratisch' noch 'visuell' beschrieben werden kann. Simmels Texte erinnern manchmal an Etikettenbücher für das Bürgertum seiner Zeit, finden Sie nicht?[19]

***

Feuilleton writers carry out a sociological analysis, though often without explicit references to theory; it is implied rather than spelled out. They take their distance from the scientific language and style. Joseph Roth, for instance, writes on a least two occasions: 'scientific, meaning boring' ('*Wissenschaftlich, also langweilig*', [1913] 1921, [1927] 2006). The newspaper sociologists share the results of their analysis in an ironic fashion. Kracauer, for instance, ironizes about the language of science by playing with 'mathematical laws', things being 'inversely [*umgekehrt*] proportional to another' or formulas like 'the more x, the more z … /the less …'

This deliberately light-footed theory is expressed through catchy formulas.

Tucholskys Formeln sind wie Ohrwürmer![20]

Here is where I find the most explicit reference to Simmel. It is often in formulas that Simmel unveils a form, a type of theoretical abstraction.[21] One can, for example, think of fashion as imitation and distinction; the stranger as proximity and distance; sociability as 'freedom of bondage'; coquetry as an offer rescinded, or consent and denial. More than merely catchy, these formulas have 'the tendency to differentiate and promote opposite characteristics', part an aspect of every form of sociation and one of 'the most fundamental traits of the modern order' (Levine, 2017, p. 397 [my translation]).[22]

Das ist eine typische Simmel'sche Haltung, das Nebeneinander von zwei Tendenzen, das ist ganz zentral zum Feuilletonschreiben. Es erinnert im Übrigen an Simmels dritte Apriori: Das Bewusstsein des Typischen, des Untypischen – die eigene Individualität –, und deren Synthese. Die Ironie der Existenz![23]

Like Simmel, the newspaper sociologists point to the simultaneity of phenomena, of actions that are 'side by side' – *nebeneinander*, as Kracauer titled several of his pieces.

Apropos Titel: mich irritieren die Titel, gegenwärtig in der heutigen deutschen Soziologie, wie 'Rückgang oder Revitalisierung der Religion?', 'Säkularisierung oder Entsäkularisierung?'; 'oder noch die mit einem zwischen': 'Säkularisierung, zwischen Mythos und Wirklichkeit.' Es ist alles so unsimmelmässig![24]

Even if formulas are often presented as lessons, they are not moralizing. Here lies the ethics – or rather the etiquette – of the feuilleton. Bar a few exceptions, feuilleton writers do not preach. Tucholsky sometimes indulges in it and then becomes a reference, a source for life maxims and 'calendar philosophy'.

***

The feuilleton is often playful, entertaining, ironic about scientific language. It is attentive to forms and, in a way, to theory and cultural analysis. Those features were ground enough for criticism. In their commentary to their anthology of 1920s–1930s feuilletons on the theme of feuilleton writing, Kernmayer and Schütz (2017, p. 125) stress that those I call the newspaper sociologists were confronted with three recurrent stigmas – being French (or feminine), Jewish, and coquettish – attacks which, in turn, fuelled a defensive attitude.

If one might argue that the authors embraced the 'coquettish' attitude towards theory, swinging between opposing viewpoints, between yes and no, there remained a tension around criticism, a trait that might be constitutive of the feuilleton as a genre and that stands at the heart of its political function. Often, unmasking authorities through irony and poking fun at them were not deemed powerful enough strategies to bring forth criticism. At the same time, authors were mindful of the context in which they were using them, and assessed their chances with their readers: 'in more abstract articles [as opposed to articles on particular events, concrete details] our principled radicality would have been visible, and with a clarity that did not seem appropriate' (Kracauer in a 1931 letter to Gubler, quoted in Volk, 1996, p. 10 [my translation]).[25]

Hum ... Der Einfluss Simmels auf Kracauer und Benjamin, z. T. sicherlich auch auf Adorno ist gewiss schon darin zu sehen, dass sie sich wechselseitig versicherten, so wie Simmel und seine mangelnde Sozialkritik könne man das nicht machen ... Erinnert stark an 'anxiety of influence'.[26]

The feuilleton authors pretend not to take themselves too seriously (Fritzsche, 1996, p. 44), say that their interpretations are not infallible, confess to doubt. They use formulations like 'it is possible that'; 'as far as I can see'; 'I don't know for sure'; 'probably'; 'might it be superstition of not ...' or raise a question: 'I don't know if the other spectators ... had the same impression'; 'Or I am mistaken?' Like Simmel who often titles his texts 'Essays' (*Versuch,* in the French sense of 'trying'), study, sketch, excursus, the feuilleton authors insist on the provisional character of their texts.[27]

Eins muss ich hier anmerken: Es gibt eine wichtige Spannung zwischen dem vorläufigen Charakter der Texte und deren Reproduktion im Buchformat. Wenn die gleichen Texte, die für den Tag in Zeitungen geschrieben waren, als Sammlungen erscheinen – oder wenn sie mit Kritik konfrontiert werden – neigen die Autoren jedoch dazu, deren anhaltenden Wert zu betonen.[28]

***

Towards the end of the 1920s, Kracauer moved from philosophical essays to more empirical, sociological ones. Simmel seems here to be a 'gateway to reality' (*'Wirklichkeitserschließer'*) from whom he distances himself with time, finding his own style (Kracauer, [1919] 2004, p. 280]; Frisby, 1986, p. 118 f.). More generally, there is increasing dissatisfaction toward a particular style of writing deemed convoluted, neither condensed nor straightforward enough (Tucholsky, [1926] 1985, p. 400). In obituaries published after Simmel's death, we read praises of the author, but also criticisms: most of all, he is presented as difficult, blamed for using an inaccessible language (see for instance: Joël, [1918] 1958; Levinsohn, [1918] 1958). The obituaries published in newspapers echo Tucholsky's quote at the beginning of this text, and his plea for a better and simpler way to write: 'Simmel's texts and lectures often stand out for their original, indeed stunning thought processes, although their expression makes them sometimes difficult, and only after repeated examination, understood' (*Neues Wiener Tagblatt*, 29.09.1918, N.N., [1918] 2000, p. 371 [my translation]).[29]

Dennoch sollte man Simmel natürlich nicht über Bord werfen. Vielleicht sollte man eben den kurzen essayistischen und narrativen Texten Simmels, die in Zeitungen und Magazinen erschienen sind, mehr Aufmerksamkeit schenken. Sie sind eben zugänglicher. Wär's nicht eine Idee für ein Seminar mit Studenten?[30]

***

Let us go back to the opening question: 'What was Simmel's influence on journalists of the 1920s and 1930s?' Thinking about perspectives, a specific attitude toward theory, and writing, we can argue that the newspaper sociology draws from, or at least share an affinity with, the Simmelian way of thinking about society;[31] yet those authors developed their mode of writing partly in opposition to his style. On another level, they also reacted to Simmel who was not a modern thinker throughout, and who believed – in the field of art, for instance – in great and singular individualities or personalities.

This still seems to hold true. Today's exponents of the sociological feuilleton, a sociologist like Tilman Allert, for instance, who writes for the *Frankfurter Allgemeine Zeitung* und the *Neue Zürcher Zeitung*, often refer – explicitly or implicitly – to Georg

Simmel. In Allert's collection of feuilletons, *Latte Macchiato. Soziologie der kleinen Dinge* (2015) and *Gruß aus der Küche. Soziologie der kleinen Dinge* (2017), Georg Simmel is one of the most quoted authors. He hints at his formulas, which he then reformulates for his readers. Today's feuilleton writers read Simmel as a kind of 'warm-up' before writing, for his way to think about society as an ambivalent and simultaneous process. They draw on his themes (sociability, the city, the quantitative aspects of the group, a figure like the stranger) and theoretical insights. They often remember a small detail that sticks with them – more so than a general idea. They still find his texts brilliant, but often difficult to sum up. And when they need inspiration for the form, the rhythm, or a writing technique, they tend to turn to authors like Kracauer and the journalists from the 1920s and 1930s.

The feuilleton makes us see, talk, and reflect; it 'mobilizes the reader's imagination' (Fuchs, 2017, p. 73), without making us forget the critique.[32] This is what I have called the 'feuilleton effect' (Thériault, 2017). You know you've written a feuilleton when a person – be it an experimental German professor (a composite of several real individuals and reactions) – experiences heightened self-reflexivity and feels compelled to comment on what s/he hears: '*Es fällt mir ein*' (this reminds me); '*übrigens*' (by the way), '*Apropos*' (on the same subject).

Ach, Sie haben mich die ganze Zeit beobachtet![33]

***

After this small exercise, I hesitate: should I start writing a feuilleton myself or go back to reading more Simmel? The feuilleton writer – and its reader – grows impatient with use. I doubt we could label her or him a *flâneur* – Kisch titles his most famous collection of texts *Der rasende Reporter*, the racing reporter ([1924] 1990; also Tucholsky, [1925] 1985, pp. 48–49). Like Tucholsky, s/he is racing too ([1924] 1985, p. 409 [my translation]):

The doctor says, I should move more.
There is this sports school…
Old things still lay on the floor,
I should have brought them to the poor a long time ago!
Was I at my father's grave?
I plan to – and never do it.
I always wanted to read the yellow book,
and also Simmel's *Sociology*.[34]

Notes

1 '*Heiliger Simmel! Man kann gewiß nicht alles simpel sagen, aber man kann es einfach sagen. … und ich lese und lese und gebe es, erschöpft, dreiunddreißigmal wieder auf und fange von neuem an und werde ohnmächtig hinausgetragen*' (Tucholsky, [1926] 1985, pp. 398–403).
2 See Kracauer (2011a) for reviews of books published in 1922 and 1923.
3 Tokarzewska (2010) shows how Simmel played both with narrative and essayistic forms before settling for the latter.
4 'Dear Ms. Thériault, this is a highly interesting topic! There is hardly any secondary literature on it'.
5 On Tucholsky, see Kracauer's letter to Adorno ([16.01.1964] 2008, p. 639).
6 See Tucholsky ([1925] 1985, pp. 48–49); Kracauer ([1929] 1998, p. 32).
7 Journalistic feuilleton writing has also known variations in different linguistic contexts. In Poland, for instance, the genre has been popular for over a century, and the anthology edited by Mariusz Szczygieł in 2014 attests to the prominence of the reportage, one more literary than sociological.

Reading the more famous exponents of the genre, one could put forward that Egon Erwin Kisch plays for the Polish tradition a similar role than that of Simmel for Germany's.

8 'Write it down, Ms. Thériault!'

9 For instance, in 'Number girl' ('*Nummernmädchen*') Kracauer focuses on a girl in a variété theatre. Although not part of the official program, she makes several appearances: she has the more menial task of announcing the numbers ([1930/1964] 2009, pp. 159–160).

10 Not 'masses', though there are important exceptions (see Kracauer's 'Mass Ornament', [1927/1963] 1995, 2011b). Kracauer also wrote some longer philosophical essays (*Haltungsaufsätze*, Volk, 1996, p. 10). He published most of his 'sociological' texts as editor at the *Frankfurter Zeitung* in Berlin at the beginning of the 1930s (see *Berliner Nebeneinander. Ausgewählte Feuilletons 1930–33*, Kracauer, 1996, A. Volk, Ed.). Most of them are about three pages long while some shorter ones are more literary in nature (see *Straßen in Berlin und anderswo*, Kracauer, [1964] 2009).

11 'Indeed! In "The Poet in the Department Store" Kracauer only mentions the name of the poet, Heinrich Mann, at the end; instead, he describes the public and the space' ([1930/1964] 2009, pp. 186–189).

12 'Doch das momentan Gegebene war für Simmel immer nur Anlaß zum Schürfen in die zeitlosen Untergründen des Lebens' (Levinsohn, [1918] 1958, p. 169).

13 Looking back at his life, Kracauer devalued the importance of his journalistic work and longed to be seen and remembered as a theoretician (see his letter to Adorno, 01.04.1964, Adorno, 2008, p. 659).

14 In a letter to Kracauer (26.06.1915) about a text the younger scholar had sent him, Simmel suggests he publishes one part of in a journal, another part in a newspaper, and that he scraps the rest (GSG 23, pp. 529–530).

15 In stressing Simmel's lack of a stable university position, Thouard (2012) makes a similar argument. He attributes his style to the nature of the life of a *Privatdozenten*: the necessity to publish to make a living and the absence of assistants. One could also point to Simmel's conception of society as a process, which is more in tune with the newspapers as a continuous gaze on the contemporary world.

16 See Lindner ([1990] 2007).

17 'Yes, yes, the 1903 text "Metropolis and Mental Life" ([1903] 1950) is of course essential when one is interested in Simmel's influence on sociology, my colleague Srubar and many others have written on that. And this reminds me: do you know Lindner's book: *The Reportage of Urban Culture: Robert Park and the Chicago School*? He connects, for the same time period, journalism, Simmel's essay and the early American sociology'.

18 'weitab von den ausgefahrenen Straßen der schulmäßigen Systematik' (Levinsohn, [1918] 1958, p. 171).

19 'That's right, like selfies. They are also part of mass culture. Simmel, on the other hand, can neither be described as "democratic" nor "visual." Simmel's texts remind sometimes of etiquette books for his days' bourgeoisie, don't you think?'

20 'Tucholsky's formulas are like earworms!'

21 In his text on Simmel, Kracauer himself underscores this point: 'Simmel enters into the spirit of artistic creations with utmost ingenuity and then struggles to establish formulas capable of conveying the specific content of the phenomena in questions' (Kracauer, [1920/1963] 1995, p. 229)/'Mit äußerster Geschmeidigkeit lebt er sich in die künstlerischen Erscheinungen ein und ringt dann nach Formeln, die den eigentümlichen Gehalt der betreffenden Phänomene in sich zu bergen fähig sind' (Kracauer, [1919] 2004, p. 214).

22 Here are some examples. For Kracauer: 'Das Radio ist schuld daran, daß die Öffenlichkeit verwaist. Zu einer Zeit, in der die Politik aus den Bürgerhäusern auf die Straße gedrungen ist, treibt es während entscheidender Stunden die Menschen von der Straße in die guten Stuben zurück' ('Am Abend des Wahltags', [1932] 2011, p. 64-65).

'Statt einen Pauschalangriff gegen verdächtige Inserate zu machen, sollte man lieber behutsam unter ihnen sichten. Erscheint die Tugend nicht in Gesellschaft des Taktes, so triumphiert sie auf einem Leichenfeld' ('Kampf gegen die Kuppelanzeigen', [1931] 1996, p. 161).

And Tucholsky's definition of the bourgeoisie: 'Menschen, die mehr verdienen, als es die Notdurft erfordert, und nicht genug, um Standesansprüchen zu genügen, die sie übernommen haben, ohne sie zu verstehen' ('Die Glaubenssätze der Bourgeoisie', [1928] 1985, p. 252).

23 'This is a typically Simmelian attitude, being two things at the same time, that is at the heart of the feuilleton writing. It recalls Simmel's third a priori: the typical, the untypical – one's individuality – and their synthesis. The irony of existence!'

24 'Yes, the titles. I can't bear what is omnipresent in German sociology, titles like "Decline or Revival of Religion?," "Secularization or De-secularization?," or the ones with a "between": "Secularization, between Myth and Reality?" This is all so unsimmelian!'

25 '... weil in allgemeinen Aufsätzen unsere prinzipielle Radikalität zutage getreten wäre, und zwar mit einer Deutlichkeit, die uns nicht oft als opportun erschien'.

26 'Hum ... Simmel's influence on Kracauer and Benjamin, and certainly also partly on Adorno is already to be seen in the fact that they tell each other one shouldn't adopt Simmel's attitude toward social criticism ... This strongly recalls an "anxiety of influence"'.

27 Thouard (2012) underscores that Simmel kept coming back to his themes, constantly reworking and rewriting his texts.

28 'One should add one thing here: there is an important tension between the provisory character of the texts and their reproduction in a book form. When the texts that were written for the day in newspapers were collected in book form – or when they were confronted with criticism – the newspaper sociologists often stressed their long-lasting value'. See Kracauer letter from 25.05.1930 to Adorno (2008, pp. 214–215); also: Schütz (2017, p. 39).

29 'Die Schriften und Vorlesungen zeichnen sich durch die Fülle origineller, ja oftmals verblüffender Gedankengänge aus, wenn sie auch durch ihre mitunter schwierige Diktion nicht leicht verständlich sind und nur nach wiederholtem Studium erfaßt werden können'.

30 'Of course, However, one should of course not to throw Simmel overboard. One should perhaps pay more attention to Simmel's essayistic and narrative texts published in newspapers and magazines. They are more accessible. Couldn't it be an idea for a seminar with students?'

31 For a similar argument about the Chicago School, see Lindner ([1990] 2007, p. 85).

32 As the novel might (see Kracauer's review of Fallada, [1931] 2011; Bourdieu, [1992] 1998) or films (Kracauer, [1925/1963] 1995).

33 'Ah, you've been observing me!'

34 'Der Arzt sagt, ich soll mir Bewegung machen. Da gibt es so eine Schule für Sport ... Auf dem Boden liegen noch alte Sachen, die sollten doch längst für die Armen fort! Bin ich an Vaterns Grab gewesen? Ich nehm es mir vor – und dabei wirds nie. Das Gelbbuch wollte ich immer mal lesen, das und Simmels Soziologie'.

References

Adorno, T. W. ([1958/1974] 1984). The essay as form. *New German Critique 32* (Spring–Summer), 151–171.

Adorno, T. W. (2008). *Briefwechsel, 1923–1966/Theodor W. Adorno, Siegfried Kracauer*. In W. Schopf (Ed.). Frankfurt/Main: Suhrkamp.

Allert, T. (2015). *Latte Macchiato. Soziologie der kleinen Dinge*. Frankfurt/Main: Fischer.

Allert, T. (2017). *Gruß aus der Küche. Soziologie der kleinen Dinge*. Frankfurt/Main: Fischer.

Barthes, R. (1980). *Chambre claire. Note sur la photographie*. Paris: Seuil.

Bourdieu, P. ([1992] 1998). *Les règles de l'art. Genèse et structure du champ littéraire*. Paris: Seuil.

Bussiek, D. (2011). *Benno Reifenberg 1892–1970. Eine Biographie*. Göttingen: Wallstein.

Coser, L. A. (1958). Georg Simmel's style of work: A contribution to the sociology of the sociologist. *American Journal of Sociology, 63*(6), 635–640.

Frisby, D. (1986). *Fragments of modernity*. Cambridge, MA: MIT Press.

Fritzsche, P. (1996). *Reading Berlin 1900*. Cambridge, MA and London, UK: Harvard University Press.

Fuchs, A. (2017). Short prose around 1900. In A. J. Webber (Ed.), *The Cambridge companion to the literature of Berlin* (pp. 71–88). Cambridge: Cambridge University Press.

GSG 11. Simmel, G. ([1908] 1992). *Soziologie. Untersuchungen über die Formen der Vergesellschaftung*. O. Rammstedt (Ed.). Frankfurt/Main: Suhrkamp.

GSG 17. Simmel, G. (2005). *Miszellen, Glossen, Stellungnahmen, Umfrageantworten, Leserbriefe, Diskussionsbeiträge 1889–1918*. K. C. Köhnke (Ed., with C. Jaenichen & E. Schullerus). Frankfurt/Main: Suhrkamp.

GSG 23. Simmel, G. (2008). *Briefe 1918-1918*. Band II, O. Rammstedt & A. Rammstedt (Eds.). Frankfurt/Main: Suhrkamp.

Habermas, J. ([1983] 1986). Simmel als Zeitdiagnostiker. In G. Simmel (Ed.). *Philosophische Kultur: über Abenteuer, die Geschlechter und die Krise der Moderne. Gesammelte Essais* (pp. 7–18). Berlin: Wagenbach.

Jäger, C., & Schütz, E. (Eds.) (1994). *Glänzender Asphalt. Berlin im Feuilleton der Weimarer Republik.* Berlin: Fannei & Walz.

Joël, K. ([1918] 1958). Erinnerungen an Simmel. In K. Gassen & M. Landmann (Eds.), *Buch des Dankes an Georg Simmel. Briefe, Erinnerungen, Bibliographie* (pp. 166–169). Berlin: Duncker und Humblot.

Jost, H. U., Utz, P., & Valloton, F. (Eds.) (1996). *Littérature 'bas de page.' Le feuilleton et ses enjeux dans la société des 19e et 20e siècles.* Lausanne: Éditions Antipodes.

Kernmayer, H., & Schütz, E. (Eds.) (2017). Oberfläche unterm Strich. Zur Geschichte und Poetik der kleinen Form. In *Die Eleganz des Feuilletons. Literarische Kleinode* (pp. 119–135). Berlin: Transit.

Kisch, E. E. ([1924] 1990). *Der rasende Reporter.* Berlin and Weimar: Aufbau-Verlag.

Kracauer, S. ([1919] 2004). Georg Simmel. Ein Beitrag zur Deutung des geistigen Lebens unserer Zeit. In I. Belk (Ed., with the collaboration of S. Biebl), *Werke, Bd. 9.2: Frühe Schriften aus dem Nachlaß* (pp. 139–280). Berlin: Suhrkamp.

Kracauer, S. ([1920/1963] 1995). Georg Simmel. In T. Y. Levine (Ed.), *The mass ornament* (pp. 225–257). Cambridge, MA and London, UK: Harvard University Press.

Kracauer, S. ([1925/1963] 1995). The little shopgirls go to the movies. In T. Y. Levine (Ed.), *The mass ornament* (pp. 291–304). Cambridge, MA and London, UK: Harvard University Press.

Kracauer, S. ([1927/1963] 1995). The mass ornament. In T. Y. Levine (Ed.), *The mass ornament* (pp. 75–86). Cambridge, MA and London, UK: Harvard University Press.

Kracauer, S. ([1929] 1998). *The salaried masses. Duty and distraction in Weimar Germany.* London: Verso.

Kracauer, S. ([1930/1964] 2009). Dichter im Warenhaus. In *Straßen in Berlin und anderswo* (pp. 186–189). Frankfurt/Main: Suhrkamp.

Kracauer, S. ([1931] 2011). Politik in der Kleinstadt. Rez. Hans Fallada, Bauern, Bonzen und Bomben. Berlin: E. Rowohlt. In I. Mülder-Bach (Ed., with the collaboration of S. Biebl, A. Erwig, V. Bachmann & S. Manske), *Essays, Feuilletons, Rezensionen, 1928–1931*, 5.3 (pp. 742–745). Berlin: Suhrkamp.

Kracauer, S. ([1932] 2011). Am Abend des Wahltags. In I. Mülder-Bach (Ed., with the collaboration of S. Biebl, A. Erwig, V. Bachmann & S. Manske). *Essays, Feuilletons, Rezensionen, 1932–1965*, 5.4 (pp. 63–65). Berlin: Suhrkamp.

Kracauer, S. ([1964] 2009). *Straßen in Berlin und anderswo.* Frankfurt/Main: Suhrkamp.

Kracauer, S. (1996). *Berliner Nebeneinander. Ausgewählte Feuilletons 1930–33.* A. Volk (Ed.). Zürich: Epoca.

Kracauer, S. (2011b). Das Ornament der Masse. In I. Mülder-Bach (Ed., with the collaboration of S. Biebl, A. Erwig, V. Bachmann & S. Manske), *Essays, Feuilletons, Rezensionen. Werke*, 5.2 (pp. 612–624). Berlin: Suhrkamp.

Kracauer, S. (2011a). *Essays, Feuilletons, Rezensionen. Werke* (5.1, 5.2, 5.3). I. Mülder-Bach (Ed.). Berlin: Suhrkamp.

Levine, D. N. (2017). Georg Simmel: Toujours à suivre. In D. Thouard & B. Zimmermann (Eds.), *Simmel, le parti-pris du tiers* (pp. 381–399). Paris: CNRS Editions.

Levinsohn, R. ([1918] 1958). Erinnerungen an Simmel. In K. Gassen & M. Landmann (Eds.), *Buch des Dankes an Georg Simmel. Briefe, Erinnerungen, Bibliographie* (pp. 169–170). Berlin: Duncker und Humblot.

Lindner, R. ([1990] 1996). *The reportage of urban culture: Robert Park and the Chicago School.* New York: Cambridge University Press.

Lindner, R. ([1990] 2007). *Die Entdeckung der Stadtkultur. Soziologie aus der Erfahrung der Reportage.* Frankfurt and New York: Campus.

N.N. ([1918] 2000). Professor Dr. Georg Simmel gestorben. In D. Frisby (Ed.), *Georg Simmel in Wien. Texte und Kontexte aus dem Wien der Jahrhundertwende. Simmel-Texte u. Rezensionen aus dem Wiener Milieu* (p. 371). Wien: WUV Universitätsverlag.

Rammstedt, O. (2006). Georg Simmels 'Henkel-Literatur'. In W. Braungart & K. Kauffmann (Eds.), *Essayimus um 1900* (pp. 177–193). Heidelberg: Universitäts-Verlag Winter.

Roth, J. ([1913] 1921). Feuilleton. In H. Nürnberger (Ed.), *Ich zeichne das Gesicht der Zeit. Essay – Reportagen – Feuilletons* (pp. 24–28). Zurich: Diogenes.

Roth, J. ([1927] 2006). *Juden auf Wanderschaften.* München: dtv.

Schütz, E. (2017). Unterm Strich. Über Grenzverläufe des klassischen Feuilletons. In H. Kernmayer & S. Jung (Eds.), *Feuilleton. Schreiben an der Schnittstelle zwischen Journalismus und Literatur* (pp. 31–50). Bielefeld: transcript.

Simmel, G. ([1903] 1950). The metropolis and mental life. In K. H. Wolff (Ed.), *The Sociology of Georg Simmel* (pp. 409–424). Glencoe, IL: The Free Press.

Simmel, G. ([1903] 1995). Die Großstädte und das Geistesleben. In R. Kramme, A. Rammstedt, & O. Rammstedt (Eds.), *Aufsätze und Abhandlungen 1901–1908* (pp. 116–131), Band I, GSG 7. Frankfurt/Main: Suhrkamp.

Srubar, I. (1992). Zur Formierung des soziologischen Blickes durch die Großstadtwahrnehmung. In M. Smuda (Ed.), *Die Großstadt als Text* (pp. 37–52). Paderborn: Schöningh.

Szczygieł, M. (2014). *100/XX. Antologia polskiego reportażu XX wieku.* Wołowiec: Czarne.

Thériault, B. (2017). Das Feuilleton. Biographie eines Genres inspiriert von Siegfried Kracauer. *trivium*, *26*(2). Available at: https://trivium.revues.org/5490 (accessed 2 February 2020).

Thouard, D. (2012). Comment lire Simmel? *Sociologie et sociétés*, *44*(2), 19–41.

Tokarzewska, M. (2010). *Der feste Grund des Unberechenbaren. Georg Simmel zwischen Soziologie und Literatur.* Wiesbaden: VS Verlag.

Tucholsky, K. ([1924] 1985). Zu tun! Zu tun! In M. Gerold-Tucholsky & F. J. Raddatz (Eds.), *Gesammelte Werke, Bd. 3 1921–1924* (p. 409 f.). Reinbek bei Hamburg: Rowohlt.

Tucholsky, K. ([1925] 1985). Der rasende Reporter. In M. Gerold-Tucholsky & F. J. Raddatz (Eds.), *Gesammelte Werke, 1925–1926*, vol. 4 (p. 48 f.). Reinbek bei Hamburg: Rowohlt.

Tucholsky, K. ([1926] 1985). Der neudeutsche Stil. In M. Gerold-Tucholsky & F. J. Raddatz (Eds.), *Gesammelte Werke, 1925–1926*, vol. 4 (pp. 398–403). Reinbek bei Hamburg: Rowohlt.

Tucholsky, K. ([1928] 1985). Die Glaubenssätze der Bourgeoisie. In M. Gerold-Tucholsky & F. J. Raddatz (Eds.), *Gesammelte Werke, 1928, Bd. 6* (pp. 251–255). Reinbek bei Hamburg: Rowohlt.

Volk, A. (Ed.) (1996). Zu dieser Ausgabe. In Kracauer, S., *Berliner Nebeneinander. Ausgewählte Feuilletons 1930–33* (pp. 7–11). Zürich: Epoca.

18

GEORG SIMMEL AND CRITICAL THEORY

Vincenzo Mele

Introduction: traditional and critical theory

A well-known aphorism contained in Simmel's *Posthumous Diary* goes:

> I know that I will die without spiritual heirs (and this is fine). My inheritance resembles cash to be divided among many heirs, each of whom invests his share in a manner according to his nature, without concerning himself with the origin of such inheritance.
>
> *(GSG 20, p. 261)*

Therefore, tracing Simmel's influence on his direct disciples as well on others whom he inspired can be a very difficult, often paradoxical, enterprise. In many cases, Simmel's reception is truly a 'cash legacy', limited to specific concepts or partial aspects of his thought.

Herein we will investigate Simmel's influence on the first to fourth generations of critical theorists of the so-called 'Frankfurt School': Walter Benjamin and Theodor W. Adorno, Jürgen Habermas, Axel Honneth, and Rahel Jaeggi. This choice appears justified for a number of reasons. Firstly, these authors represent a school characterized by both a thematic and an intellectual affinity. Secondly, in our view, these authors challenged Simmel directly, and we believe that some productive insights can be drawn from such challenges. Finally, for reasons of space, we do not delve into Simmel's influence on proponents of so-called 'Western Marxism', such as Lukács, Ernst Bloch, and Siegfried Kracauer, who were also direct disciples of Simmel's, as doing them justice would require dedicated in-depth research.

Before proceeding in this comparison, there is an important historical and conceptual premise to be made. Often comparisons in social theory and philosophy are conducted within the empty space of an imaginary contemporaneity. Authors belonging to different historical and political contexts are envisioned to carry on a dialogue in the void of an imaginary contemporaneity. On the contrary, here we must be well aware of the different historical, philosophical, and political constellations which Simmel and the early Frankfurt School belonged to. They lived through different moments in European intellectual history, diverse philosophical seasons, and hence sought to respond to disparate cultural and social urgencies. Georg Simmel and the early generation of the Frankfurt School assume two representative standpoints on 20th-century thought regarding the relation between subjectivity and mass society, symbolically represented by the *metropolis* as its characteristic social and cultural manifestation. Their visions of modernity are largely the result of perspectives that are respectively *on the threshold* and *internal* to 20th-century philosophical and sociological discourse on modernity. The most important parts of Simmel's intellectual experience *precede* 'the short 20th century' (Hobsbawm, 1994), and are hence significant for their *otherness* with respect to the period's affairs and tragedies: indeed, Simmel died in 1918, when the tragedy of the First World War (on which he had taken an activist stance for intervention) and the consequent cultural crisis marked a definitive turning point with respect to the previous era. Benjamin's, Horkheimer's, and Adorno's perspectives on modern society and culture, on the other hand, were cultivated in complete awareness of the *one-way street* (from the title of Benjamin's book) that European civilization was taking, which, unless some sort of 'emergency brake' was engaged, would inevitably lead it to the catastrophes of fascism and the Second World War. The different historical settings for their reflections could not but have had consequences on their political-philosophical orientation. This is reflected in the very concept of 'critique' and 'criticism' that is implicit in Simmel's and the early Frankfurt School's philosophical thought. While Simmel works in continuity with Kant's notion of critique in the sense of an analysis of the validity and limits of human reason and judgement, the early Frankfurt School – as Max Horkheimer shows in his famous essay *Traditional and Critical Theory* (Horkheimer, 1937, 2002) – intends 'critique' in the sense of Hegel's 'negative determination' and, more specifically, as the 'materialistic turn' imparted by Karl Marx to Hegel's dialectic, as exemplified by his *Critique of Political Economy*. 'Critique' in this sense does not have a merely cognitive and epistemological meaning, but it confronts concepts with their historical realizations and 'sublates' them – the famous crucial German verb used by Hegel is 'aufheben', meaning both to cancel (or negate) and to preserve at the same time – as both logical and practical determinations of a given historical process. In this sense 'critique' is not just an epistemological and cognitive concept, but also a political one. As Horkheimer stated, a 'critical' theory may be distinguished from a 'traditional' theory according to a specific practical purpose: a theory is critical to the extent that it seeks human 'emancipation from slavery', acts as a 'liberating … influence', and works 'to create a world which satisfies the needs and powers of human beings' (Horkheimer, 2002, p. 246). This normative orientation will remain constant through the different personalities and generation of critical theorists, albeit animated by differences in philosophical backgrounds. Although Simmel did not neglect the major political movements of his time – socialism, the women's movement (Simmel, 1892, 1896a, 1897) – and took a moderate social reformist stance (Frisby, 2002, pp. 73-76; Köhnke, 1996, p. 301 f.), his sociological and philosophical work was not inspired by a normative vision of history. On the contrary, he openly criticized the concept of historical and sociological laws, including those in the positivist version (Comte, Spencer) or in historical materialism (Marx). Simmel forged his intellectual path in an academic environment where Hegel had almost disappeared and which was dominated – albeit not exclusively – by neo-Kantianism (Köhnke, 1991). However, as we will see, Simmel's major importance for the early Frankfurt School lies in his *Kulturpessimismus* and the concept of 'tragedy of culture' – probably the most important inheritance in Horkheimer's social theory (Ruggieri, 2017, p. 66) – as well as in his critique of Kant's logicism. For Simmel, Kant's concept of 'experience' (*Erfahrung*) was rooted in the natural sciences and was inadequate to grasp the 'lived experience' (*Erlebnis*) of human beings. The aesthetic sphere, in particular, seemed the ideal grounding place for potential reconciliation of the *aporia* and the contradictions so rampant in the broader cultural context of the German *Gründerjahre*. Simmel turned his inquiry towards a new artistic style that could overcome the division between traditional art, by now autonomous, and the rationalized spheres of daily life. It is in this framework that Simmel's undertaking to formulate a 'sociological aesthetics' matured, as can be gleaned from his 1896 work of the same name (Simmel, 1896b, 1968, 1992). He introduced a design for sociological aesthetics, whose *means* was the literary form of the essay, and whose *end* was the creation of an experimental frame within which different styles of thought and research could be combined fruitfully. It was precisely from the convergence of the aesthetic experience of modernity and the sociological analysis of some particular manifestations of social life, generally city life, that it was possible to decipher the epoch-making nature of modern life, with all its contradictions, conflicts, and paradoxes. This, however, without recourse to a 'Project of modernity' (Habermas, 1992, 2018), based on a normative philosophy of history and the characteristic trust in progress, which was slowly eroding as the popularity of positivism was waning. Simmel's entire social and aesthetic thought cannot be easily grouped under the heading of 'sociological aesthetics' – though it can be said that *Philosophy of money* is a *Capital* written in dialogue with Kant's *Transcendental Aesthetic* instead of Hegel's *Logic*. Moreover, Simmel's choice to base the nascent discipline on inquiry into 'forms of association' is clearly of (neo)Kantian derivation, given the certainly aesthetic (in Kant's sense) lineage of the concept of *a priori* forms of social interaction. It must, however, be emphasized that Simmel's project for a *sociological aesthetics* did not represent a form of sociology of art. Nor can it be regarded as one of those specialist branches of sociology that proliferated subsequently (e.g., the sociology of literature, work, communication), thanks mainly to the ever-growing influence of sociology itself in academic circles. Instead, Simmel's essays, written over a period of nearly thirty years, exhibit all the qualities of a true *aesthetics of modern life*, focusing on a specific 'point of indifference' between art and the sphere of social interactions, and revealing the specific modern nature of the 'reciprocity' between the aesthetic sphere and the social sphere. The result is a research style that focuses on particular day-to-day manifestations of modern social life endowed with a specific aesthetic character and 'epoch-making' significance. He was thus able, for instance, to correlate the social character of the decorative arts to consumer art, and vice versa, highlight the specific aesthetic dimension of certain aspects of social life and, as such, describe them both as a single, identical form of experiencing modernity. Simmel was convinced that only the aesthetic sphere can fully capture and represent all modern experience of reality, especially when the focus of attention is not limited exclusively to traditional, autonomous artwork.

Although during the different phases of his thought Simmel maintained the (neo-Kantian) distinction between metaphysics, science, and theory of knowledge (*Erkentnistheorie*), his project for a 'sociological aesthetics' emerges even in the preface to his major work, the *Philosophy of money,* in which he advocates for an original 'third position' between art and philosophy. Whereas philosophy tends to 'the totality of being', art has 'the great advantage' of setting itself 'a single, narrowly defined problem every time: a person, a landscape, a mood'. In his work on money, conversely, Simmel is attempting 'to regard the problem as restricted and small in order to do justice to it by extending it to the totality and the highest level of generality' (Simmel, 1989, 1990, pp. 53-54).

Therefore it can be stated that Simmel's philosophical and sociological enterprise is characterized by what later – in another philosophical context – would be called the 'world disclosure function of language' (Harrington, 2005; Lehtonen & Pyyhtinen, 2008). Simmel's thought is constantly searching for opposite 'dualisms' (*Kant and Goethe, Schopenhauer and*

Nietzsche, Nietzsche and Kant) and 'problems' (*Hauptprobleme der Philosophie, The Problem of Sociology, The Problem of Style*): to these polarities, his own thinking provides a 'third' that proves an underlying unity between the opposite poles and preserves the tension in all its vigour. The 'third' does not, however, exist independent of dualism, as it manifests itself only in the relation between opposites, or becomes relativized into new dualisms in a never-ending process. Simmel's approach is still topical where 'problem solving' oriented approaches to language actually fail, as they overlook the 'world disclosing' functions of language. 'World-disclosure', a term drawn from the philosophy of Martin Heidegger, indicates the revealing of contexts of existential inter-relatedness among things in the world – a revealing that imparts truth in the sense of total holistic illumination. Insofar as such world-disclosure is held by Heidegger to refuse any agency of rational critique and simply said to 'happen' as an ontological 'event' in which language speaks above the heads of individuals, it is a dangerous philosophical confection whose obscurantism Adorno was right to expose (Adorno, 1973). But if we are able to define this idea as a dimension of semantic aesthetic plentitude in language-use capable of opening up novel horizons of perceptual orientation in the world that at the same time *depend on* and *enrich* problem-solving attitudes to language, it must be concluded that it has been undeservedly neglected by pragmatist and rationalist philosophies. Arguably, without Simmel's pioneering work, the conceptions of many eminent authors, such as Siegfried Kracauer, Ernst Bloch, Walter Benjamin, and even Theodor Adorno and Georgy Lukács would never have been possible. The work of Jürgen Habermas, Axel Honneth, and Rahel Jaeggi also found – or could have found, in the case of the neglected reception of Habermas – inspiration from Georg Simmel's work. It is therefore well worth the effort to reconstruct Simmel's connections and influence with the different generations of critical theorists.

Simmel and early critical theory: Walter Benjamin and Theodor W. Adorno

The similarity between Simmel and Benjamin's perspectives on modernity and metropolitan life is significant, yet at times deceptive. Thanks to David Frisby's fundamental work of rediscovery, Simmel has been interpreted in 'Benjaminian' (and 'Lukácsian') terms: Frisby (Frisby, 2013), beginning with the choice of the metaphors of the '*flâneur* sociologist' and 'sociological impressionism', reads (and criticizes) Simmel through Benjamin. However, Benjamin's contact with Simmel's work took place throughout his life, even if in a fragmentary and probably not determinant way. Although Benjamin's friend and mentor Gershom Scholem confirms that Benjamin attended Simmel's classes in Berlin prior to the First World War (Scholem & Benjamin, 1982, p. 61) and that in 1920 he hoped to apply for admission to 'Troeltsch's seminar on Simmel's philosophy of history' (even if just as a means to use the library!), traces of Simmel's influence on Benjamin's early work are difficult to find (Mičko, 2010, pp. 23–50). One important source is *The Origin of German Baroque Drama*, wherein Benjamin draws the fundamental concept of 'origin' (*Ursprung*) from Simmel's study on *Goethe* (Simmel, 1913). Goethe's morphological and metaphorical thinking would, however, establish an important 'elective affinity' between Simmel and Benjamin (Dodd, 2008): in the incomplete notes of Benjamin's *Passagenwerk* (1924-1940), Simmel is cited, often critically, on many occasions. Benjamin and Adorno's first critical engagement with the work of Georg Simmel takes place precisely in a correspondence regarding the development of the *Arcades Project*. In 1938 Benjamin intended to extract and publish an independent piece centred on the figure of Charles Baudelaire from the project on the *Arcades* of Paris. The result of this effort was a long essay, almost an independent book, entitled *The Paris of the Second Empire in Baudelaire*. However, this study was destined never to be published in the journal of the Institute for Social Research, which had commissioned it, and was subjected to a barrage of harsh criticism by Adorno, who focuses particularly on Benjamin's affinity with Simmel. This episode furnishes some interesting insight into the methodological differences between the different approaches to the theory of culture, with Adorno's strand of thought constituting an undeniably more traditional development of Marx's method of the 'critique of ideology', whereas Simmel and Benjamin were more rooted – with some differences – on what Simmel called 'sociological aesthetics', or in other words, an aesthetical paradigm of knowledge.

Adorno's reaction, upon receiving Benjamin's essay *The Paris of the Second Empire in Baudelaire*, was one of utter dismay, as he expressed to Benjamin in a lengthy letter written in November 1938, which can be summed up as an accusation of naive behavioural sociologism. He argued that Benjamin tended to derive facts belonging to the cultural 'superstructure' directly from phenomena of an economic nature:

> Let me express myself here in as simple and Hegelian manner as possible. If I am not mistaken, this dialectic lacks one thing: mediation ... This basis, however, is nothing other than that I consider methodologically unfortunate to give conspicuous individual characteristics from the realm of the superstructure a 'materialistic' twist by relating them to corresponding characteristics of the substructure in an unmediated and even causal manner. The materialistic determination of cultural characteristics is possible only when mediated by the *total process*.
>
> *(Benjamin, 1994, p. 581 f.)*

Adorno then provides further details, pointing a finger more directly at Georg Simmel, whom Benjamin had cited explicitly. Adorno particularly objected to the Arcades in which 'in-depth theoretical arguments' were replaced by 'metaphor', based on simple analogical associations among phenomena: in other words, the most harshly criticised elements were precisely those that Benjamin shared with Simmel's style of thought and research and which he had promptly espoused. In fact, the phrase Adorno frowned upon was indeed a citation from Simmel's *The Sociology of the Senses* (one of the most brilliant *excursus* of the whole of the *Sociology*), in which Simmel dwells on the issue of seeing and hearing in the city. What is of significance here is not so much Simmel's brilliant and innovative flashes of intuition, as rather the fact that Adorno – unlike Benjamin – did not appreciate what can be considered the innovative aspect of Simmelian *sociological aesthetics*, which resided in laying the groundwork for a general theory on society by starting out from elementary aspects of everyday life, often elements of an aesthetic and sensory nature. What Adorno criticises as deriving from Simmel is precisely 'the appeal to concrete modes of behaviour' (ibid.) for theoretical explanations, which in his view characterised Simmel. In Adorno's vision the interpretation of cultural phenomena (and thus also the attempt at a 'materialistic' formulation of the metropolitan lyricism of a poet) can be undertaken only through the mediation of global historical-social processes. Any 'immediate inference' as regards a link between economic and spiritual phenomena endows phenomena with precisely the type of spontaneity, concreteness, and compactness they have lost in the capitalist context. Adorno argued that cultural criticism should not pursue 'the innocuous illustration of concepts through colourful historical objects as Simmel did when he depicted his primitive metaphysics of form and life in the cup handle, the actor, Venice' (Adorno, 1983, p. 231).

What Adorno specifically objects to in this approach to social reality is the manner in which the preoccupation with the fragment and the exemplary instance – shared by Benjamin as well – never leads to their historical concretion but rather to their reduction to the eternal realm, to 'simply interchangeable examples for ideas' (ibid.).

Benjamin replied to Adorno's harsh criticism in a well-known letter in December 1938. He made few concessions to Adorno's critique which – in Benjamin's opinion – was caused by the fact that he had chosen to work on the second part of the Baudelaire study without developing the first or the methodological aspects of the whole construction. Above all, Benjamin put up a strong defence of Simmel's quotation, as well as of Simmel's work in general:

> You look askance at Simmel – . Is it not high time to give him his due as one of the forefathers of cultural Bolshevism (*Kulturbolschewismus*)? ... I recently looked at his *Philosophy of money* [*Philosophie des Geldes*]. There is certainly good reason for it to be dedicated to Reinhold and Sabine Lepsius; there is good reason that it stems from the time in which Simmel was permitted to 'approach' the circle around George. It is, however, possible to find much that is very interesting in the book if its basic idea is resolutely ignored. I found the critique of value of Marx' value theory remarkable.
>
> *(Benjamin, 1994, p. 599)*

Kulturbolschewismus is the term which the Nazi minister of culture Goebbels used to define 'degenerate art' (*entartete Kunst*), that is, the practices and movement of the avant-garde, expressionism in particular. With this reference Benjamin intended to highlight the radicalism of Simmel's position, which was substantially different from the 'dialectic mediation' that forged Adorno's line of reasoning. In this regard, it is in this philosophical space of the description - at once *metaphorical* and *empirical* - of the modern experience where Benjamin met Simmel. Just as is the case of the *Philosophy of money*, in Benjamin the shift from one sphere of experience to another occurs by metaphorical leaps, which shed a constantly new light on reality. It is for this reason that while Adorno's sociological work becomes trite if it is shorn of its dialectical pathos, the works of Simmel and Benjamin are still full of life. In a later essay (1965) dedicated to a parallel comparison between Simmel and Ernst Bloch, Adorno reconsidered his sharp early judgement in this way:

> Georg Simmel ... was, for all his psychological idealism, the first to accomplish the return of philosophy to concrete objects, a shift that remained canonical for everyone dissatisfied with the chattering of epistemology or intellectual history. If we reacted so strongly against Simmel at one time, it was only because he withheld from us the very thing with which he enticed us.
>
> *(Adorno, 1992b, p. 213)*

This ambivalent judgement reveals that his critique stemmed from an original affinity with Simmel's thought. In fact, looking at Adorno's sociological works, it is surprising to find Simmel mentioned on more than one occasion. In a recently discovered lecture on *Simmel's Theory of Individual Causality*, delivered in 1940 at Columbia University, New York, during his exile in America, Adorno discussed the foundations of the '*Kulturwissenschaften*' (Adorno, 2003). In it he posits that Simmel's intuition of 'individual law' in his *Metaphysics of Life* (1918) is the best example of the paradoxical objectivity that can be reached in cultural analysis. The theory of 'individual law' is a law that has necessity and objectivity only in one case. Adorno considers Simmel's hypothesis (formulated to make Kant's ideal of categorical imperative productive) to be important also in the epistemology of social sciences, even if it may be difficult to transpose them into workable research methods. What one would need in order to deal with such a difficult (nearly impossible) task beyond the limits of causal objectivity is '*Theory*' (*Theorie*, his italics): 'the unity of theory functions as a substitute for the universality of the causality theorem' (Adorno, 2003, p. 54). Theory, in other words, compensates for the lack of scientific evidence by replacing the 'necessity of substance' with the 'necessity of thought' which imposes itself in a specific situation. Here it appears clear that Adorno shares with Simmel the model of aesthetical objectivity that – contrary to natural science objectivity – concerns the singularity of one aesthetic event: a normativity which derives from the vital process and unity of individual life itself, like a form of '*poiesis*'.

Twenty years later Adorno mentions Simmel's as the *only* alternative model of non-reductionist sociology in the celebrated dispute on *Dialectics and Positivism in Sociology*, held in Germany in the 1960s. Here, defending his dialectical vision of society *vis-à-vis* positivism – which demands greater 'micrological' attention to individual concrete elements – Adorno himself always holds the aesthetical approach in high esteem. In Adorno's view unregulated experience is the first condition for the possibility of sociological knowledge. Indeed, he argued that 'Knowledge of society which does not commence with the physiognomic view is poverty-stricken' (Adorno, 1976, p. 33). Adorno's empirical sociological analysis (*On Jazz* as well as *The Authoritarian Personality*) essentially consists of an attempt, by means of a stylized ideal-typical construction of the surface appearances of our form of life, to draw out its fundamental property, the social deformation of our rational endowments. But the concept of 'physiognomy' also possesses a further-reaching meaning connected to Adorno's conviction that mental abilities are reflected in the corporeal nature of human beings: gestures, mimicry, modes of practical intercourse in and with the world are always as much an expression of the special profile of rational activity as they, in turn, represent reaction formations to the pressures of nature. Because nature and mind are restricted in this way, for Adorno what is needed is an expansion of social analysis beyond the traditional object domain. In contrast to Simmel and Benjamin, he tried to formulate his own model of sociological aesthetics or physiognomy, drawing inspiration not from art imagery, but from musical composition. As a composer and musicologist, he clearly found his own experience to be prototypical of cognitive experience in general. However, Adorno remains firmly convinced that aesthetic models, whether in music or art imagery, cannot carry the whole weight of rational practice. Aesthetics can provide a corrective measure for positivism and pseudo-scientific rationalism (which Popper was also right to denounce in the *Positivist Dispute*), which did violence to the individuality of objects by consuming them within an abstract conceptual schema. Philosophical interpretation cannot go beyond the immediate appearances of reality without the theory and concepts developed by the sciences. For Adorno, science and art, concept and image, analysis and expression form the two poles of rationality.

The lacking reception of Jürgen Habermas

One generation later, Jürgen Habermas dedicated to Simmel only one meaningful essay (Habermas, 1983a), a fact that can be probably understood as a form of compensation for Simmel's exclusion from his major work, *Theory of communicative action* (Habermas, 1984). However, we will see that Simmel's theory is more important for what could it have brought to Habermas' theory than for what it has actually brought. As David Frisby rightly stated

... had Habermas taken up Simmel's theory of modernity, he would have been confronted with a conception of modernity that sought to demonstrate the grounding of the aesthetic sphere in the modern life-world, rather than establish its separation from other spheres of life.

(Frisby, 1985, p. 52)

Habermas' highly proceduralist and rationalist conception of public opinion could have benefitted from Simmel's conception of sociability. In other words, what Habermas' theory of public opinion seems to neglect is the emotional, aesthetic complexity of everyday social interaction. There can be at least a double reason for Habermas neglecting Simmel's sociology. *First*, Habermas' fundamental research question is quite distant from Simmel's: following Horkheimer and Adorno's *Dialectic of Enlightenment* (2016), he set at the very centre of his philosophical and sociological investigation the *rationality* of modernity. Even though Habermas would put increasing distance between his project for critical theory and that of the first generation of the Frankfurt School, his project would not call into question a normative concept of reason (on a communicative and pragmatist base), which remained quite distinct from Simmel's approach. *Second*, Habermas, in contrast to his philosophical master Adorno, dedicated relatively few, sporadic writings and little attention to art and aesthetics. However, this does not mean that Habermas' attention to aesthetics is irrelevant in the general economy of his thought. After a remarkable essay on Walter Benjamin of 1972, entitled 'Consciousness-raising or Redemptive Criticism' (Habermas, 1972), Habermas retreats from any thematically central role for aesthetics (Duvenage, 2003, p. 29). In these years his work enters a second phase marked by his working on the neo-Kantian theory of validity-domains for which he is best known. When Habermas extends his discussion of modernity beyond the aesthetic realm ('Modernity – an incomplete project', 1983b), he relies upon Max Weber for his definition of cultural modernity (Frisby, 1985, p. 52). Weber sees cultural modernity as having its origins in the modern separation and differentiation of 'the values-spheres' of science, ethics, and art which were earlier bound together. Consequently, in *Theory of Communicative Action*, art is relatively demoted in importance to the circumscribed sphere of 'aesthetic-expressive validity', alongside the more conceptually dominant spheres of 'scientific-theoretical validity' and 'moral-practical validity'. A third phase of Habermas' thought on aesthetics is represented by his 1984 work *The Philosophical Discourse of Modernity*. This study can be considered Habermas' personal version of Lukács '*The Destruction of Reason*', this time directed against contemporary philosophers such as Jacques Derrida, Michel Foucault, Jean-François Lyotard, George Bataille, Deleuze, and Guattari, all heirs of Nietzsche's 'totalizing aesthetic critique of reason'. In this book, an important chapter is dedicated to highlighting the substantial difference between literature and philosophy, which all French post-structuralist authors tend to overcome. It is therefore clear that from the standpoint of a rigorous neo-Kantian theory of validity-domains (reinforced by Popper's three-worlds theory of knowledge), Habermas could hardly accept Simmel's aesthetic approach to social reality. In this sense, the 'postscript' Habermas dedicated to the new German edition of Georg Simmel's *Philosophische Kultur* in 1983 is quite symptomatic of the orientation Habermas' thought took. This can be summed up as privileging the problem solving function of language (deriving from Popper and the positivist dispute) over the 'world disclosure' attempted in various ways by Simmel, Benjamin, and Adorno. Habermas' opinion in this essay is that Simmel – as compared to the other prominent intellectuals of his generation such as Wilhelm Dilthey and Henri Bergson, who similarly initiated *Lebensphilosophie* (philosophy of life), or Durkheim (born in the same year as Simmel, 1858), George Herbert Mead (born in 1863) and Max Weber (born in

1864) – did not manage to become a 'classic' precisely because his essayistic and aesthetical intellectual orientation did not predestine him to be so. In this regard, Habermas writes 'Simmel was a creative although not a systematic thinker – a philosophical diagnostician of the times with a social-scientific bent rather than a philosopher or sociologist solidly placed in the academic profession' (Habermas, 1996, p. 405). Habermas was aware that it was not just this intellectual attitude that created a 'disturbed' relationship with the world of the German universities; accusations of relativism and anti-Semitism played an important role. However, 'what distanced him from the academic world was Simmel's mentality' (ibid.). Habermas, in other words, recognized – sharing Adorno's appreciation – Simmel as the precursor of the scholarly essay and that it was he who encouraged students to think 'concretely', while at the same time accusing him of remaining *undecided* between essay and scientific treatise, between the spheres of 'aesthetic-expressive validity' and 'scientific-theoretical validity'. What Habermas seems to exclude is that there can be a meaningful relationship between these two spheres, in other words, that aesthetic experience can stimulate and become a source of theoretical scientific knowledge. Embracing and making definitive the distinction between science and literature, Habermas – as his intellectual production shows, with his definitive renouncing of the essay as a form and with the synthesis of his work produced in *Theory of communicative action* – clearly orients himself toward the Parsonian scientific model of the sociological treatise, whereas an important part of American sociology (Charles Wright-Mills's *Sociological Imagination*, Randall Collins, Lewis Coser and, above all, the Chicago school's ethnographic approach) and authors in English cultural studies (David Frisby, Mike Featherstone) would follow and creatively continue Simmel's heritage.

Some questions can be raised about Habermas attributing less importance to sociological aesthetics in general and, consequently, to Simmel's approach in particular. For example, why is this sphere of human experience less prominent in his work in comparison to the earlier Frankfurt School? Would aesthetics have undermined the internal consistency of the theory of communicative action? What role could have been played in this reception by Simmel, who among the classics – in contrast to Max Weber – sought to demonstrate the grounding of the aesthetic sphere in the modern life-world, rather than establish its separation from other spheres of life? In Georg Simmel's sociology we can find more than one stimulus to integrate Habermas' rationalistic, discursive theory of the public sphere. Simmel constantly shows how boundaries between public and private are uncertain and regulated by emotions such as shame, discretion, courtesy, and other emotions. In Simmel's *sociology* of 1908 we find an important chapter entitled *The Secret and the Secret Society*, whose essential message can be summarized as follows: 'If human interaction is conditioned by the ability to speak, it is shaped by the ability to keep silent' (Simmel, 2009, p. 340). The importance of this chapter is to counterpoise Habermas' philosophical interest toward the ideal condition of communication, which is based on the more or less explicit metaphysical assumption of truth in human relationships. For Simmel, on the other hand, the social actor is a being who hides truth, instead of revealing it. As stated by Simmel:

> all that which we share with another in words or perhaps in some other way, even the most subjective, the most impulsive, the most intimate, is a selection from the actual mental totality whose absolutely accurate disclosure in terms of content and sequence would bring any person – if a paradoxical expression is permitted – into the insane asylum.
>
> *(Simmel, 2009, p. 310)*

Simmel is very well aware that the space for secrets is becoming progressively restricted in modern society, but at the same time he opines that the progress of science and intellectualism in general does not necessarily mean progress in rational communication, transparency, and understanding. Moreover, in modern life there is ever-increasing space for trust. One important consequence of the 'tragedy of modern culture' for Simmel is that 'things' became much more cultivated than 'people', with the consequence that we live in a world made of technical artefacts – including social forms and interactions – that we only partially understand and dominate. Habermas was aware of this when he spoke of the colonization of life worlds and 'expert knowledge'. However, Simmel can help us to better orientate in the modern world of 'fake news' and technical untransparency. For Simmel uncertainty and ignorance are the foundations of social world. Thus, *truth*, understanding, and consensus cannot be the bases of social life. Agreement, consensus, and truth constitute a status that is quite rare to find in social life: Simmel observes that only overt religions and secret societies are actually interested in sharing 'truths'). In most societies – included the modern one – what counts is the existence of 'common sense' as a form of general trust about the existence of things, structures, and values that most people do not really know and which they are even not interested in knowing. Social forms are *opaque*, and human beings – except for very rare and exceptional experiences such as *love* or *mysticism* - do not really know each other, but have interactions *mediated* by typifications, generalization, etiquette, etc. At the same time, personal knowledge always presupposes maintaining secrecy and is concretely manifested through the complex tactics of discretion, shame, tact, etc. In his pivotal essay on the *Sociology of sociability* (GSG 12, 177-193; Simmel, 1949), Simmel gives us another example of an aesthetic, emotional, not merely proceduralistic and problem-solving oriented conception of public sphere. Drawing from Simmel's theory, Richard Sennett in *The Fall of Public Man* (Sennett, 1977) argues that the growth and decline of the public sphere must be linked to the individual's ability to express emotions in public. The fundamental concept of 'society as a theatre' has always aimed to fulfil a fundamental ethical function: to separate human 'nature' – intended as the authentic essence of the individual – from social action. The theatre separates the alleged 'natural identity' from the 'role', because an actor's performance in another work or in another scene appears to us under a completely different guise and thus reveals a completely different personality. In Sennett's opinion, the consumeristic nature of modern cities tends to remove the artistic dimension from daily life, which renders the individual 'an actor deprived of his art', subject to the 'tyranny of intimacy'. Such intimist tyranny manifests itself in contemporary culture through the substantial atrophy of the public sphere and its roles, together with an ever more widely spreading culture of narcissism which encounters difficulty in expressing 'passions' in the public sphere. Thus, he arrives at the hypothesis that theatricality has a special, hostile relation to intimacy, while theatricality has an equally special, friendly relation to a solid public sphere (Sennett, 1977, p. 37). Simmel's essays on the actor (published posthumously) reveal that he was well aware of the special 'social' importance of theatrical art. So much so that he dedicated a specific study, which upon close inspection can be seen to enhance and complete his analyses of sociability and 'play-forms of association'. Above and beyond the opposition between reality and appearance, Simmel expressed great praise for the actor: 'the creator of a new world' (Simmel, 2017, p. 36).

> While every other art transports the reality of life into an objective, otherwordly creation, the actor does just the opposite … his task now is to make this purely ideal, purely spiritual work of the play real, to reconvert it into an expression of reality.
>
> *(ibid.)*

What is freeing about the actor's art is the same thing that the 'thoughtful man' feels in sociability, that is, just as art and play are pretences, so is sociability, but it is nevertheless an expression of life to the fullest. It sublimates life and distils it into an extract endowed with greater wealth and autonomy than 'true life' itself. If we wanted to translate Simmel's observations into psychoanalytical language, we would state that the actor projects his own drives onto the public sphere of interactions with others, into social forms and conviviality; he practices the necessary art of living in society.

The late recognition of Axel Honneth and Rahel Jaeggi: paradoxes of individualization in postmodern culture and the critique of life forms

The 'third' and the 'fourth' generation of the Frankfurt School, which can be identified with its leading figures Axel Honneth and his student Rahel Jaeggi, were certainly more receptive of Simmel's thought, since they tried to redirect critical theory out of the 'ice-desert of abstraction' (Adorno, 1992a, p. 224) and proceduralism back to social philosophy and a possible concept of 'good life'.

Honneth took seriously the characterization of Simmel as *Zeitdiagnostiker* (already recognized by Habermas) and set Simmel's *Fragestellung* (fundamental research question) at the very centre of his investigation: the pathologies of individualization in the contest of modern and postmodern life. Honneth considered Simmel's focus on individuality in the ambivalent game of interaction as a distinctive characteristic amongst the classical sociologists. However, unlike many sociologists and *Kulturkritiker* of the early 20th century, Simmel does not limit himself to issuing the umpteenth lament over the end of the individual or the dominion of *techné*, but inquisitively analyses what individuals do to live up to the possibilities offered by the 'luxuriant development of the objective culture' ('The metropolis and mental life', GSG 7, p. 128). In a brief, but highly cogent and well-documented essay, Axel Honneth delineated the 'fragments' (*Bruchstücke*) of a 'sociological diagnosis of the time' containing some essential aspects elaborated by Simmel in the *Philosophy of money* with particular regard to 'style of life' in the monetary culture. Honneth re-elaborated this concept to include the three fundamental circles of experience that describe the phenomenon of the 'aestheticization of daily life'.

Firstly, the technological innovation that came about in the late 20th century, together with the extensive process of internationalization of capital, has led to a massive entry of culture into the processes of economic evaluation, whose most prominent manifestation is the growth of mass media and advertising. This, in turn, has led to a phenomenon that has become daily experience for modern westerners (and not only), that is, the ever-increasing flow of electronically produced information and images that enters our homes daily through TV screens and computers. One result of this is the 'trend to erosion of the aesthetic means of communication of the world of social life' (Honneth, 1994, p. 12). To put it in other, simpler terms, cultural activities lose their particular nature as the means to communicate a symbolic representation of the living world of men, and instead take on the characteristics of an electronically reproduced 'technical environment' designed exclusively for amusement and entertainment. Secondly, this process of erosion of the media goes hand in hand with a process of erosion of the normative bonds of the world of social life itself, a phenomenon that the French philosopher Jean-François Lyotard has described perfectly as 'the end of the great narrations'. Finally, this 'erosion' of the social also involves a weakening of individuals' communicative and relational capacities, which indicates a tendency towards the 'atomization' of the individual and erosion of the social bonds through which social groups expressively and normatively reproduce. The definitive 'erosion' (*Auflösung*) within the 'social' milieu has some important consequences on the development of individual subjectivity: in contemporary reality, instead of traditional 19th–20th-century models of *self-realization*, based upon more or less sound interior subjective motivations, fictitious biographies are constructed aesthetically through the virtual culture of electronic media. Thusly defined, the transition to the postmodern represents nothing more than the pessimistic cultural diagnosis that Adorno and Horkheimer formulated in the chapter on the *Cultural Industry* of the *Dialectic of Enlightenment* (Adorno & Horkheimer, 2016). The difference, however, resides in the fact that, contrary to these latter, postmodern authors judge the cultural erosion and loss of individual authenticity positively. Hence, according to Honneth, the transition from the *Dialectic of Enlightenment* to *post-modern* theories and cultural diagnosis can be meaningfully compared to what Simmel had already stated regarding the cultural transition from *Schopenhauer to Nietzsche* (described in his 1907 book):

> While one [Schopenhauer] still remains oriented to the idea of an objective goal (Zweckgebundenheit) of human life, in the light of his definitive insolubility, but also in the pessimism of his Metaphysics of the will, the other [Nietzsche] can free himself from such negativism by dissociating himself from the idea of fulfilment of human life and internalizing it to the mere growth of its possibilities; in place of an idea of 'self-realization', the image (*Vorstellung*) emerges of an experimental invention of the self (*Selbsterfindung*).
>
> *(Honneth, 1994, p. 15 f.)*

If we accept the scheme proposed by Honneth and consider Schopenhauer and Nietzsche as two points of fundamental oscillation of the cultural dialectics of the 20th-century modern and postmodern - from both the general philosophical point of view as well as the sociological point of view due to its effects on what has been defined as an 'erosion' of the social (or 'aestheticization of daily life') - then Simmel provides the necessary reference points for delineating the models, sometimes converging, other times diverging, regarding representation of the individual and its possible autonomy in the context of the postmodern 'metropolization of social life'. In a later article on *Organized Self-Realization: Some Paradoxes of Individualization* (2004) Honneth completes his analysis of the pathologies of the 'postmodern' form of social life. With the help of Simmel, Honneth differentiates four different meanings of the notion of individualization: the growing individualization of biographies and life styles made possible by the modern money economy; the growing isolation of individual actors, related to the tendency of individuals to become even more lonely as the network of anonymous social contacts expands; the increase in individuals' powers of reflection; increasing personal autonomy. Considering what the distinctive characteristics of individualism are nowadays, Honneth states that individuals seem to be confronting the new burden of 'authenticity' and compulsion to 'self-realization'.

The individualism of self-realization, which Simmel traced to Romanticism, re-emerged over the past fifty years to become an instrument of economic development in the context of postmodern consumer-oriented capitalism, spreading standardization and fictionalized lifestyles under whose consequences individuals today seem more likely to suffer than to prosper. The ideal of a style of life, the idea that one's life should be as creative and original is possible, was constantly reinforced thanks to consumerism and electronic media. It is therefore not entirely improper to discern in these processes the tendency to transform the mounting claim to self-realization into a productive force in the capitalist economy. Honneth's thesis is that we are faced with a 'paradox' (which is actually typical of Simmel's thought): the cultural and economic processes of modernity that once promised greater qualitative freedom have been reversed in an ideological legitimation of de-institutionalization, with the emergence of forms of pathological individualism, such as feelings of inner emptiness, superfluousness, and the absence of purpose. Increasingly, individuals have been confronted with the social expectation of being 'flexible' and willing to develop themselves if they want to succeed in their profession. Honneth arrived at the conclusion that we are currently faced with the rapid rise of what Simmel described more than one century ago as 'exaggerated individualism':

> urged from all sides to show that they are open to authentic self-discovery and its impulses, there remains for individuals only the alternative of simulating authenticity or of feeing into a full-blown depression, of staging personal originality for strategic reasons or of pathologically shutting down.
>
> *(Honneth 2004, p. 475)*

Drawing from – and renewing – Honneth's analysis of the social pathologies of recognition, Rahel Jaeggi attempts to elaborate a *Critique of forms of life* (Jaeggi, 2018; Ruggieri, 2019). Jaeggi is convinced that Habermas' exclusive attention to the question of ethics and normativism has produced an analytic neutralisation toward any form of individual life and all its potential emancipative properties. Her critique begins precisely where problems, crisis, and conflicts arise, even if they are not overtly manifest. Within this conceptual frame the critique of form of life is not conducted from an external authoritarian perspective, but from an immanent perspective. Like Simmel, we should consider the forms of social life as arising from the reciprocal relations of intentional individual actions. In every form there is an 'immanent transcendence', strictly connected to the process of life: the dialectics of 'more life' – the immanent side of life – and 'more-than-life' – the transcendent one. These are two complementary aspects of life within a dialectical scheme which is open and tragic, since it never ends, and has no final synthesis. Even if Jaeggi seems to disempower Simmel's possible contribution to an immanent critique of forms due to her pragmatist approach in terms of a 'problem-solving' attitude towards life – life is viewed as a process of accumulated experiences that does not know 'springs' or 'new beginnings' – at the same time her form of criticism intends to be immanent and transformative: it is immanent because it starts from the immanent crisis of social practices and institutions; it is transformative, as it allows for a transcendence of context.

References

Adorno, T. W. (1973). *The jargon of authenticity*. Evanston, IL: Northwestern University Press.

Adorno, T. W. (1976). *The positivist dispute in German sociology*. London: Heinemann.

Adorno, T. W. (1983). A portrait of Walter Benjamin. In *Prisms* (pp. 227–240). Cambridge, MA: MIT Press.

Adorno, T. W. (1992a). *Note to literature*, vol. II. New York: Columbia University Press.

Adorno, T. W. (1992b). The handle, the pot, and early experience. In *Notes to literature*, vol. 2 (pp. 211–220). New York: Columbia University Press.

Adorno, T. W. (2003). Über das Problem der individuellen Kausalität bei Simmel. *Frankfurter Adorno-Blätter*, *8*, 42–59.

Adorno, T. W., & Horkheimer, M. (2016). *Dialectic of enlightenment*. London: Verso Books.

Benjamin, W. (1994). *The correspondence of Walter Benjamin. 1910–1940*. Chicago, IL: The University of Chicago Press.

Dodd, N. (2008). Goethe in Palermo: Urphänomen and analogical reasoning in Simmel and Benjamin. *Journal of Classical Sociology*, 8, 411–445. https://doi.org/10.1177/1468795X08095206

Duvenage, P. (2003). *Habermas and Aesthetics: The Limits of Communicative Reason*. Cambridge, UK: Polity Press.

Frisby, D. (1985). Georg simmel: First sociologist of modernity. *Theory, Culture & Society*, 2(3), 49–67. https://doi.org/10.1177/0263276485002003006

Frisby, D. (2002). *Georg Simmel*. Revised edition. London and New York: Routledge.

Frisby, D. (2013). Sociological impressionism. In *Sociological impressionism (Routledge Revivals)*. London: Routledge.

Habermas, J. (1972). *Bewußtmachende oder rettende Kritik — Die Aktualität Walter Benjamins* (S. Unseld, Ed.). Frankfurt a.M.: Suhrkamp.

Habermas, J. (1983a). Simmel als Zeitdiagnostiker. In *Philosophische Kultur* (pp. 243–253). Berlin: Wagenbach.

Habermas, J. (1983b). Modernity: an incomplete project. In H. Foster, ed. *The anti-aesthetic: Essays on postmodern culture*, (pp. 3–15). Seattle, WA: Bay Press.

Habermas, J. (1984). *The theory of communicative action. Reason and the rationalization of society*. Boston, MA: Bacon Press.

Habermas, J. (1996). Georg Simmel on philosophy and culture: Postscript to a collection of essays. *Critical Inquiry*, 22(3), 403–414.

Habermas, J. (2018). Die Moderne - ein unvollendetes Projekt. In W. Welsch, ed. *Wege aus der Moderne* (pp. 177–192). Berlin: De Gruyter. https://doi.org/10.1515/9783050071374-015

Harrington, A. (2005). Book review: Habermas and aesthetics: The limits of communicative reason. *European Journal of Social Theory*, 8, 379–382. https://doi.org/10.1177/136843101004002005

Hobsbawm, E. (1994). *The age of extremes: The short twentieth century, 1914–1991*. New York: Vintage.

Honneth, A. (1994). *Desintegration – Bruchstücke einer soziologischen Zeitdiagnose*. Frankfurt: Fischer.

Honneth, A. (2004). Organized Self-Realization: Some Paradoxes of Individualization. *European Journal of Social Theory*, 7(4), 463–478.

Horkheimer, M. (1937). Traditionelle und kritische Theorie. *Zeitschrift Für Sozialforschung*, VI(2), 245–309.

Horkheimer, M. (2002). Traditional and critical theory. In *Critical theory. Selected essays* (pp. 188–243). New York: Continuum.

Jaeggi, R. (2018). *Critique of forms of life*. Cambridge, MA: Harvard University Press.

Köhnke, K. C. (1991). *The Rise of Neokantianism: German Academic Philosophy between Idealism and Positivism*, trans. by R. J. Hollingdale. Cambridge/New York: Cambridge University Press.

Köhnke, K. C. (1996). *Der junge Simmel in Theoriebeziehungen und sozialen Bewegungen*. Frankfurt a.M.: Suhrkamp.

Lehtonen, T.-K., & Pyyhtinen, O. (2008). On Simmel's conception of philosophy. *Continental Philosophy Review*, 41(3), 301–322.

Mičko, M. (2010). *Walter Benjamin und Georg Simmel*. Wiesbaden: Harrassowitz Verlag.

Ruggieri, D. (2017). Georg Simmel and the 'relational turn'. Contributions to the foundation of the Lebenssoziologie since Simmel. *Simmel Studies*, 21(1), 43–71. https://doi.org/10.7202/1041336ar

Ruggieri, D. (2019). 'Constructing a new storey beneath historical materialism': Georg Simmel and the foundations of a 'relational' critical theory. *Berlin Journal of Critical Theory*, 3(2), 61–89.

Scholem, G., & Benjamin, W. (1982). *The story of a friendship*. London: Faber.

Sennett, R. (1977). *The fall of public man*. New York: Alfred A. Knopf.

Simmel, G. (1892). Ein Wort über soziale Freiheit. *Sozialpolitisches Zentralblatt*, 2, 283–284.

Simmel, G. (1896a). Der Frauenknogreß und die Sozialdemokratie. *Die Zukunft*, 17(2–10), 80–84.

Simmel, G. (1896b). Soziologische Ästhetik. *Die Zukunft*, (17), 204–216.

Simmel, G. (1897). Soziale Medizin. *Die Zeit (Wien)*, 10.

Simmel, G. (1913). *Goethe*. Leipzig: Klinkhardt & Biermann.

Simmel, G. (1949). The sociology of sociability. *American Journal of Sociology*, 55(3), 254–261.

Simmel, G. (1968). Sociological aesthetics. In P. K. Etzkorn (Ed.), *The conflict in modern culture and other essays* (pp. 68–80). New York: Teachers' College Press.

Simmel, G. (1989). *Philosophie des Geldes* (GSG 6; D. K. K. C. Frisby, Ed.). Frankfurt: Suhrkamp.

Simmel, G. (1990). *The philosophy of money* (trans. T. Bottomore & D. Frisby, Eds.), Second Enlarged Edition. London and New York: Routledge.

Simmel, G. (1992). Soziologische Ästhetik. In D. Dahme & H. J. Frisby (Eds.), *Georg Simmel Gesamtausgabe*, vol. 5 (pp. 197–214). Frankfurt: Suhrkamp.

Simmel, G. (2009). *Sociology. Inquiry into the construction of social forms.* (A. J. Blasi, A. K. Jacobs, & M. Kanjirathinkal, Eds.). Leiden and Boston, MA: Brill.

Simmel, G. (2017). Toward the philosophy of the actor. In *The king and the poor wretch* (pp. 36–65). CreateSpace Independent Publishing Platform.

PART VII

Topics of debate

19

FREEDOM

An open debate

Monica Martinelli

Introduction[1]

Freedom is crucial in the field of the social sciences. Simmel well understood that relationships, patterns, and forms of social life originate from and develop around the idea of freedom. Despite the centrality of freedom, Simmel did not write a specific book concerning this topic. Probably for this reason his lesson has long remained largely unexplored. Yet, in the wide-ranging debate of modernity on the background of the process of individualization and objectivation, Simmel offers a valuable contribution to understanding freedom. He starts from its inner nature: its relational matrix that reflects the structure of the bearer of freedom, the individual.

Simmel explicitly dedicated several texts to freedom. Two are significantly at the beginning and end of Simmel's intellectual work: namely, the chapter on *Die Freiheit* (GSG 4, pp. 130–283) in the *Einleitung in die Moralwissenschaft. Eine Kritik der ethischen Grundbegriffe*, published in two volumes in 1892–1893 (GSG 3, 4). This multifaceted text included in an important book is the context for the young Simmel to address crucial issues for the humanities and social sciences. The second contribution is the essay *Über Freiheit*, published in 1922 in the magazine *Logos*. Simmel delivered his work to the editor shortly before his death (GSG 20, pp. 80–115). This was originally intended as an essay draft; however, ultimately he could not complete it. In between these texts are the fourth chapter of *The Philosophy of Money*, 1900 (GSG 6, pp. 7-716), entitled *The Individual Freedom*, and the essay *The Individual and Freedom* (GSG 20, pp. 249-258), presumably written no earlier than 1913 and subsequently reworked.

In this chapter, I focus on some crucial points that Simmel addressed in his analysis of freedom along the following trajectories: freedom is an anthropological issue; its conception presupposes and shapes a certain idea of the human being. Moreover, freedom is a moral issue, as it is related to responsibility, human actions, and life. These paths can be rediscovered in the subsequent debates and reflections by various authors in the 1900s. Among them, particular attention is paid to Isaiah Berlin and Zygmunt Bauman. Berlin offers one of the most influential contributions on freedom of the second half of the 20th century with his well-known distinction between 'negative freedom' and 'positive freedom'. He insisted precisely on the anthropological dimension as well as Simmel, even if the latter does not consider negative and positive freedom as two different liberties but rather as a duality of freedom itself. Bauman takes up the Simmelian centrality of responsibility at the basis of freedom, and he shares with Simmel the framework of the discourse.

Simmel's perspective

By rethinking freedom from a relational viewpoint – i.e. starting from a certain view of the human being and in relation to life, beyond any dualism – Simmel provides valuable points in a debate that is still open. Simmel's starting point is the awareness of the distance in the path of philosophical, modern thought and the social sciences debate between the 'idea' and the 'experience' of freedom, which includes the separation between different human dimensions.

The idea of freedom has been repeatedly invoked as an ideal and imperative of a Self, defined as a complete totality, so that its determination is self-determination, therefore freedom. The experience of freedom, in turn, has sometimes been made to coincide with the fight against restrictive customs and any kind of bond, so stressing only the negative side of freedom. According to Simmel, theoretical and empirical absolutizations remain imprisoned in a deterministic scheme. In the first case, the Self encloses the world in itself: its actions are defined by the obligation for the reason and the will to be free. In the second case, the possibility is not excluded that individuals are at the mercy of different perceptions, impulses, and moods in a perpetual flux.

In order to build a different frame, Simmel underlines the importance of considering freedom in the light of historical-social processes in which it emerges, in turn, as a process. The circularity between the concept of metaphysical freedom and the empirical one clearly emerges, if the *Einleitung in die Moralwissenschaft* and the fragment *Über Freiheit* are read together. In the former, Simmel first criticizes the basic principles of morality as they are insufficient to explain freedom, precisely because they are not considered in relation to the experience (*Erlebnis*) of the subjects, while in the fragment he stresses the need to connect the empirical experience of freedom to a metaphysical level – i.e. to life, '*the original fact*' (Simmel, 1971, p. 380) – so that it does not sink into the arbitrary nature of pure subjectivism.

Freedom does not exist in the first instance in itself, as it were, the owner of a loner Self that, only secondarily, enters into a relationship with what is other than itself. Simmel's stance recognizes the human being as an essentially open and relational structure, which is focused on reciprocity, so that 'individual freedom is not a pure inner condition of an isolated subject, but rather a phenomenon of correlation' (Simmel, 2004, p. 372). Indeed, he declared that it is impossible to analyze freedom without considering the idea of the human being: freedom is not 'a spontaneous force' that acts of its own accord without an 'I'; nevertheless, it 'remains to be clarified what this "I" is', so that we must 'carry the analysis a bit further' (GSG 4, p. 181) – which Simmel does by re-examining the idea of the subject within modern philosophy (Martinelli, 2011). For Simmel, the issue of individuality is as crucial as it is awkward (Müller, 2018a).

Freedom as an anthropological issue

Beyond the scission between 'pure-I' and 'empirical-I'

Simmel moves away from the road marking the separation between the different dimensions of the human being, which are clearly visible, when looking at freedom. In fact, with the intention of firmly stating his complete autonomy, the attempt has been made to render him not subject to commands deriving from something other than himself. Walking as in a dead-end street, it has been determined that only reason constitutes the true Self.

In this division,

> heteronomy is not avoided, but only transferred from a relationship with the outer world to an inner one between reason and sensuousness. Only through the undemonstrated, naively dogmatic claim that that rational, universally valid part of us is the 'true' I, the essence of our essence, can Kant support the illusion that when reason commands sensuousness we thereby 'give ourselves' the duty-imperative. Herein is expressed the moralistic megalomania – which is, by the way, endemic to the history of morals – that sensuousness does not properly belong to the 'I'.
>
> (Simmel, 2010, p. 106)

Simmel distances himself decidedly from this orientation that has led to bringing the dualism between *freedom and determinism* close to that between *reason and sensitivity*, so that freedom has been associated with reason, and the constraint with sensitivity. In this frame the situation is defined as unfree where the will is subject to sensory impressions, until the action submitted to them is made to more closely resemble physical causality. According to Simmel, in the 'identification of actions determined by the senses with action devoid of freedom resides the fatal misunderstanding – which runs through all the history of moral doctrine – of sensibility in the theoretical and practical sense' (GSG 4, p. 144 f.). He talks of the 'crude displacement that, because the object of sensuousness admittedly lies outside the ego, sensuousness itself does not belong to it either' (Simmel, 2010, p. 106).

Moving away from the traditional philosophical thought means for Simmel overcoming the deception driven less by the fact that the Self is recognized as the principle of will and action, but rather by believing that it coincides with an abstract and pure Self. In this framework, the Self is a free reality, since it is totally self-referential to the point of thinking that 'under equal physical, political, economic, etc. conditions it has the power to impose its will' (GSG 4, p. 152). For Simmel the sensible dimension has a quite different meaning (Nedelmann, 1988; Sabido Ramos, 2007). It leads us towards the object and, at the same time, into the subject: thanks to it, we reach the other and return into ourselves through the subjective resonance that the other produces in us, setting off a movement of reciprocity. In particular, 'in very different measures and mixes ... these developments of sense impression construct our relationship to the other' (Simmel, 2009, p. 571).

The pure rational and universal Self, placed beyond historical multiplicity and psychological stances, has laid the premises for the idea of absolute freedom: a condition whereby freedom, detached from any bond, seems to ensure its fulfilment but to the detriment of its deeper meaning as it refers to a subject that is divided in itself. Simmel believes that the very definition of freedom would be the least superficial once the concept of the human being reached its proper position, being therefore recognized as a harbinger of psychological relativities as well as the bearer of rationality and will, and consequently able to progress across the multiplicity of life – ideas, experiences, and interpersonal ties. Human beings cannot be defined unilaterally: they are 'a complex of quality, thoughts, feelings, perhaps even something metaphysical' (GSG 4, p. 135).

Beyond the scission between individual and social dimension

Simmel distances himself from the dualism between individuality and the social dimension, too. The individual, even if he is a whole in himself, does not coincide with a monad, as he is embedded in social bonds. At the same time, the individual is not completely defined by social ties and roles: societal forms do not exhaust individuality; socialization could not aspire to totally include individuals, as they are more than their social belongings and roles.

Simmel outlines the risk of a possible fracture between the individual and the social dimension in his analysis specifically devoted to the two forms of modern individualism described with reference to the 18th and 19th centuries: 'quantitative individualism' or 'individualism of singularity' and 'qualitative individualism' or 'individualism of uniqueness' (GSG 16, p. 146; 1950a, p. 81; see also GSG 7, pp. 49–56; GSG 13, pp. 299–306; Simmel, 1971, pp. 217-226).

Both forms take shape from the modern man's cry for freedom that emerges in the middle of the Enlightenment, and even before, in the Italian Renaissance: a historical period characterized by a process of liberation that marks the exit from a hierarchically stratified society and the transition to a society that is horizontal and functionally differentiated (GSG 2, pp. 109–295). The output has meant the widening of social circles, associated with 'a more meaningful characterization of the individual member within the whole space of his being, and greater freedom of his movements' (GSG 4, pp. 169–170). For Simmel, however, the question was still open about what really was the Self in need of release, and for what it should determine itself. The main problem is that both forms of modern individualism tend to polarize on extremes, strengthening a dualistic anthropological perspective.

The theorists of the first kind of individualism have assumed that we should look at the ties imposed by group identities and by institutions as the cause of inequality and absence of freedom. These ties must therefore be eliminated, so that the 'true' man can emerge, namely a man who is free from all historical determinations and spurious elements of human experience with its contingencies and belongings. In this frame, only *nature* becomes the place of absolute equality with all individuals. Modern liberalism arises under the auspices of this individualism.

The key point of the second type of individualism is the consideration of every person as 'fundamentally different from the others with whom fate has brought him into contact' (Simmel, 1971, p. 223). The theorists of this individualism affirmed the irreplaceability of being 'that man' and not 'the' type of man in general. Such an individual type seems to configure a block of many incomparable peculiarities that accept being held together by an entity which merely coordinates the functions within an organic system: the individual is linked to others only through the role that he plays within the division of labour. Here, freedom becomes a merely inner, private experience. For Simmel, both forms of individualism obscure freedom even though they emerged from its desire. On the one hand, relying on the concept of the human being in general, a mechanistic view emerged and, as such, contributed to cancel freedom: the individual person is the receptacle of the universal one, and his treatment is like a piece of material that, beyond its form, retains within itself the material laws to be understood in the broad sense (Simmel, 1950a). On the other hand, the relational dimension tends to become nothing more than a sort of protection from loneliness.

Simmel wants to safeguard both the individual – without slipping into a kind of abstract individualism – and the relational dimension of the subject and its sociability, without impoverishing individuality. Moreover, he intends to overcome the idea of society as a mere sum of many separate individuals or as a *sui generis* entity, i.e. an organism that absorbs its members. He sees the two poles tragically moving away, reinforcing a sterile dualism. One pole is represented by the individual – who, on the one hand, only given his singularity, claims to stand himself as the representative of humanity, by abstracting himself from reality; and on the other hand, given his uniqueness, claims to be incomparable, devoid of extension. The other pole is formed by his social environment and relational dimension that, on the one hand, is taken into account only after the individual has established himself and, on the other hand, appears as a sort of reassuring expedient of isolated parts in search of a unifying element.

Both forms of individualism are noteworthy for the profound internal divide between these poles: as if the opening up to what is external to the individual (the otherness of reality, of the world, of another 'I', etc.), may come about only 'after' the construction of individual identity; or as if society were 'an absolute entity which must first exist so that all the individual relationships of its members … can develop within its framework' (Simmel, 2004, p. 174).

Significantly, Simmel speaks of 'the whole man': not the remainder left over when one takes away from him everything that he shares with others (GSG 12, p. 463).[2] This subject in its entirety is one of the fundamental ideas in Simmel's writings (Völzke, 1986). He is an individual whose 'wholeness' does not come from the combined parts: in fact, the category of 'whole' and 'parts', 'as it applies to the inanimate, is not applicable to life at all', and therefore not to the individual who is a 'form' of life, 'a whole as a unity' (Simmel, 2010, p. 134) – a vital, concrete unity.

The 'whole man' does not coincide with a heroic Self, but is aware of his 'bridge' position (located between individuality and sociality, freedom and bond, form and life), in which the tension between the rivers is not dissolved: indeed, it is in this position that the paradox and the challenge of freedom implies that the subject is a unit, without losing the connection and, at the same time, remaining itself (GSG 12, pp. 417–470). The interaction with the world constitutes 'the premise of any experience and of any action, of any thought': this is 'the fundamental experience' of the human being (GSG 14, p. 80).

Starting from these crucial premises, freedom proceeds in the direction of the increase of both personal autonomy and adherence to social life as well as of creating the social conditions able to host human freedom. Simmel places the debate about freedom in the anthropological framework: this is in line with his sociology, which can be delineated as 'sociological anthropology' (Fitzi, 2019). The interest in the anthropological dimension can be seen in many threads of the debate about freedom during the 1900s.

The common anthropological concern in different paths: Berlin and Simmel

Even though I. Berlin does not explicitly quote Simmel in his writings on freedom, he calls him 'a really great man' (Berlin, 2004, p. 642). He could probably be considered one of the thinkers who, without being evident successors of Simmel, reflect some of his concerns. As is known, in his essay *Two Concepts of Liberty* (2002), Berlin introduces the distinction between 'negative freedom' and 'positive freedom', considered with regard especially to the political arena and as two different liberties. Simmel refers to the idea of negative and positive freedom, too. But he mostly focuses on the existential level and not as if they were two different liberties – stressing instead the affirmation or denial of freedom as a relational experience as such. The two levels – the political and the existential – are in any case connected especially through the idea of the 'human being'. Berlin seems to follow Simmel's draft: 'conceptions of freedom derive directly from views of that which constitutes a self, a person, a man'; so that 'enough manipulation of the definition of man, and freedom can be made to mean whatever the manipulator wishes' (Berlin, 2002, p. 181). According to both authors, the anthropological issue remains the most useful frame for the debate on freedom.

To some extent, Berlin's idea of positive and negative freedom can be connected to the Simmelian categories of modern individualism, even if the latter do not strictly overlap one or the other conceptions of freedom. Berlin's proposal can be summarized as follows. The notion of negative freedom 'means liberty "from"; absence of interference' (ibid., p. 174). The positive conception of freedom *is* 'freedom "to" – to lead one prescribed form of life' in which the individual is his own master (ibid., p. 178). The two concepts take shape around the instances that are considered to be the conditions making freedom possible. According to the *negative* one, freedom is determined by the context, whereby its absence is due to interferences by the latter. With reference to the classical liberal thinkers, Berlin recalls their defence of a boundary which must on no account be violated. Where it is to be drawn has been a matter of haggling over the centuries. The *positive* concept insists on the fact that the source of freedom is the individual himself: its absence arises from some impediment coming from the context of will and decisions. Here the idea is crucial of an autonomous individual striving to be governed by reason and reason alone. In this frame, the following hypothesis is also accepted: if society is a project constructed according to rationality, then we freely surrender all the parts of our life to it.

From a descriptive point of view the two notions of freedom seem to reflect the features first and foremost of the anthropological background of the 'individualism of singularity' described by Simmel. Negative freedom recalls the idea of 'man as such' because it insists on the eliminations of external interferences (historical bonds); while the centrality of self-mastery in positive freedom recalls the rationality of the Self, given that it insists on the elimination of internal interferences (the emotions) thanks to reason. Since it is principally in the case of positive freedom that Berlin sees the risk of losing liberal beginnings, he concentrates the thorniest points on this type of freedom. He shows the risk here of a dangerous splitting of the individual that takes place between the rationality elaborating the principles of conduct and the empirical bundle of desires to be disciplined. This domination is accepted to guarantee freedom and may, however, take on, politically, the appearance of a fictitious collective person who nonetheless engulfs individuals.

On one side, we find here some elements of Simmel's 'individualism of singularity' in his striving for rational self-domination that devalues emotion. On the other side, the risk perceived by Berlin recalls what Simmel highlights regarding the destiny of the 'individualism of uniqueness'. Because of the need to belong that guarantees the individual the recognition, which his uniqueness needs, he is willing to relegate his freedom only to the interior sphere with the risk of being absorbed by some organic entity. For Berlin, too, the desire for recognition, which derives from the necessary integration because 'men are largely interdependent' (ibid., p. 171), cannot be made to coincide with freedom: it could lead to a preference for authoritarian social and political forms.

Some other points of contact between the two authors emerge concerning the consequences observed for the internal scission of the Self. Berlin draws attention especially to two: 'self-abnegation' and 'self-realization'. 'Self-abnegation' is a consequence of the strategic retreat into 'an inner citadel – my reason, my soul, my "noumenal" self' (ibid., p. 182), that neither external blind force can touch. It is a safe place, to which he retreats to avoid the uncontrollable yoke of the passions but also of society, obeying only his own laws. Freedom thus ends up coinciding with resistance to (or escape from) unachievable desires, and as independence of the sphere of causality. Simmel, for his part, in his concern for the consequences of all forms of reductionism of the subject, states that, while the 'pure I' is without quality when separated from the sensitive and affective dimensions (GSG 9, pp. 7–226), the individual separated from the relational dimension becomes the 'average man': an individual who does not let himself be touched by reality (2010, p. 84). On the one hand, we are dealing with a figure 'produced' by the system, in particular by the modern economy with its powerful 'objective culture' which pushes for unbridled individualization, obliging the individual to retreat into a corner and to exaggerate to make himself heard, even by himself (Simmel, 1971, pp. 324-339). On the other hand, the 'average man' is the bearer of a thought that has insisted on the modern idea of the Self without a world: 'one has the impression … that the world touching' him 'passes through him in some measure' without changing him, as he remains indifferent (Simmel, 2010, p. 84). The 'average man' and the individual closed in the 'inner citadel' end up being assimilated into systems of domination.

The other consequence of the internal scission of the Self consists in the 'self-realization' as a planning of life in conformity with the will. The risk highlighted by Berlin is that freedom, if seen as self-direction or self-control, cannot fail in the end to want what is rational. Such an individual – for Simmel – paradoxically risks imploding into a deterministic view.

Also because of these risks, Berlin prefers the negative freedom, which has made it possible to safeguard individuals from 'exploitation and humiliation' throughout history (Berlin, 2002, p. 175). However, he draws attention to a possible tension running through the individual: negative freedom forges an individualistic approach of the human being that could overshadow the fact that we are inserted into *necessary* relationships with others. If we read Berlin's two notions in the light of Simmel's analysis, it emerges that the separation between the individual dimension and the social/relational dimension characterizing the two kinds of modern individualism is present in both negative and positive freedom. The negative view (as in the case of the 'individualism of singularity') tends to consider the social as a reality subsequent to individual identity and as the place where various kinds of interference take shape threatening freedom. In the case of positive freedom, social relations and the forms arising from them risk being considered as something already given, independently of the individual who can only legitimize them if these entities guarantee us those rational aims of our true nature towards which we must strive. In fact, the advocates of positive freedom justify the instituted forms by considering them functional to safeguard its members: and freedom is freedom to do and to want what is rational and, therefore, right. For its part, the 'individualism of uniqueness' tends to justify the established forms, according to an organic view of society, which guarantee that recognition the Self needs.

Berlin argues that the two notions of freedom have developed historically in divergent directions, configuring two different freedoms. Moreover, he attributes to negative freedom the attention for the private or individual arena, and to positive freedom the attention towards the public or collective one.

In Simmel, it is not a question of two different freedoms: the negative and positive ones are two different dimensions of liberty itself. Simmel defines the premises to overcome any presumptive dualism – within the individual as well as within freedom. Moreover, the scissions they forge in the subject – present in both kinds of individualism (reason/emotions and individual/social) – affect both the public and the private sphere.

Both Berlin and Simmel perceive the tension between our freedom as individuals and our freedom as members of a political community. For Simmel, however, the *type* of relationship imagined between the individual and the social dimension constitutes the important precondition for a positive exercise of freedom *versus* its negation. For this reason, he insists on the possibility that freedom occurs in an affirmative sense, as if the confusion concerning the concept of freedom resulted from failure to understand fully the conditions under which freedom is intelligible. These 'conditions' are related to the anthropological horizon that in

Berlin's work seems not to be fully explored. Starting from the vision of the human being, it is possible to better outline relationship as well – and a 'specific' kind of relationship. In this sense, for Simmel the analysis of freedom can be driven forward, offering useful cues for the thorny issues emerging in the following debates.

Topics under discussion and possible horizons

Open questions

The distinction between negative and positive freedom feeds the debate of the 1900s and its open questions. In this framework, Simmel's thought continues to be crucial. It would be worth considering, for example, the following aspects: firstly, the absence of interferences postulated by negative freedom could obscure not only the constitutive social dimension of the individual, but also the question of the complex relationship between freedom and other social values. Secondly, the positive freedom might 'justify' the social with its instituted forms without considering the link between freedom and the moral dimension. The thorny arguments offered here can hardly be considered within the confines of these pages. They are, however, strongly connected with the anthropological frame we are discussing.

When Simmel argues that freedom does not exist without social implications, thus also becoming a social project, he means to state that freedom concerns not merely self-mastery. There are objective conditions that contribute to its realization, as is also indicated by the view of negative freedom presented by Berlin. However, Simmel believes that freedoms 'accorded by liberal doctrines which, though they certainly do not hamper the individual from gaining goods of any kind, do however disregard the fact that only those already privileged in some way or another have the possibility of acquiring them' (2004, p. 444). There is therefore a tension between freedom as absence of interference (often emphasized by those who experience satisfactory, social conditions) *and* equality (which becomes a particularly delicate condition when we consider the possibility of having and developing some personal resources). What H. Arendt (2018) explains in terms of tension between 'liberation' and 'freedom': liberation *from* injustice and oppression, fear and inequality/poverty; freedom *to* live a political life, to participate in public affairs, to take the floor and to act in public. Liberation is a crucial passage toward freedom: to free people to be free not as a privilege of the few.

In the analysis of the two types of modern individualism, Simmel had seen the problem of the conflict between freedom and other social values, in particular equality that was amply contradicted by the dominant social stratification. Not by chance,

> it was an instinctive sense for this that resulted in the extension of the demand for *liberté* and *égalité* to include *fraternité*. For it was only through the voluntary act of renunciation as expressed in this concept that it would be possible to prevent *liberté* from being accompanied by the total opposite of *égalité*.
>
> *(Simmel, 1971, p. 222)*

For Simmel, the synthesis of freedom and equality is always precarious and destined to break in two directions, which he designates as equality without freedom and freedom without equality. The first one characterizes the ideal of socialism as well as the organicistic doctrines of the 19th century, while the second direction concerns the forms of social organization (emerging with the new monetary economy starting from the 18th century) which completely detach the individual from the group.

The problem underlying this conflict of values is, once again, the one on which Simmel insists in his analysis. Sandel (1984) and Taylor (1992) seem to take it up when they state that the basic question ultimately concerns the relationship between the social dimension in its giving or not giving a sense to individual freedom *and* the individual dimension in its posing itself, within modern affairs, as the epicentre of value. In Simmelian language, the question refers to the identity of the individual and of the social, and to thinking of them in relation according to 'specific' modalities. In *Sociology*, Simmel significantly states that

> for an individual who does have relations with other individuals, freedom has a much more positive significance. For him, freedom itself is a *specific relationship* with the environment … Freedom is not a solipsistic existence but sociological action. It is not a condition limited to the single individual but a relationship.
>
> *(1950b, p. 120 f.)*

For this reason, rather than accepting the absence of interferences and the idea of an individual in perennial contradiction within itself, Simmel distances himself from an individualistic view of the world that loses the horizontal extent of freedom with the related resources and limits. He distances himself also from organicist visions and from the hypothesis of a completely, rationalized society. Both these views lose the relational side of freedom as well. He is interested to understand what is that '*specific relation* with the environment' – as if to say that the problem is not simply the *tout court* relationship, but the '*type*' of relationship, able to express freedom as a relational experience of the 'whole man'.

In fact, relational dynamics are not in themselves a guarantee of moral actions and therefore – for Simmel – of freedom. In other words, the relational dynamics certify that the subject is bound by others and binds others, but the nature of this bond needs to be specified when freedom is at stake. And it is on this point that Simmel's thought continues to be useful, setting the premises to go beyond the misunderstanding deriving from the tacit presumption that individuals can be free or not free *simpliciter*, and the relationship can be good or threatening in itself. Outlining the human being as a 'whole man', on the one side, he liberates freedom from being an absolute idea concerning an abstract subject (as if the other social values were futile), and, on the other side, he liberates the individual from subjectivism and its degenerations (as if it were logically possible for a person to be free to do everything, also something immoral). Thus, keeping the centrality of the subject's relational identity and focusing on the 'specific' relation with its environment, Simmel firmly criticizes both the viewpoint of individualism (that stresses the negative freedom in Berlin's words) and that conception of positive freedom according to which liberation is forcing empirical selves into the right, rational pattern of social life. Both viewpoints shape an 'idea of freedom as if it were the individual's power, subsisting in itself, upon which, in a relatively random and independent way, the responsibility of this individual emerges' (GSG 4, p. 209). As if freedom were not a moral issue.

Before focusing on this point, it is useful to recall Simmel's proposal, relating to the '*specific relationship*' the subject may experience.

The polar opposition

For Simmel – unlike Berlin – the social dimension is intrinsic to the individual identity itself. Not something that is simply to be accepted because of a certain 'necessary' level of integration into the context in which one lives. The singular and the unique individual, like negative and positive freedom, are permeated, for Simmel, by the same misunderstanding with respect to the co-originality of the individual and social/relational dimension. Outside this co-originality, dualism arises and produces misunderstandings, lighting up a self-referential logic: the alterity typical of the opposite pole is walled in negativity. In this frame, the core of the individual lies not in sociability but in auto-centred self-realization, and the core of society must not be sought within limits but in the radicalization of the system's demand to incorporate individuals inside it. Thus, the resolution of the tension between the opposite poles is sought in the exclusion of one of the poles. The idea is that unity does not conceive oppositions or alterity. This point brings us into Simmel's philosophy of life, i.e. the *terrain* on which freedom – as a 'specific relationship' – can flourish, without being imprisoned in abstract, mechanistic views.[3] Simmel's philosophy of life lays the foundations for a different idea of unity, beyond the one whereby origin is supposed to coincide with a uniform and unformed unity (GSG 14, pp. 7–157; GSG 7, pp. 84–91). In the attempt to describe unity, Simmel speaks of 'dual unity' or 'unified duality' (1997c, p. 60). It is a unit that is intrinsic to life, 'the original fact' and to the life experience of individuals.

At the metaphysical level, life is, in fact, at the same time boundless continuity and form/limit: 'a real unity' of 'more-life' and 'more-than-life' (Simmel, 2010, p. 13). For this reason, human experience is originally located within a scenario of alterity where relation arises not *in spite of*, but rather *because of* opposites. At the phenomenological level, it is life itself that generates and enables the diversity of its manifestations without being fragmented by these heterogeneous expressions (GSG 20, p. 106). Only *life* transcends the sterile alternative between unity and multiplicity: owing to its intimate nature, it permits that 'unity expresses itself in multiplicity and multiplicity gathers in unity' (GSG 14, p. 93). Individuals – as peculiar 'forms' of life – experience that 'indescribable unity' in their existence.

For Simmel, because of our failure to acknowledge alterity already lying in unity, thought, and practice tend to affirm unity in an absolute way – which is made to coincide each time with one of the opposite poles of a relationship (rationality or sensibility, individual or social, matter or spirit, life as flow or life as form, etc.). Social life tends to flee multiplicity and turn towards dogmatism – this means escaping pluralism and losing the experience of freedom. This involves a closure that traps life in static and sterile views – as expressed through the crisis of modern culture analyzed in depth by Simmel (1997a, 1997b).

Criticizing the modern, cultural attitude to consider human existence in a dualistic frame as only socialized (i.e. to be socialized) or only individualized (i.e. to unbind from anything), Simmel affirms that the form of sociability that characterizes the 'whole man'

> belongs to the fundamental, decisive, and irreducible category of a unity which we cannot designate other than as the … simultaneity of two logically contradictory characterizations of man – the characterization which is based on his function as a member … of society; and the opposite characterization which is based on his function as an autonomous being, and which views his life from its own center.
> *(1971, p. 17 f.)*

In this sense, the experience of freedom reveals recognizing, on the one hand, the typical needs of organized coexistence (we are not free in abstract terms, but always inside an environment), and, on the other hand, distancing from the totalitarian claims of society, through 'a struggle that must be renewed after each victory and that requires time, reflection, suffering, in order not to accept cheap compromises' (GSG 4, p. 165). Freedom is therefore not residual (as in the case of negative freedom): it does not coincide with the absence of causes and constraints but refers to the human being taken as a whole. Moreover, freedom recognizes that life is not linear (as positive freedom thinks) but flows into a dynamic movement marked by calculation and unpredictability, constraints and absence of constraints, duties and creative acting, needs and events.

For Simmel, what clearly distinguishes the development of our existence is that it is creative because of its co-originality of different poles: it 'generates something that is not simply a combination of what already exists, and cannot therefore be calculated' (GSG 20, p. 81).[4]

On this point, H. Arendt (1958) stresses enough that human beings are born to begin, and human natality is the condition *sine qua non* of all politics. In her essay on what freedom and revolution mean, she indicates 'one more aspect of freedom', after having explained the relationship between liberation and freedom: 'it is that idea of freedom … of making a new beginning', to 'start something new' (Arendt, 2018, p. 382). In this frame we can catch Simmel's statement: 'the fact that man is the being who dares is solidly connected with his freedom. The one who is determined cannot dare anything, even though his behaviour externally demonstrates this character' (GSG 20, p. 111).

Objective culture, in its instrumental view of life, no longer admits the possibility of unexpected novelty that relations of a certain 'type' generate, i.e. relations that arise because of polar oppositions. Among them, there are relations like that of 'taking-giving', of gratitude, friendship and love (Simmel, 1950b). Precisely these relationships seem to be indicated by Simmel as fundamental to sociality, as they express 'specific' modes of relationship between the individual and other than itself – modes that are able to reflect the dual unity of life, able to let something new emerge. Perhaps it is to such relational 'modes' that he refers when he observes disconcertedly the fact that people have always tried to answer the problem of freedom

> starting from methodological axioms, affirming or negating the problem, and have not consulted the enormous empirical material about human relationality understood, however, not in the sense of the experiences that can be deduced from the latter, or at least not only in this sense, but with reference to experiences that are extraordinarily much more profound and secure, on which this relationality moreover is based
>
> *(GSG, 20, p. 87)*

– revealing that 'specific relation' that freedom is.

Freedom as a moral issue

The moral principle of freedom

Freedom is initially analyzed by Simmel in a text dedicated to morality. And this is not by chance. Jankélévitch (1925) emphasizes how his concern is to subtract morality from dogmatism to bring it back to a context where the choices of the subjects are possible, and so therefore are their responsibility and freedom. In this effort aimed at de-intellectualizing morality, Simmel elaborates a 'moral principle of freedom' from revisiting Kant's categorical imperative. This principle – 'act in such a way that the freedom you exercise, along with the one your acting leaves or prepares for others, would produce the greatest' (GSG 4,

p. 246) – combines two fundamental requirements: an objective configuration of things and a subjective attitude.

Simmel insists that the subject is not a self-referential unit, and freedom is not without constraints or limits. Freedom needs something that stands in front of it – a 'Gegenwurf' (ibid., p. 134), i.e. the *ob-jectum*, a friction that calls into question the subject's ability to choose at the confluence of different and often contradictory factors and of polar tensions, in their reciprocal conditioning. Freedom consists in letting reciprocity be achieved: 'there is no freedom in the purely negative sense; it always has a positive action as its content', an action that extends to objects and with effects on others (ibid., p. 237). And if the freedom of a subject or a group means merely that they exercise an influence on other/s without reciprocity, then this means dominating. The reciprocity takes shape through the renouncement of considering the other as something that is at the disposal of the Self without the latter being simultaneously for the other. In fact, in the experience of freedom, 'the free development of the person is all the more true freedom the more it is demonstrated in the relationship with other free persons' (ibid., p. 259). Freedom is such when the subject allows the *per se* of the other to exist, the existence of the other's 'you' as other than the 'I' (GSG 16, pp. 151–179). Simmel states that 'the symptom of human freedom is that the individual gives freedom to others … There is a deep connection between one's own freedom and the freedom of others' (GSG, 20, p. 109).

Through the moral principle of freedom, Simmel transfers the ethical discourse from the absolutism of the law and the imperatives to the empirical concreteness of social ties. In fact, the subject – as we have seen – does not represent a compact, self-referential entity: its free will does not respond mechanically to a single categorical imperative, where the agreement of reason with itself excels unquestionably, but reacts, in the concreteness of social action and interaction, to an interweaving and complex set of historical circumstances, psychological motivations and social facts. However, Simmel does not renounce an objectivity of morality: faced with the alternative of a morality made to derive now from individual conscience and now from the supra-individual law, 'I believe a third way exists: the objective Ought of this very individual, the demand imposed from "his" life onto "his" life and in principle independent of whether he really recognizes it or not' (Simmel, 2010, p. 142). In this context he elaborates the 'law of the individual':[5] if moral law derives from the unitarity of life, then it is not detached from my *responsibility* understood as a *response* within a relationship with life. This law, therefore, cannot fail to be valid for my existence. Quite the opposite, 'the categorical imperative suppresses freedom because it suppresses the unity of life in favour of atomized actions, which, evaluated according to a conceptual system, bend life under themselves, determining its meaning in defining their own one' (GSG 12, p. 434).

The *law of the individual* is such, precisely because of its vital connection: it means that man's decisions and actions are the expression of the totality of his existence, i.e. of his reality and ideality. In fact, 'in all our behaviour the whole man is productive and not only, as rational morality thinks, the pure "I" or the sensitive one' (GSG 12, p. 445). The *law of the individual* overcomes, in a certain sense, the hypothesis of a split between 'negative' and 'positive' freedom. It enhances both the horizontal development of the relational nature of freedom (the latter is not absence of interferences) as well as the transcendence movement of its relational nature, i.e. its taking distance from the defined, rationalized social arena (freedom is related to morality, i.e. to responsibility which is 'the innermost spring of man's nature'; Simmel, 1950a, p. 69). If we do not wish to paralyze the development of freedom, free action acquires its ethical value only in its *responding* to life, and not in depending on external, abstract norms.

Human being is moral, therefore free: Simmel and Bauman

Simmel leads freedom, also taking the discourse from the point of view of morality, out of the mechanistic schemas whose way of thinking proceeds by 'cause-effect'. In the frame of responsibility that for Simmel is the fundamentals of freedom, the reference paradigm becomes another one, i.e. what Bauman would outline as the one of 'appeal-response', where the appeal for both authors comes from life. In fact, in this frame we find all Bauman's analysis of modernity – an author who recognizes himself as deeply, intellectually indebted to Simmel. In him Bauman sees a sociologist able to gather aspects of reality that escape most people. Also by reason of his Jewish origins (common to both), Simmel was forced to a marginal position.[6] However, precisely from that position, Simmel developed a sociology far from unilateral views and resistant to managerial utilization. In this sense, for Bauman (1991), Simmel is able to foresee the deceptions of an epoch – modernity, whose tension to utilitarianism enclosed in the 'objective culture' and in its claim to build a perfect and rational society, does not guarantee against results as tragic as they are inhuman. Simmel had spoken of decadence produced by the 'malaise of our culture' (1997b, p. 98) and of the war as the result of that pervasive objectivation (GSG 16, pp. 7–58). Some decades later, Bauman faces another huge tragedy, the Holocaust: trying to reinterpret that drama, he comes to the conclusion that all human degradation and humiliation are the by-product of the obsessive search for order. The controlling, designing, and rationalizing dreams of modernity 'gave birth to institutions which serve the sole purpose of instrumentalizing human behaviour to such an extent that any aim may be pursued with efficiency and vigour, with or without ... moral approval on the part of the pursuers' (Bauman, 1989, p. 93).

Bauman rejects the traditional interpretation of the Holocaust: it is not only the *failure* of a civilization but also its *product*. Modernity has created the conditions whereby moral judgement is considered as external to the action of the subjects, offloading onto another the responsibility for one's own actions. Instead of attending to the morality of one's own conscience – or, as Simmel would put it, to the 'law of the individual', in which morality comes from life – individuals were induced to believe that obeying the rule means being moral. Along this road we enter what Bauman calls a condition in which we are performers, abdicating freedom.

In a society that structures itself around the hypothesis of the humanizing influence of social organization, as if moral attitudes were produced socially, most individual actions have a tenuous logical connection with the final result: the outcome is what he delineates as 'adiaphorization' – a social action that is morally indifferent. Simmel had defined it earlier as an overturning of reality, given that 'the will itself is ethical, not the value and the content detached from it' (GSG 21, p. 815). In fact, 'we are not responsible for the question of whether we obey an existing law or not', but mostly for the law's existence (Simmel, 2010, p. 151).

For both authors morality is not a social product. Taking up in particular E. Lévinas, Bauman (1993) speaks of moral responsibility, which is always 'for' the other and forms the basis of freedom: this is the essential structure of subjectivity without which the individual would not even exist. Here we find again the same orientation as Simmel: 'the idea is not that morality has its own life ... Rather, the devotion of the "I" to the "thou" (in the singular or plural) is the very idea, the definition, of the moral' (1950b, p. 260).

Thus, according to Simmel and Bauman, morality is a typical feature of the human being. Simmel writes that morality

> is not oriented according to some externally established value point ... rather it is, as it were, the rhythm in which life pours forth from its deepest wellspring; it is the tone not only of what are called actions, perhaps not even only of the will, but of the whole being, and resides in every thought and the manner of its utterance, in glances and words, in the feeling of joy and the bearing of grief ... the person is moral (and not only does the moral thing).
>
> *(2010, p. 109)*

And Bauman states that the question 'why should I be moral?' is the end and not the beginning of morality, because it would deprive the individual of his responsibility, while freedom is not seriously addressed. Simmel sees in the condition of the moral being the *proprium* of the 'whole man' thanks to his response to life: a situation of continual hesitation, of continual choice and assumption of responsibility for the consequences of one's choices in a context of inevitably incomplete knowledge. Simmel writes in fact:

> what we call 'coercion' always means simply that we decide for one side of an alternative and that the possibility would not at all be excluded of taking a decision for the other side, provided that we wanted to pay the price required by this other decision. But the fact that certain costs, according to the customary scale of values, are not, as it were, even taken into consideration, to us seems to want to exclude a priori the corresponding actions of freedom, thus forming the so-called 'situation of coercion'.
>
> *(GSG 20, p. 97)*

Or, as Bauman will say, that 'no possible alternative' that becomes a dead-end street – which, over time, tends to reduce choices to those coming only from the institutionalized order, to the point of restricting freedom as it is considered as an enemy of good. Neither Simmel nor Bauman marvel at this, given that freedom, resting on responsibility, arouses concern due to its unpredictability.

Simmel insists on the priority of responsibility beyond a deterministic view. Responsibility is not covered either by the thought of absolute, abstract freedom or by the most consistent form of determinism – i.e. two contradictory conceptions that are both present in modernity and go in the same direction separating responsibility and freedom. With regard to the onus of responsibility then, excluding any positive, inner force that produces the will of a subject, it would be a coincidence that one thing or another occurred, and the subject cannot be made responsible for that. In the latter case, because, in the presence of total causality, anything becomes predictable in a cause-effect chain, well outside the scope of the actor. What emerges is a hetero-direction that relieves the subject of its own responsibility and freedom, at the same time, creating a situation of widespread irresponsibility.

Bauman seems to echo Simmel's indications: he insists that being human means opposing the drift of irresponsibility. And seeing that there have been those who, in certain extreme situations, have opposed and refused to follow the rules of rational calculation, putting others' lives before their own, it is possible to open a different road. For Bauman, those who have widened the measure of responsibility were humans who realized they were free and through their freedom could rediscover their humanity. For both authors freedom can remain an empty and fundamentally negative experience, if it is not combined with a choice that in turn prepares freedom for others, becoming a moral act itself as it never falls back to itself 'but runs in the forward-striving direction of life as such' (Simmel, 2010, p. 150).

Conclusion: freedom, a matter of spirit

Modern traditions of thought about freedom above all considered it in terms of its ability to dissolve and unbind from external interferences, from others, from the internal influences of the individual that threaten his self-mastery. The risks of absolutizing such positions have led to degenerations of freedom, often based on reductive and dualistic visions of the individual. In this way, freedom ended up affirming itself at the expense of other social values. Simmel's contribution goes in the direction of rethinking freedom starting from its inherent nature: its relational matrix which, on the one hand, reveals the constitutive relationality of the human being itself ('the whole man'), and on the other hand, indicates that the social is not something already defined regardless of freedom and responsibility of individual's actions.

Simmel's contribution could be summarized as follows: freedom is a matter of spirit. While it unbinds, freedom binds, according to a 'specific' relationship: freedom 'unbinds' in the sense of 'liberation from' – a crucial step towards freedom where the subject is in conditions of stringent external constraints, especially the systemic ones. Freedom 'binds', in the sense of giving life to a certain type of social bond. For this reason, as H. Arendt also points out, freedom continually implies a process of liberation which needs to be realized in favour of those who, within society, continue to lack freedom. In this sense, Berlin's emphasis is useful when it highlights the 'positive' aspect of 'negative' freedom: freedom as liberation 'from' interferences that prevent the deployment of freedom. Simmel would call this orientation the positive, i.e. affirmative side of freedom. The work of liberation is never finished and involves various levels of social life: the institutional, the economic and social, the cultural and intersubjective.

However, as indicated by Simmel's considerations about some outcomes of modern revolutions as well as by Arendt's accurate analysis on the same topic, this movement of freedom as 'liberation from' can lead to new forms of domination and oppression if freedom is thought just as a process of liberation only for the independence of the 'I', and not as an expression of that morality which is 'the innermost spring of man's nature' (1950a, p. 69; see also Wolff, 1995). Both Simmel and Bauman insist on this point. The Simmelian 'law of the individual' represents the possibility of a view of freedom that precisely considers that 'innermost spring' related to life.

In this framework, freedom is therefore, at the same time, freedom 'from' and freedom 'to':

> freedom is something completely other than the repudiation of relationship, than the untouchability of the individual spheres by those located nearby. It follows from that very simple idea that a person is not only free but indeed also wants to use that freedom for something.
>
> *(Simmel, 2009, p. 81)*

The logic of freedom is dynamic and not static, relational and not individualistic. Freedom occurs in relationships among free people and accomplishes in generating the freedom of others. Freedom is freedom to give birth to something new, to dare, to begin – unless we consider human existence and social life within a mechanistic frame.

Responsibility, which Simmel considers as a fundamental of freedom, is related to this movement: in fact, it is not 'an echo that mechanically appears only when an outer movement has occurred' (2010, p. 76).

As we have seen, Simmel's contribution lies above all on the anthropological level. Starting from the idea of the subject, he distances himself from all the dualisms that split the subject into itself and with something else. The dualistic imbalance implies the risk of the pathologization of freedom. He is concerned to highlight the co-originality of those polar phenomena, which are typical of our 'spiritual-vital existence', and ultimately of life itself. Life is in fact, for Simmel, the original phenomenon related to which freedom is a relational experience, which reflects life's specific relational style. In this frame, the freedom of the 'whole man' cannot but be relational: the meaning of this adjective refers not only to the inter-individual social level (social interaction), but to the constitutive nature of life and of our existence. It is, in fact, the dynamism of the 'self-transcendence' of life that generates the space of relationship: it outlines the *modus* of this relationship. It is as a 'third space' beyond duality and unity where simultaneity of life as a process *and* of life as a form is safeguarded; and, at the phenomenological level, the simultaneity of polar elements is safeguarded (for example, reason *and* feelings, individuality *and* sociability, autonomy *and* bond). This *tertium* shapes a way of relating, and making sure that the polar elements will not be absorbed by each other: it is the womb for the free generative movement of life. Human existence is forged by this structural relationship with otherness, and thereby its freedom is the custodian of alterity (Tyrell, 2011).

Significantly, Simmel defines our existence as '*lebendig-seelisches Dasein*': it is the 'spiritual-vital existence' that 'at any moment should produce the new in a creative way, and therefore one not calculable … not repeatable … Every stage of our spiritual condition is a new stage that can only be awaited' (GSG 20, pp. 82, 84). The adjective '*seelisch*' includes the term '*Seele*', i.e. 'soul'. For Simmel, the soul here is the memory of life's self-transcendence (Susman, 1959). Not by chance the Simmelian '*Seele*' constitutes his final defence against the ongoing process of dissolution taking place in modernity. The main reason for this diagnosis rests, on the one side, on the modern, scientific and positivistic attitude interested in socializing the spirit (and the human existence) conceiving human actions and mind as a product, or a by-product, of society or of material processes of our brain, nevertheless dissolving freedom (GSG 18, pp. 167–202). On the other side, it rests on the emerging powers – such as the technical systems, which immanentize our experience, not only flattening life to a merely instrumental dimension but also filling up our constitutive openness and freedom, with abstract views that reduce reality to a mere representation – i.e. something to dominate; or with the mere liberation of impulses in an eternal flux which dissolves individuals within an irrational vitalism – until they are unable to choose; or with a strong network of means, and means of means, until ends gradually disappear. Simmel wishes to preserve the 'soul' of freedom. Life, which is a continuous transcending movement, marks freedom as a constitutive relationality – a '*specific*' relationality, able to break the immunity typical of all closed systems, and to generate other freedom, i.e. to let human 'spiritual-vital existence' flourish.

Notes

1 Unless otherwise specified, all English quotes are the author's translation.
2 This term appears also in the *Einleitung* (where he speaks of the 'global-I'; GSG 4, p. 143) and in the chapter about *The Law of the Individual,* cf. Simmel (2010, p. 147) (where he speaks of the 'whole person').

3 For in-depth analysis, see Jankélévitch (1925); Fitzi (2002, 2018); Oelze (2006); Böhringer (2018).
4 'We are shaped in such a way that we can understand a creative generation only through a duality of original and active elements' (GSG 14, p. 90). This point is interesting enough in order to rethink social life (and socio-economic models of development) in a generative framework, precisely on the basis of a certain idea of freedom (see Magatti, 2018; Martinelli, 2018).
5 The essay of 1913 (GSG 12, pp. 417–470) was incorporated in *Lebensanschauung*, 1918 (GSG 16, pp. 346-425).
6 For a collocation of Simmel within the anti-semitism of his time, see Müller (2018b).

References

Arendt, H. (1958). *The human condition.* Chicago, IL: The University of Chicago Press.
Arendt, H. (2018). 'The freedom to be free'. The conditions and meanings of revolution. In H. Arendt (Ed.), *Thinking without a banister. Essays in understanding. 1953–1975* (pp. 368–386). New York: Schocken Books.
Bauman, Z. (1989). *Modernity and the holocaust.* Cambridge: Polity.
Bauman, Z. (1991). *Modernity and ambivalence.* Cambridge: Polity.
Bauman, Z. (1993). *Postmodern ethics.* Oxford: Blackwell.
Berlin, I. (2002). Two concepts of liberty. In I. Berlin (Ed.), *Liberty* (pp. 166–217). Oxford: Oxford University Press.
Berlin, I. (2004). *Letters. 1928–1946.* Cambridge: Cambridge University Press.
Böhringer, H. (2018). In der Unentschiedenheit des Lebens. Simmel Lebensphilosophie. In H. P. Müller & R. Reiz (Eds.), *Simmel-Handbuch. Begriffe, Hauptwerke, Aktualität* (pp. 844–853). Berlin: Suhrkamp.
Fitzi, G. (2002). *Soziale Erfahrung und Lebensphilosophie.* Konstanz: UVK.
Fitzi, G. (2018). Life and forms. The sociological meaning of a metaphor. *Simmel Studies, 22*(1), 135–155.
Fitzi, G. (2019). *The challenge of modernity. Simmel's sociological theory.* London: Routledge.
Jankélévitch, V. (1925). Georg Simmel, Philosophie de la vie. *Revue de Métaphysique et de Morale, 32*(2), 213–257.
Magatti, M. (Ed.) (2018). *Social generativity. A relational paradigm for social change.* London: Routledge.
Martinelli, M. (2011). *L'altra libertà. Saggio su Georg Simmel.* Milano: Vita e Pensiero.
Martinelli, M. (2018). Georg Simmel's life and form: A generative process. In M. Magatti (Ed.), *Social generativity. A relational paradigm for social change* (pp. 63–90). London: Routledge.
Müller, H. P. (2018a). How is individuality possible? Georg Simmel's philosophy and sociology of individualism. *Simmel Studies, 22*(1), 15–33.
Müller, H. P. (2018b). Einführung. In H. P. Müller & R. Reiz (Eds.), *Simmel-Handbuch. Begriffe, Hauptwerke, Aktualität* (pp. 11–90). Berlin: Suhrkamp.
Nedelmann, B. (1988). 'Psychologismus' oder Soziologie der Emotionen? Max Weber Kritik an der Soziologie Georg Simmels. In O. Rammstedt (Ed.), *Simmel und die frühen Soziologen* (pp. 11–35). Frankfurt/M.: Suhrkamp.
Oelze, B. (2006). Über einige Motive der Lebensphilosophie Georg Simmels. *Simmel Studies, 16*(2), 135–159.
Sabido Ramos, O. (Ed.) (2007). *Georg Simmel. Una revisión contemporánea.* Barcelona: UAM-Azcapotzalco/Anthropos.
Sandel, M. (1984). *Liberalism and the limits of justice.* Cambridge: Cambridge University Press.
Simmel, G. (1950a). Fundamental problems of sociology (Individual and society). In G. Simmel (Ed.), *The sociology of Georg Simmel* (pp. 3–84). Glencoe, IL: The Free Press.
Simmel, G. (1950b). *The sociology of Georg Simmel.* Glencoe, IL: The Free Press.
Simmel, G. (1971). *Georg Simmel. On individuality and social forms.* Chicago, IL: The University of Chicago Press.
Simmel, G. (1997a). The concept and tragedy of culture. In D. Frisby & M. Featherstone (Eds.), *Simmel on culture* (pp. 55–75). London: Sage.
Simmel, G. (1997b). The crisis of culture. In D. Frisby & M. Featherstone (Eds.), *Simmel on culture* (pp. 90–101). London: Sage.

Simmel, G. (1997c). The personality of God. In G. Simmel (Ed.), *Essays on religion* (pp. 45–62). New Haven, CT and London: Yale University Press.

Simmel, G. (2004). *The philosophy of money*. Edited by T. Bottomore & D. Frisby. London: Routledge.

Simmel, G. (2009). *Sociology: Inquiries into the construction of social forms* (2 Volumes). A. J. Blasi, A. K. Jacobs, & M. Kanjiranthinkal (Eds.). Leiden and Boston, MA: Brill.

Simmel, G. (2010). *The view of life. Four metaphysical essays with journal aphorism*. Chicago, IL: The University of Chicago Press.

Susman, M. (1959). *Die geistige Gestalt Georg Simmels*. Tübingen: Mohr Siebeck.

Taylor, C. (1992). *Sources of the self. The making of the modern identity*. Cambridge: Cambridge University Press.

Tyrell, H. (2011). Georg Simmels 'große' Soziologie (1908). Einleitende Bemerkungen. In H. Tyrell, O. Rammstedt, & I. Meyer (Eds.), *'Georg Simmels große Soziologie'. Eine kritische Sichtung nach hundert Jahren* (pp. 9–68). Bielefeld: Transcript Verlag.

Völzke, E. (1986). *Das Freiheitsproblem bei Georg Simmel*. Tübingen: Kleine Verlag.

Wolff, K. H. (1995). Hingebung und der Andere. In F. Dörr-Baches & L. Nieder (Eds.), *Georg Simmel zwischen Moderne und Postmoderne* (pp. 189–201). Würzburg: Königshausen & Neumann.

20

GEORG SIMMEL'S THEORY OF RELIGION

Volkhard Krech

Introduction

Along with Max Weber and Émile Durkheim, Georg Simmel has long been considered a classic in sociology. The topic of religion plays a central role in the work of these three authors. But while Max Weber's and Émile Durkheim's approach to the sociology of religion has been widely studied, this does not apply to the same extent to Simmel's theory of religion. In the following analysis, I will sum up several of Simmel's main considerations on religion and further develop some aspects that I did not elaborate upon in my previous research (Krech, 1998).

The work context

Georg Simmel did not write a systematic theory of religion. Nonetheless, his contribution contains stimuli for a theory of religion based on the sociological, cultural-theoretical and philosophical layers of his work.

Religion in the context of the sociological approach

Simmel's sociological approach is based on the 'regulative world principle' of universal interaction (*Wechselwirkung*). In the process of universal interaction, however, there are 'crystallizations' and 'states of aggregation', which Simmel calls social forms and world formations. They are the result of social differentiation. Thus, the task of academic study is to discern which summarization is appropriate 'to provide comprehensive knowledge by individually studying the interactions of each of these with all other beings' (GSG 2, p. 130). The elements that make up society therefore do not need to be empirical units. Rather, 'individual' and 'society' are *'methodical concepts* – whether they divide given events and states among themselves or consider two aspects of their unity which we cannot examine directly' (GSG 11, p. 860). They are therefore not ontological items. Rather, they are to be used as a pair of complementary concepts for heuristic purposes.

Simmel is often referred to as a 'theorist of individuality'. This is certainly true, but in this characterization one must not forget that he also assumes the primacy of sociality. The individual is an *entity of attribution*, and emphatic individuality is a *phenomenon of deviation*. In contrast to an idealistic philosophy of consciousness, the individual is not constituted by his or her 'direct self-awareness', but first and foremost is the result of social addressing. The fact that individuality in the emphatic sense is a process of deviation from what is socially given is expressed both by the second *a priori* condition of Simmel's sociological epistemology and the philosophical concept of qualitative individualism. While the first *a priori* condition covers typification, the second deals with the fact 'that every member of a group is not only a part of society but also something else besides' and 'that the individual is in certain respects not a member of society' (Simmel, [1908] 2009, p. 45). In contrast to quantitative individualism, which refers to the degree of freedom made possible by the intersection of social circles, qualitative individualism means 'that each individual is separated from others, that one's being and activity with regard to form or content or both suits only that person and that this being different has a positive meaning and value for one's life' (Simmel, [1908] 2009, p. 637). In this sense the individual is the final and creative 'source of world affairs' (GSG 15, p. 154).

The two determinants of the concept of the individual – as an entity of social attribution and as a phenomenon of deviation and incommensurability – are in a relationship of tension. The individual stands within sociation processes and outside them at the same time. Simmel characterizes this double position as the 'the relationship of a single member to the whole, even though that single member still desires to be a whole himself' (Simmel, [1912/1906] 1997f, p. 157). This is where religion comes into play, because the tension between sociation and individuation processes is its reference. Religion takes its origin in these 'religioid' social circumstances, i.e. social conditions that are 'religious semi-products'. It creates its own world, theorizing these circumstances, and, aided by its symbolism, leads them to a solution. Simmel traces this process in his essay on religion (Simmel, [1912/1906] 1997f).

Religion in the context of cultural studies (Kulturwissenschaft)

Around 1900, Simmel increasingly turned to cultural studies and thus expanded the sociologically limited subject area. In general, Simmel's concept of culture refers to the sum of all those domains that shape 'people's relationships to one another and to themselves' (Simmel, [1900] 2004, p. 451). Objective cultural domains include science, art, religion, morality, law, politics, economics, and technology. The following two aspects are characteristic of these objective cultural domains, which Simmel often calls 'series of purposes' (*Zweckreihen*). First of all, each of these domains is subject to an 'autonomous ideal' (Simmel, [1900] 2004, p. 452), which gives its contents an objective meaning, creates an internal connection among its individual elements, and thus leads to internal coherence and autonomy. As a consequence, the individual cultural domains are sharply differentiated from one another and may even stand in contrast to one another.

The idea of culture, however, can by no means be merged into various series of different purposes that proceed on their own rules. The aforementioned domains shape the actual purposes in life. From the point of view of a higher cultural ideal, however, they constitute only the cultural *contents*, which in turn are formed by a sequence encompassing them, i.e. the cultural series. It is not merely the factual meaning within the series of purposes that constitutes a cultural value. Rather, the domains mentioned are cultural values only when they are inserted into the cultural series beyond their immanent purpose and thus gain 'their significance for the overall development of individuals and society at large' (Simmel, [1908] 1997d, p. 43).

This understanding of culture produces a double meaning of its concept, i.e. objective and subjective culture. While objective culture signifies 'things, extended, enhanced and perfected as described above so as to lead the soul to its own perfection, or to constitute a part of the road to higher life of the individual or the community' (Simmel, [1908] 1997d,

p. 45), subjective culture denotes 'the degree of personal development thus attained' (ibid.). Both aspects of the concept of culture are interdependent. Simmel staunchly opposes the view that subjective culture is a concept that can be subsumed under objective culture. Rather, the process called cultivation follows the opposite direction: 'subjective culture is the overriding final goal, and its measure is the measure of how far the spiritual process of life has any part in those objective entities and their perfection' (ibid.). From this axiomatically-valued point of view, it follows that there can be no subjective culture without objective culture. On the one hand, the concept of culture is determined by the 'self-development of the spiritual centre'. On the other, self-development requires more objective and external means: 'Culture comes into being ... by the coincidence of two elements, neither of which contains culture in itself: the subjective soul and the objective intellectual product' (Simmel, [1911] 1997a, p. 58). Therefore, if there is no subjective culture without objective culture, then, conversely, objective culture can achieve relative independence from subjective culture (Simmel, [1908] 1997d, p. 45). This possibility resulted in the 'preponderance of objective over subjective culture that developed during the nineteenth century' (Simmel, [1900] 2004, pp. 453–454), and this explains the problems and 'disharmony of modern life' (Simmel, [1908] 1997d, p. 45). In his essay 'The Concept and Tragedy of Culture' (Simmel, [1911] 1997a), Simmel specifies the dualism of objective and subjective culture as a *tragic* conflict of modernity, because the dualistic development of culture follows an *inherent* logic.

The perspective of cultural studies has essentially been determined by the problem of lost ultimate purpose. In his *Einleitung in die Moralwissenschaft* ('Introduction to the Science of Morality'), Simmel had already mentioned pessimism and the 'feeling of emptiness and worthlessness of life' as characteristic features of modern culture (GSG 4, p. 30). In terms of both content and form, 'we are losing the unshakeable value of life, the ideals that provide us with firm objectives' (ibid.). This process can be traced to the fact that 'faith is disappearing more and more and criticism is destroying our devotion to traditional political, religious and personal ideals' (ibid.). Formally, this disorientation is due to the development of modern society, as a result of which 'the fast pace and restless rhythm of modern life does, in a sense, not allow such ideals to manifest' (ibid.). At the same time, however, and this is the point of Simmel's diagnosis, the ultimate purpose has not eliminated the need for it (ibid.). Simmel described the age he lived in as a time of transition; he diagnosed a habitual backlog of orientation patterns that have not yet adapted to the changed living conditions (ibid.). In his explanations in *The Philosophy of Money*, he discerns that, in modern times, money has taken the place of absolute purpose, which had formerly been held by God (Simmel, [1900] 2004, pp. 237–242). At the same time, however, the relativistic worldview, which finds its purest expression in today's monetary system, terminated the metaphysical need for absolute values. Simmel outlines the history of Europe's cultural development, which begins with the Christian concept of the salvation of the soul and the Kingdom of God at the turning point in time, and ends with the mere *formal* need for an absolute, ultimate purpose as the sign of the cultural situation at the time, and he comes to the conclusion: 'the need has outlived its fulfilment' (Simmel, [1900] 2004, p. 363). Against this background, Simmel can understand '[t]he weakening of religious sentiments and, at the same time, the vital reawakening need for such sentiments' as 'a consequence of the fact that modern man is deprived of an ultimate purpose' (Simmel, [1900] 2004, p. 363 f.).

The cultural value of religion is measured by whether, and if so how, religious ideas – still or again in a different way – affect the personal culture and in this way can form a life-immanent, ultimate purpose. In this context, theism and the Christian concept of the soul play an important role. According to Simmel, the idea of God as a personality can be understood as a religious cipher that symbolizes the unity of being and, *at the same time*, the individual being as a whole. From the perspective of cultural studies, the cultural value of theism consists in the fact that it exercises a constitutive function of constituting individuality in anthropological terms. The subjective side of the idea of God is symbolized by the Christian *topos* of the salvation of the soul, which unites both dimensions of the concept of personality, namely personality as form and as regulative idea. Thus, the salvation of the soul advances to the ultimate purpose of life, which, according to Nietzsche whom Simmel follows in this respect, is of course founded in life itself.

Religion in the context of the philosophy of life approach

Even if religion manages to mediate the tension between sociation and individuation as well as between objective and subjective culture, two contradictions remain:

a)   The sociological paradox lies in the fact that on the one hand, the individual functions as a constitutive element of everything that is societal, while on the other hand society questions the autonomous existence of the individual.
b)   The contradiction observed in cultural studies lies in the notion that subjective culture should be the ideal ultimate purpose of culture, but it is absent as a result of the autonomy and heterogeneity of objective cultural domains.

Simmel tries to resolve these aporia by scaling the concept of freedom with a philosophy of life approach and formulating the meta-ethical principle of 'individual law'. In contrast to material ethics, the philosophy of life is concerned with the mediation of what is and what should be done in the dimension of *unseparated life*. Simmel's central argument is to understand limitation not negatively, but as a *constitutive* of freedom (GSG 15, pp. 147–148).

In his philosophy of life approach, Simmel determines the religious function in conveying the fundamental tension between freedom and obligation, which – as a distinction between form and process – underlies sociation as well as cultural processes. In its general version, religion deals with the subject of demarcation and the transgression of boundaries. In order to emphasize the dynamic, form-dispersing aspect of religion, Simmel distinguishes between *religion* as an autonomous world of dogmas and institutions on the one hand and *religiosity* as a function of life itself on the other. His philosophy of life approach to the concept of religion becomes particularly clear in the conception of *being* religious in contrast to *having* religion:

> The religious mode of existence, however, is not simply a static, tranquil state, a *qualitas occulta,* a symbolic once-and-for-all like the beauty of some natural phenomenon or a work of art. It is a form of life in all its vitality, a way in which life vibrates, expresses itself, and fulfills its destinies.
>
> *(Simmel, [1911] 1997g, p. 14)*

The difference between a permanent need for an ultimate purpose and a lack of fulfilment of this need can therefore be overcome by the possibility 'that religion returns from its substantiality, from its attachment to transcendent contents to a function, to an inner form of life itself and of all *its* contents, or that it emerges from it' (GSG 14, p. 380). From a philosophy of life perspective, religiosity mediates the fundamental opposition of life between process and form. In this sense, Simmel reinterprets the Christian idea of the salvation of the soul as the realization of the ideal of the inner self (Simmel, [1903] 1997e, p. 30). The idea of the salvation of the soul stands for the idea that 'nothing needs to be added or affixed to it from outside, but it really needs only to cast off a shell and fulfill its inner being' (Simmel, [1903] 1997e, p. 31).

The systematization of Simmel's theory of religion from a sociological perspective

The following explanations are an attempt to understand the sociological approach as the nucleus in which cultural studies and philosophy of life are already laid out or from which they virtually unfold in this sense. I also read the works that are not explicitly sociologically oriented through a sociological lens, as it were. I subscribe to Landmann's view that 'Simmel's philosophy of life is also philosophy of culture' (Landmann, 1987, p. 9) and like to extend it by Rammstedt's thesis (1995) that Simmel's cultural studies is sociology at the same time – admittedly, in the broader sense. While the brief embedding of the history of Simmel's works in the first chapter is based on the diachronic sequence, in the following I will be dealing with the systematic unity of Simmel's theory of religion from a synchronic perspective. Schematically, the two readings can be represented as follows (Table 20.1 and Figure 20.1):

Table 20.1 Thematic-diachronic perspective

	Sociology	*Cultural studies*	*Philosophy of life*
object	sociation processes	culture	life
guiding difference	individual /society	subjective culture/objective culture	form /process

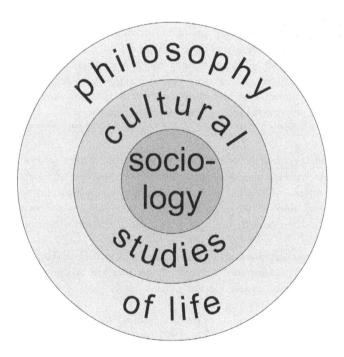

Figure 20.1 Systematic-synchronic perspective

The main point of reference of the systematic reconstruction is the monograph on religion in the second edition (Simmel, [1912/1906] 1997f). The starting point of the monograph is the abstract problem of determining the relationship between part and whole. After Simmel presented his epistemological point of view, three areas are named in which religion becomes thematic: the individual's relationship to external nature, to destiny, and to society. Having briefly reflected on the first two fields, Simmel concentrates on the third complex of themes, i.e. on 'the relationships of human beings to the human world and to the currents of religion that flow within them' (Simmel, [1912/1906] 1997f, p. 151). The general problem of the relationship between part and whole is substantiated in sociation processes as the double position of the individual towards society, i.e. in 'the relationship of a single member to the whole, even though that single member still desires to be a whole himself' (Simmel, [1912/1906] 1997f, p. 157). Simmel gains a specific sociological perspective on religion by drawing an analogy between the attitude of the individual towards God and the behaviour within sociation processes. By drawing this analogy, Simmel systematizes his early sociological approach to religion. While in his 1898 essay on the sociology of religion all three themes – faith, unity, and analogy – were equal examples for the development of religion from social circumstances (Simmel, [1898] 1997b), now the structurally comparable relationship between the individual to God, on the one hand, and to a social community on the other, takes a heuristic priority, and faith as well as the concept of unity become concretions of this abstract relation. It seems as if it was precisely the *philosophical* preoccupation with religious ideas that led Simmel to elaborate his *sociological* approach to religion.

Simmel explains his understanding of analogy and conceptualizes the term and the respective method:

> analogies are not to be regarded as some random similarity of unconnected phenomena. Rather I wish to interpret the parallels between the two spheres as follows. The religious category is a spiritual way of living and of experiencing the world, and is a force that searches, acts, feels, and takes hold of the content of existence. This allows it to create an objective world for itself. Religion stands juxtaposed to religiosity, which is in itself a *state* or a spiritual rhythm lacking any object. Among those contents which religiosity pervades or takes control of are the sociological formations whose structure predestines them to be ideal raw material for the development of religious life.
>
> *(Simmel, [1912/1906] 1997f, p. 165)*

The method of analogy thus denotes a mode of knowledge within an attitude towards the world. Intertwined with the analytical distinction between content and form, the immanent forming of the material of human interaction and the transcendent shaping into religious imagination are two kinds of the same function of religiosity; they derive 'from a single, common root that determines their shape' (ibid.) and differ only in terms of the content they incorporate.

Likewise, more precisely than in the 1898 essay, the function of the religious category is now determined in a social respect, namely as an increase in the consciousness of the individual within a sociation process, so that

> the acquisition of a sense of solemnity and stability for what is socially required, expressing its full social significance in a particular key and with a force not otherwise possible. Thus, the social norm reaches a new stage in its development.
>
> *(Simmel, [1912/1906] 1997f, p. 155)*

As an illustration, Simmel uses the cases he already presented in the socio-religious essay of 1898. The religious category works in sociation processes where social integration means individuation at the same time: the religiously tinged social processes induces 'an inclusion of the subject in a higher order, though he senses it as something inward and personal' (Simmel, [1912/1906] 1997f, p. 161).

Furthermore, a look at the analogous structure of religiously tinged sociation processes and dogmatic contents of religion provides an insight into the process of differentiation of religion into an independent ideal world. The religious category takes shape in social processes, the transcending and objectification of which then gives rise to the world of religion; in turn, religion can, as a differentiated domain, have an effect on social processes in the above-mentioned way of increasing consciousness and thereby enable both social integration and personal individuation. Simmel already advocated the thesis of the relationship between socialization processes and the differentiated world of religious ideas as interactions in his sociological essay on religion of 1898 (Simmel, [1898] 1997b). In his monograph on religion of 1906, Simmel was able to substantiate and specify this assumption by synthesizing the results of sociological analysis with epistemological reflection: religion can fulfil the function of raising consciousness, because religious faith primarily focuses not on its content, but rather denotes the subjective – and therein no less social – process in the sense of an attribution to a person (cf. already Simmel, [1902] 1997c). From that point on, the terms 'faith' and 'unity' become clear to Simmel: he defines faith as a 'a spiritual state: though oriented toward an exterior object, this orientation itself is nonetheless an inner, spiritual quality' (Simmel, [1912/1906] 1997f, p. 167). Thus, the bond of union faith possesses both an integration function and – as the unification of consciousness on the basis of its intentional character – an individuation function at the same time. In the faith in God, the process of believing then releases from its attachment to a social counterpart in order to constitute absolute faith in its transcendent form.

The concept of unity initially (and above all in early epochs of the history of religions) becomes thematic in the social sphere. The collective is the place where individual members can be observed as a unity. At the same time, however, social unity becomes problematic because the individual also wants to understand him- or herself as his or her own unity:

That the freedom of the individual will always try to detach itself from the unity of the group, and that even in the simplest and most naive social entities such unity does not develop as readily as the unity of an organism and its parts – this in particular must have raised human awareness of social unity as a distinct form or energy of being (Simmel, [1912/1906] 1997f, p. 174).

The concept of unity thus sheds special light on the analogy between socialization processes and differentiated religious ideas: 'That the individual's sense of social belonging to his group always entails a mixture of enforcement and personal freedom, as alluded to earlier, now reveals itself as the most profound formal link between social and religious life' (Simmel, [1912/1906] 1997f, p. 182). The social conflict between society and individual, both of which take on a unity for themselves, is thus *structurally comparable* to the religious question of this relationship: whether the Divine totally determines humanity or the individual has a certain autonomy. Based on this insight, Simmel turns to the dogmatic contents of the pantheism-theism issue and the associated question about the personality of God as well as the concept of the salvation of the soul. It is not the case that he tried to reduce the subjects of religious imagination to a socially conditioned fact; Simmel had already rejected the question of the origin of religion as well as its mono-causal derivation in his sociological essay on religion of 1898 (Simmel, [1898] 1997b), although the sociological perspective on religion could not sufficiently ward off the danger of a causal derivation. By explaining his heuristic procedure of analogy formation in more detail, it seems Simmel recognized this danger and tried to counteract it. Religiously connoted social facts and the differentiated world of religion have a common source in the religious category. Only from this realization of what is common can the difference between the two phenomena be presented in detail. Using the method of comparison, Simmel is able to demonstrate the substantial content *beyond the social* in the world of religious mindscape:

> In confronting God, however, there is more at stake than specific details or the mere concordance or opposition of our actions in relation to His will; what is at stake is the principle of freedom and independence in its purely inner meaning.
>
> *(Simmel, [1912/1906] 1997f, p. 187)*

The heuristic starting point of Simmel's sociology of religion therefore is the demonstration of analogies between sociation processes and the religious mindscape. Based on structural similarities, Simmel concludes that there is common ground underlying both elements of comparison, which he identifies in the religious category. The comparative perspective can be represented schematically as follows (Figure 20.2):

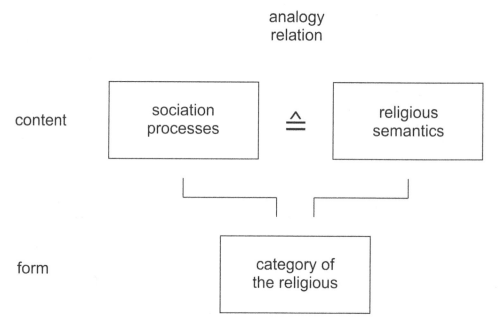

Figure 20.2 Systematic analogy relation

Now, however, Simmel does not stop at this systematic comparative perspective, but he deduces from it a development of religion from sociation processes. This diachronic perspective of a theory of differentiation can be depicted schematically as follows (Figure 20.3):

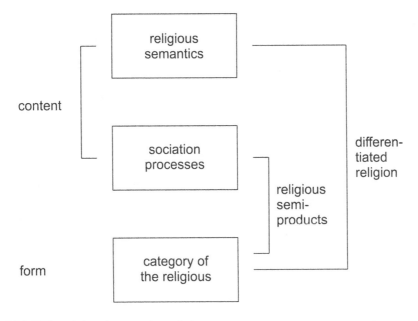

Figure 20.3 Differentiation-theory analogy relation

The second edition of *Religion* appears in 1912, having been modified and expanded by about a third. The sociological framework outlined above is retained and extended by philosophical passages. First, the question of religious truth is reflected in more detail than in the first edition, in contrast to theoretical knowledge and practical experience. In doing so, Simmel draws on considerations he had made in his essay 'A Problem of the Philosophy of Religion', published in 1905. By drawing a distinction between content and form, according to which the religious category is in principle able to take up any content, Simmel identifies the elements of truth in religious ideas not in objective statements, but in a disposition of human existence, which is characterized by '[t]he need to find completeness in the fragmentary nature of man's existence, to reconcile conflicts within the individual and between men' (Simmel, [1912/1906] 1997f, p. 142). Employing the concept of life, Simmel now focuses more strongly on the process character of the religious function: 'Religiousness in its pure essence, free of all empirical material, is a *life*; the religious person is somebody who *lives* in a certain way peculiar to himself' (Simmel, [1912/1906] 1997f, pp. 143–144). If the insight into the formal character of the religious is originally owed to the reception and extension of Kant's theory of categories, then this determination now becomes part of a philosophy of life. Numerous expressions from the semantic field of movement can be cited as indications of this change, some of which are linked to the concept of life, such as 'religion … as impulses within life' (*religiöse Lebensbewegtheiten*) (Simmel, [1912/1906] 1997f, p. 144), 'autonomous life world' (ibid.), 'religious process' (Simmel, [1912/1906] 1997f, p. 147), 'religious current' (Simmel, [1912/1906] 1997f, p. 144), 'life process that is religious as such' (Simmel, [1912/1906] 1997f, p. 162), 'religious life' (Simmel, [1912/1906] 1997f, pp. 141, 153, 158, 165, 182, 209), etc. The distinction between form and content is not abandoned but superimposed by the distinction between life (as a process) and form (as an objective structure).

The emphasis placed on the addition of the 1906 text indicates a stronger emphasis on the cultural and life-philosophical perspective. However, it will hardly be possible to draw the conclusion from this that the entire ductus shifts in favour of philosophy. Rather, it becomes clear that assumptions on the philosophy of religion are made on the *basis* of sociological analysis. In his sociological presentation of the conflicting claims to wholeness by society and the individual, Simmel inserts a passage that makes the philosophical perspective appear as an extended sociology. In the very first edition, after analogizing social circumstances with the contents of differentiated religion, he comes to the conclusion that the tension between compulsive determination and personal freedom that characterizes the sociation process 'reveals itself as the most profound formal link between social and religious life' (Simmel, [1912/1906] 1997f, p. 182). Simmel consolidates this insight in the second edition by shedding light on both the analogical method and the relationship between sociological and philosophical approaches: the 'constant intertwining of freedom and obligation, even if it is only symbolic, is one of the social formative processes that is ideally suited to adopting and shaping fundamental religiousness, which otherwise exists merely for itself' (Simmel, [1912/1906] 1997f, p. 185). Religious unity is now located on the pre-empirical level of unseparated life, and this shift serves as a reason for identifying religious unity in the sphere of inter-individual relations:

> The self-contained stare of religious being, that unity which knows no otherness, finds a form of expression in the interplay between freedom and obligation as displayed in empirical human relationships: by describing this religious state as a duality, it is as if we were giving it the words which it can describe itself, even though these words belong to a foreign language. In the categories of freedom and dependence, which religion as a spiritual quality seems to presage, it can pour forth its energies to generate a relationship to the absolute. The state of religious being would not be capable of groping toward the absolute unless it could find the contents capable of being assigned a religious form.
>
> *(ibid.)*

As far as the systematizing integration of the different layers in Simmel's theory of religion is concerned, the following conclusion can be drawn: due to the fact that the revised and newly received passages of the second edition of the monograph on religion reflect the life-philosophical change, the second edition turns out to be a product that uses all of the three layers of Simmel's works as sources. In this way, the second edition provides a unifying perspective for the many different approaches – both in terms of method and content – that Simmel pursues in his individual essays. The result of the synthetizing is a concept of religion that is composed of the following four constitutional elements:

a) The *empirical derivation* of religion from social processes by means of the paradigm of differentiation, the resulting distinction between religion as an autonomous world of ideas, and the 'religioid' (Simmel, [1912/1906] 1997f, p. 158), which can already be found in social processes, serves as a starting point.

b) However, in order to avoid materialistic reductionism, Simmel uses *transcendental philosophy* to establish the religious as an a priori category of consciousness. In this way, religion can be understood as derived from the social, but at the same time, the religious category is placed before the sociation processes: 'It is not empirical contents that are exaggerated to form religious phenomena; instead, the religious components within the empirical world are given special emphasis' (Simmel, [1912/1906] 1997f, p. 145).

c)   Simmel meets the resulting need to explain the loss of importance of religion in modern times in two ways. Firstly, he uses a *historical-philosophical approach* to relativize religion's universal claim to interpretation and states that the validity of a value is bound to certain epochs. Secondly, Simmel analyzes the assertion of the need for religion of today's individuals; a need which, of course, cannot easily be fulfilled in modern times, especially not in the classical way religion used to do it.

d)   Finally, Simmel explores the empirical fact that, despite religion's loss of importance, religiosity in modern times still endures and even enjoys a kind of comeback; he does so in his *life-philosophical approach* by nuancing the religious function as a process, which he understands as centration of the individual consciousness on itself, in view of increasing fragmentations due to ever more complex sociation processes.

The synthetizing of the individual components into a uniform concept of religion sheds light on the relation between epistemology, empiricism, and speculation as well as the relation between sociology and philosophy in Simmel's work. As a sociologist, Simmel first emphasizes the double connection between society and religion in the shape of the religious in the social as well as the social in the religious. On the one hand, through the analogy between the relationship of the individual to his or her group and the relationship between the individual and his or her God, Simmel realizes 'that religious behaviour is not exclusively bound to religious contents, but is a generally human form, which is realized not only in transcendent objects, but in some other emotional motives as well' (GSG 16, p. 75). On the other hand, a sociologist who studies religion may discover 'that a self-contained religious life also has moments which are not specifically religious but social in nature' (ibid.). Sociological analysis of these social moments on the basis of religious sentiments led to the insight that 'what in terms of religious behaviour may be regarded as the purely religious elements – and as such indifferent to everything that is social' (GSG 16, p. 75)'. From a sociological perspective, religion seems to be something derived from the social realm; the philosophy of religion, however, can refer to the autonomy of religious ideas independent from the social realm. From the perspective of philosophy-oriented sociology, Simmel is able to write: 'All purely factual meanings in which our soul somehow participates … the domains of religion and nature – all these things, as far as we come to own them, have essentially nothing to do with "society"' (GSG 16, p. 126). It is only on the basis of the sociological paradigm of differentiation that the necessity and object of the philosophical perspective of religion can be determined, which means analyzing whether religion as a differentiated world can have a retroactive effect on the social sphere. Against the background of sociological analysis, activating the potential for sociologically analyzed pathologies of modern society becomes a genuine task of philosophical reflection on religion and religiosity.

Thus, the fact that the perspectives of sociology, cultural studies, and the philosophy of life complement each other should be made clear. All of these perspectives are connected to each other precisely in the subject of religion. The systematic reason for this lies – as Simmel concludes – in the double position of the individual as the common starting point of sociological analysis as well as of philosophical considerations. The inside and the outside in the relationship between society and individual is, as was mentioned above, a concretion of the relationship between part and whole, which religion deals with in a more abstract and therefore also purer form as a relation between God and the world or the individual soul. Both sociology and philosophy throw light upon two sides of one and the same fact – in accordance with Simmel's dictum that every form is capable of absorbing any content.

Starting from this common basis, sociology and philosophy therefore distinguish themselves from one another with regard to their respective epistemology: while the sociology of religion analyzes religious aspects of different sociation processes, the philosophy of religion focuses on the function of religiosity in life processes. Sociology highlights the religious form as a function of social integration, philosophy in turn emphasizes the unifying aspect of · religion for individual consciousness. The double position of the individual, analyzed sociologically and reflected philosophically, is the reason for the twofold achievement of the religious category: the social integration function as well as the function of the individuation of each consciousness.

Without explicitly mentioning the complementarity of sociological analysis and philosophical reflection, Simmel nevertheless suggests that both approaches refer to each other by pointing out the respective limits demarcated by aporia. Although the sociological description of social *existence* does not make the synthesis of social integration and individuation of the individual subject seem unthinkable in principle, it does ascribe to it a utopian character in terms of realizing it in the social domain. Philosophy of religion, on the other hand, is not bound by the constraints of empirical conditions and can – on the level of *what should be done* – focus on speculative ideas that offer a solution to the abstract problem of the relation between part and whole in the form of defining the relationship between the transcendent God and the immanent world. However, the aporia in the philosophy of religion arises where the pure function of religiosity, in order to be able to realize itself at all and take on a historical form, has to refer to social reality. For this reason, at least in the perspective of the monograph on religion of 1912, the philosophical approach on religion is linked back to the initial sociological problem. From the theistic conception of a personal God, the world of religious ideas can again have an effect on sociation processes by anticipating the synthesis of social integration and personal individuation as a regulative idea beyond the social realm, but related to it, in an ideal and pure way. The empirical insight: 'We are all fragments, not only of humanity in general but also of ourselves' (Simmel, [1908] 2009, p. 44) is countered by the utopian concept of a solution to the paradox of uniformity and totality of individual consciousness and – at the same time – the individual's position in social processes, which takes shape in the transcendent religious ideas and their repercussions on sociation processes. In this sense, Simmel's theory of religion is based on his sociology, which is then complemented by philosophical aspects and transformed into cultural studies informed by sociology. Sociology in the narrower, formal sense negotiates the effects of the religious form on the social structure, which is shaped by the difference between 'individual' and 'society'. In the course of the differentiation process, religion then develops into an ideal autonomous world with its own contents. Simmel's plurality of perspectives is therefore based on the distinction between social structure and semantics; while formal sociology analyzes the social structure, philosophy deals with semantics. As the religious contents have a retroactive effect on the social structure, they can also be understood as the object of sociological analysis.

However, it must be taken into account that Simmel is not interested in presenting religious ideas as mere projections of social processes. What matters more to him is to understand the purely formal category of religion as the basic form of human consciousness, which can be actualized both in social facts and in genuinely religious ideas. These in turn interact with each other. On the one hand, the inter-individual forms of social life often provide content for religious ideas (Simmel, [1912/1906] 1997f, p. 160 f.). Social unification may provoke a religious reaction, because 'the former contains inherent shaping forces that lead the human being beyond his immediate empirical existence and impose mystical interpretations on all social life that transcends the individual' (Simmel, [1912/1906] 1997f, p. 182). On the other hand, religious ideas that have been made absolute might also have an effect on social matters in that they symbolize them; religious ideas can even advance social engagement. The transformation of religiously formed social contents into religious contents occurs by way of the religious category. Transcendence is the purest, most highly enhanced realization of what must remain fragmentary in society. According to this perspective, God represents the formula or the symbol of the social problem of the individual's attachment and freedom. The function of religion is therefore to intensify the unity-building interaction between individual and society by semantic means and to bring special focus on the relationship between individual and society as the intertwining of social inclusion and exclusion.

From a comparative perspective, religious semantics can be understood as a special instance of reflection on the relation between individual and society. However, since the method of analogy consists in seeing what is common in distinction to what is not common, there also need to be differences. Differences between religious semantics and social structures seem to consist in the concept of the pure form of religion in the sense of the Kantian idea of regulative goals setting the standard towards which the realization of the idea of unity should be oriented. Religion has its roots in social life, but it is not absorbed in it. As a form, religion is 'more-than-life'. The 'more' radiates in the ideal, transcendent conception of unity back to the social existence of the individual, so lending it an orientation towards an end point, which by transcending the striving for unity as a basic need of the soul reacts upon the figure of the absolute from outside.

This 'more' becomes concrete in different ways – from intensified engagement in social relationships to asceticism. The idea of unity, which is realized in the interaction between devotion and reception in social interaction processes, is advanced in the religious practice of asceticism and the related notions of merit. On the one hand, sacrifice, which consists in renouncing things and practising asceticism, binds practitioners to the transcendent divinity for whose sake they practise asceticism, because: 'The more sacrifices we have made for a cause, the more capital we have invested in it, the greater our interest in it is; by making personal sacrifices, we virtually melt into it, negating the barrier between us and it' (GSG 3, p. 215). At the same time, however, all the credit given to the ascetic causes his or her personality to grow (GSG 3, p. 219), because 'defeating inner resistance [seems] to bring with it a feeling of spiritual expansion and a strengthening of power' (GSG 4, p. 220). Thus, ascetic practice can be seen as an enhancement of normal social interaction processes, which are always about giving and taking, commitment and freedom, socialization and individuation. By transforming a social practice of giving and taking into a religious one, new potentials for action are created that ordinary interactions are unable to produce. But even if asceticism as an extreme form of a religious act is not practised, religious formation may lead to the intensification of social interaction processes. This is the case, for example, in religiously conceived professional ethics. If individuals understand their activity as an imposed, religiously motivated duty, they might exercise their profession even more diligently. At the same time, they are integrated into society and simultaneously individualized by maintaining their personal status within the entire order. This fact, incidentally, corresponds to Simmel's third sociological *a priori* condition, namely '[t]hat every individual is directed according to one's own rank in a definite position inside of one's social milieu' (Simmel, [1908] 2009, p. 50). In religiously motivated sentiments of duty and profession, religious doctrines as transcendent contents might affect the social conditions from which they have developed by intensifying social processes with the 'pure' reflection on the problem of freedom and attachment.

Life's 'axial rotation'

In his *Lebensansschauung* (*The View of Life*), Simmel makes a final attempt to mediate the paradoxes of part and whole, individual and society, as well as objective and subjective culture. To this end, he differentiates between vital processes and established forms. In *The View of Life*, Simmel argues that a vital process constitutes ideal worlds that transcend life but at the same time remain part of it. In this way, the distinction between part and whole is transcended in favour of a multi-valued logic.

> Just as life's transcendence, within the plane of life itself, of its current, delimited form constitutes more-life (although it is nevertheless the immediate, inescapable essence of life itself), so also its transcendence into the level of objective content, of logically autonomous and no longer vital meaning, constitutes more-than-life, which is inseparable from it and is the essence of spiritual life itself.
>
> *(Simmel, [1918] 2010, p. 16)*

Simmel was aware of the logical challenges when he wrote: 'Life finds its essence, its process, in being more-life and more-than-life; its positive is as such already its comparative' (Simmel, [1918] 2010, p. 17). He meets the logical challenge in the following way:

> This self-alienation of life, this confronting of itself in an autonomous form, can only appear as a contradiction when a rigid boundary is established between its within and its without, as though they were two self-centered substances, rather than conceiving of it as a continuous movement whose unity at every point is divided into those opposing directions only by the spatial symbolism of our expression.
>
> *(Simmel, [1918] 2010, p. 16)*

Life makes an 'axial rotation' (*Achsendrehung*) (Simmel, [1918] 2010, p. 25), revolving around itself and at the same time transcending itself. This view is based on a threefold concept of transcendence. In the first sense, transcendence encompasses vital processes beyond conventions and routines. There is no life without established, fixed forms. However, the transcendence of 'more-than-life' repeatedly explodes these forms. The second meaning of transcendence refers to the constitution of ideal worlds. Life constantly generates contents that are objectified, but which in turn have an effect on vital processes. The third meaning of transcendence refers to religion as a special domain that consists of dogmas and institutions. Through 'the turning point of form out of its vital and into its ideal validity' (Simmel, [1918] 2010, p. 26), the particular objective forms of life 'are now the dominant ones, they absorb the stuff of life and it must yield to them' (Simmel, [1918] 2010, p. 25 f.). According to Simmel, the 'axial rotation' can best be studied with regard to religion:

> Here perhaps more completely than anywhere else has occurred the rotation around forms that life produces in itself in order to give its contents *immediate* context and warmth, depth and value. Now, however, these forms have become strong enough no longer to be defined by these contents, but rather to define purely of themselves; the object shaped by them, corresponding to their no longer finite measure, can now take charge of life.
>
> *(Simmel, [1918] 2010, p. 54)*

Consequently, the specifically religious mode of transcendence transcends the other modes of transcendence.

Simmel's distinction between individual and society, freedom and social attachment, objective and subjective culture, the specific and the general, process and form, etc. find their most general expression in the distinction between the relative and the absolute. Both refer to one another. Their unity denotes the concept of 'absolute life' (Simmel, [1918] 2010, p. 16). All vital processes take place as single events that oscillate between the two poles of the relative and the absolute (Figure 20.4).

The first rotation occurs through transcendence as more-life; the second rotation through transcendence as more-than-life in the shape of ideal forms that emerge from vital processes. They lead a life of their own, but also have an effect on the life processes – for example, by shaping one's way of life through fostering certain habits. Ideal forms are relative entities because they compete with one another with respect to their own claims to rationality. Each form creates an entire world and has, in principle, the capacity to absorb everything in life. The movement of the ideal forms towards the absolute and their effects on the process enables life to move between the relative and the absolute. Every single event and every individual life is a punctualization within the three-dimensional space of life oscillating between the relative and the absolute.

As previously noted, Simmel considers religion to be perhaps the best example of axial rotation. As his writings on religion show, the relationship between the soul and

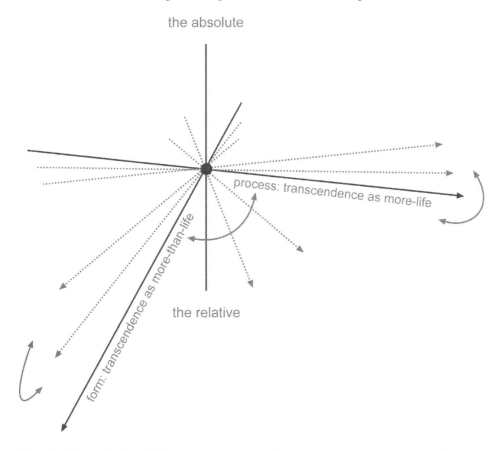

Figure 20.4 The oscillation of life

God is a religious symbolization of the abstract relation between the relative and the absolute. As an idealized form, religion can retroactively affect a religiously determined life as an 'immanent transcendence' and mediate the paradox between the relative and the absolute (Figure 20.5).

Religion oscillates between the relative, symbolized by the soul, and the absolute, symbolized by God. The axial rotation takes place through the objectification of religion, which then affects the religiously determined life. However, Simmel doubts 'whether the religiosity of *average types* can in fact make a turn from the substance of the heaven of gods and the transcendent "facts"; a turn towards shaping life itself in a religious way' (GSG 14, p. 383). Despite these reservations, Simmel diagnoses a tendency of religion towards a 'radical turn', which would like to offer undeniable religious energies

> another form of activity and, so to speak, utilization, as the creation of transcendent structures and the relationship to them – and which will perhaps restore the metaphysical value to the religious existence of the soul, which has released it from itself and yet also lives within it as *its* life.
>
> *(GSG 14, p. 384)*

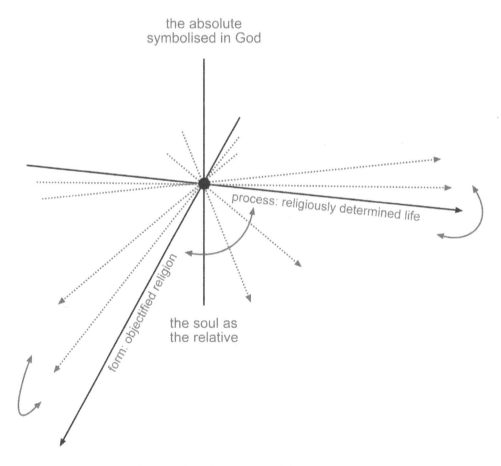

Figure 20.5 The oscillation between objectified religion and the religiously determined life

The axial rotation leads to a religiosity beyond objectified religion, to an 'immanent transcendence'. Whether religion has a future in this transformation remains to be seen.

References

Krech, V. (1998). *Georg Simmels Religionstheorie*. Tübingen: Mohr Siebeck.

Landmann, M. (1987). Einleitung. In M. Landmann (Ed.), *Das individuelle Gesetz: Philosophische Exkurse* [Neuausgabe mit einem Nachwort von Klaus Christian Köhnke] (pp. 7–29). Frankfurt a.m.: Suhrkamp.

Rammstedt, O. (1995). Soziologie und/oder Kulturwissenschaft. Georg Simmels theoretische Zugänge zum Gesellschaftlichen. In B. Schäfers (Ed.), *Soziologie in Deutschland: Entwicklung, Institutionalisierung und Berufsfelder, Theoretische Kontroversen* (pp. 99–107). Opladen: Leske + Budrich.

Simmel, G. ([1898] 1997b). A Contribution to the sociology of religion. In *Essays on religion* [Edited and translated by Horst Jürgen Helle in collaboration with Ludwig Nieder. Foreword by P. E. Hammond] (pp. 101–120). New Haven, CT: Yale University Press.

Simmel, G. ([1900] 2004). *The philosophy of money* [Translated by T. Bottomore & D. Frisby from a first draft by Kaethe Mengelberg] (3rd ed.). London and New York: Routledge.

Simmel, G. ([1902] 1997c). Contributions to the epistemology of religion. In *Essays on religion* [Edited and translated by H. J. Helle in collaboration with L. Nieder. Foreword by P. E. Hammond] (pp. 121–133). New Haven, CT: Yale University Press.

Simmel, G. ([1903] 1997e). On the salvation of the soul. In *Essays on religion* [Edited and translated by H. J. Helle in collaboration with L. Nieder. Foreword by P. E. Hammond] (pp. 29–35). New Haven, CT: Yale University Press.

Simmel, G. ([1908] 1997d). On the essence of culture. In D. Frisby & M. Featherstone (Eds.), *Simmel on culture: Selected writings* (pp. 40–45). London: Sage.

Simmel, G. ([1908] 2009). *Sociology: Inquiries into the construction of social forms*. 2 Volumes [Translated and edited by A. J. Blasi, A. K. Jacobs & M. Kanjirathinkal. With an introduction by H. J. Helle]. Leiden and Boston, MA: Brill.

Simmel, G. ([1911] 1997a). The concept and tragedy of culture. In D. Frisby & M. Featherstone (Eds.), *Simmel on culture: Selected writings* (pp. 55–75). London: Sage.

Simmel, G. ([1911] 1997g). The problem of religion today. In *Essays on religion* [Edited and translated by H. J. Helle in collaboration with L. Nieder. Foreword by P.p E. Hammond] (pp. 7–19). New Haven, CT: Yale University Press.

Simmel, G. ([1912/1906] 1997f). Religion. In *Essays on religion* [Edited and translated by Horst Jürgen Helle in collaboration with L. Nieder. Foreword by P. E. Hammond] (pp. 137–214). New Haven, CT: Yale University Press.

Simmel, G. ([1918] 2010). *The view of life: Four metaphysical essays, with journal aphorisms* [Translated by J. A. Y. Andrews & D. N. Levine. With an introduction by D. N. Levine & D. Silver and an appendix, 'Journal Aphorisms, with an Introduction', edited, translated, and with an introduction by J. A. Y. Andrews]. Chicago, IL and London: University of Chicago Press.

21

GEORG SIMMEL

War, nation, and Europe

Patrick Watier

Introduction[1]

Simmel's war writings put their readers in an unusual situation. What is their status? Are they just isolated remarks, unrelated to his sociological and philosophical works? Or are they somehow connected to these? If so, how? Simply confronting the work will not settle the question. On the one hand, the letters and texts that deal directly with the war suggest that the personal experience shared by many intellectuals and artists gave a particular colour to their cultural pessimism, and to the paths to salvation they imagined. On the other, they suggest that such experience reinforced a personal aspiration towards a sense of the collective and a concern with membership in a body which exceeded any individual, invoking a new man which the war had forged and brought into the world.

I approach these different components on three levels. The first is Simmel's correspondence, where they find immediate expression. They take a less emotive, less personal form in the texts published in *Der Krieg und die geistigen Entscheidungen* (GSG 16, pp. 7-58). The first of these levels therefore involves Simmel's personal experience, while the second involves what we must recognise as propaganda. The third level consists of academic texts, some written long before the war, some just prior to its outbreak, and some as it was still ongoing. These include *The philosophy of money* (GSG 6) and *Das individuelle Gesetz* (GSG 12, pp. 417-470).

How are we to understand both Simmel's nationalist exultation, which never descends to jingoism, and the hope he places in Europe as a community which would once again open its doors to its prodigal son when the war was over? For there could be no Europe without Germany, Simmel thought, and it may even have had a distinct and unique role within it, as Nietzsche's 'good European'.

Like others, Simmel's individual experience took on a religious cast. He left his self behind – an ecstasy which gave him the sense of being immediately one with every other person, of living history rather than being its product. In his *Diaries*, Musil describes this as the 'great experience' (Musil, 1981, p. 419).

The correspondence

We encounter such a feeling in Simmel's correspondence,[2] which offers an intimate expression of his lived experience of the situation. A first example comes in a letter written on 8 August 1914, to Hugo Lippman, a psychiatrist and philosopher who, with his wife Agathe, had been friends with the Simmels since 1907:

> I have the feeling that the German people is going to deploy power which has never reached so far in the history of the world. I believe each person must feel that *an absolute situation is present*, of the sort encountered only rarely in existence – a situation in which relativities and dependencies no longer matter. It is a phenomenal and quite new experience.
>
> *(GSG 23, p. 365)*

The tone is set. All of Simmel's writings on the beginning of the conflict use the same register, combining enthusiasm and terror – particularly since those living in Strasbourg could sometimes hear artillery fire in the distance, the fortifications on the border were under siege, and there was no traffic except for military vehicles. Letters provided the only link with the outside world. On 9 August, a week after the beginning of hostilities with France, Simmel wrote to his old friend Margarete von Bendemann, whose pen name was Margarete Susman:

> It's a whole new experience when a people, 65 million strong, from the Kaiser down to the proletarian's child, is faced with the question of whether to be or not to be. Everything I experienced up to this date as distress now seems flimsy and insubstantial in comparison. There is no space in the present moment for any mention of individual fate. But I believe that, as a result, the force of the people will be deployed in a way that global history has yet to experience ... If we survive this war, we will in a radical sense be new men.
>
> *(GSG 23, p. 367)*

He wrote to von Bendemann again on 22 August:

> Yes, these are great and terrible days: life is now settled on an entirely new foundation, whose breadth and depth I had not understood before. It is inconceivable that it could return to its former condition of naïveté in our lifetimes. It is an entirely new experience to feel the heat of the whole cultural world's destiny as entirely personal – no longer as a part, but as both absolutely insignificant and at the same time as the bearer of the whole and of each fragment.
>
> *(GSG 23, p. 372)*

But Simmel soon felt sharply just how unbearable the war's consequences were. In another letter to Agathe and Hugo Lippman on 23 March 1915, he used two stories to illustrate the situation's catastrophic nature. One is closer to our topic: he asked if they had heard of Péguy,

> a young French writer who is producing the deepest sort of work, among the best being done today.

His writing has been translated by a *Privatdozent* from Strasbourg, Stadler, who I met one summer – a very interesting, deeply human man. The two found themselves twenty meters away from each other in the trenches. Stadler sent a note across the lines which Péguy couldn't read or understand. But he responded: *Mon ami je ne vous comprends pas, mais je vous aime* [My friend, I can't understand you, but I love you]. And a few days later both of them were killed. I don't know any other example or anecdote [*Einzelheit*] that provides such a complete symbol of what is truly unbearable about this war.

(GSG 23, p. 507)

Se non è vero è ben trovato, perhaps, but the example is a very good illustration of the suicide being committed by a Europe of culture and spirit. This is undoubtedly how Simmel came to write 'The Idea of Europe' (GSG 13, pp. 112-116). Before doing so, however, he defended the German nation and the German people. One last example from his correspondence shows this explicitly. Simmel simply saw the antagonisms of the period's culture as a dead end, and felt that the effervescent sense of a new beginning – which was undeniably present on both sides – promised a new relationship and connection between form and content, the birth of a new life. In a letter to Marianne Weber on 14 August 1914, he wrote:

What is unique in the present moment is that finally, at last and once and for all, the needs of the present and of the Idea are one and the same. This can only really be experienced intuitively or, far better, in practice. Lukács has not had this experience, and one cannot demonstrate it to him. He therefore sees militarism everywhere – whereas we see it as liberation rather than militarism, because the former strips the latter of its self-sufficiency (characteristic of it in peacetime), making it a form and means of the total exultation of life.

(GSG 23, p. 422)

A less exalted mind might remark that there were, surely, more appropriate ways to manifest life's potential than in the 'great butchery' of war. Words lose their precise sense here. Simmel had claimed that war serves the vital flux, and that a new German and a new man would emerge with a fresh awareness of the fundamental values: food, courage, skilfulness, *élan vital*. This was the only reason

that the soldier, at least when engaged in vigorous action, feels this action to be an enormous increase in the quantity of life, so to speak, and to be in more direct proximity to its surging dynamism than he is able to feel in his usual working activities.

(GSG 16, p. 50)

But what appears just as clearly in this letter to Marianne Weber is that, once the tragedy of culture is surpassed and idea and reality were no longer two unconnected parts of the same fabric, the eternal conflict between life and form would be resolved, and there would be a reconciliation between 'the need to love what is, because as such it is nonetheless the reality of the Idea – and the need to hate it, because being reality it cannot be the Idea as such' (GSG 23, p. 422).

The wartime texts

The wartime texts reflect an 'absolute situation' – a term Simmel used, Susman notes, to describe the period, one that also requires absolute decisions.

Among Simmel's wartime writings, I shall focus especially on his short book *Der Krieg und die geistigen Entscheidungen* (GSG 16, pp. 7-58), dedicated to his friends in Strasbourg, which reproduces a lecture Simmel gave in the hall of the Aubette in Strasbourg on 7 November 1914. The lecture was part of the *Strassburger Reden zum Weltkrieg*, which were delivered by professors at the University of Strasbourg and published by Trübner in 1915. The book also contains '*Die Dialektik des deutschen Geistes*' (GSG 13, pp. 224-230), originally published in the newspaper *Der Tag* on 28 September 1916, 'The crisis of culture' (GSG 13, pp. 190-201), a lecture given in Vienna in 1916, and finally 'The idea of Europe' (GSG 13, pp. 112-116), which exists in two versions, from 1915 and 1917. Issues discussed in *Philosophy of Money* recur emphatically in these texts, sometimes implicitly and sometimes explicitly, as in 'The crisis of culture'. It is as though the war had led Simmel to re-evaluate certain descriptions of ways of living, and to devalue others. There had been a balance between critical and positive elements in *Philosophy of Money*, and issues involved in the monetary economy had interacted: growth in individual liberty, Simmel argued, had brought with it a growth in indifference, and the emergence of the multifaceted personality and its individualisation had established new relationships between individuality and society conceived as a totality. But now only the negative elements were retained: the pursuit of wealth, world-weariness, and cynicism. Only the firm spiritual decision symbolised by war offered a way out.

Simmel believed that, with the war, he had discovered and witnessed with his own eyes a life-sized *analogon* of that which Weber could (rightly, in general) perceive only very mutedly in modern society: 'a prophetic pneuma, which in former times swept through the great communities like a firebrand, welding them together' (Weber, 1946, p. 155). In other words, his themes were the relationship between community and society, the meaning of the relationship between individuals and the whole, and, in Durkheim's terms, the role of social effervescence in the constitution of social wholes. Simmel believed a new man would emerge from this maelstrom.

This question of the role of effervescence in the constitution, consolidation, and perpetuation of social connections is fundamental in the sociological tradition. Simmel was faced with precisely such an experience. As his assistant Hauter reports, 'Simmel saw war as a life achievement' (Becher, 1984, p. 5): the war enabled the consolidation of a nation's life in the face of danger. As Hauter also remarks, such a view of enthusiasm was associated with Berlin; Simmel might have thought differently if he had been living in Strasbourg for longer.

These great themes converged in two texts by Simmel, '*Bergson und der deutsche "Zynismus"*' (GSG 17, pp. 121–123) and '*Deutschlands innere Wandlung*' (GSG 15, pp. 271–285). As we will see, the two appeared in quick succession, indicating that their contents were closely related. Simmel believed his generation was faced with a choice: 'To rebuild a life in a new atmosphere and on new hypotheses or, if we lack the strength, to return to indecision and survival' (GSG 16, p. 13). Most important in this internal change was the feeling of a new whole, a collective being which lay between individual and nation. It is as though Simmel was reintroducing his thoughts about the role of conflict in giving groups cohesion and self-awareness. In a sense, events had confirmed his theory.

What lots of us perhaps knew theoretically – that, in individual existence, the individual himself possesses only a small portion which is truly individual – does not receive any clear and differentiated awareness in times of calm, because in such moments the sole things that prevail are those which differentiate men: practical interests and activities.

(GSG 16, p. 14)

This shared foundation appears in situations of disturbance and shock, when the almost spatial separation between the shared and the individual disappears: the individual becomes part of everything and feels himself responsible for everything. That is why life had become so grand and weighty: 'each thought and feeling is attached to a supra-individual totality' (GSG 16, p. 15). A solution to the problem of relations between the all-embracing community and the individual lay in the meaningful social space around them. Such unity would put an end to the period of disorientation: the individual and the general would interpenetrate at each point, producing a unity of life. Individual life would be filled with totality, and social unity would be fixed in place by the sense of a new life and of having experienced a historic turning point. This is clearly just a wartime translation of an existing discourse of cultural pessimism, one we will see further illustrated by Simmel's criticism of the rise of mammonism in the moments leading up to the war (Watier, 1991). Returning to a simplified version of the themes in *Philosophy of Money*, Simmel emphasised the role played by money, which had become not just the means for acquiring commodities, but an ultimate value and an end in itself. Money enables the realisation of psychological desires, and is an adequate and convenient means for fulfilling the demands of everyday existence. Mammonism, however, involves a further step: Simmel says that it is an elevation of such phenomena to the metaphysical and objective level, where the deepest danger lies. In 'The turn toward ideas', the second chapter of the *View of Life* (GSG 16, pp. 236-296), he described the wholly negative consequences of the new power of the monetary economy, which, in Chapter 4 of *Philosophy of Money*, was still counterbalanced by the increasing individual liberty that accompanied it. It is not so much the means by which the economy operates (including money) which are fundamental – means that can become ends. Rather, there may occur no change in principle whatever; all thereby remains in the same level and only changes the psychological accents. But the complete rotation through which the economy really becomes a world unto itself surely does arise as soon as it becomes a process occurring according to purely objective, material-technical regularities and forms, a process for which living persons are only bearers, agents of the norms immanent to it and necessary on its account; and the owner and manager are, no differently from the labourers and errand-boys, slaves of the production process. The violent logic of its development does not depend on the will of the subjects, nor on the meanings and necessities of their lives. The economy now goes its necessary way, entirely as though men were there for its sake, but not it for the sake of man (GSG 16, p. 293).

Simmel had emphasised the importance of intermediary groups, and the key role of their intertwining for individual liberty and the development of culture. He had been a relativist, emphasising the positive and negative consequences of phenomena. But now he had allowed himself to be seduced by a simple opposition between part and whole, between individual and society. Society was no longer all those forms of association which allowed for the growth of public spirit, the nation-state, conceived as a community – a community which, as we will see, was not all-embracing towards individuals. At present, these individuals were pursuing goals which exceeded them, and which freed them from all the torments of modernity.

The *Petit Parisien* carried remarks by Bergson attacking the cynicism underlying Germany's entry into the war, which he saw as the sign of a return to barbarism. In an article in the *Strassburger Post* (Nov. 1914), Simmel returned to the argument he had made on 7 November in 'Deutschlands innere Wandlung' (GSG 15, pp. 271–285), that the war had instead enabled a break with cynicism. Simmel had corresponded politely with Bergson, and had introduced him in Germany – something Bergson, who himself had helped Simmel's work to be published in France, thanked him for in June. While feeling he had to respond to Bergson, Simmel could now see the world only through a prism Margarete Susman described as totally unreal – one characteristic of the approach of many German intellectuals.

The mutual misunderstanding is clear. Like Durkheim, Bergson condemned the invasion of Belgium and Germany's disregard for treaties as cynical. Simmel demonstrated how far dialogue had become impossible: he immediately deployed his own critique of cynicism and world-weariness, which operated on an entirely different level, to argue that Bergson did not understand the German situation. Simmel was thinking of the cynical conception associated with the monetary economy: 'We are reproached for our cynicism, but this age's primary signature is precisely the rejection of all cynicism' (GSG 17, p. 12). The argument unfolds on a different plane, one having nothing to do with fact. Like Bouglé, what Bergson called cynicism were the policies of two prey empires (*empires de proie*) which disregarded treaties, popular will, and the principle of nationalities. 'Belgium may have claimed to remain "neutral and loyal", but a sneering Germany walked all over its body' (Bouglé, 1918, p. 13). The Manifesto of the Ninety-Three justified the action by a policy of prevention: if we hadn't done it, the Allies would have been happy to do so instead (Fulda et al. ([1914] 1985). In Simmel's view, Bergson had failed to understand that

> the German form of existence had been thrown into the crucible, and that was the strongest motivation behind this incredible shock, even in the first moments of the conflict – the recasting people experienced was far stronger than any political danger or any danger associated with the war.
>
> *(GSG 17, p. 122)*

The central enemy was defined ideologically, both in 'Bergson und der deutsche "Zynismus"' and 'Deutschlands innere Wandlung': it was mammonism, the worship of Mammon. Any pride in the individual or the class disappeared with the war – a pride for which the idea of the whole had become chimerical, and even the joy-giving aestheticisation of existence had disappeared. Simmel wrote that 'those roots and fruit associated with cynicism have now been extirpated from the German image of life – which is worth a single phrase: *après nous le déluge*' (GSG 17, p. 123).

Ultimately, the liberty the world seemed to provide was a useless one. And it was all the more to be condemned because of its attachment to cynicism and world-weariness. What appeared most clearly was the sovereignty of a generalised equivalence of signs, values, objects, and ideas circulating in modern communication and culture without any fixed point, and the disappearance of virtue. The centre of the knot was duty, a form of decency or politeness towards oneself. It seems to me, then, that Simmel's discourse on war and his article with reference to the *Petit Parisien* show how he in turn abandoned the yes and the no, refusal and acquiescence. Instead, as he himself signalled in his chapter on conflict in *Soziologie*, he allowed himself to be wholly taken over by the war. War was the only conflict which seized the whole content of existence, submitting it to its sole sovereignty in order to transform life – life which should in some unknown way become other, resolve this atmosphere, and dissolve this moment where, for any action, we are always presented with conflicting motivations, one after the other. Simmel's critique of the current way of living recalls *Untimely Meditations*, where Nietzsche argues that the present is the site of an 'sacred coercion' which no longer allows us to compromise or to be invaded by a historicist awareness, which has become weakened by understanding everything (Nietzsche, [1873] 1964, pp. 266, 334). The comprehension of power is now substituted for the power of comprehension.

It was as though the war had made clear that the problem of knowledge should make room for the problem of life – a life, one could be confident, would give birth to the new, and whose mark was 'patriotic' enthusiasm. Simmel's Strasbourg lecture is explicit about history: whereas, in *Untimely Meditations*, Nietzsche gave a historical formulation of the problem of the meaning of living, Simmel believes that we are situated at that point where our conscience knows 'that we are truly living history' (*dass wir jetzt wirklich* Geschichte *erleben*), rather than simply being produced by it (GSG 16, p. 16).

The background of cultural criticism

Simmel relied on elements of cultural criticism from his earlier writing, particularly *Philosophy of money* (GSG 6). By simplifying the stakes, war would now give meaning back to the ultimate goals, and the relationship between ends and means would no longer be lost in the infinite. Simmel was consciously helping to legitimate the state of war by giving the conflict a meaning for Germany. He argued that France had an idea, revenge, which acted as its central value, giving it a distinctive force and unity and, in a sense, an immediate advantage. Similarly, in 1870, Germans had had the idea of their national unity to defend. But what was there in Simmel's day? He gave a historical reconstruction of the current situation: in 1870, the external enemy provided the means to unite Germany economically; now, it was the means to unite the same community spiritually. The ruling idea forged in and by this war therefore had to be the defence of, and participation in, this developing spiritual community from which the new man would emerge. The text's emphasis on the importance of firm decisions contrasts with a passage in his chapter on Rodin in *Philosophische Kultur*. There, Simmel discussed the shift from the spirit of the Renaissance, characterised by 'an oscillation between melancholy and drunkenness, between cowardice and courage, between faith and unbelief', with each of these positions remaining substantial and *sui generis*, to the modern spirit, characterised by a 'simultaneity of yes and no, rather than an alternation between yes and no' (GSG 19, p. 256). Simmel's lively, positive description of the charms of modern fluidity had transformed into its opposite. Uncertainty was finally coming to an end; we must take a decision and hold to it, and stop playing games with reality.

In this sense, the war placed the individual in an absolute situation in which uncertainty was impossible. The war effort meant that the firm and certain will had to discard all that fluidity which seemed to provide modernity with its distinctive charm. In 'Deutschlands innere Wandlung', Simmel wrote:

> I dare to put forward the claim that most of us have only now experienced was we could call an absolute situation. All the circumstances in which we typically functioned had something relative about them, and presupposed deliberations to be made between more and less, which were conditioned by one side and the other. There is no more question of this now. We are … facing absolute decision, in

which there is no more oscillation between sacrifice and gain, when and but, no more compromise, no more quantitative point of view.

(*GSG 16, p. 22*)

The situation was interpreted in terms of victory, of what truly mattered compared to the softness of peacetime. It is striking how far the same themes recur, in a more intellectualised form, in 'The Crisis of Culture' (GSG 13, pp. 190–201). Simmel's support for the war was explicit in the Strasbourg lecture. His position in 'The Crisis' is less clear-cut, but the arguments are the same: money finally becomes a means and self-preservation is put in service of a higher end rather than being the ultimate goal – in short, the normal hierarchy of ends and means is re-established.

Studying Germany's past enabled Simmel to present a hypothesis he claimed to be explanatory, located between the modern man, the one we know, and a new and different man: we do not yet know what he will be like, but he will deliver us from the antinomies of the modern soul. Modernity had created man, but this man was only a figure, a content to be replaced, establishing a new relationship between form and content in which the links between part and whole, individual and general, would be reworked. In this sense, a shift was occurring from the modern man to a new one, with the latter corresponding – like Rousseau's natural man – to a new conception, to an *idea*. War became the means leading to this new man. The conditions and symbol of this search lay in the fact that only in this war had 'our people finally become a unity and a totality, and it is as such that we have crossed the threshold of a new Germany' (GSG 16, p. 29).

Turning the question towards the domain of culture: what about the aim and possibility of appropriating the cultural labour of previous generations? What vision of the future would this serve? The bridge linking past and future was collapsing under the pressure of goals which were already being renewed, but the appropriation of what had already been surpassed had not taken place. Furthermore, the precedence of means over ends was a product of technique, and provided us with a connection to technique and its autonomous development. It is clear that the events of the present were being analysed against a background of philosophical-cultural interpretation. In '*Die Dialektik des deutschen Geistes*' (GSG 13, pp. 224–230), Simmel referred explicitly to his book *Rembrandt*, where he had described the Latin and German minds (GSG 15, 305-515). Exploring '*Die Einheitsart der religiösen Bilder*' in *Rembrandt*, Simmel had expressed his idea of the relationship between individual and society, noting that the sociology of Rembrandt's group paintings poses 'a subtle problem' (GSG 15, p. 466). Usually, when several people are grouped together in a frame, we feel a unity superior to, and irreducible to, the sum of its parts. The state is something other than the sum of its citizens, and the will of a totality is something more than the composition of individual wills: we are dealing here with a unity located beyond its particular components. By contrast, as Simmel had already shown for 'The Night Watch', in Rembrandt's painting:

unity weaves itself immediately out of the living spheres of the individual acting persons ... it is not an autonomously all-embracing whole mingling the figures, as it were, merely as limbs. This applies to the religious painting, too ... [T]his mood has its origin entirely in the individual, the unity of the whole stemming exclusively from the combined effect of these purely personal spheres easily realised in their substantial equality. The whole remains bound to the personal elements in their individuality, and their unity demands no reduction of the latter ... [Rembrandt] requires no levelling reduction or elevation of the persons because from the start, they all live in the same mood.

(GSG15, p. 466 f.)

This idea was initially expressed about painting, but could now apply to the enthusiasm of August 1914, seen as the representation of an ideal unity where each person was immediately connected to the others.

Simmel was clear that the foundations of these thoughts on the crisis of culture – which belong to cultural history and the philosophy of culture – had been laid in *Philosophy of money*. He raised doubts about the growth of technique, 'which leaves us bogged down in a web of means and means of means' (GSG 13, p. 190). At the same time, he hoped that, through soldiers' experience of it, the war will create closer links between the individual and the whole, and so a *form* of reconciliation – 'the relationship between party and whole … between *cause* and *person*' (GSG 13, p. 194). His conclusion was to reject those periods where there is no distinction between the unimportant and the essential. Such periods had lost their significance: it was necessary to align oneself clearly with the defence of a Germany which was no longer the old Germany, but the one being constructed in these decisive moments, and whose signs – like enthusiasm or ration tickets, which put a vital question front and centre – showed that final ends had once again assumed the cardinal position they should never have lost.

If we agree with Dumont (Dumont, 1983, p. 130 f.), who argues that societies in which individualism plays a major role have difficulty lending consistency to a representation of their 'intra- and inter-social unity', the question becomes even more pressing for supranational groups. This is the very problem Europe faces today, which neither economics nor a sort of European constitutional patriotism seems able to resolve. In other words: what is the fundamental idea?

The idea of Europe

I admit here that, while I can understand the collective enthusiasm, I have a far harder time grasping the 'predestination through perversion', to quote the historian Heinrich Winkler, (Winkler, 2006, p. 585) which saw the construction of Europe as Germany's special mission. The text 'The Idea of Europe', which had two versions – the second, from 1917 (GSG 16, pp. 54–58), is slightly shorter than the first, from 1915 (GSG 13, pp. 112–116) – remains to some extent enigmatic. This theme is not exclusive to Simmel, having been developed by others, including the painter Franz Marc.

We should begin with a point of terminology. The idea of Europe is a concept of a whole which surpasses any possible experience. Simmel relies here on Kant, who defines 'idea' as follows: 'by the idea of a necessary concept of reason, I understand one to which no congruent object can be given in the senses' (Kant, [1781] 1998, p. 402).

This idea has no definite content and cannot be defined logically. It is a historical idea, corresponding to an effort to move towards the spiritual values of the past and the present. The idea of Europe is inseparable from the cultural values which, Simmel argued, were still revered by the man of culture in his own time. It is a specific dialectic between individual national life and the ideal site of common values produced by national beings. What is still worth thinking about in Simmel's text, beyond the conditions under which it was produced, is the tension it identifies in the production of an idea which lies beyond the particularities of individual nations, but which nonetheless draws from each one, and which resolutely refuses any internationalism. Indeed, internationalism can be characterised as an abstraction of many nations in which 'each renounces its own value'. Applying the schema of *Bildung*, we could say that Europe as Idea is the conquest of a cosmos of spiritual values: in each instance, it is the individual journey each person makes towards Europe on the basis of their own national being, and by which they are transformed. Such a process is not free from crisis or conflict. *Bildung* is part of the vital process of a spiritual entity, a human person, a society, a historical tradition. It does not involve an educator transmitting information, but instead a conflictual process, through what Hegel calls experience, in which a spiritual being discovers its own identity and seeks to actualise this through the process of discovery. It corresponds to a particular complex of spiritual goods revered by the man of culture, and is distinct, for instance, from the Greco-Roman spirit of Antiquity or the Christian civilisation of the Middle Ages.

The second version of 'The Idea of Europe' is more measured about responsibility for the war, which is no longer simply produced by Germany's enemies, but is now attributed to 'the blindness and criminal frivolity of a minority of men across Europe'. In this sense, the work is better aligned with the hope for reconciliation expressed in its conclusion. Even setting aside the critique of internationalism as an abstraction, the text has many grey areas. It is supposed to be a plea for Germany and Austria to return to the whole they form a part of. But in what sense is Germany so distinctive that it is destined to show Europe the way? Since at least Fichte, the idea that the human race in Germany possessed a distinctive capacity for founding new institutions had developed in opposition to French universalism. We find traces of this in Simmel's text. As conceived by its intellectuals, Germany was a regenerative force in the world.

But if it was a matter of Germany's being finding a complement in its other, and if Germany was unique among its kind, it is difficult to see how this European culture – not just a treasure, but a project providing new configurations and new arrangements – could develop. Marc gave a good illustration of the sort of circular argument which gave Germany a cardinal place:

> We, the Germans, should avoid nothing with greater passion than narrowness of heart and of national will. They will ruin everything for us. He who has control will receive: it is by this motto alone that we will keep our place as spiritual victors and will be the first Europeans. The next type of European will be the German one, but the German must first of all become a good European.
>
> *(Marc, 1978, p. 160)*

Towards the end of his life, on 20 May 1918, in a letter to Gertrud Kantorowicz, Simmel asked: 'How long will this insane suicide last? … [E]verything the war seemed to promise has long since disappeared, and the final outcome will be American domination, a shift in global power westwards' (GSG 23, p. 960). The same theme appears in a letter to Keyserling on 25 March 1918, where Simmel wrote that America, the *tertius gaudens*, would undoubtedly emerge as the conflict's great victor. Civilisation would triumph over culture. He believed the final hope could be discerned in the passionate desire, within the youth movement, for the spiritual to take on life and for life to become spiritual. This movement was in some sense the bearer of this aspiration towards the new man, and Simmel bestowed on it the task of overthrowing bourgeoisism, the restricted values of the bourgeoisie. Beyond the lived experience they contain and their well-founded remarks about Europe's suicide, it may be that these texts, despite appearances, demonstrate an extraordinary denial of reality: as Otto Baumgarten would say, they are *wirklichkeitsfremd*; as Susman would say, they are *unwirklich*. Susman also offers us a plausible key to understanding why this is the case. Germany had appeared to Jewish intellectuals not just as a home, but as that very homeland they had longed for, and their sincere patriotism was connected to this sense of belonging (Susman, 1958, p. 290). As Simmel said, he ascribed qualities to Germany, and loved it as a person.

And, in this moment of patriotic exultation, what was and has always been sharpest in Simmel's method – the illumination it provided in many dimensions, its succession of conditioning and conditioned points of view – was lost.

Notes

1 Translated by Mark Cadenza. Unless otherwise specified, all English quotes are the author's translation.
2 All references to Simmel's correspondence are to Simmel, G. (2008). *Briefe, 1912–1918*. Otthein and Angela Rammstedt (Eds.) (*Gesamtausgabe* vol. 23). Frankfurt am Main: Suhrkamp.

References

Becher, Heribert (1984). Georg Simmel in Strassburg. *Sociologia Internationalis*, *22*(5), 3–17.

Bouglé, Célestin (1918). *Dans le 'secteur' de Jeanne d'Arc: Conférence faite à une ambulance en Lorraine*. Paris and Neuchatel: Attinger Frères.

Dumont, Louis (1983). *Essais sur l'individualisme*. Paris: Seuil.

Fulda, Ludwig, Reicke, Georg, Riehl, Alois, & Sudermann, Hermann ([1914] 1985). Aufruf an die Kulturwelt. In W. M. Calder & H. Flashar, III & Th. Lindken (Eds.), *Wilamowitz nach fünfzig Jahren* (p. 718). Darmstadt: Wissenschaftliche Buchgesellschaft.

Kant, Immanuel ([1781] 1998). *Critique of pure reason* [trans. and ed. Paul Guyer and Allen W. Wood]. Cambridge: Cambridge University Press.

Marc, Franz (1978). *Schriften*. Köln: DuMont.

Musil, Robert (1981). *Journaux*. Tome 1. Paris: Seuil.

Nietzsche, Friedrich ([1873] 1964). *Considérations inactuelles – Unzeitgemässe Betrachtungen* I–II, Collection bilingue. Paris: Aubier Montaigne.

Susman, Margarete (1958). Erinnerung an Simmel. In K. Gassen & M Landmann (Eds.), *Buch des Dankes an Georg Simmel. Briefe, Erinnerungen, Bibliographie* (pp. 278–291). Berlin: Duncker & Humblot.

Watier, Patrick (1991). The war writings of G. Simmel. *Theory, Culture & Society*, *8*(3), 219–233.

Weber, Max (1946). Science as a Vocation. In M. Weber, *From Max Weber: Essays in Sociology* (pp. 129–158). New York: Oxford University Press.

Winkler, Heinrich (2006). *Germany: The long road west. 1933–1990*. Oxford: Oxford University Press.

22

SIMMEL'S COSMOPOLITANISM

Austin Harrington

Undoubtedly, it is right to speak of Simmel as a 'cosmopolitan' thinker and indeed in some sense as a theorist of 'cosmopolitanism' in modern European social thought. As readers know well, Simmel is the author who writes unceasingly of reciprocity or *Wechselwirkung* between actors and identities in world history, of boundaries always crossed and blurred, of intersecting social circles, of 'bridges and doors', of money and money-analogues as sinews of communication between multiplex time-space locations, and famously of the figure of 'the stranger' as a constitutive moment of every putative community. As Simmel tells us in 'The Metropolis and Mental life' and *The philosophy of money*, modern social and economic exchange by means of money enables formal commonality and equality between interacting parties and at the same time also potentially unending differentiation of parties from one another (GSG 6, pp. 655-60; GSG 7, pp. 116-31; Simmel, 1978, pp. 470-74; 1997a). Global divisions of labour in world trade draw nations and groups inexorably into communication with one another and at the same time generate constantly shifting patterns of identity and selfhood. Modernising developments in the transformation of values from substantial to functional relations drive a process in which the 'greatest individualization' joins with the 'greatest extension of the circle', such that durable identities in Simmel's thinking emerge only in effects of constant social interaction and intersection (GSG 11, p. 843; Simmel, 2009, p. 640 f.).

Yet one issue arises in this thematisation that requires some clarification – which is namely that in the relatively few places in which Simmel explicitly deploys the term 'cosmopolitanism' and its cognates (*Kosmopolitismus, kosmopolitisch, Weltbürgertum, weltbürgerlich*), his tone of writing is in fact largely hostile. It is true that in the passage in which Simmel refers famously to the metropolis as the 'seat of cosmopolitanism', as well as in the passages of the final chapter of *Sociology* of 1908 in which he links Stoic cosmopolitan values to the 'extension of the group and the formation of individuality', his tone is positive – or at least neutral (GSG 7, p. 126; GSG 11, pp. 814-16; Simmel, 1997a, p. 181, 2009, p. 640 f.). However, in the few significant value-laden instances in which he draws on these terms, he does so in his writings from the years of the First World War in the context of an attack on attitudes to life that most of his readers at this time would have associated with the political cultures and worldviews of Germany's enemies after 1914 – namely Britain, France, and America. In both 'The Idea of Europe' from March 1915 and the lightly revised version of this essay he published in 1917, Simmel uses the term *Weltbürgertum* essentially synonymously with the term 'internationalism' (*Internationalismus*) and quite pointedly gives the reader to understand that by the latter he means in practice, in one respect, international socialism and, in another respect also, the emerging concept and plan for a League of Nations, as promulgated during the war largely in Britain and famously towards its end by US President Woodrow Wilson. Here Simmel refers quite derisorily to both 'internationalism' and 'cosmopolitanism' as merely 'find-sounding names ... given to rootlessness in order to make men deaf to its reality' (GSG 16, p. 58; Simmel, 1976, p. 270). 'Internationalism', he writes, stands, at least 'in its grotesquely heightened form', for 'mere globetrotting ... a hotchpotch, a characterless, indiscriminate mêlée of interests and ideas, at most something abstracted from many nations by disregarding their particular individual values' (GSG 16, p. 55 f.; Simmel, 1976, p. 268 f.). And similarly in the essay entitled 'The Dialectic of the German Spirit', from 1916, Simmel declaims against any ethos of 'expanding the soul to all the world and finding nothing human alien to it' or 'thinking of the "world" like the globetrotter, in a washed-out exoticism, in a blind overvaluation of everything merely "different"' (GSG 13, p. 229; Simmel, 2007a, p. 69).

Unquestionably, these outbursts complicate our understanding of Simmel as a 'cosmopolitan' thinker. As is well-known, Simmel fell in line with the call to war in its early months after August 1914, and, like so many others of his world and milieu, including many German-Jewish writers from assimilated families, felt a passionate sense of identification with the sense of a war for German national *Kultur*. The war, he wrote in November 1914, had purged the Augean stables of commercialised society, flushing out everything effete and superfluous from the experience of life (GSG 15, pp. 271-85). The call to arms created an 'absolute situation', a sublime hour of reckoning that fused past, present and future time in a resolute experience of historicity (GSG 15, pp. 275, 279). Even as late as March 1918, in a letter to Hermann Graf Keyserling, Simmel affirmed that war would have to be fought 'not only for German power and economy' but most of all for 'the to-be or not-to-be of the German Spirit' (Simmel, 1968, p. 243).

Nonetheless, it is important to recognise that during the war Simmel also published several more reflective statements on nationhood and Europe, all of them suggestive of a more temperate political turn of his thinking in these years. For the most part, Simmel's apparent hostility to cosmopolitanism at this time needs to be set against the background of his thinking and career as a whole and read largely only as reacting negatively to what might be seen as certain 'thin', 'abstract' or hollowed-out appropriations of cosmopolitan discourse, void of a more sociologically honest and perspicuous sense of political, economic, and historical power-realities. In general, Simmel's positive ethical and political vision of cosmopolitanism can be construed as the view that while universalising normative values must be upheld against phenomena of particularistic group marginalisation and stigmatisation of minorities – including, notoriously, uses of the word 'cosmopolitan' as anti-Semitic code for Jewish financiers and intellectuals – cosmopolitanism must be steadfastly distinguished and valorised differently from any sense of an internationally dominant consensus of structures of elite power or from any kind of predominantly material mercantile culture of global lifestyle mobility or ethos of world trade.

This contribution addresses three interrelated foci of Simmel's statements in these connections. After a brief résumé of Simmel's statements on Germany, nationhood, and Europe from the war years, the discussion turns to his pronouncements on relations of Europe and America from the same period. A final part then moves to the wider sociological significance of Simmel's account of relations of the 'Germanic' and 'classical

Romanic' cultural worlds in European art history and literature since the Renaissance, as presented in his monograph of 1916 on Rembrandt and related essays. In each of these areas, the main proposal of this chapter is that in common with some of his contemporaries, including the two brothers Max and Alfred Weber and figures such as Max Scheler and Ernst Troeltsch and numerous literary personalities, Simmel can be seen as entertaining an idea of Europe as the cipher of a possible cosmopolitan community of nations, national cultures, and nation-states – but one that remains resistant to prospects of false or coercive assimilation of differences of regional life into common invariant types of lawful conduct on the world stage.[1]

Nations, nationalism, Europe, and America

It must be admitted that, by any measure, Simmel's statements from the first months of the war seem to confirm a pattern typical of German national literary sentiment at the outbreak of the war, marked by a precious act of uncoupling of *Kultur* and *Geist* from 'mere politics' – including especially from perfidious 'English politics'. Having first anathematised all Germany's enemies in the early autumn months, Simmel proceeded to proclaim in May 1915 that while reconciliation might be found in the end with Germany's 'political enemies' – meaning in the first instance France – never could there be pardon for the detractors of Germany's sacred *Geist*, namely with Britain (GSG 17, pp. 128–131).

Yet repeatedly from the spring of 1915 onwards, Simmel appealed to a German sense of membership in a wider European house of nations, counselling against 'chauvinism and nationalist blinkeredness' and insisting that 'Europeanism' (*Europäertum*) should be considered 'no mere external pendant to the German character' but part of its 'innermost vital essence' (GSG 16, p. 57 f.; Simmel, 1976, p. 270). A cult of sacrifice for the fatherland, he warned to a large audience in Vienna in January 1916, could be 'highly misleading' and sheer 'emotionalism' (GSG 16, p. 57 f.; GSG 13, p. 198; Simmel, 1976, p. 270, 1997b, p. 98). The total subjection of human lives to a nation's ends exceeded any moral justification, and the countless thousands of deaths of men at the front only revealed 'with maximum clarity that the self has lost its status as an ultimate end' in the present age (GSG 13, p. 198; Simmel, 1997b, p. 98).

In his text of 1917, *Der Krieg und die geistigen Entscheidungen*, a pamphlet composed of four lightly revised essays published over the previous three years, Simmel assembled much of his thinking about the war and Europe. Beginning with an encomium to Germany and ending with a revised statement of 'The Idea of Europe', the sequence of these pieces suggests something significant about the direction of his thinking over the course of the war. A definite 'idea of Europe', Simmel urged, challenged the belligerent nations to rise above themselves in a higher nexus of association, in whose breast each might become most true to itself by transcending its own separate existence. In Europe, he reiterated, these nations, without disavowing their own native traditions, might realise themselves by rediscovering themselves in something greater than their own isolated particularity – for Europe existed only in and through its member nations, not apart from them (GSG 16, p. 57; Simmel, 1976, p. 270). Europeanism enabled Europe's national societies to surmount their own belligerent forms of myopia by furnishing them with a more concrete feeling of the general moral norm beyond national particularity. Whereas internationalism, Simmel argued, negated nationalism only by substituting an abstract sameness, Europeanism mediated national-cultural individuality in a more coherent and more meaningful manner with a sense of the moral-legal universal order.

In this sense, the idea of Europe subsumed 'the subtlest essence of what is intellectually mature without cutting it off from its national roots'. It allowed nationality to be 'an inalienable possession without being a blinkering limitation' (GSG 16, p. 55 f.; Simmel, 1976, p. 268 f.).

In the second item in the compendium, 'The Dialectic of the German Spirit', Simmel urged that any 'German spirit' became itself only in negation of itself (GSG 13, pp. 224-30; Simmel, 2007a). There was, Simmel maintained, a 'yearning of the German people for that which both completes and differs from them', for 'something redemptive in something antithetical … in the foreign'. Lacking a determinate, ready-formed essence, Germans remained a people of incompleteness: 'late-comers to form', late to unity, integration, and self-enclosure. But this was 'not because form essentially eludes us' but because Germans 'always encounter a particular form only by breaking it apart and feeling behind it the ideal claim, possibility and value of its antithesis as a supplement to it' (GSG 13, p. 225; Simmel, 2007a, p. 66). Just as Hegel's cardinal thought had been that 'everything seeks its opposite and that only in becoming its opposite does each thing complete itself', so Germans strove for 'a way of intensifying the direction of our ideal existence by assimilating the opposite of this ideal and completing ourselves only in and through this opposite'. A 'dialectic' of the German mind differed in this sense from any unstable Faustian duality, dualism or 'problematic vacillation'. The ideal of the Frenchman was 'the complete Frenchman' as the ideal of the Englishman was 'the complete Englishman' – whereas Germans sought 'the complete German *and* at the same time its opposite, its other, its supplement' (GSG 13, p. 224; Simmel, 2007a, p. 65).

Unmistakable in these remarks is Simmel's sense of an essential dynamic of reciprocity or *Wechselwirkung* in the formation of both national and transnational identities – the term *Wechselwirkung* also notably being the key operative word in Goethe's influential maxim on the impossibility of 'patriotic art', allied to the poet's famous late reflections on the idea of a 'world literature' or *Weltliteratur*.[2] Every national culture lived through a flow of historical experience structured by forms and shapes of interaction with others, in a constant cycle of exchange and objective challenges. Just as self-education and self-formation of the person depended on qualities of concourse of the person with others, so all nations with an interest in self-enlightenment and refinement lived in states of exchange and sociability with others; and just as identities of individuals grew from 'meeting-points in social circles', so all national identities became and overcame themselves only in processes of reflective interaction. In this sense in 1915 in 'The Idea of Europe', Simmel named Goethe, Beethoven, Schopenhauer, and Nietzsche (and then later, in 1917, also Darwin, Tolstoy, and Bergson) as personalities who 'have been to an extreme degree men of national character' but who also became 'creators of "Europe" by developing specifically national qualities to their extreme limits' (GSG 16, p. 56; Simmel, 1976, p. 269). These men's intellectual and artistic achievements, Simmel declared, stood for exemplary instances of European national self-overcoming. They showed how each nation stood to learn from others 'in every cultural domain', and how

> when civilized peoples [*Kulturvölker*] succeed in rising from their own national soil to a new and unprecedented height, they begin to make contact with one another, to grow with one another, and to become indispensable to one another, entirely from their own volition.
>
> *(GSG 17, p. 129)*

Nations realised their moral idea by rising to higher levels of reflective self-understanding, by affirming experiences of their own trans- and supra-national formation.

In a second article for the newspaper *Der Berliner Tageblatt* from May 1915, Simmel turns to the significance of news of deliveries of munitions from the United States to Britain in the early months of the year 1915 (GSG 13, pp. 138–142; Simmel, 2004). A keen sense of *Realpolitik* here animates Simmel's argument that while Germany and France tore themselves to pieces, not England but rather America stood waiting in the wings, now dealt a golden opportunity to act as *tertius gaudens* – as third keeper of the peace in Europe's affairs. These events, Simmel declared, were 'the first great practical manoeuvre with which America hopes to turn the hands on the clock of world history toward the West'. As third-party beneficiary of Europe's *harakiri*, nothing in America's policy of neutrality precluded an American interest in exacerbating Europe's internal war of all against all; and in truth, nothing stood between this interest and the 'humanitarian ideals it has been preaching incessantly' (GSG 13, p. 139 f.; Simmel, 2004, p. 70).

Admittedly, America in Simmel's thinking in this essay might seem simply to replace Germany's national enmity to England with a new transatlantic enemy to Europe – the New World functioning as the symbolic vehicle for the production of a pan-European feeling. The United States, Simmel writes, now sees 'a chance to place itself at the head of world events'.

> [It] waits in the wings, like a lurking heir at the death-bed of the rich father. … As Europe dispatches to America a not insignificant portion of its strenuously acquired fortune, it blows itself up with its purchases and hands over to America the accession to the throne of world domination. … America deals the European peoples the weapons with which they are to destroy themselves to its advantage, and gets itself paid for them in immeasurable riches. At a stroke, America contrives Europe's enervation in two ways: a masterpiece of world-historical speculation!
>
> *(GSG 13, p. 139; Simmel, 2004, p. 70)*

Clearly, Simmel's rhetoric of America as a 'lurking heir at the death-bed of the rich father' carries a strong sense of European foreboding: an almost Oedipal fear of approaching usurpation of the crown of civilisation. Yet Simmel seems nevertheless to have mused that *Wechselwirkung* between cultures applied not only to relations between European nations but also no less urgently to European relations to America and to the world *in toto*. In another late letter to Hermann Graf Keyserling, Simmel averred that it was questionable whether Europe should have 'a permanent lease on the inheritance of Culture' (Simmel, 1968, p. 245). Perhaps in future, he wrote, there would

> come a time when Europe will be to America as Athens to the later Romans: a travel destination for the young in search of culture, a place full of interesting ruins and great memories, a source of supplies for artists, scholars and chattering literati.

Nothing in this prospect contradicted the possibility of a future 'American world culture'. As frightful as this might seem to some Europeans, its inconceivability might be no greater than the imaginability of the modern nation-state from the perspective of the ancient Egyptians (ibid.). Europe's situation vis-à-vis America might have resembled the great migrations and mixings of peoples of the first millennium after the birth of Christ. These developments 'to the civilized peoples of antiquity must have seemed mere senseless destruction and incomprehensible despoliation' – yet they 'nevertheless created the conditions for a vitality and productivity of infinite value' (GSG 16, p. 54; Simmel, 1976, p. 267). In short, Simmel insisted, Europeans had 'placed too much trust in the security of their relations' (GSG 13, p. 141; Simmel, 2004, p. 71). The war had made a mockery of the notion of Europe as some kind of point of happy 'equilibrium' between West and East. It showed that the continent had entirely 'forfeited the concept of the "good European" in which we of the older generation believed we had some share' (GSG 16, pp. 55, 57; GSG 13, p. 141; Simmel, 1976, pp. 268, 270, 2004, p. 71). A future wellspring of culture far beyond the horizons of old Europe was therefore not to be dismissed. 'For far too long', Simmel underlined, 'we have assumed the course of world history to unfold on Europe's shores alone, the crest of its waves leaving Asia millennia in the past and now coming to rest for ever in our continent' (GSG 13, p. 142; Simmel, 2004, p. 71).

For Simmel and for many of his contemporaries, America is in many respects the figment or foil for a European fear and discourse of total industrial encroachment over life. Yet Simmel is also critical of this outlook, again urging in his letters to Keyserling that German vitalistic youth movements that swore a 'mortal hostility to bourgeois complacency and to all mechanization and Americanization' contained much that was 'opaque, seething and shamelessly aggressive' (Simmel, 1968, p. 246). Failing to rise to the true challenges of the hour, these movements forgot that life in the present could not subsist without the commodities and forces of the global industrial civilisation they despised. As Simmel observes in *The philosophy of money* and reiterates later in essays such as 'The Crisis of Culture', individuality of the self might have been threatened by massifying effects of life in the modern industrial metropolis but strength, vitality, and integrity of individual character could also be enhanced by constant change and exchange in multiple social circles. Objectivity, sobriety, and impartiality of worldview as characteristic of urban money cultures were the preconditions of claims to distinction and individuality. It may have been that a 'lack of something definite at the centre of the soul' impelled a 'search for monetary satisfaction in ever-new stimulations, sensations and external activities', but the principle remained that money in its correlation with intellectuality 'facilitates the growth of individuality and subjectivity', insofar as its 'unchanging uniformity, its qualitatively communistic character, leads to each quantitative difference becoming a qualitative one' (GSG 6, pp. 612, 675 f.; Simmel, 1978, pp. 440, 484). Again and again, Simmel urges that in light of ever widening effects of interpenetration of social circles, modern collective identities retain meaning only against the background of the dissolution of substantial reference-points of life and the fragility and questionability of notions of the unity and wholeness of the group in any traditional sense.

Cosmopolitanism, 'concrete' and 'abstract'

Yet these considerations for Simmel still do not preclude a need to understand and safeguard conditions for maintaining and nourishing ethically durable identities of life over time. Here an important question remains for Simmel as to how differences and distinctions of the self and the group can be recovered from within the teeth of equality and formally consistent treatment of parties on the global plane of law and market exchange. It is in this sense that in 'The Crisis of Culture' – the third of the four items he republishes in *Der Krieg und die geistigen Entscheidungen* – Simmel dwells on some of the difficulties that nations and societies frequently confront in recognising themselves in the products of their own shared agencies of exchange (GSG 13, pp. 190-201; Simmel, 1997b). In experiencing these products as increasingly alien to themselves, modern populations and individuals find themselves ever less readily equipped to discern natively meaningful relationships to the foreign. Increasingly less able or adept at weaving together the fibres of their existence into organic figurations, individuals, and groups, Simmel can be read as saying, struggle to determine expressive relations to the foreign as their *own* relationships, rather than as mere adjustments to extraneous-seeming protocols of behaviour. As expressive life becomes more and more objectified, peoples confront a multitude of disparate elements seemingly bereft of organic *Gestalt*. The spectre becomes one of an apparent 'chaos of disjointed individual elements devoid of any common style', a 'chaos of fragmentary vestiges of form' – an 'abundance of heterogeneous and infinitely seductive traditions and resources'. National collectivities, like persons, need to be able to craft themselves into coherently structured figurations from these 'disjointed elements'; for only on this basis are they able to enter into trusting relations with others and with foreignness as such (GSG 13, pp. 194, 199, 200; Simmel, 1997b, pp. 94, 99, 100).

It is in this light that Simmel's thinking can be read fruitfully with an eye to his concurrent writing during the war about concepts of 'individual law' in ethical social life. Though admittedly only explicitly formulated as a thesis holding at a level of individual persons rather than collectivities, Simmel's thinking about 'individual law' in his last great work, his *Lebensanschauung*, arguably also carries a certain implied significance for his conception of the position of the kinds of collective social entities he refers to by the name of 'nations' (GSG 16, pp. 346-425; Simmel, 2010, pp. 99-154). In this sense for Simmel, any law for an individuality, including 'international law', must be this individuality's *own* law, and not merely and exclusively another's law – such as a law of an abstract foreign power or colonial-imperial force or alien global commercial apparatus of market exchange. Even in a context of post-traditional identities, a question persists for Simmel of how qualitative differentiation can return justifiably and non-arbitrarily in a world whose systematic organising principle is one of quantitative equivalence. The challenge for Europe's national groups in this sense for Simmel is to respond to a rule of law that is formally consistent and general in its application as well as *individual* in its application – individual in the sense of responsive to ethical uniqueness as the inviolable foundation of the equality of each participant to every other.

As Simmel repeatedly makes clear in his earlier writings from the turn of the century, to violate individuality as a value was to force all to become qualitatively the same or 'indifferent' (*gleichgültig*) to one another – to assimilate; to subsume under a single invariant rule, type, or standard of valid conduct (GSG 7, pp. 49-56; Simmel, 1950). Therefore important was not only the emancipation or liberation of individuals from constraints and oppressions but also the expressive free self-realisation of individuals in an acceptance of inescapably concrete finite contingent placement of life in given historical orders. The task of present times lay in seeking freedom of the individual not in abstract opposition to historical particularity but rather in reflective distance from it. The tendency of many Western European (Franco-British) strains of political thought since the eighteenth century had been to confuse particularistic institutional inequalities (*die bestehenden, sinnlosen Unterschiedenheiten*) with qualitative difference in general (*Ungleichheit überhaupt*) (GSG 7, p. 50; Simmel, 1950, p. 60). The more Germanic 'qualitative' strand of thinking about individuality that descended from Goethe via Schleiermacher and romanticism to Nietzsche may have had its 'mystical and fatalistic features', which were to be avoided; however, its basic insight perdured and was to be respected, namely that, as Goethe had taught, the 'universally human' consisted not in a single world in which each individuality occupied an allotted place but only in a plethora of individual worlds, in a plenitude of 'individualities' (GSG 7, p. 55 f.; GSG 15, p. 170; Simmel, 1950, p. 83 f.).

In the context of Simmel's political essays from the years of the First World War, it can be argued that this thinking implied on the collective level a question of the non-separatist difference of Germany within a common house of equal European responsibilities before the law, and that the challenge for Germans in this sense for Simmel was to discern an appropriately self-critical way of articulating this difference. Indeed it is this that can be said to be at play in Simmel's writings on relations of 'Germanic' ethical styles of life to 'classical Romanic' ethical styles in his statements on individuality and social form in European painting and literature of the early modern period. In numerous statements, including in passages of his monograph on Rembrandt and related essays, Simmel's reflections turn to questions of how particular national-cultural figurations can be both 'common to' and 'different from' others and how Germanic cultural heritage in particular can be both 'part of' and 'set apart from' that of Western Europe (GSG 13, pp. 299-306, 313-320; GSG 15, pp. 305-515; Simmel, 2005, 2007b, 2007c).

Until recent times, Simmel considers, classical Romanic understandings of the moral place of individuals and individuality in society have 'been able to grip much wider circles of humanity and to play a much larger part in the formation of the European ideal of civilization than Germanic individualism' (GSG 13, p. 301; Simmel, 2007b, p. 72). Classical republicanism bequeaths to European self-understanding a precept of the formal equality of human beings under the rule of law; and in the cultures of the court societies and city-states of early modern Europe, this precept shows itself in a 'feeling that only peers can acknowledge each other', in a sense of the 'noble closure of the circle' and of the 'inner parity' of its members (GSG 15, p. 393; Simmel, 2005, p. 64). Over the centuries, this sense of parity gradually comes to be extended to all men and women as bearers of rights; and Western Latinate ideas of the individual since the early modern period consequently come to appear 'closer to the universally human' than those of the more Germanic nations. In this sense, classical Romanic civilisation appears to 'open a relatively wider gate and [to] admit an indefinite number of others to an understanding and appreciation of itself' (GSG 13, p. 320; Simmel, 2007c, p. 58). But this apparent greater universality of Western Latinate ideas of the individual, Simmel urges, is not to be regarded as resting on an intrinsically more authoritative form of universality than other historically distinctive understandings of the moral integrity of individuals in society. Representations of the individual in Germanic culture might appear more obscure, more resistant to intelligible access and in this sense more 'particularistic' in character. A more introspective style of individuality in Germanic culture might seem to make the 'Germanic mind difficult of access for other peoples' (GSG 13, p. 320; Simmel, 2007c, p. 58). But, Simmel insists, none of this should be interpreted as meaning that Germanic style in representations of the individual in society remains essentially any less universally morally authoritative than classical Romanic style. It should only be seen as indicating that Germanic style expresses a different – not a lesser – understanding of the universal moral worth of individuals and individuality in relation to moral-social law.

Important, Simmel underlines, is that none of these remarks are to be seen as implying any wholly negative ethical verdict on Romanic style as something resting on 'a "merely extraneous" … choice of values' (GSG 13, p. 319; Simmel, 2007c, p. 57). The predominance of a socially self-conscious 'way of being-for-others' in classical Romanic style, Simmel stresses, has nothing inherently to do with any atmosphere of superficiality or insincerity (GSG 13, p. 320; Simmel, 2007c, p. 58). But the fact remains that classical Romanic style tends to withdraw from inner 'motion and mutability' in order to bestow on form 'a validity beyond the life that first flows into it' and produces in this way 'a kind of supra-individuality' manifest in an aspect of 'radiant outward display' (GSG 13, pp. 317, 318; Simmel, 2007c, pp. 55, 56). The friezes of the Parthenon, Leonardo's and Titian's portraits, classical French drama, and the novels of Balzac, all evoke in this sense a distinct manner of placement of the individual in society, different from that of northern seers such as Rembrandt, Goethe, or Shakespeare. The former tend to convey presentations of individuals as members of recognisable social types: 'different kinds of membership of definite genres of human being', in which human figures are 'suffused by a more general ideal sphere' (GSG 15, p. 394 f.; GSG 13, p. 301; Simmel, 2005, p. 67, 2007b, p. 73). The contrast, Simmel considers, is that Germanic individualism in art tends to show how individuals owe their existence 'perhaps to the cosmos, to society, to the divine order', but not to 'a shared and ideal formal law'; it exhibits a sense in which the sources of individuals' feeling of moral calling lie 'solely within the unique self' (GSG 13, p. 304 f.; Simmel, 2007b, p. 75). Individuals in Germanic culture appear to be 'left to their own devices, in a solitary feeling and consciousness of self', in a consciousness of 'being-alone-with-oneself in the ground of the world'. It is in this sense, Simmel comments, that Rembrandt's figures exhibit 'an inner universality', a feeling of an individual passage of experience 'in which life forms itself wholly from within', where individuals 'live only from the centre of their individuality and within this centre, not by dint of any typical conduct' (GSG 13, pp. 303, 306, 314 f., 319; Simmel, 2007b, pp. 74, 76; 2007c, pp. 54 f., 57). In the same way, Goethe's literary characters, Simmel writes in 1913, affirm a vision of the 'qualitative uniqueness of the essentially non-equivalent'. Each 'individuality' in Goethe constitutes a 'world of its own'; universality inheres in the plurality of worlds as such, not in any single world that makes each expressive phenomenon a mere point within a more encompassing and subsuming matrix (GSG 15, pp. 152, 169 f.).

In sum, Simmel's account of German relations to the West in his statements on Rembrandt and European painting differs from anything like the purely nationalist celebration of Rembrandt as a Germanic cultural icon presented by Julius Langbehn in a popular book first published in 1890.[3] Within the Romano-Germanic nexus of European cultures, Simmel holds, a Germanic ethical style of the individual fundamentally learns from and incorporates classical Romanic form, even as it also struggles with it and asserts its difference. The universal ethical norm that Germanic culture shares with other European as well as non-European cultures remains a 'concrete' rather than an 'indifferent', 'abstract' or invariant one. On the plane of transnational relations, 'individual law' in Simmel's commentary implies that any national individuality can and must be capable of recognising itself and others as 'individual' in the law and under the law, and thus the question arises for him as to how character, distinction, or individuality, whether personal-singular or group-collective, can be rescued from a monetarised world of functions and functionality without illusion, anachronism, or atavisms, and of how in this sense particularities can return in the cancellation of their historically obsolete substantial forms. Across the domains of intellectuality, money, and law, the question of the age remains for Simmel as to how individuality is to be recovered in a form different from sheer atomism or egoism and of how in this sense the placelessness of cosmopolitanism can nevertheless return in some relationship to place, to delimitation and boundedness – beyond utopia.

Here as elsewhere, it is impossible to see Simmel as having espoused anything like an agenda comparable to Hugo von Hofmannsthal's subsequent image of Franco-German spiritual comity in 'Das Schrifttum als geistiger Raum der Nation' of 1927. Nothing in

Simmel's essays compares with Hofmannsthal's and the Conservative Revolution's declared longing for restored wholeness of European life in the face of perceived dismemberment and decay. In the spirit of Goethe's metaphysics of eternal alternation between oneness and division, equilibrium and polarity, Simmel writes of a modern European universe of constant Heraclitean flux, of oneness always in a coeval relation to difference and diremption (GSG 6, p. 713 f.; GSG 15, pp. 61-150; Simmel, 1978, p. 510). Like other advanced voices in German letters during and after the war, Simmel can be read neither as a nationalist thinker nor as a Eurochauvinist one but one keen nonetheless to explore the precise extent and limit to which peculiarities of collective cultural and historical identities can be explored and affirmed, without obscurantism. In this perspective, cosmopolitanism for Simmel encompasses a meaning of endless 'Heraclitean' differences of the subject on a plane of global circulation, but always in relationship to some kind of provisionally unitary standpoint or *Mittelpunkt* of the self, to a concrete particular 'individuality' – including in some sense to a collective, national or group individuality. The transnational in this sense is not the abstract negation or subsumption of the national but the inflection and elevation of the national to a higher power of reflexive agency and awareness. The cosmopolitan universal is the universal confronted rigorously and relentlessly with its own potential geo-historical particularity and relativity in the flux and flow of life. Though dying very shortly before the end of the war, Simmel in this sense can be seen as consistent in political worldview with an advanced strand of writing in German social and political thought of the early Weimar years that engages in a certain note of 'protest' of the 'German mind' against etiolated empty 'Western' 'internationalist' discourse in world politics – but one that does not seek to make any kind of apology for Germanist nationalism or in any way to break in principle with universalist moral and legal norms in the international sphere. Not unconnected to but also importantly not simply reducible to the nationalist positions of figures such as Oswald Spengler in *The Decline of the West* and Thomas Mann in *Reflections of an Unpolitical Man*, another, fragile strand of Weimar German cosmopolitanism arises in German discourse of these years – one which in the end fails to survive the convulsions of the Republic and the rise of National Socialism but one which still stands today as one world-historically significant symbol of a horizon of possible 'alternative modernity' within European history that *might have been* and that might still assert its legitimate normative voice in relations of memory and action on the plane of world politics today.

Notes

1 Further at length: Harrington (2016, pp. 141–227). For one valuable survey and synthesis of debates in contemporary cosmopolitan theory, see Held (2010); also Delanty (2009).
2 'There is no patriotic art and no patriotic scholarship. Both belong, like all things good, to the entire world and can only be fostered through the general free interaction [Wechselwirkung] of all living things, in continual concern for those elements of the past that have been handed down and made known to us' (Goethe 1998, p. 93 [*Wilhelm Meisters Wanderjahre*, 1829, 'Aus Makariens Archiv', para. 74]; cf. Curtius, 1948 [epigraph]).
3 *Rembrandt als Erzieher: von einem Deutschen* (1890); reviewed by Simmel in 1890 (GSG 1, pp. 232-42; cf. Hughes, 1958, pp. 43-5; Stern, 1961, pp. 97-181).

References

Curtius, E. R. (1948). *Europäische Literatur und lateinisches Mittelalter*, Bern: Francke/ *European literature and the Latin middle ages*, tr. W.R. Trask. Princeton, NJ: Princeton University Press, 1953.
Delanty, G. (2009). *The Cosmopolitan imagination: The renewal of critical social theory*. Cambridge, UK: Cambridge University Press.

Goethe, J. W. (1998). *Maxims and reflections*, tr. E. Stopp. London: Penguin.

Harrington, A. (2016). *German cosmopolitan social thought and the idea of the West: Voices from Weimar.* Cambridge, UK: Cambridge University Press.

Held, D. (2010). *Cosmopolitanism: Ideals and realities.* Cambridge, UK: Polity Press.

Hughes, S. (1958). *Consciousness and society: The reorientation of European social thought, 1890–1930.* New York: Knopf.

Simmel, G. (1950). Individual and society in eighteenth and nineteenth-century views of life, tr. K.H. Wolff. In K. H. Wolff. (Ed.), *The sociology of Georg Simmel* (pp. 58–84). Glencoe: The Free Press.

Simmel, G. (1968). Briefe an den Grafen Hermann Keyserling [1914-18]. In M. Landmann (Ed.), *Georg Simmel: Das Individuelle Gesetz: Philosophische Exkurse* (pp. 237–53). Frankfurt am Main: Suhrkamp.

Simmel, G. (1976). The idea of Europe, tr. P.A. Lawrence. In P. A. Lawrence. (Ed.), *Georg Simmel: Sociologist and European* (pp. 267–271). New York: Barnes and Noble.

Simmel, G. (1978). *The philosophy of money*, tr. T. Bottomore, D. Frisby and K. Mengelberg. London: Routledge.

Simmel, G. (1989-2015). *Georg-Simmel-Gesamtausgabe (GSG)*, 24 vols. Frankfurt am Main: Suhrkamp.

Simmel, G. (1997a). The metropolis and mental life, tr. K. Wolff. In D. Frisby & M. Featherstone (Eds.), *Simmel on culture* (pp. 174–85). London: Sage.

Simmel, G. (1997b). The crisis of culture, tr. D. E. Jenkinson. In D. Frisby & M. Featherstone. (Eds.), *Simmel on culture* (pp. 90–101). London: Sage.

Simmel, G. (2004). Europe and America in world history, tr. A. Harrington. *European Journal of Social Theory, 8*(1), 63–72.

Simmel, G. (2005). *Rembrandt: An essay in the philosophy of art*, tr. A. Scott and H. Staubmann. New York: Routledge.

Simmel, G. (2007a). The dialectic of the German spirit, tr. A. Harrington. *Theory, Culture & Society, 24* (7/8), 65–9.

Simmel, G. (2007b). Individualism, tr. A. Harrington. *Theory, Culture & Society*, 24(7/8), 71–6.

Simmel, G. (2007c). Germanic and Classical Romanic style, tr. A. Harrington. *Theory, Culture & Society*, 24(7/8), 53–8.

Simmel, G. (2009). *Sociology: Inquiries into the construction of social forms*, 2 vols., tr. A. Blasi, A. Jacobs, & M. Kanjiranthinkal. Leiden: Brill.

Simmel, G. (2010). *The view of life: Four metaphysical essays with journal aphorisms*, tr. John A. Y. Andrews & Donald N. Levine. Chicago, IL: The University of Chicago Press.

Stern, F. (1961). *The politics of cultural despair: A study in the rise of the Germanic ideology*, Berkeley, CA: University of California Press.

23

ECONOMIC PATHOLOGIES OF LIFE

Arthur Bueno

Introduction[1]

Simmel's diagnosis of modernity has been many times recognised as one of the most important aspects of his oeuvre. Such an assessment has, in fact, played a crucial role in the renewed interest experienced by his writings since the late 1960s, so much so that Jürgen Habermas was no more than conveying a spreading view when he praised Simmel's 'phenomenologically precise description of the modern way of life' (Habermas, [1983] 1996, p. 410; cf. Landmann, 1968; Blumenberg, 1976; Frisby, 1978, Frisby, 1981; Dahme & Rammstedt, 1984). In the wake of the twenty-first century, Axel Honneth took a step further by claiming that 'the perspicuity with which Georg Simmel observed the social and cultural transformations of his times' not only provided for an illuminating analysis of modernity but also contained a 'presentiment' of our contemporary situation, in which psychological malaise and suffering came to increasingly manifest themselves in the form of depressive symptoms (Honneth, [2002] 2004, p. 475).

One may sense, indeed, a striking resemblance between Simmel's depiction of modern life and recent analyses of our social psychological condition. Our society, as Simmel's, can be seen as marked by the widespread occurrence of 'feelings of tension, of expectation, of unresolved urgency', in tandem with equally frequent experiences of 'deadly boredom and disappointment' and the impression 'that the core and meaning of life slips through our fingers again and again, that definitive satisfactions become ever rarer, that all the effort and activity is not actually worthwhile' (Simmel, [1889] 1997, p. 236, [1896] 1997a, pp. 251, 249).[2] These affective states, widely addressed today with terms such as depression and burnout (cf. Ehrenberg, 1998; Rosa, 2011; Neckel & Wagner, 2013), were then summarised under the notion of 'neurasthenia', a social psychological condition marked by the oscillation between urgency and exhaustion, saturation and insufficiency, 'hyperesthesia' and 'anesthesia' (GSG 5, p. 214).

From very early on, the consideration of modern experience in terms of a widespread neurasthenia occupied a central place in Simmel's writings. Such a diagnosis constitutes, indeed, the common thread running through a number of essays from the 1890s and early 1900s in which he addressed several phenomena of his time: from the dull 'one-sidedness' of modern production to the 'multifariousness' of art consumption and the 'blunting of sensibility' that comes with it (Simmel, [1890] 2015, pp. 88, 90); from 'the feverish chase of daily work' to the search for 'orgiastic and sensually intoxicated' forms of nightlife entertainment (Simmel, [1893] 1997, p. 260); from the 'momentary rapture' of the journeys to the Alps and the 'variety of fleeting impressions' of the Berlin trade exhibition to the 'blasé attitude' experienced in the metropolises (Simmel, [1895] 1997, p. 220, [1896] 1997b, p. 255, [1903] 1997, p. 175; cf. Bueno, 2013; Svartman & Bueno, 2016).

Equally crucial is the fact that such a characterisation of modern life as neurasthenic also underlay Simmel's initial attempts to analyse the money economy and its wide-ranging implications (cf. GSG 5, pp. 212–14). In 'On the Psychology of Money' and 'Money in Modern Culture', modernity was seen as characterised by an enormous expansion of the teleological series, i.e., the extensive and intensive development of institutions (understood as 'means' for action) through which a growing number of purposes can be ever more indirectly achieved. Such a process of technical (in the broad sense) rationalisation of culture is, however, inherently ambivalent: it brings about a specific form of irrationality which Simmel called the 'psychological interruption of the teleological series' or the 'colonisation of ends by means' (Simmel, [1889] 1997, p. 235, [1896] 1997a, p. 250). In a context where chains of action have become so extended and our final purposes so mediated and distant, it is only understandable that – on the basis of the 'principle of conserving energy [*Kraftersparnis*]' – the more remote goals sink away from consciousness and we concentrate our effort upon the immediately present means, which may then gain an autonomous significance and become itself an ultimate end (Simmel, [1889] 1997, p. 235; cf. GSG 2, pp. 109–295). The more intricate and elaborate the technique of all domains of life becomes, 'the greater [the] danger is of getting stuck in the labyrinth of means and thereby forgetting the ultimate goal' (Simmel, [1896] 1997a, pp. 250–51).

Such a process affects the whole of modern culture, but has become especially prominent in the money economy: 'never has a value which an object possesses only through its convertibility into others of definitive value been so completely transferred into a value itself' (Simmel, [1889] 1997, p. 235). As a consequence, both this dynamic and its affective implications are made particularly visible in certain 'manic' economic behaviours:

> It is interesting, therefore, to see how this psychological interruption of the teleo-logical series appears not only in direct greed and miserliness, but also in its appar-ent opposite, the pleasure in simply spending money as such … Herein are the stages of the teleological process: the rational ultimate goal is, indeed, only the enjoyment from the use of the object; the means to it are: first, that one has money, second that one spends it, and third that one possesses the object. Purpos-ive consciousness can stop at any one of these three stages and constitute it as an end in itself; and in fact, so forcibly, that each of its three components can degen-erate into manias.
>
> *(Simmel, [1889] 1997, p. 235)*

From the standpoint of Simmel's psychology of money, economic attitudes such as greed, miserliness, and squandering are thus crucial for understanding the problematic features of modernity: in them, it becomes clear how the colonisation of ends by means may give rise to that oscillation between saturation and insufficiency which he characterised with the notion of neurasthenia. So much so that the analysis of these 'hypertrophied' or 'pathological' behaviours – as he later designated them – was to become a central part of *The philosophy of money* (Simmel, [1900/07] 2004, pp. 239, 242).[3] With the shift from a psychology to a philosophy of money, however, the process of interruption of the teleological series came to be understood within a broader conceptual framework: one in which those phenomena were considered not only from an action-theoretical perspective but also as manifestations of life's fundamental oppositions.

Dialectics of monetary life

The new scope of Simmel's project is announced in the first pages of *The philosophy of money*. At the core of the book is the notion that, from a philosophical standpoint, money can be viewed as a symbol of the totality of life: 'The unity of these investigations ... lie[s] ... in the possibility ... of finding in each of life's details the totality of its meaning' (Simmel, [1900/07] 2004, p. 53). But what is to be understood here by 'life'? In *The philosophy of money*, as in his other works, Simmel postulates an ontological relativism according to which all the elements of the world are involved in an ongoing and shifting entanglement of reciprocal effects (*Wechselwirkungen*). This is what allows him to approach 'the totality of [life's] meaning' on the basis of its 'details': since all of these are reciprocally intertwined, one can start with any particular element and explore its connections with the others so as to progressively obtain an image of the whole, moving from the 'surface of existence' to 'the ultimate decisions concerning the meaning and style of life' (Simmel, [1903] 1997, p. 177).

The philosophy of money is in this sense a philosophy of life – one whose 'problem is nothing less than the totality of existence' (Simmel, [1900/07] 2004, p. 54).[4] In principle, such an approach could devote itself to any particular object and unravel its connections with others in order to obtain an image of the whole. For Simmel, however, money presents an object particularly well-suited to such an endeavour. Being 'indifference itself, in that its entire purposive significance does not lie in itself but rather in its transformation into other values', money consists in the most 'superficial and insubstantial' of all elements and, at the same time, the most effective bearer of the *Wechselwirkungen* one must unfold in order to approach the 'inner substance of life' (Simmel, [1900/07] 2004, p. 53). If the task of philosophy is to explore the connections between the 'most superficial phenomena' and the 'most profound currents' of life, money can appear as a 'symbol of [its] essential forms of movement' for it constitutes the point at which those two poles most radically oppose each other and, at the same time, where they most closely meet (ibid.). Simmel's relativism is thus dialectical in a crucial sense: it relies on the notion that the totality of life – at least when viewed from the standpoint of money – finds its most significant expression where its oppositions reach a peak, where they present themselves as unresolved contradictions. This is what *The philosophy of money*, in each of its different parts, offers: an image of life in the form of a 'dialectics without reconciliation' (Landmann, 1968, p. 16).

It is on the basis of such a philosophical perspective that Simmel returns, in the third chapter of the book, to his previous analysis of the colonisation of ends by means. Such a process is now grasped, dialectically, as the unfolding of a central tension inherent to human action: that between the 'relativity of our aspirations' and 'the absoluteness of the idea of final purpose' (Simmel, [1900/07] 2004, p. 236). On the one hand, we are driven by an infinite series of purposes which can never reach a standstill; each enjoyment is followed by a new demand, each accomplishment of an ideal is followed by the awareness of its incompleteness. From this perspective, it does not seem possible to speak of an ultimate end: 'no gain or condition attained grants us the final satisfaction which is logically bound up with the concept of an ultimate purpose' (ibid.). Our aspirations are, in this sense, inescapably *relative*.[5] At the same time, while acting we cannot avoid designating 'one moment as the ultimate end, for which everything preceding it is only a means' (ibid.). Even if a final purpose in the sense of something attainable does not exist, in each of our practical endeavours we cannot but strive for something *absolute*. The notion of ultimate end operates then as a 'regulative principle': a prospect never attained but always present, as the horizon in relation to 'the earthly paths that always lead towards it, yet which, after the longest wanderings, never seem to be any closer than at the outset' (ibid.).

For Simmel, the tension between these two poles reaches its peak in monetary actions. Being an equivalent of the value of potentially everything, money may come to be perceived as the ultimate purpose par excellence, the value of all values. It presents us, in this regard, with the most accomplished crystallisation of the notion of *absolute* end. At the same time, it has no inherent purpose and offers itself as nothing but a crossing point between things. It consists, for that matter, in the most *relative* means we know of. Money thus symbolises – 'with the flawlessness of a textbook example' – the fact that even the most relative 'means of life' can be converted into the most absolute 'purpose of life', and vice-versa (ibid.).

It is from such a standpoint that Simmel now returns to those actions that were previously described as 'manic'. In monetary attitudes such as greed, avarice, and squandering, as well as in seemingly non-monetary behaviours such as ascetic poverty, cynicism, and the blasé attitude, one can find different ways of dealing with the tension between the 'relativity of our aspirations' and 'the absoluteness of the idea of final purpose'. Each of them reveals, in different form, the teleological contradictions of money as well as the psychological consequences of the advancement of the money economy in modernity.

Greed and avarice

The first cases addressed by Simmel in his typology of hypertrophied behaviours are greed and avarice. Both are grasped initially as instantiations of a 'remarkable psychological mania for accumulation' which is also manifested, for example, in the behaviour of individuals who 'pile up precious collections of any kind without getting any satisfaction from the objects themselves' (Simmel, [1900/07] 2004, p. 239). The collector is moved by a paradoxical drive towards accumulation: even while shutting away his valuables from everyone else and watching most jealously over them, he does not do so for the sake of enjoying them. What appears to him as valuable is not the object in its specific quality – the 'subjective reflex' associated to its use, as Simmel puts it – but the simple fact of its acquisition and possession, i.e. a certain form of 'supra-subjective' relationship between the owner and the owned:

> Here it is not the quality of the object that is the genuine bearer of value ... The real value, at which the teleological sequence comes to an end, lies ... in this own-ership by the subject which exists as an objective fact.
>
> *(Simmel, [1900/07] 2004, p. 240 f.)*

Now, such a drive towards mere objective accumulation may surface even more intensely when the object involved is itself defined by a tendency towards abstraction, when it is 'indifference itself' (Simmel, [1900/07] 2004, p. 53). Consisting in an abstract means which provides access to other things but cannot be itself consumed, money offers an exceptional occasion for that supra-subjective 'mania for accumulation' which the collector exerts with regard to concrete things:

> The abstract character of money, its remoteness from any specific enjoyment in and for itself, supports an objective delight in money … The miser loves money as one loves a highly admired person who makes us happy simply by his existence and by our knowing him and being with him, without our relation to him as an individual taking the form of concrete enjoyment.
>
> *(Simmel, [1900/07] 2004, p. 242)*

For the greedy and the miser, money presents thereby the possibility of an 'abstract form of enjoyment which, none the less, is not enjoyed' (Simmel, [1900/07] 2004, p. 243).[6] Such a paradoxical form of (non-)enjoyment can only take place insofar as money is not treated simply as a means to other things, but converted into an end in itself, i.e. into something which 'makes us happy simply by [its] existence' (Simmel, [1900/07] 2004, p. 242). Two of its features are therewith intensified and achieve their most extreme opposition to one another. Money offers, on the one hand, the promise of unlimited possibilities for enjoyment. It constitutes, in this regard, 'the *absolute* means'. On the other hand, it does not offer in itself any form of concrete enjoyment. It is, in this sense, 'the absolute *means*'. By holding onto money without spending it, the greedy and the miser experience these two aspects at once: they sense the infinite possibilities money provides even while leaving them 'as yet completely untouched' (Simmel, [1900/07] 2004, p. 243). That psychological mania for accumulation takes here the form of an enjoyment which is *unlimited* precisely because it is *never realised*.

The conversion of money into an ultimate purpose may lead, then, to a heightened sense of one's own potential. This is premised on the specific manner in which two opposite features of potentiality are combined in the monetary means. On the one hand, being capable of something involves more than the mere mental anticipation of a future event; it already implies a certain given state: 'whoever "can" play the piano, even if he does not do so, is different from someone who is unable to do so, not only in a future moment, but even at the present moment' (ibid.). On the other hand, a potential is also inherently characterised by a moment of uncertainty: 'this state of ability, which in itself contains nothing of the future, leads to the realisation of what can be done only by meeting with further conditions whose occurrence we are unable to predict' (ibid.). In money, as experienced by the greedy and the miser, these two dimensions of potentiality are presented in their most acute form. Money is, on the one hand, an 'absolute *capacity*' – i.e., nothing but potential. 'What one really possesses at the precise moment of [its] possession is nothing' (ibid.). Here the present owes all its meaning to the future to come; money is *absolutely nothing* without its actualisation. Yet it is also, on the other hand, an '*absolute* capacity' – i.e., the most effective potential. Money is that which can be potentially concretised in *absolutely everything*, so that 'the degree of certainty that it will materialise at the right moment' is much more comprehensive than in other capacities (ibid.).

This explains why the conversion of money into an ultimate end can become particularly attractive even while – or precisely *because* – it does not lead to any concrete enjoyment. Taking to their extreme those two dimensions of potentiality, the focus on the mere acquisition or possession of money may appear as a way of avoiding all frustration:

> money is not expected to achieve anything for the greedy person over and above its mere ownership. It is a thing absolutely lacking in qualities and therefore cannot … conceal within itself any surprises or disappointments. Whoever really and definitely only wants money is absolutely safe from such experiences.
>
> *(Simmel, [1900/07] 2004, p. 244 f.)*

Money seems, then, to present us with the ultimate end par excellence, the object in which 'the absoluteness of the idea of final purpose' is fully realised in the form of unhindered enjoyment. It can only do so, however, in an abstract and empty manner: it only safeguards us against all frustration on the condition that it provides us with no enjoyment at all.

> If our wish does not extend beyond money towards a concrete goal, then a deadly disappointment must follow. Such a disappointment will always be experienced where monetary wealth, which has been passionately desired and considered an unquestionable happiness, reveals what it really is after it has been acquired: money is merely a means, whose elevation to an ultimate purpose cannot survive after it has been acquired.
>
> *(Simmel, [1900/07] 2004, p. 244)*

Money is revealed, then, to be nothing but an empty means, the most accomplished bearer of 'the relativity of our aspirations'. These contradictions explain why the search for 'objective delight' in its acquisition or possession may give rise to an oscillation between feelings of saturation and insufficiency: while promising unlimited possibilities for enjoyment, money does not contain in itself any concrete enjoyment; while offering a way of avoiding all frustration, it is also the source of a deadly disappointment.

Squandering

As the experiences of the greedy and the miser reveal, the attempt to convert money into an absolute purpose and to find unhindered enjoyment in its acquisition and possession cannot but fail: despite its promise of fulfilling each and every desire, money can only provide for an 'abstract form of enjoyment which, none the less, is not enjoyed' (Simmel, [1900/07] 2004, p. 243). Seeking to establish money as the actual bearer of 'the absoluteness of the idea of final purpose', the greedy and the miser end up finding in it the most radical symbol of 'the relativity of our aspirations'. Now, once money's position as a relative means comes to the fore, the question arises as to where 'the absoluteness of the idea of final purpose' could find a new ground. This is a problem that will be, as it were, bequeathed to the squanderer. Acknowledging money's relativity, he seeks for an absolute purpose precisely in the next stage of the teleological sequence: its expenditure. His behaviour acquires thereby a distinctive aspect, as exemplified in a story narrated by Hippolyte Taine and viewed by Simmel as 'typical of the wild extravagances of the *ancien régime*':

> When Prince Conti sent a diamond valued at 4,000–5,000 francs to a lady and it was returned to him, he ordered it to be crushed so that he might use it as writing sand for the letter he wrote to her in reply. Taine adds to this story the following remark about the conventions of that period: 'The less one cares about money, the more a man of the world one is'.
>
> *(Simmel, [1900/07] 2004, p. 249)*

As this example indicates, the spendthrift looks for something which is, at first sight, completely opposite to what is aimed by the greedy and the miser: he is not oriented towards accumulation but rather towards disposal. Instead of seeking an absolute purpose in the appropriation of a valued object, he does so through the opposite move of setting himself both *apart* from and *above* such a thing. For Prince Conti, having a diamond crushed meant positing it as something utterly unimportant and, by the same token, affirming his distance and superiority in relation to it (as well as to the woman whose love the diamond was supposed to stand as an equivalent for). This indicates how squandering is first and foremost a *value* relation: significant here is not the fact that such or such thing was destroyed, but rather that an equivalent of 4,000–5,000 francs was disposed of with indifference. The 'pure function of squandering' consists in a move towards self-valuation through devaluation (ibid.).

Now the implications of such an act can only be intensified when it is directed not simply to an equivalent of value – as Prince Conti's diamond – but to the bearer of abstract value itself, i.e. money. Here is where the pure function of squandering is most radically displayed: 'the indifference towards money value … constitutes the essence and attraction of extravagance'. And yet, as Taine's story indicates, such an indifference 'presupposes … money value as something experienced and appreciated; for, obviously, throwing away what is indifferent would itself be completely indifferent' (ibid.). The spendthrift's own value can only be affirmed on the condition that he assumes that what is being squandered possesses great value: 'the conscious and emphatic negative attitude towards money is based – as in a dialectical process – on its opposite, which alone can give it significance and attraction' (ibid.).

This brings his experience closer to that of the greedy and the avaricious, despite their apparent opposition. 'To the spendthrift money is as important as it is to the miser, though not in the form of owning it but in squandering it' (ibid.). Just as in greed and avarice the affirmation of money value becomes an end in itself detached from any concrete enjoyment, in squandering the negation of money value is converted into an absolute purpose whatever the concrete results of such an endeavour: 'instead of seeking out the enjoyment of real entities', which are by definition limited, the squanderer as much as the greedy and the avaricious look 'for the intangible, which extends to the infinite and has no external or internal reasons for its restriction' (Simmel, [1900/07] 2004, p. 250). These behaviours are hence marked by a peculiar '*Maßlosigkeit*' (a lack of moderation, a boundlessness, a tendency to move beyond any reasonable measure) which is connected to the inherent excessiveness of the object on which they rely:

> Because of its close relationship to money, extravagance very easily gains an immense increase in momentum and robs those who are subject to it of all reasonable standards, since the regulation that is given through the measure of receptivity of concrete objects is lacking.
>
> *(ibid.)*

Such a structure manifests itself in different ways according to the stage of the teleological sequence at which action is interrupted. In greed and avarice, the sequence is interrupted before the moment of expenditure, so that money's inherent tensions come to be expressed in the form of a contradictory relation between *potentiality* and *actuality*. Now, to the extent that money is spent and that such an act becomes an end in itself, those tensions change shape and come to be expressed in the form of a contradiction between *necessity* and *superfluity*. The more an object appears to us as necessary, Simmel says, the more the desire for it is felt as urgent but also as limited. In turn, something superfluous is experienced as less urgent but also as unlimited:

> The scale of our needs moves between these two poles: either it is one of immediate intensity but then certainly limited by nature, or else it is the need for luxuries, in which case the lack of necessity is replaced by unlimited possibilities for their expansion.
>
> *(Simmel, [1900/07] 2004, p. 252)*

Most cultural goods, Simmel claims, 'exhibit a certain mixture of these extremes, such that the approximation to the one corresponds to a growing distance from the other' (ibid.). Money, however, combines the maximum of these two poles: it is the most indispensable object since it provides the means for the most basic needs of life; yet it is also the most dispensable object for, in itself, it cannot satisfy any necessity. To that extent, money associates the *intense urgency* of the most basic needs with the *extensive unlimitedness* of the most superfluous desires. It gives rise, then, to the paradoxical experience of an urgent need that cannot be satisfied, a luxury that nevertheless appears as indispensable. Here again, life takes on the neurasthenic form of an oscillation between feelings of saturation and insufficiency:

> The spendthrift is indifferent towards the object once he possesses it; his enjoyment is doomed never to find repose and permanency; the moment of his possession of an object coincides with the negation of its enjoyment. In this respect, life has the same demonic form as for the avaricious: every goal attained arouses a thirst for more which can never be satisfied, for this whole tendency searches for satisfaction, as it flows out of an ultimate purpose, within a category that denies any purpose from the outset and limits itself to the means and to the penultimate moment.
>
> *(Simmel, [1900/07] 2004, p. 251)*

Ascetic poverty

The greedy, the miser, and the squanderer hence remain within the circle of influence of money and its inherent contradictions. Yet the spendthrift is distinguished by the fact that he already intends to move beyond money, even if such an attempt is doomed to fail. Now there is a figure that takes such negation of money to a further degree; one which seeks not merely to devalue it but also to counteract it with a definite ideal: 'poverty as a positive value, poverty in itself as a self-satisfying purpose of life' (Simmel, [1900/07] 2004, p. 252). Fundamentally characterised by a refusal of money, such a stance only gains its full meaning in the context of an advanced money economy. This is due, above all, to the transformations that the expansion of monetary transactions brings about in moral experience: 'Humane and sympathetic feelings towards poverty', says Simmel, 'are more easily aroused where what the poor lack and what one can help them with is ... what is most immediately necessary to them' – e.g., food and clothing (Simmel, [1900/07] 2004, p. 253). In strictly monetary relationships, however, those sympathetic feelings have to make a detour before they reach their final objective and, for this reason, often flag. The possession of money may then come to be detested as the most dangerous temptation or the primary evil, in contrast to which poverty can appear as a positive and indispensable means for the salvation of the soul – and the more so, the more central money becomes.

Monetary insensitivity and idealised poverty thus develop hand in hand. At first, the positive valuation of poverty can take the form of a mere indifference towards worldly enjoyments and interests: 'The first Christians may frequently have behaved in this way, that is, not directly antagonistic and aggressive towards tangible goods, but simply lacking any relation to them' (ibid.). But the more the money economy expands, the less it becomes possible to sustain a mere dismissal of material interest and the more asceticism has to acquire resolute forms: 'since one continually confronts [money] on the road to the most indispensable and since its acquisition requires more attentiveness and activity of the will than the resultant concern with subsistence', the ascetic person must 'not permit the smallest amount of his consciousness to be distracted' (Simmel, [1900/07] 2004, p. 253 f.). Under these circumstances, the 'indifference to everything external ... will easily transform itself into real hatred' and money may appear as a dangerous temptation:

> Because it is ready to be used at any moment, it is the worst snare of a moment of weakness, and since it serves all activities, it offers the soul its most tempting aspect at that time. ... Hence for ascetic modes of sensibility it becomes the real symbol of the devil who seduces us under the mask of innocence and simplicity, so that the only safeguard against both the devil and money is to keep them at a distance and reject any relation to them.
>
> *(Simmel, [1900/07] 2004, p. 254)*

The more central money becomes to our lives, the more resolute must be its rejection on the part of the ascetic, the more emphatically poverty comes to appear as its positive counterpoint. According to Simmel, such a process reached a peak in the early Franciscan friars, who elevated poverty to 'an *autonomous* value and a correlate of the deepest innermost needs' (Simmel, [1900/07] 2004, p. 255; emphasis added). For them, poverty was not simply a *means* for the salvation of the soul, a 'possession which ... mediated the acquisition of the supreme goods, performing for the latter the same service as money does for worldly and contemptible goods' (ibid.). It was first and foremost an *end in itself*:

> poverty was already quite clearly one side or expression of the fact that the world belongs, in a higher and supreme sense, to he who renounces; he does not really renounce, but rather in poverty he possesses the purest and finest extract of things, just as the avaricious possesses the same in money.
>
> *(ibid.)*

Converted into an absolute purpose, poverty seemed then to have lost its ascetic nature: it no longer consisted simply in a condition for the salvation of the soul, but rather presented its immediate fulfilment and enjoyment. At the same time, such an ideal was defined by a radical form of asceticism and renunciation. The Franciscans' motto – *nihil habentes, omnia possidentes* – expresses in the clearest manner the contradiction inherent to the elevation of poverty to an ultimate purpose: definitive possession is sought precisely in the abstention from all possession. The radical renunciation of the one who does not really renounce hence mirrors that abstract form of enjoyment which is not enjoyed. Poverty as an ethical ideal displays the same contradictory structure of the monetary means, only in an inverted form. It attests, instead of refusing, the latter's power:

> The tremendous and wide-reaching power of the process by which money is elevated from its intermediary position to absolute importance is best illuminated by the fact that the negation of its meaning is elevated to the identical form.
>
> *(ibid.)*

As with squandering, the conversion of poverty into an absolute purpose is premised on the money value it intends to negate, and thus becomes equally involved in an unresolved contradiction: aiming to provide one with the realisation of 'the absoluteness of the idea of final purpose', it reveals itself to be entangled – as much as the monetary means – in 'the relativity of our aspirations'. Here, as before, life takes on a 'demonic form' inasmuch as every renounced goal 'arouses a thirst for more [renunciation] which can never be satisfied' (Simmel, [1900/07] 2004, p. 251).

Cynicism and the blasé attitude

This poses an important problem, which will be taken up by the next figure in Simmel's typology of hypertrophied behaviours. The acknowledgement that even a value that seemed entirely opposite to money – poverty as an ideal – relies on the assumption of the latter's absolute value leads to a relativisation not only of that ideal, but potentially of all values. Seeking to escape money's contradictions, the idealisation of poverty has resulted in an extension of the latter's relativity to the entire sphere of value: 'The negativity of the teleological sequence, which money had already brought about in extravagance and the desire for poverty', may now come to seize upon 'the particularity of values, which are merely crystallised in money' (Simmel, [1900/07] 2004, p. 256).

Such is the position defended by modern cynicism, which, as Simmel argues, is remarkably different from the Greek philosophy from which the term originates. While ancient cynicism deemed all distinctions between higher and lower values to be irrelevant, this stance did not lead to the abolition of value but was rather premised on the affirmation of 'an entirely positive ideal in life: the unconditional strength of the soul and the ethical freedom of the individual' (ibid.). In comparison with the latter, all other ideals would pale into insignificance and 'precisely in their indifference the existence of this absolute value would be revealed' (ibid.). For the modern cynic, however, such a positive ideal has vanished:

> In the attitude which we nowadays characterise as cynical, it seems to me decisive that here too no higher differences in values exist and that, in general, the only significance of what is highly valued consists in its being degraded to the lowest level, but that the positive and ideal ethical purpose of this levelling has disappeared.
>
> *(ibid.)*

In modern cynicism, the levelling of every particular value no longer leads to the affirmation of an absolute ideal, but simply to the notion that there is no difference at all between values. Such an attitude, for Simmel, consists in a 'subjective reflex' of the objective dominance of the money economy in modernity:

> The more money becomes the sole centre of interest, the more one discovers that honour and conviction, talent and virtue, beauty and salvation of the soul, are exchanged against money and so the more a mocking and frivolous attitude will develop in relation to these higher values that are for sale for the same kind of value as groceries.
>
> *(Simmel, [1900/07] 2004, p. 256 f.)*

This description might make it seem that cynicism is constituted by a purely negative moment: here 'the absoluteness of the idea of final purpose' appears to have disappeared, insofar as all particular values are considered relative. But things are not exactly so. Modern cynicism refuses the *difference* between values, but not the *existence* of value: 'the cynic is still moved to a reaction by the sphere of value, even if in the perverse sense that he considers the downward movement of values part of the attraction of life' (Simmel, [1900/07] 2004, p. 257). Some notion of the absolute is retained here, even if in the very reduced form of a mere confirmation – through the debasement of all particular values – that value still exists. Such is the contradiction inherent to modern cynicism: it affirms the existence of a value sphere at the same time – and precisely *to the extent* – that it brings about a levelling of all differences between values.

The relativisation of the differences between particular values can lead, however, to the conclusion that things in themselves have no value at all. This is the position of the blasé person, who takes such levelling even further than the modern cynic and has completely lost the feeling for value: 'He experiences all things as being of an equally dull and grey hue, as not worth getting excited about' (ibid.). Unlike the cynic, who still finds an 'attraction of life' and 'a definite pleasurable sensation' in the devaluation of everything, the blasé person no longer allows himself to be moved by anything. More than just levelling the differences between values (*Verschiedenwertigkeit*), he is indifferent to the differences in the nature of things themselves (*Verschiedenartigkeit der Dinge*) and is thereby robbed from 'the whole liveliness of feeling and volition' (ibid.).

In the blasé attitude, the 'negativity of the teleological sequence' thus reaches its peak: in connection with the extension of money's logic beyond the economic realm, the 'relativity of our aspirations' seizes upon not only the particularity of values but the existence of values as such. Here the 'absoluteness of the idea of final purpose' seems to have vanished, leading to a radical form of meaninglessness in which 'all possibilities of attraction are destroyed' (Simmel, [1900/07] 2004, p. 258). Yet the blasé attitude has, in fact, its own form of absolute purpose: once it is no longer possible to find an 'attraction of life' in the sphere of value, the individual may seek it in the mere quantitative increase in excitement. Here is where the oscillation between anesthesia and hyperesthesia takes on its most acute form, where 'the relativity of our aspirations' has acquired an unprecedented extension and 'the absoluteness of the idea of final purpose' has been reduced to the search for mere stimulation in things – 'without thinking it important for us to find out why these stimulate us' (ibid.).

> Out of this there emerges the craving today for excitement, for extreme impressions, for the greatest speed in its change … The satisfaction of such cravings may bring about a temporary relief, but soon the former condition will be re-established, though now made worse by the increased quantity of its elements. … A money culture signifies such an enslavement of life in its means, that release from its weariness is also evidently sought in a mere means which conceals its final significance – in the fact of 'stimulation' as such.
>
> *(Simmel, [1900/07] 2004, p. 258 f.)*

Conclusion

As we saw, in *The philosophy of money* Simmel took up his early analysis of the psychological interruption of the teleological series and further developed it into a typology of hypertrophied or pathological behaviours. Each of the latter presents a specific instantiation of that wide-ranging process, responding each time differently to the action-teleological tension between 'the relativity of our aspirations' and 'the absoluteness of the idea of final purpose'. These behaviours are hence central for a philosophical investigation for which life manifests itself most tellingly where it takes the form of a 'dialectics without reconciliation'.

For the greedy and the avaricious, that tension appears as one between *potentiality and actuality*: they look for the absolutely actual in the acquisition or possession of a potential (e.g., money) which cannot, however, be actualised. In squandering, such an actualisation does take place; money is spent and converted into something else. Yet the tension remains, now taking the form of an opposition between *superfluity and necessity*: the spendthrift looks for the absolutely necessary in the dissipation of a superfluous object (e.g., money) which cannot, however, be dispensed with. For the ascetic poor, money is not something that can be disposed of; it rather appears as an evil or dangerous object that should be morally renounced for the sake of religious salvation. His experience is hence marked by a tension between *renunciation and redemption*: he looks for absolute redemption in the renunciation of something (e.g., money) which cannot, however, be fully renounced. While the modern cynic does not renounce, he devalues that which he comes to possess. His experience is marked by a tension between *levelling and distinction*: he looks for absolute distinction in the levelling of all particular values (e.g., through money) and this, however, cannot but lead to the levelling of value distinctions themselves. The blasé person, in turn, abstains from the search for distinction; he is indifferent towards value itself and hence towards the qualitative differences among things. His experience is marked by a tension between *indifference and stimulation*: he looks for absolute stimulation in sheer impressions made by objects whose specific qualities are, however, indifferent to him (as they are to money).

Insofar as they constitute particular cases of the colonisation of ends by means, these types of action present life in a 'demonic form': each of them displays in a different guise that ceaseless oscillation between (hyperaesthetic) saturation and (anaesthetic) insufficiency which Simmel viewed as characteristic of 'the phenomena of modern culture as they are determined by the money economy' (Simmel, [1908] 2009, p. 46). Through an investigation of hypertrophied or pathological behaviours, *The philosophy of money* hence not only discloses a set of general tensions inherent to teleological action but also illuminates a crucial feature of modern social psychological experience. In both these regards, the book provides more than just an analysis of a set of economic attitudes. Revealing oppositions that are implicated in every human action and not only in those which involve money, it also discerns types of behaviour which go beyond the economic realm and can be seen to permeate modern social life as a whole. If this was so when Simmel wrote *The philosophy of money*, it is even more at a time, like ours, marked by a wide-ranging marketisation of social relations as well as by the proliferation of abstract media of valuation and exchange (rankings, ratings, etc.). In such a context, it comes as no surprise that one can find variations of the greedy, the miser, the squanderer, the ascetic, the cynic, and the blasé person well beyond strictly economic relations. Nor is it shocking that, in such conditions, social experience may often take on the form of what Simmel called neurasthenia and we nowadays associate with notions such as depression and burnout.

Notes

1 This work was generously supported by the Alexander von Humboldt Foundation, the Coordination for the Improvement of Higher Education Personnel (CAPES), the German Academic Exchange Service (DAAD), and the National Council for Scientific and Technological Development (CNPq).

2 Simmel's writings are referenced in this text according to their English translations, whenever these are available. All quotations were compared with the German originals (as published in the *Georg Simmel Gesamtausgabe*) and occasionally modified for the sake of precision.

3 By characterising those behaviours as 'pathological' or 'hypertrophied', Simmel was not aiming primarily at an *individual* psychological diagnosis but rather pointing to the fact that such forms of action consisted in instantiations of the wide-ranging 'paradoxes', 'dissonances', 'internal contradictions' or 'pathologies' of modern *culture* (Simmel, [1908] 1997, pp. 44, 45, [1911–12] 1997, p. 66, [1917] 1997, pp. 91, 92).

4 This is not to say that Simmel presents here a *Lebensphilosophie* as the latter was understood at his time (cf. Fitzi, 2002). Nor does it mean that *The philosophy of money* can be interpreted, without further ado, along the lines of his late metaphysics of life (Simmel, [1918] 2010). In this chapter I consider only the path from Simmel's psychology of money to his *Philosophy of money*. On the differences between such a philosophical perspective and the one developed in his late works, cf. Bueno (2018).

5 This points to a crucial difference between the analyses developed in 'On the Psychology of Money' and *The philosophy of money*. Whereas Simmel's early assessment of the interruption of the teleological series relied on a substantive notion of 'rational ultimate goal' – understood as 'the enjoyment from the use of the object' and thus as something actually attainable (Simmel, [1889] 1997, p. 235) – in his 1900 book he sets out by addressing precisely the problematic aspects of such a conception.

6 Enjoyment (*Genuß*) is a crucial figure in Simmel's theory of teleological action as well as in his value theory: as 'a completely undivided act', a 'psychological condition [that] is not yet, or is no longer, affected by the contrast between [a desiring] subject and [a desired] object', it constitutes the horizon of every human action (Simmel, [1900/07] 2004, p. 62 f.). Hence the paradoxical character of a form of enjoyment that retains the distance between subject and object and thus is not actually enjoyed.

References

Blumenberg, H. (1976). Geld oder Leben. Eine metaphorologische Studie zur Konsistenz der Philosophie Georg Simmels. In H. Böhringer & K. Gründer (Eds.), *Ästhetik und Soziologie um die Jahrhundertwende: Georg Simmel* (pp. 121–134). Frankfurt am Main: Klostermann.

Bueno, A. (2013). Simmel e os paradoxos da cultura moderna. In A. Bueno (Ed.), *O conflito da cultura moderna e outros escritos. Georg Simmel* (pp. 145–182). São Paulo: Senac.

Bueno, A. (2018). Rationality – Cultivation – Vitality: Simmel on the pathologies of modern culture. *Dissonancia: Critical Theory Journal*. Advance online publication, 1–36.

Dahme, H.-J., & Rammstedt, O. (1984). *Georg Simmel und die Moderne. Neue Interpretationen und Materialen.* Frankfurt am Main: Suhrkamp.

Ehrenberg, A. (1998). *La fatigue d'être soi. Dépression et société.* Paris: Odile Jacob.

Fitzi, G. (2002). *Soziale Erfahrung und Lebensphilosophie. Georg Simmels Beziehung zu Henri Bergson.* Konstanz: UVK.

Frisby, D. (1978). Introduction to the translation. In G. Simmel (ed.)., *The philosophy of money* (pp. 1–49). London: Routledge.

Frisby, D. (1981). *Sociological impressionism. A reassessment of Georg Simmel's social theory.* London: Heinemann.

Habermas, J. ([1983] 1996). Georg Simmel on philosophy and culture: Postscript to a collection of essays. *Critical Inquiry, 22* (3), 403–414.

Honneth, A. ([2002] 2004). Organized self-realization: Some paradoxes of individualization. *European Journal of Social Theory*, 7(4), 463–478.

Landmann, M. (1968). Einleitung des Herausgebers. In M. Landmann (Ed.), *Das Individuelle Gesetz. Philosophische Exkurse* (pp. 7–29). Frankfurt am Main: Suhrkamp.

Neckel, S., & Wagner, G. (Eds.). (2013). *Leistung und Erschöpfung. Burnout in der Wettbewerbsgesellschaft.* Berlin: Suhrkamp.

Rosa, H. (2011). Beschleunigung und Depression. Überlegungen zum Zeitverhältnis der Moderne. *Psyche, 65*, 1041–1060.

Simmel, G. ([1889] 1997). On the psychology of money. In D. Frisby & M. Featherstone (Eds.), *Simmel on culture: Selected writings* (pp. 233–243). London: Sage.

Simmel, G. ([1890] 1989). Über sociale Differenzierung. Sociologische und psychologische Untersuchungen. In *Georg Simmel Gesamtausgabe, Band 2: Aufsätze 1887 bis 1890* (pp. 109–295). Frankfurt am Main: Suhrkamp.

Simmel, G. ([1890] 2015). On art exhibitions. *Theory, Culture & Society, 32*(1),87–92.

Simmel, G. ([1893] 1997). Infelices possidentes! (Unhappy dwellers). In D. Frisby & M. Featherstone (Eds.), *Simmel on culture: Selected writings* (pp. 259–262). London: Sage.

Simmel, G. ([1895] 1997). The Alpine journey. In D. Frisby & M. Featherstone (Eds.), *Simmel on culture: Selected writings* (pp. 219–221). London: Sage.

Simmel, G. ([1896] 1992). Soziologische Aesthetik. In *Georg Simmel Gesamtausgabe, Band 5: Aufsätze und Abhandlungen 1894–1900* (pp. 197–214). Frankfurt am Main: Suhrkamp.

Simmel, G. ([1896] 1997a). Money in modern culture. In D. Frisby & M. Featherstone (Eds.), *Simmel on culture: Selected writings* (pp. 243–255). London: Sage.

Simmel, G. ([1896] 1997b). The Berlin trade exhibition. In D. Frisby & M. Featherstone (Eds.), *Simmel on culture: Selected writings* (pp. 255–259). London: Sage.

Simmel, G. ([1900/07] 2004). *The philosophy of money*. London: Routledge.

Simmel, G. ([1903] 1997). The metropolis and mental life. In D. Frisby & M. Featherstone (Eds.), *Simmel on culture: Selected writings* (pp. 174–187). London: Sage.

Simmel, G. ([1908] 1997). On the essence of culture. In D. Frisby & M. Featherstone (Eds.), *Simmel on culture: Selected writings* (pp. 40–46). London: Sage.

Simmel, G. ([1908] 2009). *Sociology. Inquiries into the construction of social forms*. Leiden and Boston, MA: Brill.

Simmel, G. ([1911–12] 1997). The concept and tragedy of culture. In D. Frisby & M. Featherstone (Eds.), *Simmel on culture: Selected writings* (pp. 55–75). London: Sage.

Simmel, G. ([1917] 1997). The crisis of culture. In D. Frisby & M. Featherstone (Eds.), *Simmel on culture: Selected writings* (pp. 90–101). London: Sage.

Simmel, G. ([1918] 2010). *The view of life. Four metaphysical essays with journal aphorisms*. Chicago, IL: University of Chicago Press.

Svartman, B., & Bueno, A. (2016). Economia monetária, economia psíquica: Simmel, Freud e o esquematismo da subjetividade moderna. In M. Checchia (Ed.), *Combate à vontade de potência: Ensaios sobre psicanálise e dominação* (pp. 153–190). São Paulo: Annablume.

PART VIII

Lines of reception

24

SIMMEL'S AMERICAN LEGACY REVISITED

Milos Brocic and Daniel Silver

Introduction

Simmel's early influence on American sociology is well-documented by now (Levine et al., 1976a, 1976b; Jaworski, 1997; Goodstein, 2017). Albion Small, the founder of America's first sociology department at the University of Chicago, and Robert E. Park, the influential pioneer of the 'Chicago School', both engaged with Simmel while studying in Germany, importing his sociology into America, and applying it to domestic concerns. His influence continued among later generations of scholars at the University Chicago, in the works of Everett Hughes, Donald Levine, and Erving Goffman, among others (Jaworski, 1997; Low, 2008). Since then, American sociology continued to return to Simmel's work as a source of inspiration, with his legacy unfolding into a rich and diverse stream of scholarship across many of the discipline's major subfields (Levine et al., 1976a, 1976b, Brocic & Silver, Forthcoming).

According to Murray S. Davis (1981, p. 1193) 'Simmel's most important contribution to modern social science was not procedures (as was Durkheim's) or substance (as was Weber's) but inspiration'. It is unsurprising then that the trajectory of this inspiration has itself been the focus of scholarship. Simmel's reception has offered scholars an occasion to reflect on larger disciplinary issues within American sociology, whether its theoretical assumptions (Levine, 1991), disciplinary boundaries (Goodstein, 2017), or even the strategic value it offers for political projects (Jaworski, 1997). A critical tone is not uncommon among these assessments, however. Simmel's appropriation in the discipline is widely regarded as fragmented and piece-meal. Though some scholars identify this scattered interpretation as an opportunity for creative uptake (Coser, 1956; Jaworski, 1997), for others, it reflects a failure to grasp the full richness of Simmel's thought (Levine et al., 1976b; Goodstein, 2017). According to Goodstein, sociology's early monopolization of Simmel's American uptake narrowed the reception of his ideas, with restrictive disciplinary conventions violating the boundary-defying nature of his thinking. This critique is not without merit. Simmel first and foremost considered himself to be a philosopher. Indeed, his initial exposure to America was in through a review of his work in *The Philosophical Review*. Moreover, prior to his publications in the *American Journal of Sociology*, his essay, 'Moral Deficiencies as Determining Intellectual Functions' was already published in *The International Journal of Ethics* in 1893. Despite these earlier more explicitly philosophical contributions, Simmel came to be overwhelmingly embraced as a sociologist in America. As translations of sociological writings proliferated, and his ideas became centrally featured in Park and Burgess' *Introduction to the Science of Society* – the famous 'green bible' that constituted the first sociology textbook – Simmel's broader work as a philosopher and cultural critic was to some degree neglected.

Developments since the 1970s have been favorable for a renewed and more wide-ranging reception of Simmel's work, however. New translations have emerged exposing Simmel's fuller oeuvre to a broader English-speaking audience (Kemple, 2012). *The philosophy of money*, widely regarded in Germany – and by Simmel himself – as his *magnum opus*, was translated into English in 1978. *The view of life* – Simmel's final work which represented the culmination of his philosophy of life – was translated into English in 2010. Though selections from *Sociology: Inquiries into the Construction of Social Forms* had been previously published in various journals and collections, a complete translation of the book was only published in 2009. Outside of these major works, Simmel was also a prolific essayist, being among Berlin's most important cultural critics at the time (Leck, 2000). Over the past fifty years, dozens of translations of these essays have been published (Kemple, 2012). In tandem with these new translations, developments within academia appear encouraging as well. The emergence of cultural studies towards the end of the 20th century offers renewed opportunity for interdisciplinary Simmelian influence, continuing his thread through the Frankfurt tradition. Even some sociologists have moved to correct the narrow reception of Simmel, emphasizing the more vitalist, aesthetic and metaphysical elements of his work that tend to be neglected by sociologists (Weinstein & Weinstein, 1989; Leck, 2000; de la Fuente, 2008; Silver & Lee, 2012; Silver & O'Neill, 2014; Silver & Brocic, 2019).

These developments provoke new questions about Simmel's reception: what new trends have emerged in Simmel's American legacy? What is the interdisciplinary uptake of Simmel? How do these developments advance our interpretative understanding of Simmel's work? In this chapter, we explore this reception of Georg Simmel in America across different disciplines and seek answers to these questions. After reviewing prior accounts of this legacy that have primarily focused on Simmel's early reception by the Chicago School sociologists and via Frankfurt School critical theorists (primarily associated with the New School for Social Research), we highlight trends since the 1970s. To do so, we use a mix of computational and traditional scholarly methods. The former consists in comparative decade-by-decade co-citation networks of articles that cite Simmel, contrasting: (a) US Sociology journals; (b) US philosophy journals; (c) US Cultural Studies journals; and (d) all other journals. This method allows us to pinpoint the diversity of scholarly conversations in which Simmel has figured centrally, and to compare the nature of these conversations across fields and time. Close scholarly examination of other authors and texts associated with Simmel across time and subfield allows us to determine who Simmel's champions have been, and which of his ideas they have selectively advanced, reinterpreted, or ignored. After assessing these trends, and how Simmel's reception compares across disciplines, we conclude by reflecting how this enhances our understanding of his legacy.

Simmel's early reception in America

Simmel's integration into American Sociology began at the University of Chicago. Though Simmel never visited the USA himself, early pioneers of the discipline became acquainted with his work while studying in Germany. Simmel was an important figure in Berlin's vibrant cultural life (Leck, 2000). Despite being marginalized by academic institutions, he nonetheless enjoyed considerable popularity, holding widely attended lectures, and publishing a prolific body of work. According to Karl Mannheim, Simmel was the most important philosopher of Wilhelmian Germany (Leck, 2000, p. 281). During Small and Park's time in Germany, however, Simmel's interests lay primarily in sociology, seeking to articulate a research program for the nascent discipline. Simmel championed a neo-Kantian formal approach to sociology, coupled with a commitment to uncovering the dynamic forms of association that held the more visible 'organs' of society together. Social life was portrayed by Simmel as fragmented, processual, and essentially incomplete. This put him at odds with Durkheim's vision of sociology, which featured collective representation and solidarity centrally, and pursued examination of collective 'social facts' that stand above and against individuals (Pietilä, 2011). Still, Simmel's sociology resonated with Small and Park, who found inspiration in his formalism and interactionism, importing it into America to apply to domestic concerns. Upon return, Small founded the *American Journal of Sociology*, and translated numerous of Simmel's essays, which became an early staple in the journal.

Simmel's work left an important and lasting imprint on sociology at the University of Chicago. For Park, Simmel's forms of social interaction – conflict, domination, competition, and the like – informed his own theorizing of integrative processes in city life, while social types like 'the Stranger' influenced his own ideas on the 'Marginal Man'. Simmel's portrait of the city, including its alienating qualities and the pervasive blasé attitude it evoked among inhabitants, moreover, became an important early insight for urban sociology through its incorporation in Louis Wirth's seminal article 'Urbanism as a Way of Life'(1938). Outside of urban sociology, Simmel's neo-Kantian emphasis on the selectivity of our perceptions lived on in the work of Everett Hughes. Hughes found inspiration in Simmel's concept of social distance for articulating the protective function of etiquette; the social front it offered to individuals, where convention could conceal the inner life, and shield it from vulnerability (Rock, 1979; Jaworski, 1997). This fragmented understanding of the individual, meticulously managing their impressions to find relief from social pressures, continued in the work of Goffman. Though Goffman's references to Simmel were few and far, scholars have noted their close affinity (Smith, 1989; Jaworski, 1997). This is true for Mead and Blumer as well, where Simmel's influence and affinity has been observed (Low, 2008).

Simmel was not incorporated equally across American sociology, however. Most notably, his brand of sociology conflicted with that of Talcott Parsons. Simmel's relationalism stood in sharp contrast to Parsons' more voluntaristic conception of social action. His formalism, moreover, left little room for Parsons' interest in normative values. Excluding Simmel from his influential book *The Structure of Social Action*, Parsons effectively blocked Simmel's early incorporation into the canon (Arditi, 1987; Levine, 1989; Camic, 1992; Aronowitz, 1994). Still, Parsons' aversions did not extend to his students, most notably Robert K. Merton. In developing his ideas on the role set, and the multiple and often competing affiliations that individuals occupy, Merton drew on Simmel's understanding of the fragmentary character of social life (Coser, 1975). He regarded Simmel as among the most important inspirations for his work. This enthusiasm continued among his own students as well. Upon Merton's advice, Lewis Coser wrote his dissertation on the fourth chapter of Simmel's *Sociology*, 'Conflict'. Coser's (1956) *The Functions of Social Conflict* situated Simmel's conflict-cohesion dialectic within a functionalist framework, ultimately becoming a landmark treatment of conflict in the field.

This early reception overwhelmingly drew on selections from Simmel's *Sociology*, a book that offered a treasure trove of insights, but was notoriously regarded as unsystematic. Unsurprisingly, a selective and piece-meal appropriation of Simmel's followed. Mostly stripped of their connection to broader themes of modernity, his work became incorporated into the dominant Mertonian 'middle-range' framework, mined for inventive propositions and sharp insights, and applied to radically disparate social domains (Coser, 1956; Turner, 1975). This was hardly reflective of Simmel's broader body of work, however. Among Simmel's German contemporaries, he was most influential for his diagnosis of modernity, and his philosophy of life (Goodstein, 2017). According to Leck (2000), a deep anti-bourgeois and countercultural current guided Simmel's work, as he would regularly draw in the most radical students. Frankfurt School pioneers, Georg Lukács and Ernst Bloch, were among Simmel's closest students, and both were deeply influenced by his writings on alienation in *The philosophy of money*. Lukács' *History and Class Consciousness* – an important book in the development of Western Marxism – contains many traces of his mentor's ideas on rationalization and objectification in modern life. Simmel has also been identified as an often unrecognized predecessor of Walter Benjamin (Frisby, 1986; Jameson, 1999; Symons, 2017). The latter's portrayal of the shocking sensory experience of city life which fractured the subjective lives of urban dwellers recalled Simmel's depiction of nervous overstimulation in 'The Metropolis and Mental Life'. Benjamin, indeed, explicitly acknowledged Simmel's importance in his writings on Charles Baudelaire. At the same time, Simmel's ideas were foundational for 20th century continental philosophy and phenomenology, through his influence on Martin Heidegger. Indeed, Heidegger attended Simmel's lectures on the philosophy of life in which Simmel prefigured core Heideggerian ideas such as finitude and mortality, even if Heidegger barely acknowledged the influence publicly (Grossheim, 1991). This subterranean influence, however, has been uncovered in more recent interpretations (Gadamer, 1965, 1986; Grossheim, 1991; Krell, 1992; Jalbert, 2003).

Some version of this Simmel, as the predecessor of the Frankfurt School, and as a philosopher of life and modernity, continued in America. This was mostly through the New School of Social Research, and particularly through the efforts of Albert Salomon. Acutely aware of the narrow formalist reception of Simmel's work in American sociology, Salomon sought to correct this interpretation by highlighting the unity between Simmel's philosophy and sociology, and positioning him within the phenomenological school of thought, among thinkers like James, Bergson, and Schutz (Jaworski, 1997, 1998). Salomon attended Simmel's lectures in Berlin in 1910, experiencing Simmel's brilliance firsthand. The American reception of Simmel was in his view 'scandalous' (Jaworski, 1998, p. 10). Scholars at the New School thus championed an interpretation of Simmel that challenged Merton's structuralist interpretation dominant at the neighboring Columbia University. Against the empiricist orientation of American sociology, however, a more humanistic and philosophical version of Simmel confronted considerable obstacles. Indeed, Levine et al.'s 1976 review of Simmel's influence on American sociology found little evidence of this Simmelian uptake.

As discussed above, however, recent developments suggest that the room for redeeming a more rounded interpretation of Simmel has expanded. New translations have introduced English audiences to Simmel's more philosophical writings, while new fields like cultural studies open renewed opportunity for drawing on his more critical cultural writings. In the next section we examine Simmel's American reception over the past fifty years. How has it changed, how has this stayed the same, and what does this reveal to us about Simmel?

Simmel's American reception since 1970

Influence is a slippery concept and tracing it is a notoriously difficult task. Sometimes scholars are not forthright about their influences. Others claim indebtedness not as a reflection of genuine inspiration, but as a signpost to perennial concerns. Simmel's case presents added challenges. The incredibly variegated, disjointed, and non-cumulative use of his ideas means there is no single lineage to follow. Simmel himself was presciently aware of this. He predicted his influence would be like 'a cash legacy divided among many heirs, and each converts his share into whatever business suits his nature, in which the provenance from that legacy cannot be seen' ([1918] 2010). To partially overcome these challenges and capture the diverse strands of his use, we adopt a combination of newer computational methods along with traditional scholarship. We downloaded from the Web of Science bibliographies and abstracts of all articles published from 1970–2019 that included at least one citation to Simmel's work. Given our focus on the American reception, we restricted our sample to only articles where at least one author reported an affiliation to an American institution.

With these citations we used a Python script developed by Neal Caren to create a network of co-citations and to identify the different clusters making up separate networks. Specifically, given our interest in Simmel's interdisciplinary use, we generated citation networks for Simmel's use in sociology journals, cultural studies journals, philosophy journals, and all other journals. The nodes in each network are comprised by sources cited in the bibliographies of the Simmel-citing articles. The citation of two sources in the same Simmel-citing article forms the network's edges. To identify the major clusters within this larger network, the Python script relied on the Louvain community detection method. Each of these clusters were organized hierarchically according to their most central citations. These central citations reveal the organization of those American articles which cite Simmel into different clusters, and the different traditions upon which these clusters draw.

Tables 24.1–24.3 below provide summaries for these different disciplinary uptakes of Simmel. Though there is some use of Simmel among American philosophers, the instances of these are very few. Our analysis finds no clustering in this discipline, and thus we do not present a table here. The other disciplines, however, do reveal clustering along coherent subdisciplinary topics. In what follows we draw on these results to reflect on the new trends in Simmel's reception since 1970; how his appropriation varies across disciplines; and finally, what this reveals about Simmel's legacy more generally.

Diagrams which visualize the citation networks can be found on the online appendix at https://legacyofsimmel.weebly.com/.

Simmel in sociological research since 1970

The last comprehensive review of Simmel's sociological reception and empirical application in America was by Levine et al. in 1976. Using this assessment as a benchmark, we consider continuity and change in the sociological uptake since 1970. Our results reveal some familiar terrain for Simmel's adoption. Two major clusters we find – urban sociology and conflict – build on important traditions that carried on since Levine et al.'s review. In the urban sociology cluster, we find continuity with the early Chicago School appropriation. Wirth's (1938) 'Urbanism as a Way of Life', in particular, continues to mark Simmel's integration in the field. Simmel is often used by scholars to reflect on the alienating conditions of urban life; how interpersonal relationships become more distant in dense environments, and the implications this has for subjective well-being. The insights from 'Metropolis and mental life' become incorporated into the 'Community lost' thesis framework (Mayhew & Levinger, 1976; Welch, 1983; Bell, 1992). A similar pattern recurs in the conflict cluster. Again, Simmel's appropriation remains tied to his early champion, Lewis Coser. Scholars draw on Simmel in tandem with Coser to explore the role of conflict

Table 24.1 Sociology

Networks:	**Urban Sociology**:

Networks:

Building off Blau's structuralist interpretation of Simmel, networks scholars continued to rely on Simmel to for understanding affiliations among actors. Simmel's form vs. content distinction sets the agenda in this cluster. Geometric metaphors such as 'webs of affiliations', 'distance', 'dyads', and 'triads' offer theoretical perspective to network scholars pursuing empirical inquiry on the formal properties of social ties.

Key ideas:

Exchange
Homophily
Duality
Structural Holes
Social Distance
Multiple Group
Affiliations

Key Texts:

Conflict and the Web of Group Affiliations
'The Quantitative Conditioning of the Group'
'The Intersection of Social Circles'

Theory:

Simmel is central to several, often competing, theoretical traditions in sociology. Simmel has been described as 'the classical sociologist most deeply committed to relational theorizing' (Emirbayer, 1997) and is often juxtaposed to Parsonian normative functionalism. He was also an early influence for symbolic interactionism from the Chicago School, offering pioneering insights on the phenomenological social dimensions of everyday life. For others though, he is 'the father of quantitative sociology' (Blau, 1977a), laying the foundation for formal sociology.

Key ideas: **Key Texts:**

Relational Sociology   *Sociology of Georg Simmel*
Symbolic   'The Problem of Sociology'
Interactionism   'How is Society Possible'
Formalism

Culture:

Despite his emphasis on form over content, American sociologists have found purchase in extending Simmel's formal insights into the cultural domain. Scholars use network analysis to examine cultural tastes and explore a more fluid interaction between culture and networks. Apart from the research on culture and networks, Simmel's writings on fashion have also been influential. Simmel is often cited alongside Veblen, narrowly positioned as representing a the 'trickle-down' approach to taste where elite culture is mimicked by the lower classes – a legacy of Blumer's interpretation of Simmel's essay on

Urban Sociology:

The urban sociology cluster represents perhaps the oldest Simmelian tradition in American sociology, with Simmel being a formative influence on the pioneers of the Chicago School. Still, the literature in this cluster reveals important developments. Louis Wirth's seminal piece 'Urbanism as a Way of Life', which drew on Simmel to emphasize the alienating qualities of the metropolis, remains the central citation in the cluster. Earlier articles, especially the 1970s, continued to draw on Simmel in a similar fashion. Into the 1980s, this 'community-lost' thesis lost favor to a more networked approach to urban communities that emphasized connectedness over alienation. Simmel nevertheless remained relevant in offering perspective to this approach.

Key Ideas: **Key Texts:**

Blasé Attitude   'The Metropolis and
Community-lost   Mental Life'
Marginal Man   'The Stranger'

Conflict:

Conflict represents an older tradition of Simmel's uptake in American sociology. Lewis Coser's, *The Functions of Social Conflict*, introduced Simmel's insights to a broader audience when it was published in 1955. Since then, scholars have continued to draw on Simmel's duality of conflict and solidarity to explore the associative consequences of conflict. While earlier studies tended to focus on ethnic conflict, more recent work also explores the associative and dissociative tendencies behind political polarization.

Key Ideas: **Key Texts:**

Solidarity   'Conflict'
Polarization
Cross-Pressures

(Continued)

Table 24.1 (Cont.)

fashion. Overall, though, Simmel's sociology offers
a relational approach to culture.

Key Ideas:	Key Texts:
Trickle-down Taste	*Individuality and Social Forms*
Sociability	'Sociability'
Cultural Networks	'Fashion'

as a source of internal group solidarity (Turner, 1975; Olzak & West, 1991; Balser, 1997; Gould, 1999). According to this perspective, Simmel is often juxtaposed with more rational-choice models of collective action; rather than instrumental considerations, the process of conflict itself inspires group solidarity and identification, drawing in individuals as affectively-charged collective rather self-interested actors (Hirsch, 1990; Olzak & West, 1991; West, 1995).

Despite this apparent continuity, closer decade-by-decade analysis also reveals evidence of change. Simmel's appropriation alongside Wirth in urban sociology was especially prominent during the 1970s. As the subfield moved away from emphasizing the alienating qualities of urban life, Wirth's appeal declined. Simmel's application, however, did not. Instead, as new scholars began emphasizing the freedoms offered by urban life, the opportunities to express and cultivate attachment to likeminded people and cultural scenes (Fischer, 1982; Silver & Clark, 2016), and the interconnected dependencies that outlasted the *Gemeinschaft* community (Granovetter, 1973; Wellman, 1979; Wellman & Wortley, 1990), Simmel's writings nevertheless remained vital. Similarly, the Simmel-Coser agenda, while resurgent in the 1990s, finding renewed application for rising ethnic violence following the fall of communism, has declined more recently. And yet Simmel continues to offer insights for scholars of conflict, particularly for those studying polarization, and the simultaneous clustering and division among the public (DiMaggio et al., 1996; Axelrod, 2016; Baldassarri & Gelman, 2008; Baldassarri, 2011).

In both cases, the drift away from Simmel's earlier champions was accompanied by a shift towards an emerging structuralist interpretation of Simmel. Here, the Mertonian approach to Simmel's work blossomed. Perhaps the greatest champion of Simmel's work in this domain, in fact, is a student of Merton's – Peter Blau. Although Levine et al. (1976a) already noted Blau's usage of Simmel in his writings on exchange, it was with the publication of *Inequality and Heterogeneity* in 1977 that Blau introduced Simmel to a new and broader audience. Simmel, according to Blau (1977a, p. 26), was 'the father of quantitative sociology'. In Simmel's work, Blau found the elements to articulate a formal approach to social structure defined primarily according to group size as well as the level of differentiation within and between these groups. This included weaving together Simmel's insights from the second chapter of *Sociology*, 'The quantitative conditioning of the group', as well as Simmel's situating of individuals within intersection of multiple and overlapping social circles guided by homophily, taken from *Conflict and the Web of Group Affiliations*. For scholars of the ecology of affiliations, his ideas provided both a theoretical foundation and a research agenda (McPherson & Rotolo, 1996; Popielarz & Neal, 2007; Bruch, 2014). Moreover, as noted above, this interpretation informs scholarship on polarization, which proceeds by examining cross-cutting interests, affiliations, and their numerical distribution (DiMaggio et al., 1996; Baldassarri & Gelman, 2008; Baldassarri, 2011).

Table 24.2 Cultural studies

Modernity:	Space:
Though American social scientists often draw on Simmel's insights from *The philosophy of money* (POM), it fails to form a coherent cluster in the citation analyses of sociology and other disciplines. Within cultural studies, however, POM inspires a more organized discussion. Indeed, much of this is indebted to the work of David Frisby, who both worked on the English translation, and wrote extensive exegetical texts on the book, as well as on Simmel's contemporaries who were inspired by it. Ultimately, POM offers scholars perspective on modernity. Scholars draw on it for insights on modern life's characteristic processes. The role of money in the rationalization of life, its potential for estrangement, but also in facilitating the generation of value and moral meaning through exchange are often emphasized. Relatedly, his discussion on objectification and the relationship between creative subjective life and emergent forms which inspire and constrain this vitality offer scholars perspective on alienation. His essays 'The Conflict in Modern Culture' and 'On the Concept and Tragedy of Culture' see Simmel move beyond sociological formalism and offer cultural critique on the tragic character of modern life. The writings of Lukács – a favorite student of Simmel's – often enter these discussions, with his writings on reification deeply influenced by Simmel's philosophy of life. As scholars operating within cultural studies grapple with the dynamics of modern life, as well as its relation to the historical figures who inspired early interpretations of these processes, Simmel becomes both a source of insight and an important figure within the historical narrative.	While Simmel's insights on urban life and space are often mined for testable propositions in the social sciences, in cultural studies, it is Simmel's sociological impressionism that resonates. The nervous energy and hyperstimulation of the metropolitan life that Simmel vividly describes inspires scholars' own musings of the experience of space. Instead of Louis Wirth and the scholars of the Chicago School, Walter Benjamin and Baudelaire appear much more frequently – the former's insights on the shock and sensory fragmentation of urban life resonating closely with Simmel's own observations. These discussions often move beyond sociological treatment of the transition from rural to urban society. Instead, fragmented phenomenological impressions of the metropolis become a window into modernity's core ethos: a dialectical condition rife with tensions animating city life and its inhabitants with combustive energies and liberating – though often overwhelming – potential.

Modernity Key Ideas:	Key Texts:	Space Key Ideas:	Key Texts:
Individuality	*The Philosophy of Money*	Hyperstimulus	'The Metropolis and Mental Life'
Value	*On the Concept and Tragedy of Culture*	Blasé Attitude	'Space and the Spatial Ordering of Society'
Alienation		Crowd	
Objectification	*The Conflict in Modern Culture*		
Life and Form			

Consumption:

Scholars writing in cultural studies journals about consumption often draw on Simmel for insight. In certain regards, his uptake here is similar to his sociological use. Simmel's essay 'Fashion' offers perspective on the process of distinction and imitation which informs the dynamic of fashion cycles. But while sociological uptake of this work often emphasizes the implications for class stratification, treatment of this work in cultural studies goes beyond. Theorists often rely on Simmel to explicate the importance of aesthetics in modern life more generally. Simmel's flâneur represents the potential for aesthetic self-realization in a fragmented and disorderly urban environment; more than a matter of inequality, fashion cycles highlight the tempo and rapid obsolescence of form; his writings on jewelry and adornment are used to articulate the role of objects in managing impressions.

Consumption Key Ideas:	Key Texts:
Distinction	'Fashion'
Aesthetics	'Adornment'

Table 24.3 Interdisciplinary (not including sociology/cultural studies/philosophy)

Conflict:

Like in sociology, Simmel's writings on conflict largely became integrated into American disciplines outside of sociology by way of Coser's exegetical work. Whereas sociological interest in Simmelian approaches to conflict began to wane into the 1990s, however, research from political science continues to build on his pioneering insights. Simmel's conflict-cohesion hypothesis is the basis for the study of 'diversionary effects' – the strategy wherein politicians wage conflict as a strategy to rally public morale and divert attention from issues which threaten their power. Simmel's theory of triads, furthermore, is applied to international relations, underpinning game theory propositions that inform dynamic relationships and alliances. Overall, outside of sociology, Simmel's formalism appears to share an affinity with a *Realpolitik* framework, offering analytical tools for understanding relationships among elements (state, public, foreign entities, minorities etc.) not according to their moral contents but their social form.

Social Networks:

With social networks being a multidisciplinary field, Simmel's pioneering insights for networks inspire non – sociologists as well. These include scholars especially management and organizational behavior scholars. The 'Simmelian Tie', in particular, is a widely cited concept in these fields that was introduced by David Krackhardt. Drawing on Simmel's insights on triadic relationships, Krackhardt posits the Simmelian tie to emphasize the emergent constraint that arises when three nodes have strong ties among one another. Positioned as an alternative to Burt's structural hole (which also drew on Simmel), Krackhardt emphasizes the restriction that being enveloped in a clique entails. Overall, though, despite publishing in different journals and coming from different schools, the uptake of Simmel here is very much the same as his use in the sociological analysis of networks.

Key Ideas:	**Key Texts:**	**Key Ideas:**	**Key Texts:**
Conflict-cohesion	*Conflict and the Web of*	Structural Hole	*Conflict and the Web of Group*
Diversionary Tactics	*Group Affiliations*	Simmelian Tie	*Affiliations*
Rally effect	'The Quantitative Condi-	Social Distance	'The Quantitative Conditioning
Triad	tioning of the Group'	Stranger	of the Group'
Two-Against-One			'The Intersection of Social Circles'

Culture and Consumption:

Much like the study of social networks, sociology does not have a monopoly on the study of culture and consumption either. Still, the use of Simmel across different disciplinary areas which address these topics, whether in anthropology or marketing, is very much the same. Again, Simmel's insights from 'Fashion' are often narrowly construed as representative of the 'trickle-down approach'. That said, more nascent Simmelian programs in sociology of culture have not yet permeated other disciplines. Though scholars often rely on Simmel to make basic statements regarding the importance of taste and in distinguishing social groups, research blending culture and networks that we find in sociology has not entered other disciplines to the same degree.

Urban Studies:

Continuing the pattern from preceding clusters, the interdisciplinary nature of urban studies means considerable overlap with sociology in ideas and authors, albeit published in different journals. Again, 'Metropolis and the Mental Life' is the primary reference for Simmel in this cluster, although some scholars also draw on 'Sociability' to conceptualize leisurely spaces in the city. Though Simmel is often referenced in discussions concerning the anomic conditions of urban life, at the same time, many authors recognize the liberation and freedom that cities also offer – perhaps to a greater degree than in sociology. While the backlash to the 'community-lost thesis' was facilitated through social networks research in sociology, here we find scholars drawing on Simmel's dualistic understanding of the metropolis to emphasize the social psychological consequences of urban life outside of alienation – including creativity, efficacy, and freedom.

(Continued)

Table 24.3 (Cont.)

Key Ideas:	Key Texts:	Key Ideas:	Key Texts:
Trickle-down Taste	'Fashion'	Freedom	'The Metropolis and Mental Life'
		Blasé Attitude	'Sociability'
		Community-lost	

Blau's interpretation of Simmel gained a strong foothold in the field, persisting in the more formal interpretations of Simmel's work. This is especially true in research on social networks – the largest cluster in our analysis. Simmel offered networks theorists their most explicit theoretical statement (Scott & Carrington, 2011). Against the Parsonian emphasis on norms as well as the methodological individualism of rational-choice theorists, Simmel regarded social relations as primary. Society was understood neither as a substantive whole, a normative authority, or a collection of isolated individuals, but as a constellation of interactions. A strong interpretation of Simmel's distinction between form and content became foundational for network theorists. Following Simmel, networks theorists regarded the formal structure of relations as the proper object of sociological inquiry, abstracting social dynamics from varied contents of life, and emphasizing the causal priority of these relational configurations over individual motivations, beliefs, values, and emotions. The geometric metaphors that interspersed Simmel's *Sociology*, such as dyads, triads, circles, webs, or distance, provided a template for methods, with analysts applying greater mathematical rigor and precision in operationalizing concepts like brokerage, tie strength/weakness, density, homophily, etc.

Simmel's influence is apparent in some of the subfield's most influential articles. Ronald Breiger's (1974, 1990) theorizing of the duality between persons and groups, as well as the blockmodeling approach (White et al., 1976) drew on Simmel's mutual constitution of individuals and social groups, where individuals are located in the unique social circles they intersect, and social groups are emergent from these interconnected individual interactions. Granovetter's (1973) seminal article, 'Strength of weak ties', moreover, resonated with Simmel's account of the integrative role of secondary affiliations. Indeed, an early draft of the article was premised on challenging Wirth's depiction of modern relations as alienating, citing Simmel for alternative perspective. His influence is perhaps clearest, however, in Ronald Burt's (1992) work on structural holes. For Burt, it was not the strength/weakness of a tie that mattered so much as its location among other ties; specifically, if a tie bridged over two clusters that are otherwise weakly connected. Drawing on Simmel's idea of *tertius gaudens*, Burt's key point is that in addition to the novel information offered by this network position, bridging this 'structural hole' positioned the actors as a broker between the two clusters. The structural hole assumes a triadic configuration, setting the stage for *tertius* strategies. Actors can control channels of information and resources to manipulate their network positions for advantage. Burt's argument is among the most highly-cited in the social science literature, introducing Simmel's propositions to a broad audience, and leading scholars to return to Simmel in developing networks concepts further (Krackhardt, 1999; Vedres & Stark, 2010; Small, 2017).

Although the growth of social networks analysis since the 1970s and the incorporation of Simmel within this agenda points towards the triumph of the Mertonian Columbia school interpretation, this portrait does not capture his legacy completely. The second largest cluster in our analysis reveals Simmel as a fixture within broader theoretical discussions in the field. In this discussion, Simmel is variously cast as a pioneer of formalist (Erikson, 2013), relational (Emirbayer, 1997), postmodern (Weinstein & Weinstein, 1991), and, significantly, phenomenological sociology (Rock, 1979; Low, 2008). In fact, while Levine et al. (1976a) noted some use of Simmel as a sociologist of 'everyday life', it was only later in the 1970s, when phenomenological sociology coalesced into a more coherent program under the banner of symbolic interactionism, that Simmel's influence became fully appreciated. As in networks research, Simmel is regarded as a precursor to the pioneers of the discipline – a 'classic of classics' – whose neo-Kantian sociology opened inquiry into forms governing micro-level interactions. Here, he is also embraced for his formalism, yet it is pursued in a very different direction than in social networks analysis (Rock, 1979; Zerubavel, 1980; Snow et al., 2003). Rather than a quantitative appraisal of ties and their interrelations, for symbolic interactionists, relational forms are abstracted from the dynamics of immediate interactions instead. Social distance, for example, refers not to the number of overlapping ties between nodes in a network, but rather to the fragmented portrayal of self and the incompleteness of what we reveal in interactions (Goffman, 1959; Gurevitch, 1989; Arditi, 1996). Consistent with recent hermeneutic appraisal of the varied 'forms of form' used in Simmel's work (Silver & Brocic, 2019), the sociological uptake thus manifests in different ways. Simmel's role as a classic in two often competing traditions (Erikson, 2013) reveals his American sociological uptake is more varied than is often given credit (Goodstein, 2017). Simmel is at once both a rich source of testable propositions for empirical scientists, and an important inspiration for more interpretative researchers.

That said, despite important differences between social networks and symbolic interactionism, in both cases Simmel is received for his formalism. His broader cultural critique of modernity, his theory of alienation, and his philosophy of life continue to be marginal among sociological journals. This is apparent in how Simmel is used in the study of culture. Whereas the European tradition has often drawn on Simmel's critique of modern culture, articulated in *The philosophy of money*, American sociologists of culture tend to use him much more narrowly. In his writings on fashion, for instance, Simmel uses the cultural form to illustrate modernity's rapid obsolescence and the fragility of the insider/outsider identities it inspires. In the reception in US sociology, however, Simmel's ideas are predominantly interpreted as representing the 'elite-to-mass', or 'trickle down' model of consumer imitation, where lower classes imitate elites, who consequently change their style in an effort to maintain distinction (Davis, 1991; Woodward & Emmison, 2001; Aspers & Godart, 2013). Simmel has also figured prominently in recent sociological research connecting culture and networks. Here the common association of networks with form and culture with content is flipped on its head, with scholars seeking form in culture (Erickson, 1996; Schultz & Breiger, 2010; Lizardo, 2016, 2019). Rather than an outcome of networks, scholars explore how culture shapes the formation of networks. While this research has produced intriguing empirical work, it is firmly within the formalist interpretation. Again, Simmel's insights are stripped from their broader, more critical, implications.

The absence of a cluster on Simmel's more philosophical themes does not mean this work is non-existent in American scholarship; only that it is marginal within the mainstream Simmel appropriation. Indeed, there are efforts to redeem Simmel's philosophical sociology. The work of Silver, in particular, has drawn on *The philosophy of money* to reassess alienation theory (Silver, 2019), and to explore suggestive linkages between Simmel's ideas about money and his metaphysical writings about religion (Silver & O'Neill, 2014), while also turning to Simmel's writings from *View of life* to develop connections between self-relations and social relations (Silver & Lee, 2012). Economic sociologists have increasingly also turned to insights from Simmel's *The philosophy of money* as well, using his emphasis on objectification as theoretical foil to advance their own arguments (Zelizer, 1994), and his interactional approach to value as theoretical foundation (Fourcade, 2011; Polillo, 2011; Dodd, 2014). Overall, though, the reception of Simmel's philosophical work mostly lacks substantive engagement in American sociology. This weak reception, according to Goodstein (2017), is symptomatic of core issues in American sociology, as Simmel's key theoretical and methodological achievements are not only neglected or misconstrued, but worse, they are illegible within its disciplinary imagination. This raise the question of the uniqueness of Simmel's reception in sociology, and how reception may differ across disciplines. In the next section we consider this interdisciplinary reception in the US.

Simmel beyond sociology

Our citation analysis of Simmel's reception outside of sociology was organized by considering his uptake in cultural studies, philosophy, and all other journals separately. The results reveal Simmel as an important thinker outside of sociology. His reception is uneven, however. Though Simmel is prominent in interdisciplinary discussions, and is an important figure in cultural studies, he has yet to break through in philosophy. As mentioned above, the citations to Simmel from philosophy journals fail to coalesce into a coherent cluster. When he is used, it is commonly by sociologists writing in philosophy journals (Weigert, 1975; Plekon, 1980; Wolff, 1989), or philosophers seeking insights into social phenomena – especially modernity.

This pattern is apparent in the cultural studies reception of Simmel as well. *Theory, Culture, and Society* emerges as the major forum for more holistic discussions among mostly sociologists engaging with Simmel's views on modernity (Breiger, 1990; Lechner, 1991; Weinstein & Weinstein, 1991; Capetillo-Ponce, 2005; Swedberg, 2005; Kettler, 2012; Lee & Silver, 2012). Often, these scholars enter dialogue with the work of David Frisby and his interpretation of Simmel's 'impressionistic' sociology. According to Frisby (1981), Simmel resembled Benjamin's *flâneur* – an idler who strolled around the city, making disparate though stimulating observations about life, yet avoiding deep convictions and retreating from important questions. In Frisby's view, Simmel de-totalized modernity, failing to offer a coherent account that would meaningfully engage with issues of power. This critique recalls the sentiments of Simmel's students, Lukács and Bloch, who abandoned their advisor as they moved towards Marxism and class struggle. The search for an overarching statement motivating and organizing Simmel's thought beyond passing observations has been a persistent concern in hermeneutic analysis. Frisby's sentiment is shared by Fredric Jameson (1999), for whom Simmel's reliance on dualisms led to a relativistic approach lacking conceptual synthesis needed for real social critique. Simmel and Oakes (1980) also observes that Simmel's theory of forms tends to undermine unity, totality, and closure. Although Weinstein and Weinstein (1989) agree that Simmel's work is scattered and unsystematic, they reach less critical conclusions. Rather than a *flâneur*, Simmel is said to be a postmodernist *bricoleur*. Though far-ranging and varied, his observations are appropriate to the postmodern context he is embedded in – conditions which demand a relativistic and patchwork approach to understanding social life.

While this impressionistic portrayal of Simmel tends to distance him from serious philosophy, it nevertheless casts his work in a more humanistic light, bringing him closer to cultural figures. Capetillo-Ponce (2005) for instance, discusses Simmel's influence on Mexican poet, Octavio

Paz, the two sharing a similar fragmentary style and penchant for disclosing social types and forms. Swedberg's (2005) analysis of Rodin's *Burghers of Calais* also puts Simmel in discussion with the arts, drawing on Simmel's appraisal of the statue – how it embodied the vital movements of modernity – to articulate its aesthetic appeal. Beyond cultural connections, impressionistic interpretations of Simmel also tend to highlight the distinctiveness of his writing style. Sometimes, this appraisal is critical. Kettler (2012), for instance, regarded Simmel's essayist style to be determinantal to his philosophy, suggesting the precedence of style over substance. For others, though, it is regarded as generative. Precisely because of his essayistic literary style, Felski (1995) argues that Simmel is exceptional as a facilitator of cross-dialogue between literary and sociological texts on the topic of gender and modernity. Green (1988) offers perhaps the most thorough analysis of Simmel's style, in the context of a broader treatment of sociological texts as literary works by applying postmodern literary methods to them. He finds that Simmel's reception is marked by recurrent 'epithets' related to his style of composition: 'multi-faceted,' 'modern,' and 'marginal'. In Green's reading, these epithets have their source in the fact that Simmel's writing style is 'simultaneously dialectical, reflexive, and deconstructive' (Green, 1988, p. 175). Taken together, these works highlight insights and debates that a humanistic approach to Simmel's work generates, closely associated with emphasizing his role as a creative stylist and writer.

This humanistic and postmodern interpretation of Simmel is not accepted by all American scholars, however. Levine (1991, 2012) challenges the perception that Simmel's thought lacks a critical edge and is without a unifying framework. A deep devotion towards the flourishing of human individuality and personal integrity, according to Levine (1991), is the undercurrent motivating Simmel's thought. Far from an escapist without conviction, Simmel is said to champion the cultivation of authentic individuality. His writings on the alienating consequences of the money economy and modernity are tragic insofar as they inhibit individual self-realization. Simmel carried out these convictions as an educator as well, offering a novel approach to education that was critical of current conventions (Levine, 1991; Leck, 2000). Regarding the systematicity of his corpus, furthermore, Levine (2012) contests the neat fracturing of Simmel's work into three stages of Darwinism, Kantianism, and Goethean/Bergsonian Life-Philosophy, arguing that notions of life and form are the conceptual thread running through his work. Goodstein (2017) also rejects as misleading the notion that Simmel's work lacks coherence. She argues that a 'comprehensive metaphysical principle' underlies Simmel's work: a '"living reciprocity" of elements epitomizes his phenomenological strategy for coming to terms with the ethical and epistemological challenges of a world marked by incessant transformation' (Goodstein, 2017, p. 84 f.).

Overall, then, it is apparent that the discussion of Simmel in cultural studies transcends his narrow treatment in sociology. The discussions here tend to engage with and interrogate holistic understandings of Simmel's work. Among seekers of a comprehensive philosophical outlook, Simmel's emphasis on individuality, as well as the link between his vitalism and form, become highlighted as unifying threads. While impressionistic interpretations tend to neglect these currents, they still aim towards a holistic appraisal of his work, emphasizing its overall fragmentary style. The loose appropriation of propositions and selective insights that guide sociological inquiry is largely absent here. Instead, this approach is often traded in for more critical approach concerned with parsing out linkages to the vicissitudes of modernity. Still, it is important to note that the bulk of this work is by sociologists writing in cultural studies venues. Rather than an issue of unenlightened readings of Simmel, the marginalization of his philosophical sociology more likely represents challenges in accommodating these dualities within the more empirically oriented interpretative framework of mainstream sociology.

Surveying the interdisciplinary reception of Simmel outside of sociology, philosophy, and cultural studies reveals that the formalist interpretation of Simmel is not unique to sociology. Here, the same major clusters emerge: conflict, networks, culture, and urban studies. The uptake among these clusters generally mimics his sociological uses. Simmel is primarily used for his formalism. The prominence of these clusters does vary, however. Whereas sociological interest in a Coser-Simmel approach to conflict began to wane into the 1990s, research from political science continues to build on his pioneering insights, with the conflict cluster being the largest. Simmel's conflict-cohesion hypothesis is the basis for the study of 'diversionary effects' – the strategy wherein politicians wage conflict as a strategy to rally public morale and divert attention from issues which threaten their power (Levy, 1989). That conflict can increase group solidarity and presidential popularity regardless of the basis of conflict or wisdom of policies, is a widely accepted proposition within the field, with researchers articulating the conditions which either promote or deter this effect. Outside of the Coser tradition, Theodore Caplow's use of Simmel in (1968) *Two Against One: Coalition in Triads*, where Simmel's triadic dynamics were situated within a *Realpolitik* framework, also continues to influence literature in international relations (Schweller, 1998; Crawford, 2003). For these scholars, Simmel's formalism shares a provocative affinity with Machiavellianism, approaching relationships among actors (states, public, foreign entities, minorities etc.) according to the consequences of their formal configurations and not their moral contents. Randall Schweller (1998), for instance, draws on Simmel in explaining the outbreak of World War II. Departing from the narrative of moral failings of political leaders and the public, Schweller's emphasizes the role of the tripolar structure of the international system between Germany, the Soviet Union, and the United States, highlighting formal dynamics of this triadic configuration.

While these strains of Simmel-indebted research programs remain vital in a way that is not the case in sociology, the *modus operandi* of Simmel's appropriation remains very similar: Simmel is received as a formalist, and a prolific generator of propositions. This is mostly true for the other clusters in this interdisciplinary reception as well. Returning to Goodstein's (2017) critique of the limitations of the sociological reception of Simmel, our analysis thus offers some insight. While Simmel's reception in American sociology is narrow insofar as it neglects his work as a theorist of modernity, there appears to be more diversity of Simmel's reception *within* sociology than there is *between* the social science disciplines; whether political science, economics, anthropology etc. Indeed, Simmel is an inspiration for different, often competing, traditions within the field, whether symbolic interactionism or social networks. He is variously a functionalist, a postmodernist, a pioneer of relationalism, phenomenology, and even quantitative sociology! Furthermore, where Simmel's philosophical sociology is redeemed – primarily in cultural studies – it is in large part owing to the efforts of individuals employed by sociology departments. Overall, while Simmel's work fits uneasily within disciplinary boundaries, it is apparent that the spirit of his work transcends these confinements, expanding his vital and everchanging legacy across fields.

Concluding remark

Taking stock of Simmel's American reception since 1970, we find that his work continues to inspire new directions. With the arrival of social networks, and the coalescing of the symbolic interactionist agenda into the 1970s, Simmel's pioneering insights became claimed by each of these important streams of research, being *the* classic behind each of the subfield's classics. Furthermore, while older subfields like conflict and urban sociology continue to be part of his reception, the trajectories here reveal considerable dynamism as well. Though Simmel was an important early influence on narratives emphasizing the alienation of urban life (Wirth, 1938), later urban theorists who challenged this account nevertheless continued to turn to Simmel for insight (Granovetter, 1973; Wellman, 1979; Wellman & Wortley, 1990). Finally, as research on culture blossomed in the field, Simmel's work continued to find traction. Though his disinterest in the contents of life suggest an uneasy fit with analysis of culture, Simmel writings have nevertheless informed research on dynamics of fashion distinction (Davis, 1991; Woodward & Emmison, 2001; Aspers & Godart, 2013), and his formalism has been extended to cultural tastes as well (Erickson, 1996; Schultz & Breiger, 2010; Lizardo, 2016, 2019). Overall, his legacy is varied and rich with dialectical tensions, with scholars often unwittingly turning '*Simmel against Simmel*' in their attempt to propel research forward.

Efforts to integrate a more holistic understanding of Simmel mark a further development in the US reception of Simmel since the 1970's. Scholars have attempted to redeem Simmel's philosophical sociology through hermeneutic appraisal. Some accommodate his oeuvre's scattered and contradictory nature by emphasizing its postmodern and humanistic affinities (Simmel & Oakes, 1980; Weinstein & Weinstein, 1989; Jameson, 1999), while others stress his normative commitment to individuality (Levine, 1991), the vitalism in his view of life (Silver et al., 2007), or his reliance on reciprocity as a methodological strategy (Goodstein, 2017) as sources of unity. Despite these differences, this scholarship, through its holistic appraisal of Simmel's work, and in treating him as a theorist of modernity, nevertheless distinguishes itself from the mainstream appropriation of Simmel.

That being said, though the more piece-meal and propositional uptake of Simmel does not explicitly engage with his broader oeuvre, it nevertheless offers important insights on the matter. That Simmel keeps inspiring novel, though scattered, propositions, should not be trivialized or dismissed for its unfaithfulness to his broader corpus. Instead, it is a remarkable testament to the virtue of his formal method. His unfolding legacy is a living embodiment of the sort of dialectical tension and perpetual overcoming processes that informed his philosophical approach (Silver et al., 2007). A broadly shared interpretation of Simmel's work and (inter)disciplinary position may remain elusive, as fundamentally incompatible appropriations abound. However, rather than looking for a single unifying synthesis, the analysis here suggests that the whole of Simmel exists in the distributed collection of Simmelian ideas set in motion within and across disciplines. Indeed, in this contradictory reception, the Simmelian ethos may paradoxically reveal itself most faithfully.

References

Arditi, G. (1987). Role as a cultural concept. *Theory and Society, 16*(4), 565–591.

Arditi, J. (1996). Simmel's theory of alienation and the decline of the nonrational. *Sociological Theory, 14*(2), 93–108.

Aronowitz, S. (1994). The Simmel revival: A challenge to American social science. *Sociological Quarterly, 35*(3), 397–414.

Aspers, P., & Godart, F. (2013). Sociology of fashion: Order and change. *Annual Review of Sociology, 39*, 171–92.

Axelrod, R. (2016). The dissemination of culture: A model with local convergence and global polarization. *Journal of Conflict Resolution, 41*(2), 203–226.

Baldassarri, D. (2011). Partisan joiners: Associational membership and political polarization in the United States (1974–2004). *Social Science Quarterly, 92*(3), 631–655.

Baldassarri, D., & Gelman, A. (2008). Partisans without constraint: Political polarization and trends in American public opinion. *American Journal of Sociology, 114*(2), 408–446.

Balser, D. B. (1997). The impact of environmental factors on factionalism and schism in social movement organizations. *Social Forces, 76*(1), 199–228.

Bell, M. M. (1992). The fruit of difference: The rural-urban continuum as a system of identity. *Rural Sociology, 57*(1), 65–82.

Blau, P. M. (1977a). A macrosociological theory of social structure. *American Journal of Sociology, 83*(1), 26–54.

Blau, P. M. (1977b). *Inequality and heterogeneity: A primitive theory of social structure.* New York: Free Press.

Breiger, R. L. (1974). The duality of persons and groups. *Social Forces, 53*(2), 181–190.

Breiger, R. L. (1990). Social control and social networks: A model from Georg Simmel. In C. Calhoun, M. W. Meyer, & W. R. Scott. (Eds.), *Structures of power and constraint: Papers in honor of Peter M. Blau* (pp. 453–476). New York: Cambridge University Press.

Brocic, M., & Silver, D. (Forthcoming). The influence of Simmel on American sociology since 1975. Submitted to *Annual Review of Sociology.*

Bruch, E. E. (2014). How population structure shapes neighborhood segregation 1. *American Journal of Sociology, 119*(5), 1221–1278.

Burt, R. S. (1992). *Structural holes: The social structure of competition.* Cambridge, MA: Harvard University Press.

Camic, C. (1992). Reputation and predecessor selection: Parsons and the institutionalists. *American Sociological Review, 57*(4), 421–445.

Capetillo-Ponce, J. (2005). Deciphering the labyrinth: The influence of Georg Simmel on the sociology of Ocatvio Paz. *Theory Culture & Society, 22*(6), 95–121.

Coser, L. A. (1956). *The functions of social conflict.* New York: Free Press.

Coser, L. A., & Merton, R. K. (Eds.). (1975). *The idea of social structure: Papers in honor of Robert K. Merton.* New York: Harcourt Brace Jovanovich.

Crawford, T. W. (2003). *Pivotal deterrence: Third-party statecraft and the pursuit of peace.* Ithaca: Cornell University Press.

Davis, F. (1991). Herbert Blumer and the study of fashion: A reminiscence and a critique. *Symbolic Interaction, 14*(1), 1–21.

de la Fuente, E. (2008). The art of social forms and the social forms of art: The sociology-aesthetics nexus in Georg Simmel's thought. *Sociological Theory, 26*(4), 344–362.

DiMaggio, P., Evans, J., & Bryson, B. (1996). Have American's social attitudes become more polarized? *American Journal of Sociology, 102*(3), 690–755.

Dodd, N. (2014). *The social life of money.* Princeton, NJ: Princeton University Press.

Emirbayer, M. (1997). Manifesto for a relational sociology. *American Journal of Sociology, 103*(2), 281–317.

Erickson, B. H. (1996). Culture, class, and connections. *American Journal of Sociology, 102*(1), 217–251.

Erikson, E. (2013). Formalist and relationalist theory in social network analysis. *Sociological Theory, 31*(3), 219–242.

Felski, R. (1995). *The gender of modernity.* Cambridge, MA: Harvard University Press.

Fischer, C. S. (1982). *To dwell among friends: Personal networks in town and city.* Chicago, IL: University of Chicago Press.

Fourcade, M. (2011). Cents and sensibility: Economic valuation and the nature of 'Nature'. *American Journal of Sociology, 116*(6), 1721–1777.

Frisby, D. (1981). *Sociological impressionism: A reassessment of Georg Simmel's social theory.* London: Heinemann.

Frisby, D. (1986). *Fragments of modernity: Theories of modernity in the work of Simmel, Kracauer, and Benjamin.* Cambridge, MA: MIT Press.

Gadamer, H.-G. (1965). *Wahrheit und Methode: Grundzüge einer philosophischen Hermeneutik* (2. Aufl., durch einen Nachtrag erweitert). Tübingen: Mohr.

Gadamer, H.-G. (1986). Erinnerungen an Heideggers Anfänge. *Dilthey-Jahrbuch Für Philosophie und Geschichte der Geisteswissenschaften, 4,* 13–26.

Goffman, E. (1959). *The presentation of self in everyday life.* Garden City, NY: Doubleday.

Goodstein, E. S. (2017). *Georg Simmel and the disciplinary imaginary.* Stanford, CA: Stanford University Press.

Gould, R. V. (1999). Collective violence and group solidarity: Evidence from a feuding society. *American Sociological Review, 64*(3), 356–380.

Granovetter, M. S. (1973). The strength of weak ties. *American Journal of Sociology, 78*(6), 1360–1380.

Green, B. S. R. (1988). *Literary methods and sociological theory: Case studies of Simmel and Weber.* Chicago, IL: University of Chicago Press.

Grossheim, M. (1991). *Von Georg Simmel zu Martin Heidegger: Philosophie zwischen Leben und Existenz.* Bonn: Bouvier Verlag.

Gurevitch, Z. D. (1989). Distance and conversation. *Symbolic Interaction, 12*(2), 251–263.

Hirsch, E. L. (1990). Sacrifice for the cause: Group processes, recruitment, and commitment in a student social movement. *American Sociological Review, 55*(2), 243–254.

Jalbert, J. E. (2003). Time, death, and history in Simmel and Heidegger. *Human Studies, 26*(2), 259–283.

Jameson, F. (1999). The theoretical hesitation: Benjamin's sociological predecessor. *Critical Inquiry, 25*(2), 267–288.

Jaworski, G. D. (1997). *Georg Simmel and the American prospect.* Albany: State University of New York Press.

Jaworski, G. D. (1998). Contested canon: Simmel scholarship at Columbia and the New School. *The American Sociologist, 29*(2), 4–18.

Kemple, T. M. (2012). A chronology of Simmel's works in English. *Theory, Culture & Society, 29*(7/8), 317.

Kettler, D. (2012). Introduction to 'Soul and Culture'. *Theory, Culture & Society, 29*(7–8), 279–285.

Krackhardt, D. (1999). The ties that torture: Simmelian tie analysis in organizations. *Research in the Sociology of Organizations, 16*(1), 183–210.

Krell, D. F. (1992). *Daimon life: Heidegger and life-philosophy.* Bloomingto, IN: Indiana University Press.

Lechner, F. J. (1991). Simmel on social space. *Theory, Culture & Society, 8*(3), 195–201.

Leck, R. (2000). *Georg Simmel and avant-garde sociology: The birth of modernity, 1880–1920.* Amherst, NY: Humanity Books.

Lee, M., & Silver, D. (2012). Simmel's law of the individual and the ethics of the relational self. *Theory, Culture & Society, 29*(7–8), 124–145.

Levine, D. N. (1985). *The flight from ambiguity: Essays in social and cultural theory.* Chicago, IL: University of Chicago Press.

Levine, D. N. (1989). Simmel as a resource for sociological metatheory. *Sociological Theory, 7*(2), 161–174.

Levine, D. N. (1991). Simmel and Parsons reconsidered. *American Journal of Sociology, 96*(5), 1097–1116.

Levine, D. N. (1995). *Visions of the sociological tradition.* Chicago, IL: University of Chicago Press.

Levine, D. N. (2012). Soziologie and Lebensanschauung: Two approaches to synthesizing 'Kant' and 'Goethe' in Simmel's work. *Theory, Culture & Society, 29*(7–8), 26–52.

Levine, D. N., Carter, E. B., & Gorman, E. M. (1976a). Simmel's influence on American sociology. I. *American Journal of Sociology, 81*(4), 813.

Levine, D. N., Carter, E. B., & Gorman, E. M. (1976b). Simmel's influence on American sociology. II. *American Journal of Sociology, 81*(5), 1112.

Levy, J. S. (1989). The Diversionary Theory of War: A Critique. In Manus I. Midlarsky (ed.), *Handbook of war studies* (pp. 259–88). Ann Arbor, MI: University of Michigan Press.

Lizardo, O. (2016). Why 'cultural matters' matter: Culture talk as the mobilization of cultural capital in interaction. *Poetics, 58*, 1–17.

Lizardo, O. (2019). Simmel's dialectic of form and content in recent work in cultural sociology. *The Germanic Review: Literature, Culture, Theory, 94*(2), 93–100.

Low, J. (2008). Structure, agency, and social reality in Blumerian symbolic interactionism: The influence of Georg Simmel. *Symbolic Interaction, 31*(3), 325–343.

Mayhew, B. H., & Levinger, R. L. (1976). Size and the density of interaction in human aggregates. *American Journal of Sociology, 82*(1), 86–110.

McPherson, J. M., & Rotolo, T. (1996). Testing a dynamic model of social composition: Diversity and change in voluntary groups. *American Sociological Review, 61*(2), 179–202.

Olzak, S., & West, E. (1991). Ethnic conflict and the rise and fall of ethnic newspapers. *American Sociological Review, 56*(4), 458–474.

Pietilä, K. (2011). *Reason of sociology: George Simmel and beyond.* London and Thousand Oaks, CA: Sage.

Plekon, M. (1980). 'Anthropological contemplation': Kierkegaard and modern social theory. *Thought: Fordham University Quarterly, 55*(3), 346–369.

Polillo, S. (2011). Money, moral authority, and the politics of creditworthiness. *American Sociological Review, 76*(3), 437–464.

Popielarz, P. A., & Neal, Z. P. (2007). The niche as a theoretical tool. *Annual Review of Sociology, 33*(1), 65–84.

Rock, P. E. (1979). *The making of symbolic interactionism.* London: Macmillan.

Schultz, J., & Breiger, R. L. (2010). The strength of weak culture. *Poetics*, *38*(6), 610–624.

Schweller, R.L. (1998). *Deadly imbalances: Tripolarity and Hitler's strategy of world conquest*. New York: Columbia University Press.

Scott, J., & Carrington, P. J. (2011). *The SAGE handbook of social network analysis*. London: SAGE.

Silver, D. (2019). Alienation in a four factor world. *Journal for the Theory of Social Behaviour*, *49*(1), 84–105.

Silver, D., & Clark, T. N. (2016). *Scenescapes: How qualities of place shape social life*. Chicago, IL: University of Chicago Press.

Silver, D., & Brocic, M. (2019). Three concepts of form in Simmel's Sociology. *The Germanic Review: Literature, Culture, Theory*, *94*(2), 114–124.

Silver, D., & Lee, M. (2012). Self-relations in social relations. *Sociological Theory*, *30*(4), 207–237.

Silver, D., Lee, M., & Moore, R. (2007). *The view of life*: A Simmelian reading of Simmel's 'Testament'. *Simmel Studies*, *17*(2), 265–290.

Silver, D., & O'Neill, K. (2014). The significance of religious imagery in *The philosophy of money*. *European Journal of Social Theory*, *17*(4), 389–406.

Simmel, G. (1893). Moral deficiencies as determining intellectual functions. *International Journal of Ethics*, *3*(4), 490–507.

Simmel, G. (1955). *Conflict and the web of group affiliations*. New York: Free Press.

Simmel, G. (1971). *Georg Simmel on individuality and social forms*, edited by D. N. Levine. Chicago, IL: University of Chicago Press.

Simmel, G. ([1900] 1978). *The philosophy of money*, trans. T. Bottomore & D. Frisby. London: Routledge.

Simmel, G. ([1908] 2009). *Sociology: Inquiries into the construction of social forms* (2 Vols) ed., trans. A. J. Blasi, A. K. Jacobs, M. Kanjiranthinkal, intro. H. J. Helle. Leiden and Boston, MA: Brill.

Simmel, G. ([1918] 2010). *The view of life: Four metaphysical chapters with journal aphorisms*, trans. A. Y. Andrews & D. N. Levine, intro D. Silver. Chicago, IL: University of Chicago.

Simmel, G., & Oakes, G. (1980). *Essays on interpretation in social science*. Totowa, NJ: Rowman and Littlefield.

Small, M. L. (2017). *Someone to talk to*. New York, NY: Oxford University Press.

Smith, G. (1989). *A Simmelian Reading of Goffman*. Unpublished Doctoral Dissertation, University of Salford.

Snow, D. A., Morrill, C., & Anderson, L. (2003). Elaborating analytic ethnography: Linking fieldwork and theory. *Ethnography*, *4*(2), 181–200.

Swedberg, R. (2005). Auguste Rodin's the burghers of Calais: The career of a sculpture and its appeal to civic heroism. *Theory, Culture & Society*, *22*(2), 45–67.

Symons, S. (2017). *More than life: Georg Simmel and Walter Benjamin on art*. Evanston, IL: Northwestern University Press.

Turner, J. H. (1975). Marx and Simmel revisited: Reassessing the foundations of conflict theory. *Social Forces*, *53*(4), 618–627.

Vedres, B., & Stark, D. (2010). Structural folds: Generative disruption in overlapping groups. *American Journal of Sociology*, *115*(4), 1150–1190.

Weigert, A. J. (1975). Substantival self: A primitive term for a sociological psychology. *Philosophy of the Social Sciences*, *5*(1), 43–62.

Weinstein, D., & Weinstein, M. A. (1989). Simmel and the dialectic of the double boundary: The case of the metropolis and mental life. *Sociological Inquiry*, *59*(Winter 89), 48–59.

Weinstein, D., & Weinstein, M. (1991). Georg Simmel: Sociological flâneur bricoleur. *Theory, Culture & Society*, *8*(3), 151–168.

Weinstein, D., & Weinstein, M. (2012). *Postmodernized Simmel* (1st edition). London: Routledge.

Welch, K. (1983). Community development and metropolitan religious commitment: A test of two competing models. *Journal for the Scientific Study of Religion*, *22*(2), 167–181.

Wellman, B. (1979). The community question: The intimate networks of east Yorkers. *American Journal of Sociology*, *84*(5), 1201–1231.

Wellman, B., & Wortley, S. (1990). Different strokes from different folks: Community ties and social support. *American Journal of Sociology*, *96*(3), 558–588.

West, E. (1995). Organization building in the wake of ethnic conflict: A comparison of three ethnic groups. *Social Forces*, *73*(4), 1333–1363.

White, H. C., Boorman, S. A., & Breiger, R. L. (1976). Social structure from multiple networks. I. Blockmodels of roles and positions. *American Journal of Sociology*, *81*(4), 730–780.

Wirth, L. (1938). Urbanism as a way of life. *American Journal of Sociology*, *44*(1), 1–24.

Wolff, K. H. (1989). From nothing to sociology. *Philosophy of the Social Sciences*, *19*(3), 321–339.

Woodward, I., & Emmison, M. (2001). From aesthetic principles to collective sentiments: The logics of everyday judgements of taste. *Poetics*, *29*(6), 295–316.

Zelizer, V. A. R. (1994). *The social meaning of money*. New York: BasicBooks.

Zerubavel, E. (1980). If Simmel were a fieldworker: On formal sociological theory and analytical field research. *Symbolic Interaction*, *3*(2), 25–34.

25

GOFFMAN, SCHUTZ, AND THE 'SECRET OF THE OTHER'

On the American sociological reception of Simmel's 'das Geheimnis des Anderen'[1]

Gary D. Jaworski

Introduction

Reflection on the reception of Georg Simmel in American sociological thought can be said to have begun with Albion W. Small, founding chairman of the Department of Sociology at the University of Chicago. Having translated, published, and lectured about Simmel for years – that is, having institutionalized the study of Simmel in his department and the larger discipline – Small expressed disappointment with the results of his efforts. Writing in the context of a review of Nicholas J. Spykman's (1966) book, *The social theory of Georg Simmel*, Small (1925, p. 84) wrote: 'the Americans who have given indubitable evidence of having considered Simmel thoroughly might be counted on the fingers of one hand'.

Fifty-one years later, Donald N. Levine and his colleagues found that the situation had changed. In two long articles surveying the American Simmel reception, they found not neglect but fragmentary incorporation into a wide variety of sociological fields of inquiry (Levine, Carter, & Gorman, 1976). Whilst traces of Simmel can be found in varied subject areas, the incorporation of his writings in sociological thought was, and is still, largely instrumental and unsystematic. My own work in this area (e.g., Jaworski, 1997, 1998) filled in some of the missing chapters of the story of Simmel's American reception and showed that Simmel was good to theorize with not only for scientific reasons but for extra-theoretical reasons as well. The moral implications of Simmel's thought have been as important to its American reception as its sociological insight.

Throughout the 1990s, there was sustained interest in understanding Talcott Parsons's non-reception of Simmel in *The Structure of Social Action* (e.g., Jaworski, 1990; Levine, 1991; Alexander, 1993; Lidz, 1993; Buxton, 1998). This work reaffirms the value of open debate, and of archival research, for settling questions of intellectual reception.

More recently, Elizabeth S. Goodstein (2017, p. 256), addressing what she calls Simmel's 'appropriation by fragments', takes everyone to task – sociologists and philosophers alike –

for 'a history of misreading that has obscured Simmel's achievements as a thinker'. Simmel was a 'liminal figure', Goodstein maintains, and as such had one foot in philosophy and another in sociology. As these disciplines evolved, however, Simmel was eventually 'occluded and excluded' from both, forgotten as a philosopher and marginalized as a sociologist. The result is a reception characterized by highly selective readings of Simmel as opposed to deep understanding of his thought. Goodstein's study leads one to the possible conclusion that Albion Small's lament remains true after all, at least for American sociology. Goodstein admits, however, that these selective readings of Simmel have 'genealogical interest' and thus have 'a good deal to teach us about the theoretical and historical stakes of the genesis of the modern disciplinary order as a whole' (Goodstein, 2017, p. 305). The present investigation stands on the shoulders of all the above analyses and aims to serve precisely the 'genealogical' purpose that Goodstein identifies.

In their examination of the American reception of Simmel's writings on secrecy, Levine and his colleagues made special mention of the works of Erving Goffman. They report that much of Goffman's work 'is grounded on Simmel's notion that persons are surrounded by a variable sphere of traits, possessions, and sentiments, which constitute their private domain' (Levine, Carter & Gorman, 1976, p. 1119). Further, they point to the ways in which Goffman's discussion of deference and demeanor, as well as his analyses of the numerous ways in which people act to preserve their private spheres, demonstrate a profound appreciation for Simmel's thought. In the spirit of this insight, the present author has conducted an extensive examination into Goffman's interest in secrets and secrecy (Jaworski, 2019). This in-depth study has revealed that Goffman's intellectual concern for secrets is expressed in his earliest writings and indeed endures and develops throughout his career. If there was anyone who considered Simmel thoroughly, it was Erving Goffman.

This chapter offers an interim report on the findings of this larger investigation. It examines the reception of one of Simmel's (1908, p. 348) tacit concepts, '*das Geheimnis des Anderen*' ('the secret of the other'), by Erving Goffman and Alfred Schutz. Despite the introduction of this Simmelian term by two masters of the craft of sociology, via widely read books – Goffman's *Interaction Ritual* and Schutz's *The Phenomenology of the Social World* – those ideas remained refractory to dominant disciplinary assumptions and failed to take root. What was gained and what lost in the bargain?

Erving Goffman on secrecy and society

An interest in secrets is revealed in Goffman's dissertation, 'Communication Conduct in an Island Community' (Goffman, 1953). The conceptual apparatus is preliminary and examples are limited to the community in the Shetland Islands he was studying, but the basic ideas that Goffman would develop throughout his career can be found in those pages. This is not the place to analyse in detail the steady bearings that the dissertation provided for Goffman; but it is possible to note the way in which this text adumbrates his later writings on the subject of secrecy and society.

It should be said at the outset that the years of Goffman's graduate study (1945–1953) were heady times for the field of communication. Consider alone the handful of books that were published during and after the war and which decisively shaped communication theory and practice: Norbert Wiener's *Cybernetics* (1948), Shannon and Weaver's *The mathematical theory of communication* (1949), Gilbert Ryle's *The concept of mind* (1949), Rausch and Bateson's *Communication* (1951), von Neumann and Morgenstern's *Theory of games and economic behavior* (1944). These books provided a context of intellectual innovation and offered answers to vexing questions of the time, such as the problem of rational behavior in uncertain times. All of the books would become important to Goffman, several are cited in the dissertation, and one was decisive. In the 'theory of games' Goffman found truths that were consistent with the interactional worlds he was inhabiting.

Goffman borrowed the basic terms of information theory and employed them in his study of the island community. He writes of 'senders' and 'recipients', of 'messages' or 'signs', 'noise' and 'coding'. But more than the terminology, he contemplated and answered the key question of the intellectual era: where is rationality to be located (Erickson et al., 2013)? In answering this question, Goffman gave primacy to 'information about others'. The greater the knowledge of others, Goffman contends, the more likely a person is to predict their behavior and prepare for it and indeed even control it. Moreover, the actor can learn what is expected of him and thus 'determine for himself who and what he is' (Goffman, 1953, p. 72). This is pure Meadian symbolic interactionism, but Goffman goes beyond Mead by adding in ideas from others. From the 'theory of games' Goffman took the idea of interaction as a tactical and calculated game and persons as rational manipulators. From this perspective, both sender and recipient are engaged in tactical control of information by sharing only so much information about themselves that meets their needs, whilst scrutinizing the other for as much information as they can gain. Goffman calls this a game of concealment and search (Goffman, 1953 p. 84), a formulation that echoes the 'search problem' of the wartime years, that is, how to find and destroy German submarines (Leonard, 2010, p. 271).

Yet Goffman was cognizant of the limitations of von Neumann and Morgenstern's model. The 'rational man' concept advanced by the theory is inadequate on its own. It allows for an understanding of social interaction that transcends context, but, Goffman contends, interpersonal communication is by its nature situated conduct. This is shown by the 'expressive component' of communication – the part that is spontaneous, emotive and, to an extent, uncontrollable. With philosopher Gilbert Ryle, Goffman considered the view that 'our knowledge of other people' relies so much on 'unstudied talk', that is, on the part of one's communication that is 'spontaneous, frank and unprepared' (Ryle, 1949, p. 181). Goffman writes: 'It would seem that the unthinking impulse aspect of interaction is not a residual category that can be appended as a qualification to the rational model of communication; the spontaneous, unthinking aspect of interaction is a crucial element of interaction' (Goffman, 1953, p. 244 n2). These ideas Goffman would develop throughout his career.

In thus prioritizing the region of 'information of the other', Goffman also entered the complex territory of interpersonal communication: of innuendo, bluffing, calculated display, etiquette, feigning and deceit, and secrets – all of which are mentioned or discussed in the dissertation. As such, the subject of secrets was, in part, a natural extension of the focus on interpersonal communication. It becomes more when Goffman turns information theory in a sociological direction through a discussion of several strongly institutionalized social roles which aid in the communication process. He discusses the 'drafter', such as a secretary, a person who assists the sender with formulating a message. Another institutionalized role is the 'relayer', such as a stenographer (Goffman was writing in the 1950s), a person who receives the sender's message and codes it for transmission. Finally, there is the 'courier', such as a messenger or postal worker, the person who delivers the message. All of these specialized roles, Goffman contends, face a 'strong moral prohibition not to take advantage of the position in which their occupational duties place them' (Goffman, 1953, p. 108). Despite these prohibitions, abuses occur, and people make 'inappropriate use' of the information with which they are entrusted. An example: 'on the island, persons who use the telephone and telegraph tend to allow for the fact that messages may not remain a secret' (Goffman, 1953, p. 107). In other words, someone may be eavesdropping and using the information received for their own interests.

These ideas are considerably extended and deepened in Goffman's first book, *The presentation of self in everyday life* (Goffman, 1956, 1959) (hereafter referred to as *Presentation*). There Goffman presents his view of social interaction as an endless round of face-to-face performances on a 'stage' with audiences of people, and often with the help of 'teams' who sustain the impressions that are being fostered. This social interaction order is a moral order, where idealized impressions are offered, sustained, and occasionally threatened. The matter of secrets is introduced in a chapter titled 'Discrepant Roles' where Goffman discusses a 'basic problem' for many performances as one of information control. For performances to be accepted, certain information – what Goffman now calls 'destructive information' – must be excluded. 'In other words', Goffman writes, 'a team must be able to keep its secrets and have its secrets kept' (Goffman, 1959, p. 141).

Goffman begins by presenting a typology of secrets and, with it, a nascent sociology of information control in modern societies (1959, pp. 141-143). 'Dark secrets' refers to information that a team knows and conceals that is incompatible with the image that the team is attempting to maintain before its audiences. The name of this type of secret is suggestive, and one expects a revealing analysis. In fact, Goffman gives it very little attention other than to refer the reader to another part of the book where marital secrets are discussed. 'Strategic secrets' – Goffman mentions as examples the practices of business and the military – denotes information that a team may use in the future against the opposition. The key difference between dark and strategic secrets is that the former is a dangerous or discrediting secret that one 'holds on' to, perhaps forever, and the latter is one that is used, or potentially used, in some imminent or future strategic interaction. By 'inside secrets' Goffman means the kind of information that serves the function of exclusion, helping one group to distinguishes itself from others. Secrets are not, however, only about the concealed information that a group or team has about itself. They may also denote information that one group has about another. Here Goffman compares 'entrusted secrets', information that one is granted and obligated not to share, and 'free secrets', or information that one learns from means other than entrusted sharing, such as through independent discovery or indiscreet admission.

The chapter follows with an examination of 'the kinds of persons who learn about the secrets of a team and with the bases and the threats of their privileged position' (Goffman, 1959, pp. 143-144). Here Goffman takes up themes, such as those discussed above, of the opportunities of 'drafters' and 'couriers' to inappropriately use the information with which they have been entrusted. It also reprises his even earlier pre-dissertation article on 'Symbols of Class Status' (1951), where he writes of 'curator groups', those whose work with elites – as personal assistants, hair dressers, butlers, nannies, among many others – gives them a privileged 'back stage' view. To quote Goffman (1959, p. 153) 'they learn the secrets of the show'. But in *Presentation*, Goffman takes these themes in a darker direction by exploring a wider range of roles with access to 'destructive information'. In addition to 'drafters', 'couriers' and 'service specialists', Goffman now writes of 'informers', including traitors, turncoats, and spies. He writes of 'shills', those who are secretly in league with the performer, including 'protective agents' and 'spotters'. He writes of the 'go-between' or mediator. He writes of the 'non-person', people who are present in a region but who are treated as though they were not there. He writes of the 'confidant' and of 'renegades'.

Goffman on 'Simmel's *Dictum*'

As one reads Goffman on secrets, it is instructive to consider the sociological analysis of secrets and secrecy written by Georg Simmel, the German philosopher and sociologist.[2] Simmel occupies a uniquely central place in the intellectual traditions of the University of Chicago, where Goffman took his Ph.D. There is a clear and well-established line of thought from Georg Simmel to Albion W. Small, founding chair of the Department of Sociology, to Robert E. Park, the intellectual leader after Small, and then to Everett C. Hughes, who was primus inter pares among post-World War II Simmel scholars, and then to Erving Goffman, among others (Levine, Carter & Gorman, 1976; Jaworski, 1997). Indeed, Simmel's essay 'The Secret and Secret Societies' (hereafter referred to as 'The Secret') first appeared in print in the *American Journal of Sociology* (Simmel, 1906) in an English translation by Albion W. Small. Two years later, Simmel included the final and somewhat longer version of that essay as the fifth chapter of his magnum opus *Soziologie* (Simmel, 1908). But it was Kurt H. Wolff's English translation of the chapter, published in *The Sociology of Georg Simmel* (Simmel, 1950), that made the ideas broadly accessible to scholars in English-speaking countries. Wolff translated Simmel's often complex German into readable English, compared to Albion W. Small's sometimes inelegant phrasing, and he broke out Simmel's longish paragraphs into multiple sections with subject headings. These changes turned Simmel's daunting chapter into an essay with easily digestible parts. Goffman's doctoral dissertation is replete with Simmel quotations from the Wolff translation (Smith, 1989, pp. 431-444), including several from the chapter on 'The Secret'. This encourages an examination of their respective views on the subject.

Near the end of his doctoral dissertation, Goffman cited a line from 'The Secret' that he calls 'Simmel's dictum' – namely, that

> discretion consists by no means only in the respect for the *secret of the other*, for his specific will to conceal this or that from us, but in staying away from the knowledge of all that the other does not expressly reveal to us.
>
> *(Goffman, 1953, p. 320, emphasis added)*

Simmel uses different words a little later on when he writes about 'an ideal sphere that lies around every human being'. As with the research by Levine and colleagues (Levine, Carter, & Gorman, 1976), most of Goffman's commentators (e.g. Burns, 1992, p. 39; Manning, 1992, p. 86) have noted Goffman's reference to Simmel's phrase the 'ideal sphere' surrounding every human being. They have rightly pointed out that the reference signals Goffman's explicit interest in the inherent dignity of persons, a theme that he explored pointedly in *Asylums* (Goffman, 1961) and *Stigma* (Goffman, 1963). They have also identified Goffman's Durkheimian bearings on this matter. Goffman tells us as much in his early article on 'The Nature of Deference and Demeanor'. 'In this paper', he writes, 'I have suggested that Durkheimian notions about primitive religion can be translated into concepts of deference and demeanor' (Goffman, 1967c, p. 95). There is no question, however, that Goffman found something valuable in Simmel's analysis of 'discretion' found in his chapter on 'The Secret' (Simmel, 1950, pp. 320-324). He refers to 'Simmel's dictum', quoted above, not only in his dissertation but also later in 'On Face-Work' (Goffman, 1967b, p. 16 n10). And he 'refines' (Burns, 1992, p. 39) Simmel's idea of an 'ideal sphere' into his own notion of 'civil inattention'.

For Simmel, discretion is the duty to stay away from 'all that the other does not expressly reveal to us' – one's secrets. As such, prying into those secrets cannot be done without destroying the 'personality value of the individual'. Simmel himself employs an analogy to explain his point: the analogy of private property. People rightly consider their material goods to be an expression of their personalities and, further, they expect the right to keep that property inviolate. Similarly, Simmel argues, one's 'intellectual property' is also highly personal and must not be violated through theft or invasion. To do so – to engage in the 'avid, spying grasp' of another's every word – is to violate a person to the core. Still, Simmel appreciated the complexities of modern life and the numerous invasions they entail. Even the most decent person can come across information that another would not willingly share. (Goffman included this source of information in his original typology of secrets, discussed above, when he wrote of 'free secrets'.) More importantly for Simmel, the 'interests of interaction and the interdependence of members of society' constantly challenge the duty of discretion. There is no general norm that can be relied upon to answer the question about how much knowledge of the other is appropriate. Without clear moral guidelines, Simmel says, this question must be answered by individual decision on a daily basis.[3]

The phrase 'secret of the other' may be too poetic to enter the general sociological lexicon. In his post-dissertation writings, Goffman cited it only in a footnote and developed his ideas primarily through the analogy of ritual: of 'avoidance rituals', 'presentational rituals', 'face-work', and the like. But the phrase encourages the present effort to understand Goffman's views on secrecy. Like Simmel, Goffman was not only, or even primarily, interested in 'destructive secrets' or 'dark secrets' and the like. For both Simmel and Goffman, secrets are not inherently aligned with moral badness or sociological dysfunction. In fact, secrets can also be aligned with the greatest good – with a person's dignity and worth, with respect for a person's honor, with the preservation of respect for the other. These views Goffman shared not only with Simmel but also with his early mentor, Everett C. Hughes (Jaworski, 2000). To quote Simmel (1950, p. 331): 'the secret has no immediate connection with evil, evil has an immediate connection with secrecy: the immoral hides itself for obvious reasons'.

Alfred Schutz and the 'secret of the other'

Additional perspective on Goffman's references to 'Simmel's dictum' may be gained by comparison to the relevant writings of Alfred Schutz. To approach this idea, first a brief detour.

Elsewhere, this author has reported on efforts by Albert Salomon, one of the original faculty members of what was first called the 'University in Exile', to interpret Simmel as a vital precursor to the phenomenological philosophy that the Graduate Faculty of the New School for Social Research in New York City was championing (Jaworski, 1998). As a part of this effort, in the early 1960s, Salomon led a seminar on 'Simmel and Schutz as Sociologists'. The seminar on Simmel and Schutz 'explored the affinities between the two figures, including their common background in the philosophy of Bergson and the similarity of the intellectual problems on which they worked' (Jaworski, 1998, p. 11). Despite the fundamental differences between their intellectual worlds, Salomon maintained that Simmel and Schutz displayed an 'inner affinity'. This inner affinity included their mutual concern for 'the secret of the other'.[4]

Evidence of this inner affinity is found in Schutz's appreciation of 'Simmel's excellent analysis of the sociology of the letter' (Schutz, 1964, p. 112 n12). Simmel's analysis of the letter is found in *Soziologie* as the 'Excursus on Written Communication' within the chapter on 'The Secret', though in Kurt H. Wolff's English translation the text is included as just another section named 'Written Communication' (Simmel, 1950, pp. 352-355). Simmel's analysis of the letter contrasts face-to-face communication with communication through the written word. He explores the paradox of written communication: it enhances the logical clarity of communication whilst magnifying the ambiguity surrounding an understanding of the individual. Because the reader of a letter does not have immediate access to the visual and audible signs of delivery, the letter is more open to interpretation and also to misunderstanding. Hence, what Simmel calls the 'secret of the other' – the inner thoughts and emotions of ones most intimate life – whilst potentially available through face-to-face interaction, is concealed in written communication (Simmel, 1950, p. 355).

Schutz first references Simmel's 'secret of the other' in his early study *Der sinnhafte Aufbau der sozialen Welt* (Schutz, 1932), translated into English as *The Phenomenology of the social world* (Schutz, 1967). Like Goffman, he cites Simmel's notion in a footnote (Schutz, 1932, p. 233 f. n1, 1967, p. 204 n69). Schutz's famous book, the only one published during his lifetime, is foundational for phenomenological sociology around the world. As such, no adequate summary can be offered in the space available here. But a key distinction may be noted for present purposes. Schutz distinguishes between directly experienced social reality, as may be found in a face-to-face situation, and indirectly experienced reality, such as our relationship to individuals and groups with whom we have no direct social contact – in Schutz's terms the larger classes of our 'contemporaries', 'predecessors' or 'successors'. Schutz's phenomenological sociology privileges the 'directly experienced social relationship of real life' (Schutz, 1967, p. 164). In such a situation, I am in direct spatial and temporal experience of the other, what Schutz calls 'simultaneity'. I can look in the person's eyes, ask him or her a question, hear the tone of voice, and watch the person's bodily movements. In all this, I am aware of this other human being as a person. The situation is very different for someone who only indirectly observes another. In these circumstances, we know people only as types. Among the examples cited is Simmel's text on the letter. Here, Schutz cites several key sentences from Simmel's 'Excursus on Written Communication', which in the English language edition employs Kurt H. Wolff's translation. In this translation Simmel writes:

> One may say that, whereas speech reveals the secret of the speaker by means of all that surrounds it – which is visible but not audible, and which also includes all the imponderables of the speaker himself – the letters conceals this secret. For this reason, the letter is clearer than speech where the secret of the other [*das Geheimnis des Anderen*] is not the issue; but where it is the issue, the letter is more ambiguous. By the 'secret of the other' [*das Geheimnis des Anderen*] I understand his moods and qualities of being, which cannot be expressed logically, but on which we nevertheless fall back innumerable times, even if only to understand the actual significance of quite concrete utterances.
>
> *(Schutz, 1967, p. 204 n69, quoting Simmel, 1950, p. 355)*

For Schutz, these ideas underscored the errors of straying too far from the concrete individual in his or her uniqueness. For, as one moves away from the concrete individual, one never confronts the subject as a real person; people are known only as types.

Schutz (1945) extends these ideas in his incisive wartime essay in social psychology, 'The Homecomer', first published in the *American Journal of Sociology* in March of 1945. World War II would end only months later. Schutz defined the 'homecomer' as 'one who comes back for good to his home' (Schutz, 1964, p. 107). Employing basic concepts in phenomenology that he was developing at the time, Schutz analyses the returning veteran as a special case of a subject's experience of growing up at home, of being away, and of returning home again. This was an experience that Schutz himself had had after World War I (Barber, 2004).

In the face-to-face relations of the 'pure we-relation' at home, each person 'participates in the onrolling inner life of the Other' (Schutz, 1964, p. 110). Further:

> In the face-to-face relation I can grasp the Other's thoughts in a vivid present as they develop and build themselves up, and so can he with reference to my stream of thought; and both of us know and take into account this possibility. The Other is to me, and I am to the Other, not an abstraction, not a mere instance of typical behavior, but, by the very reason of our sharing a common present, this unique individual personality in this unique personal situation.

Such 'pure we-relations', Schutz admits, reveal manifold degrees of intimacy and anonymity. 'In the highest form of intimacy', Schutz writes quoting Kipling, we know the Other's 'naked soul'. But separation and return changes all that. The 'absent one' experiences a significant shift in the 'system of relevance' and in the degree of intimacy. The aspirations and values that a person had at home may shift considerably. Moreover, what counts now – in the case of the veteran, the military group to which one belongs and the attitudes of the officers and comrades – are not shared by 'those left at home'. For them, understanding the one who left home is no longer formed by face-to-face interaction; rather, wartime propaganda builds up stereotypes of the soldier, which do not reveal an individual's personal, unique experiences. For those at home, for example, stories of wartime courage abound in the media, whereas for the soldier conduct in battle may be seen merely as acts of survival or the performance of duty.

Communication from home via the letter manifests this same shift from intimacy to distance, and from uniqueness to stereotype. 'Many a soldier in the combat line', Schutz writes, 'is astonished to find letters from home lacking any understanding of his situation, because they underscore the relevance of things which are of no importance to him in his actual situation' (Schutz, 1964, p. 112). Moreover, Schutz asserts,

> when the soldier returns and starts to speak – if he starts to speak at all – he is bewildered to see that his listeners, even the sympathetic ones, do not understand the uniqueness of these individual experiences which have rendered him another man.

Conclusion

The above analysis shows that both Goffman and Schutz made room in their work for the ideas that Simmel expressed in his notion of 'secret of the other'. Schutz's phenomenologically informed sociology made conceptual space for the individual's uniqueness and ineffable personal experiences. This perspective gave him a strong position from which to critique those social developments, such as wartime propaganda, that turned the individual into a means toward wartime ends – 'to increase the efficiency of war production or the subscription to war bonds' (Schutz, 1964, p. 114). Goffman also emphasized the dignity of the individual and leveled strong criticism at those social arrangements, such as total institutions, whose effect was to destroy individual dignity and uniqueness. Though Goffman traded in the types and typifications that social scientists make – he was the Linnaeus of sociology – he grounded his analyses in face-to-face interactions. Moreover, for Goffman as for Schutz, the critique of 'what is' implied a vision, however tacit, of 'what should be', an imagined society where persons matter.

Interestingly, Goffman and Schutz both cited Simmel's notion in a footnote, a likely admission that the idea, however insightful and revealing, was refractory to the discipline in which they were writing – philosophy and sociology for Schutz and sociology and anthropology for Goffman. Further, both cited the idea early in their careers, a time perhaps before disciplinary norms had fully taken hold. Still, despite their recognition of Simmel's idea it seems that others have not followed their lead. This is all the more striking in that the two sociologists were in the vanguard of the anti-positivist intellectual movement in mid-20th century social thought.

It is revealing that Goffman's commentators, when discussing Simmel's notion of human dignity, are open to referencing his idea of an 'ideal sphere' surrounding an individual; however, the related Simmelian term 'secret of the other' is ignored. The notion of an 'ideal sphere' locates personal dignity outside the individual – in a domain that 'surrounds' a person. The 'secret of the other', on the other hand, directs us decisively inside the individual. Considered in this way, it is understandable that Simmel's 'secret of the other' was not accepted by positivist sociology; but neither did it gain a foothold in interpretive or phenomenological sociology. Was this just a missed opportunity or had disciplinary domain assumptions and boundaries denied further interest? Whilst this central question cannot be pursed here, it is worthy of further study.

The importance of this kind of tacit knowledge was championed by chemist and philosopher Michael Polanyi in his notion that 'we can know more than we can tell' (1958, 2009, p. 4) in books that explored the role of tacit knowledge in scientific thinking. In contrast, Simmel's 'secret of the other' might be rendered 'we are more than we choose to reveal or say', an idea that underscores the role of the tacit dimension in social interaction. This was an idea that enticed Goffman throughout his career. Simmel's term, more fully considered, attempts to convey the idea that individuals have qualities that are difficult to articulate but that, nevertheless, inform our understanding of them; that those qualities are the preserve of the individual and, if withheld, must not illegitimately be extracted; and that those qualities – those 'secrets' – are a part of our fundamental humanity and provide both a condition and a limit to our knowledge of the other. Thus considered, the term's critical and constructive theoretical potential, though unrealized at present, remains open for development.

A final thought. Though Goffman was no phenomenologist (Psathas, 2014), his own 'inner affinity' with Simmel reveals, also, an affinity with Schutz and the philosophical tradition he developed. On this matter, it is appropriate to heed the words of Schutz himself when he wrote that 'the attempts of Simmel, Max Weber, [and] Scheler to reduce social collectivities to the social interaction of individuals is, so it seems, much closer to the spirit of phenomenology than the pertinent statements of its founder' (Schutz, 1970, p. 39).[5] In this respect, Simmel, Schutz and Goffman each stand firmly within the 'spirit of phenomenology' and as champions of human dignity and individual uniqueness.

Notes

1 Acknowledgements: The author thanks Andrew Abbott, Philip Manning, Larry Nichols, Dmitri Shalin, and Yves Winkin for their encouragement and counsel during the early stages of the larger project on Goffman and secrets. For critical readings and helpful advice, the author thanks Michael D. Barber, Guy Oakes, and Greg Smith. Any errors of fact or interpretation are the author's alone.
2 The relation between Simmel and Goffman has been a continuing subject of scholarly interest. Among the most valuable sources are Smith (1989), Smith (1994), Davis (1997), Jaworski (1997) and Gerhardt (2003). Marx and Muschert's (2009) essay 'Simmel on Secrets' is a missed opportunity to examine Simmel's writing on secrecy in relation to Goffman. Its main contribution is not an explication of Simmel's writings on secrets, as one might expect from the title. Instead, its aim is to extract from Simmel's chapter on secrets an inventory of propositions for future research. See

Jaworski (1998) for an examination of when and how 'scholarship' on Simmel was supplanted by the 'research program' style of work that this essay exemplifies.

3 These views on secrecy encourage reflection on Goffman's own practices of secrecy: sealing of his private papers, objecting to including his photograph on book jackets, etc. Winkin (1999, p. 19) reflects on these matters when addressing the ethical implications of his own research. See also Jef Verhoeven (1993) for reflection on the reasons for publishing his revealing interview with Goffman. In addition, see the 'Marx-Shalin Exchange on the Goffman Project' (Marx & Shalin, 2008). Elsewhere, Marx (2011) refers to Descartes' motto – 'he lives well who is well hidden' – and avers that 'it might also have been Erving Goffman's [motto]'.

4 Salomon makes this argument about the 'inner affinity' of Simmel and Schutz, and characterizes that kinship using Simmel's notion of 'secret of the other', in his seminar notes to 'Simmel and Schutz as Sociologists' (Salomon, 1962). The phrase 'the secret of the other' is the translation that both Albion W. Small and Kurt H. Wolff use for the original '*das Geheimnis des Anderen*' (e.g., Simmel, 1908, p. 348) and is clearly the only appropriate translation.

5 This quotation was brought to our attention by an essay by Lester Embree (2010, p. 4). Ebree's citation, however, is incorrect. The quote from Schutz is in *Collected Papers III* (1970, p. 39) not *Collected Paper II* (1964). The author thanks Professor Michael D. Barber for providing the correct citation.

References

Alexander, J. (1993). Formal sociology is not multidimensional: Breaking the code in Parsons's fragment on Simmel. *Teoria Sociologica, 1*(1), 101–114.

Barber, M. (2004). *The participating citizen: A biography of Alfred Schutz*. New York: SUNY Press.

Burns, T. (1992). *Erving Goffman*. New York: Routledge.

Buxton, W. (1998). From the 'missing fragment' to the 'lost manuscript'. *American Sociologist, 29*(2), 57–76.

Davis, M. (1997). Georg Simmel and Erving Goffman: Legitimators of the sociological investigation of human experience. *Qualitative Sociology, 20*(3), 396–398.

Embree, L. (2010). Founding some practical disciplines in Schutzian social psychology. *Bulletin d'Analyse Phénoménologique, VI*(I), 1–11.

Erickson, P., et al. 2013. *How Reason Almost Lost Its Mind*. Chicago: University of Chicago Press.

Gerhardt, U. (2003). Of kindred spirits: Erving Goffman's oeuvre and its relationship to Georg Simmel. In J. Treviño (Ed.), *Goffman's legacy* (pp. 143–165). NJ: Rowman & Littlefield.

Goffman, E. (1951). Symbols of Class Status. *The British Journal of Sociology, 2*(4), 294–304.

Goffman, E. (1953). *Communication conduct in an island community*. Ph.D., University of Chicago.

Goffman, E. (1956). *The presentation of self in everyday life*. University of Edinburgh Social Sciences Research Centre. Monograph No. 2.

Goffman, E. (1959). *The presentation of self in everyday life*. New York: Anchor Books.

Goffman, E. (1961). *Asylums: Essays on the condition of the social situation of mental patients and other inmates*. New York: Random House.

Goffman, E. (1963). *Stigma: Notes on the management of spoiled identity*. New York: Simon & Schuster.

Goffman, E. (1967a). *Interaction ritual*. New York: Random House.

Goffman, E. (1967b). On face-work: An analysis of ritual elements in social interaction. In E. Goffman (Ed.), *Interaction ritual* (pp. 5–45). New York: Random House.

Goffman, E. (1967c). The Nature of deference and demeanor. In E. Goffman (Ed.), *Interaction ritual: Essays on face-to-face behavior* (pp. 47–95). New York: Random House.

Goodstein, E. (2017). *Georg Simmel and the disciplinary imaginary*. Stanford: Stanford University Press.

Jaworski, G. (1990). Simmel's contribution to Parsons' action theory and its fate. In M. Kaern et al. (Eds.), *Georg Simmel and contemporary sociology* (pp. 109–130). Boston, MA: Kluwer.

Jaworski, G. (1997). *Georg Simmel and the American prospect*. New York: SUNY Press.

Jaworski, G. (1998). Contested canon: Simmel scholarship at Columbia and the New School. *The American Sociologist, 29*(2), 4–18.

Jaworski, G. (2000). Erving Goffman: The reluctant apprentice. *Symbolic Interaction, 23*(3), 299–308.

Jaworski, G. (2019). Secrecy and society in Erving Goffman and other post-World War II sociologists. Unpublished manuscript.

Leonard, R. (2010). *Von Neumann, Morgenstern and the creation of game theory.* New York: Cambridge University Press.

Levine, D. (1991). Simmel and Parsons reconsidered. *American Journal of Sociology, 96*(5), 1097–1116.

Levine, D., Carter, E., & Gorman, E. (1976). Simmel's influence on American sociology I & II. *The American Journal of Sociology, 81*, 813–845, 1112–1132.

Lidz, V. (1993). Parsons and Simmel: Convergence, difference, and missed opportunity. *Teoria Sociologica, 1*(1), 130–142.

Manning, Ph. (1992). *Erving Goffman and modern sociology.* Stanford: Stanford University Press.

Marx, G. (2011). In Gratitude: The Right Chemistry, Timing, Place and Organization. http://web.mit.edu/gtmarx/www/sssp.html.

Marx, G., & Muschert, G. (2009). Simmel on secrecy: A legacy and inheritance for the sociology of information. In C. Rol & C. Papilloud (Eds.), *Soziologie als Möglichkeit: 100 Jahre Georg Simmels Untersuchungen über die Formen der Vergesellschaftung* (pp. 217–233). Wiesbaden: Verlag für Sozialwissenschaften.

Marx, G., & Shalin, D. (2008). Marx-Shalin exchange on the Goffman project. In *Bios sociologicus: The Erving Goffman archives* (pp. 1–28), available at: https://digitalscholarship.unlv.edu/goffman_archives/85.

Polanyi, M. (1958). *Personal knowledge: Towards a post-critical philosophy.* Chicago, IL: University of Chicago Press.

Polanyi, M. (2009). *The tacit dimension.* Chicago, IL: University of Chicago Press.

Psathas, G. (2014). Goffman and Schutz on multiple realities. In M. Staudigl & G. Berguno (Eds.), *Schutzian phenomenology and hermeneutic traditions* (pp. 201–221). New York: Springer.

Ruesch, J., & Bateson, G. (1951). *Communication: The social matrix of psychiatry.* New York: Norton.

Ryle, G. (1949). *The concept of mind.* Chicago, IL: University of Chicago Press.

Salomon, A. (1962). Lecture notes to 'Simmel and Schutz as sociologists'. Salomon Papers. Sozialwissenschaftliches Archiv, Universität Konstanz, Mappe Number 29.

Schutz, A. (1932). *Der sinnhafte Aufbau der sozialen Welt.* Vienna: Julius Springer.

Schutz, A. (1945). The homecomer. *The American Journal of Sociology, 50*(5), 369–376.

Schutz, A. (1964). *Collected papers II: Studies in social theory.* A. Brodersen (Ed.). The Hague: Martinus Nijhoff.

Schutz, A. (1967). *The phenomenology of the social world.* Evanston, IL: Northwestern University Press.

Schutz, A. (1970). *Collected papers III: Studies in phenomenological philosophy.* I. Schutz (Ed.). The Hague: Martinus Nijhoff.

Shannon, C., & Weaver, W. (1949). *The mathematical theory of communication.* Urbana, IL: The University of Illinois Press.

Simmel, G. (1906). The sociology of secrecy and of secret societies. Translated by A. Small. *American Journal of Sociology, 11*(4), 441–498.

Simmel, G. (1908). *Soziologie: Untersuchungen über die Formen der Vergesellschaftung.* Leipzig: Duncker & Humblot.

Simmel, G. (1950). *The sociology of Georg Simmel.* Translated, edited and with an Introduction by K. H. Wolff. New York: Free Press.

Small, A. (1925). Review of Nicholas J. Spykman, *The social theory of Georg Simmel. American Journal of Sociology, 31*(1), 84–87.

Smith, G. (1989). *A Simmelian reading of Erving Goffman.* Ph.D, University of Salford.

Smith, G. (1994). Snapshots 'Sub Specie Aeternitatis': Simmel, Goffman and formal sociology. In D. Frisby (Ed.), *Georg Simmel: Critical assessments III* (pp. 354–383). New York: Routledge.

Spykman, N. (1966). *The social theory of Georg Simmel.* New York: Atherton Press.

Verhoeven, J. (1993). Backstage with Erving Goffman: The Context of the Interview. *Research on Language and Social Interaction 28*(3), 307–315.

von Neumann, J., & Morgenstern, O. (1944). *Theory of games and economic behavior.* Princeton, NJ: Princeton University Press.

Wiener, N. (1948). *Cybernetics: On control and communication in the animal and the machine.* Cambridge, MA: MIT Press.

Winkin, Y. (1999). Erving Goffman: What is a life? The uneasy making of an intellectual biography. In G. Smith (Ed.), *Goffman and social organization studies in sociological legacy* (pp. 19–41). London: Routledge.

26

TRACES OF SIMMEL IN LATIN AMERICA

Modernity, nation, and memory[1]

Esteban Vernik

Transatlantic transferences

The work of German philosopher and sociologist Georg Simmel first reached Latin America in 1923. The Universidad de Córdoba in Argentina published philosopher Carlos Astrada's translation of '*The conflict in modern culture*' (*Der Konflikt der modernen Kultur*), the lecture that Simmel had delivered in Berlin in 1918, with an introductory study by the translator.

The lapse between the lecture's delivery and its publication on the other side of the Atlantic is strikingly short: just five years, at a time when transoceanic communication was nowhere near as fast as it is today. Furthermore, Simmel's work was little known in the Spanish-speaking world.[2]

The contexts of the original publication and of its translation in Córdoba were quite different, and there is no clear motivation for the transfer of ideas. As the *Literarisches Zentralblatt für Deutschland* of 17 August 1918 relates, '*The conflict in modern culture*' was first published between 31 July and 6 August 1918 – just a few weeks before Simmel's death on September 28 (GSG 16, p. 436 f.). It was a reworked version of the lecture Simmel had given at the Institute of Marine Science[3] in Berlin on the evening of Thursday, 3 January 1918 (currently in GSG 16, pp. 181–207). A report on the lecture was published the morning after its delivery in the liberal Berlin daily *Vossische Zeitung*. It was one of three lectures that Simmel – who had been living in Strasbourg in a sort of self-imposed exile for four years – gave in Berlin in early January 1918. The other two were 'Mechanical worldview' and 'On the essence of historical understanding'. Upon returning to Strasbourg, the philosopher and sociologist wrote in a letter to a friend 'I have given three great lectures that draw on an array of sources. They were all very well attended and received a great deal of attention. I have not lost my touch'.[4] Simmel would deliver the lecture two more times, once in February and once in March of that same year. The first time was in Amsterdam at the invitation of the Amsterdam Students' League; at the lecture's close, it was considered, in Simmel's words, 'a spark of the German spirit'.[5] The second time, in Strasbourg, was to the League of Women Patriots. The *Strasburger Post* wrote of the 'great success' of the lecture '*The conflict in modern culture*'. Both Simmel's description of the response in Amsterdam and the name of the venue where he gave the lecture for the third time in

Strasbourg suggest the cultural atmosphere in that final year of the War: European intellectual life, like its culture, was steeped in crisis.

Meanwhile, on the other side of the Atlantic and in the Southern Hemisphere, there was a general sense of jubilation at the Universidad de Córdoba in response to what is known as the *Reforma Universitaria* (University reform). Students mobilised alongside industrial workers to strike and take over the Dean's Office. The *Reforma Universitaria*'s Latin Americanist and anti-imperialist ideas soon spread to Peru, Mexico, and Cuba, with long-lasting effects on the democratisation of cloisters of knowledge.[6] Carlos Astrada, along with Deodoro Roca and Saúl Taborda, emerged as one of the leaders of the movement as he was beginning to lay the basis for what would be one of the most original and prolific bodies of work in South American philosophy – one that is, nonetheless, little recognised by the academic canon. In 1921, Astrada greeted the Soviet process with his article 'The Rebirth of Myth,' a humanist and vitalist interpretation of the October Revolution.[7] And, in 1923, as stated above, he translated and edited *The conflict in modern culture*.

Free and agile thinking against reification

> Nothing is more devoid of dogmatism than Simmel's thought. No crystallized concept intercepts its free and lively movement.
>
> *(Astrada, 1923, p. 6)*

Simmel's thinking and philosophical attitude were met, in Latin America, with fascination. In addition to the care and seriousness of Astrada's edition, his insightful introduction to Simmel is a vitalist philosophical exercise in its own right.

In his prologue, Astrada describes '*The conflict in modern culture*' as 'one of the most recent expressions of the interesting and original speculative work of this subtle and deep thinker' (Astrada, 1923, p. 5). Simmel's work is called 'the expansion of a rich and sensitive soul inclined to pondering transcendent questions. Astir in his penetrating analysis is, we sense, the philosopher's living thought' (ibidem). From that overarching perspective, Astrada underscores the mobile nature of Simmel's analyses, pointing out that

> It is not surprising that work fruit of such flexible and bold thinking, work with an array of novel perspectives, expands from the valuable and suggestive observation at its base into different spheres of culture, different problems of a philosophical nature whether in relation to the sociological or the moral, the metaphysical or the artistic.
>
> *(ibidem)*

Astrada calls Simmel a 'uniquely sharp analyst, with criteria at once wide and exact. Rather than attempt to solve the problems arising from his vigorous thinking, he chooses to delve into their content, underscoring his hypotheses, ideas, intuitions' (Astrada, 1923, p. 6). He looks to Simmel's own words to evidence his philosophical attitude:

> At stake is not what content philosophy shall address but what form it shall take; not differences between dogmas, but the oneness of the movement of thought that underlies all those differences until they congeal in a dogma and impede any communication, any crossover, between all philosophy's paths, resulting in isolation, in failure to participate in the rich possibilities of different movements. Only insofar as

attitude of spirit can philosophy be brought into philosophical culture, because it does not demand that the spirit adhere to a certain line for the sake of a concept; it leads, rather, to the berth that holds all possible strains of philosophy. That is the only way philosophy can truly delve into existence in its entirety.

(ibidem)

Astrada sees in Simmel an 'almost extreme' hermeneutical relativism. His always provisional and reworked positions are guided by unwavering restlessness. Astrada argues, then, that Simmel's intellectual production was the expression 'of a curious and inquisitive spirit that eagerly pursued new developments and attempted to capture unusual points of view, always provisional positions on the indefinite perspective of constantly reworked thought and life' (Astrada, 1923, p. 7).

And this first introduction of Simmel by the young Astrada – he was just twenty-eight years old at the time – concludes with two points that would mark the reception of the German thinker from the beginning. The first is a reference to an episode in Simmel's life. 'Simmel was a heretic for orthodox professional philosophy, for the establishment philosophy that Schopenhauer so energetically criticised. It should come as no surprise, then, that Heidelberg University did not open its doors to him or grant him a professorship' (ibidem). That fact, which is today better known amongst Simmelian scholars,[8] seems almost like an augur of what would happen to Astrada at the end of his academic career. Opposed to the liberal professors that took over the Universidad de Buenos Aires Philosophy Department after the coup ousted Perón in 1955, Astrada had to seek refuge in the distant and then-new Universidad Nacional del Sur in Bahía Blanca (we will get back to that experience shortly).

The second, and perhaps more substantial, point is the characterisation of Simmel as a thinker of the modern, as one who grappled with his times. Astrada considers Simmel the most legitimate representative of a philosophy that interrogates the spirit of a time, a philosophy whose essential traits are 'hints, fragments, premonitions, and not yet formulated metaphysical fundaments' (Astrada, 1923, p. 8). Astrada would absorb Simmel's way of doing philosophy, his philosophic attitude.

That first contact with Simmel would influence Astrada's thought at different stages of his prolific and original work.[9] The aforementioned early writing on the Russian Revolution celebrated the emergence of new vital forms of expression that transcended dogmas and hardened values. Indeed, Astrada looked to Simmel frequently, from his first works to his final writings. His 'La deshumanización de Occidente' (The dehumanisation of the west), an article written in 1925, is grounded in the text by Simmel he had translated and edited two years earlier, specifically when it speaks of the fragmentary and scientific-technical nature of the times and condemns the reduction of man to the useful ends of the system, to cog in the all-embracing mechanism of power (Astrada, 1925). Similarly, his 1933 book *El juego existencial* (The existential game) places Simmel in the saga of Heidegger's existentialism. Astrada looks to Simmel's 'Tragedy of modern culture' in his pioneering phenomenological description of the cultural industries of film and radio (Astrada, 1933). Two decades later, in *El marxismo y las escatologías* (Marxism and Eschatologies), Astrada once again cites Simmel to rebuke evolutionist visions of history in the Marxist field (Astrada, 1957).

If previously Astrada had drawn on Simmel the philosopher's theories of culture, art, and history,[10] in 1959, in a sociology class he gave at the Universidad Nacional del Sur in Bahía Blanca, he turned to Simmel's *große Soziologie* (GSG 11) to provide a detailed explanation of the German thinker's theory of sociology. In class notes currently being reconstructed, we can see the central place that Simmel's sociology occupied in that course. It was explained after Tönnies's theories in a line of thought that extended to Leopold von Wiese's formalist sociology. Astrada traced Simmel's conception of sociology in the first chapter of *Soziologie*, which he later illustrated with examples taken from other chapters. While later in the course he looked to other authors, he mentioned Simmel's sociology again, as well as forms of socialisation (*Vergesellschaftung*) as his object of study, and the separation Simmel draws between forms and contents as his method of abstraction.

This course attests, then, to the central place of Simmel's sociology in these lessons. Simmel is more important in them than Durkheim and no less important than Max Weber – and that went against the grain of sociology at Argentine institutions at the time. In 1957, the Universidad de Buenos Aires Sociology Program and Institute were created. Under Gino Germani, an Italian immigrant who lived most of his life in Argentina, sociology was re-founded. At its core was developmentalist modernisation that revolved mostly around North American structural-functionalist sociology. Influenced by Talcott Parsons, Germani would leave little room for Simmelian sociology, which for many years was considered 'impressionistic'; it was seen as prior to and lesser than modern scientific sociology. As a result, the centrality of Simmel's theory in the sociology course Astrada gave in 1959 would be the last thorough explanation of the German's thinker's work to be given at an Argentine university for almost three decades.

Simmel was similarly left out of university social science curricula in other incipient sociology departments in the region (this was the case in Brazil, Colombia, and Mexico). The leading figures at those departments were dismissive of Simmel's work, which they considered unscientific.

The circulation of Simmel's writings in Latin America

It is possible to distinguish, in sweeping terms, three periods in the history of editions of Simmel's work in Latin America. During the first, 1923–1959, Simmel exercised considerable influence on major Latin American essayists writing about the nature of the region's new nation states. During this period, much of the Berlinese philosopher and sociologist's work was translated into Spanish and published in the region and in Spain. The second period, 1960–1985, witnessed the institutionalisation of the social sciences in the region. During this period, unlike the earlier one, Simmel's writings were fairly marginal. In the third period, from 1986 to the present, Simmel's work has been revalorised. Especially in the later part of this period, the renewed appreciation for Simmel has led to a great many publications and translations of his work, a growing presence on university curricula, and more discussion of his ideas both within the region and in relation to production outside of it. What follows is greater description of each of the three periods.[11]

1923–1959

Crucial to this first period are José Pérez Bances and Carlos Astrada, the first two translators of Simmel into Spanish. Even today, their translations are among the most widely read; they are the vehicles through which Simmel's ideas circulate in their respective countries and in the larger Spanish-speaking world. A modern philosopher of the emancipation of Indo-American peoples, Astrada – as discussed above – engaged many facets of Simmel's work as he wrote his own. In Madrid, Pérez Bances, an intellectual close to José Ortega y Gasset, would go on to translate a number of other works by Simmel.

It was in Pérez Bances's translations that *große Soziologie*, a work so lauded by Ortega, reached Latin America. The first Spanish-language edition of that work was published in six volumes – each one containing two chapters of the original treatise. It was released in Spain in 1926 and 1927. In 1939, another edition of Bances's translation of *große Soziologie* was published in two volumes in Buenos Aires by Espasa-Calpe (Simmel, 1939). The Spanish-language edition of *Philosophische Kultur* that Ortega so encouraged travelled a similar path. It was first published in Spain in 1934 under the title *Cultura femenina y otros ensayos* (Feminine Culture and Other Essays) and later, in 1938, in Argentina. Significantly, Ortega visited Argentina a number of times in those years at the invitation of cultural patron Victoria Ocampo, the director of *Sur* journal, one of the main venues for cultural debate in the thirties, forties, fifties, and sixties.[12]

But if in Spain there were no publications of Simmel's work after the thirties – with the exception of the 1946 edition of *Hauptprobleme der Philosophie* (Simmel, 1946) – in Argentina there was a wealth of new publications that reached its height with five titles by Simmel published in just two years (1949 and 1950): a new translation of *Schopenhauer and Nietzsche* by Francisco Ayala (Simmel, 1950a); *Goethe*, in an edition that included as well the monograph *Kant und Goethe. Zur Geschichte der modernen Weltanschauung*; *Rembrandt. Ein kunstphilosophischer Versuch*; *Die Probleme der Geschichtsphilosophie*, based on the third and definitive edition published in 1907, but with the addition of the late essays by Simmel entitled *Das Problem der historischen Zeit*, *Die historische Formung*, and of a valuable critical study of the author and his work; and *Lebensanschauung. Vier metaphysische Kapitel*. The final four were meticulous editions put out by Nova (Simmel, 1949, 1950b, 1950c, 1950d). In addition, there was Marcelo Schulzen and Susana Molinari's translation of *Hauptprobleme der Philosophie* for Editora del Plata (Simmel, 1947). Those twelve publications of Simmel's work in Argentina were joined by *El problema religioso* (The religious problem) released in 1953 by Argos. The introduction speaks of 'the striking analogy between Simmel's concept of "death immanent to life" and Martin Heidegger's very recent concept of "being for death"' (Simmel, 1953, p. 9).

Mexico was, during this period, a force in publishing, thanks in part to Spanish intellectuals living there who translated a great deal of German philosophy: Wenceslao Roces's translations of *Capital* and other works by Marx, and of *Subject-Object* by Ernst Bloch; José Gaos's translations of *Being and Time* and other works by Heidegger; and the team coordinated by José Medina Echavarría's translations of *Economy and society* by Weber and the complete works of Dilthey. It is startling, then, that no translations of Simmel's work were published in Mexico during these years. Regardless, the ideas of the Berlinese philosopher and sociologist did have followers there. Olga Sabido Ramos identifies a first phase in the forties when Simmel's work reached Mexico at the hand of exiled Spanish intellectuals (Luis Recaséns Siches and Leandro Azuara Pérez, for instance, engaged Simmel's thinking from the perspective of judicial philosophy) (Sabido Ramos, 2016, p. 7 f.). In Colombia, Simmel's essay 'The Ruin' was published in the Sunday supplement to the Bogotá-based newspaper *El tiempo* in 1946. There were no publications of Simmel's work in Brazil – the only Portuguese-speaking country in the region – during this period. Traces of Simmel did make themselves felt, however, in the work of the most clear-sighted social scientists in that tropical country: anthropologist Gilberto Freyre and historian Sérgio Buarque de Holanda looked in 1933 to Simmel in works fundamental to Latin American social thought like *Casa Grande e Senzala* (Large House & Senzala) (Freyre, 1985) and 1936 in *Raizes do Brasil* (The Roots of Brazil) (cf. Freyre, 1964). Sérgio Buarque de Hollanda very likely took the clear distinction between form and content – a distinction of unquestionably Simmelian extraction – from Gilberto Freyre. Leopoldo Waizbort (2007) sees Gilberto Freyre's thought as clearly anchored in Simmel, specifically in relation to the sociological abstraction between form and content, on the one hand, and, on the other, shared themes like fashion, women's role, the social space, and distinction. Freyre's work *Sociología. Introducción al estudio de sus principios* (Sociology: An introduction to the study of its principles), which was ground-breaking in Brazil, makes frequent reference to Simmel (Freyre, 1942). Finally, in Peru, José Carlos Mariátegui – considered the writer who most deeply engaged the problems central to Latin America – was very interested in parts of Simmel's work. We will get back to that later.

1960–1985

In the following decades, there was a marked silence in the region on Simmel's work. At the end of this period in Spain, though, a re-edition of Simmel's *Grand Sociology* (*Sociology: Inquiries into the construction of social forms*) (Simmel, 1977a) and a translation of *Filosofía del dinero* (*The philosophy of money*) (Simmel, 1977b) were both published the same year. Also at the end of this second period, a major collection of essays by Simmel was published in Brazil, giving Portuguese-speaking readers access to parts of *große* and *kleine Soziologie*, as well as a chapter of *Vom Wesen des historischen Verstehens* and an introductory study that traces the Simmelian origin of conflict theory (Moraes Filho, 1983).[13] In addition, sociologist Gabriel Cohn's worthy book on Max Weber discusses his relationship to Simmel (Cohn, 1979). Other than that, there was little mention of Simmel in social science teaching in Latin America with the exception of the occasional reference to some of the topics in *Sociology* like the phenomena of 'the poor man' and 'the secret' or – in the field of urban sociology – to the essay *Die Großstädte und das Geistesleben*, which circulated in the problematic form of a translation to Spanish based on an earlier translation from English.

1986–2018

At the beginning of this period, there was renewed interest in Simmel in the framework of the debate on modernity/postmodernity. Careful translations by Salvador Más and Gustau Muñoz of *El individuo y la libertad* (The individual and freedom), a collection of essays of cultural criticism preceded by *Brücke und Tür* (Simmel, 1986), and of *Philosophische Kultur* (Simmel, 1988) – the 1911 book that reappeared in Spanish after the German edition from the eighties with preface by Jürgen Habermas – reached the region from Barcelona.

In Mexico in 1986, a translation by Francisco Gil Villegas of Max Weber's 'Georg Simmel as Sociologist' was published, as was, in 1990, the compendium *Georg Simmel* by English sociologist and architect David Frisby. That book would have as much influence on new Spanish-language readers as its original had had on the English-speaking world four years earlier. Other interpretations of Simmel include Brazilian Leopoldo Waizbort's *As Aventuras de Georg Simmel* (The adventures of Georg Simmel) (Waizbort, 2000), a book that, at nearly six hundred pages, is as voluminous as it is well documented. That work is still the major point of reference for readings of Simmel in Brazil. Two years later, Donald Levine's compilation *On individuality and social forms* was translated in Argentina – a book important less because of the selection of texts by Simmel included (most of them were already available in Spanish) than because of its introduction (Simmel, 2002a). During these same years, works by the Simmel study group at Bielefeld University began to reach Latin America; that team, conducted by Otthein Rammstedt, started publishing the first volumes of GSG in 1989.

During this period, Simmel's work once again became an object of inquiry at Latin American universities. In 1996, the Universidad de Buenos Aires School of Social Sciences started offering a year-long course on Georg Simmel; every year, a group of students delve into readings of and on Simmel. As a result of an ambitious course geared to the spread and study of Simmel's work, titles once unavailable have been republished with new introductory studies. This is the case of *The view of life* (Simmel, 2001) and *The conflict in modern culture* (Simmel, 2011), but – more significantly – a group of books translated to Spanish for the first time with critical additions has benefitted from cooperation with scholars from around the world. Consider titles like *Cuestiones fundamentales de sociología* (Fundamental questions of sociology), *Estudios psicológicos y etnológicos sobre música* (Psychological and ethnological studies of music), *Imágenes momentáneas* (Fleeting images), *Sub specie aeternitatis, Roma, Florencia y Venecia* (Rome, Florence, and Venice), *Pedagogía escolar* (School pedagogy), *La religión* (Essays on religion), *Sobre la diferenciación social* (On social differentiation), and *La cantidad estética* (Aesthetic quantity) (Simmel, 2002b, 2nd edition 2003, 3rd edition, 2018; Simmel, 2003, 2007a, 2007b, 2008, 2nd edition, 2018, 2012, 2017, 2018).

In conjunction with the renewed recognition and study of Simmel's work at academic institutions, international encounters held in the region strengthened ties between Simmel scholars. The four editions of the *Jornadas Internacionales Actualidad del pensamiento de Simmel* were held in Buenos Aires in 2002 and 2015, in Mexico City in 2006, and in Medellín in 2011.[14] The lively lectures given by Professors Otthein and Angela Rammstedt before large audiences at the 2002 and 2011 meetings were particularly impressive. Similar international encounters on Simmel were also held in Brazil, specifically in Belém do Pará in 2006 and 2018. They helped to broaden the horizons of debate on the relevance of Simmel's work in that country. Three years before the international meeting on Simmel held in Medellín in 2011, the *Seminario Internacional Georg Simmel, a 150 años de su nacimiento* was held in Bogotá. Together, those seven encounters on Simmel in Latin America represented a major boost to studies of his work during this period.[15] In the framework of these encounters, the *Red latinoamericana de estudios sobre Georg Simmel* was created in 2014. Housed at the Universidad de Antioquia in Medellín, its website[16] not only provides information about scholarly events on Simmel, but also acts as a venue for the exchange of ideas and reflections.

This third period, then, has witnessed a resurgence of Simmel's work in Latin America thanks to new editorial and critical efforts. No less important to this new panorama are the treatises by Simmel that have been re-released and, hence, made available to a growing number of readers: in 2013, Capitán Swing press in Madrid republished Ramón García Cotarelo's translation of *The philosophy of money* with introduction by David Frisby; and in 2014, the Fondo de Cultura Económica in Mexico re-released José Pérez Bances's translation of *gran Sociología* (Sociology: inquiries into the construction of social forms) with introductory study by Gina Zabludovsky and Olga Sabido Ramos. Similarly, Prometeo press in Buenos Aires re-released earlier translations of *Schopenhauer y Nietzsche* (Schopenhauer and Nietzsche), *Problemas fundamentales de la filosofía* (Main problems of philosophy), *Goethe, Rembrandt* (Rembrandt: An essay in the philosophy of history), *El problema religioso* (The religious problem) with forwards by Daniel Mundo.

Esteban Vernik

What is a Latin American nation?

As we have shown, translations and editions of Simmel's writings have circulated in Latin American intellectual circles since the twenties. The region's intellectuals brought Simmel's reflections on modernity to bear on their own inquiries. They looked to parts of Simmel's thinking as they pursued an autonomous line of reflection on the cultural and existential meaning of Latin America and its lived reality.

Which is the significance of society units as Peru, Brazil, and Argentina? Which is the relation between the South American modernity and the West cultural heritage? Should we look at Europe's modernity as well in order to inquire about the identity of Latin American emerging nations? How do telluric factors coming out from the South American landscape operate on the emergence of an autochthonous – yet in discussion with the latest trends – thought?

In sweeping terms, works by, among others, Peruvian thinker José Carlos Mariátegui (1895–1930), Brazilian Gilberto Freyre (1900–1987), and Argentine Carlos Astrada (1894–1970) revolved around the problem of the region. By different means, all three of them looked to Simmel, quoting him, remarking on and drawing sustenance from his work. Those three authors representative of a Latin American way of grappling with the problem of nation evidence the early influence of Simmel's thought.

Their task was to interrogate the social, cultural, and political nature of Latin America's large territories, with its jungles, sierras, and plains. They grappled with the processes of European colonial expansion as those who were, ultimately, 'the masters of the earth' set out to exploit the region's natural resources by bringing over slaves from Africa and reducing to servitude, if not exterminating outright, native peoples. The question of colonialism has been central to Latin American social writing since the very early twentieth century, and – in a process not without setbacks – it pervaded incipient social science institutions in the region as well. As crucial as concern with the colonialism foundational to Latin American societies were reflections on the 'implantation' of European modernity, that is, the expansion of the capitalist market, the emergence of classes and nation states, and the spread of lifestyles more and more coveted by the monetary economy and technology.

It was in that framework that, in the first half of the twentieth century, Latin American writers-turned-sociologists like Mariátegui, Freyre, and Astrada – figures essential to understanding the idea of Latin America or, rather, of what they called Indo-America in an attempt to underscore the importance of native peoples to American nations – tied their meditations to Georg Simmel's work on the meaning of modern life.

Of the three, José Carlos Mariátegui is the one whom the history of Latin American social thought remembers most. He wrote, in 1928, *Siete ensayos de interpretación de la realidad peruana* (Seven Interpretative Essays on Peruvian Reality) (Mariátegui, 1969), a treatise crucial to understanding the problems facing Latin American societies. In his short life, Mariátegui wrote a very original body of work that joined Indigenism and European avant-garde symbolism with significant injections of ideas taken from Marx, Nietzsche, Weber, Croce, and Sorel. Mariátegui does cite Simmel on occasion in a reflection on Dada and Futurism; in an essay written in 1924, he addresses Simmel's *Philosophie der Mode* at some length (Mariátegui, 1982, pp. 463–481). Mariátegui, who conceived that Peru's main problem was the contradiction between the big landowners latifundium property system and the four-fifths parts of the population living in terrible exploitation and poverty, proposed a transformation in the ownership of the land regime as well as the restoration of the indigenous sovereignty over their land, the restoration of the identity and the sense of membership, of the 'legal popular feeling', Sorel talked about. In his '*Seven essays of interpretation of the Peruvian reality*', he puts forward the creation of a Peruvian socialism, whose main actor would not be the industrial working-class, but the vast proportion of mobilised indigenous and peasants. This mobilisation demanded – through the ancient Inca mythologies – the indigenous conscience restoration. And furthermore it requested the analysis of the contradictions common to the Peruvian situation, yet in permanent dialogue with Western techniques, methods, and ideas. As a manifesto, we read: 'I have learned and studied in Europe and I think there is no salvation for Indo-America without European and Western science and thought' (Mariátegui, 1969, p. 12).

Gilberto Freyre was the first thinker to grapple with the specificity of Brazil, and its relevance, on the basis of an analysis of its history and social formation. As mentioned above, Freyre – author, in 1933, of a classic book of Brazilian sociology – was the one who introduced Simmel's work to the next generation of Brazilian modernist thinkers. His work, which includes the emblematic *Interpretación del Brasil* (Brazil: An interpretation) (Freyre, 1964), makes a steadfast effort to delineate a 'tropical' Brazilian social type, one that differs from the mild European character but that also assimilates that European type to yield a specific mode of being. At stake is critical absorption enriched by a vast range of human traditions. And that comprehensive characterisation of the Brazilian and the Latin American draws on figures from Simmel like the adventurer and the great metropolis.

In his idea of Indo-America, Carlos Astrada – who, as we have shown, was influenced by Simmel from the time he was young – imagines the political potential of a nation to be grounded in the hermeneutics of its origin myth. He argues that every nation has such a myth – it is a secret to be deciphered and a prospective utopian call to be fulfilled as the nation's fate. A nation, Astrada writes,

> is not only the result of a physical process that takes place within a certain socio-geographic framework. [A nation] is born insofar as political; it is devoted to a fate it must fulfil, to a mission to be performed according to universality.
>
> *(Astrada, 1972, p. 7)*

Hence, for Astrada, the idea of nation entails a relation between the particular of the 'nation that we are' and the universal of the humanity; terms which involve a relation of double interpretation between them. Its translation inside the nation: as constant realisation of the nation foundational myth, as critical restoration of the national heritages and traditions. And its translation outside the nation: as birth form towards the past and the future by means of a politics, which we could well name, of philosophical cordiality among the nations.

The identity-in-the-making of the new Latin American nations meant a critical interrogation of the relationships between cosmopolitanism and nation, and between avant-garde and popular culture – indeed, it still does. Astir in the work of all three of these authors is the notion that the Latin American subject arises from complex cultural processes where the indigenous, the European, and the African cross. That hybridisation occurred from the very inception of these nations, from the time of the European conquest and the exploitation of African slaves and indigenous populations – when they were not exterminated outright, that is.

In closing, we will take a look at Ernest Renan's celebrated *What is a nation* (1882). His answer to that question is tied to a collective determination enacted every day to remember and forget history while projecting into the future (Renan, 2010). But a nation is also – we must add, pursuant to our overview – a body of translators. Translators of founding myths, and of the latest novelty to arrive from overseas. It is in that framework that we look to the Latin American tradition of Simmel readers.

Astrada, Mariátegui, and Freyre delved in the Latin American myths with the aim to re-found its nations in a prospective and utopian way. Whilst they tested the most radical questions about the Latin American existence and the influence of the natural, cultural, and historical landscape on it, they were stimulated by the work from Georg Simmel, a work they have, likewise, published and examined by means of those questions.

Coda: nation and memory

If, as Renan asserts, a people is in fact a spiritual principle that requires equal measures of memory and forgetting, as well as 'common glories in the past and a will to continue them in the present' (Renan, 2010, p. 64), then it is, to a large extent, a question of collective memory. In Latin America, it was in the late nineteen-eighties and early nineties that the question of memory and sites of memory arose as problem central to philosophical-political reflection and to social research agendas. It is associated with the period of transition to democracy after decades of totalitarian regimes – whether under dictatorship or limited democracies – had riddled almost all the countries in the region.

At that juncture, in the context of debates on memory and nation in the social sciences in Latin America, a body of relevant works reached the region. They included, chiefly, Maurice Halbwachs's *On collective memory* (Halbwachs, 2004), a book clearly rooted in Durkheim but that draws inspiration from Bergson, and Pierre Nora's *Les lieux de mémoire* (Nora, 2008). While neither of those books is directly tied to Simmel's work, which itself does not make explicit reference to the question of memory, Simmel has – as we have seen – been read in Latin America in relation to the idea of nation. Though not one of his core concerns, the problem of nation crops up in a number of passages in his work: his dissertation on the origins of music (GSG 1, p. 45-89), the chapter on history in his *Schulpädagogik* (School Pedagogy) (GSG 20, pp. 311-472), and his writings during the war collected in *Der Krieg und die geistigen Entscheidungen* (The War and the spiritual decisions) (GSG 16, pp. 7-58). How does Simmel address the question of memory? Does his work contain theoretical elements useful to that fertile field of research and reflection?

Though we have not been able to find writings in Latin America that apply Simmel's ideas to memory, we believe that his diagnosis of modernity does contain elements pertinent to it, and to its study.

To that end, we will turn to the problem of technology. In the closing chapter of *The Philosophy of Money*, Simmel concludes that in modern times the means take precedence over the ends; he warns of the dangers of technical progress, of 'making final ends illusory' (GSG 6, p. 670). The modern subject is immersed in a teleological network that upholds as absolute the contradiction contained in the fact that the means are greater than the ends. He observes that 'If we consider the totality of life, then the control of nature by technology is possible only at the price of being enslaved in it and by dispensing with spirituality as the central point of life' (GSG 6, p. 672). Because of the alienating nature of the proliferations of means, 'Man has thereby become estranged from himself; an insuperable barrier of media, technical inventions, abilities and enjoyments has been erected between him and his most distinctive and essential being' (GSG 6, p. 674). Technology, then, leads to the forgetting of memory. Simmel pays attention to phenomena like the expansion of transportation and its growing speed, the proliferation of the telegraph and telephone, the laying of electrical wires. He observes a modern culture that has exceeded the confines not only of space but also of time. Everything is more mobile and quicker. The stuff of life speeds up to keep pace with the circulation of money. Simmel's images of modernity seem so current that they lead more to forgetting than to remembering …

Notes

1 Translated by Jane Brodie.
2 Only one text by Simmel had been translated previously: the book *Schopenhauer y Nietzsche* was translated into Spanish by José Pérez Bances in Madrid in 1915, while Simmel was still alive.
3 The now-defunct *Institut für Meereskunde* was located at 34–36 *Georgenstraße* in Berlin before being destroyed in World War II. It was founded in 1900 in order to 'further understanding and knowledge of the sea and coastlands, and to raise awareness of the national and economic importance of maritime interests'. It was, without question, a public cultural initiative tied to the defense of the colonialist interests of the Second German Empire (1871–1918).
4 Letter to Margarete von Bendemann, 17 January 1918 (GSG 23, 907–908).
5 Letter to Margarete von Bendemann, 27 February 1918 (GSG 23, 909–910).
6 There is a vast bibliography on the Reforma Universitaria, cfr. Riquelme, M. & A. Rigi Luperti (2019).
7 'Russia … is the myth that has fertilised the world's consciousness, that consciousness that lay buried under the rubble of inhuman values. From her like an echo of legend, the voice of her greatest prophets – Dostoyevsky, Tolstoy, Gorky, Lenin, Lunacharsky – reaches us, the voice that utters Man's eternal gospel' (Astrada, 1921, p. 2).
8 Simmel was rejected for a professorship in Heidelberg three times, in 1908, 1915, and 1916 – this final time after having been given a professorship in Strasbourg in 1914.
9 Astrada's work encompasses some sixteen published volumes that range in content from commentaries on Hegel, Marx, Nietzsche, and Heidegger to an attempt to compose a philosophy of the Indo-American being that considers the particularities of Latin American nations. Though Astrada is one of his country's most original and prolific philosophers, he has been relatively marginalised in its history and criticised harshly by the philosophy and sociology establishment. That is partly because of his proximity to Martin Heidegger, with whom he studied in Freiburg starting in 1927 (he was a close disciple of Heidegger throughout his life), and partly because of his political leanings. He was an early sympathiser with Peronism; then a member of the Communist Party, which he left after a disappointing spell in Moscow; and finally a Maoist. See David (2004) and Bustos (2019).
10 The books from Simmel Astrada explicity makes use in his own writings until that moment, are: *Der Konklikt der modernen Kultur, Philosophie der Mode, Hauptprobleme der Philosophie, Rembrandt. Ein Kunstsphilosopher* and *Probleme der Geschichtsphilosophie.*
11 The list of publications by Simmel that follows does not set out to be exhaustive. There are two thorough bibliographies of his works published in Spanish, but they need to be updated since many more works have been published since they were put together. See Lazcano and Mutiloa (2000) and Cataño (2008).
12 In addition to Ortega, the other figures close to Simmel whom Ocampo encouraged to travel to Argentina include Count von Keyserling (1951). He was dazzled by his hostess, whom he described as 'the most remarkable woman I've met in my life'. He dedicated fiery pages to her in his book *Viaje a través del tiempo* (The Travel Diary of a Philosopher). Years later, at Victoria Ocampo's initiative, first Spanish-language versions of authors like Hans Freyer, Walter Benjamin, Theodor Adorno, and Max Horkheimer were translated by *Sur.*
13 The title of the essay is 'The Sociological Formalism and the Theory of Conflict' and on its cover is a photograph of soldiers putting down a group of protesters – which tells us a great deal about what the publication of this collection of texts by Simmel meant in the context of the Brazilian dictatorship.
14 For a detailed analysis of the results of the four meetings, as well as their 'exchanges of effects' (*Wechselwirkungen*) from the perspective of field and network theory, see Sabido Ramos (2016).
15 For the results of these meetings, see Vernik and Fressoli (2002); Sabido Ramos (2007); Tejeiro Sarmiento (2011); Díaz Aldana (2015); Vernik and Borisonik (2016).
16 http://www.redsimmel.org

References

Astrada, C. (1921). *El renacimiento del mito*. Buenos Aires: Cuasimodo.
Astrada, C. (1923). Nota preliminar. In G. Simmel (Ed.), *El conflicto de la cultura moderna* (pp. 5–7). Translated and prefaced by C. Astrada. Córdoba: Facultad de Derecho y Ciencias Sociales, Universidad Nacional de Córdoba.

Astrada, C. (1925). *La deshumanización de Occidente*. La Plata: Sagitario.

Astrada, C. (1933). *El juego existencial*. Buenos Aires: Babel.

Astrada, C. (1957). *El marxismo y las escatologías*. Buenos Aires: Procyon.

Astrada, C. (1972). *El mito gaucho*. Buenos Aires: Kairós.

Bustos, N. (2019). *El humanismo de la libertad de Carlos Astrada*. Doctoral Thesis. Universidad de Buenos Aires.

Cataño, G. (2008). Bibliografía de Georg Simmel en castellano. *Revista Colombiana de Sociología*, *31*, 83–89.

Cohn, G. (1979). *Crítica e resignacao, fundamentos da sociología de Max Weber*. Sao Paulo: Queiroz.

David, G. (2004). *Carlos Astrada. La filosofía argentina*. Buenos Aires: El cielo por asalto.

Díaz Aldana, G. (2015). *Una actitud del espíritu. Interpretaciones en torno a Georg Simmel*. Bogotá: Universidad Nacional.

Freyre, G. (1942). *Sociología. Introduccao a seus principios*. Río de Janeiro: José Olimpo.

Freyre, G. (1964). *Interpretación del Brasil*. Translated by T. Ortiz and M. Aguilera. México: Fondo de Cultura Económica.

Freyre, G. (1985). *Casa Grande y Senzala*. Caracas: Biblioteca Ayacucho.

Frisby, D. (1990). *Georg Simmel*. Translated by J. Pérez Carballo. México: Fondo de Cultura Económica.

GSG 1: Simmel, G. (2000). *Psychologische und ethnolgische Studien über Musik*. Edited by K. C. Köhnke. Frankfurt am Main: Suhrkamp.

GSG 6: Simmel, G. (1989). *Philosophie des Geldes*. Edited by D. Frisby & K. C. Köhnke. Frankfurt am Main: Suhrkamp.

GSG 16: Simmel, G. (1999). *Der Krieg und die geistigen Entscheidungen and Der Konflikt der modernen Kultur*. Edited by G. Fitzi & O. Rammstedt. Frankfurt am Main: Suhrkamp.

GSG 20: Simmel, G. (2004). *Schulpädagogik*. Edited by T. Karlruhen & O. Rammstedt. Frankfurt am Main: Suhrkamp.

GSG 23: Simmel, G. (2008). *Briefe 1912–1918. Jugendbriefe*. Edited by Otthein and Angela Rammstedt. Frankfurt am Main: Suhrkamp.

Halbwachs, M. (2004). *Los marcos sociales de la memoria*. Translated by M. Baeza & M. Mujica. Postface by G. Namer. Barcelona: Anthropos.

Keyserling, C. (1951). *Viaje a través del tiempo*. Buenos Aires: Sudamericana.

Lazcano, D., & Y. Mutiloa (2000). Los escritos de Georg Simmel. *Revista Española de Investigaciones Sociológicas*, special issue on Centenary of *The Philosophy of Money*, 269–286.

Mariátegui, J. (1969). *Siete ensayos de interpretación de la realidad peruana*. Lima: Amauta.

Mariátegui, J. (1982). La civilización y el cabello. *Obras Completas de José C. Mariátegui*, *2*, 463–471. La Habana: Casa de las Américas.

Moraes Filho, E., (Ed.) (1983). *Simmel. Sociología*. Translated by C. Pavanelli. Sao Paulo: Ática.

Nora, P. (2008). *Les lieux de mémoire*. Translated by L. Masello. Preface by J. Rilla. Montevideo: Trilce.

Renan, E. (2010). *¿Qué es una nación?* Translated by A. Kuschnir and R. González. Preface by A. Smith. Buenos Aires: Hydra.

Riquelme, M., & A. Rigui Luperti (Eds.) (2019). *A cien años de la Reforma Universitaria. Tensiones entre la Nación, la Universidad y les estudiantes*. Río Gallegos: Ediciones Unpaedita.

Sabido Ramos, O. (Ed.) (2007). *Georg Simmel. Una revisión contemporánea*. México: Anthropos/UAM-Azcapotzalco.

Sabido Ramos, O. (2016). El significado de la obra sociológica de Georg Simmel en lengua castellana como efecto de una red (2002–2015). Reporte de investigación. Departamento de Sociología, september 2016. Available at: www.academia.edu/31341759/El_significado_de_la_obra_sociol%C3%B3gica_de_Georg_Simmel_en_lengua_castellana_como_efecto_de_una_red_2002-2015_._Reporte_de_investigaci%C3%B3n?auto=download (Accessed: 16 February 2019).

Simmel, G. (1915). *Schopenhauer y Nietzsche*. Translated by J. Pérez Bances. Madrid: Beltrán.

Simmel, G. (1923). *El conflicto de la cultura moderna*. Translated and Preface by C. Astrada. Córdoba: Facultad de Derecho y Ciencias Sociales, Universidad Nacional de Córdoba.

Simmel, G. (1939). *Sociología. Estudios sobre las formas de socialización*. Translated by J. Pérez Bances. Buenos Aires: Espasa-Calpe.

Simmel, G. (1946). *Problemas fundamentales de la filosofía*. Translated by F. Vela. Madrid: Revista de Occidente.

Simmel, G. (1947). *Problemas fundamentales de la filosofía*. Translated by S. Molinari and E. Schulzen. Buenos Aires: Editora del Plata.

Simmel, G. (1949). *Goethe*. Translated by J. Rovira Armengol. Buenos Aires: Nova.

Simmel, G. (1950a). *Schopenhauer y Nietzsche*. Translated by F. Ayala. Buenos Aires: Anaconda.

Simmel, G. (1950b). *Rembrandt. Ensayo de filosofía del arte*. Translated by. E. Estiú. Buenos Aires: Nova.

Simmel, G. (1950c). *Problemas de filosofía de la historia*. Translated by. E. Tabernig. Buenos Aires: Nova.

Simmel, G. (1950d). *Intuición de la vida. Cuatro capítulos de metafísica*. Translated by J. Rovira Armengol. Buenos Aires: Nova.

Simmel, G. (1953). *El problema religioso*. Translated by J.I.K. Buenos Aires: Argos.

Simmel, G. (1977a). *Sociología. Estudios sobre las formas de socialización*. Translated by J. Pérez Bances. Madrid: Revista de Occidente.

Simmel, G. (1977b). *Filosofía del dinero*. Translated by R. García Cotarelo. Madrid: Instituto de Estudios Políticos.

Simmel, G. (1986). *El individuo y la libertad. Ensayos de crítica de la cultura*. Translated and Preface by S. Mas. Barcelona: Península.

Simmel, G. (1988). *Sobre la aventura. Ensayos filosóficos*. Translated by G. Muñoz y S. Más. Posface by J. Habermas. Barcelona: Península.

Simmel, G. (2001). *Intuición de la vida. Cuatro capítulos de metafísica*. Translated by. J. Rovira Armengol. Preface by E. Vernik. Buenos Aires: Altamira.

Simmel, G. (2002a). *Sobre la individualidad y las formas sociales*. Translated by E. Vernik. Edited and Preface by D. Levine. Bernal: Universidad Nacional de Quilmes.

Simmel, G. (2002b). *Cuestiones fundamentales de sociología*. Translated by. Á. Ackermann Pilári. Preface by E. Vernik. Barcelona: Gedisa.

Simmel, G. (2003). *Estudios psicológicos y etnológicos sobre música*. Translated by C. Abdo Férez. Preface by E. Vernik. Buenos Aires: Gorla.

Simmel, G. (2007a). *Imágenes momentáneas. Sub specie aeternitatis*. Translated by R. Ibarlucía y O. Strunk. Preface by E. Vernik. Posface by O. Rammstedt. Barcelona: Gedisa.

Simmel, G. (2007b). *Roma, Florencia y Venecia*. Translated by O. Strunk. Preface by N. Cantó Milá. Posface by E. Vernik. Barcelona: Gedisa.

Simmel, G. (2008). *Pedagogía escolar*. Translated by C. Abdo Férez. Preface by K. Heuter. Posface by E. Vernik. Barcelona: Gedisa.

Simmel, G. (2011). *El conflicto de la cultura moderna*. Translated and Preface by C. Astrada. Introduction of E. Vernik. Córdoba: Universidad Nacional de Córdoba/ Encuentro.

Simmel, G. (2012). *La religión*. Translated by L. Carugatti. Preface by E. Vernik. Posface by O. Sabido Ramos. Barcelona: Gedisa.

Simmel, G. (2014). *Sociología. Estudios sobre la socialización*. Translated by J. Pérez Bances. Introduction of G. Zabludovsky and O. Sabido Ramos. México: Fondo de Cultura Económica.

Simmel, G. (2017). *Sobre la diferenciación social. Investigaciones sociológicas y psicológicas*. Translated by L. Lewkow. Preface by E. Vernik. Barcelona: Gedisa.

Simmel, G. (2018). *La cantidad estética. Ensayos de filosofía del arte*. Translated by C. Díaz Isenrath. Preface by E. Vernik. Barcelona: Gedisa.

Tejeiro Sarmiento, C. (Ed.) (2011). *Georg Simmel y la modernidad*. Bogotá: Universidad Nacional.

Vernik, E., & H. Borisonik (Eds.) (2016). *Georg Simmel, un siglo después. Actualidad y perspectiva*. Buenos Aires: CLACSO/IIGG.

Vernik, E., & M. Fressoli (Eds.) (2002). *Reporte del Coloquio 'Actualidad del pensamiento de Simmel'*. Buenos Aires: Mimeo-Universidad de Buenos Aires.

Waizbort, L. (2000). *As aventuras de Georg Simmel*. Sao Paulo: Editora 34.

Waizbort, L. (2007). Simmel no Brasil. *Dados*, *50*(1), 11–48.

Weber, M. (1986). Georg Simmel como sociólogo. Translated by F. Gil Villegas. *México: Sociológica*, *1*(1), 81–85.

INDEX

CPSIA information can be obtained
at www.ICGtesting.com
Printed in the USA
BVHW010332170522
637022BV00004B/28

9 780367 277239